TREKKING
NEPAL

Above: *Annapurna 1 and Annapurna South from Ghorepani*
(Photo by Tokozile Robbins)

Previous page: *Upper Pisang in foreground with lower Pisang below*
(Photo by Tokozile Robbins)

Below: *Horseback riding in Langtang* (Photo by R.C. Sedai)

Chorten *en route to Kilcho Lake, a full-day side trip from Braka Village*
(Photo by Tokozile Robbins)

Above: *Dry goods vendor* (Photo by Tokozile Robbins)

Below: *Experience the coziness of a homestay hearth.* (Photo by Tokozile Robbins)

Above: *Tea estate in Eastern Nepal* (Photo by Mark Jackson and Susan Bergin /SAFA Himalaya Collection/Nepal)

Below: *Traditional houses in Dongme* (Photo by R.C. Sedai)

A herd of bharal, *or blue sheep*
(Photo by Tokozile Robbins)

Delphinium tatsienense
(Photo by Tokozile Robbins)

Great Mormon swallowtail on a
Himalayan meadow primrose
(Photo by Tokozile Robbins)

Beware of raised stakes on some improved trails.
(Photo by Tokozile Robbins)

Yak in the alpine heights (Photo by Mark Jackson and Susan Bergin/SAFA Himalaya Collection/Nepal)

Scenic Pharak lies alongside Phewa Lake and is the staging point for a journey to the Annapurnas. (Photo by Tokozile Robbins)

Looking up at Manang village from the Marsyangdi River (Photo by Tokozile Robbins)

Above: Above: *Typical child carriers for the trails are woven bamboo baskets.*
(Photo by Matt Freedman)

Opposite: *Hillside in Pharek below Khumbu* (Photo by Matt Freedman)

Below: *Hiker along trail on terraces* (Photo by Matt Freedman)

Above: *Thamserku silhouettes* (Photo by Pat Morrow)

Below: *Buying jewelry at a market in Kunde* (Photo by Pat Morrow)

Above: *The village of Dongme has the snowy Himalaya as a backdrop.* (Photo by R.C. Sedai)

Below: *The Sun Kosi River* (Photo by R.C. Sedai)

Above: *Male guardian deity at north end of Kagbeni village* (Photo by Tokozile Robbins)

Below: *Monks sort mushrooms for drying, Upper Pisang.* (Photo by Tokozile Robbins)

Next page: *Small Buddhist* gomba *of Tal village*
(Photo by Tokozile Robbins)

Inside Thubten Chholing Gomba (Photo by Matt Freedman)

Rai woman giving a namaste, *the traditional greeting* (Photo by Pat Morrow)

Lamas *along the Indigenous Peoples Trail* (Photo by Mark Jackson and Susan Bergin/SAFA Himalaya Collection)

Gomba and remains of fortress at Dzong (Photo by Tokozile Robbins)

Farmer near Shivalya (Photo by Mark Jackson and Susan Bergin/SAFA Himalaya Collection/Nepal)

Manang girl returning from gathering dung for fuel (Photo by Pat Morrow)

Hiking to Tsergo Ri viewpoint with Langtang Lirung (23,711 ft, 7,227 m) in the background (Photo by Alonzo Lyons)

TREKKING
NEPAL

a traveler's guide

eighth edition

**Stephen
Bezruchka**
and
Alonzo Lyons

THE MOUNTAINEERS BOOKS

THE MOUNTAINEERS BOOKS
*is the nonprofit publishing arm of The Mountaineers Club,
an organization founded in 1906 and dedicated to the exploration,
preservation, and enjoyment of outdoor and wilderness areas.*

1001 SW Klickitat Way, Suite 201, Seattle, WA 98134

© 2011 by Stephen Bezruchka and Alonzo Lyons

First edition 1972; second edition 1974; third edition 1976; all published by Sahayogi Press, Kathmandu, Nepal.
Fourth edition 1981; fifth edition 1985; sixth edition 1991; seventh edition 1997; eighth edition 2011; published in the United States by The Mountaineers Books, Seattle, Washington.

Distributed in the United Kingdom by Cordee, www.cordee.co.uk
Manufactured in the United States of America

Copy Editor: Jane Crosen
Cover, Book Design, and Layout: Peggy Egerdahl
Cartographer: Pease Press Cartography

Cover photograph: *Ama Dablam is one of the attractions in the Everest region.*
    © Kai Pak Patrick Yeung

Library of Congress Cataloging-in-Publication Data
Bezruchka, Stephen.
  Trekking in Nepal : a traveler's guide / Stephen R. Bezruchka and
Alonzo L. Lyons. — 8th ed.
    p. cm.
  Includes bibliographical references and index.
  ISBN 978-0-89886-613-1 (pbk.)
  1. Hiking—Nepal—Guidebooks. 2. Nepal—Guidebooks. I. Lyons, Alonzo L.
II. Title.
  GV199.44.N46B49 2010
  915.496—dc22
                        2010045517

ISBN (paperback): 978-0-89886-631-1
ISBN (e-book): 978-1-59485-410-1

CONTENTS

section one: PREPARING TO TREK

section two: THE ROUTES

appendixes

FOREWORD

My introduction to trekking in Nepal came in 1982 when, as the official photographer for the first Canadian expedition to attempt Mount Everest, I joined my teammates for the walk to base camp.

Unlike today's commercial expeditions that fly almost to the mountain, allowing precious little time for acclimatization and orientation, we deliberately chose to walk almost all the way from Kathmandu along the trail system that the British had taken during the first ascent of the mountain in 1953. This paid off as the entire team was perfectly acclimatized after almost three weeks of gradual ascent. But what I didn't realize until much later was that the extra time that we spent on the trail affected the way I came to regard foot travel in the Himalaya.

Prior to that trek, I had focused only on the challenges and perceived dangers of the climb. Never having been to the Himalaya, I had no idea of the rich diversity of the natural and human landscape. By going the extra distance, I discovered the biggest reward of all, the hill people.

I also had the good fortune to have as a tent mate the expedition doctor, Stephen Bezruchka. I can't think of a better authority to initiate a neophyte to the mightiest mountain range on Earth than the person whose book *Trekking in Nepal* was already considered to be the bible of guidebooks for the region.

Since that wonderful introduction to the Nepal Himalaya, I have trekked most of the established trails and many of the more obscure tracks in the country. Given this perspective, I can say without exaggeration that the welcoming nature of the hill people of Nepal, and the integrity of their trail system, is without equal.

In 1989 my wife Baiba and I joined Stephen on a magical trek in western Nepal. Stephen used the opportunity to add this trek as a chapter in his book. I'll never forget the image of him striding up the trail, tape recorder in one hand, stopwatch in the other, asking occasionally for directions in fluent Nepali, totally at ease in the mountains he had chosen as his second home. On all our other treks when we weren't graced with Stephen's company, this book was a constant companion. In 1994, with our friend Ang Nima Sherpa of Kunde village, we linked six treks into one. Starting at Pokhara in the west, we looped around Annapurna, and continued another 80 days and 600 kilometers to arrive on the sunlit patio at Ang Nima's guesthouse in Kunde village where we sipped *chang* and admired the stellar view of Ama Dablam. There were sections along that route that were covered in Stephen's book that even Ang Nima hadn't been on.

Over the years, this book has continued to evolve, adding even more tips on how best to interact with and understand the wonderful denizens of this former Himalayan kingdom. In the seventh edition, Stephen announced that it was time for someone else to take over the onerous, but rewarding task of revising *Trekking in Nepal*. Fortunately, Alonzo Lyons stepped forward, and in this eighth edition you will find an up-to-date guidebook for greater Nepal with the most current descriptions for Annapurna, Everest, Langtang, and Helambu, along with enticing new details on side trips in these areas.

Pat and his wife, Baiba, with the still unclimbed South Face of Dhaulagiri and the Kali Gandaki valley to the right behind them (Photo by Pat Morrow)

Alonzo has also added The Trails Less Traveled. This chapter will beckon to people hoping to get away from the popular venues and closer to the heart of this remarkable culture.

The best advice I can offer to the independent trekker who wants to acquire valuable insight into Nepal and in so doing, themselves, is this: Arm yourself with the 35+ years of distilled wisdom that are contained within and use this book as a cultural and geographical reference as much as a directional guide. By following the book's basic tenets for helping to minimize tourism's impact on the local people and the environment, you'll come to enjoy the hospitality of this unique country as much as I have.

  —*Pat Morrow*
    Mountain photographer, filmmaker, author, and the first person
    to climb the Seven Summits—the highest peaks on all continents

PREFACE

But in the end, guidebooks, like textbooks, are no substitute for the real world. They tell you what to expect from an endeavor—travel—in which the greatest pleasure is the unexpected.

—Thomas Swick, travel editor,
Fort Lauderdale Sun-Sentinel

Peter Whittaker has said, "There are certain spots in the world where you can stand that will change the way you look at things forever." For many, Nepal is that place. Adventure used to be for the elite or crazy, but now "adventures" are undertaken by ordinary people in economically rich countries—perhaps a disease of the complex, modern, postindustrial society.

Trekking in its various styles is an increasingly popular activity, with over 100,000 participants in Nepal annually. Especially along the popular routes, there have been many changes over the span of more than forty years that Stephen has been fortunate to be involved with Nepal.

Trekking is so popular because of the landforms in this remarkably varied country and because of the nature of the Nepali spirit. What can be done to enhance the experience of both the visitor and the Nepali host? Clearly it is understanding on both sides that is necessary. With the remarkable quality of Nepali tolerance, there is little that needs to be said about that aspect. But for the visitor, there is much to be learned about the way of Nepal if you want to be respected by your hosts. That is the purpose of this book. Whether you are going with an agency, organizing your own portered trip, or going it alone, this book will help you have an experience that is remarkable, memorable, and close to the heart of Nepal. For even though you might surmise that the larger numbers of tourists will dilute the hospitality of the Nepali people, the opposite is true. The more you are sensitive to the ways of Nepal, the more intimate and wonderful your experience. This will set you apart from the others.

The purpose in writing this guidebook was to provide visitors with the information they needed to be culturally appropriate and environmentally sensitive guests in this remarkable country and to keep them on the correct trails. Some tourists who come to Nepal want to be served in ways they can't in their own country because they can't afford it. Such tourism is neocolonial imperialism and, although you can't entirely escape elements of it in your travels, we try to show you ways to get beyond this mode. Today it is still possible to have the same wonderful, intimate experience with Nepali people that Stephen had forty years ago; however, there are now options, such as extensive lodges built specifically for tourists, and packaged tours that make it easier to not have this opportunity. This book will help you avoid these options if you wish a different experience than suggested by the glossy adventure travel brochures.

In this atypical guidebook, we try to provide various insights to the riches of this perhaps most diverse spectrum of peoples and terrain in the world. Numerous sidebars are scattered through the book to help enhance your understanding of the country and to tease your intellect and sharpen your powers of observation. Most likely, on your return home, it will no longer be difficult to understand why this relatively tiny country continues to have a profound impact on foreigners.

This guidebook, faced with a physical and political climate that is constantly changing, is bound to be out-of-date in some places and in error in others. Over the years, many trekkers to Nepal have sent information, and this has resulted in substantial improvements to the book. Please keep the comments and letters coming: mbooks@mountaineersbooks.org.

CHANGES AND CHALLENGES

As a result of security concerns from the Maoist movement in Nepal (see "Backgound" for a more detailed look at Nepal's history), the polyregicide that wiped out most of the royal family June 1, 2001, and the responses to September 11, 2001, many people have written in about the risk of travel to Nepal. During the first decade of this century there have been few reports of serious harm to tourists, although those who traveled during the civil war were often asked to make donations to the Maoists. During the first half of that decade, tourism to Nepal declined considerably. It began growing again, especially after a peace accord was signed in 2006, and despite recent global economic upheaval the industry continues to grow. The Nepal Tourism Board has initiated a Visit Nepal 2011 campaign with the hopes of doubling the current 500,000-plus annual visitors. In most rural areas you might visit outside of the popular trails, you are more likely to

Terraced rice fields greet you at every turn in the mid-hills.
(Photo by Mark Jackson and Susan Bergin/SAFA Himalaya Collection/Nepal)

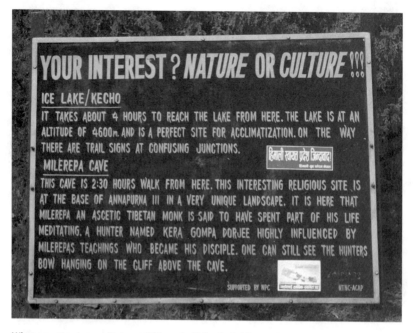

What are your aims and interests? (Photo by Tokozile Robbins)

find a Nepal with fewer tourists, enabling you to have more personal encounters with Nepalis on your travels.

The decision to travel to Nepal depends on how much of an unknown but small and different risk than you are exposed to at home you are willing to accept. Visitors can keep up with the latest U.S. travel precautions at http://travel.state.gov, and check with respective embassies in Nepal for the current political backdrop and advisories. The U.S. Embassy is at http://nepal.usembassy.gov.

Of course, the challenges facing the world are magnified in developing countries and particularly Nepal. An abundance of glaciers, rivers, and forests make this region especially susceptible to distortions in climate, and although far from clear, some data indicate that Nepal's Himalaya might be heating up at a more pronounced rate than the global average. The fertile Indo-Gangetic plain, from areas of Pakistan in the west across southern Nepal and northern India to include Bangladesh, is a densely populated area and home to one-ninth of the world's people. The people of this plain as well as in Tibet rely on Himalayan runoff for survival. The majority of Nepal's population is agrarian. Obviously, weather imbalances can have dramatic consequences; the region has already seen disruption in monsoon timings and the marked retreat of some glaciers. Nepal has been dealing with decreasing food security, hunger really, particularly in the far west because of the former insurgency and prolonged drought and unusual rainfall patterns that disrupt usual growing seasons.

As well as environmental challenges, Nepal has been through mercurial political changes in the last fifteen years, especially since the monarchy was formally abolished in May 2008 (after 239 years) and Nepal became a democratic republic. It is now up to the people to choose the way forward. With its rich resources of willing, able, and talented people, Nepal is approaching the development summit for which it is aiming, but at the same time has a long way to go. It is improving on many fronts but ranked 143rd in the watchdog group Transparency International's Autumn 2009 Corruption Perception Index, and corruption has and continues to severely hamper development. Political factions spend valuable time and effort currying favor for personal advantage, and venality stifles most areas of progress and taints the inordinate amount of financial "aid" that pours in every year. For example, the World Bank committed a monstrous $782 million to Nepal for 2010 and 2011, with nearly 45 percent of that being grants and the rest loans. However, in this day and age of widespread sharing and availability of information, it is becoming more difficult to conceal misdeeds. Advances in technology will help to expose deficiencies in governance and open up the system to improvements to spur positive growth in Nepal as elsewhere.

Although Nepal is changing swiftly along with the rest of the world, trekking continues to be an experience of a lifetime. Please allow this book to be your guide to cultural and ecological sensitivity along the way.

Nepal is there to change you, not for you to change it. Lose yourself in its soul. Make your footprints with care and awareness of the precarious balance around you. Take souvenirs in your heart and spirit, not in your pockets. Nepal is not only a place on the map, but an experience, a way of life from which we all can learn.

A NOTE ABOUT SAFETY

Safety is an important concern in all outdoor activities. No guidebook can alert you to every hazard or anticipate the limitations of every reader. Therefore, the descriptions of roads, trails, routes, and natural features in this book are not representations that a particular place or excursion will be safe for your party. When you follow any of the routes described in this book, you assume responsibility for your own safety. Under normal conditions, such excursions require the usual attention to traffic, road and trail conditions, weather, terrain, the capabilities of your party, and other factors. Keeping informed on current conditions and exercising common sense are the keys to a safe, enjoyable outing.

Political conditions may add to the risks of travel in Nepal in ways that this book cannot predict. When you travel, you assume this risk, and should keep informed of political developments that may make safe travel difficult or impossible.

—*The Mountaineers Books* ◈

ACKNOWLEDGMENTS

Many people have helped Stephen in updating previous editions. Thanks go to Line Antonsen, Chris Beall, Robin Biellik, Rachel Bishop, Rupert Blum, Gunter Boch, Cherie Bremer-Kamp, Bruce and Ellen Campbell, Susan Clark, Norm Coleman, Mary Ann Davis, Don and Aiko Diehl, Thiley Lama Domaray, Ed Earl, Carl Flannagan, Jim and Isabel Foster, Lori Green, Carl Harrison, Roger Hoehfurtner, Eric and Ingred Holzman, Carol Inskipp, Inu K.C., Liesl Messerschmidt, Patricia Knox, Wendy Brewer Lama, Steve LeClerq, Jim Litch, Eugene Marguilis, Tom Manery, Don Messerschmidt, Julie Nassif, John Peirce, Edmund Potter, Rachel Rosen, Daniel Schelling, David Schensted, Joan Settin, Surendra Sharma, Ang Rita Sherpa, Kazi Sambu Sherpa, Lhakpa Norbu Sherpa, David Shlim, Tenzing Tamang, Jean Thomas, Kay Timms, Eric Wolf, and Laura Ziemer. Mary Anne Mercer facilitated the previous edition in countless ways. Stephen's porters taught him most of what he knows about Nepal. He is especially grateful to Chandra Pal Rai. The production staff at The Mountaineers has been very helpful. Thank you all.

Stephen's work on this edition has been as an overseer. His time in Nepal is mostly spent talking to Nepalis about the work they are doing to change the country for the better. He no longer keeps notes or times on the trails and is delighted that Alonzo has taken the baton. He thanks Nepal, the land and its people, for giving him visions he never could have dreamed of.

Alonzo gives thanks with all his heart to the following people for providing inestimable guidance, friendship, and continual support during his Nepal peregrinations: Ram Chandra Sedai (an invaluable source of information, assistance, and friendship), Tokozile Robbins (for valorous perseverance in extraordinary conditions and frequent sprinklings of otherworldly wisdom), Daniel T. Flynn (an endless source of guidance and heroism), Kumar Kaedel, Durga Tamang, Sudarsan Pradhan, D. B. Gurung, Tek Gurung, Phulmaya Moktan, Pushpa Raj Yolmo, Arun Shrestha, Prabin Paudel, Prakash Giri, Jim Duff, Declan Murphy, Aiko Yamazaki, Basanta Dawadi, Ratna Bhirsing, Keshav Bista, Romi Pradhan, Chunu Shresta, Narayan Neupane, Akabir Bairagi, Ujwal Thapa, Richard Bull, Aman Nakarmi, Chandra Jewan Shahi, Kashi Raj Bhandari, Tej Bohara, Shankar Rai, Santosh Gurung, Kanchha Tamang, Lila Bahadur Baniya, Sanil Sharma, Nima Gombu Sherpa, Pradam Prasad Bhusal, Rabi Jung Pandey, Arjun Limbu, Shanta Khadka, Sangita Thapa, Nyima Tamang, Jyoti Adhikhari, Colin Smith, Devika Gurung, Marcus Ivarsson, Amber Syangdan, Phyllis Lyons (his lovely *Aamaa*), Shirley O'Neil, Ellen Santiago, Annie Hickerson, Katie Lyonsmith, John Lyons, and infinite others along the way. Special thanks to Jane Crosen and the good folk of The Mountaineers Books. With highest gratitude to Stephen for the opportunity and guidance to "wear his moccasins" for a short while to follow some of his visionary footsteps.

Opposite: ACAP signs dot the Annapurna region.
(Photo by Gail Robson)

BACKGROUND

A hundred divine epochs would not suffice to describe all the marvels of the Himalaya.

—Sanskrit proverb

What kind of experience will you have in Nepal? Think of waking up early one morning and directing your gaze to the north. It is quite cloudy, but for some reason you lift up your eyes. There it is—the triangular rock-and-snow face of Machhapuchhre (Fishtail Peak), glistening in the sun through a hole in the clouds, a relatively small Himalayan peak that is not even 23,000 feet (7000 m) high! How could it look so big? Or you are walking along the trail when you suddenly hear, "Good morning, sir," spoken in perfect English. You turn around, astonished, to see an ordinary-looking Nepali. Yes, the speaker is a Gurkha soldier, retired from the British Army. The two of you pass many miles talking together. Or, it is the day's end and you are resting after the walk, looking at a Western book or magazine that you carry. Soon you are surrounded by children who gaze intently at the photographs. You want to tell them that the world those pictures represent is not better than theirs. Or it is spring and you have toiled to get far above the valley. The rhododendrons make the mountains look like a paradise. The blooms are red in many places, yet the colors can be light, and even beautifully white. Every day there will be many times like these when you will forget the miles you have yet to go, the vertical feet yet to climb, the load on your back. And you will vow to return.

Nepal is a land of unparalleled variety. Climatically, the country has subtropical, temperate, and alpine regions, determined by elevation (as detailed in Chapter 1), and contains examples of most of the vegetation zones of the world. Imagine a trapezoidal shape, 500 by 150 miles (800 by 240 km), divided lengthwise into three strips. The northernmost strip is the Himalaya, meaning "abode of snow," and includes eight of the ten highest mountains in the world. The Himalayan region is sparsely settled by people who speak languages of the Tibeto-Burman family and practice Tibetan Buddhism. The southernmost region, called the Tarai, is an extension of the Gangetic plain of northern India, containing jungles with elephants, rhinoceroses, and tigers. These inhabitants contrast markedly with the yaks and snow leopards less than 100 miles (160 km) to the north. The Tarai is populated by people who speak Indo-European languages and practice Hinduism. Between the two outer strips lies an interface of hills and valleys. The inhabitants speak languages of both the Tibeto-Burman and Indo-European families, and generally practice Hinduism with Buddhist, animistic, and shamanic influences. This "religion of the hills" (more on this in Chapter 3) defies categorization. This middle region, the hills, is the unexpected treasure of Nepal.

On the shoulders of Ganesh Himal (Photo by Pat Morrow)

HISTORY OF NEPAL

The country known as Nepal is a conglomeration of as many different ethnic groups, languages, and cultures as it is biogeographic regions. This hostile terrain was settled by peoples fleeing invaders from all directions (see "Before the Gorkha Conquest" sidebar). They found solace in remote valleys and eventually became incorporated into myriad small kingdoms, until one sovereignty, Gorkha, led by Prithvi Narayan Shah, politically unified the country in the 1760s. Subsequently, for over a hundred years, until 1951, Nepal was authoritatively ruled by a sequence of hereditary prime ministers, the Ranas who overmastered the monarchy. During this period Nepal was essentially cut off from outside influences. Because of its forbidding mountains to the north and deadly malaria endemic in the Tarai to the south, Nepal was never successfully invaded by a major power. After an attempt at democracy in 1959, which threatened the status quo, political parties were outlawed; the country was said to be ruled by a system of participatory councils, but real power was vested in the king and his personally chosen secretariat.

BEFORE THE GORKHA CONQUEST

The Himalaya has always been viewed, it seems, as a safe haven for immigrants and refugees. One large movement of peoples into Nepal dates from the twelfth to fifteenth centuries CE, when many Hindus—particularly of Rajput origins—fled the Indian plains during the Mughal invasion. (CE, "Common Era," is a secular designation identical in numbering of years to AD, "Anno Domini." CE can also be thought of as "Current Era" or "Christian Era." BCE refers to before the Common Era and is identical to BC in the "Anno Domini" form.) Some refugees settled in the Kathmandu valley, but great numbers remained more rural, populating the lower valleys and hills all across the land. The PahAARi or hill people of the adjacent India hills (Kumaon and Garhwal, west of Nepal) are culturally, physically, and linguistically the "cousin-brothers" of the Nepali caste hill people who date from this refugee invasion.

The refugee arrivals were mostly Brahman (priest caste) and Chhetri (warrior caste, known as Kshatriya in India), along with low-caste craftspeople and menial laborers. They encountered a local population of Khas people and many ethnic groups, with whom they intermixed to various degrees—linguistically, economically, religiously, and socially. The caste Hindu migrants brought certain strong social and cultural traditions—a status hierarchy, language, religion, and a rice- and cattle-based economy that, blended with the local lifestyle and world view, formed what is today's unique Nepali national culture.

Nepali history until the Gorkha Conquest of the eighteenth century CE is one of petty principalities. These small hill kingdoms fell into two groups—the *baaisi raja*, or twenty-two kingdoms, of western Nepal, and the *chaubisi raja*, or twenty-four kingdoms, of central Nepal (between the Kali Gandaki and the Trishuli rivers). Many treks of central and western Nepal pass through these former kingdoms, and if you are observant you can see remnants of fortresses (*koT*) on many of the higher hilltops. The most famous fortress, now a sacred temple site, is the "Gorkha Darbar" (Gorkha palace) above Gorkha Bazaar in central Nepal. Other fortresses are found in high places along the Marsyangdi Khola trail (e.g., Lamjung Darbar, just west of Besisahar), near Pokhara (Kingdom of Kaski), and along the Kali Gandaki just north of Beni (Rakhu). The famous Malla Kingdom of far west Nepal encompassed parts of western Tibet and was so strong that it influenced political events as far east as the upper Kali Gandaki valley. The west Nepal Mallas (not to be confused with the later Malla rulers of Kathmandu's three city-states) ruled from about the twelfth to fourteenth centuries CE. They were apparently related to the Khas people, an ancient group whose presence as a power in the region had profound effects on all of Nepal's subsequent social history. They ruled simultaneously with the arrival of the migrant Rajputs. The fighting forces for these Nepali kingdoms were conscripted from local ethnic populations, such as the Magar and the Gurung.

It should be noted that various kingdoms of western Tibet, Ladakh, and Kashmir also had influence on northern Nepali affairs, particularly in the region of Jumla (far northwest) and Mustang (north central). Many Tibetan fortresses (*dzong*) may be seen in the northern border areas. The history of these regions is being rediscovered by scholars. The ancient alliances and influences of these many principalities, Nepali and Tibetan, are still felt in the internal political workings of the present-day nation of Nepal. And the silent and empty ruins speak to a rich and yet little-studied feudal past—part of its untapped sociohistorical and archaeological heritage. ❖

In early 1990, popular support for democracy again surfaced. The movement never had grassroots-level backing throughout the country, but was led by students and the educated in the large cities. Encouraged by the quest for democracy throughout the world at that time and the threat of more uprisings, the *jana andolan*, "people's movement," was able to overthrow monarchical rule and promulgate a new constitution with a constitutional monarch, but with real power vested in a popularly elected parliament.

However, rural people understood little of the new word, "democracy," and in the ensuing decade the blatant corruption of the new system was apparent to all. The systems of patronage and corruption that date back at least to the century of Rana rule have been maintained in the political mechanism with little change in Nepali society and politics. In 1990, few would have believed that two decades hence so little would be accomplished in the first twenty years of democracy. None of the governments since the 1990s has lasted more than two years.

In the mid-1990s, as a hierarchical class structure developed in place of the previously caste-based one, fraudulent elections became widespread. Globalization made promises to everyone but only delivered to the well-off. Many if not most rural and urban families became more impoverished but survived by going into debt and sending members abroad to support them by cash remittances. The mood of the country had regressed from optimism to frustration.

Among the political parties were several variations on communism. One splinter group declared a People's War in 1996 and managed to gain local support in the western part of the country, and the Maoist "People's War" subsequently spread throughout much of the country.

Young women found that waging a People's War was preferable to traditional oppression. Because there were so few state agencies in the rural areas, the Maoists could work relatively unhindered. Eventually, state reprisals resulted in many deaths of civilians as documented by human rights organizations. Terrorism has occurred on both sides (more deaths are attributed to police violence than to the rebels). Generally, tourists were not bothered, but there was a time when Maoists charged a fee and issued their own permits in some trekking areas in addition to the government-issued permits.

In late 2005, the Maoists came to the table and joined a coalition of seven leading parties to oppose the king who had dissolved parliament and was trying to reassert royal rule. In early 2006 widespread protests began. During this second people's movement, *jana andolan* II, hundreds of thousands of people marched in the capital defying martial law. The king capitulated, which eventually led to a formal dismantling of the monarchy and an end of the ten-year civil war.

Nationwide elections were held at the beginning of 2008. The Maoists unexpectedly won the highest number of parliamentary seats. The new government formally declared Nepal a democratic republic in May 2008 with none other than the leader of the Maoists, Pushpa Kamal Dahal, nicknamed Prachanda ("the fierce one"), as the first Prime Minister and leader of the republic.

Since that brief period of extraordinary cooperation, the factions quickly regressed to former times with spiteful bickering and soliciting of adversaries for power swaps. Prachanda resigned in May 2009 following a spat with the president over control of the military, and a tenuous coalition government was then formed with the Maoists in opposition and stalemate ensued.

Stagnation has resulted despite a mandate that the elected constituent assembly complete a peace process that had been agreed to by the coalition. Additionally, the assembly was supposed to write the republic's constitution within a two-year deadline but

THE GORKHA CONQUEST

The small central hill kingdom of Gorkha eventually became the most famous under its eighteenth-century leader Prithvi Narayan Shah. His grandiose plans were to unify the Himalaya into a great mountain state. In the 1760s he laid siege to the Malla Newar city-states of Kathmandu–PaaTan and BhatgAAU (Bhaktapur) and ultimately went on to control a vast territory, from Bhutan on the east to Kashmir on the west, parts of southern Tibet on the north, and territories of the British East India Company in the south. By the early 1800s, however, this Gorkha conquest was halted by the British, and the Gorkha domain was cut back to approximately its present boundaries, losing nearly a third of its land in the process. The British were so impressed with the fighting abilities of the Gorkha hill people, however, that they chose not to subjugate the kingdom. Instead, they allowed it to remain independent and a source of the warriors of Gorkha, whom they called Gurkhas, for the British Army. Around 200,000 Gurkhas fought for Britain during World Wars I and II, and more than 45,000 Nepalis have died in British uniform. Presently, some 3500 are serving in Britain's army.

During recruiting season nearly 20,000 Nepali applicants are pared down to around 300 to join the esteemed Gurkhas. The first cut is the hardest, a written test which reduces those eligible to under 1000, who are then put through rigorous physical tests and medical examinations. The former Shah kings of Nepal were the direct descendants of Prithvi Narayan Shah of Gorkha. Their dynasty ended after 239 years in May 2008 when Nepal became a democratic republic. ❖

---

failed, leading to a last-hour extension on May 28, 2010, of the assembly's term by a year.

Political feuding continues, with no easy solutions on the horizon. In much of the country outside of Kathmandu, particularly in the Tarai (southern plains), systemic corruption and the prolonged weakness and even absence of government has led to deterioration of the rule of law. A new constitution will hopefully set the agenda for a more functional government and prosperous Nepal, notwithstanding what the historical track record might otherwise suggest.

All the while, trekkers continue to travel, often in a modest style, and enjoy Nepali hospitality.

RESOURCES AND DEVELOPMENT

The economy is based on subsistence agriculture. Nepal has statistical characteristics of the world's poorest countries in terms of per capita gross domestic product, literacy, and infant mortality. Reductions in child mortality have been significant, but high maternal mortality continues. The population is aging. But the high rate of population growth—doubling time was about thirty years—has declined considerably. Local food production can't meet the needs, and hunger continues. Another serious problem is deforestation, especially in the Tarai, where after malaria was controlled forests were cut to clear land for agricultural use to feed the increasing population. Nepal's population is nearly 30 million (the world's fortieth largest), growing at over 1.6 percent a year.

Nepal, closed to foreigners and foreign influence until 1951, did not officially open its doors to tourists until a few years later. Nowadays, over 500,000 tourists visit the country each year, and a massive amount of foreign aid has been pushing Nepal on the road to "development." Major contributors of aid have been India, Japan, Germany,

France, China, and the United States. Having observed this process over many years, we see development along Western European and North American lines as basically counterproductive if not exploitive, but it is hidden by euphemisms that donors and recipients put forth. Throughout the world, aid is often tied to the purchasing of products and services from donor countries, and much of the funding pays generous expatriate salaries for work Nepalis could do themselves. Funds and activities of few projects trickle down to benefit the disadvantaged. Only 10 percent of development assistance is said to reach the lower class. Much of the funding leaks, finding its ways into the pockets of the nouveau riche—it has been estimated that anywhere between 10 to over 50 percent of flows get lost. This fosters a donor mentality in the government, NGOs, and INGOs (with over 27,000 and 223 organizations registered in 2009, respectively) and breeds unhealthy resentment in much of the population. A look at the burgeoning wealth of the middle class in Kathmandu, where homes cost more than in Western cities, attests to the leakage of funds. Thanks to structural adjustment policies carried out as a condition of receiving World Bank and International Monetary Fund loans, which resulted in devaluation of the rupee, foreigners receive excellent value for their hard currency in Nepal, while the poor there continue to suffer. One could remark that countries that have had modern "development" are worse off than countries that have not. Look at Korea, Taiwan, Japan, and China as examples of Asian miracles. They escaped the development process and prospered.

Producing rice in the monsoon has men plowing and women transplanting seedlings.
(Photo by Alonzo Lyons)

On the basis of outside advice and funding, Nepal has set aside the largest percentage of land relative to any other country in the world as national parks, 20 percent, with plans of increasing it to 25 percent, a process begun in 1973. Although the concept supposedly creates a haven for tourist needs, it has conflicted with resident people who have sometimes been resettled far from their villages with disastrous results. Discord between the needs of local peoples, with their increasing numbers, and those of businesses that cater to the tourism industry will continue.

Nepal's greatest economic resource is said to be the hydroelectric potential of its vast rivers fed by the Himalaya. Attempts at massive international development of this treasure have been thwarted so far, but numerous small projects electrify parts of the country. India would like to have a control in this asset and use it to help power the billion-plus people sitting south.

An unrecognized major asset is the self-respect (*ijat*) of the hill peasant, who was never subjugated by an external power. He or she works hard and, if away from the development mainstream, does not dwell on being economically poor. Only near the imbroglio of progress do you find people monetarily much wealthier talking about how poor they are. An insidious fault of "development" is that it teaches poverty.

In spite of this, many outsiders (the authors included) and Nepalis are strongly committed to trying to improve the situation in Nepal. Many work at the grassroots level and in organizations making significant changes. These efforts look at the bigger picture, recognizing the powerful forces at work, and try to change them through individual and group effort.

With an understanding of these harsh realities for the bulk of a resilient Nepali people, we hope to provide you with information to travel within this glorious, unforgettable country and to limit your perpetration of the bad effects of "development." As a typical visitor, physically isolated from the major problems of the world, but ever more exposed to them via an interconnected media, you will have on your trek an opportunity to come face to face with the inequities and dilemmas of some consequences of development. You may choose to shut the door and never venture forth again, or "help" some individuals which might do nothing more than assuage your own guilt while compounding a problem, or look at the big picture and then work for global change and an end to the hegemony of those who abuse power, within nations and among nations. Or you may effect some combination of these responses: "Be the change you want to see in the world" (M.K. Gandhi).

Rai girl met on the way to Khumbu
(Photo by Matt Freedman)

DISCOVERING NEPAL—ON FOOT

This land of contrasts beckons those who are willing to travel, as the majority of Nepalis do, on foot. Although there is a rapid amount of road building taking place, walking is the usual means of reaching most rural destinations. Nepal's road network is still one of the lowest in the world of mileage in proportion to area or population. The trails that trekkers use are also the transportation and communication routes for the local people.

Trekking, as described here, means travel by foot for many days. The term originated from a Dutch word for travel and came to be an Afrikaans word meaning a migration by oxcart. As far as the hills of Nepal are concerned, travel is by foot, not oxcart, and is essentially hiking or backpacking along extended routes that generally have facilities for food and lodging. Trekking routes pass through rural, sparsely settled areas, the home-land of the Nepali people. During a trek, travelers can spend nights in recently con-structed hotels, simple lodges, or they can camp by themselves or stay in the homes of local people. This last option is little used by tourists these days but still is the most hos-pitable form of travel available. Travelers can eat either local food or westernized food that is brought in by porters or trekkers themselves. Most of Nepal is not wilderness as the term is understood in the West. Visitors need to be cognizant of the local values and culture, a subject expanded upon in Chapter 3.

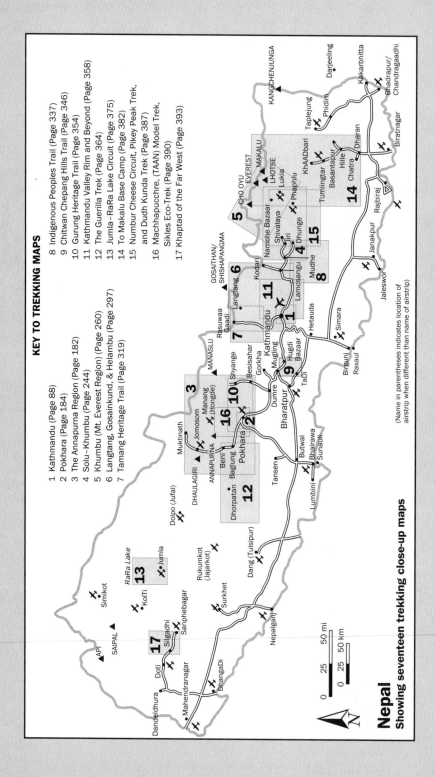

Nepal

Showing seventeen trekking close-up maps

KEY TO TREKKING MAPS

(Name in parentheses indicates location of airstrip when different than name of airstrip)

1

TREKKING STYLES AND DESTINATIONS

It's the richest banquet imaginable. For anyone with an appetite for fantastic legends, a thirst for color (especially red), and a general craving for utter theological wonder, visiting Nepal is a case study in all-you-can-eat.

—Jeff Greenwald, *Shopping for Buddhas*

Before trekking in Nepal, some basic decisions need to be made early. This chapter outlines the most important ones—namely, how, where, and when to trek. It also includes a summary of treks that will give you an idea of the best trek for you.

TREKKING STYLES AND RELATED ACTIVITIES

There are three basic approaches to trekking, but within each there are many variations as well as some related activities that can be enjoyed during treks. The style you choose depends on your budget, time available, and personal preferences. The areas you wish to visit dictate certain choices. Finally, your choice depends on what you want from your trek. An abundance of special-interest activities are available these days, focusing on areas of art, health matters, natural history, meditation, religion, flora and fauna, and beyond. Additionally, adventure sports include rock climbing, mountain biking, rafting, canyoning, kayaking, paragliding, bungee jumping, and more. These activities can be arranged at agencies that abound in Thamel, Kathmandu, and Lakeside, Pokhara.

Certain areas, such as the regions around Kangchenjunga, Upper Mustang, Manaslu (including Tsum valley), Humla and Mugu (northeastern Nepal), Dolpo, and Nar Phu (within ACAP), are only open to trekkers going through an agency. This is said to be an attempt by the government to lessen the environmental impact; however, financial reasons play an important role, too. Regulations are constantly in flux, and there is pressure to change the rules to make these areas more accessible to all tourists, a move that would help to spread the wealth to the local economy rather than the bulk going to a trekking agency. However, until then, these areas are considered "restricted" by the government and require not only involvement of an agency, but a minimum of two customers and special permits from the Immigration Department.

TREKKING WITHOUT A GUIDE

Trekking without a guide, also known as the "live on the land" approach, is popular among budget-conscious travelers. There is a popular phrase among trekkers, "No porters, no guides, no hassles!" If you are an independent-minded trekker wishing to travel without a guide or porter, then by all means do so. You will do fine, especially along

Trails that tourists use are also local routes; the majority of Nepalese travel on foot.
(Photo by R.C. Sedai)

the classic venues of Annapurna, Everest, and Langtang, Gosainkund, and Helambu, as these main routes receive the most trekkers and are well-established and a guide is not usually necessary for routefinding. However, consider hiring a guide in the short term for side trips within these areas and for the less-traveled routes.

Along the popular trails, enterprising Nepalis have established hotels and lodges that provide rooms for trekkers and offer international menus. Locals are very likely to run after you or at least shout if you take the wrong turn on a trail. It is easy for people to travel without a guide, carrying their own small loads. Along the popular routes, your main human contacts are with other, similar-minded trekkers. Local porters can usually be hired anywhere along a trek. (For more information on hiring and outfitting porters, see Chapter 2.) If you have porters, they can keep you on the right trails. This is a good way to learn Nepali, too, especially if traveling off the popular routes. Daily costs on the popular routes, not including any porters, can average $10 to $15 USD or more per person, depending on the amounts spent on food and accommodation, with rates increasing with elevation and remoteness. (With a porter, add another $10 a day and $15 for a guide; see the "Money" section of Chapter 2 for other estimated costs of trekking.) Disadvantages of this mode of travel can include spending time in Kathmandu organizing affairs, getting lost occasionally—especially when traveling off the standard routes—and being more limited in the areas you can travel to. The more trekkers in the party, the less interaction there will be with the local people, and the less intimate your experience with Nepal will be. Two trekkers are probably the limit for a close interaction with the people, unless most participants speak Nepali.

Trekkers who choose to travel without a guide are more likely to be disappointed in meeting some of their expectations than those who have their treks catered through a professional agency, although most people manage quite well. Trekkers who arrange travel with an agency to popular areas often remark they could have done it on their own and plan to next time. The advantage of trekking without a guide is that learning to deal without the cultural props you grew up with can be an educational and enlightening experience. Attempting to view the world through Nepali eyes may be the best lesson trekking in Nepal has to offer.

TREKKING WITH A GUIDE

Trekking with a guide can mean arranging and outfitting a large trek just as a professional agency would do, or it might mean simply hiring a guide to accompany a small group. A guide can keep the party on the correct trails and may sometimes cook, carry a load, or attend to other chores. Many guides are quite knowledgeable and can be a valuable resource to explain things seen, and not seen. Porters—that is, people hired strictly for load-carrying—can be taken on along the trail when necessary or hired in Kathmandu before starting a trek. The guide can take care of this. Parties may camp all the way; or they may eat and sleep in hotels and camp only where necessary. Camping is a good way for older people to travel as well as those wishing less uncertainty about the quality of food and accommodation, providing they bring along enough equipment and food for comfort. Many trekkers hire a guide for themselves if alone or for their small party, and travel using lodges and restaurants for accommodation and food. They enjoy the association with the guide and the company of other trekkers.

Recognize that if you have a staff of more than, say, four, it is unlikely that fast times can be made over long distances. The larger the party, the more likely that it will move at the customary pace for specific treks.

A guide can be hired either privately (sometimes at specific points along a trek for difficult portions), by asking at the hotel in Kathmandu or out in the hills, or through a trekking agency. The agency can also make other arrangements, such as organizing air and overland travel and providing equipment and porters. With the large number of agencies competing for business, they try to accommodate desired trekking arrangements even if the trek is less than completely organized.

Parties wishing more of a spirit of adventure—and a savings on wages—can hire an inexperienced guide. Such a person may be a seasoned trekking or mountaineering expedition porter or a young person eager to break into the business. Such people can be excellent and will often do much more than guide—they are often willing to cook, carry, and help in other ways. On Stephen's first trek in Nepal in 1969, he hired Nima Thundu, a young inexperienced Sherpa. They both learned a great deal and enjoyed themselves immensely. Nima went on to start the first company in Nepal producing trekking food.

In hiring a guide, one of the benefits may be a visit to the family's home. This is highly worthwhile even if a considerable detour is necessary. Oftentimes, trekkers discover it to be the highlight of their journey, especially if this takes place after the bulk of the trek. They experience wonderful hospitality and usually maintain a rewarding friendship with this individual and his or her family after they leave the country.

The advantage of trekking with a good guide is that it can allow considerable flexibility in the choice of route, diversions, and scheduling. However, be aware that there are instances where a guide (and sometimes a porter) reduces the freedom of movement and choice among lodges, schedules, stopping points, and more. This can result in frequent disagreements between the guide and guest, which is obviously undesirable, especially in remote, serene environments. Often, guides receive a commission for bringing trekkers to certain lodges and restaurants and become insistent about patronizing these establishments. It is important to set out guidelines before travel begins as to who will decide the extent of the daily schedule, including when and where you will stop, and expenses. It often helps to have something in writing to refer back to if necessary. Furthermore, it is important to read the trail descriptions to be able to decide route details for yourself.

With a guide along there is a greater opportunity for interacting with the local people encountered en route, especially if the party is small. Keep in mind that it is best to have a guide who is actually from the specific area that you will be visiting. However, arranging a guide after arriving in Nepal can be time-consuming, frustrating, and somewhat difficult. It can be helpful to seek the assistance of a local trekking agency. Trekking in a modest style is a good means of getting money into the hands of people in the hills of Nepal because the villagers, who provide food, run the inns, and work as porters, benefit directly. This is a true form of economic assistance, with less chance of leakage compared to top-heavy international aid projects. Costs for this style are considerably less than for professionally arranged treks and depend on the number of assistants hired. Independently hired guides usually ask for at least $10–$15 USD per day, and porters ask for the moon but usually will accept $8–$10 per day. Costs will begin at least 25 percent higher if going through an agency, and the porters and guides will receive appreciably less than these amounts.

For more about trekking with guides and porters, see Chapter 2.

TREKKING WITH A PROFESSIONAL AGENCY

If you go with an agency headquartered outside Nepal, most of your arrangements will be made with them. If you decide to go with a Nepali agency, then more preparations are needed, including the obvious one of getting to Nepal (air and bus travel are covered in Chapter 2). Flights to Kathmandu are usually heavily booked during the major tourist seasons of spring and autumn, and the sooner you start this process the better. If you plan to utilize a Nepali agency, contact several before choosing the one that fits your needs and seems responsible. A list of trekking agencies that are members of the Trekking Agents Association of Nepal (TAAN) can be found at their website, www.taan.org.np, as well as other useful information on trekking, mountaineering, and tourist-related activities.

Mountain Travel was the first trekking agency, founded in 1965 by the late Himalayan veteran Lt. Col. James Roberts, considered the father of trekking in Nepal. Agencies operate within Nepal today with few standards, as the industry is largely unregulated— although TAAN and the Nepal Association of Tour and Travel Agents (NATTA) are trying to change this by organizing and forming a powerful lobby. The recent economic downturn affected almost every place in the world, with acute effects in the tourism and travel industry. Frequently, businesses in Nepal close or change hands, and standards of performance vary widely. There are about 600 to 700 trekking agencies in Nepal. Some are shoestring operations, yet trekkers report satisfaction from even the smallest agency, and we recommend hiring locally when possible.

You may be able to get in touch with an agency over the Internet to arrange the kind of trip you desire. Most agencies have a website, making it possible to contact one that appeals to you to organize a trek. Be specific and clear in your correspondence, asking questions and stating your needs in a point-wise fashion. This should include dates, routes, equipment, food, staff, and so forth. Include plenty of information about your party, such as ages and experience. Some trekkers wait until they arrive in Nepal, visit various agencies, and shop around to see what can be organized for them at short notice. For one or two trekkers not planning a route far off the beaten path, this can work out fine. Some have done this in a day, but plan on two or three days, especially during peak times.

There is a trend for female travelers to hire female guides and porters, with increased satisfaction and the elimination of the potential of harassment. Additionally, a ruling by Nepal's Supreme Court in 2007 guaranteed the rights of gay, lesbian, bisexual, and transgender people, and tour companies have emerged that cater to this community. In fact, Nepal is home to one of South Asia's first openly gay lawmakers, Sunil Babu Pant. Some agencies cater to people with disabilities. Itineraries tend to take trekkers to less-visited areas, an added attraction. Information about such agencies might best be obtained from travel agents in your own country.

Many trekking agencies and organizations based in other countries operate treks for groups to various regions of Nepal. Be advised, there can be no congruence in the names of such agencies—for example, Gonzo Treks based in Truth or Consequences, New Mexico, may not operate through Gonzo Treks in Kathmandu. Glossy brochures present superlatives. The actual treks are usually subcontracted to one of the trekking agency operators in Nepal. You can deal directly with the Nepali agency from home beforehand and thereby have more of your money go directly to services in Nepal.

This mode of travel is expensive, starting at a minimum of $20–$25 USD per day of trek, but offers a degree of luxury that is not often available in the other modes. Treks are organized for both large (ten to fifteen people) and small (one to two people) groups and are usually conducted by Sherpa guides called sirdars, some of whom are famous for their mountaineering exploits on Himalayan expeditions. The guides speak sufficient English to allay fears of language difficulties. A large retinue of porters ensures that nothing essential to the comfort and well-being of trekkers is left behind. The parties usually camp in tents near villages and skilled cooks prepare fine meals. (If you prefer to eat Nepali fare rather than bringing along canned and packaged goods, suggest this to the agency. Eating locally might even reduce costs as well as reduce waste and impact on the environment.) Trekkers camping in cold, high places, however, will not be as warm as those who stay in lodges where some heat source typically exists.

The trek parties often have someone with medical knowledge along, and emergencies can usually be handled more quickly than in noncommercial groups. There is also no need to spend time planning for all these arrangements in Kathmandu. Trekking with an agency means there is an avenue for complaint if there are problems, something that is important to some visitors. Response is usually better when complaints are made through an agency in your own country.

Agency trek parties usually have to stick to a predetermined route and schedule, so there is less leeway for interesting diversions or layovers. The maximum distance covered per day is usually limited by how far a laden porter can go. Members of large parties generally keep together. Trekkers in these professionally organized parties are usually rather insulated from the local people encountered en route. Participants tend to relate exclusively to one another, to the guides, and to other employees of the trek. In groups where you don't know the other travelers beforehand, personality clashes and acrimony can develop.

If going with an agency, ask how many rest days are built into the schedule at high altitude. Also ask about flexibility in the schedule should a member of the party develop altitude illness. Be aware that most of the serious cases of altitude illness develop among group trekkers, because these parties try to stick to a predetermined schedule, and peer pressure pushes people beyond their limits. If the party will sleep above 14,000 feet (4270 m), do the guides carry oxygen, and do they have an altitude chamber? (For details, see "Altitude Illness" in Chapter 5.) What is the name of the agency's liability insurance company and the amount of insurance it carries? The standard is at least $1 million. Has the staff had wilderness medical care training?

Given the scarcity of firewood in Nepal, it is necessary for the trekker going with an agency to choose one that minimizes its impact on the environment. Ask how they handle garbage. Do they carry out non-burnables? Has the staff attended the Kathmandu Environmental Education Project (KEEP) workshop on responsible trekking, as attested to by a certificate? (For more on KEEP, see the sidebar in Chapter 4.) Ask whether all the cooking, including meals for the porters, is done on kerosene/gas. Ask whether porters are provided with sufficient equipment so they don't need to huddle around fires at night to keep warm. Inspect the porters' equipment to verify. The following additional questions for trekking companies are suggested by the International Porter Protection Group (IPPG):

1. Does the company follow IPPG's five guidelines on porter safety (see "Guides and Porters" in Chapter 2)?
2. What is their policy on equipment and health care for porters?
3. What do they do to ensure the trekking staff is properly trained to look after porters' welfare?
4. What is their policy on training and monitoring porter care?
5. Do they ask about treatment of porters in their post-trek feedback questionnaire to clients?

Furthermore, ask the prospective outfitter for references so you can talk to the people who have taken the trip that interests you. Much of the experience is leader-dependent, so talk to people who have been with that leader. Talk to him or her directly and get a sense of what your experience with that person will be like. Question background, wilderness and medical skills, language ability, and so forth. Going with a leader who has particular expertise in your area of interests would be an important factor in choosing a trek with an agency. These days, to save costs, many agencies use a local leader, and contacting that person from home may be more difficult. Find out about the subcontractor and exactly what is included in the price. Often extra expenses are tacked on later. Determine your responsibilities. With some discount agencies, you have to do your share. Ask whether or not the agency screens the clients for potential health problems and level of physical fitness (or just for the size of their pocketbook).

Some agencies offer teahouse/trekker lodge-style treks. In these, accommodations and food are contracted out to the various establishments en route. This results in a cheaper trek, compared to the traditional camping style. A guide is along to take care of logistics and interpret features about the countryside. This mode is suitable for small groups heading for the popular trails. With increasing competition among the many agencies operating today in Nepal, you can negotiate partial arrangements with an agency. This could include as little as getting permits and arranging a guide, or perhaps porters. The costs, exclusive of airfares and charters, run from about $20–$25 USD to over $100 USD per person per day and vary according to the length of the trek and the number of people in the party. This kind of travel is especially suited for those

Landing in Simikot in Humla will bring you to Nepal's most remote district.
(Photo by David Citrin)

who have neither the time nor the desire to make their own arrangements but wish to enjoy the scenery of the country. In contrast to people who prefer other styles of trekking, those who embark on this type of trek are paying for comfort and security.

Some people argue that an agency trek is preferable because your food is carried from Kathmandu and does not deplete local resources. Similarly, when the trekkers' food is prepared on kerosene stoves, there is less pressure on local wood resources. On such treks, however, all of the food for the porters is purchased along the route, and some food for trekkers may be purchased locally, as well. The argument that sirdars for trekking groups will get the best prices for local foods does not hold up. When the primary concern is that the trek go well, cooks and sirdars pay high prices for food items. As a consequence, the price for villagers can increase, too. Porters almost always use local wood, and for big treks there are many more porters than trekkers. So the net impact of such travel is found to be less environmentally and economically friendly than small-scale treks.

There is little sharing of profits with the locals on agency treks, and a considerable portion of the money to support these treks leaves Nepal to pay for imported food and equipment. One estimate suggested that 67 percent of Nepal's earnings from packaged tourism is spent to import goods and services required by visitors. It is something to consider; however, we do not mean to discourage travel with an agency. It is best to be clear on your hopes, needs, and means and travel accordingly.

CHOOSING A TREKKING STYLE

It is basically true that "anybody" can trek in Nepal—if they try to match level of experience to the difficulty of the journey. Given the tremendous travel expense, time commitment, and, for many, a once-in-a-lifetime opportunity, ambition can easily outstrip ability. Trekking in the Himalaya was once considered at the high end of the spectrum of hiking, backpacking, and mountaineering. Often, mountaineers experienced in ranges such as the Alps, Rockies, or Sierra become "mere" trekkers in the Himalaya, where routes carry them thousands of feet above the summits of their home ranges.

But these days, less experienced hikers elect to undertake harder treks. Walking in the mountains is a skill that requires training and experience. The number of tourists who have fallen from trails (fatally and nonfatally) is up dramatically. Inexperienced hikers have become incapacitated by severe musculoskeletal problems that could have been prevented by adequate training.

Trekking should be regarded as an expedition: you are often far from any form of outside help. Unless you are experienced and confident of your self-sufficiency skills, first treks should be on established tourist trails that offer a minimum of difficulty and no dangerous passes. The scenery in Nepal is no less exotic because other outsiders have seen it before you. As your experience, skills, and confidence grow, you can plan more challenging, isolated, and adventurous treks.

There is a laudable worldwide movement afoot to promote what is variably known as "ecotourism," "alternative tourism," "discerning tourism," "gentle tourism," or "tourism with insight." Advocates try to promote travel that is consistent with local needs and attempt to maintain local cultural values and remain environmentally sensitive. Agencies may advertise such travel, but it can certainly be done outside of an organized trek—and done better.

More Time Than Money. If you crave adventure, have plenty of time but limited money, want to adapt your schedule to circumstances, and want to interact with local people as much as possible, then organize your own trek.

More Money Than Time. An organized trek with one of the well-known agencies may be for you if you have a limited amount of time yet want to cover a major route and can accept limitations in flexibility. An agency trek may be an attractive option if you enjoy the idea of camping in Nepal with food prepared to familiar tastes and with all arrangements made for you. One disadvantage of such treks is the relative lack of close contact with the local people. Others may not like the seeming colonial relationship between the tourists and the staff.

Of course, the dichotomy is not quite so cut and dried. Many agencies allow some flexibility in scheduling, and with increasing competition they try to adapt treks to your needs.

Another "decision tree" for the first-time trekker to Nepal is the following: If you are on a tight budget, basically go trekking on a popular route and stay in local inns. If you enjoy carrying a pack, you need not hire a porter—but if you do not want to be inhibited with anything heavier than a day pack, hire a local porter. Those with more funds, and perhaps more anxiety about doing it themselves, often hire a guide and porters, usually through an agency in Kathmandu, and stay in local hotels.

If you have more money to spend and have your own group, organize a trek through an agency and stay in tents. If you do not have a group and are willing to travel with strangers, join an organized group through one of the agencies in Kathmandu or Pokhara. Those with a lot of money and wanting as few inconveniences as possible should join an organized trek from their home country.

TREKKING ALONE

Trekking alone—that is, without other foreign companions—is the best way to get to know Nepal. Those trekking alone would be wise to hire a guide or a porter, especially on trails with few foreigners. Take time and ask around. You should be able to find someone suitable, not necessarily English-speaking, which will be an opportunity to learn some Nepali. If traveling alone along the popular trails without a porter, you will find it easy to meet up with similar-minded people and travel together. It is also easy to meet and join up with other trekkers in Kathmandu. People advertise for trekking partners on bulletin boards at the Kathmandu Environmental Education Project (KEEP) office and in tourist-frequented places (see Chapter 2 for directions to KEEP and other key locations in Kathmandu).

Women especially should not travel alone but should try to find a female guide or porter. Nepalis find it difficult to understand why foreigners, especially women, would travel alone—indeed, most Nepali women would not. As unpleasant as it may sound, local people may consider a woman walking alone to be a witch or person of low morals. An agency in Pokhara, Three Sisters Adventure Trekking (www.3sistersadventure.com), has worked since the mid-1990s to empower Nepalese women and has trained over 700 women, providing female guides and porters for female trekking parties. (Chapter 2 looks more closely at the status of women in Nepal and efforts to create equitable opportunities for women through employment.)

The same caution applies to men, although sometimes one may see a Nepali man traveling alone. On a trek in which Stephen went with three porters, Tupi Pasang, a yak herder, remarked to him, "You must be a poor man in your country; you're traveling alone and with few porters or supplies."

There have been instances of attacks on trekkers, usually those who are alone in remote areas. Unfortunately, we can no longer state that you are perfectly safe from human harm in Nepal, but if you follow the principles outlined in Chapter 3 and are sensitive to your hosts, you should have few problems. Although lawlessness is on the rise, particularly in the southern plains, due to a succession of weak governments, travel in Nepal is certainly safer than in almost every other country, including your homeland.

TREKKING WITH YOUR FAMILY

Children need not be left at home in order for the adults of a family to enjoy a trek in Nepal. Certainly a trek with children will be different from one without children, but it need not be any less enjoyable or memorable. In fact, children can be social icebreakers in an alien land; they provide a common link with which the local people can identify.

When Stephen first came to Nepal in 1969, no one trekked with children except occasional expatriates working there; now you often see families along the popular trails. The Nepali village people are open and friendly, and the sight of a trekking family will interest them. While you eat, they will often care for the child, holding, comforting, and playing with him or her. Although a small child may initially be overwhelmed by the interest of outsiders, an exciting cultural exchange can be encouraged if the child becomes accustomed to the local people. Flexibility in the itinerary is particularly important if the family hopes to achieve this communication. Many of the difficulties encountered in trekking with children in Nepal can be overcome if the family first tries some overnight excursions near home. In fact, we would not recommend that a family attempt trekking in Nepal if they have not done overnight hikes together at home. Chapter 4 looks more closely at food, lodging, trail activities, and other day-to-day aspects of trekking with children, and Chapter 5 includes an important section on health care for children. Those sections should be read concurrently with this one.

It is best not to travel with very young children, perhaps those under five years of age, unless parents have prior trekking experience in Nepal. If a child is over five, it is advisable to have more than one child along for companionship. Families who wish to trek independently of an agency will find it easiest to take one of the popular routes where lodges cater to trekkers.

Do not assume that treks must be modest in scope. One family with children aged four and six trekked with another family with a child of six. They covered almost 500 miles (800 km) in fifty-five days, from Pokhara to Baitadi in the extreme western part of Nepal. This trek was more ambitious than most people would choose to undertake with children of that age, but for them it was a wonderful, unforgettable experience. The two families, by carrying moderate packs themselves weighing 30–50 pounds (13–23 kg) and living off the land insofar as possible, were able to get by with only two porters. They never carried any of the children except across streams or rickety bridges. The pace was slower than that of normal adults, but they compensated for this by increased attention to peripheral activities, such as photography and bird-watching. The children thrived on the physical exercise. They received a lot of personalized attention from their parents and were constantly stimulated by new sights and activities. At the end of the day, they had little energy left and usually fell asleep soon after dinner.

It may not be inappropriate to consider taking older children out of school for a trek. Understanding school officials will probably agree that what the children learn on the trip far outweighs any loss in classroom learning. You can bring materials to home-school during the time away. Stephen did this with his daughter, Maia, and when she returned she was ahead of her class! Parents can help children keep journals of their activities and adventures, which will aid them with their writing and provide fascinating memories of the trip, a resource for later use.

Younger children need not be left at home. Infants can trek, though we would recommend that only breast-fed infants be taken. One trekking family with a two-year-old found it most convenient that the child was still breast-feeding (not exclusively, of course). In Nepal children nurse at their mothers' breasts until they are comparatively quite old. Certainly this is the most sanitary method of feeding, and it has many other health benefits.

There are many practical and cultural ideas to consider to make your family trek both fun and full of pleasant memories. These are discussed in Chapter 4.

TREKKING WITH DISABILITIES

There is increased recognition of the benefits of outdoor activities for those with physical and mental disabilities who face challenges different from the usual. Quadriplegics, amputees, the blind, the hearing-impaired, and many others have enjoyed travel off the road in Nepal. Such people should have had some experience in their home country first in order to adapt equipment and procedures. Many of the trekking agencies will be helpful in fine-tuning the adaptations for Nepal. While some risks are heightened by trekking in Nepal, the benefits may be greater, especially in terms of increased self-esteem and broadened perspectives. Nepali society is very understanding of people with disabilities, as such individuals have always been accepted into the fabric of daily life.

Two quadriplegics who undertook a three-day trek north of Pokhara came back with very positive impressions. The trekking agent prepared special *Doko* (woven baskets) to carry the individuals and organized three porters per person who switched off on steep ascents while much longer stretches were covered on more moderate terrain. Local attitudes and those of the staff were not patronizing and were fully supportive.

Individuals with chronic medical problems or debility can undertake treks providing they understand the lack of access to modern medical facilities. Seniors on popular treks can undertake short daily distances, interspersed with frequent rests, and have all the duffel carried by porters. Although many such individuals travel with agencies, there is no reason why you could not do it independently and stay in people's homes, rather than in lodges, the book's prescription for ensuring an intimate experience in Nepal.

TREKKING IN THE MONSOON

The monsoon has routinely begun toward the beginning of June and usually lasts through September; normally, it arrives first in eastern Nepal and works its way westward. Although many consider it out of the question, the joys of trekking during the rainy season have been discovered by a select few "Nepalophiles." There are several reasons to consider joining these eccentrics. Many people can come to Nepal only during the Western summer holidays, which correspond to the monsoon. Some want to trek when popular trails are not packed with foreigners, or they are interested in the plant and animal life that is most spectacular at this time, as are the waterfalls. Although there is plenty of cloud cover, it is undeniably a beautiful time of the year—a season when the

Vegetation is lush and waterfalls are at their grandest during the monsoon.
(Photo by Gail Robson)

heavy haze, sometimes referred to as the Asian Brown Cloud, that now reaches up to Himalayan heights is absent (see the sidebar later in this chapter). During the monsoon, everything is lush and green and the air is oxygen-rich. The clouds perform dramatically and periodically part to reveal the splendor of spectacular vistas. Mist-shrouded mountain views during the monsoon are unforgettable. The high country is alive with activity as people pasture their animals on the lush upper slopes.

During the monsoon, Nepal is much like it was years ago, except that now there are better bridges, solar panels, mobile phones, portable radios, more supplies available, and children who may be out of the habit of asking for a rupee, pen, or sweet when they see you. There will be occasional downpours throughout the day. When a deluge arrives, find the nearest shelter and wait it out, as cloudbursts usually do not last long— although some can last for several days. You can plan your route to get either behind (north of) the Himalaya in the so-called rain shadow (north of Pokhara), or to the far west, or into the Everest Region (Khumbu) to experience less rainfall. See the climatological data in "Weather," in the following section.

There are problems, however, with trekking during the monsoon. Everything tends to get soaked. Trails are often muddy, usually wet, and sometimes treacherously slippery. It can be hot and muggy at low altitudes, although more comfortable higher up. Distant views are clouded most of the time. Roads, trails, and bridges may wash out, necessitating time-consuming and difficult detours. What may have been a trickle in the dry season becomes a deep, fast torrent in the monsoon. Travel often involves fording streams or even rivers. At times you may have to wait a day or two for the water level to drop enough for a safe ford. To make matters worse, hordes of leeches tyrannize the forests above 4000 feet (1200 m) (see the "Animal Bites" section, Chapter 5, and the sidebar on leeches in Chapter 6), while mosquitoes are a menace at lower elevations.

Yet, just as you can adjust to trekking in Nepal during the dry season, so you can adapt to the monsoon. Certain items of equipment are essential: a waterproof cover for your pack, sheets of plastic for the porter loads, an umbrella, a hat, ski poles, and footwear with good traction, preferably running shoes or cross-training shoes, or boots with flexible soles. Light skirts for women, preferably with a hem about calf length, and long shorts for men are the most practical clothing. Waterproof rain parkas are not very useful—if you do not get wet from the outside, you might soak in sweat from the inside. Gear made of fabric that breathes yet is waterproof (such as Gore-Tex), if kept clean, is suitable for the higher altitudes. Jackets with underarm vents allow considerable ventilation, as do such pants with side vents. Fleece (synthetic pile) clothing or garments of synthetic downlike material are useful in the wet high altitudes.

In planning a monsoon trek, do not plan on covering too much distance in a short time. It is difficult to equal dry-season trekking times. Many of the trails will be different during the monsoon. Drier ridges are usually taken instead of the flooded valley bottoms. Take time to enjoy village life, to sample the fruits and vegetables in season, and to enjoy the prodigious plant life. And do not tell too many people how much you enjoyed it lest the secret get out!

MOUNTAINEERING

According to the Nepal Tourism Board, there are currently some 326 peaks in Nepal open for mountaineering. Climbing permits for expedition peaks including eight of the world's ten highest mountains are issued by the Mountaineering Section of the Ministry of Culture, Tourism, and Civil Aviation. Besides the many expeditionary peaks, the highest mountains, there are thirty-three minor peaks, so-called "trekking summits," that can be attempted by obtaining permits issued by the Nepal Mountaineering Association (NMA). Eighteen of these are the original trekking peaks, opened in 1981, and are categorized as Group B. An additional fifteen peaks were added in September 2002 and are referred to as Group A peaks.

The fact that they are called trekking summits in no way implies that they are trivial. Some are difficult and dangerous, and some have only had a few ascents. These high-altitude tourist summits are not suitable for trekkers who do not have substantial experience in alpine climbing. In one tragedy, eleven people (ten clients and a Sherpa) were killed when a climber presumably slipped on a steep, icy slope and brought down the rest in domino fashion. Poor judgment and technique accounted for the disaster, one of the largest in deaths in a single climbing accident in the Himalaya. Further information on the eighteen Group B climbs can be obtained from Bill O'Connor's book *The Trekking Peaks of Nepal,* and more from mountaineering journals, trekking agencies, and the climbing community.

If you have been to Kala Pattar and other high-altitude trekking destinations in Nepal and are looking for new "summits," are trekking peaks for you? If you are not a mountaineer, by and large the answer is no. Although some are not technically difficult, they do involve mountaineering skills, unlike almost all the treks described in this book, which require just walking. Considerable familiarity with climbing on rock, snow, and ice, camping on snow, and the understanding of objective hazards is necessary.

To attempt one of these peaks, apply to the Nepal Mountaineering Association (NMA), located in Naxal, Nag Pokhari, Kathmandu (www.nepalmountaineering.org). Fees, payable at the time of application, are nonrefundable. Climbers can apply after they arrive in Nepal. There are specific regulations to follow. Although it is not necessary to use a trekking agency, most climbers do, and having an NMA guide along is a requisite.

WHERE AND WHEN TO TREK

In choosing a trek, consider the following: the time available, the strength and ability of the members of the party, and the desires of the trekkers. Certain treks offer majestic mountain scenery, others a glimpse of hill life in Nepal, and still others spectacular floral displays. Routes can be linked to provide many different experiences. Some entail entering potentially dangerous mountain terrain. Finally, the time of year is very important, as certain treks are difficult if not impossible during heavy snowfalls. Some trekkers are very uncomfortable in the pre-monsoon heat. If nature is your primary interest, see "Observing Plants and Animals," later in this chapter, for suggested best times to visit. Read the introduction to each region under "Where to Go" for a sense of the area.

With the increased popularity of trekking, lodges abound in places where there are no villages and where no Nepalis would otherwise be living. This is outside of normal seasonal migrations from higher, cooler areas to lower, warmer areas and vice versa. That is, in some places, lodges exist solely to cater to tourists. Recognize that in such areas, as well as in highly visited regions and urban areas, you will have less opportunity to sample Nepali life as it was, and still is, under the influence of normal routines. The most popular times to trek, in decreasing order, are October, November, March, April, December, February, January, September, May, August, June, July.

In making a choice, understand that the first few days of a trek get you used to the rhythm. Little may be gained by the neophyte Nepal visitor who is out for just a couple of days. People do undertake such brief treks, but we suggest you aim for at least a week on the trail for starters.

CLIMATOLOGICAL DATA FOR SELECTED TREKKING TOWNS

(First line: Precipitation [mm]. Second line: Temperature—Max/Min [°C])

Town (Altitude [meters/feet])	Jan.	Feb.	March	April	May	June	July	Aug.	Sept.	Oct.	Nov.	Dec.
Kathmandu	18	11	33	54	83	270	383	338	160	62	7	2
(1336/4383)	19/2	21/3	25/7	28/10	30/14	29/18	28/19	28/19	27/17	27/12	23/7	20/2
Trishuli	20	23	29	57	90	319	463	474	265	107	14	5
(541/1775)	22/7	25/8	30/13	34/17	33/19	33/21	32/20	32/20	31/18	30/15	27/12	23/8
Langtang	10	20	30	25	60	80	175	215	90	10	5	5
(3500/11,483)	2/-11	3/-10	8/-6	14/-2	17/2	18/7	19/9	18/8	16/7	15/2	9/-8	8/-10
Pokhara	26	25	50	87	292	569	809	705	581	224	19	1
(827/2713)	19/6	21/8	26/12	30/15	30/18	29/20	29/21	29/21	28/20	26/17	23/11	20/7
Lumle	28	45	52	194	318	902	1522	1339	932	294	23	2
(1615/5300)	13/5	14/6	19/10	22/13	22/14	23/17	22/17	23/17	21/16	20/14	16/9	13/6
Marpha	14	13	27	22	26	44	63	58	45	58	7	2
(2667/8750)	10/-1	12/0	15/3	18/5	19/7	21/11	21/12	21/12	20/11	17/7	14/2	12/0
Jomosom	20	18	23	15	11	17	41	54	35	37	2	2
(2713/8900)	12/-3	13/-1	16/2	20/4	23/7	25/12	25/14	25/14	23/11	19/5	15/1	13/-2
Chame	3	71	72	—	50	106	182	145	65	59	8	24
(2615/8580)	9/-3	13/1	14/1	20/7	19/6	21/11	21/10	21/10	19/10	17/6	14/1	11/-3
Jumla	32	40	43	27	40	70	162	173	92	39	1	4
(2329/7640)	11/-2	13/-3	17/0	22/3	24/6	24/13	23/15	24/15	23/12	24/6	19/-4	15/-5
Jiri	18	20	47	71	139	381	599	605	337	93	15	3
(1905/6250)	13/0	15/1	19/4	22/8	22/12	23/16	23/17	23/17	22/15	20/10	17/4	14/1
Namche Bazaar	26	23	34	26	41	140	243	243	165	78	9	39
(3446/11,300)	7/-8	6/-6	9/-3	12/1	14/4	15/6	16/8	16/8	15/6	12/2	9/3	7/-6
Tengboche	13	24	23	25	29	95	280	265	140	72	9	2
(3867/12,887)	4/-9	5/-9	9/-6	12/-4	14/-1	14/3	14/5	14/4	13/2	12/-2	8/-7	6/-7
Taplejung	15	32	55	111	243	335	448	400	271	82	14	4
(1783/5850)	14/4	15/6	19/9	22/2	23/14	24/17	24/18	24/17	23/16	22/13	18/8	15/5
Ilam	10	8	18	62	139	321	463	280	215	81	8	2
(1300/4265)	16/9	18/10	23/14	25/16	25/17	25/18	25/18	25/19	25/17	25/16	21/12	18/8

INCHES

```
0          1          2          3          4          5          6
|ıııı|ıııı|ıııı|ıııı|ıııı|ıııı|ıııı|ıııı|ıııı|ıııı|ıııı|ıııı|
|     |     |     |     |     |     |     |     |     |     |     |
0          ·     50               100              150
```
MILLIMETERS

TEMPERATURE

```
°F
-40                    32          98.6
|        0             | 40            80          | 120
|        |             |  |           |            |  |
-40      -20           0             20           40
°C                                                 37
```

WEATHER

The usual trekking season lasts from October to May. In October and November the skies are generally clear with outstanding views. This is the most popular time for trekking. Although the monsoon usually begins in June, it has of late been slow to start. It is usually over by the beginning of October, but sometimes it has dragged on for much of that month. Occasional short storms may dump considerable snow at high altitudes, and above 10,000 feet (3050 m) the temperature often goes below freezing at night.

December and January are the coldest months, but there is little snowfall. Excellent clear views at altitude are common, although haze often sits in valleys more than it used to and reaches the upper heights, too, obscuring the clarity of views. Much of this air pollution arises from the northern plains of India, one of the most densely populated regions on the planet. Haze drifts north from fires lit there as well as in Nepal for winter warmth and cooking, the burning of fields, general industrial output, especially brick making, and the incineration of rubbish, a common practice in Asia. Temperatures constantly plunge below freezing at night above 10,000 feet (3050 m) and below 0°F (−18°C) at altitudes above 14,000 feet (4300 m). Some inhabitants of the northern Himalayan region head south for the winter at this time. It can be a hauntingly beautiful time of the year to trek.

February and March bring warmer weather but more frequent storms and considerable snowfall at higher altitudes. Birds and flowers, especially rhododendrons, are seen at the lower altitudes. Toward the end of March, the haze—caused by air pollution and

CLIMATE

Nepal has a monsoon climate, but there are fears that it is being disrupted by global climate change. The heavy rains of the monsoon, originating in the Bay of Bengal, usually occur from June to September and begin in the eastern parts—two to three weeks can separate the onset of the monsoon in the east from that in the west. More rain falls in the east, which is closer to the moisture source. At high altitudes, above about 20,000 feet (6000 m), there is snow rather than rain. In addition, a less well-defined winter monsoon occurs from December to the end of March. This precipitation takes the form of snow at altitudes above about 8000 feet (2440 m).

The monsoon is caused by the movement of moist air north and west from the Bay of Bengal. As the moist air rises, it cools and condenses as rain. This precipitation falls on the southern side of the main Himalayan range. Generally, there is less precipitation at higher altitudes, because the clouds have already released moisture at the lower altitudes. When the resulting dry air mass crosses the Himalaya, it has little moisture left to deposit on the northern sides. A rain screen thus exists on the north sides of the Himalaya, producing the xerophytic conditions in Dolpo and Mustang.

The winter rains enable Nepalis to grow a second crop at lower altitudes. Generally, these crops are grown up to the altitude at which clouds hang during the monsoon, as the clouds limit the amount of sun available then. Rain falling on north and west faces evaporates less, so there tends to be greater variety in the flora in these areas. Shady areas also have more varied vegetation. While trekking, observe the changes in vegetation on different terrain, and try to predict local climatic factors that produce them. ❖

dust, mostly from the Gangetic plain of India—often obscures distant views. In addition, it becomes much warmer in the regions below 3000 feet (1000 m).

April and May are less suitable for trekking because of the heat—sometimes 100°F (38°C)—at altitudes below 3000 feet (1000 m). Also, haze mars distant views of the peaks. During these months, however, you encounter many species of plant and animal life not seen at other times. As the season progresses, the magnificent rhododendrons bloom at higher and higher altitudes until the flowers reach tree line. Occasional pre-monsoon storms pass through and clear the haze and cool the atmosphere for a few days. While temperatures below freezing can be encountered above 12,000 feet (3600 m), it becomes warm below 8000 feet (2500 m) and almost oppressive below 3000 feet (1000 m).

Heavy snowfalls, especially during January, February, and March, limit travel on passes, such as Thorung La in Annapurna, the Trashi Labsta, Cho La, Renjo La and Kongma La in Khumbu, the Laurebina La near Gosainkund, Ganja La between the upper Langtang valley and Helambu, and the high route from Pokhara to Jumla.

As noted earlier, trekking in the monsoon (June through the end of September) can be undertaken by the keen or experienced. Rain, mist, and fog can be expected almost daily, making the rarefied air more oxygen-rich than it would otherwise be, and clouds part occasionally to give spectacular views of the mountains. The flora is usually at its most colorful, and the mid-elevation meadows and forests are teeming with butterflies. Troublesome leeches also abound in forested areas above 4000 feet (1200 m) and must be dealt with during the monsoon (see the "Animal Bites" section, Chapter 5, and the sidebar on leeches, Chapter 6).

Mountain weather is highly unpredictable. Classic signs of a storm approaching, such as a cirrus-clouded sky or a fall in barometric pressure, can be misleading. Occasionally, unexpected heavy storms can wreak havoc. In October 1987, November 1995, October 1996, and October 2005 surprise storms dumped several feet of snow in all the high areas, resulting in some trekker deaths.

The table above gives precipitation and maximum and minimum temperatures for various trekking locations. You can estimate temperatures for other nearby locations by a simple formula: For every rise of 100 meters the temperature falls 0.65°C; or for a rise of 1000 feet it falls 3.5°F. Metric units are used; conversion scales are given below the table.

WHERE TO GO

First-time trekkers on one of the popular routes are often surprised to discover that travel in Nepal is neither a wilderness experience like they are used to back home nor a stark cross-cultural experience. The Ministry of Tourism, Nepal Tourism Board, the Annapurna Conservation Area Project, and other agencies are working hard to create food and accommodation standards that agree with tourist tastes. The Nepal of legend is there but not on the popular trails—at least not without effort to find it.

Some people do not want to be one of a hundred trekkers in Lobuche (Khumbu) in early November. Others delight in meeting travelers encountered everywhere on the trek. Use the information in this book to choose a route and a time when you will not meet many other trekkers if this is your inclination. On a popular route, if you want to find an experience out of the ordinary, hang around in less popular sites, hire a local guide (not one from Kathmandu), and stay in people's homes rather than in lodges.

Certain areas, such as the regions around Kangchenjunga, Upper Mustang, Manaslu (including the Tsum valley), Mugu and Humla (northeastern Nepal), Dolpo, and Nar Phu (within ACAP), are only open to trekkers going through an agency. These

SUBCONTINENTAL POLLUTION

Asian Brown Cloud (also known as Atmospheric Brown Cloud) is a layer of airborne pollutants up to 2 miles thick that covers much of the Indian subcontinent in the dry season. It is estimated that 75 to 80 percent of the smog is anthropogenic and is particularly heavy and noticeable from November to April when precipitation that would otherwise scrub the air is scant. The contaminants can reach halfway around the world within a week. A similar bloc of particulate air, referred to as Asian "Dust," occurs over East Asia, carrying the pollutants from industry and human activity and fine sand particles from the Gobi Desert and steppes of the Mongolian Plateau. The combined effect of these masses of airborne pollutants on health in Asia, which has over half of the world's population, is a cause for growing concern, as is the effect on global weather patterns.

The southern Tarai of Nepal is part of the Indo-Gangetic plain, which has one of the highest population densities in the world. People in Nepal, India, Bangladesh, and Pakistan regularly use unclean fuels such as wood, coal, and kerosene for domestic cooking fires, and often burn garbage produced from everyday commerce, including plastics. Other practices that produce smog include the burning of harvested fields and industrial processes such as combustion in kilns for brickmaking. The problem becomes compounded in the winter and dry seasons, when cleansing rain is scarce and more wood and garbage are burned for warming fires.

The haze from the activities of this dense aggregate of humanity is considered a cause for extreme weather events. The dark layer of smog absorbs sunlight, causing it to warm up, and thus affects the regional climate and beyond. An increase in average global temperatures might even be more pronounced at high elevations as some data suggest, and some Himalayan glaciers are retreating at an alarming rate. Carbon deposits on snow and ice result in more solar absorption and exacerbate the problem.

Although Nepal is said to be one of the lowest-per-capita emitters of greenhouse gases, haze, especially in the cold season, haunts the air up to Himalayan heights and even spoils views. Two rivers that run through Kathmandu, the Bagmati and Vishnumati, have become extremely polluted open sewers. These and other water sources throughout Nepal are routinely used for general disposal as well as toilet activities and are thus infected with fecal and other contaminants. It is doubtful that defiling of waterways, burning of fields and rubbish, and use of cooking fires are fully included in the popular carbon footprint calculations that put developed countries in a bad light versus developing regions; however, there is no doubt of the adverse impact on the environment. Obviously, the United States and other industrialized nations also have a lot of ground to cover for climate transgressions and neglect of the environment.

In any event, we do not need to rely on the phlegmatic machinations of government to legislate change that will (dubiously) make everything better. In the long run, transitioning to a post-carbon economy, a green economy, will be necessary. Some parts of the world are making better progress than others on the policies that would underpin such a transition. In addition, tackling global warming requires individual participation en masse. Rather than looking at what others are contributing and waiting for worldwide consensus to mandate a plan, we can adjust personal behavior by limiting the amount of garbage that we produce, especially on the trails. At the same time, simply reducing or eliminating the consumption of meat might be all that is needed to greatly diminish the human element in climate, as suggested by Albert Einstein: "Nothing will benefit human health and increase chances for survival of life on Earth as much as the evolution to a vegetarian diet." ❖

Consider forgoing Western amenities in these mountains. (Photo by Don Messerschmidt)

restrictions are subject to change; however, due to the current strict requirements, especially that visitors must have a guide, these areas have less call for coverage and hence will not be described in this guidebook. However, many less prohibitive options abound, some of which are mentioned in Chapter 9, as well as the classic venues of Annapurna, Solu–Khumbu (Everest), Langtang and Helambu, and sensational side trips therein.

Annapurna

The Annapurna region in the area north of Pokhara has traditionally been the most popular with trekkers, sometimes seeing over 80,000 visitors a year (over 75,000 tourists visited the Annapurna region in 2009, whereas less than 2000 visited the adjoining Manaslu region). The mountain scenery is as spectacular as any in Nepal. However, with new roads being built, particularly near or coinciding with the Round Annapurna Circuit Trek, this may change, although alternate routes are outlined in this guidebook. The many different ethnic groups encountered are as interesting, if not as famous, as the Sherpas of Khumbu. Some of the areas provide perhaps the finest native cuisine in rural Nepal. Those searching for the best food along the trails of Nepal will find it up the Kali Gandaki river. The area is most suitable for those traveling without guides or porters. Most of the treks in this region traverse through many different ecological zones. They begin with the customary terraces of the hills, encounter rain and deciduous and pine forests, pass through arid desert-like country similar to the Tibetan plateau, and even reach alpine areas. Remarkable transitions through different areas, each with its customary animal life, can be made in a few days to a week.

The most famous trek follows a trade route from Pokhara to the Kali Gandaki river, rising through one of the deepest gorges in the world—that between Annapurna and Dhaulagiri—to Jomosom, the administrative center of the Mustang District and beyond to Kagbeni and Muktinath, a renowned, ancient pilgrimage site. The region north of the narrowest portion is called Thak Khola, the ancestral home of the Thakali people. Although a motor road runs to Jomosom, susceptible to monsoon washouts, and another is being built from Tibet, this walk is still breathtaking, and there exist alternate routes to following the road. Ten days is the minimum time for a round-trip to Jomosom. The quickest and least strenuous way to enjoy this area is to fly to Jomosom and walk to Tatopani or out through the lookout point at Poon Hill near GhoRepani. The whole trip would take a week or less.

Annapurna Sanctuary, the otherworldly basin southwest of Annapurna that is the source of the Modi Khola, is a fine objective for those who wish to trek only a short time yet venture into alpine country. The Gurung villages en route are spectacularly colorful. A week to ten days is the minimum time depending on acclimatization.

Manang, the region north and east of the Annapurna massif, is a third worthwhile objective north of Pokhara. The people of the villages of Manang are traders and, many of them, world travelers. Beyond the villages a high pass, Thorung La, leads over to Muktinath, allowing a complete circuit of the Annapurna massif without backtracking. You can travel across Thorung La during the popular season without bringing food or shelter. Facilities exist 2300 feet (700 m) higher on the eastern side, making it easier to cross from east to west, Manang to Muktinath. Another advantage to crossing counterclockwise is that you gain altitude along the way gradually, to better allow for acclimatization. Combining Manang and Thak Khola in a circuit covers more than 135 miles (215 km) and requires almost three weeks, or longer if you take our recommended side trips. The Thorung La usually cannot be crossed from December to March without mountaineering skills because of winter conditions.

Annapurna Conservation Area, 1030 square miles (2660 sq km), north of Pokhara, spans the Himalayan biogeographical divide, the Kali Gandaki valley, supporting species from both the eastern and western Himalaya, as well as flora and fauna typical of the trans-Himalayan zone. A total of 441 bird species has been recorded. A wide variety of mammals occur, including the lesser panda, snow leopard, Himalayan musk deer, and *bharal* (blue sheep).

Lomanthang, the fabled hidden kingdom of Mustang north of Kagbeni, has been opened up to limited agency treks for those willing to pay the high fees ($500 USD for the first ten days, among other requirements). The area is stark, arid, and strikingly beautiful.

Solu–Khumbu (Everest) Region

Solu–Khumbu, the district south and west of Mount Everest, in northeast Nepal, is populated by Sherpas, an ethnic group that has achieved fame from exploits on mountaineering expeditions. Khumbu, the northern half of this region, includes the highest mountain in the world, Mount Everest, 29,028 feet (8848 m), known locally as Chomolongma (Tibetan) or Sagarmatha (Nepali), and three other 8000-meter (26,247-foot) summits, Lhotse (27,890 feet, 8501 m) and Cho Oyu (26,906 feet, 8201 m), part of Sagarmatha National Park, and Makalu (27,765 feet, 8463 m) of the bordering Makalu-Barun National Park.

Situated in the Khumbu area of the Solu–Khumbu district, Sagarmatha National Park (445 square miles, 1148 sq km) is a World Heritage Site (Natural). The attractions are the majestic mountains, the villages in the high mountain valleys, the associated monasteries, and the legendary inhabitants. The park is home to high-altitude wildlife, mostly elusive, although Himalayan monal pheasants, Tibetan snow cocks, and musk deer are often seen. The area has been the second most popular trekking area in Nepal, seeing just over 29,000 visitors in 2009, but due to the road construction north of Pokhara it is likely to replace the Annapurna region as most popular. However, it is still likely that fewer people a year visit Khumbu than crowd into small areas of well-known European and North American mountain parks during busy weeks. Cuisine ranks second below the Annapurna region.

Travel choices to and from Khumbu include walking from Jiri, Shivalaya, or possibly Bhandar depending on road conditions, or flying from Kathmandu to Lukla, a high-altitude airfield (9350 feet, 2850 m) located one to two days south of Namche Bazaar, the entrance to Khumbu. Trekkers who land at high altitudes such as at Lukla (or, even worse, charter helicopter service to Shyangboche at 12,205 feet, 3720 m) and venture into the rarefied altitudes are at greater risk of altitude illness. Our preference is to walk to Khumbu and then fly out.

Two weeks is the minimum time recommended for Khumbu if your goal is the foot of Everest or Gokyo. If you walk from Jiri and fly back from Lukla, the entire trip takes three to four weeks. Walking to and from Khumbu makes that part of the trip almost two weeks. Many trekkers find the walk to Khumbu from Jiri more memorable than the destination of Everest itself. Ethnic groups encountered along the way include the Hindu castes, Tamang, Jirel, and Rai. For those with less time for a full walk-in, an option is to fly into Phaphlu (8103 feet, 2470 m), an airstrip near the district headquarters of Solu–Khumbu, Salleri, and join the main Jiri–Lukla trail at Ringmo in a few hours. The benefit of this option is that it avoids the daylong bus ride to Jiri/Shivalaya and saves two to three days' walking time. Another attractive route is to walk to or from the southeast and the Arun drainage, crossing several valleys, to Tumlingtar where there is an airfield and jeep service to Hille, which has bus service.

Langtang, Gosainkund, and Helambu

The popular trekking region most accessible to Kathmandu includes Helambu, Gosainkund, and Langtang, all north of the capital city. The region is the third most popular area of the three classic trekking venues. Helambu is typical of hill Nepal near

The West Face of Dhaulagiri from Jaljala (Photo by Stephen Bezruchka)

Kathmandu, with Yolmo (Sherpa) populations higher up, Tamang lower down, and Hindu castes in the valleys. The lake at Gosainkund is a holy pilgrimage site, while Langtang is an alpine valley nestled in the Himalaya. Both are within Langtang National Park (660 square miles, 1710 sq km), containing a wide range of habitats, from subtropical to alpine.

Upper temperate and subalpine species include pheasants, the red panda, Himalayan musk deer, and Himalayan tahr. Spring and summer bring a rich variety of butterflies and flowers. The three regions are linked by trails, and can be visited as time and conditions permit. The minimum time for a brief trek is a week. Two weeks would allow you to combine two of the regions, and in three weeks you could enjoy the entire area. Food and lodging are available except for the difficult Ganja La crossing linking Langtang and Helambu, which requires mountaineering skills and full self-sufficiency. The Gosainkund–Helambu link involves a moderate pass, the Laurebina La (15,121 feet, 4609 m), with facilities along the route available during the popular season.

The Trails Less Traveled

Outside of the three most popular areas outlined above are regions less visited by trekkers, and some treks in these places are covered in Chapter 9. Along these routes, trekkers will encounter a wide variety of ethnicities, mostly Hindu or Buddhist practitioners whose beliefs influence the shamanist and animist practices of other groups. Unlike the popular routes, these treks have few lodges or facilities set up strictly for tourists, and trail sections to distant villages through remote areas may be difficult to follow. Physical comfort may be at a minimum. The rewards are trekking through pristine areas and meeting the hill people in traditional settings, largely unaffected by modernization. The mental solace, interactions, and cultural insights could be the most memorable of your visit to this unforgettable Himalayan country. The routes through these areas are not for everyone. Considerable resilience is needed, along with a spirit of adventure and an open mind. It is perhaps best to consider a first trek on a more established tourist trail. As your experience grows, you can take on these more adventurous treks.

Western Nepal

In general, if this is your first visit to Nepal, choose one of the other treks unless you have some specific reason for wanting to trek in western Nepal. On the other hand, if you are a veteran trekker and are looking for new, exciting, interesting experiences, go west.

Generally, the part of Nepal west of the Kali Gandaki river is not often visited by trekkers. Facilities are few and distances are great. Very few roads are suitable for launching treks, and air transportation is more difficult. Food is sometimes unavailable. Except

for treks near the Dhaulagiri Range, few trails provide views of spectacular mountains. In fact, Dhaulagiri (26,795 feet, 8167 m) is the only 8000-meter peak in Nepal west of the Kali Gandaki. The feeling of being right in the mountains, as in Khumbu (Everest), is rare. The country is rugged and, in the northern reaches, has a feeling of openness. The farther west you go, the less contact the Nepali people have had with Westerners.

One trekker destination is a circuit from Jumla to RaRa Lake, Nepal's largest and the site of a national park (41 square miles, 106 sq km) dominated by magnificent coniferous forests.

A sadhu from Simikot lives in a cave nestled against the border with Tibet up in the northwest corner of Nepal. (Photo by Pat Morrow)

Jumla might be reached by a hard-going seasonal road that regularly washes out or by scheduled planes from Kathmandu, but it is easier to connect through airfields in Nepalganj or Surkhet and then fly into Jumla. You might share the plane with heavy bags of rice from the Nepal Food Corporation and U.N. Food Program, as this area is regularly short on food. RaRa is a three-day trek from the Jumla. An option on the way out is to trek to KolTi airport in Bajura District in three days along a route built locally through the U.N.'s food-for-work program. Scant facilities along the way provide the bare minimum in food and a place to sleep. Rather than fly out from KolTi, you could continue south to Khaptad National Park or to Sanphebagar in Accham District and meet another airstrip and the roadway as well.

Few trekkers visit RaRa and this region (only 146 in 2009). Ethnic groups encountered on this trek include BhoTiya, Thakuri, and the Hindu castes. Like the rest of western Nepal, RaRa Lake National Park is relatively species-poor compared to the east. However, because the west is under-recorded, a visit should prove exciting, as there is a good chance of finding something unexpected. RaRa also provides opportunities to see some exclusively western Nepal birds such as the cheer pheasant and white-throated tit. The lake is a popular staging point for migrating waterbirds overflying the Himalaya. Grasslands bordering the lake are full of colorful flowers in spring and summer.

PHYSIOGRAPHIC CHARACTERISTICS OF INHABITED REGIONS

Features	Tarai	Siwalik Hills	Middle Mountains	High Mountains	High Himalaya
Elevation in feet (m), approx.	300–1000 (100–300)	650–5000 (200–1500)	2000–8000 (600–2500)	3300–13,000 (1000–4000)	6500–17,000 (2000–5000)
Climate	Tropical	Subtropical	Cool temperate	Alpine	Alpine to arctic
Major natural vegetation	Sal and mixed hardwoods	Sal and mixed hardwoods, pine	Pine and mixed hardwoods, oak	Fir, pine, birch, rhododendron	Open meadow, tundra
Major crops	Rice, maize, wheat, mustard, sugarcane, tropical fruits	Rice, maize, wheat, millet, radish, mango	Rice, maize, wheat, millet, barley, pulses, potato	Oats, barley, wheat, potato, buckwheat, yam	Grazing (monsoon)
Livestock	Cattle, buffalo	Cattle	Cattle, sheep, buffalo, pigs	Cattle and crosses, sheep, goats	Yaks and crosses, sheep, goats
Textile materials	Jute, straw, grass	Bamboo	Nettle, hemp, bamboo, sheep's wool	Nettle, bamboo, sheep's wool, yak and goat hair	Sheep's wool, yak and goat hair
Ethnic groups	Tharu, Hindu castes, migrants, Musalman	Tharu, migrants from middle mountains	Gurung, Magar, Tamang, Newar, Rai, Limbu, Hindu castes	Thakali, Sherpa, Tamang, Chhetri, BhoTiya, Gurung	Sherpa, BhoTiya

(After Dunsmore, 1993.)

HILL AND MOUNTAIN PEOPLES OF NEPAL:
ASSOCIATION AND DIVERSITY

Nepal is a land of great diversity. Its social, cultural, religious, geographical, floral, and faunal varieties fascinate and challenge the imagination. The diversity across the land is quickly seen and felt by trekkers. In a relatively short distance (although it may be days of arduous walking), a trekker can leave the low, subtropical Tarai forests and ascend northward into the high alpine meadows. The Tarai-walla (a person of the Tarai) is left behind for the PahAARi (hillsman), the Lekhali (person of the high country), the goThaalo (alpine herdsman), and the BhoTiya (Tibetan) of the hills and mountains.

Variations in social and cultural expression seem to parallel the physical, geographic, and biotic changes associated with altitude and latitude. The trekker sees an ever-changing variety of farmsteads, villages, and bazaars; passes the shrines of Hindu, Buddhist, and animist; encounters farmer, trader, storekeeper, pilgrim, innkeeper, and herder; and notes changes in the architecture of homes and religious edifices. The colorfully diverse expressions of human adaptation to the Himalaya are unexpectedly fascinating for a land to which some visitors might expect only spectacular mountains, smiling guides, yak herds, and pagoda-like temples.

Nepal has dozens of ethnic and caste groups, each differentiated by unique aspects of language, dress, locale, lifestyle, house style, economy, and religion. At one level of analysis, however, certain elements of uniformity tend to knit all the diversity together. Take language. It divides Nepalis into two major camps: those who speak Nepali as their mother tongue—primarily the caste groups—and those who speak languages identified by linguists as part of the Bodic division of Sino-Tibetan (sometimes called Tibeto-Burman)—that is, the hill ethnic groups and those of close Tibetan affinities. At another level, however, language draws them together; most Nepalis, regardless of local dialect, speak Nepali in the public forums of trade, education, government, and daily encounters with outsiders. (In some places, English has become the second major language of the land.)

Another of the more visible attributes of uniformity in Nepal is a marked association between cultural groups and the altitude/latitude where they traditionally live. Each distinct group can be identified in great part by the ecological niche it occupies. Each niche is characterized by similarities in dress, house style, religious expression, patterns of trade, and subsistence. Caste groups, for example, tend to occupy the lower valleys in dispersed settlements, where they cultivate rice on irrigated paddy fields. Ethnic groups tend to cluster in nucleated villages on higher, more northerly ridges, where they raise upland crops such as millet, corn, barley, and wheat. Each depends on the other for exchange of produce and for other economic, social, and religious interaction. In addition, Nepal's rich cultural heritage has been heavily influenced and sometimes irrevocably changed by the recent influx of tourism, education, technology, mass communications, work migration, and other aspects of modernization. ❖

Other Treks

Most of Nepal is now open for trekking, although previously noted restricted areas require special fees, a minimum party of two, and organizing your journey through a trekking agency. Many areas outside of the formal trekking areas are worth exploring including much of the mid-hills. Most visitors find that areas that are without spectacular mountain views are at least as enjoyable as the famous areas. Consider linking several treks. Some wanderers head from Kathmandu to Khumbu, then to Makalu, and on from there. You could essentially traverse all the Himalaya in Nepal. Peter Hillary (Sir Edmund's son) and Pat Morrow have done this to a great extent, and recently Robin Boustead produced a beautiful photo-journal, *The Great Himalayan Trail*, of an eponymous high route along the spine of the Himalaya (see also, www.thegreathimalayatrail .org). His book focuses on the Nepal section, with plans to expand east and west to include the whole range. Before venturing into some of the more remote, less popular areas, we recommend doing one of the standard treks.

A typical small shop in the mid-hills (Photo by R.C. Sedai)

TREKS AT A GLANCE

Section II of the book covers the famous trekking regions of Annapurna, Solu–Khumbu (Everest), and Langtang, Gosainkund, and Helambu, plus several more routes that can be done by independent trekkers. You will find not only current descriptions of the popular routes, but several remarkable side trips along these classic treks. Chapter 9 provides routes for the more adventurous traveler and even some for seasoned trekkers looking for something entirely unique. Below is a brief outline of travel segments and treks covered in depth in Section II (with chapter number, where relevant, in parentheses), summarizing difficulty, time, and features.

DIFFICULTY

Easiest

Indigenous Peoples Trail (9)
Kathmandu Valley Cultural Trail (9)
Tatopani (or Beni or even Pokhara)
  to Jomosom along the Kali
  Gandaki/Thak Khola (river valley
  forming western half of the Round
  Annapurna Circuit) (6)

Moderate

Annapurna Sanctuary (6)
Chitwan Chepang Hills Trail (9)
Gosainkund (8)
Gurung Heritage Trail (9)
Helambu (8)
Khaptad National Park (9)
Langtang (8)
Naya Pul to Jomosom via GhoRepani
  and Poon Hill (6)
Pikey Peak Trek (9)
Side trip to Milarepa Caves from
  Braga village (6)
Tamang Heritage Trail (9)

More Difficult

Annapurna Circuit over
  the Thorung La (6)
Dhaulagiri Icefall (6)
Dudh Kunda Trek (9)
GhoRepani to Khopra Ridge
  viewpoint (6)
"Guerilla" Trek (9)
Khumbu side trips to Kala Pattar,
  Gokyo Ri, and Island Peak
  Base Camp (7)
Khumbu/Everest region's Cho La
  and Renjo La (7)
Langtang side trips from Kyangjin
  Gomba to Kyangin Ri/Menchamsu,
  Tsergo Ri, and Langsisa Kharka (8)
Makalu Base Camp (9)
Manang's high-altitude side trips of
  Tilicho Tal, and Kicho "Ice" Lake (6)
Mardi Himal Trek (9)
North Annapurna Base Camp (6)
Numbur Cheese Circuit (9)
Panch Pokhari and Bhairab Kund (8)
Tamang Heritage Trail side trips from
  Naagthaali to Taaruche
  viewpoint and from Briddam
  Village to Gottegang Kharka (9)

(CONTINUED)

TIME	FEATURES

Shortest (a few days to less than a week)
Chitwan Chepang Hills Trail (9)
Flying to Jomosom and walking to
   Birethanti (6)
Flying to Lukla, Hongde (Manang),
   or Jomosom, walking a day or
   two without altitude gain, and
   flying back (6, 7)
Gosainkund (8)
Gurung Heritage Trail (9)
Helambu (8)
Indigenous Peoples Trail (9)
Initial part of almost any trek
   (starting out and returning after
   a day or two)
Kathmandu Valley Cultural Trail (9)
Langtang (8)
Pokhara to Ghandruk circuit (6)
Pokhara to GhoRepani circuit (6)
RaRa Lake circuit (9)
Tamang Heritage Trail (9)

A Week or More
"Guerilla" Trek (9)
Annapurna Sanctuary (6)
Dudh Kunda Trek (9)
Khaptad National Park (9)
Mardi Himal Trek (9)
Numbur Cheese Circuit (9)
Panch Pokhari and Bhairab Kund (8)
Pikey Peak Trek (9)

Two Weeks or More
Combining two or three areas
   north of Kathmandu (8)
Lukla to Everest Base Camp
   and Kala Pattar or Gokyo (7)
Makalu Base Camp (9)
To Manang and back from
   Besisahar (6)

Three Weeks or More
Annapurna Circuit (6)
Khumbu with plenty of side trips
   or walking from Jiri (or even
   Kathmandu or Tumlingtar)
   and back (7)

Most Spectacular Mountain Scenery
Annapurna Circuit (6)
Annapurna Sanctuary (6)
Dudh Kunda Trek (9)
Khumbu (7)
Makalu Base Camp (9)
Numbur Cheese Circuit (9)
Gosainkund (8)
GhoRepani to Khopra Ridge
   viewpoint (6)
Manang's high-altitude side trips of
   Tilicho Tal, and Kicho "Ice" Lake (6)
Upper Langtang Valley (8)

New Adventures
Trek during monsoon season—even
   in areas you have visited before in
   the dry season
Go on a far-west or far-east trek
Rewalk a trek you did ten or more
   years ago
Trek with few if any other trekkers
   on a less popular route
Take your family (spouse, parents,
   or children)
Don't go with an agency if you have
   done so previously
Don't hire any guides or porters who
   speak English
Focus on a specific interest, such as
   flowers, birding, local crafts,
   photography, or architecture
Go on a pilgrimage at the time
   Nepalis visit pilgrimage sites
Climb a trekking peak if you have
   the requisite mountaineering
   experience

NATURAL HISTORY OF NEPAL

Nepal provides marvelous food for thought. A manifold society with almost unfathomable ethnic diversity is layered over landscapes varying from tropical rain forest to snowy heights and desert.

Paradoxically, the forces that shape Nepal are essentially simple: its people endeavor to survive, while the land attempts to self-destruct through natural erosive forces. The majority of the population lives in the more hospitable fertile plains in the south as well as the mid-hills and valleys which lie between the plains and the Himalaya to the north.

Nepal's wide-ranging landscape, from near sea level to 29,028 feet (8848 m), the top of Everest, was formed by the Eurasian plate working against the Indo-European plate. The major rivers of Nepal cut from north to south, the way they had been running before the earth was lifted by tectonic collision to create the world's loftiest range. As the land slowly lifted to form mountains, the rivers kept their position through erosion.

Beyond the mighty mountains lies a trans-Himalayan landscape that rarely sees the rain that is abundant to the south of the peaks. It is a stark, arid, high-altitude desert, sparsely populated. However, people, plants, and animals have adapted to the wide

Looking down on buckwheat fields in the Marsyangdi River valley from the route to Kicho Lake (Photo by Tokozile Robbins)

Langur monkeys can be found from the Tarai to 13,100 feet (4000 m).
(Photo by Stephen Bezruchka)

geologic scope that accompanies the abrupt elevation differences. Visitors will be enthralled by both the geologic scope of Nepal and the biological differences encountered due to variations in landscape.

GEOLOGY OF NEPAL

While the Himalayan orogeny has been active for the last 55 million years, the present-day landforms of the Himalaya are the result of tectonic and erosional activity that has taken place during the last 1.6 million years (the Pleistocene and Holocene epochs). This includes the glacial activity that has carved out the mountain slopes and the U-shaped valleys of the Higher Himalaya and the Tibetan Marginal Range above approximately 12,500 feet (3800 m); the erosional activity of water that has produced the deep, V-shaped valleys of the Higher and Lesser Himalaya, including the Arun and Kali Gandaki valleys, which vie for the honor of "deepest valley in the world"; the recent uplift of the Mahabharat Lekh, which has forced all the rivers of Nepal, except the Arun Khola, to turn abruptly from their north–south orientations to east–west orientations as they flow out of the Higher Himalaya or Tibetan Marginal Range; and the formation of, and subsequent drying up of, a number of lakes lying on the north side of the Mahabharat Lekh, including the Quaternary Kathmandu Lake, which has been uplifted and drained during the last 10,000 years to form the Kathmandu valley.

Of particular interest are the numerous major rivers that originate on the Tibetan plateau and within the Tibetan Marginal Range that cut through the High Himalaya. Why doesn't the highest mountain range in the world, the Himalaya, form a hydrologic divide? These Himalayan rivers were flowing southward off of the Tibetan plateau onto the plains of north India prior to the uplift of the Higher Himalaya. The erosive power of these rivers has kept pace with the uplift of the Himalaya, cutting spectacular gorges through the Higher Himalaya as fast as the tectonic forces of the region could lift up the summits of the great Himalayan peaks. The Kali Gandaki, Arun, Bramhaputra, and Indus are all examples of rivers that have maintained their original positions, and cut impressive valleys, during the uplift of the Himalaya.

FOUR PHYSIOGRAPHIC REGIONS

According to the theory of plate tectonics, between 75 and 80 million years ago the Indian subcontinent, containing present-day India, Pakistan, Nepal, Bangladesh, and Sri Lanka, broke away from Antarctica and began its northward "drift" toward Asia. The Indian Ocean, which separates India and Antarctica, began opening up through the seafloor-spreading along the mid-Indian Ocean Ridge at this time. India and Antarctica traveled away from each other at an initial rate of about 16 cm per year, separating the two continents a distance of 2000 miles (3200 km) over the next 20 million years. To the north of the Indian continent, a vast ocean, the Tethys Sea, was closing and the oceanic crust underlying the Tethys Sea was being subducted (consumed) beneath Tibet.

About 55 million years ago, the Indian subcontinent began plowing into Tibet and southern Asia. Seafloor-spreading has continued in the Indian Ocean since the collision, and India has continued to move northward relative to Tibet and Asia. With the Indian subcontinent smashing into Tibet and southern Asia, something had to give. The result has been the crumpling-up, folding, faulting, and uplift of the northern margin of the Indian subcontinent to form the Himalaya, as well as the uplift of the Tibetan plateau by the Indian subcontinent being thrust under it.

The northern boundary of the Tibetan Himalaya is the Indus–Tsangpo Suture, along which the Indus and Tsangpo rivers flow. The Indus–Tsangpo Suture is the actual collision zone and boundary between the Indian subcontinent and the Tibetan microcontinent. Along some sections of the Indus–Tsangpo Suture, oceanic crust and the subcrustal mantle have been squeezed up between the Indian and Tibetan continents and thrust over the oceanic sediments of the Tibetan Himalaya. This oceanic crust, along with the Tethyan sediments of the Tibetan Himalaya, is all that remains of the Tethys Sea today.

The Tibetan or Tethys Himalaya lie between the Indus and Tsangpo rivers to the north and the high summits of the Higher Himalaya, which form the backbone of the Himalayan range (for example, Mount Everest, Annapurna, and Dhaulagiri), to the south. The Tibetan Himalaya include the Tibetan Marginal Range, a range of mountains that lies to the north of the High Himalayan peaks and includes the Dolpo, Mustang, and Manang regions of central Nepal as well as the Tingri region of southern Tibet. The Tibetan Himalaya are composed of Cambrian to Eocene sediments, which were deposited in the Tethys Sea between 500 and 55 million years ago on both the northern margin of the Indian continent (the continental platform underlain by Higher Himalayan rocks) and in the deep ocean basin between the Indian and Asian continents. These oceanic sediments include limestones, sandstones, and shales and contain abundant fossils, including brachiopods, oysters, occasional plant fossils, and the famous Upper Jurassic ammonites found in profusion around the sacred area of Muktinath. The Nilgiri Limestones (named after the peak of Nilgiri in the Annapurna region) were deposited in the Tethys Sea during the Ordovician period (500 to 435 million years ago); they presently form the summits of Nilgiri and the Annapurnas, and are found on the northern flanks of Dhaulagiri. Similar early Paleozoic sediments cap the summits of Mount Everest, Lhotse, Kanjiroba, and Nanda Devi; thus, it is true that many of the highest summits of the world are capped by rocks that were once deposited in an ocean. Because these early Paleozoic Tethyan sediments in the Annapurna and Everest regions lie at the base of a 7.5-mile (12-km)-thick sequence of Tethyan sediments, and because the summits of these mountains are presently over

← (CONTINUED)

5 miles (8 km) high, these sediments have been uplifted some 12.4 miles (20 km) since the onset of the Himalayan orogeny (mountain-building event) 55 million years ago. During the Himalayan orogeny, the Tethyan sediments have been extensively faulted and folded; this can be seen between Marpha and Muktinath and north of Manang in the Annapurna region.

The physiographic Higher Himalaya includes the high mountains of the Himalaya proper (for instance, Kangchenjunga, Makalu, Everest, Cho Oyu, Shishapangma, Manaslu, Annapurna, Dhaulagiri, Kanjiroba, Api, and Saipal) and the valleys within the high mountains. The Higher Himalaya are generally considered to include those regions with altitudes over 13,000 feet (4000 m) that lie south of the Tibetan plateau and the Tibetan Marginal Range. Geologically, the Higher Himalaya consist of highly metamorphosed and extensively deformed schists and gneisses (crystalline rocks). These rocks were the original Precambrian continental crust of the northern margin of the Indian continent. (The Tethyan sediments of the Tibetan Himalaya were deposited upon these Higher Himalayan rocks.) About 25 million years ago, a deep, east–west-trending fracture formed within the Indian continental crust. The continental crust on the north side of the fracture (the Higher Himalayan rocks) was shoved over the continental crust and its sedimentary cover rocks south of the fracture (the Lesser Himalayan rocks). The Higher Himalayan crystalline rocks (to the north) were thrust over the Lesser Himalayan sedimentary rocks (to the south) along a fault known as the Main Central Thrust. The Main Central Thrust is the geological boundary between the Higher Himalaya and the Lesser Himalaya. Higher Himalayan rocks have been thrust over the Lesser Himalayan sediments a minimum of 100 km into eastern Nepal. Between 25 and 10 million years ago, at about the same time as thrusting was taking place along the Main Central Thrust, very high temperatures in the Higher Himalayan rocks melted the schists and gneisses, forming large granite bodies in many of the Higher Himalayan Peaks. These granites can be seen on Makalu, Everest, Lhotse, Shishapangma, and Manaslu.

The physiographic Lesser (or Lower) Himalaya is divided into two distinct regions in Nepal: the Middle Mountains and the Mahabharat Lekh. South of the Higher Himalaya lie the heavily inhabited Middle Mountains, from which almost all treks to the Higher Himalaya begin. Elevations in the Middle Mountains range from a few hundred meters in the valleys—for example, Tumlingtar at an elevation of 1500 feet (457 m)—to 13,000 feet (4000 m) on the ridges. The Middle Mountains are dissected by major south-flowing rivers, such as the Karnali, Kali Gandaki, and Arun rivers. The ridges that come off of the southern flanks of the Higher Himalaya also trend roughly north–south. The Mahabharat Lekh, an east–west-trending range of hills with summit elevations of 6500 to 8000 feet (2000 to 2500 m), runs the whole length of Nepal south of the Middle Mountains and north of the Siwalik Hills. The Mahabharat Lekh can be seen south of Kathmandu and the Kathmandu–Pokhara road and is breached by the Trishuli-Narayani river, along which the road from Kathmandu to Narayangarh and India runs.

Much of the physiographic Lesser Himalaya are underlain by rocks belonging to the geologic Lesser Himalaya. The geologic Lesser Himalaya consist of variously metamorphosed and deformed sediments that were deposited in an inland basin from Precambrian times (more than 570 million years ago) up to about 50 or 60 million years ago. The original sediments of the Lesser Himalaya included shales, sandstones, conglomerates, limestone, and some acid-volcanic rocks. During the last 25 to 30 million years, these were metamorphosed to form the slates, phyllites, metaquartzites, marbles, →

← FOUR PHYSIOGRAPHIC REGIONS (CONTINUED) →

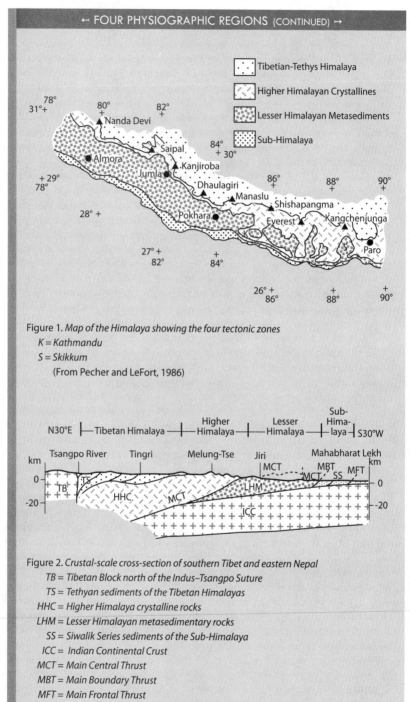

Figure 1. *Map of the Himalaya showing the four tectonic zones*
K = Kathmandu
S = Skikkum
    (From Pecher and LeFort, 1986)

Figure 2. *Crustal-scale cross-section of southern Tibet and eastern Nepal*
TB = Tibetan Block north of the Indus–Tsangpo Suture
TS = Tethyan sediments of the Tibetan Himalayas
HHC = Higher Himalaya crystalline rocks
LHM = Lesser Himalayan metasedimentary rocks
SS = Siwalik Series sediments of the Sub-Himalaya
ICC = Indian Continental Crust
MCT = Main Central Thrust
MBT = Main Boundary Thrust
MFT = Main Frontal Thrust
        (From Brunel, 1986, and Schelling, 1989)

and granitic augen-gneisses that make up the Lesser Himalaya today. Practically no fossils are seen in the Lesser Himalayan metasediments. It is interesting to note that the hills encircling Kathmandu, and the Mahabharat Lekh in eastern Nepal, which belong to the physiographic Lesser Himalaya, are actually composed of Higher Himalayan rocks—schists, gneisses, and granites—that have been thrust over the Lesser Himalayan sediments along the Main Central Thrust.

The Sub-Himalaya is the geologic name for the Siwalik Hills, the foothills of the Himalaya lying between the Mahabharat Lekh to the north and the Indo-Gangetic plains of north India to the south. These hills rarely exceed 4000 feet (1200 m) in elevation. The Siwalik Hills are composed entirely of shales, sandstones, and conglomerates less than 20 million years old, which are the product of the erosion of the rising Himalaya to the north. Thus, the Siwalik Series sediments record the uplift of the Himalaya. The Siwalik sediments contain scattered fossils of crocodiles, rhinoceroses, and elephants, all present-day inhabitants of the few wild regions left in the Himalayan foothills, such as Chitwan National Park. Presently, the Lesser Himalaya, including the Mahabharat Lekh, are being uplifted and thrust southward over the Sub-Himalayan Siwalik Hills; the Siwalik Hills are being uplifted and thrust southward over the Ganges plain. ❖

MAJOR HABITAT TYPES

Nepal's major natural habitat types are forests, grasslands, and wetlands. Nepal has rather few wetlands, but their ecological diversity is great. For instance, a total of over 160 indigenous species of fish have been recorded. There are three major river systems, which are fed by the Himalayan snows and glaciers: the Kosi, Kali Gandaki, and Karnali. Other wetlands include a number of small lakes scattered throughout the country. The Kosi Barrage area, a large expanse of open water, marshes, grasslands, and scrub lying in the Kosi's floodplain in the far eastern lowlands, is by far the most valuable wetland in the country. It is internationally important as a staging point for migrant water birds. Over 50,000 ducks are estimated to be there in February. The barrage was built in 1964 with India's assistance to help control floods and provide irrigation to farms. However, the Kosi has an extremely high sediment load, which raises the height of the waters, and it regularly floods surrounding areas, often toward the end of the monsoon season. The river is known as the "Sorrow of Bihar" for the damage it has caused in the Indian state to the south. Most recently, the Kosi burst its banks in August 2008, displacing millions of people.

Only small areas remain of the country's lowland grasslands, and almost all of these lie within protected forest areas. They are important for a number of threatened animals, including the swamp deer, the greater one-horned or Indian rhinoceros (*Rhinoceros unicornis*), and two of the world's most endangered bustards, the Bengal and lesser floricans. In spring and summer, a mass of colorful flowers bloom on alpine grasslands. A number of mammals, such as the *bharal* or blue sheep and common goral, depend on these grasslands for grazing and in turn they form the vital prey of the threatened snow leopard (*Panthera uncia*) with an estimated Nepal population of 300–400.

Forests form the major natural vegetation of Nepal. In his classic work *Forests of Nepal*, Adam Stainton identified thirty-five different forest types—an extraordinarily high number for such a small country. (Nepal is 58,826 mi^2 (147,181 km^2), ninety-third

Buckwheat fields blossom near the Mountain of Heaven, also known as the Great Wall of Pisang. (Photo by Tokozile Robbins)

in the world and about the size of Arkansas.) These include dry coniferous forests on the northern Himalayan slopes, rhododendron shrubberies in the subalpine zone, temperate oak forests draped in mosses, and lush, wet tropical jungles. The main reason Nepal is of great value for birds is because of its forests. There are as many as 124 species of breeding birds for which the country may hold significant world populations. Nearly all of these are dependent on forests. Nepal's forests also support a rich variety of mammals, although those in the Himalaya have been little studied so far. Relatively few species have adapted to habitats heavily modified or created by people, such as gardens, scrub, and cultivation. Most that have adapted are widespread and common, such as the Asian magpie robin and jungle crow, while many animals dependent on natural habitats are declining.

NEPAL'S SPECIES RICHNESS

Nepal has a remarkably high diversity of flora and fauna considering its small size. There are some 863 species of birds, more than 650 of butterflies (as well as over 3900 moths), and about 6500 of flowering plants. Between 1998 and 2008, 353 new species

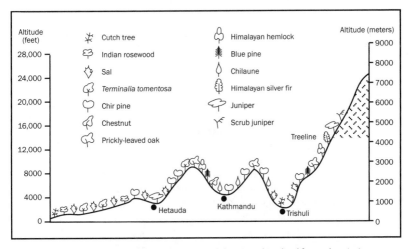

Figure 3. North–south profile through central Nepal showing altitudinal forest descriptions.

were found in the Eastern Himalaya (comprising Nepal, Bhutan, northeastern India, northern Burma, and southern Tibet). The discoveries include 242 plants, 16 amphibians, 16 reptiles, 14 fish, 2 birds, 2 mammals, and 61 invertebrates. Of the birds, Sykes's nightjar (*Caprimulgus mahrattensis*) was discovered in Nepal's Kosi Tappu Wildlife Preserve in January 2008.

Nepal's species richness can be partly attributed to the country's extremely varied climate and topography. The altitudinal range is extreme, ranging from almost sea level at Kanchan Kalan (230 feet, 70 m) to the highest point on Earth, Mount Everest (29,028 feet, 8848 m). In the lowlands, such as in Chitwan National Park, there are tropical forests, which support the greatest number of species. Here can be found some of the Indian subcontinent's large mammals, including the greater one-horned or Indian rhinoceros and tiger (*Panthera tigris tigris*). The World Wildlife Fund (WWF) recently estimated that there are 121 adult tigers in four protected areas of the Tarai.) At the other extreme is the alpine zone of the high peaks, which holds the smallest number of species. Among these is the Tibetan snow cock, a large gamebird that normally summers above 14,760 feet (4500 m).

The other major factor contributing to Nepal's species richness is its position of overlap between Asia's two great biogeographic realms—the Oriental and Palearctic, produced by the collision of the Indian subcontinent and Asia. Palearctic species originating in Europe and northern Asia are dominant in the Himalaya. For example, birds include accentors, redstarts, and rosefinches. Primulas, gentians, and edelweiss flower in the alpine grasslands, attracting Apollo butterflies. Oriental species are the most common in the tropical and subtropical zones of southern Nepal. Hornbills feed in large fruiting trees of the forest canopy, while gaudy pittas search the leaf litter below, and large, colorful butterflies, such as the yellow and black birdwings, flutter past.

The natural history sidebars scattered throughout the "Routes" chapters of Section II offer information on plants and animals encountered by the trekker. Common and scientific names are given with Nepali equivalents, in brackets, that are consistent with *Glossary of Some Important Plant and Animal Names in Nepal* (listed in Appendix A).

OBSERVING PLANTS AND ANIMALS

Flowers The main season when flowers (*phul*) are blooming in the Himalaya is from mid-March to the end of May, while the period between November and late March is a good time to look for flowering plants in the lowlands.

Birds

The period between mid-March and the end of May is excellent for birds (*charo*) because many residents and summer visitors are at a peak of activity. Late May is the best time to bird-watch on the high-altitude treks, such as those to Langtang and Solu–Khumbu. Although it is very hot, late April is exciting for bird-watching at Chitwan, and probably other lowland forests, because large numbers of migrants are passing through the lowlands on their way to the hills and most summer visitors have arrived, while a few winter visitors still remain.

Between December and mid-March is a very interesting time due to Nepal's numerous winter visitors. Look for birds while you trek to the Thak Khola and around Annapurna. In October and November, small numbers of passage migrants can be seen flying south along the Himalayan valleys. In recent years, thousands of birds of prey have been reported northwest of Pokhara, moving west along the southern edge of the Himalaya.

When bird-watching, remember that most birds are active early in the morning and that their movements are affected by the sun. Slopes bathed in sunshine attract birds away from slopes in the shade, except during hot midday periods, when birds tend to be inactive. When walking in forest you may hardly see any birds for several hours. This is because most birds from one area of forest often join together to form a fast-moving party of different species. (A worthwhile website for Nepal bird-watchers is www.birdlifenepal.org.)

Mammals

In general, mammals can be seen throughout the year, although the best months are March to May in the lowland, protected areas of Chitwan, Sukla Phanta, Bardia, and Kosi Tappu. During these months, the regrowth of grasses after the annual grass-burning attracts large numbers of herbivores and with them their predators.

Unlike birds, wild mammals (*janaawar*) are usually difficult to see in Nepal. Many of them are only active at night and are usually silent. The first two- or three-hour period after sunrise is a productive time to look for nocturnal mammals. They are often still active then and the trail is more likely to be undisturbed. Most mammals are shy and wary of people, and it is best to wear clothes that blend in with the surroundings. Greens or browns are suitable in forest, and pale colors in the Himalaya when they are snow-covered. Remember to be silent and to walk lightly, with slow body movements. Large carnivores and some other mammals are potentially dangerous and should never be approached.

Insects

June to September is the best time for insects (*kiraa*), but the monsoon weather will present difficulties in finding them. Many species can be seen in other months—for example, many butterflies (*putali*) emerge in March and April, becoming abundant by May and June. There are at least six butterfly species endemic to Nepal, that is, believed to be found only in Nepal. ❖

2

PREPARATIONS AND TRAVEL

All obstacles are blessings of the guru.

— A BhoTiya saying

Remember this saying when in Nepal, for despite all your careful preparations, some "serendipitous accident" may occur. The message in this chapter is "Be prepared" but, most of all, be prepared to be flexible and to make the best of all circumstances. Trekking in Nepal, like any other activity, is usually more successful if the participants are ready and if they have some idea of what to expect.

Once you decide to go to Nepal and have a departure date in mind, purchase an airline ticket. Flights to Nepal are heavily booked in autumn and spring, and if you are going independently, it helps to plan ahead. Nepal is five and three-quarters hours ahead of Greenwich Mean Time (GMT), whereas New York City or Eastern Standard Time (EST) is five hours behind GMT (four hours behind GMT during Daylight Savings Time, i.e., from the second Sunday in March until the first Sunday of November). That means that if it is 12:45 PM in Nepal, then on the East Coast of the United States it is 2 AM (3 AM during Daylight Savings Time).

The country telephone code is 977 with city area codes of 01 for Kathmandu and 061 for Pokhara (omit the zero if calling from outside these cities). Nepal follows two calendars, both the solar-based Gregorian calendar followed in the west and the luni-solar Bikram Samvat (BS) calendar which is roughly fifty-six years, eight months, and fifteen days ahead; for example, the year 2010 CE (AD) corresponds to 2066–67 BS. The Bikram Samvat calendar begins at the start of the solar new year in mid-April. Supposedly, the advent of this calendar marked the victory of an emperor in India over invaders in 56 BCE and was initiated as the beginning of a new era. Nepal adopted this calendar during the reign of the Rana regime, oligarchs who ran the country from the mid-1800s CE until 1951 CE.

VISAS AND PERMITS

Visas for travel to Nepal can be obtained from one of the Nepali Embassies and Consular Services in thirty-seven countries throughout the world. The visas are valid for up to one month. Two passport-size photographs are necessary for the application, and travelers should bring a dozen or so to Nepal for use in formalities including permits to trekking areas. Passport photos can be readily made in Kathmandu.

Visas valid for fifteen, thirty, and ninety days are issued on arrival at entry points to Nepal. The costs change frequently; as of June 2010 a fifteen-day visa was $25 USD payable in Nepalese rupees, U.S. dollars, or other convertible currency; $40 USD for a thirty-day visa; and $100 USD for a ninety-day visa.

Indians do not need a visa, and a thirty-day gratis visa is available for citizens of other South Asian Association for Regional Cooperation (SAARC) bloc countries of Bangladesh, Bhutan, the Maldives, Pakistan, and Sri Lanka. However, nationals of the following countries are not granted visas on arrival: Nigeria, Ghana, Zimbabwe, Swaziland, Cameroon, Somalia, Liberia, Ethiopia, Iraq, Palestine, and Afghanistan.

Nepal is a landlocked country bordered by the Tibet Autonomous Region of China to the north and India to the east, west, and south. The common eight entry points are (1) Kathmandu, for those arriving by air; (2) Kodari, along the Nepal–Tibet border; (3) Birgunj across from Raxaul, India, on the main road from India to Kathmandu; and (4) Belahia across from Sunauli, India, near the town of Bhairawa on the road from India to Pokhara and close to Lumbini, the birthplace of Prince Siddhartha Gautama who later took on the title of Buddha. Other border points with India, less used by tourists, are (5) Kakarbhitta on the far eastern border with India, (6) Nepalganj and (7) DhangaDi in the far west, and (8) Gaddachauki/Mahendranagar along the far western border with India. Travelers coming by private vehicle need a *carnet de passage* for their vehicles. Otherwise, without a *carnet de passage,* a daily fee is charged with a maximum of one month allowed in-country for foreign-registered motorcycles and other vehicles. There is bus service on the main roads linking the entry points.

Bringing extensive electronic equipment through customs in Nepal can be problematic if discovered, especially if you have more than one item per category, such as two laptops. They may ask you to pay fees and to give assurance that you will take the items with you on departure.

Although the initial entry visa is valid for fifteen, thirty, or ninety days, extensions for fifteen days to a month at a time are granted at the Central Immigration Office of the Home Ministry (www.immi.gov.np), at Maitighar, in Kathmandu (south of the compound that houses parliament, Singha Durbar; see map of Kathmandu, later in this chapter). To get to the Immigration Department, head right/south from the entrance to Singha Durbar on Ram Shah Path road (also known as Babbar Mahal), which will take you past several large government buildings. Shortly after crossing an intersection, head left/east away from the main road and up on a smaller road that dead-ends near the Immigration Department. Extensions are processed on the second floor. Sometimes they require U.S. dollars and sometimes rupees, usually depending on which is stronger at the time, and a poor exchange rate is given. Visa extensions are also granted at the Immigration Department office in Pokhara near Ratna Chowk in the southern area of town west of the airport (see map of Pokhara, Chapter 6).

The maximum limit for a stay in Nepal on a tourist visa is 150 days per calendar year; however, the last 30-day extension (that is, from days 120 to 150) might require presenting an airline ticket with a confirmed departure date within the 150-day time limit. There are fines and penalties for overstaying a visa, roughly $3 USD per day for short overstays. Overstays of less than a week can be processed at the airport or land exit point upon emigration. Border crossings are open seven days a week; however, the Immigration Department and all government offices are closed on Saturdays and sometimes Sundays and on other frequent holidays. Otherwise, hours are supposed to be from 10 AM to 4 PM (Friday, 10 AM to 3 PM). Applications are processed the same day. Applications can be submitted until 3 PM (earlier on Friday) and then picked up before closing. During slow times, you may be able to get everything processed in a single visit, that is, without having to return later in the day; sometimes (unofficial) extra fees are requested to expedite processing.

NATIONAL PARK, CONSERVATION AREA, AND RESTRICTED AREA PERMITS

National park and conservation area permits are issued at the National Parks and Conservation office in Brikutimandap, Kathmandu (see map of Kathmandu later in this chapter), and the cost ranges from 1000 to 2000 NRS (Nepali rupees). Bring your passport, or a photocopy and photographs, for the processing of these permits.

Separate charges are levied for restricted areas which include Kangchenjunga, Manaslu, ACAP's Nar Phu, Upper Mustang, Dolpo–Shey Phoksumdo, Mugu, and Humla, and permits obtained from the Immigration Department are required. A minimum of at least two people are necessary, and arrangements for a visit to these areas must be made through an agency—that is, a guide is required. An unfortunate result of these rules is that little of the cost of an organized trek to these areas reaches the local people. Regulations are constantly in flux and subject to change, especially with pressure to allow greater access to these areas and to increase local benefits rather than the majority of funds going to the government and city-based trekking agencies. Permits will be checked at national park and conservation area entry points and often at police check posts along the routes. It is advisable while trekking to check in at these places and become aware of any trail updates and advisories. Some police posts may have you write your passport details in a log, so carry at least a copy of your passport.

TREKKER INFORMATION MANAGEMENT SYSTEM (TIMS) CARDS

The old trekking permit system used for decades no longer exists. There is an attempt to institute a Trekker Information Management System (TIMS) registration for which you get a card to present at checkpoints along with conservation area or national park entry permits. For independent trekkers, TIMS cards are available at a separate TIMS counter at the Nepal Tourism Board (NTB) office in Bhrikutimandap near the counters where national park and conservation area permits are obtained, as well as at the offices of the Trekking Agencies' Association of Nepal (TAAN) in Kathmandu (Maligaon) or Pokhara.

Is it necessary to obtain and carry a TIMS card for each trek?

NTB and TAAN collect information on trekkers via these cards. Previously, these cards were distributed free of cost (despite some agencies charging a fee). Some people suggested that the cards were merely a ploy for collecting marketing data which cleverly required a visit to a trekking agency, giving them a chance to pitch services. However, NTB apparently realized the potential windfall of money and wanted a larger portion (they are also recipients of the hefty "departure tax" implemented in 2005 to be paid by all travelers departing Nepal from Tribhuvan International Airport, 1356 NRS for travel to SAARC countries and 1695 NRS for all other countries. Note, there is no such departure tax for overland exits). That is, as of spring 2010, TIMS cards cost $20 USD per card/trek for each independent trekker on top of conservation area, national park, and restricted area fees (and $10 USD/head for people trekking through an agency).

When the cards were free, there was little to no enforcement at checkpoints and some trekkers did not bother to obtain one. With the assignment of fees, NTB and TAAN have a financial incentive, and monitoring will likely be stepped up and obtaining the cards enforced. Nevertheless, changes to trekking policy occur frequently, and it is difficult to predict how this will settle out and what adjustments will be made. In any case, although checkpoints will not likely be placed outside of popular routes, it is recommended to obtain a TIMS card for each trek to avoid bureaucratic hassles. For more information, see www.timsnepal.com, a website put up by TAAN.

EMBASSY REGISTRATION

The final recommended formality is to register in Kathmandu with your embassy or consulate, which can also be done for free at the Kathmandu Environmental Education Project office (KEEP) in Jyatha, Thamel, as well as at the Himalayan Rescue Association (HRA). HRA has a second-floor office in the Sagarmatha Bazaar complex in the center of Thamel along one of Nepal's few "walking streets" (no vehicles allowed). Attend HRA's altitude lecture, too. If there is no consulate, find out which country, if any, represents your country in Nepal. This can be determined from the state department or corresponding institution in your own country.

The essential information needed by the consulate is your name, a contact number back home, your passport number, and itinerary. Bring the phone numbers of the appropriate individual to contact if help is needed while on a trek. The many benefits of this process include making it easier to carry out a rescue and to contact you if there is a family emergency back home.

NATIONAL PARKS, CONSERVATION AREAS, AND WILDLIFE RESERVES

Nepal has an extensive conservation system. The protected area now safeguarded is the highest percentage of any country, over 20 percent of the landscape, and the government plans to increase this to 25 percent, aiming to conserve representative samples of the country's ecosystems.

Nepal's Department of National Parks and Wildlife Conservation (DNPWC) has designated nine areas as national parks and five as conservation areas, along with three

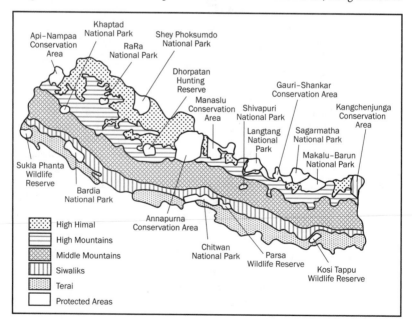

Figure 4. *Nepal's protected areas and main physiographic zones*

ACAP sign along alternate route from Tukche to Jomosom (Photo by Tokozile Robbins)

wildlife reserves and Dhorpatan Hunting Reserve. The areas, from west to east, include Api–Nampa, Khaptad, Bardia, RaRa, Shey Phoksumdo, Annapurna, Chitwan, Manaslu, Langtang, Shivapuri, Gauri–Shankar, Sagarmatha (Everest), Makalu–Barun, and Kangchenjunga. (Api–Nampa and Gauri–Shankar were proposed as the newest conservation areas on December 4, 2009, at a cabinet meeting held atop Kala Pattar, Khumbu, staged to highlight global warming concerns in the Himalaya ahead of the Copenhagen summit on climate change.)

Foreigners wishing to visit protected areas must pay a fee, obtain a permit at the entrance or in Kathmandu, and follow the regulations (it is better to obtain permits beforehand, as some areas, such as the Annapurna Conservation Area, charge double the usual fee at entry points). Buying wood from locals or taking it from the forests is illegal in the parks. All travelers doing their own cooking are required to carry stoves and fuel. The flora and fauna are protected too, and violators can be arrested and fined.

Nepal's national conservation strategy aims to strike a balance between the needs of the local people, trekkers, and the natural environment—needs that are ultimately the same. However, the task of protecting such a large proportion of the country is formidable. Many areas are remote and are only accessible by air or on foot. The rugged terrain of the Himalayan-protected areas makes coverage problematical. Practicing conservation education in a country where most of the population lives in widely dispersed small villages is very difficult.

The National Trust for Nature Conservation is responsible for managing the Annapurna and Manaslu Conservation Areas. The measures the trust is taking are both innovative and successful. The trust, established in 1982, is a nongovernmental, non-profit, independent organization aiming to conserve and manage natural resources in order to improve the quality of life of the Nepali people.

Wildlife reserves and conservation areas are alternatives to designating an area as a national park. The funds collected for visiting the conservation areas are earmarked for sustainable development projects for the residents of the region, as well as the conservation of natural resources in an attempt to balance the effects of tourism with development for its residents. This seems to have worked well in the Annapurna area where the Annapurna Conservation Area Project (ACAP) has improved trails, built toilets and garbage pits, organized litter collection, standardized menus, and set prices at lodges. ACAP has produced useful publications, and has visitor centers throughout the area as well. With national parks, the entrance fee goes into the general government treasury and rarely reaches local residents.

Additionally, outside of the publicized and regulated trekking areas, much of Nepal is not covered in guidebooks. Especially enticing is the mid-hills region between the plains and Himalaya and spanning nearly 500 miles from east to west. However, before venturing into new areas, we recommend doing one of the standard treks or at least one of the trails less traveled introduced in Chapter 9. The rest is up to you to discover.

MAPS

Maps are an integral tool for travel in Nepal providing vital route information and terrain characteristics. Especially important are features of elevation and settlement locations. The maps in this book, drawn to scale, show the villages and trails described in the text, and help the reader visualize the descriptions. Except for major ridge features and drainage systems, little else is depicted. Those wishing to explore an area further should acquire a more detailed, smaller-scale map.

Nepal-produced, adequate maps of the Himalaya and trekking routes are available at bookstores in Nepal, especially in Thamel, Kathmandu, and Lakeside, Pokhara. Trails, villages, and some contours are shown on most of them; however, many of these have been drawn by people who have not trekked. Be aware that accuracy is sometimes limited. Excellent topographic maps might be available; however, most series were published long ago and might be difficult to find. A map titled *Mount Everest*, of both the north and south sides of the mountain, was published by the National Geographic Society in November 1988. On a scale of 1:50,000, it has details not present on the *Khumbu Himal* sheet of an Austrian series and is helpful for trekkers heading from Pangboche on up. It is sometimes available in Kathmandu.

Map sellers handling maps of Nepal (including those published in Nepal) can be contacted online at the following links:

Aree Greul (Germany), www.mountain-bookshop.de

Chessler Books (U.S.), www.chesslerbooks.com

Cordee Outdoor Books & Maps (U.K.), www.cordee.co.uk

Himalayan Map House (Nepal), www.himalayan-maphouse.com

Pilgrims Books (Nepal), www.pilgrimsonlineshop.com

Stanfords (U.K.), www.stanfords.co.uk

Maps are also available at online stores, such as www.mapsworldwide.com and www.omnimap.com.

EQUIPMENT

Camping and mountaineering equipment used by Sherpas, other trekkers, and climbers on Himalayan expeditions is often available for sale or rent in Kathmandu, Pokhara, Namche Bazaar, and popular waypoints along the routes. You may even find new gear that went unused on expeditions. While much of it is designed for climbing, the equipment is often suitable for trekking as well. The road forming the southern border of Thamel in Kathmandu is a good place to find shops with expedition gear, and do not be surprised if the owner of the shop with whom you are bargaining is a prolific climber. Prices vary from cheap to outrageous, and quality is not uniform. Some trekkers sell equipment by means of notices in restaurants, hotels, and at KEEP (see the sidebar in Chapter 4). Packs, jackets, and many other items are locally manufactured (not under license), complete with a counterfeit foreign label. Such gear might only last one trek, but some is durable and excellent. There are now genuine outlet stores along Tridevi Marg in Thamel and Durbar Marg, the road that leads from the former royal palace, now the Narayanhiti National Museum. Some people are able to pick up everything they need in the city, but it is safer to arrive at least minimally prepared.

If you don't own items such as a good down or synthetic sleeping bag, jacket, sleeping pad, and pack, or if you have other travel plans that make it difficult to bring your own equipment, then plan to rent. Again, be aware that quality is variable and a sleeping bag with an advertised rating of –20°C might not come near to matching expectations. We would not advise renting footwear. At least bring bring your own shoes and boots, first wearing them at home to break them in lest they "break you" on the trail (new boots are notorious for causing blisters). When renting equipment, don't leave your passport as collateral—you may need it. Cash, either Nepali rupees or hard currency, is usually left as a deposit. Sometimes a guide well known to the shopkeeper can vouch for your return of the gear. Such trust in Nepal may surprise you.

If traveling to remote places where there are no lodges, you can outfit your party for excursions by renting tents, sleeping bags, and cooking and climbing gear. Inspect any equipment carefully before you rely on it for a prolonged period in the high country. Equipment can be rented in Kathmandu, Pokhara, or in popular high-altitude destinations such as Namche Bazaar (Khumbu), Kyangjin Gomba (Langtang), Jomosom (Annapurna Circuit), Manang (Annapurna Circuit), and Chomrong (Annapurna Sanctuary).

FOOTWEAR

Comfortable footwear is a must. Look for good traction, shock absorbency, waterproofness, breathability, good foot and ankle support, light weight, durability, and a separate, perhaps shock-absorbent, insole. A variety of good and bad designs appear in trekking stores in Kathmandu.

Running shoes, cross-trainers, and the like are popular and quite suitable below the snowline. But make sure they provide adequate traction, and consider the need for ankle support, especially if carrying a pack. Good shock-absorbing heels are excellent for downhill travel. This type of footwear is not suitable for snow. If you plan to cross high passes, take along substantial boots for snow and cold or face the risk of serious frostbite. Substantial leather-and-fabric hiking boots with shock-absorbing heels are good for the hills—if they are strong enough to last. Individuals prone to ankle sprains should always wear boots that go over the ankle and provide support. Those troubled with knee problems, especially when going downhill, should wear boots or shoes with shock-absorbing heels. Trekkers carrying a heavy pack are better off with a more substantial boot. For high-altitude treks, you might consider taking two pairs of boots, a light, flexible pair and a more substantial pair for rugged terrain. For the substantial pair, make sure there is enough room to comfortably accommodate an extra pair of socks for the cold regions. Bring spare insoles. In snow or wet weather, appropriate waterproofing material is needed. For high-altitude ventures where you might encounter sections of ice such as on frozen streams, consider traction devices to attach to the soles of your boots. While crampons might be the choice for mountaineers, gripper products such as Yaktrax, Microspikes, or STABilicers could be useful for hikers. Try the footwear out at home on terrain similar, if in lesser scale, to that in Nepal.

Lightweight foam or rubber sandals can be ideal to change into at the end of the day. They can also be used for some limited trail walking, and such footwear with Velcro or other easily attachable straps that do not come between the toes are unexcelled for wading streams.

If boots or shoes are irritating your feet, determine what the problem is. Does the foot move relative to the shoe or boot and create friction? If so, try using the laces in a creative way to decrease the movement. Try lacing loosely to the instep, and then tying a knot and lacing tightly the rest of the way, especially for downhill portions. Boots with locking lace hooks make this easier. On some boots, avoiding some of the first lacing holes while lacing vertically may prevent painful infolding of the leather. Try adding padding, such as moleskin, in layers to the area where friction is occurring to redistribute the stresses. If your footwear has removable insoles, carry a spare pair and change them frequently. Bring spare laces or nylon cord which can also be used in an emergency to provide added traction to cross snow or icy or otherwise slippery sections by tying them around the sole of the boot.

Once you have a well-fitting, comfortable shoe, the secret of foot care is in the socks. The outer pair, which should be soft and woolen to absorb the moisture, should be changed frequently. Avoid thick outer socks made of synthetic material (acrylic or nylon) because they do not absorb sweat well and often lead to blisters. Wick-dry socks are preferred by some. Synthetic socks as thinner inners worn under heavier outers allow the feet and the inner socks some movement inside the outer socks, decreasing stress and preventing blisters. (For prevention and care of blisters, see Chapter 5.) We recommend wearing wool socks over a light, thin pair of synthetic socks. A plastic bag over the inner sock may prevent the inside of the boot from getting wet from sweat and, as a vapor lock, can help keep feet warm in cold, snowy conditions. If forced to use inadequate footwear in unexpected snowy conditions, use of this vapor-barrier technique may save toes from frostbite. Change socks twice a day or more, keeping a pair drying outside the pack, if you are having trouble with your feet. Take enough pairs, say four to six, for the journey. In the high frosty regions, gaiters are useful in keeping snow out of boot tops.

CLOTHING

Loose, quick-drying trousers for men, long skirts for women, and shirts with pockets are good basic garments. Pants with zip-off legs are a good choice for variable temperatures. To understand why skirts are *de rigueur* for women, see the "Dress" section in Chapter 3.

While traveling in the Himalaya, layering is essential. Nepal's steep terrain can cause a swift buildup of internal heat, especially while carrying a pack on sun-drenched uphill sections. However, the high altitude also means that you and the environment can cool quickly, especially in the shade of the mighty Himalaya and when the sun has set or is behind the clouds, and more so if your clothes are wet from sweat. Therefore, it is important to have the ability to remove or add items easily. Clothes made of all-cotton material, though comfortable, are not the best choice as cotton absorbs and tends to hold moisture.

Long thermal underwear is necessary at higher altitudes, especially during the winter months. This first layer of clothing should keep you dry by being able to wick moisture away from the skin to the next layer. There are many brand specialties in this area. Thermals made with polypropylene, a petroleum-based synthetic, might be a good inner layer, although it has a reputation of becoming stinky (hence the nickname, "poly-phew"). Nylon is a durable material; perhaps something blended with cotton would do well. Some find that merino wool underwear next to the skin is the non-malodorous ideal for warmth and versatility. Silk is lightweight yet needs extra care and easily comes apart at the seams. Animal rights activists will be happy to know that there are silks available that do not rely on mass killing of production caterpillars. These include *ahimsa* silk (also known as peace silk and vegetarian silk) and *tussah* (or wild) silk.

The next layer should provide warmth. Wool clothing is traditionally chosen for the cold because it feels warm when wet. A sweater or synthetic fiber-insulated fleece (pile) jacket works well in wet weather and also dries quickly. One with underarm vents or "pit zips" that allow you to slip off the sleeves while walking can be the ultimate insulator.

The outer layer should not only add warmth but keep you dry as well. A down jacket can be a light, efficient choice, but down is useless when wet. A waterproof, breathable shell that is soft and light works well. Aim for something either with a zip-out liner or large enough to cover a sweater or fleece jacket. Keep in mind that the more waterproof the material, the less breathable it will be. Garments made of genuine Gore-Tex have a good reputation, and there are other similar materials on the market. Check to ensure that the seams have been properly sealed.

Down pants or fleece-lined pants for sitting around in the cool high campsites are also good. Most important is a windproof outer pant to wear inside drafty lodges and in the high country. We recommend a waterproof, breathable outer pant with leg zippers that can be worn over pants—or, for women, worn under a skirt. Garments that can be easily put on over other clothing are the most versatile. In short, a layered system with suitable underwear, leggings or fleece pants, and jacket, covered with a waterproof and breathable jacket and pants, provides versatility for almost all conditions. Wear the underwear and the outerwear for active situations, adding the fleece in severe cold. It takes practice to adjust clothing, donning and doffing it when necessary to keep from overheating and then freezing in your sweat, or from getting too cold when you stop.

A hat, especially a balaclava, is important on cold days to conserve body heat (otherwise considerable heat can be lost from the scalp due to the head's abundant blood supply). A visor to shade the eyes from the sun is an ideal addition. Dark UV-protective glasses or goggles are also essential at high altitudes, especially on snow. Such eye protection should have eye shields to prevent light from coming in from the sides. Sunglasses should absorb all ultraviolet light and at least 90 percent of visible light. If you or someone else is stuck on snow without them, fabricate an emergency pair by making slits in a strip of cardboard, paper or cloth and wrapping it around the eyes. Long hair combed over the eyes can also help. If you wear eyeglasses or contact lenses, bring a spare pair and a copy of the refraction prescription. Consider bringing disposable contact lenses to solve the problem of cleaning them in Nepal.

Insulated mittens are better than gloves for cold weather. Fingerless gloves, or ones made of thin silk or synthetic material, are good for operating cameras or attending to other intricate details in the snow. Liner mitts with pockets for heat packs might work for those who get cold fingers yet need to operate equipment in the cold. Finally, for snow or winds up high, a waterproof or at least wind-resistant outer mitt is necessary. An unexpected snowfall, falling and getting mittens wet, and numerous other situations can result in finger loss from frostbite. (See the previous section for sock recommendations and frostbite prevention for toes.) If you are stuck, and inadequately equipped, use spare socks as mittens, and cover them with plastic bags or stuff sacks, to save your fingers.

It is difficult to stay dry while walking in rainy weather. Those wearing waterproof garments tend to sweat inside them. Gore-Tex or similar breathable jackets and pants with vents or zippered areas under the arms and down the legs are preferable, because they have better ventilation. In the 100 percent humidity of an intense rainfall, no clothing can breathe, so you will get wet from the inside no matter what. In those circumstances, light clothes and an umbrella or loose-fitting poncho may be the best compromise. Trekkers can also use umbrellas for shade in the hot sun as well as for privacy while answering nature's call.

Men should bring knee-length shorts for the hot, low altitudes. A bathing suit can be useful, and modesty should prevail at all times (see Chapter 3 for more on bathing customs).

You may feel chilly in the morning, when it could be well below freezing, yet sweat later in the day while active in the sunshine. The climatological data for Nepal in Chapter 1 should help you plan what to bring.

SLEEPING GEAR

A down or synthetic-fiber mummy sleeping bag is usually necessary for comfort at temperatures below freezing. A bag with a full zipper is more versatile because it is comfortable at cool, high altitudes and in warm, low country. A washable sleeping bag liner solves some hygiene problems, and the liner alone may be all you'll need during the

Journals written en route will become treasured mementos. (Photo by Pat Morrow)

monsoon season at low altitudes. Trekkers not spending time in the cold heights may bring a bag that is too thick and hence too warm. Unfortunately, sleeping bags do not have removable layers of insulation. Many lodges have quilts, comforters, and blankets, but you can't always count on their presence, adequacy, and cleanliness, especially during busy times. Hotels where clean sheets are changed daily are not part of trekking in Nepal. Many trekkers along the popular routes manage without a sleeping bag, but we wouldn't advise this on high-altitude routes.

In lodges along the popular trekking trails, you usually get a mattress and a pillow to sleep on, but not everywhere, especially during the high season when late arrivers sometimes have to sleep in a dining hall. Although most lodges will have foam padding, those who are camping will need an air mattress, foam pad, or inflatable pad for a comfortable night's sleep. The short models, extending from the knees to the shoulders, weigh less and can be sufficient. Some people carry inflatable pillows. If you bring an inflatable pad or pillow, carry a repair kit. A sheet of plastic or ground cloth helps keep sleeping gear clean and dry and prevents dampness from being wicked up from the ground.

The lightest, most versatile combination for all but the highest elevations is a light, rectangular sleeping bag with a full zipper and a removable bottom sheet with slots for an air mattress or pad. The combination bottom sheet, zipped to the top bag, makes a light, comfortable bed for two, especially when the air bed or pad is installed. The unzipped bag, with sheet attached, can be used as a blanket for two in the warmer zones. The bottom sheet can be zipped to make a single cool cloth bag for low elevations. This cloth bag can be installed in the regular sleeping bag as a liner for individual use up high. Wearing plenty of clothing in this case can make it suitable at higher elevations, if you choose a bag size large enough.

SHELTER

Your route and preferred style dictate whether you need a tent. If you prefer to camp, or desire privacy where there aren't trekker lodges, a tent is necessary, as it is at high altitudes where there might not be facilities or shelter. Generally, having one large enough to sit up in and to house other people such as porters in an emergency is best. Weight, seasonality, and ease of setting up are factors to consider. A three-season tent with ventilation and a rain fly over the opening(s) is versatile enough for most trekkers. Make sure that the seams are properly sealed. Check out the setup instructions, and practice before you depart and do not forget a groundsheet. A lightweight "emergency blanket" (aluminized polyester), bivouac shelter, or plastic sheet can be carried for emergency shelter.

PACKS

Many well-designed packs are available. Choose one that will store items requiring easy access in pockets and can expand capacity when necessary. Carry a spare plastic buckle at least for the waistband and perhaps for the straps (keep buckles engaged while not wearing the pack to protect them from being stepped on). Equipment and supplies that the porters carry can be packed in sturdy, bright-colored duffel bags, preferably ones that can be locked. A waist or chest pack, worn in front, can keep camera and other frequently needed items easily accessible.

While we understand the "carry it all yourself" philosophy, it makes little sense to burden yourself down like a pack animal and then wear yourself out carrying the load. There may be little for you to enjoy except the feeling that you did it. In this case, we recommend hiring porters to ease your load and provide employment, and greatly enhance the journey in the process. (See the "Guides and Porters" section later in this chapter.)

COOKING GEAR

For those organizing their own cooking kits, gear is available in Kathmandu. Regulations require that all trekkers and their porters, cooks, and guides be self-sufficient in the national parks. Trekkers should use stoves powered by kerosene, propane/butane, or other fuel rather than wood, especially in the high-altitude areas, national parks, and conservation areas. One group that Stephen encountered, crossing Thorung La after a heavy snowfall on the last day of November, was wise in bringing a stove. They were able to melt snow and have a hot drink up high. On the same day there, another un-prepared trekker sustained serious frostbite. Even if you are eating in lodges, carrying a lightweight, portable stove and fuel canister along with bags of your favorite tea or other brew can be a life-saver in the high country as well as provide a tasty, invigorating drink.

Kerosene is the only fuel available in the hills, although some shops on the main routes may have mixed-fuel canisters (such as Primus) for sale. It is better to buy canis-ters at trekking shops in Kathmandu that also sell stoves capable of using both portable canisters and kerosene. There are kerosene depots available along the popular routes so you can periodically replenish supply. The impure kerosene available usually clogs up most stoves, so periodic cleaning of the fuel jet becomes necessary. Become familiar with the stove's operation before you trek and carry a repair kit or spare parts.

MISCELLANEOUS GEAR AND PERSONAL ITEMS

A medical kit is essential (see Chapter 5).

Take enough stuff sacks to store all your gear and to make it easier to keep track of your goods. Light, zippered, nylon bags in various colors can be used to store small items. They can be packed in a duffel bag or a porter's *Doko*. A sturdy, zippered duffel bag that locks is ideal for a porter to carry. Get a heavy nylon or canvas model—light nylon wears too quickly. A bright-colored bag makes it easy to spot from afar and can help locate your porter. On long treks during the monsoon, we use large plastic garbage bags (brought from home) to protect the contents of those duffel bags that don't need to be unpacked too often; small plastic bags inside stuff sacks are useful for other gear. It's a good idea to bring another lockable piece of luggage in which to store extra gear at a hotel while you trek. Small combination locks are convenient to use, although keyed, Chinese-made locks are widely available in Nepal.

An ingenious device that converts a sleeping pad into a comfortable seat (such as Therm-a-Rest's Trekker Lounge or Chair) may be especially useful for those staying in tents, or in Nepali homes where they are floor-bound, and want a seat to read or write for some time.

Consider what might break down, and carry appropriate spare parts and repair tools. A sewing kit is indispensable, as is a sewing awl for heavier items. Epoxy glue can repair most things if used discriminately and a small roll of duct tape can be invaluable. A flex-ible contact cement, such as Barge cement, is useful on boots. A pair of pliers can be good to have; the Leatherman or Swiss Army gadget combination can be useful but unnecessarily heavy unless the multi-functional tools are needed. Often a simple pocket knife will do. Nylon (parachute) cord has many uses, including lashings, makeshift shoe and boot laces, or clothesline.

Ski poles, walking sticks or *lauro*, and the like have become commonplace. The tele-scopic ski poles adjust to various lengths and collapse to a small size. People customarily use them for steep descents to shift weight from the lower body to the upper, thus easing the impact on their knees and hips and possibly lessening fatigue. Trekking poles also help you maintain purchase on steep ascents and on difficult trails. Consider rigging a carabiner and sling to each pack strap to attach to the wrist loops of collapsed poles, to secure them when you want to photograph or do not want to hold them. A jury-rigged screw head on the ski pole handle can provide a monopod for your camera.

For most trekkers we advise carrying poles, or bamboo versions found in tourist areas and along the trails, and using them occasionally on difficult stretches. They may prevent stumbles leading to injurious falls. On the other hand, constant use of a walking stick wastes energy and tires the arms and shoulders. As well, your sense of balance relaxes, and in precarious situations where you can't use poles, or on easy terrain without them, this could be dangerous. In difficult, extremely steep situations, you are better off holding onto the ground for support and balance. Sticks or ski poles are ideal for crossing streams on ice-covered rocks, for snow drifts on high passes, on slippery monsoon trails, on slippery moraines, and on icy trails after snowfalls. Those with severely arthritic hips or knees find them useful on descent. As a slight assist, one pole is adequate, but people with disabilities should use two, kept in close to the body. Practice before relying on them.

An ice ax is advisable for steep snow or glacier travel, but only if you know how to carry and use this potentially lethal device.

Bring several handkerchiefs or bandannas. A bandanna can be useful as a makeshift face mask in windy, dusty areas and during vehicle travel, and to dry cups, plates, and hands, as well as for the usual runny nose that accompanies colds and upper-respiratory infections—or learn to blow your nose Nepali style, covering each nostril in turn and blowing out the other. (The use of toilet paper for nose blowing creates disposal problems.) Petroleum jelly, chap stick, and balm are good for cold-weather chapping. For women, a reusable menstrual cup (such as the Mooncup) as an ecologically sound alternative to tampons and sanitary napkins can be ideal for travel and lasts for years. It is recommended that you become familiar with using and cleaning it before relying on it during a trek. Otherwise, tampons should be the variety that can be inserted without an applicator that then must be discarded.

A water bottle of at least 1-quart (liter) capacity should be carried for each person in the party. Your local hospital emergency department might be able to provide empty one-liter plastic bottles that were used to hold irrigation fluids. Plastic and lightweight stainless-steel or aluminum containers can be found in trekking shops in Nepal. Stainless-steel or aluminum bottles can be ideal for storing water that has been boiled and is still hot. Encasing the bottle in a clean sock or hat or wrapping another item of

This bamboo comb removes lice nits, and ghiu *(used as hair oil) suffocates the critters—part of hygiene for Nepalis.*
(Photo by Stephen Bezruchka)

clothing around the container will enable you to use it as a source of heat that can be kept close to the body or even placed in a sleeping bag for added warmth. Some trekkers find a wide-mouth "pee bottle" useful in a cold tent or lodge at night. Wide-mouth Tupperware containers with good lids work well for women. Women might also find a portable female urinary device (such as Shewee) to be useful along the trails.

Pack biodegradable soap, a washcloth or towel, and a toothbrush. Bring a headlamp or small flashlight (torch)—the plastic kind is warmer to handle in cold weather. An LED headlamp is ideal for keeping the hands free, particularly if you like to read and write after sundown. Bring rechargeable rather than disposable batteries. They can be charged in many places now, especially along the main routes. However, carry spares and keep in mind that less-frequented trails might only offer solar power which might not have the accessories to fit recharging devices. There are no battery recycling facilities in Nepal, and it is considered environmentally ethical to bring spent cells back to your home country for proper disposal.

Consider earplugs (several pairs, as they are not only easily lost but in high demand) for noisy hotels, buses, and the occasional obstreperous dog in the depths of the night. A combination lock can secure hotel room doors without keys or as a backup to hotel locks and allow several people to enter independently. Such locks can also be used for duffel bags and pack pockets.

It is wise to have at least one GPS device or compass in the party for high mountain travel. Magnetic declination in Nepal is less than 2 or 3 degrees west in most places and can be overlooked for most map work. GPS can be unreliable in sections of Himalayan drainages where steep gorges diminish satellite reception. A pair of binoculars, an altimeter, and a thermometer can be helpful. For those wishing to have a convenient multipurpose instrument, there are now several watches that combine an altimeter and compass with the timekeeper.

Trekkers wearing contact lenses are advised that the risks of infectious complications are probably greater here than at home. Bring plenty of sterilizing/disinfecting solutions, and don't exceed advised recommended wearing times. Use boiled water for cleansing when water is called for. At the first sign of any problems, remove the lenses and wear glasses. Follow the treatment for conjunctivitis outlined in Chapter 5. Disposable extended-wear contact lenses are probably the best choice for a trek.

Insects are not usually a problem in the high country, and malaria is very rare in trekkers to Nepal, but those trekkers traveling extensively in the lowlands during the warmer months or during the monsoon could use mosquito netting while sleeping and insect repellents while traveling. Repellents with picardin and DEET (or N,N-diethyl-meta-toluamide) are effective against mosquitoes, or try natural repellents such as citronella or eucalyptus oil–based repellents. Insecticide sprays and powders (those containing pyrethrins or permethrin are safest) may help in the sleeping bag and can be applied to the netting. Anti-leech oil can be found in Kathmandu for monsoon treks. Some people attract bedbugs and other critters that wreak havoc in the night, especially in some lodges. Repellents, nets, and insecticides help.

Consider taking a recording device to capture the local music and other sounds of Nepal. Many compact efficient models are available. An external microphone enhances recording quality. You might consider using a dictation recorder for your voice impressions as you walk. A pocket attached to a pack strap can carry small electronic devices and more.

If you are a musician who plays a portable instrument, consider bringing it along. A harmonica, recorder, or flute can help break the ice in a village and elicit good will.

Consider other social and entertainment skills that you may have that you could share with people in Nepal. Perhaps you juggle, draw, or can play games with string, or perform magic tricks.

Most trekkers carry reading matter (high-content magazines are lightweight), and writing materials, and hotels along the popular routes often have paperbacks to sell or trade. Rereading a journal kept on a trek can be very rewarding. A pack of cards or miniature versions of popular board games (such as Scrabble) can be a good way to liven up a restaurant and get to know fellow trekkers.

Bring a picture book about your country to show to special Nepali people you encounter. Rural Nepali folk especially appreciate looking at pictures of farm scenes, horses, cows, sheep, goats, and produce. Assemble a small photo album of family and farm-related activities. Viewing this will be a gift to share.

Trekkers likely to visit monasteries en route might acquire *kata*, or ceremonial scarves, to present to *lamas* or adorn sacred objects. These can be purchased in Kathmandu, but you can often get them on site at a monastery by asking a monk.

This gaaine *or minstrel wanders from town to town singing and playing the* saarangi. (Photo by Stephen Bezruchka)

For the rare situation in which you may have to deal with the bureaucracy in rural Nepal, especially off the main trekking routes, a supply of business cards and letterhead stationery can be valuable. Rubber stamps and, especially, embossed seals can also help get things done.

For anything absolutely indispensable that you could not replace on the trail, consider taking a spare. You might also bring items to barter or trade on your trek. Warm clothes, booties, almost any kind of clothing, including designer labels, are valuable currency, particularly along the well-trekked trails. See Chapter 3 for gift suggestions and appropriate circumstances.

Nowadays, there are outdoor outfitters with stores that resemble warehouses with a vast variety of products all aimed at increasing comfort and style while exploring the outdoors. For many reasons, including some important ones to be discussed later, be reasonable in what you bring and keep most of it packed until needed. Trekkers who carry their own equipment often find on return that they lugged many non-emergency items that were never used. Often they end up leaving things along the way. Review your equipment list, and pare it down beforehand.

EQUIPMENT LIST

In the following equipment list, **R** indicates items you may be able to rent in Nepal, and **P** indicates items you can hope to purchase in Nepal, though you may not be able to count on the quality.

R	P	ESSENTIAL FOR ALL TREKKERS
	•	Walking shoes, well broken in, and spare insoles if appropriate
	•	Socks: several pairs of heavy synthetic or wool outer socks and a few pairs of nylon inner socks, plus a clean pair of either for sleeping in while at higher elevations
	•	Skirts: midcalf to above the ankle for women
	•	Pants: baggy ones are best
	•	Shirts, blouses, T-shirts
	•	Underwear (including sports bra for women)
	•	Hat with wide brim (or visor)
•	•	Sleeping bag adequate for temperatures encountered (may be provided by some trekking agencies). Ratings for bags made in Nepal are unreliable. Consider a sleeping bag liner as well for added warmth
		Repair kit to deal with all your gear
	•	Water-purification materials (see Chapter 5)
	•	Water bottle; at least 32-ounce (1-liter) capacity per person
•	•	Backpack with outside pockets to handle smaller items
	•	Nylon stuff sacks for organizing equipment
	•	Medical kit (see Chapter 5)
	•	Headlamp (recommended) or flashlight (torch)
	•	Rechargeable batteries, charger, and universal adapter
	•	Handkerchief or bandanna (more than one): useful as makeshift face mask in windy, dusty areas, and to dry cups, plates, hands, as well as for usual runny nose that accompanies high, cold areas
	•	Toiletries: biodegradable soap (ayurvedic soap is readily available in Nepal), washcloth, towel, toothbrush and paste, dental floss, comb, hand sanitizer
		National park or conservation area permit, if required
	•	This book
		Verified phone numbers for your embassy or consulate, trekking agency (home number of managing director), and helicopter services, to use in case of needing a rescue
	•	Rupees in a variety of denominations
		U.S. dollars, enough for an air ticket fare if your route takes you near airstrips and plans change so you want to fly out
	•	Pen or pencil, ink, paper (letterhead if possible), envelopes (to write an emergency message should the need arise), and business cards
	•	Pocket knife, perhaps with scissors and more
	•	Plastic bags: several sizes with rubber bands or twist ties, especially useful for keeping gear dry in inclement weather
		Elastic bands, nylon line (parachute cord): for lashings, hanging laundry, makeshift shoestrings, or for wrapping around sole of shoes when extra traction is needed on icy, or otherwise slippery trails
	•	Blister materials (see Chapter 5)

EQUIPMENT LIST (CONTINUED)

R	P	
	•	Lubricant for chapped lips and skin
		Feminine hygiene: women can consider bringing an environment friendly, re-usable menstrual cup (e.g., Mooncup) that collects menstrual fluids, as an alternative to carrying absorbent, disposable tampons or other materials
		Plastic trowel to bury feces
	•	Matches or cigarette lighter for toilet paper
	•	UV-protective sunglasses
		Spare eyeglasses or contact lenses if you wear them
	•	Umbrella if traveling in warm sunny lowlands or in the monsoon
		Earplugs, more than one pair (rooms in lodges can have remarkably thin walls, buses often have blaring stereos, and unruly dogs bark deep into the night)
	•	Pair of flip-flops, sandals, or other lightweight foam footwear: for use after the day's hike is over, around the room, lodge, and village; especially useful in toilet and shower areas
		Smiles

FOR TREKS TO COLD, SNOWY, AND HIGH PLACES

R	P	
•	•	Wool or fleece hat; balaclava
•	•	Wool sweaters or fleece or down/synthetic down jacket
•	•	Wool or fleece pants
	•	Long underwear of polypropylene, nylon, wool, or silk
	•	Sleeping bag liner
•	•	Mitts (possibly gloves) with water-resistant shell and warm, light inner lining for dexterity
•	•	Windproof outer garments, pants, and jacket
•	•	Boots, well broken in and waterproofed
	•	Gaiters to keep snow out of boots
•	•	Ice ax, rope, and crampons for glacier travel
	•	Glacier goggles with spares, including enough for Nepali employees
	•	Sunscreen; zinc oxide and lip balm for lips

IF TREKKING WITH AN AGENCY
(Check with the manager regarding items in the other categories)

R	P	
	•	Duffel bag (sturdy, zippered, lockable with all your gear stowed inside) to give to your porter
		Phone numbers of the agency, including the home phone of the managing director

IF TREKKING INDEPENDENTLY AND RELYING ON LODGES

R	P	
	•	Toilet paper, if you are not inclined to use water
	•	Makeshift shelter: emergency blanket (aluminized polyester), plastic sheeting, or bivouac shelter
	•	High-energy food for contingencies
	•	Sleeping bag liner for use between lodge's sheets/blankets

EQUIPMENT LIST (CONTINUED)

IF TREKKING INDEPENDENTLY AND CAMPING/COOKING FOOD (Occasionally)

R	P	
•	•	Tent
	•	Air mattress or foam pad
	•	Plastic ground sheet (especially if up high)
	•	Toilet paper
	•	Sturdy duffel bags, zippered and lockable, for gear
•	•	Stove
	•	Fuel containers, fuel filter if using kerosene
•	•	Cooking pots
	•	Cups, plates, spoons
	•	Scouring pad
•	•	Shelter, warm clothing, and cooking facilities for your employees if you will be in remote areas
	•	Food, packed appropriately
	•	Water bag for carrying large quantities from a distant source

MONSOON TREKS

R	P	
	•	Running, jogging shoes with good traction
	•	Umbrella
•	•	Collapsible ski poles
	•	Waterproof-breathable (Gore-Tex or similar) jacket with underarm vents, or a rain poncho or cape large enough to cover self and pack
	•	Pack cover (ones made in Kathmandu are a good value)
	•	Waterproof rain chaps or pants (optional)
	•	Large, heavy-duty plastic bags and several smaller ones
	•	Plastic sheeting for covering porters' loads and other uses
	•	Insect repellent: picardin, DEET (available at CIWEC), essential oils of eucalyptus or citronella or longer-lasting candles, pyrethrin
	•	Anti-leech oil (available at KEEP and some pharmacies in Kathmandu)
		Patience
		Adaptability

OPTIONAL GEAR

R	P	
	•	Specialty food items: protein-dense items like spirulina or Vegemite/Marmite, perhaps garlic bulb/powder
	•	Bathing suit
	•	Shorts for men
	•	Shaving paraphernalia for men
	•	Altimeter
	•	Universal adapter for recharging batteries/electronic devices
	•	GPS
	•	UV water purifier (e.g., SteriPEN)
		Microbiological water filter
	•	Compass
	•	Thermometer
	•	Watch with a chronograph and alarm (possibly an altimeter)

		EQUIPMENT LIST (CONTINUED)
R	P	OPTIONAL GEAR (CONTINUED)
•		Binoculars
•		Spotting telescope and tripod
•		Maps
		Star chart
		Credit/debit card
•		Vacuum bottle
		Candle lantern
•		Candles
		Female urination device (Shewee allows women to urinate while standing)
•		Reading material (magazines are lightweight)
•		Journal, diary, or pocket notebook to record observations
•		Stationery, air letters, postcards, stamps
•		English-language learning materials to use with porters (buy in Kathmandu)
•		*Kata* or ceremonial scarf to give to a *lama* or to adorn sacred object
		Picture book or postcards about your country or favorite activities
		Picture book of farms, farm activities, and animals
		Photographs of your family, friends, and activities
•		Camera, spare memory cards, appropriate spare lithium batteries
•		Audio recorder, external microphone, lithium batteries
•		MP3/Ipod
•		Mobile phone/Blackberry
•		Musical instrument
		Board games
•		Badminton set
•		Belt bag, waist pack, or chest pack, for easy access to selected items while walking
•		Knee or ankle brace
•		Collapsible ski poles

PHOTOGRAPHY IN NEPAL

"Photography is a magical process that has given Sahibs all over the world the chance to rest under the guise of business," states Ed Cronin. Inexperienced photographers should bring a small, simple digital camera. For the more experienced, a chest pack to hold the camera and several lenses for a single-lens reflex (SLR) keeps equipment close at hand. Bring necessary spare batteries (lithium is best) to power the modern camera, for outside of the main trekking routes, none will be available in the hills. It is better to have rechargeable batteries and to carry extra charged battery packs. As Nepal becomes increasingly electrified, there are many places along the popular routes to recharge. Make sure to bring a universal adapter. Electricity averages 220 volts/50 cycle in Nepal. Entrepreneurs in areas with electricity may sometimes take a fee to charge your batteries. Keep batteries warm to prolong their life, perhaps using a pocket close to body heat during the day and storing them under your blanket or inside the sleeping bag at night. Remember to bring extra memory cards.

Jim Elzinga once remarked that if you are walking along a trail in Nepal with a camera, lose your step, and fall, and in the process accidentally trip the camera shutter, you will get a good photograph. It does take a little more work, a lot more if you want top images, but Nepal is very photogenic. Problems in getting good results stem from the immense scale of the terrain, light contrasts, and poorly lit interiors. In Nepal the range of light intensities in bright sun makes good results almost impossible except in the early morning or late in the day. For best results restrict your photography to the oblique filtered light close to sunrise and sunset. Consider using a standard ultraviolet (UV) or a skylight filter, and perhaps a polarizing or a graduated filter for landscape shots. Bring a tripod if you are serious about mountain light.

Useful principles for bringing back memorable photos are to take pictures of large-scale overviews, then focus on the subject, and finally get some close-up detail of features. Modern small digital cameras excel technically at close-ups and telephotos, but often lack wide-angle capabilities without accessory lenses. Getting in close with a wide-angle lens is an underappreciated photojournalistic skill. Variable light sensitivity that covers a huge range, image stabiliziation, as well as flip-out screens that allow composition from a variety of positions are features of many modern cameras that enhance photographic capabilities today. It can be helpful to bring along the instruction manual unless you know your camera's capabilities well or it is a very simple model (which few are these days).

FOOD

In lodges catering to trekkers, an international menu of greatly varying quality is available. Where possible, stick to the local meals, often *daal bhaat tarkaari* (lentils, rice, and vegetables), which is more energy-efficient to prepare and uses local resources. Packaged quick-cooking noodles have become more commonplace in shops and inns throughout much of the country as a fast food. However, they are usually not satisfying as a meal replacement and often contain monosodium glutamate (MSG); vegetarians will be interested to know that the flavor packets usually contain animal by-products. Often the plastic packaging is tossed indiscriminately or burned and adds to pollution problems.

The expeditionary trekker, organizing food to cook along the way, can find considerable variety in Kathmandu, where many Western processed and packaged foods are now available in the large "supermarkets" that have sprung up, mainly to cater to the new Nepali middle class and expatriates. Dehydrated foods produced in Kathmandu, suitable for trekking and mountaineering expeditions, are available. These foods are of good quality, are quite reasonably priced, and require less fuel to cook than many other foods. You may want to bring along nuts and dried fruits as a nutritious supplement, and combined with a bit of chocolate you can get an energy boost. Fresh fruit is rarely to never available higher up.

The type of food available in the hills varies depending on the place and the season. Weekly markets, a great source of supplies in addition to being entertaining, are often found in the hills. Staples and occasional processed foods are available. Foods taken on mountaineering expeditions find their way into shops in the appropriate areas—for instance, around Namche Bazaar and Annapurna. The variety and quality vary greatly. Cooked meals available at inns, lodges, and hotels are described in Chapter 4.

Although the metric system has been introduced and is the legal standard, the traditional system of measure given here is still used in distant locales. The metric measures used in the hills have variable standards. The Nepali beer bottle, holding about 700 milliliters or 23.7 fluid ounces (US), is often passed off as a liter or 33.8 fluid ounces (US). Volume is traditionally measured in *maanaa*. One *maanaa* equals 20 ounces or 2 ½ cups (0.6 liter). Eight *maanaa* equal a *paathi*. One *pau* equals 7 ounces or 200 grams. Be sure

Heavily loaded porter in flimsy footwear on the pebbly route from Munchi to Manang
(Photo by Tokozile Robbins)

to bring sealable containers with you on a trek to carry the foods you might buy. Small cloth bags with plastic liners are ideal.

Note that few meat items are mentioned. Most Westerners are used to meals centered around meat, but this was not traditionally so in Nepal, and is even changing in the West for health reasons. Along trekking and main travel routes, meat, chicken, goat, or buffalo is often available at extra cost. For more on food and nutrition, see Chapters 4 and 5.

GUIDES AND PORTERS

Having an informed guide can make all the difference on a venture into the Himalaya. He or she can share a wealth of knowledge and insight on the route and culture, assist in arranging food and accommodation, and generally help to ensure your well-being. It can be an extraordinary introduction to Nepal. Conversely, having a poor guide can cause needless conflict and tension and turn the trek into a struggle. Traveling with a porter can also be a tremendous opportunity to get to know Nepal and its people. However, some tourists might be uncomfortable with the idea of allowing another person to carry their gear. In reality, having a porter should be a mutually beneficial arrangement, providing a decent wage to the person you hire in a land with a dearth of employment while allowing you more freedom and ease and enhancing the journey in many ways. Not only will the trek be more comfortable, but often long-lasting friendships are made. In any event, trekkers are indirect recipients of porter labor from the food and goods purchased along the routes hauled up by them.

Be aware, there are many instances reported where a guide (and sometimes a porter) has reduced the freedom of movement and choice among lodges, schedules, stopping points, and more. Often, guides receive a small commission for bringing trekkers to certain lodges and restaurants and become insistent about patronizing these establishments. This can result in frequent disagreements between the guide and guest. To avoid such conflict, make sure up front that both parties know what they are agreeing to, perhaps even putting the arrangement into writing. Include not only the wage, but whether that wage includes food and lodging, and whether the guest or the guide decides on the particular lodge and restaurant and the extent and limitations of the daily schedule. It is important to read the trail descriptions to be able to decide for yourself—also the section on "Accommodation" in Chapter 4.

On the popular routes in the Annapurna Region, Langtang, Helambu, and Khumbu, you can do fine without a guide or *sirdar* (guide and manager in charge of porters and personnel). People trekking in Nepal for the first time, and off the popular routes, will generally have fewer problems if they have a guide. This is especially true for a group of people who are planning to hire a number of porters for a long trek they have organized themselves. Usually, the sirdar arrives at the starting point a day or two ahead to hire the needed porters and make other arrangements. It is best to recognize one person in the group of trekkers as the leader and have the sirdar deal with him or her. The rate of pay for guides, porters, and so forth varies depending on where they are hired (rates are highest if arranged in Kathmandu, on the side of a high-altitude pass, and in western Nepal); where you are going (more is expected when you will go up high, be on snow, and other extreme conditions); the time of year (rates are higher in times when there is otherwise plenty of trekking or village work); the experience and language capabilities of the guide; and whether the trekker provides food (they usually do for guides). Find out the current rates for guides and porters from the Kathmandu Environmental Education Project (KEEP) and from other trekkers, and inquire at trekking supply shops and agencies. It is wise to ask several people to get a good estimate and make sure to pay a fair wage.

For a large party that will not be eating locally, a cook and perhaps a helper are needed, in addition to the porters, who are hired strictly for load carrying. The guide can usually suggest a cook. Porters are also hired by the guide, or by you if you do not have a guide. It is often possible to make a contract with a porter to carry the load a certain distance in contrast to a daily wage. Guides and porters can be hired through trekking agencies in Kathmandu, in areas near airstrips, restaurants, and hotels frequented by foreigners, or at staging areas for treks.

Take your time in the hiring process. Do not immediately hire the first person who approaches you. Trust your impressions of people, and talk to several to find those you seem to get along with. Some people prefer to hire guides and porters who have not worked mostly for trekking groups and who dress in simple clothes.

Some porters on the large treks prefer the companionship of their friends to that of the trekkers. Look for porters who might enjoy interacting with trekkers. For a small group of, say, two trekkers and two porters, eating locally, it is more efficient to eat together. Generally, there is a two-tiered pricing system where Nepalis receive large discounts relative to foreigners. However, you may want to set a limit for the daily cost of the food, to minimize the risk of incurring large bills for alcohol and snacks. This allowance should be increased in high and remote areas where everything is more expensive.

It is important that you ensure that hired porters and even guides have adequate clothing for the conditions you will face (see Dr. Jim Duff's recommendations in "The Nepalese Porter"). However, guides sometimes demand excessive amounts of equipment, and seeking another person in this circumstance is recommended. Experienced guides do not carry loads and usually do not cook; they confine their activities to guiding, hiring porters, and attending to various logistical matters. Most guides speak some English, and some speak varying degrees of French, German, Korean, Japanese, and other languages. Be aware that if you ask someone to arrange hiring porters at a site, the porter may have to pay a percentage of the wages to the "agent." Patronage is an old concept in Nepal. So consider being your own contractor if you don't go through an agency, and the porter will likely benefit more. Sometimes younger people with little experience or knowledge of English, who are nevertheless enthusiastic and quite capable, can be more desirable, especially for the trekker who wants as few assistants as possible and wants to learn some Nepali. Sometimes these workers may carry a porter's load and do some cooking in addition to guiding.

In the Annapurna Conservation Area region and in Sagarmatha National Park, a requirement that guides (*sirdars*) be hired from recognized trekking agencies may be enforced. This is sometimes monitored at police check posts, where a guide might be asked to produce a letter from an agency. Trekkers who have hired independent guides might do well to be processed apart from their guides at check posts and to state that they are their own guides, if this regulation appears to be enforced. Alternatively, if you have hired a guide with the help of a trekking agency, then be sure to have a letter stating his connection with that company.

Women as well as men can be good porters, and some women have become guides. Female travelers and families with children might especially be interested in hiring female crew. Three Sisters Adventure Trekking, in Pokhara, has worked since the mid-1990s to empower Nepalese women, and the agency provides female guides and porters for female trekkers (www.3sistersadventure.com). Uneducated, often oppressed women from the hills who find employment as a porter are opened to economic and other opportunities that are unheard of for many Nepali women who usually live sheltered existences determined by patriarchal societal mores. Traditionally in Nepal, boys are valued more than girls, and girls are often the last to eat during daily meals and the first to be removed from school if work is needed in the home or fields. There are large gender gaps in literacy, with some differences between males and females greater than 30 percent in rural areas and 25 percent in urban areas. Tragically, it is estimated that up to 15,000 girls are sold each year by their parents for labor and even to the flesh trade in India. A 2008–09 study of eight of Nepal's seventy-five districts found that the maternal mortality rate had been halved since 1991, however, there was an alarming rise in the suicide rate of women of reproductive age, making suicide a leading cause of death among women in the examined districts. Sometimes female porters and guides have been taken advantage of by disreputable agencies and not paid. Check on this if you have any doubts, and use whatever means you can to get them their salary. The legal system characteristically supports employers rather than laborers

Large groups organized by trekking agencies commonly follow day-to-day itineraries or "camps," stopping at agreed-upon points. Porters hired for such routes may insist that you pay them the daily rate for the usual stages—a fixed sum for the distance to be covered—instead of the days you actually walk. It is often likely that a small, fit group will cover ground faster than at the camp rate. Sometimes you may not be able to get around paying the camp rate, but because this amount often does not include pay for the return journey, it may work out to be similar to a daily rate.

All transportation costs such as bus or plane fares to the actual beginning of the trek are the responsibility of the trekker. In addition, if the trek does not leave an employee at his home or point of hiring, you are obligated to pay for his return, usually at half the daily rate. Travel is faster on the return trip, so the number of days the journey will take should be agreed upon in advance.

If you hire a porter or guide from a trekking agency and pay the agency the salary, be aware that a substantial part of that pay will go to the agency, as overhead. Trekkers on organized treks are sometimes surprised to discover how little salary their staff make. Inquire from the porters, and compare the wage scales with the land costs you paid. Some trekkers concerned with the inequitable distribution of the funds they paid for their trek have on future treks arranged a flat fee with the agency to obtain the porters and then paid the porters themselves.

Do not give an unknown guide a large advance—perhaps two or three days' wages at the most. Even if your guide is looking after the porters, you should, at the start of a trip, make the wages clear with them yourself to avoid possible misunderstandings later. An advance of two or three days' wages may be paid to the porters so that they can purchase needed items. Have the guide keep an account book. Also, do not loan your guide or porters money in contrived circumstances if you expect to get it back. If you feel insecure about your potential guide, ask for references and try to verify them. There are stories of guides whose primary purpose is to embezzle from their clients. This is unlikely with guides who come from agencies or a reliable source.

Portering in Nepal takes place for four reasons: (1) to replenish a family's domestic supplies including water, firewood, and staples; (2) to stock shops of hill merchants; (3) to bring in materials for development projects; and (4) to support tourist groups. Keep in mind that Nepalese porters have traditionally been exploited. Things are changing for the better with groups like International Porter Protection Group (www.ippg.net), Porters Progress U.K. (www.portersprogress.org), Community Action Nepal (www.canepal.org.uk), International Mountain Explorers Club (www.mountainexplorers.org), and KEEP (www.keepnepal.org) raising awareness and setting up clothing banks, shelters, and aid posts among other programs and resources for porters. However, porters are at the lower end of a hierarchical society. In Nepalese terms, people in this position rarely complain, even at times when physical harm may be occurring. Thus, you as the employer, either directly or through an agency, need to keep a watch on the safety of the porters along the way to help ensure that the pattern of neglect and exploitation does not continue. That said, we would like to reiterate that properly engaging a porter and guide, if you are so inclined, can greatly enhance your experience while providing them valuable income. In fact, if you travel without a porter or guide you might be missing an extraordinary opportunity to get closer to Nepal.

Porters carry their loads—usually around 65 pounds (30 kg)—by means of a tumpline or *naamlo*, a band going around the load and around the forehead. Even if you give your porters a modern pack to carry, some may disregard the straps and waist belt in favor of a tumpline, which supports the weight from their foreheads. This may be the most efficient and comfortable way to carry a heavy load. Try a tumpline with your pack and gradually increase the weight it supports to get an idea of how it feels. All bags carried by porters should be locked to prevent pilfering and possible recriminations.

Locks and cheap duffel bags are available in Kathmandu. Or use, as porters do, a *Doko*, a conical basket available throughout much of Nepal. Anything can be carried in it, and an outer wrapping of plastic can keep the load dry when it rains. Items carried by porters receive rough treatment, and it is best to carry fragile items yourself.

In the past, when there was more respect for portering, *chautaaraa* (trailside resting platforms) and other aids for the porter were built and maintained, but these are less predominant now. Historically, portering was used by the state to extract value from villages that did not produce a taxable surplus. Tamang, an ethnic group from the hills near Kathmandu, served as porters in the service of central elites and were guarded from recruitment to the Gurkhas.

Some trekkers prefer to bring reliable people with them from Kathmandu. Porters hired locally may be Sherpas or Tibetans in Khumbu, Tibetans in Pokhara, Gurung north of Pokhara, Tamang in Kathmandu, or people of other ethnic groups, depending on the area; however, these days, porters are just as likely to be lowlanders in search of available work. People often find that the lowland, often Hindu caste, porters and guides are less satisfactory than the hill ethnic groups.

If you have a group of porters and feel that they are taking too many rests, check to see that their loads are not too heavy. Sometimes, rather than staying with them, shadowing them, it may turn out to be more efficient to agree on a destination for lunch or that evening, and walk independently of them, especially after a trusting relationship has developed. You might also travel ahead and arrange to have food cooked for them at a hotel or *bhaTTi*, a traditional inn. Then it is ready when they arrive.

Recognize that as outside wealth has come to Nepal, portering, never a job with status, has become even more menial. People who work as porters do so to supplement family income. Porters are treated disrespectfully by status-conscious Nepalis as a rule. By rising above this, the trekker can gain friends and learn much about Nepal. Those who have traveled in the Karakorum will know that the Balti porters there have tried to gain a measure of control over their labor. Some visitors there may resent their strikes and disputes, but these acts are a resistance against domination. What does this mean for Nepali porters and our relationship with them?

There are good ways to share your satisfaction with porters on the trip and to show your appreciation for their efforts at its end. English lessons are much valued. You could buy some appropriate language materials in Kathmandu or bring them from home. Practical gifts include used clothing, pocket knives, pencils, crayons, paper notebooks, sewing needles, and strong thread.

Do not overlook the possibility of using ponies or even yaks to carry loads. This is especially feasible in Khumbu and other northern regions. Stephen has used a yak and a *zopkio*—the sterile male offspring of a cow mated with a yak. These animals are remarkably sure-footed; the *zopkio* has a much better disposition than the yak, which requires pulling and pushing at times, but the yak can withstand cold more than the *zopkio*. In some areas horses can be used. Animal use depends on the availability of fodder, so high passes will not be feasible during the late fall and winter but quite appropriate in the monsoon.

THE NEPALESE PORTER: TOUGH, PROUD, VULNERABLE

Literally thousands of porters carry loads for trekkers in Nepal every season, either directly for independent trekkers or trekking companies, or indirectly by supplying trekkers' lodges. In addition they carry loads to expedition base camps. These subsistence farmers are not from the tiny and famous ethnic group the Sherpas, but are from the valleys of the middle hills. As a result they are not acclimatized to high altitude, and are less aware of the dangers of altitude illness and hypothermia than most trekkers.

Trekking agencies are in cutthroat competition for your business, and it is the porters who suffer most from price-cutting. The middleman, guide, or sirdar will often take a cut of their wages and any tip of cash or gear you might leave at the end of your trek. The only way to counter this is to be aware and witness or handle these transactions personally.

"Overloading" is a new concept to porters who traditionally carried as much as they could possibly manage. While unavoidable in some situations, overloading is generally dangerous, exploitative, and reduces the number of jobs available. In Nepal 65 pounds (30 kg) is considered reasonable and is the legal maximum.

Before signing up with a trekking agency, ask about their policy on porter clothing, food, shelter, and wages, and complain if you see any mistreatment while up in the mountains and on return.

IPPG (International Porter Protection Group) recommends the following guidelines:

1. Clothing appropriate to season and altitude must be provided to porters for protection from cold, rain, and snow. This may mean: windproof jacket and trousers, fleece jacket, long johns, suitable footwear (boots in snow), socks, hat, gloves, and sunglasses. (KEEP in Thamel, Kathmandu, has a clothing bank where the above items can be borrowed for porters' use and garment and gear donations are accepted, too; see the sidebar in Chapter 4.)
2. Above the tree line porters should have a dedicated shelter, either a room in a lodge or a tent (the trekkers' mess tent is no good as it is not available till late evening), a sleeping mat, and a decent blanket or sleeping bag. They should be provided with food and warm drinks, or cooking equipment and fuel.
3. Porters should be provided with life insurance and the same standard of medical care as you would expect for yourself.
4. Porters should not be paid off because of illness/injury without the leader or the trekkers assessing their condition carefully. The person in charge of the porters (sirdar) must let their trek leader or the trekkers know if a sick porter is about to be paid off. Failure to do this has resulted in many deaths. Sick/injured porters should never be sent down alone, but with someone who speaks their language and understands their problem, along with a letter describing their complaint. Sufficient funds should be provided to cover cost of rescue and treatment.
5. No porter should be asked to carry a load that is too heavy for their physical abilities (maximum: 20 kg on Kilimanjaro, 25 kg in Peru and Pakistan, 30 kg in Nepal). Weight limits may need to be adjusted for altitude, trail, and weather conditions; experience is needed to make this decision. Child porters should not be employed. ❖

—Dr. Jim Duff, founder and Director, IPPG (International Porter Protection Group, www.ippg.net)

AIR TRAVEL

Flying in Nepal is exciting, for the pilots are skilled at landing in remote airstrips and fly in seemingly impossible monsoon weather without benefit of IFR beacons. The old adage that they don't fly when there are clouds because "the clouds have rocks in them" doesn't seem to hold these days, especially where the route is reasonable. Their safety record is enviable.

Small STOL (short-takeoff-and-landing) aircraft provide service to small airstrips in many parts of Nepal. Helicopters can also provide service to trekking sites. There is increasing helicopter access to other places in the hills, not just airstrips but district centers. Many of these sites are not popular with trekkers but can be useful for jumping off. Flights and charters are arranged in Kathmandu through the offices of Nepal's flagship airline, Nepal Airlines, or any of the many private airlines and the agents that abound.

Trekking and travel agencies in Kathmandu can take care of dealing with domestic flights and with international carriers, even if you don't arrange a trek with them. There are fewer inconveniences with air travel within Nepal for trekkers in the last few years as more carriers compete for tourist traffic. Some suggestions for further minimizing hassles with flights in Nepal include making sure you have a return reservation back home before you arrive in Nepal. If you do, then once you arrive, reconfirm it in person at that airline's office. Otherwise, make sure you book a flight back before trekking.

Local flights usually must be paid for in hard currency. If you have a return ticket to Kathmandu or some other destination in Nepal, when you arrive at the remote location, take time to reconfirm at the airline's local station, and see that your name is on the passenger list. If your flight is bumped, then patiently go daily to the office and try to make arrangements to get on a flight. Be aware that each flight has seats reserved for government officials. Travelers with legitimate, documentable reasons can sometimes get clearance from government officials such as the Chief District Officer (CDO) to be issued these seats. This process is begun by writing a letter (on letterhead if possible) explaining the reason to the responsible official.

Many flights to remote areas leave from hubs such as Biratnagar, Dharan (for helicopters), Pokhara, or Nepalganj, and transportation from Kathmandu must be arranged. Once there, getting to the airport from your hotel can be problematic, so scout out the options the day before, and arrange something. Baggage allowance is usually limited to 15 kg (32 ½ pounds) per person; excess baggage charges then apply to anything over that. Sometimes everything, including carry-on luggage, is weighed, especially on flights into high-altitude areas. Comply with these regulations so the plane is not overloaded. Crashes from overloading have resulted from people's insistence to carry everything!

Trekking parties are cautioned not to wave at low-flying helicopters, as this is an invitation to be rescued. Such activity has confused rescue pilots trying to locate the stricken party.

BUSES, TRUCKS, AND CARS

In the 1970s studies showed road building in Nepal to have a net negative effect on economic development. This is long forgotten and there is a frenzy of road building, with little budgeted for maintenance. New roads will increase the popularity of other areas for trekking, though it may take a few years after completion for the word to get out. Landslides and washouts will continue to make getting anywhere in the hills problematic, and perhaps the old trails will still be useful. Any road described in this book may not be passable by vehicle at the time you access it, or you may have to walk across a slide to board a different vehicle on the other side.

Roads in Nepal are hazardous and should be approached with some fear.
(Photo by Alonzo Lyons)

Private bus companies provide service over Nepal's main roads. The routes most often used by trekkers are Kathmandu to Jiri, Shivalaya, or Bhandar for treks east into Solu–Khumbu; Kathmandu to Dhunche and Syabrubensi for treks north; and Kathmandu to Pokhara and Phedi or Naya Pul for treks north of Pokhara. There are several categories of bus service, with no uniform standard. Tourist buses are supposed to make fewer stops and have reserved seats. Tickets for them can be purchased from the various travel and trekking agencies, and they often leave from Kantipath, five minutes down/south from Thamel's Tridevi Marg road or other convenient sites. To find local buses, go to the bus parks in Kathmandu, the Old Bus Park (also known as Ratna Park) for Jiri and Dhunge, and near Baleju (Nayaa Bas Park or New Bus Park) for Dhunche, Hugdi Bazaar, Syabrubensi, and Pokhara. You can purchase the ticket a day early, but often a seat can be had on the day of travel. On the day of travel, buses and mini-vans can also be found at an intersection or *chowk* along the west side of Kathmandu's ring road named Kalanki. Kalanki *chowk* is at a crossroads for vehicles departing the valley via the Thangkot escarpment; all transport vehicles heading out of the Kathmandu valley to the east, west, and south use this route except for those going north to Tibet at Kodari and Jiri in the Everest area. This may change once new access highways are built heading directly south or east from Kathmandu, but that time is in the distant future. By buying a ticket early, you can choose a seat close to the front of the bus or mini-van and, if you are tall, try to get one with legroom. Often the seat just behind the driver is best. On the day of departure, arrive early enough to find your bus and be prepared for contingencies.

Mini-vans are more expensive and, as smaller vehicles, are usually faster. However, those prone to motion sickness are advised to use a bus rather than a mini-van, because the buses are larger and usually give a smoother ride. On the other hand, local buses are crammed full with people smoking cigarettes or vomiting, goats, chickens, and luggage. They stop often, and can take forever. Riding on these buses often taxes the trekker as much as trekking with a pack. Riding on top of buses is currently prohibited within the Kathmandu valley and when approaching police check posts. Most trekkers are willing to put up with the slow, pitching buses in order to save the time it would take to walk. Riding closer to the front and not eating a big meal before boarding is advised. There are night bus services between Kathmandu and many points in the Tarai. This odyssey begins in the late afternoon, and you arrive bedraggled in the morning. Observing the duties, and way of life of the bus staff, especially the drivers, with the different personnel required, can be a fascinating diversion for the weary rider. Expect any bus ride outside of the Kathmandu valley to take most of a day.

Trekkers may sometimes be able to purchase rides on trucks transporting goods; this may even be preferable to the crowded buses. If you find yourself in the back of a pitching truck, try to get your center of gravity as low and forward as you can. It may be more convenient for a large party wishing to transport all its gear, porters, and trekkers to the start of a trek to hire private vehicles. It can also be easier for small groups or individuals. Trekking agencies usually make these arrangements and provide pickup services.

A high incidence of road accidents commonly accompanies road development in developing countries; Nepal is no exception and has one of the highest fatality rates in Asia in terms of total vehicle users with an average of three people killed in road accidents per day. Roads are narrow, often made narrower by washouts, and without the substantial restraining barriers seen at home. Vehicles are often overloaded, repairs jury-rigged, good brakes a fantasy, and drivers fatigued, with alcohol compounding the problem. Speeds along the roads are increasing in spite of more frequent accidents, for all the newer vehicles are capable of rapidly plunging into obstacles. Your greatest risk of injury in Nepal, while not trekking, is from motor vehicle accidents—a substantial risk, perhaps comparable to the risk of serious altitude illness or greater. If a road accident occurs, emergency medical service and definitive care are limited at best. Avoid travel at night if possible. At all times keep your arms and head inside the vehicle rather than hanging out a window, as the roads are narrow and the passing of other vehicles and objects can be harrowingly close. Get off a vehicle if you feel a driver is behaving unsafely. Take "number 11" where possible (*eghaara nambarle*), referring to using two legs for walking.

At road heads, we advise you to sleep as far from the bus staging area as possible. Otherwise, you may spend much of the night listening to the mating calls of these metal beasts.

MONEY

Individual trekkers should take 10-, 20-, 50- and 100-rupee (*rupiyAA*) notes. For a group paying bills together, 1000-, 500-, and 100-rupee notes are also convenient. A Nepalese rupee (NRS) is equal to a little over one U.S. cent at the mid-2010 exchange rate: 73 NRS (Rs. 73) to 1 U.S. dollar ($1 USD). There are many ATMs and foreign exchange shops in Kathmandu and Pokhara. While banks do have branches in most of the district centers and a few towns, exchanging foreign currency at rural locales can be time-consuming and difficult, if not impossible, but as always Nepali bureaucracy is fascinating. There are now even ATMs along the popular routes in places such as Jomosom and Namche Bazaar, but they are not reliable. You can even get advances on credit cards for an exorbitant fee. If money has to be sent to you in Nepal, the most versatile way for U.S. citizens may be to have it sent to the State Department in Washington, D.C. They will send a transmittal letter to the Embassy allowing disbursement of U.S. cash.

Hard currency (Nepalese rupees, U.S. dollars) is necessary for purchasing air tickets, as well as for paying for trekking permits to certain areas. U.S. dollars may be handy if your trekking route takes you by an airstrip and you decide to fly out unexpectedly. Bring some hard cash and traveler's checks to Nepal, especially if not trekking with a foreign-based agency. If everything has been arranged by a prepaid trekking company, little money is needed, although bring some for tips to porters, kitchen staff, and guides.

Some trekkers barter clothes and equipment for Nepali crafts, meals, and lodging. Western goods can also be exchanged for cash at times. The local people like to obtain useful foreign goods in this way. However, we usually travel with minimal gear that is difficult to replace in Nepal, and we do most of our commerce with cash. Some people exchange, sell, or give away much of their clothing and equipment toward the end of their trek.

It is best to take new currency on your trek. Replace worn, tattered notes for crisp new ones in Kathmandu or Pokhara. People in the hills may refuse a ragged, torn note. If you are traveling without porters or guides and eating food locally, $10–$15 USD per person per day usually takes care of the necessities, although on popular routes and especially at higher elevations you may need at least $20–$25 USD per day. With a porter or guide, add at least $10–$15 USD per day, respectively, if you hire them on your own. In the Annapurna region, and in Khumbu where there are more sophisticated hotels, you can spend a great deal more. Carry enough funds for contingencies. You get incredible value for the money spent in Nepal. Don't lose that perspective. Prices are usually straightforward and posted on menus along the popular routes. See Chapter 3 for more information on how to handle transactions away from the beaten paths. There are also national park and conservation area permit costs to consider; for example, entry into Sagarmatha National Park is 1000 NRS, and for the ACAP area it is 2000 NRS (restricted areas cost much more). Additionally, since March 2010, TIMS card fees are $20 USD per person per trek ($10 for trekkers going via a trekking agency). Using these figures, a two-week trek in Solu–Khumbu would at least cost roughly the following:

Daily cost of food and lodging, at least $20–$25 USD x 14 days = between $280 and $350 USD

Sagarmatha National Park fee = roughly $14 USD

TIMS card fee = $20 USD

Total, not including transportation to and from the trailhead, frills like extra snacks or drinks, and porter or guide = between $314 and $385 USD

The prices throughout this book are based on mid-2010 rates. Although you may well find the prices higher when you reach Nepal, you'll at least have some idea of what to expect.

COMMUNICATION BY PHONE, MAIL, AND INTERNET

Calling home was once upon a time restricted to an interminable process at a single office in Kathmandu. Now international calling services are widely available and, if an Internet line is used, not to mention Skype, the cost is quite low. There are even links powered by solar cells in many remote areas. However, these rural services can be expensive. Bring extra cash if you plan to call home, as you cannot call collect. You can often get a call back; however, you will still have to pay a reduced per-minute usage charge. Nepal's telephone code is 977, with city area codes of 01 for Kathmandu and 061 for Pokhara (eliminate the zero if calling from outside these cities). When calling, keep in mind that Nepal is five-and-three-quarters hours ahead of GMT.

Internet cafés abound in Kathmandu and Pokhara where you can send and receive electronic mail. Occasionally and perhaps unexpectedly, these shops are encountered even along high trekking routes, although connections in remote places can be

Kastmandap Temple, from which Kathmandu takes its name, is located at a busy crossroads in Durbar Square. (Photo by Alonzo Lyons)

tortuously slow and unreliable. We will mention locations that might currently have service; however, service will continue to expand.

For receiving postal mail in Nepal, the best addresses to use, in order of preference, are (1) a friend living in Nepal, (2) your trekking agency, if you have one, (3) your embassy, (4) Post Restante (Kathmandu General Post Office, Kathmandu, Nepal). Kathmandu's main post office is in Sundhara, across to the west from Tundhikhel near Dharahara/Bhimsen Tower. Hours are 10 AM–4 PM, closed Saturday. (See Map 1.)

KATHMANDU

Kathmandu (4383 feet, 1336 m) is a teeming metropolis caught up in the throes of modernization. The city takes its name from a centuries-old structure,Kastmandap, which humbly translates to "wooden pavilion." Kastmandap is a temple that sits majestically in the busy World Heritage Site of Durbar Square among several other regal structures. Legend has it that the large, three-story-high structure was made from the timber of a single sal tree and was originally built at a trade crossroads in the twelfth century CE. An idol of the deity Gorkhanth, a tantric immortal, is housed within.

It would be difficult to visit Nepal without passing through Kathmandu at some point. Colloquially speaking, all roads lead to this capital city. Kathmandu is the site of Nepal's only international airport, although Pokhara is being considered for an upgrade and an international airport is planned for Bara District in the south with a major highway corridor linking that proposed airport with Kathmandu.

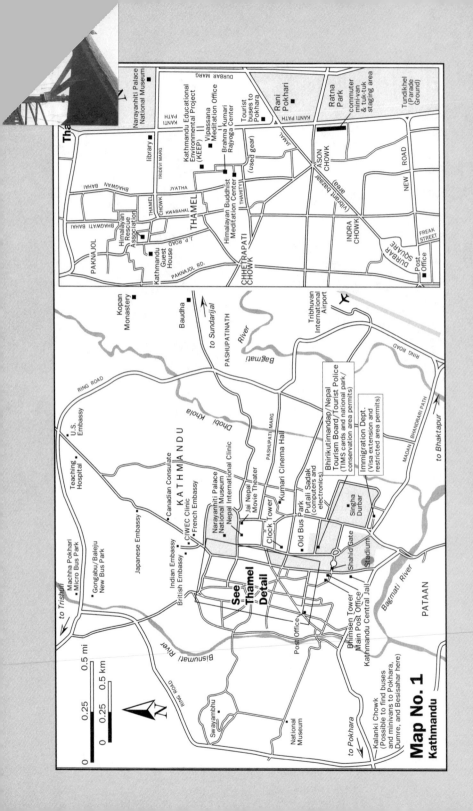

Map No. 1
Kathmandu

THAMEL

Narayanhiti Palace National Museum

library

Kathmandu Educational Environmental Project (KEEP)

DURBAR MARG

KANTI PATH

Vipassana Meditation Office

Brahma Kumari Rajyoga Center

Tourist buses to Pokhara.

Rani Pokhari

Ratna Park

commuter mini-van & tuk tuk staging area

Tundikhel (Parade Ground)

TRIDEVI MARG

JYATHA

THAMEL CHOWK

KWABAHAL

(used gear)

THAHITY

KANTI PATH

BHAGWAN BAHAL

BHAGWAN BAHAL

Himalayan Rescue Association

THAMEL

Himalayan Buddhist Meditation Center

J. P. ROAD

ASON CHOWK

(Vibrant bazaar area)

NEW ROAD

PAKNAJOL

Kathmandu Guest House

PAKNAJOL RD.

CHHETRAPATI CHOWK

INDRA CHOWK

DURBAR SQUARE

FREAK STREET

Post Office

Kopan Monastery

Baudha

to Sundarijal

PASHUPATINATH

Bagmati River

Tribhuvan International Airport

RING ROAD

Dhobi Khola

RING ROAD

U.S. Embassy

Teaching Hospital

K A T H M A N D U

Canadian Consulate

CIWEC Clinic

French Embassy

Narayanhiti Palace National Museum

Nepal International Clinic

Jai Nepal Movie Theater

Clock Tower

PASHUPATI MARG

Kumari Cinema Hall

Putali Sadak (computers and electronics)

Old Bus Park

Bhrikutimandap / Nepal Tourism Board / Tourist Police (TIMS cards and national park / conservation area permits)

Immigration Dept. (Visa extension and restricted area permits)

Singha Durbar

MADAN BHANDARARI PATH

to Bhaktapur

Machha Pokhari Micro Bus Park

Japanese Embassy

Gongabu / Baleju New Bus Park

Indian Embassy

British Embassy

See Thamel Detail

Shahid Gate

Stadium

Bagmati River

PATAAN

to Trishuli

Bisnumati River

RING ROAD

Post Office

Bhimsen Tower Main Post Office

Kathmandu Central Jail

Swayambhu

National Museum

to Pokhara

Kalanki Chowk (Possible to find buses and minivans to Pokhara, Dumre, and Besisahar here)

0   0.25   0.5 mi

0   0.25   0.5 km

N

For getting around Kathmandu, there is a public transport network of buses, mini-vans, and smaller *tempos* or three-wheeled public transportation vehicles that travel throughout the valley on specific routes. This is an inexpensive way to get around and allows insight into the lifestyle of city dwellers, but public vehicles are usually packed with people. Placards with numbers and destinations (usually written in Nepali) are posted on windshields, and the white-and-green *safaa* tempos or clean tempos run on electric power. Those seeking transport hail the driver from the roadside anywhere along a specified route. To use this system requires more effort than a casual visitor is likely to expend, and minimal language skills would be useful. That said, the conductors, mostly adolescent boys who announce routes and collect money, are usually, but not always, helpful if not amused by intrepid foreigners using this transit network. Otherwise, taxis are ubiquitous and drivers are required to use the trip meters, which are often unreliable. Nonetheless, most taxi drivers will try to negotiate an inflated flat fee. Other than walking, traveling via bicycle rickshaw is the most environmentally sound method of getting around and provides a source of income for some of the poorest inhabitants of the valley.

Many people revel in the havoc and eccentricity of Kathmandu's myriad bazaars, streets, and restaurants, while others take the first available chance to be rid of the crowds, noise, and pollution to leave for higher ground. Indeed, Kathmandu can be extremely polluted, from the ground you walk on to the air you breathe, and extra caution is needed with food and water. Tourist areas are relatively well-maintained and garbage collection now takes place, although erratically, and piles of garbage are often set alight before they can be collected, especially in the cold season where both garbage and wood are used in the city as fuel for warming fires. Wood is also widely used for cooking in the valley, too.

There are upwards of a million and a half residents in Nepal's largest city and the greater valley in which it sits, with 6 percent annual population growth. With a high density of people and a lack of adequate measures to control pollution, the joint aggregate of human activity often blankets the valley in a cloud of haze that travels all the way to the ramparts of the Himalaya and mars views. However, on windy days, or just after a rainstorm clears out, the urban sprawl reveals its magnificent setting with a broad panorama of the distant Himalaya standing guardian to the north and east. At these times, a visit to a rooftop restaurant will reward you with a scenic mountain vista.

The air quality is much better than it used to be in the days when garbage was more widely burned and swarms of diesel *tuk-tuks*, small three-wheeled taxis, roamed the lanes while inefficient kilns dotted the valley. Even still, kilns are the second largest source of air pollution in the valley, after vehicles. The valley's uninhibited growth requires 1.2 billion bricks a year. Since 2002, regulations have been implemented that reduce pollution from inefficient kilns, and with the addition of electric public transport vehicles, air quality has improved dramatically but still has a long way to go.

However, at the ground level, a constant cacophony of horns arises from vehicles plying the streets and narrow passageways, most of which are also crowded with vendors. As a necessary stop for most travelers, there are many activities to bide your time in this renowned city, and the contrast between hectic urban life and the trekking trails can make the time in the Himalaya all the more cherished. Below is a brief description of the valley and a few options for spending time there, either preparing or waiting for a journey or for general leisure. Additionally, we have included a route description for an excursion up to and beyond the ridge that forms the rim to the northeast of the valley, a three-day trek that can still be made even should a transport-halting *bandh* (nationwide strike) occur or if you otherwise need to leave the city (see "The Kathmandu Valley Rim and Beyond," Chapter 9).

CHALLENGES FACING THE VALLEY

Despite Nepal's many roaring rivers with a vast potential for hydroelectric power, Kathmandu is still hit by daily outages of electricity, especially in the winter season when demand is high and capacity is low due to less water flow at the hydropower stations. Simply put, the power supply is insufficient and Nepal has neither the generating facilities nor infrastructure, despite many foreign aid projects aimed at improving the situation. Not a few of these immoderately funded projects have been mired in corruption and failed to materialize. Kathmandu also suffers from a shortage of potable water. The daily demand is about 74 million gallons (280 million liters) while supply is 23 million gallons (86 million liters) during dry months and 28 million (105 million liters) during the rainy season. Groundwater depletion and quality is a growing concern. One solution to Kathmandu's water woes might be the harvesting of rainwater. It has been calculated that over ten times the current water demand falls on the valley's 250 square miles (640 sq km) each year.

However, the Kathmandu valley's concern over electricity and water deficits is overshadowed by a larger issue. A 2001 study listed Kathmandu as the world's most earthquake-vulnerable city, and the country is in a seismically active zone. Over 1000 earthquakes occur annually in Nepal, with magnitude range of 2 to 5 on the Richter Scale. The collision of the Indo-Australian Plate and the Eurasian Plate led to the uprising of the world's highest range and Nepal's greatest spectacle, the Himalaya (the story of Nepal's geological origins has been told in Chapter 1). The 2001 study focused on the following three criteria: building frailty, potential for landslides and floods, and the capability of local authorities for rescue, firefighting, and life-saving operations. Preparedness has not improved since 2001, and population density has increased. The tragic earthquake that struck Haiti in January 2010 has raised the call for better readiness in the valley. Should a heavy tremblor hit, it would be catastrophic given Kathmandu's overpopulation and poorly built infrastructure. Most buildings are made of poured cement and masonry and erected without regard to building code. A major earthquake struck in 1934, killing over 4500 people in the valley and destroying one-fifth of its structures. Another earthquake in 1988 in eastern Nepal claimed the lives of 721 people and 22,000 houses collapsed.

TOURIST ACCOMMODATION AND FACILITIES

The majority of tourists stay in or near an area named Thamel. To some, this area may seem like paradise, whereas to others it is the opposite. Regardless, Thamel has an overabundance of signs advertising hotels, restaurants, bars, bakeries, and more, including a broad range of shops selling everything from Tibetan *thangka* to packaged Chinese snack items. It can seem oddly incongruent with the rest of Kathmandu, not to mention Nepal, and may be overwhelming to some, especially on a return from the mountains. However, tourism is a mainstay of Nepal's economy and, despite the seeming mayhem, Thamel can be a useful place for making travel arrangements and picking up clothing and gear.

A wide range of equipment and clothing is available, although much of it is counterfeit of brand names, also known as "North Farce"; beware of poor quality (authentic outlets are along Tridevi Marg and Durbar Marg). Harder to find are shops that can supply you with genuine mountaineering gear, often run by mountaineers themselves. Some of this gear is left over from prior expeditions and some is brand-new. The road at the southern border of Thamel that lies perpendicular to Kantipath Road has several of these shops. Do not be surprised if the owner with whom you are striking a bargain has

Seasonal products are sold along the roadside.

Baudhnath Stupa in Kathmandu combines many religious elements. (Photo by Pat Morrow)

been to the summit of Everest several times, as well as other giants. The operator of a shop frequented by Alonzo has scaled Everest thirteen times at last count.

The Kathmandu Environmental Education Project (KEEP), with an associated Porter's Clothing Bank, and the Himalayan Rescue Association (HRA) both have locations in Thamel. A visit to either will provide a chance to register for free with your respective embassy. Both organizations have notice boards with valuable information for travelers, including people looking for trekking partners. KEEP is particularly worthwhile to visit for unbiased resources and materials, including trekker logbooks with the latest trail information and supplies such as water purifiers, anti-leech oil, biodegradable soap, and more (see "KEEP" sidebar in Chapter 4 for more information about KEEP). KEEP (tel. 4216775, www.keepnepal.org) is located in Jyatha, Thamel, whereas HRA (tel. 4440292) is currently located on a second floor office of the Sagarmatha Bazaar complex in the heart of Thamel, along one of the few "walking streets" (vehicles not allowed) in Kathmandu. HRA's main office is in Dhobichaur, Lazimpat, along the road to the north of the former royal palace compound.

Additional areas to stay in Kathmandu that are popular with tourists are Paknajol (which lies to the northeast of Thamel) and an area referred to as "Freak Street" in Basantapur near Durbar Square as well as the area around Baudhnath Stupa. These areas have a wide range of hotels of variable quality, restaurants, travel agencies, and other shops that cater to tourists. Several upper-end hotels are found along Durbar Marg, the road leading to the front gate of the former palace, now Narayanhiti National Museum as well as in the Lazimpat area of town and in the nearby city of PaaTan (also known as Lalitpur).

OBTAINING PERMITS FOR TREKKING

Entry permits for national parks and conservation areas as well as Trekkers' Information Management System (TIMS) cards are available at Bhrikutimandap along Pradarshaan Marg (Exhibition Road); passport-size photos are needed, two for each conservation or national park permit as well as two for each TIMS card. (TIMS cards are also available at the TAAN Headquarters in the Maligaon section of the city; however, the office is difficult to locate). Bhrikutimandap is also the location of the main offices of the Nepal Tourism Board (NTB) and Tourist Police headquarters. The NTB has a small visitor center with brochures and leaflets. There are less than forty tourist police for over 500,000 tourists who visit Nepal each year. They report that an average of 600 cases are lodged every year, and 80 percent of these cases are theft.

Exhibition Road is just down the road (to the south) from Ratna Park and the Old Bus Park and to the east of the large parade ground and open space known as TundiKhel. Farther south from Exhibition Road is Bhadrakali Temple, mounted at the center of a large roundabout. To the left/east of the temple is Prithvipath Road, which leads to the seat of parliament, Singha Durbar. Heading right/south from the entrance to Singha Durbar on Ram Shah Path Road (also known as Babbar Mahal Road) will take you past several large government buildings. Shortly after crossing an intersection, head left/east away from the main road and up a smaller road that dead-ends near the Immigration Department where visas can be renewed and permits to restricted areas are obtained.

THINGS TO DO

On the opposite side of Exhibition Road from NTB and where conservation area and national park permits are issued, is the Nepal Police Health Club. It is open for day visits for a fee; long-term memberships are available, too. Facilities include a small gym, sauna, a large swimming pool, and restaurant. Aerobics classes are given in the morning. Costs are activity-based and for non-members range from 150 NRS for swimming to 250 NRS for the fitness center.

People wishing to keep their legs in shape for the strenuous ups and downs of Nepal's trails can visit the National Stadium, about a thirty-minute walk down Kantipath Road from Tridevi Marg street in Thamel. The stadium is also known as Dashratha Rangsaalaa after the martyr Dashratha Chand, executed by firing squad in 1941 CE for initiating a protest movement against the ruling Rana family. The stadium is usually open to all comers from sunup to sundown unless an event is taking place. The track is especially alive in the early morning with joggers and martial arts practitioners, among other enthusiasts. Behind the stadium is the National Swimming Pool which guests can visit for a usage fee of 75 NRS for gents and 70 NRS for ladies. It is closed Sundays and during the winter months. Otherwise, the following three time slots are available: 10 AM– noon, 1 PM to 3 PM, and 4 PM to 6 PM. Adjoining the pool is the complex of the Nepal Tennis Association with three clay courts that can be used for a fee. Racquets, partners, and even coaches are available for temporary hire.

Along the way to the stadium from Thamel, in an area named Sundhara, to the right-hand side of a gas (petrol) station and near a large office building and shopping complex, is Kathmandu's Central Jail. At any given time, there are many foreigners housed here from around the world, and most are incarcerated for visa or drug violations. Visitations are encouraged, and a smaller women's jail is behind the men's compound.

Tourists in Kathmandu will inevitably encounter children living on the street. For guidelines on how to respond to begging, see "Victims of Kindness" in Chapter 3.

Those wishing to join a Buddhist meditation course in the land of Buddha's birth (he was born in Lumbini, in the southern Nepal district of Rupandehi) can visit the Vipassana Foundation. Regular courses are available on a donation basis. To reach their main office and a nearby meditation hall (the retreat meditation hall is on the outskirts of the valley), follow Kantipath to the right/south from Tridevi Marg. Within five minutes there is a complex with a Nepal Bank office and Hero Honda motorbike sales shop and Honda service shop. The office is inside this complex at the basement level. Courses are run by donation. Visit www.dhamma.org/en/schedules/schshringa.shtml for further information.

Another center in the Thamel area that holds daily talks on meditation and Tibetan Buddhism is the Himalayan Buddhist Meditation Center, which is under the auspices of Kopan Monastery in Baudhnath. The center is located in the Jyatha area of Thamel not far from the Kathmandu Environmental Education Project (KEEP) on a narrow road named Chhyuhaa Galli. (Additionally, just down from the KEEP office is the Brahma Kumari Rajyoga Center, which offers free week-long introductory courses in Raja Yoga.)

Narayanhiti National Museum was formerly the Royal Palace. (Photo by Alonzo Lyons)

There are many Tibetan monasteries near Baudhnath, some of which regularly hold teachings. The following institutions have courses that cater to interested foreigners: the International Buddhist Academy (www.sakyaiba.edu.np), Rangjung Yeshe Institute (www.shedra.org), and Kopan Monastery (www.kopan-monastery.com). Most monasteries in the Baudhnath area and elsewhere open their doors to visitors. Please respect that you are in a religious setting (even while some of the residents might not). If you visit during daily prayer and chanting ceremonies, you are in for an otherworldly experience, as the sing-song rhythm of the chanting along with accompanying bells, conch shell blasts, horns, drums, and cymbals can leave quite an impression. These ceremonies usually take place in the early morning or early evening. If you enter a monastery, do not sit against pillars or on cushions unless invited to do so. Obtain permission before taking photographs of the monks.

Narayanhiti, the former royal palace and site of the royal massacre of June 1, 2001, is located at the northern end of Durbar Marg in central Kathmandu. Since the monarchy was abolished in May 2008 and Nepal declared a republic, the palace has been turned into Narayanhiti National Museum. It first opened its doors to the public in February 2009. The museum entry fee is 250 NRS for SAARC and Chinese nationals and 500 NRS for other foreigners. It is closed Tuesday and Wednesday, otherwise open from 11 AM to 4 PM.

The National Museum (Rastriya Sangrahalaya) in Chhauni is also worth a visit (and the Military Museum lies on the opposite side of the road). Entry fee for the National Museum is 100 NRS, 50 NRS additional for cameras. The summer hours are 10:30 AM to 4:30 PM (closed Tuesdays; Monday hours are 10:30 AM to 2:30 PM). In winter it closes an hour earlier. The official website is www.nationalmuseum.gov.np.

WORLD HERITAGE STRUCTURES

The whole Kathmandu valley has been declared a World Heritage Site because of seven structures cited by the United Nations Educational, Scientific, and Cultural Organization (UNESCO) as demonstrating historic and artistic achievements. The World Heritage Sites of Hanuman Dhoka (Kathmandu) Durbar Square, Patan Durbar Square, and Bhaktapur Durbar Square were the respective courts of the three kings ruling the Kathmandu valley at a time before the country was unified. An entry fee is required to enter these areas.

Three other World Heritage Sites are the sacred temple of Pashupatinath honoring Shiva, near the airport, and the large *stupa* (Buddhist shrines) of Swayambhunath and Baudhnath, which are centuries-old landmarks and which also require entrance fees.

The final, seventh World Heritage Site farther out in the northeast of the valley is Changu Narayan Temple. It has elaborate carvings and is believed to have been constructed in the third century and is dedicated to Vishnu.

FURTHER SIGHTSEEING AND OTHER ACTIVITIES

The religious sites of Budhanilkantha and Namo Buddha are worth a visit. Namo Buddha is a site where the Buddha, in a lifetime former to becoming the Buddha, is said to have sacrificed his own flesh out of compassion to save the lives of a starving tigress and her cubs that were too weak to hunt on their own.

Within the valley are the cities of Bhaktapur, meaning "the city of devotees," and Patan, an upscale haven for NGOs. The national zoo is in the Jawalakhel area of Patan, should you desire to witness suffering animals kept in meager facilities.

A 12-mile (20 km) trip outside of the valley to the southwest is the village of Pharping, which existed while the Kathmandu valley was still a lake. Pharping is the site of Nepal's first hydroelectricity station (and Asia's second), built in 1912 when the autocratic Rana family was in power. Nearby are the caves of Asura and Yangleshö, said to have been used by Padmasambava, also known as Guru Rimpoche. Allegedly, his handprint is impressed on Asura's rock wall. There are many large Tibetan monasteries in this area, and practitioners often make retreats here.

The Newar are the original inhabitants of the valley and their cuisine, language, and culture are quite distinct. Visit a Newar restaurant and try *chataamari*, the Newar answer to pizza. For a look at one of city's busiest and most vibrant bazaars, visit the narrow street linking Ason Chowk and Indra Chowk and beyond to New Road and Durbar Square. This is a hectic market with an endless variety of items on sale and display, from spices to carpets and much more. However, it is not for the claustrophobic, as the alleyway is packed with vendors, shoppers, onlookers, general pedestrian commuters, and honking motorcyclists.

Kathmandu has many *dohori* restaurants that provide live Nepal folk music with repartee between traditionally costumed male and female singers. This is a staged version of a courtship tradition that still exists in villages, and you might be able to see the genuine version in the hills if you get off the beaten track. There are several large cinema halls in Kathmandu, mostly showing Bollywood productions with occasional Nepal-made films and foreign films as well. Kathmandu Guest House, a Thamel

SECULAR FESTIVALS

Several national holidays are celebrated throughout the country. The most important, from the standpoint of national culture, is GaNatantra Divash, or Republic Day, May 28. It is highlighted by parades on the Tundikhel (parade ground) in the center of Kathmandu. National ethnic groups, dancing troupes, and various peasant, class, and cooperative organizations participate, all dressed in their traditional finery. There is much pomp and splendor.

At least three different New Year celebrations are held in Nepal annually. The New Year according to the lunisolar Bikram Samvat calendar begins in the Nepali month of Baisakh (mid-April). The Tibetan New Year, called Losar, usually falls in February. It is heralded by feasting and celebration among the Tibetan community. The traditional Newar New Year falls in October and is celebrated by the preparation and sale of great amounts of sweet cakes and candies, with colorful decorations throughout the streets of Kathmandu, PaaTan, and Bhaktapur (also known as BhatgAAU).

Rural fairs or *mela* are countrywide and occur throughout the year at various locations. Many are held in the spring and in the fall after the harvest. Fairs are traditionally associated with local rural shrines, quite often for Hindus at the confluence (*beni*) of two sacred rivers or simply on the bank (*ghaaT*) of a sacred river. They usually coincide with a religious occasion and include worship at a local shrine. Some *mela*, such as Khaptad Mela held in Khaptad National Park, are quite large and last several days, attracting people from surrounding districts. Others are quite brief and limited to a small region. ❖

The fabled Swayambunath also known as The Monkey Temple is perched atop a hillock that rises above Kathmandu's bustling streets. (Photo by Alonzo Lyons)

landmark, regularly screens movies in their small hall, and in high season, informational lectures and videos documenting popular trekking routes are available in the evening for a fee.

There are plenty of book dealers, both new and used, small to behemoth, in Kathmandu, often operated by genuine aficionados of literature. Many, but not all, of these bookshops are in the tourist areas of Kathmandu. Nepal also has several daily and weekly newspapers that provide goings-on within the valley. Keep in mind that freedom of the press is under threat in Nepal, with 288 incidents of press freedom violation in 2008 (including physical attacks, imprisonment, and more) and 155 incidents in 2009. Some of Nepal's news sources can be accessed online. The following portals provide up-to-date news and more from or about Nepal: www.nepalitimes.com, www.nepalnews .com, www.thehimalayantimes.com, www.himalmag.com, www.nepalmonitor.com, and http://travel.nytimes.com/travel/guides/asia/nepal/overview.html.

PEOPLES OF THE KATHMANDU VALLEY

The early inhabitants of the Kathmandu valley were farmers and herders. The indigenous Newar are a mixture of those peoples and other migrants who found their way, over the centuries, to this fertile basin. Each conqueror of the valley, some from the eastern hills of Nepal (of Kiranti stock) and some from north India, added to the cultural heritage to make the ethnologically rich Newar culture and society of today. Newar make up the bulk of the merchants and shopkeepers (alongside more recently arrived Indian merchants) in the three cities of Kathmandu, PaaTan, and BhatgAAU (Bhaktapur). Newar are also the predominant shopkeepers in outlying rural bazaars and, throughout the country, make up a considerable percentage of the Nepali civil service.

The Kathmandu valley is also populated by large numbers of Brahmans and Chhetri. They too were farmers, and many have become professional and civil servants in the capital city.

Other peoples often seen on the streets of the capital are Hindu peddlers from the Tarai, Tamang hill people who work as day laborers, BhoTiya (including many Sherpas) from the north, Gurung and Magar from central and west Nepal, and Kiranti (Rai and Limbu) from east Nepal. Since 1959, many Tibetan refugees have also settled in the valley. Monks and other Tibetan men and women are found near the Buddhist temples and monasteries of Baudhnath and Swayambhunath, on the outskirts of Kathmandu, and at the refugee and handicraft center at Jawalakhel, PaaTan. Tibetan handicrafts—especially articles of woolen clothing and colorful carpets—are well known to tourists in Nepal and in the export marts of Europe and America.

In medieval times, Newar craftsmen developed the distinct architectural and decorative motifs and religious arts of the valley and, not insignificantly, of Tibetan Buddhism as well. They became active traders when, for centuries, a main trade route between India and Tibet passed through Kathmandu and BhatgAAU. In time, Newar extended their craftsmanship and business enterprises to Lhasa and other Tibetan trade centers. After the defeat of their valley kingdoms by the Shah rulers from Gorkha in 1769, the Newar proceeded to take economic advantage of the Gorkha conquest. As Gorkha military and administrative outposts were established to tie the new Himalayan kingdom together, Newar merchants went along to set up shops. They created many of the hill bazaars that trekkers encounter throughout Nepal, and they continue to serve as suppliers for many of the still remote government outposts.

Not all Newar are businessmen or civil servants. Members of one subgroup known as Jyapu are seen tilling the vast fields of rice, wheat, and vegetables in the valley. Others are stone and wood carvers, carpenters, potters, goldsmiths, blacksmiths, butchers, and Hindu or Buddhist temple priests. Newar peasant communities are even occasionally found in the outlying districts. Most Newar, no matter how far dispersed, try to keep kinship and ritual ties with the Kathmandu valley because it is their homeland. ❧

3

CULTURE: INTERACTING WITH NEPAL

Our hosts have more to teach us in regard to living in contentment, than we can possibly teach them. In the unfussed ways of villagers met on trek, we learn that patience, humility, and tolerance for all are virtues worth striving for.

—Kev Reynolds, *Langtang, with Gosainkund and Helambu*

This chapter provides food for thought on how to help preserve the character of trekking in Nepal. This type of tourism is now being called "tourism with insight," "alternative tourism," or "eco-trekking," among other things. We are pleased to see Nepali organizations now espousing the cross-cultural attitudes presented by Stephen in this book in 1976. What follows are cross-cultural clues for the survival of trekking in Nepal.

The fullest enjoyment of Nepal in all its myriad aspects comes to those who attempt to transcend the cultural and linguistic differences between themselves and their Nepali hosts. Such people are more easily accepted into the social framework of Nepal, and there are many rewards.

At times some trekkers have offended their Nepali hosts. Others have taken great advantage of traditional hospitality without considering the consequences. Still others, realizing how much farther their money will go in this country, have made a big display of their wealth. They have handed out large (for Nepal) sums of money and given away many of their possessions. Trekkers have disgraced religious customs and shown great disrespect for their hosts' beliefs. The local people have adapted somewhat to this breach of courtesy and ethics by these foreign invaders, even coming to expect it along popular trails. Generally, they both admire and envy foreigners yet detest such behavior. Partly for this reason, traditional Nepali hospitality is less obvious along these trails. The Nepali people will not let you know of their displeasure—it isn't their way—but among themselves they will have less respect for you and less desire to treat you as an honored guest. Should you make the effort to stand apart from the other trekkers, to respect the Nepali people and their customs, they will relate to you in positive ways you couldn't have imagined. You will find yourself more respected in turn.

There are basic rules governing acceptable behavior in Nepal that have knit the social fabric together over centuries of change. An outsider may feel vulnerable, anxious about making a fool of him or herself by behaving inappropriately. With so many different cultural traditions in this country, no Nepali is facile in more than a few. Hence an outsider, if he or she is seriously trying to be culturally cognizant, will be noticed and respected. The rules are not difficult. You need only observe what Nepalis around you are doing and act accordingly. What follows classifies and expounds on this.

This section, the most important part of this book, is an attempt to provide you, the guest in Nepal, with the information to act in ways that constitute reasonably acceptable behavior to your hosts. Most of the material here has been subtly gleaned from Nepalis or from the experiences of sensitive visitors to Nepal. If your attitudes are right, and your practices are acceptable, then a few faux pas will be overlooked. All outsiders in Nepal have, at times, acted incorrectly. That is how we have obtained most of the information presented here. But once you have learned acceptable norms of behavior, the benefits should make all the effort worthwhile. Encourage others who have your confidence to do likewise. This is essential if trekking in Nepal is to continue to be one of the supreme experiences in social-cultural peregrination.

When talking to trekkers in Nepal, compare the experience of those who are behaving in a fashion sensitive to Nepali customs with those who aren't so considerate. The thoughtful trekker invariably has a more intimate relationship with the Nepali people, encounters fewer problems, and is eager to come back.

RELIGION

Nepali religion is based on two "great" or "high" traditions—Hinduism and Buddhism—each underlain by expressions of local "little" traditions of animism and shamanism. (Of course, practitioners of the latter do not see their religion in this way; the dichotomy is only for purposes of analysis.) Because only a very small percentage of Nepalis are Muslim, or Musalmaan, and as most of them live in the Tarai, they will not be considered here. Even fewer are the number of Christians in Nepal; however, the number of Christian converts is growing due to a recent trend in proselytizing, even though it is illegal in Nepal.

HINDUISM AND BUDDHISM

"Hinduism is not a religion, but a way of life," states ethnologist A. W. MacDonald. This seems evident from observing the devout in Nepal. Hinduism is rooted in the texts of the ancient Vedas dating to 2000 BCE. As it evolved, three main deities became fo-

cal: Brahma the creator, Vishnu the preserver, and Shiva the destroyer. In their varied manifestations they pervade daily ritual and symbolize the cycle of life. There are no basic dogmas, no qualities that define a Hindu, except perhaps whether that person employs a Brahman as a priest. It is left to each individual to decide the form of his or her worship. The caste system is a fundamental aspect of Hinduism. Most Hindus believe that circumstances in this life are preconditioned by actions from former incarnations. People who perform well in their

Shakyamuni Buddha, born in Nepal's Lumbini, depicted in a trailside mani *wall* (Photo by Tokozile Robbins)

TIKAA AND OTHER RELIGIOUS ADORNMENTS

A *Tikaa* is a mark of religious and decorative significance on the forehead of Hindus. They are given and received, particularly at festival and religious occasions, to express good wishes, friendship, respect, and honor. When a Hindu visits a temple or shrine, he or she often takes *Tikaa* from the officiating priest. Formerly, one day each year, during the religious observance of DasAAI, the King would give *Tikaa* to the general populace. Outside of Kathmandu, the headman of a village has the honor. Plaiwn *Tikaa* of red or yellow powder is an essential part of *pujaa* (worship) for men and women. Black ones guard against untoward spirits. Fancy ones, commercially produced, are worn by women as decoration or makeup in urban areas today.

Colored powder, usually red and orange, is put on images of gods, thrown at Holi, and slapped on cheeks at festivals. This custom of Hindu origin is a sign of reverence that pleases the gods and delights people by expressing their connection with one another and with the gods.

Children, who need protection from the "evil eye" of witches and from ghosts and spirits, wear black *gaajal* at the eyes and black strings at the neck, wrists, ankles, and waist. Similarly, silver anklets are thought to help their legs grow straight. Amulets with *mantra* papers are worn at the neck. *Rudaaksha* (seeds of *Eleocarpus ganitrus*) are a sign of respect to Shiva, while Narasimha images of copper protect against lightning and fright. ◈

given station in this life will have a favorable rebirth. That is, an individual who aspires to rebirth in a higher caste must live a proper life in his present caste. This precept has exerted a significant stabilizing effect on Indian and Nepali societies. However, the view that one's position in life has been predetermined is considered to be an impediment to development. In other words, because of a belief in predestiny, many people are more likely to accept unfavorable circumstances rather than try to change them for the better. Caste etiquette was codified as law in Nepal in the Muluki Ain of 1854. Although this law has been repealed, it still governs behavior. Buddhism, on the other hand, is often considered as more a philosophy than a religion, although some Buddhists see the Buddha as a deity and petition to him as such. Additionally, Tibetan Buddhists ascribe suprahuman characteristics to some current and former *lamas* as well as to intercessory entities. Ritual observances and the petitioning of and devotion to these divine beings would classify this type of belief and practice as a religion by most definitions.

Siddhartha Gautama was born in Lumbini in Nepal's Tarai around 623 BCE. and came to be known by the title of Buddha. Buddhism, founded by Buddha and his disciples, is based on the four noble truths: suffering is inherent in existence, craving and attachment lead to suffering, the attainment of nirvana is an end to this suffering, and there is a path to nirvana, the eightfold way. These are: right view, right resolve, right speech, right action, right livelihood, right effort, right mindfulness, and right concentration. Nowadays, Buddhism depends on the institution of a monastery and monks and nuns. The Buddhist lay community supports a monastery and derives strength from it. Meditation and observance of moral precepts are the foundations of Buddhist practice with acts of devotion playing a role in Tibetan Buddhism. The recitation of the esoteric mantra *Om mani padme hum* and the spinning of prayer wheels are examples of meditative practice observed by the common folk.

HINDU FESTIVALS

DasAAI (Dusserah in India) lasts for ten ("*das*" means ten in Nepali) days at the time of the new moon in mid-October. This is Nepal's most important festival. It commemorates the legendary victory of the goddess Durga (Kali) over the demon-buffalo, Mahisashur, which generally symbolizes the triumph of good over evil. The festival begins with Ghatasthapana, the ceremonial setting of a jar of water in a place of worship in one's house, which symbolizes *shakti*, the primordial force of femininity or Universal Mother.

A prominent feature of DasAAI is the ceremonial decapitating of buffaloes at the *koT* (fort) near Hanuman Dhoka on the ninth day of the festival. The tenth day, called Vijaya Dasami (literally, "Victorious Tenth Day"), is the day of the *Tikaa* ceremony and symbolizes victory by extermination of the demon-buffalo by Durga. On this occasion, before the monarchy was dismantled, the former King and Queen received citizens at the royal palace, where they gave *Tikaa*. In the hinterlands, village leaders administer *Tikaa* to their constituents.

Schools and government offices are closed for long periods during the DasAAI festival, and the holiday is considered a time for family reunions all over the country. On rural trails, one will see women and children returning to their *maiti ghar* (or mother's home) during the time of DasAAI and/or during Tihaar, the festival of lights, which follows.

At this time of year, Kathmandu's Tundikhel grounds, opposite the Old Bus Park, are alive with goats and sheep brought into the valley from northern districts and with buffalo from the Tarai. These animals are for sale and are ultimately used in the sacrifices and banquets of the occasion. The whole DasAAI season is one of feasting and merrymaking.

Tihaar or Diwali is a five-day festival in mid-November. The lights of this festival represent knowledge and its victory over ignorance. During Tihaar various creatures are singled out for positive attention—on the first day, the crow; on the second day, the dog; on the third day, the cow; and on the fourth day, the bull. On the final day, Bhaai Tikaa, sisters ceremonially give their brothers *Tikaa* on the foreheads and wish them prosperity and long life, and the brothers offer a gift in return, usually money or clothing.

The third day is also Lakshmi Pujaa, dedicated to Lakshmi, goddess of wealth and associated with light. On this day, houses are cleaned starting early in the morning, and shops may get a fresh coat of paint or general facelift. →

In Nepal, Hinduism is reflected both in the system of caste, which defines social status, and in a subsistence economy based on rice agriculture and a highly ritualized cattle culture (cow worship). Buddhism, principally the Mahayana ("Great Vehicle") Tibetan form, is found among the BhoTiya people of the northern border area who incorporate Vajrayana Buddhism as well, with strong tantric expression, which is practiced by Buddhist Newar of the Kathmandu valley. Buddhism and Hinduism tend to blend in many settings, such as the Kathmandu valley, where indigenous Newar practice both religions, side by side and intermixed. Hindus consider Buddha as an avatar of the Hindu deity Vishnu and thus they frequent Buddhist temples and are accepting of Buddhists at Hindu shrines.

The various local expressions of these two faiths, and of animism and shamanism, are so conceptually interwoven that it would take much more than this short account to untangle and explain them accurately and clearly.

A young girl with a bright smile adorned for DasAAi festival with a broad Tikaa. (Photo by R.C. Sedai)

Houses are trimmed with marigold flowers, and hundreds of tiny oil lamps and candles transform Kathmandu into a beautifully lit city as dusk falls. Lakshmi's blessings are invoked, and a new business year is officially begun.

During this season, girls and boys also carol in the streets and alleyways of towns and villages. Girls carol on the night of Lakshmi Pujaa, and boys carol on the next night. Additionally, during Tihaar, public gambling is condoned, and you will see many crowds around groups of *juwaa* (cowrie shell) players, or card players.

Finally, among the Newar merchant community, Tihaar marks the beginning of their New Year, and Newar bazaars, in particular, are festooned with decorations and crowded with well-wishers and merrymakers. At this time, the sweet shops are overflowing with pastries and candy treats. A popular treat during Tihaar is the rice-flour doughnut, called *sel roti*.

Both DasAAI and Tihaar mark the end of the farming season, the bringing in of the harvest, and new beginnings. This time of year is especially joyous for individuals and families alike, and most people prefer to be at home with relatives and friends.

Shiva Ratri is a night consecrated to Shiva and celebrated on the night before and day of the new moon in February/March and a few days before as well. All-night vigils with sacred fires are held at Shiva shrines, and the largest take place at the World Heritage Site of Pashupatinath Temple, which lies along the banks of the Bagmati River. Pashupati is another form of Shiva and is considered the "protector of animals."

Shaivites and onlookers alike crowd into the Pashupatinath Temple grounds where a hearty mix of Brahman priests, ash-smeared yogis, beggars, vendors, and visitors mingle. Hindus consider it auspicious to visit Pashupatinath at some point during the festival. Pilgrims travel from afar to take place in the rituals, which include fasting, singing, tabla and sitar music, praying, chanting, reciting of holy text, and meditating, along with conspicuous consumption of cannabis which is overlooked during this devotional time.

Although Pashupatinath is focal point of this festival in Kathmandu, celebrations take place throughout the valley and country. Devotees around Nepal and India pay homage by building sacred fires and holding vigils on the night of honor to Shiva. ❖

RELIGION OF THE HILLS

Nepal is a complex social mosaic, with Hindu and Buddhist traditions of the Indo-Tibetan frontier overlaying local animistic and shamanistic beliefs. Many of the customs stem from Hindu concepts of purity and ritual pollution, with influences of Tibetan societal framework and monastic religious ideas. The hills of Nepal, as the interface, have been increasingly Indicized or Sanskritized, but Western influences are ever more present today. With the advent of political change in the early 1990s, some ethnic groups are subtly reasserting their own cultures. Though it is never easy (or welcome) to attempt simple classification of a belief system, the religion of the hills basically consists of animistic and shamanistic practices, interwoven with Hindu and Buddhist influences. Still, in the major population centers Hindu religion has predominant influence.

Animism and shamanism are concerned, respectively, with spirits that exist in nature and with the human condition, body and soul, alive or departed. Animistic beliefs and shamanic ritual permeate both of the "high" traditions of Buddhism and Hinduism (see sidebar above). At virtually every wayside shrine, in almost every religious rite, in ceremonies performed by lay people as well as by Hindu temple priests (*pujaari*), Buddhist priests (*lama*), or village shamans (*jhAAkri*), you will see some form of worship (*pujaa*) focusing on both the animate and inanimate objects of nature. Funerals, rites of passage, and curing ceremonies are all elaborately ornamented with the animist's and shaman's concern for placating local spirits and natural forces. (Various sidebars scattered throughout the book give a more detailed description of funerals, weddings, festivals, ritual healing, and other religious traditions of Nepal.)

If you happen upon a religious ceremony, your presence may be offensive (your proximity to food preparation or to hallowed ground, for example, may be deemed ritually polluting). As you observe events, be aware of the sensitivities of the officiants and participants. And open your senses to the fullness of their expression, especially to the sometimes awesome respect shown for nature—to the moon, earth, fire, water, and air; even to cow dung and smoky incense; to cow's curds and urine; to the blood sacrifice of chickens, pigeons, goats, and buffalo. Therein you will begin to glimpse a close, sacred association between villager and nature. Humans' link to nature is a necessary relationship that many people, caught up in the frenetic pace of the modern world elsewhere, seem to have forgotten or have uncaringly abandoned.

INDICIZED POLITIES	TIBETICIZED POLITIES
center–periphery relations more direct	networks looser in more severe terrain
culture heart of North Indian plains one of the most densely settled areas of world	culture heart of central Tibetan plateau, one of the most sparsely settled areas in the world
rice–cow subsistence system	cold crop, herding subsistence
dominated by Chhetri–Brahman alliances	dominated by nobility–monastic alliances
high caste landlord elite	nobility and monastic landlord elite
expansive patrilineage dynamic	less expansive system
caste hierarchy as socio-religious ideas	endogamous social groupings and monastic religious ideal
Indic calendar	Chinese calendar

—Todd T. Lewis and Theodore Riccardi, Jr., *The Himalayas: A Syllabus of the Region's History, Anthropology and Religion*

LANGUAGE

Along the popular trails, Nepalis who deal with trekkers have learned basic English, travelese, and other foreign languages to enable them to please their guests. Even off the trekker trails, some English is spoken; but in remote areas you are less likely to find translators to help communicate.

Everyone who attempts to learn some rudimentary Nepali will find his experience in the country more fulfilling. People will be friendlier and more welcoming, and they will go out of their way to help if you try to speak some Nepali.

Nepali is an Indo-European language derived from Sanskrit and is relatively easy to learn. It is used as the second tongue by half of Nepal, so people commonly hear many variations in how it is spoken. Hence your efforts to speak the national language will immediately make you welcome and help you stand out from other visitors. It is the first step in transcending cultural differences to make for a more rewarding interaction.

Whether or not you try to speak Nepali, be prepared for the questions you will be asked. They want to know: are you married? (and if not, how old are you, and who is the man or woman with you?); how many children do you have? (if none, they will be extremely puzzled); how much money do you make? (perhaps you can answer in terms of what fraction of your rent it pays); what does your camera cost? (it helps to have forgotten); can you give me some medicine? You may be surprised at how much people notice about you. Recently, a Tamang to whom Stephen was speaking in Nepali told him he was from America because of the slang expressions he was using!

DRESS

The dress code for men is as important as that for women but is often neglected. Men wearing shorts have low status in Nepal. Don't wear shorts when visiting monasteries. Men should never bare their chests, except when bathing discreetly (see below). Otherwise, wear a shirt at all times.

Women should attempt to wear full, long skirts, midcalf at least. It is important that women do not expose their legs. Wearing long underwear is helpful if your skirt is shorter than midcalf. In fact, if wearing a skirt, you can put on long underwear, leggings, or sweatpants when it gets cold and take them off quite discreetly when it warms up. Shorts are not acceptable for women. If women wear shorts, Nepali men and women tend to make rude remarks among themselves. Attire appropriate for the beaches of Cannes is not appropriate for Nepal, just as attire for Papua New Guinea Highlands is inappropriate in Perth. Skirts can allow a woman to urinate with some privacy if there aren't enough bushes around, especially if she doesn't wear underpants.

For women, a *lungi* or tube of material can be purchased in any cloth shop in Nepal and custom-sewn in ten minutes into a suitable garment. Have a pocket or two sewn in. An elastic waistband or drawstring is helpful for washing discreetly. Perhaps easier to wear is the *AAgi*, or *chubaa*, a long, sleeveless BhoTiya dress that ties in back. In Kathmandu you can sometimes purchase a ready-made cotton one, or it can be made from wool or polyester. Long skirts brought from home are also excellent. Some women have made them of denim, or with beautiful patterns. Skirts should be full (not tight) and in a lightweight fabric (cotton or synthetic) will be as cool as shorts, and definitely cooler than trousers. Wool is best for the cold. If you must wear baggy pants for the arduous part of the day's walk, change into your skirt in the evening when in a village or when dealing with Nepali people.

In Kathmandu and trekker tourist areas such as north of Pokhara and in Khumbu, you will find some young Nepali women wearing pants. This causes concern among

MUSIC OF NEPAL

The hills of Nepal are alive with the sound of music. Each of the many cultural groups has its own musical traditions, instruments, and means of aural expression. Like so many aspects of folkways, there are Tibetan influences in the north, and Indian in the south, with the hills the repository of indigenous music. In the high regions of Himalayan culture, a chorus line of shuffling and singing at festivals is common, while men may strum a lute (*damyin* or *toongna*) while singing in falsetto. In the hills, at celebrations, pairs of men and women alternate in rowdy repartees, making *dohori* folk music. During Tihaar (Diwali), the festival of lights or devotion to the goddess Laxmi, groups wander from village to village in the hills and sing. The barrel-drum, or *maadal*, is a common rhythmic accompaniment.

Music is a major part of religious expression. Tibetan Buddhist ceremonies with chanting, drumming, bells, conch blasts, horn and cymbal playing use sound as a medium for meditation and symbolic reasons. What may seem to the outsider as cacophony is highly developed, articulate expression. Shamanic rituals use drumming as a means of invoking the spirits and eliciting trance. Newar music is incredibly varied and highly developed in the Kathmandu valley. Trekkers are attracted to devotional songs by ensembles at temples, and festivals are never silent. Many varieties of drums and nasal intonement, as well as horns, percussion, and shawms (a woodwind instrument), extend musical dimensions. The tailor caste, *damaai*, provides festive music (*pAchai baajaa*) at weddings and other Hindu rites. There is different regional emphasis on the performances, unending drumming being found in the far west, while large curved horns (*narsinga*) and shawms (*sahanai*) are prominent in central and eastern parts of the country. Circular breathing is used to play the shawm continuously.

There is considerable gender division in musical expression. Women sing while they work: transplanting rice, planting potatoes, or carrying along the trails. They sing at the female wedding party in Hindu celebrations at the groom's house, while the men are at the bride's. They sing on the fasting second day of the women's festival of *tij* in August–September to commemorate when Parvati, the daughter of the Himalaya, won the hand of Lord Shiva. They travel around in groups singing and dancing, replaying Parvati's dance before Shiva.

Solo songs on themes of love, the pain of life, and contemporary issues are common among men and women in the hills and mountains. A minstrel caste, the *gaaine*, is found around Pokhara and to the north and occasionally in the Arun drainage. Individuals or groups who live near a Hindu village wander from place to place, gaining their livelihood by singing lyric, narrative, or religious songs for a donation, accompanied on a four-stringed bowed fiddle (*saarangi*). Many of their songs are full of outspoken political and social criticism, akin to that of blues and folk singers in the United States. Many simple homemade instruments, including bamboo flutes (*bAAsuri, murali*) and mouth harps (*murchunga*), are seen and heard.

However, many of these musical genres are slowly being lost, reflecting cultural change as new genres, especially from Hindi cinema, replace them. Alas, much of current change brings to mind the ideas expounded by Warren Hern, who asked whether the human species was a cancer on the planet. Look at a definition for cancer, and you will find four features: unrestrained growth, invasion of local tissues, distant spread, and dedifferentiation. Nepal provides a perfect example of this. Dedifferentiation is the process of "cells" becoming more primitive (or of human culture becoming more American!). But cultural death is a long way off in Nepal. You will discover this by listening to the sounds you hear while on the trail and in people's homes. ❖

Comfortable attire for women trekking (Photo by Stephen Bezruchka)

traditional Nepalis there (not unlike the concern voiced by older people for the younger fad in America of piercing many body parts). By wearing skirts you earn respect quickly, the reward for being a sensitive guest.

Several women on one trek reported a phenomenal difference in acceptance by Nepalis depending on whether they wore skirts, pants, or shorts. One woman in another group of women decided to not wear a skirt while her companions did. She reported that her friends received all the attention from Nepalis and she was ignored. This all changed after a visit to the tailor along the way where she had a skirt made. One woman who started trekking in a skirt decided it wasn't necessary and changed into shorts. In an hour she was accosted by a Nepali man. Another changed from shorts into a skirt and found that, rather than being stared at as a curiosity, she felt more accepted by Nepalis. A Nepali hillsman who married a trekker reported that he was attracted to her in distinction to other women because she wore a skirt.

Trekkers who have questioned Sherpas or other Nepalis about appropriate attire have countered these arguments by quoting their answers. The Nepalis usually answer to please, even though their feelings might have been offended. Donald Messerschmidt, a savvy Nepal anthropologist from whom Stephen first learned about trekking in 1969, was talking with a shopkeeper in Tirkhedhunga when a foreign couple walked by, dressed as if on the Riviera, the man in a tiny brief, the woman in a skimpy bikini. The shopkeeper asked Don what country they came from. Don, having heard them speak, told him. The shopkeeper then asked, "What's the matter, don't they have cloth in that country?" Consider how you might feel if a Papua New Guinea Highlander male, wearing only a penis shield, walked near your home and spoke to you. Would you treat him in a friendly manner and invite him inside? Nepalis feel equally put off by the dress of many foreigners. Along the well-traveled routes, they have seen it all.

JEWELRY AND BODY DECORATION

Jewelry and other body decoration is another fascinating aspect of Nepali culture that attracts the attention of visitors. As in most societies, jewelry is used for decoration. For women, it used to be their inalienable property and their dowry; currently, with seasonal economic hardship, men take their women's jewelry to pawn in the winter, hopefully to get it back in the spring. Jewelry is almost always handmade. The metal is paid for by weight, with a small fee for craftsmanship.

A married Rai woman wearing a tilhari *and nose ring*
(Photo by Stephen Bezruchka)

Such decoration shows affluence, with little individuality or idiosyncratic expression. At festivals and weddings, however, it is appropriate and necessary to wear all one has, for Nepal is very much a public culture.

Wearing jewelry is "auspicious" for women, who wear it at their ears, neck, and wrists. The religious implications are many. To honor is to adorn: men, their wives and daughters; hosts, their guests, with *kata* (scarves) and *maalaa* (flower garlands); and devotees, their gods, with red powder, *kata*, *maalaa*, and real jewelry; and *stupa* (shrines) and mountain passes, with prayer flags, *kata*, and flowers.

Many styles are borrowed freely from adjacent groups. Occasional indicators of ethnicity are found: Newar never pierce noses; caste Hindus always do; only Sherpas and other BhoTiya wear striped aprons and the big silver hook clasps to hold them.

Women pierce the nose on the left side (the female side) in the Hindu castes and insert a discreet stud. Many hill ethnic groups—Tamang, Gurung, Magar, Rai, Limbu, and Hindus—pierce the left nostril and septum. You may find a ring on the left side or a flat or dome-shaped plate of gold, with or without a colored stone. While the latter may be glass, or plastic because of its attractive color, the gold is usually real and quite pure. Brass or alloy is occasionally seen.

Ears are pierced early in life, as earrings are considered auspicious and gold helps the ears to hear *dharma* (spiritual teachings) and the mind to understand it. There is great variety in the ornaments worn on earlobes, with no clear representational design. Some earrings will have *makar* (dragon) heads on either side, similar to the fish design of old water fountains. Large, up to 3 inches (8 cm) in diameter, lightweight gold earrings, held stiff by their rim (*chepTisun*, meaning "flat gold"), are worn by Tamang, Magar, and Gurung, especially.

In the hills, many groups (except Sherpas and other BhoTiya) wear large *dhungri* ornaments through the stiff center cartilage of the ear. These may be so heavy that the ears flop over, a traditional sign of beauty among some peoples. The ear rims of some individuals may also have as many as eighteen to twenty tiny holes for carrying little rings. Some men, notably the Jyapu, pierce the right (male) ear, high up. BhoTiya men and women wear coral and turquoise on strings through the earlobes. ❖

BATHING

Trekkers often like to relax in hot springs or swim and wash in rivers or lakes. Nepalis are usually very shocked if this is done with genitals exposed. Women should not bare their breasts, especially those who have not borne children. Men may go bare-chested only while swimming or bathing. Also be modest while washing yourself within view of others. Women wearing skirts can bathe discreetly when not alone by hitching the skirt up, using it as a tent. A skirt also provides modesty when changing: clothes can be changed underneath easily, especially if your skirt has an elastic waistband or drawstring and is not too bulky. A tank suit underneath the skirt makes it easier to swim. Read the section on fuel under "Conservation" for energy-efficient ways to keep clean.

EATING

Hindus are concerned about ritual pollution of food when it is touched by anyone outside their caste or religion. As a foreigner, you are outside the caste system or considered an outcast or untouchable. Thus, do not touch any cooked foods on display, though it is usually all right to handle uncooked foods such as fruit and raw vegetables. When drinking from a container used by others, avoid touching your lips to it; pour the liquid into your mouth. Similarly, when drinking from a water bottle, do not touch your lips to it—at least not in sight of your hosts. Wait for food to be served to you rather than helping yourself. Do not give meal leftovers to your hosts, even though they may be rare delicacies brought from home. Do not offer a person anything from which you have taken a bite or sip. This is the *juTho* concept of food—if any of the food is touched by someone's mouth, the entire plate is contaminated and the utensils must be washed before anyone else uses them. By the same token, all leftover food or drink must either be thrown away or fed to animals. The only exception is that a wife may eat from her husband's plate. Hence, do not accept more food than you can eat. In a tea shop, put your empty glass where the Nepalis put theirs. Trekkers who visit Brahman houses or villages can expect to be served apart from others, usually outside their host's house. Although times are changing, usually trekkers will not be allowed inside the kitchen or to sleep in a Brahman house. In general, don't offer to share food in a group of Nepalis unless you have enough for everyone.

Don't touch food with your left hand. Nepalis use the left hand for toilet activities. It is offensive for them to see food in it. Eat with your right hand and use your left for picking up a glass or holding something not edible. Before and after meals, you will be offered water and a place to wash your hands and rinse your mouth. Wash your hands separately, or your left one not at all. Your right hand may be used to wipe your mouth, never your left. Give and receive food items with your right hand. In eating *daal bhaat* and

Nepalis never touch their lips to a container when drinking but pour the liquid down without spilling a drop.
(Photo by Stephen Bezruchka)

vegetables, where the meal is served in separate containers, keep them that way, except for small portions that you mix on your plate prior to eating. Spoons for eating are often available, but try eating with your right hand. It's fun! It's also the Nepali style and the most prevalent way of consuming food in the world.

In hotels that cater to trekkers, Western habits are more in vogue. All the same, the more a trekker is aware of customary Nepali manners, and the more he or she uses them in everyday behavior, the more comfortable a Nepali host will be with that person.

The daily routines of trekking life, including food and accommodation, are covered in Chapter 4.

BARGAINING AND BUYING

To understand the custom of bargaining, which is almost universal in Asia, one must realize that it is a game, not an impediment to friendship. Westerners, by contrast, often harbor ill feelings after the bargaining process. Yet once a price is agreed upon, it is "fixed." Language trouble can also create misunderstandings. Stephen can well remember bargaining with a taxi driver to take him to the start of a trek out of the Kathmandu valley. The driver named a price and Stephen began to bargain with him, but named a higher price, as his command of Nepali numbers in 1970 was poor. The driver quickly agreed, and it was only as the ride began that Stephen realized the mistake. Nevertheless, he paid the price he had agreed upon.

Try to find out the going price for an item before you begin bargaining. Failure to do so hurts everyone. As an example, if a Nepali will sell an egg to his neighbor for 8

Nepali rupees (NRS), but finds he can get 20 rupees from a trekker, he will be less likely to sell that egg to his neighbor. The price of eggs goes up. The Nepali is hurt, but not the trekker, to whom the difference in price is negligible. Such inflation is common. It behooves the trekker to always pay the lowest going price in any transaction, especially for something Nepalis buy also. In some tourist areas, two prices are used, one for foreigners and one for Nepalis. Although it makes sense, given how much more money foreigners generally have, it will increase prices for Nepalis.

In many places, people want Western gear, such as down jackets, windbreakers, and other items of apparel or equipment, more than they do your money. So you can either plan to bring extra to trade, or barter unneeded items toward the end of your trek.

Trekkers with their large sums of disposable currency have significant economic impact along the trail. By spending for locally produced goods and services, they can stimulate

A blind man relies upon his dog to lead him along the trail. (Photo by Stephen Bezruchka)

and support the local economy. This keeps people gainfully employed with respect and dignity, lessening the desire to move to Kathmandu (or migrate abroad) and work in sweat shops or other menial jobs there. Eat local food, buy locally produced crafts, and limit purchases and use of imported products (packaged foods, bottled drinks and sauces, souvenirs, and other items brought from Kathmandu).

Bargaining effectively takes time, so be leisurely and relaxed. Don't show too much interest in the item, and certainly don't begin by offering the top price you are willing to pay. If you are hung up over the last stages of the bargaining process, remember the monetary exchange value of the amount in dispute. Sometimes it may just be a few cents and not worth the haggle for something a local wouldn't buy, and you will not be putting pressure on local demand.

Prices are fixed for certain items, usually food and commodities, especially along well-traveled routes. In the ACAP areas, lodge management committees have standardized menus and lodging with fixed prices for foreigners. In other national park areas, this is happening to different extents. Bargaining is not recommended here, or in other areas where prices have been fixed, although some drop prices during low season. Prices increase the farther from the supply. In high-altitude areas where Nepalis don't normally go outside of seasonal animal pasturing or on trading trips, prices will be relatively steep.

Recognize that the local perception of cheap travelers is that they are fools. Moderate extravagance and generosity are appreciated by the Nepalis. Traveling cheaply, easy in Nepal, should not be the goal of your travel.

GENEROSITY AND GIFT-GIVING

In rich countries, many of us feel we can buy whatever we want, whereas Nepalis tend to make things happen by creating social obligations. Many Nepali ethnic groups exchange goods and services by reciprocal relationships without involving money, while other traditional patron-client relationships are more hierarchical. Economic reciprocal exchanges based on social bonds of caste, kinship, and family are found in many Nepali ethnic groups with modern versions used to facilitate business transactions—the so-called "source-force" exchanges, for example. This practice involves utilizing access based on these bonds to gain power—be it jobs, contracts, or other advancement.

The trekker can unknowingly enter into these kinds of reciprocity relationships. Many foreigners feel the trekking experience to be a sacred journey, requiring physical and emotional stamina in an exotic environment. Special bonds develop over the course of a trek between the trekker and his or her employees because the work involves social interaction as well as physical labor. These bonds are more like the implicit trust of kinsmen than of unrelated people and are not found in most other types of tourism exchanges. Trekkers complete this journey with overwhelming gratitude and try to express this feeling through generosity to their staff. They may do so through giving tips, or even financially sponsoring some of their employees or children in their families for education and opportunities. The staff in turn reciprocate through special ceremonies and exchanges, hoping to establish long-term bonds between the hosts and guests.

These interactions may represent an attempt to replicate the egalitarian nature of pre-tourist relationships, which have served humankind for countless millennia. Some foreigners have assumed long-term responsibilities in the relationship, even bringing some of the staff to the United States in return for assistance in their future sacred journeys. However, such associations tend to become hierarchical over time. The beneficence rarely involves the lowly porters and others who have little contact with the trekker, and this selectivity can increase the gulf between the rich and the poor, the haves and the have-nots. The lesson: Try to maintain reciprocity and egalitarianism however you can, in spite of the hierarchical nature of touristic encounters. Any attempt to maintain these equitable traditions will benefit us all.

In dealings with people, pay the going rate. Never walk off without paying. In tipping people for their services, be reasonable. Routine tipping is not a Nepali custom. Some people tip much more than the salary or cost of the service they are paying for. This only reinforces the belief that the foreigner does not know the value of his money, and thus should be relieved of as much of it as possible.

Giving to monasteries is an important tradition in Nepal and elsewhere. Buddhist cultural values are related to the number of monks and their devotion as well as the existence of teachers to carry on traditions. The decline of monasteries is more likely to affect faith and values than the pollution of sacred sites by unknowing tourists. By donating, you help conserve Buddhist culture (and gain *dharma* merit). The main way the religion continues to survive the onslaught of western culture is through charitable largesse to the monasteries. Most have a donation box. Be generous. Villagers' sense of your respecting their culture also ensues. Hinduism is less dependent on the presence of *sadhu* (holy men), but giving to them is also appropriate.

Bringing small gifts for people who have helped you along the way is a good idea. People you wish to be generous to may appreciate a look through your camera or binoculars, or at pictures in this book or others you may have. Allowing people to look through picture books from home, postcards of temples and other sights of Nepal, or photographs of your family, is a most welcome gesture. Sing songs for them, dance with them, or play a musical instrument. If you are artistically inclined, bring a sketchbook or journal and share drawings with people you come to know. Let them draw for you. One trekker brings string and plays string games with children and adults, something that is imaginative, cheap, and portable. Displays of generosity should be limited to appreciation for something extraordinary that has been done for you. When you give or receive something to or from someone, hold onto the object with both hands, a sign of respect.

Gifts should emphasize the transcendent values of friendship, knowledge, and health over material wealth. Beware of the long-term repercussions of anything you do. When Daniel Taylor-Ide, who was working in family planning in Kathmandu in 1969, suggested that Stephen distribute condoms during his treks, it seemed a great idea. Reluctant to demonstrate their proper use to adults, he blew them up as balloons for children. This was a highly successful public relations gesture, but trekkers following in his path were besieged with requests for condoms and balloons. Currently such litter abounds. Bring small useful items like strong sewing thread, needles, cloth, and rope. Whether or not you travel with small children, baby clothes will be appreciated. Consider bringing your older clothes that are out of style, or older camping or trekking equipment that is no longer used to give to porters and people as gifts, again within the grounds noted above.

BEGGING

Trekkers may sometimes encounter beggars to whom it is appropriate to give. There are few traditional beggars in the hills, but occasionally *sadhu* or *yogi*, itinerant spiritual seekers, travel through on pilgrimage with begging as part of their way of life. Monks and nuns occasionally beg. Food such as rice is an appropriate gift item for them. Sometimes destitute people are encountered and gifts of clothing, food, and occasionally money are appropriate. Note the actions of Nepalis around you when deciding whether to give.

It is instructive to watch patterns of begging develop along the trekking trails over the years. When Stephen first came to Nepal in 1969 there was no begging in the hills. Nowadays, children and others along the trekking trails accost tourists and beg for candy, money, pens, and cigarettes. A few hours' walk off these trails, people rarely to never beg at all.

Why do trekkers give money, pens, candy, and other items to children? Clearly they like the happy smiles they receive. And in Nepal, foreigners can feel generous without having to give very much. Others feel guilty about the great gulf in material wealth between themselves and Nepali people. If you are one of these, realize that you are helping to make beggars out of children who once were spontaneously happy. To encourage and support begging is an example of cultural arrogance. Do you want Nepalis to lose their self-respect? If everyone stopped reinforcing inappropriate begging, it would cease in a generation or less. To sample the experience without begging, take a trek away from popular areas. You'll be convinced.

Nepalis have had good dental hygiene in the past, due mostly to their low consumption of sugar. Don't work against this by giving candy. The amount of tooth decay in the trekker areas from consumption of sugar in the form of sweets has increased dramatically. This was the major reason to establish a dental clinic in Namche Bazaar (in the Everest region). Don't encourage smoking by handing out cigarettes. Some Nepalis will not allow smoking inside their inns! Handing out money to everyone who asks or giving money for posing for pictures is not a good idea. Parents of Nepali children are usually ashamed to learn that their children have been begging, and they try to stop it, except in areas where begging has been so reinforced that parents actively encourage it.

When approached by a beggar, ignore the person and walk away disinterested. Don't taunt or ridicule the beggar. Sarcasm is not commonplace in Nepal.

Adults are approaching trekkers asking for various opportunities such as help in getting a visa or for airfare to a foreign country (yours) or for support for their children to go to school in Kathmandu. Trekkers have been generous in these ways, and word gets around. Some trekkers enjoy a chance to help people poorer than they who have been kind to them. It would be better to seek out the truly marginalized groups in Nepal who can't interact with trekkers the way lodge owners, guides, and other tourism workers do. But this is much harder and less likely for the trekker.

Sometimes trekkers are approached to donate money for village construction projects such as schools, trails, and bridges. That may be legitimate and if Nepalis also contribute, then the trekker might give a nominal amount, too. In some places Nepalis will approach you to plant a *Tikaa* (red mark) on your forehead or garland you with flowers for which they expect you to pay. Avoid such people if you don't want to pay for the offering. Sometimes trekkers will spend several days with a family and then decide to be generous with that family in some special way. That is perfectly appropriate; it is a part of normal social human behavior. It certainly doesn't encourage the kind of begging that has sprung up on the shoulders of trekker tourism.

"Oh money come to me!" This may become the *mantra* of the future in Nepal if we who are fortunate enough to travel here don't exercise care and sensitivity.

The following sobering assessment is from Declan Murphy, a grassroots social worker and is based on longtime interactions with Kathmandu's street kids. It describes the unexpected effects of well-meaning intentions, and provides telling insight into the nature of the donor mentality that has become prevalent in Nepal and the wider consequences of giving aid. Currently, there are over 220 international non-government organizations (INGOs) operating in Nepal and nearly 30,000 registered NGOs with

VICTIMS OF KINDNESS

Initially, it may be difficult to comprehend, but the last thing street children need are more random-acts-of-kindness by well-meaning individuals, which have unwittingly contributed to children choosing to remain on the street in vulnerable circumstances. For anyone wishing to truly help these children, the solution is simple yet incredibly difficult to properly explain or practice: "Do nothing!" Unfortunately, this advice is all too often ignored, as it goes against the grain of human nature. At first look, doing nothing does little to ease feelings of helplessness when witnessing firsthand the inequality and injustice of crushing poverty, and herein lies the biggest problem.

The primary beneficiary of the gift-giving (be it a few rupees, a piece of fruit, an unfinished sandwich, or even a moment of friendship) is generally the donor, whose guilt is assuaged. These acts of compassion turn out to be problematic as the child's persistent attempts are rewarded and he or she is further encouraged to continue begging rather than seek the widely accessible assistance of numerous local organizations which exist to provide longer-term support to these children. The casual donor's short-term gifts only compete with these organizations' long-term solutions. In a young mind, the organizations' facilities and care program can pale in comparison to the boundless excitement of the streets and gifts, especially money which is often used to procure glue to sniff for its intoxicating effects.

The child's guardians too, can become insidiously aware of the child's earning potential and often promote what becomes a lucrative street-side drama performed for an ever-revolving audience of tourists. More worrying is that these children also learn the benefits of being friendly with strangers—the dangers of which often only become apparent to some of the children when it's already too late.

The desire to help is understandable and truly commendable, but the reality of the situation is such that, more often than not, it's more helpful to do nothing and simply enjoy your time in a troubled yet amazingly beautiful county of contrasts. It should never be forgotten that by being a tourist in Nepal, you already contribute in a real and meaningful way to one of the country's most valuable sources of income. An almost endless list of other service providers, both seen and unseen, *will* benefit directly from your time in Nepal. So, please, take a moment to contemplate what you *are* already doing just by being in Nepal, and consider the result of attempting to satisfy that nagging feeling of needing to do more. ❖

perhaps equal that number unregistered. Extrapolate the problems mentioned below to the foreign donor paradigm for an idea of the mixed effects of hundreds of millions of dollars of annual "aid" funds and projects.

If the desire to donate is irresistible, then the following guidelines from The Center for Responsible Travel (www.responsibletravel.org) provide valuable information for those wishing to make a difference while traveling: "Travelers' desire to help, interact, and learn from those they meet during their holiday is clearly positive. However, there are sometimes unintended consequences from these good intentions. Misguided contributions can perpetuate cycles of dependency, cause corruption, burden communities with unwanted or inappropriate donations, and require recipients to spend time and resources to handle 'gifts' they didn't request or cannot use…when, how, and what to contribute needs to be decided by the host community, not the tourist or the tourism company."

If you are serious about wanting to help in a meaningful way, then pause for a few years while you undertake critical reflection. The world has experienced close to half a millennium of colonialism in various forms. The current global situation represents an incredible gulf between those who have too much and those who are struggling to survive yet lacking basic needs of food, water, and shelter. Dealing with the economic crisis affecting much of the world in 2010 will require rethinking the nature of human and societal relations. This happened with the transition from forager-hunters to agriculture and with industrialization and the digital revolution. We have opportunities to shape the forces at work in the world, but it requires that we ponder our position in society and how that can have unintended effects. Stephen tries to get his graduate students to monitor their roles in the work world. This can be unsettling. Travelers who are touched by the inequality they see between them and Nepali children can truly make a difference but not in the way they think of first by assisting individuals they encounter. Collective action will be required.

THEFT AND SECURITY

Trekkers are often surprised to find that Nepali people are genuinely friendly and extremely honest. If you find yourself suddenly surrounded by a group of onlookers in Nepal, robbery is the farthest thing from their minds. They are curious and eager to help; they are not afraid to get involved. However, Nepal, once renowned as a place where travelers had absolutely no worries about theft and violence, is slowly entering modern times.

There is occasional theft and petty vandalism; packs and luggage left on tops of buses are easy targets, as are unattended tents (some of which have even been stealthily slit open and robbed while occupied). More people are reporting items missing from their packs, and sometimes thieves are seen rustling through packs left outside lodges or unattended along the trail. Pickpockets now work some of the popular trails. Misunderstandings have resulted in a few reported attacks, robberies, and even a rare death. There have been attacks on trekkers camping alone in areas with few people, attacks by porters, and instances where trekkers on an exposed area have been pushed off a precipice. Is there an increase in the incidence of such episodes, or are incidents more publicized as the number of trekkers increase?

Some trekkers have been insensitive to local customs, have mistreated their porters, and have behaved in a manner outside the norms of Nepali experience. Trekkers who could not afford it at home could have servants do many of the distasteful and laborious chores of camping and backpacking. Hired porters and assistants were sometimes thought of as less than human; this was evident in the lack of responsibility that many trekkers took toward their employees. There has been a change in cultural values among some Nepalis living in the areas most heavily influenced by trekking. Some Nepalis believe that trekkers don't value their money because they don't try to get the best prices. Since they are so willing to pay too much, others try to relieve them of their seemingly unvalued money and possessions.

Remember, however, that the risk of attack and robbery in Nepal is much less than in your home country. Try to prevent petty thievery by keeping a watchful eye on your possessions. Carry around exposed to view only the equipment you expect to use a great deal. Try to have all your gear stowed inside your pack and duffel bag, and keep the pockets done up. Lock items whenever possible. Discreetly inventory your gear in the morning and afternoon; it will be less likely to disappear through porter mishap. When traveling by bus with your belongings in the luggage rack on top, either have someone in the party ride with them or be watchful of people climbing on top when the bus stops. During a bus stop for lunch, it is safest to bring your carry-on items with you, out of the vehicle. It helps to keep all easily removed items buried deep inside the luggage. In populated areas, don't leave your tents unattended. Don't trek alone, especially if a woman. Treat your porters with respect. Make sure they have equipment and food sufficient for the undertaking. In lodges and hotels where the honor system is used, be honest, and never run off without paying. Where this has happened too many times, the lodge has the trekker pay for each item as it is ordered. Carry money in a money belt around the waist, or deep inside the pack, that you don't lose sight of. Don't be tempted by greed into a potential confrontation where by sleight of hand you lose your money. This happened to Stephen in Connaught Circus in Delhi and taught him a valuable lesson.

Women are reporting sexual harassment with greater frequency. This can occur in lodges as well as along the trails. Pornographic materials portraying salacious images are wrongly attributed to all foreign travelers. Police may not be sensitive or be eager to investigate. Dressing appropriately helps. Either ignore relatively minor episodes and leave, or be indignant. If this happens in a lodge, threaten adverse publicity.

In case of theft, report this to the police. Likely you will have to travel to a major police station in Pokhara, say, or Kathmandu and file a formal report. Make copies of your passport and other valuable documents should you have the displeasure of needing replacements, getting airline tickets reissued, and so forth. Usually other trekkers will be generous enough to take care of immediate needs and even loan money on goodwill terms.

Be sure to register with your country's embassy or consulate when you arrive in Nepal. This is advisable for all trekkers, even those on organized treks. Let the embassy officers know your dates and itinerary, and give them a contact person should they need to follow up.

MEDICAL TREATMENT OF LOCAL PEOPLE

In the past, medical facilities were very scarce in Nepal, and foreigners were almost the only source of Western medicines. Each passing traveler was considered a doctor and indeed, many people, both medical and nonmedical, devoted a large part of their energies to treating the ills of the local people. Today this effort is not warranted and may do more harm than good. It helps destroy confidence in health care services developing in rural areas.

Besides the facilities staffed by doctors along the trails, there are many health posts manned by auxiliary health workers. It is doubtful that ephemeral medical care such as a trekker could dispense would result in a cure or significant benefit to the sufferer. Furthermore, the idea that a little medicine might help a sick person and enable him or her to get to proper medical aid just does not hold up. Based on Stephen's personal experience as a doctor working in remote areas of Nepal and on discussions with other medical personnel, giving medicine to someone whom you wish to refer to another facility is almost certain to deter that person from acting on the referral. Finally, the idea that a little aspirin won't hurt anyone is untenable because, since it will not effect a cure, it may help destroy confidence in Western medicine. In a country with many different medical practices, it is best to introduce those aspects of medicine that definitely work.

This policy is in Nepal's best interests, several important Nepali organizations have publicly concurred.

This advice does not apply to your porters and other employees. If a problem presents itself that you can confidently manage, you should treat them to the best of your abilities. Otherwise, if the condition is serious, you are responsible for obtaining proper medical care for that person. In other situations, exercising normal humanitarian instincts and helping your fellow human is also appropriate. That is, don't walk away from the scene of an accident without rendering assistance in any way that you can.

(Health and medical problems are addressed in Chapter 5.)

MISCELLANEOUS CUSTOMS

The fire and hearth are considered sacred in Sherpa homes, in those of most other BhoTiya, and in high-caste Hindu homes. Thus do not throw any refuse, including cigarettes, into a hearth, at least not without asking. Sherpas and other BhoTiya believe that burning or charring meat offends the gods. Do not roast meat on an open fire.

Shoes are considered the most degrading part of your apparel, so keep them on the floor or ground. Remove them before putting your feet up on anything. Shoes, especially leather ones, should always be removed before entering any kind of temple, *gomba,* or monastery. Do not touch anyone with your shoes. The greatest insult you can give a Nepali is to kick him or her with your shoe. Follow the example of your host in deciding whether to remove shoes before entering a Nepali home. If in doubt, remove them. When removed, keep the soles on the ground, not overturned. When sitting or sleeping near the family shrine or in a temple or *gomba,* don't point your feet at the images.

Do not wash your feet in water that will flow into a water-driven prayer wheel. If you must wash your feet in such a stream, do it downstream, after the water has passed through the entire series of prayer wheels. The head of an adult Nepali is the most sacred or ritually clean part of the body. You should never touch it. Similarly, don't touch anyone with your left hand. Pointing your finger at someone is considered rude.

Before sitting down on the ground, you will almost always be offered a mat to sit on. When sitting, do not point the soles of your feet at anyone. Nepalis will not step over your legs and feet. Be sure to draw them up to make a path for anyone coming or going. If you and your porters, or Nepali hosts, have to sleep on the floor together, sometimes around a fire, the arrangement should be sure to avoid anyone's feet being pointed at a Nepali person's head. As you go farther north, these Sanskritized concepts of purity and pollution become more relaxed and Tibeticization influences predominate. Watch your hosts and adjust your habits accordingly.

Public displays of affection are not the custom in Nepal. Young men may hold hands walking together, and women may as well, but men and women do not customarily hold hands in public. It is best to confine your amorous feelings to private places.

While traveling, you may pass Buddhist *mani* walls containing tablets with prayers carved on them in handsome Tibetan script. Walk by them, keeping them on your right, as Buddhists would do as a sign of respect. Similar treatment is given to the *chorten* and *stupa,* commemorative mounds sometimes modeled after those at Swayambhu or Baudha. If in doubt as to whether a structure is one of these, keep it on the right as you walk by. When visiting a monastery or *gomba,* a donation of money for the upkeep is expected as a gift. In paying respects to the abbot of a monastery, you might offer him a ceremonial scarf, or *kata,* obtained from another monk. Many Hindu temples will be out-of-bounds for non-Hindus.

A traditional mud chulo *(cooking stove) modernized with a pressure cooker covered with mud paste for easier cleaning* (Photo by R.C. Sedai)

Many Western habits are offensive to traditional Nepalis. Some, such as shaking hands, using dry toilet paper, carrying around a used handkerchief, and eating without washing, seem unsanitary to them. Many of these have become more accepted in time, even commonplace, but respect for the native customs pays rich dividends to the trekker.

OTHER CONCERNS FOR THE TREKKER

Photography. Respect people's desires not to be photographed. This is now quite common along popular treks. Think how you would feel if hordes of invaders would regularly descend into your life, not say a word to you, but plunge long lenses into the midst of your daily routine and occasionally into your most private affairs. Many people, especially elderly villagers, believe that being photographed can shorten a person's life span. Flash photography inside monasteries is thought to hasten the disintegration of paint there.

Sometimes if you talk with the people whom you would like to photograph for a while, they will consent. After you show them pictures of your family, they may be more willing to be photographed. Or, let a recalcitrant subject take a photograph with your camera. After she snaps the shutter, she may change her mind and let you photograph. If you want a photograph badly enough, these techniques, respecting human dignity, work.

Don't promise to send copies of photographs to people unless there is a reasonable chance that you can do so. Sending photographs through the mail in Nepal is becoming more reliable. Write down their names and postal addresses in English, which is sufficient for the envelope. You could also send the photos with another traveler or through your trekking agency in Kathmandu. With digital cameras these days you can show people the images taken immediately afterwards. Why would you not do so? Unfortunately, this is just one more way to display the enormous economic gulf between yourself and most Nepalis. Do not take flash photographs inside *gomba* during ceremonies.

Recreational Drugs. Some people who come to Nepal are attracted by the freely available marijuana and hashish. The plant grows as a weed in much of the country.

Traditionally, older shopkeepers consumed it now and then at the end of the day. Young Nepali people never used it when Stephen first came to Nepal in 1969, at a time when *ganja* was legal and sold in government shops. Now, influenced by foreign habits, they indulge. Nepal now has a considerable hard drug problem among its natives, both as consumers and drug runners. Some trekkers smoking marijuana on the trails will offer it to wide-eyed young children. Consumption of this drug is a personal adult decision. It is illegal to carry and sell it. It is wrong to try to entice youngsters to use it.

Artifacts. Many trekkers purchase art and craft objects in the hills. Sometimes they buy valuable relic art objects, often at modest prices. This is expressly illegal; it is prohibited to remove any valuable antique items from their origins. Even transporting idols and artifacts has resulted in imprisonment to trekkers. Steadfastly deny any interest in antique art, for if you don't, you encourage Nepalis to steal old objects from sanctuaries, trails, monasteries, or temples in order to sell them to foreigners.

ECONOMIC AND CULTURAL IMPACT OF TREKKING

Tourism development proceeds through three (perhaps four) distinguishable stages. The first is "discovery," which for trekking in Nepal occurred in the 1960s and 1970s for the popular areas. Trekkers were addressed as *sahib* or *memsahib*, a colonial term of respect never heard today. There still are plenty of places in Nepal to discover today, even a few included in this book.

During the next stage, local resources are used for both traditional and touristic needs, under the control of local people. This is still happening in places visited by trekkers in small numbers. This contributes to the local economy significantly.

In the third stage, tourism is institutionalized, with standardization for services and professionalization of tourist–host relationships. With increasing numbers of tourists in this stage, loss of local decision-making occurs, and profits from the growing competition for local resources flow outside the destination area. Goods and services for the tourist are imported, and much of the economic gain leaves the area. Popular trekking areas in Nepal are either in this third stage or in a transition to it.

A possible fourth stage would be when destruction or overuse of resources leads to a decline of tourism and consequent decrease in the local living standards. Some areas have noted a decline in trekkers, presumably because of publicity regarding lack of hygiene. Furthermore, marginalized groups often become poorer as a result of inequities in distribution of income from tourism.

Trekking tourism relies on a large trail network and inexpensive labor to porter. Most peasant farmers can no longer sustain their families on the available land, so they search out seasonal work. Trekking business produces social and spatial mobility and contributes to migration to the cities and adoption of market forces and urban values. Ancestral villages become abandoned, and languages are lost. Then roadways and even helicopters put porters out of work. Some get rich, while many get poorer, losing their traditional means of support. Trekking tourism has thus radically altered conventional Nepalese society and culture; some have called it "wrecking in Nepal." It has contributed to the increasing disparity between rich and poor, the fundamental modern factor that is destroying the fabric of humankind everywhere. It doesn't have to; that is a key message of this book.

The possible fourth stage, a decline mentioned above, is becoming the norm in Nepal. Although overuse of resources is one small aspect, the effects of modernization for tourist transactions were in part responsible for the Maoist-led rebellion (briefly recounted in "Background"). Many reasons have been offered to explain the unbelievable

NEPALI DIASPORA

The decade-long war, persistent political turmoil, and a dearth of jobs have driven many Nepalis to venture abroad in search of employment. Formerly, India was the destination of choice. Nowadays, Nepalis are traveling farther afield, and some 1.2 million Nepalis are employed in over forty foreign countries other than India. In the fiscal year 2007/2008, the Statistics Department recorded that a total of 239,637 Nepalis left the country for work. Qatar, Malaysia, the United Arab Emirates and Saudi Arabia received more than 90 percent of Nepali migrant workers. (Alarmingly, Malaysia received the lowest designation in the U.S. State Department's 2009 report on human trafficking, placing it among countries who do not follow the minimum standards for opposing trafficking.)

Many of these jobs abroad are fraught with danger and involve hard physical labor in factories or on construction sites. With a weak home government and no labor representation, these Nepalis are often exploited, and this starts with the recruiting agencies in Nepal. Stories abound of people mortgaging family property against exorbitant recruiting fees, only to find on arrival in a new country that conditions are entirely different than had been promised. Passports are often held captive as workers endure inhumane, long hours in stressful jobs with low wages and little to no rights. For some, it takes years of labor to pay back placement companies.

In 2001 it was estimated that twelve Nepalis were dying every month in Middle Eastern countries due to poor conditions and mistreatment. Seventy-five percent of the recruiting agencies in Kathmandu were damaged in riots in 2004 following the deaths of twelve Nepali workers by insurgents in Iraq. In Malaysia, industrial accidents killed fifty-two Nepalis in 2005, fifty-eight in 2006, and fifty-nine in 2007, and work-site injuries harmed many more; recourse in compensation is not available to widowed families or injured workers. Nevertheless, Nepalis keep applying and are eager to work abroad due to the dismal employment scene in Nepal.

Until recently, most of these workers sent remittances home via the age-old *hawala* or *hundi* system of money brokers that was time-consuming, charged a high commission, and relied on honor rather than receipts. Nowadays, bank-to-bank transfers and remittance companies are making life at least a little easier for the Nepali diaspora. In 2004, after a steady rise, overseas remittances finally surpassed both tourism and exports combined as Nepal's biggest source of foreign income. Additionally, a network (www.helpnepal.net) was set up by Nepalis to help connect those living abroad, and together this group has been donating funds for Nepal-based development projects. ❖

transition to a civil war that engulfed Nepal for ten years. The relatively peaceful façade that welcomed foreigners for decades was covering up tremendous state repression. Police and government terrorist actions have been going on for a long time. Accounts from the 1940s through the 1960s demonstrate that even visionaries such as B. P. Koirala, who became the first elected prime minister in 1959 and whose family continues to play a key role in the political scene, were victims of state violence. Terrorism brought violent responses then as it does now.

The situation has largely stabilized since the Maoists came to the table in late 2005 and joined a multi-party alliance that ended the war. This led to the formal dismantling of the monarchy in May 2008 and the declaration of Nepal as a democratic republic. However, politcal infighting and dissolution continues while tourists continue to arrive to enjoy the natural beauty of the Himalaya and a warm reception from the resilient people of Nepal.

ESSENTIAL CULTURAL DOS AND DON'TS

Do

- Wear a shirt if you are a man
- Wear a long skirt if you are a woman
- Keep your valuables secure; locked up if possible
- Keep prayer walls and *chorten* on the right when passing them
- Pay the standard price for food and other goods
- Draw up your legs while sitting on the floor so Nepalis can pass by you
- Leave donations when visiting monasteries
- Support local handicrafts that result from traditional cultural elements
- Smile—Nepalis tend to smile to relieve possible embarrassment; a return smile quickly eases tensions

Don't

- Give to beggars unless Nepalis also do so, and give the amounts they do
- Give money or items to people who have not assisted you
- Give medicines to local people
- Point the soles of your feet at anyone
- Touch anyone with your shoes
- Touch any Nepali's head
- Give or receive food with your left hand
- Eat off another's plate
- Give food to Nepalis if you have touched it
- Touch your lips to a drinking container that is to be used by others
- Accept more food on your plate than you can eat
- Walk out of a hotel or *bhaTTi* without paying your bill
- Throw garbage in your host's fire
- Photograph people against their wishes
- Defecate or urinate indiscreetly
- Offer recreational drugs to Nepali children or adults
- Travel alone, if a woman
- Be sarcastic to a Nepali
- Be openly affectionate

4

TREKKING LIFE, FOOD, AND ACCOMMODATION

Madam, this is Nepal. In America you can be a bird in a gilded cage. Here the bird is free. And for that there is a price.

—A Nepali to an inconvenienced and angry trekker

Trekking is a healthy activity, although not without its hazards. It is strenuous and burns calories, and many overweight people shed their excess load along the trail while everyone feels his or her muscles strengthen and firm up. To be sure, there are perils and lower standards of hygiene. Furthermore, modern health care is not available in the hill and mountain areas. But when sensible precautions are taken, few get seriously sick in Nepal. To the contrary, most people find a trek in Nepal physically and spiritually enlightening.

Trekkers traveling in areas where there are few foreigners and who wish to eat local food must adhere to the local schedules. Though local schedules vary depending on the season, area, and village, the following general outline gives you some idea of what to expect.

In the hills, Nepali people get up around sunrise, sometimes have a brief snack, then work until the midmorning meal around 10 AM. Work then continues until the late afternoon and is followed by the second meal of the day. A light snack preceding this meal is not uncommon. Because activities coincide with periods of daylight, people tend to go to sleep soon after sunset; however, this is changing, with solar power lighting up much of Nepal. In the mountains, people wait until it warms up a little before engaging in much activity, and generally eat three meals a day.

Generally, most trekkers stop before 5 PM regardless of season and usually depart mid-morning, after a warm drink and breakfast. Schedules are more affected by altitude and places to stay than by length of day, which varies little from season to season at this latitude (roughly that of Florida).

Those on an organized camping trek follow a personalized daily routine. Variables such as the type of trek, the size of the party, and the area visited all affect the way you organize your daily trekking activities. The day usually begins with hot tea served in your tent before you get up. Breakfast follows, then you hike till around midday, eat lunch prepared by an advance cook team, then continue till the evening stop. Those traveling in areas where there are plenty of trekker-oriented hotels can structure the day much as they wish. Trekkers employing Nepali assistants (guide, porters) are advised to adhere to a schedule compatible with their staff.

Typical lodging along the main routes (Photo by Tokozile Robbins)

ACCOMMODATION

Depending on your trekking style, group size, and route, where you stay may range from large, well-furnished tourist hotels to simple lodges to tents and shelters to local Nepali homes. Nowadays, with a preponderance of tourist facilities, this last option is seldom tried by trekkers but is the most rewarding way to travel in Nepal and is highly recommended.

Along the popular routes, lodges can be quite comfortable, and these get crowded during the high season. Many of the bigger operations hire staff from outside the region and offer extensive menus. The older of these lodges can be more cozy and hospitable. Travelers can eat either local food, typically *daal bhaat tarkaari* (rice with lentil soup and a vegetable dish, or sometimes the rice is substituted for *roTi* or even a flour paste), which is what the staff usually eats and is more energy-efficient to cook, or Westernized food that is brought in by porters or trekkers themselves.

We make no effort to evaluate the quality of the services of the lodges. Not only do travelers have widely ranging tastes, but standards, reliability, and ratings cannot be counted on in rural Nepal. Nor can we guarantee that lodges will function when mentioned in the text. Many are open only during trekker season. Ask before proceeding to high areas, especially if in off-season times.

TOURIST LODGES AND HOTELS

Tourist lodges are located mostly north of Pokhara in the Annapurna region, north of Kathmandu in Langtang and Helambu, and on the route to and within Khumbu, the Everest region. There generally you find private and dormitory rooms with beds or sleeping platforms, covered with foam or cotton mattresses. Cotton mattress covers and pillow cases as well as blankets are provided, but these are not renewed after each traveler spends a night. The walls between private rooms are often thin, so vocal privacy is rare. Noisy parties can be disruptive, and earplugs are useful for a good night's sleep. There is usually a sunroom that serves as a central dining area, sometimes with an electric light or a bright kerosene lantern and often a wood stove for warmth. Usually, smokers are not segregated, so nonsmokers have to put up with fuming travelers. Posher rooms have attached bathrooms, but usually there is a shared latrine outside and sometimes a flush toilet, more often a pit. Most toilets will have a container in which to put used toilet paper, instead of down the hole, to keep the system from clogging. Toilet paper is almost never provided. A bucket of heated water can be requested for washing if a solar-powered shower has not been set up, both of which are sometimes charged for separately. Lodges have become quite comfortable, even in high-altitude settings, although in many places the facilities will be more spartan. Floors and walls may be built of sod blocks carved from the alpine meadows nearby.

The term *lodge* tends to mean a place to eat and spend the night, as does *hotel*, but terminology is not standardized. You can always sleep in a traditional inn or tea shop, although the amenities may be a bare minimum.

In some areas of Annapurna or in Khumbu, there are luxurious facilities with corresponding prices. Lodges may sometimes cater only to clientele with a specific travel agency; however, if bookings have been low, you may be accommodated.

There is an increasing tendency, especially in the national parks, to cook on kerosene in these lodges. In other places, mudded-in wood stoves are the norm and electric hot plates may be found, too. Kitchen facilities are usually wanting, and hoteliers, in spite of their lengthy menus, may only have one or two stoves to cook on for everybody. It makes sense to adjust your order to what is already being cooked, rather than have each person order a separate item. International menus have become commonplace in many lodges, with the quality of the food varying enormously from place to place and from time to time. Some trekkers in lodges complain when all the items they order are not served piping hot all together. If this applies to you, reread the quote at the beginning of this chapter. Prices in lodges are usually fixed; there is generally no bargaining except possibly in off-season times.

Seek out less popular lodges, or *bhaTTi* ("traditional inns"), rather than patronizing the most frequented places. Such redistribution of income will have a significant economic impact in the area. At a popular trekking stop, you may find everyone staying there, not necessarily because it is the best, but simply because it is the newest or because everyone else is there or it was mentioned in a guidebook. Avoid this herd mentality.

Lodge owners along the popular trekking routes are especially eager to please tourists. By asking about rubbish disposal, segregation of smokers, use of kerosene, and hygiene, a trekker can influence future directions for the lodges. Compliment lodge owners for the many things they do well.

PEOPLE'S HOMES

In North America and other travel destinations, bed-and-breakfasts (B&Bs) have become popular, partly because they allow the visitor a more homey atmosphere and a chance to get to know a family. Almost any home in Nepal is a B&B and offers the trekker a chance to intimately experience Nepali life. Small parties, up to four or five including porters and guides, can ask in villages, even if lodges exist, to be fed and put up overnight in a home. We have been doing this for over forty years and find Nepalis in popular trekking towns today delighted to participate in the tourist economy by offering food and lodging this way. Porters and guides find the experience enjoyable too, for they get an opportunity to experience other cultures in the mosaic of Nepal. If you speak a little Nepali, you will face little difficulty arranging this. If you don't, try to use a few phrases, or advise your guide or porter to inquire for you. We cannot more strongly support any other activity associated with trekking. This is as fun, adventurous, and memorable as it gets.

Once you or your guide has established that you will stay in someone's home, remove your shoes, bend forward so you don't hit your head, and enter. In the dim light, you will be offered a place to sit near the fire, usually on a mat of some kind. Take this place, smile, and wait for some food or drink to be prepared. Don't take the space closest to the fire in a Sherpa or BhoTiya home unless that has been offered, for that is the place of honor. Talk about your travels. Relax. If you are with other trekkers, limit the closed interactions between you and show interest in the people and place you are in. Play with children, compliment the family, and tell them a little about yourself.

Some discussion may ensue about what you eat. Ask that you eat the same food as the rest of the family. Food will appear, and you will have an opportunity to eat simple, wholesome, tasty fare. Usually you will wash your hands outside first. Don't worry about getting sick from the meal. You won't die if you have a loose movement; you've probably had a few already while being cautious. Satiated, bring out your photo album and share a little of yourself and country.

If asked what your gear or items cost in your country, you might tell them you don't remember, it was purchased so long ago. Eventually, make sleeping arrangements, usually on the floor with the rest of the family, or on benches along the walls. Morning will bring a new experience. When it is time to leave, ask how much to pay. Sometimes this will be left up to you, so pay appropriately.

You may not want to stay in lodges often after this. Staying in this traditional way provides a great window on rural Nepali life that has been described as Chaucerian, Sumerian, Ubuntu, or biblical. We urge you to take the opportunity to share this kind of experience. The authors stay in such a fashion whenever they can and began doing so long before facility with Nepali language was achieved.

CAMPING AND USING SHELTERS

If camping and stopping to cook your own food along the trail during the day, expect it to take two hours. Setting up camp with an agency trek in the evening typically takes thirty minutes, and breaking it the next morning takes an hour. Trekkers on trips organized through an agency will tend to have customary meals at the usual times. Lunch is usually prepared by the cooking staff, who then go on ahead. The staff sets up and breaks camp, and makes sure that the trekker keeps to the correct trail.

Trekkers traveling in the high country on less foreigner-frequented trails may stay at *goTh,* temporary shelters used by shepherds. Some are quite substantial structures, whereas others are only four walls without a roof or just the frames for the walls. When the shepherds bring their animals up to graze during the hot monsoon months, they bring bamboo mats or yak wool roofs to cover the frames. *Yersa* in Khumbu are groups of *goTh* used by those who pasture yak and sheep. Substantial rock overhangs are another useful form of refuge. If there is any doubt about whether these shelters will be available or if privacy is desired, it is best to carry a tent.

Those camping will find a variety of sites. Organized treks will have these all arranged. Your tents will be set up and ready when you arrive. In the morning, a hot cup of tea or coffee will be at your tent entrance, and warm wash water usually follows. On your own, look near villages for campsites on terraces that are harvested or fallow, or use school yards. Make a donation to a responsible person of the school for upkeep and supplies. Clearings in the forest, monastery courtyards, and *dharmsala* (resting houses for native travelers) are other sites. National parks and conservation areas will have designated fee camping sites near lodges. In western Nepal, where there are flat-roofed houses, you can often pitch your tent on a roof! Be sure to obtain permission to use people's land. Finding water may be difficult. Ridges and hillsides may lack water, especially before the monsoon. Trek descriptions in later chapters indicate where we know water to be a problem.

In all these situations, keep track of equipment and supplies and, when leaving, check that nothing is left behind. In lodges, look under the bed and in the corners of the room and dining area for belongings. At the first and last days of a trek, or when something unexpected happens, people tend to be more careless and may leave items behind.

FOOD

Try to eat the local diet, *daal bhaat,* which consists of a large quantity of rice with a lentil soup poured over it and usually complemented with *tarkaari,* a vegetable dish. Although consisting of the same general ingredients, there is enormous variety in taste in *daal bhaat* from place to place and even day to day at the same location. It is the safest bet on the menu for a quality meal and nearly always satisfying, and the delicious variety keeps you coming back for more. Occasionally you may be able to get an egg or some meat at an increasd cost should you so desire. Unlimited quantities of *bhaat* (rice) are generally included in the meal, but the *daal* (lentils) and vegetables are rationed. In the commercialized trekking areas, second helpings of each are usually offered but not more. The usual custom is to have it prepared fresh, and oftentimes the quantities are misjudged beforehand and more rice might not be available.

Sometimes, especially away from the popular trekking areas, rice is not available, and you may eat *saatu, dherdo,* or *piTho,* terms for roasted flour (corn, millet, or wheat) made into a thick paste by adding boiling water. Eat it with a freshly prepared sauce usually made with diced chili peppers and vegetables or *daal* if available. Many trekkers on organized treks ask the cooks to prepare this tasty, simple menu.

In Khumbu, as in most mountain areas, the traditional diet can be mostly potato based. Potatoes are made into a stew (*shakpa*) or pancakes (*riki kur*) or mashed and served with a spicy sauce (*riltok sen*), but most often they are boiled and eaten after peeling the skin off. Other features of the Sherpa diet, also common to other BhoTiya, are *thukpaa,* a noodle soup, and *tsampa* (roasted barley flour). *Tsampa* is eaten either as a watery porridge (*chamdur*), made by pouring tea over it and mixing it with a finger, or as a drier form (*pak*) poured into the tea. You will be given a half-filled bowl of Tibetan tea and the flour in a separate container, usually with a spoon. Add some, then mix with a finger, adding more, to knead it with all your fingers in the bowl and produce a thick dried plug (*pak*). Eat pieces with some stewed vegetables. This is a common early-morning start-up.

Fast food has not yet arrived in rural Nepal; the closest approximation is quick-cooking, packaged noodles, which are becoming a fast-food trail snack, their wrappers often littering the trails. You will not find these noodles in most people's homes, however. When traveling in remote high country, carry some snacks such as cookies and crackers (locally known as biscuits), dried fruit, chocolate, or nuts, to tide you over stretches without facilities. Do not eat extensively at lunch, or you may experience heartburn, especially as you tighten your pack's waistband and begin the uphill climb.

Chiyaa, or tea with milk and sugar is the traditional beverage along the trade routes in the hills. Per request, lodge owners will make it without the milk or sugar, or with lemon or ginger. In the north, Tibetan salt-butter tea (*solja*) is common, a hearty broth. You can also ask for boiling water or hot water. If the kettle has been sitting on the stove at a rolling boil or if the water comes from a vacuum bottle used to make tea, it is usually safe. Drinking this water is a good way to replenish fluids in homes and lodges in cold high places, when sweet tea is not wanted and *solja* is unavailable.

Local alcoholic drinks include *chang* (Tibetan) or *jAAR* (Nepali), beer leached from a fermented mash of corn, rice, millet, or barley; *rakshi* (Nepali) or *aara* (Tibetan), a distilled version of the above mash; and *tumbaa* (Tibetan), a drink made by pouring boiled water over a bamboo canister of fermented millet mash and sucked through a bamboo or aluminum straw. These are inexpensive, and tastes vary widely; *tumbaa* may be the safest brew. Alas, modernization has brought potent commercially distilled, bottled products, which are less expensive than beer, the rich man's drink, though little beer is consumed by locals outside of Kathmandu. There is no consistent widespread terminology for these commercial products, with the exception of *biyar* (beer).

TREKKING WITH CHILDREN

Resourceful families who have ventured into the wilderness or taken foreign trips with their children will have a good idea of what to do. Chapter 1 looked at planning a family adventure in Nepal; the following is a synthesis of practical advice for trekking with children. Like almost everything in life as a parent, there are new challenges, new insights, and many tales to tell to friends back home afterwards.

Your children may play at village work. (Photo by Robert Zimmerman)

Families with younger children have used a back- or front-style pack carrier. Other families hire a porter, the best being a woman—a Sherpani or hill Nepali. It will be difficult to hire just one woman. Two together could porter and help take care of the child. Most such women have children themselves and enjoy singing and playing with the child. They usually prefer carrying the child in a *Doko*, the conical wicker basket, using a tumpline. A foam pad for the inside and an umbrella attached to the basket rim for shade keep the child comfortable. It is not unreasonable to carry a child up to 44 pounds (22 kg) in this manner. Some children, especially active ones, may not tolerate being carried in a basket by a stranger. The method you choose depends on your personal preferences. Certainly carrying your own child can contribute to an important relationship with him or her.

Children in diapers need not be a problem. Use cloth diapers, but avoid pollution of streams when washing by using a separate pan and scattering the wash water. Bring a string for a clothesline, biodegradable soap (general pharmacies and ayurvedic shops in Kathmandu usually have a supply), and clothespins. Drying diapers is difficult in the monsoon; in fact, it is probably not advisable to trek with young children at that time. Nepali children in rural Nepal never use diapers as we know them. A few disposable diapers may come in handy in case of diarrhea, even for a toilet-trained child. Disposable diapers are not readily available in Nepal except in the upscale supermarkets in Kathmandu. Burn them out of sight of others and bury the ashes. A "potty" or chamber pot for toilet-trained children may be helpful. Otherwise, unfamiliar surroundings may make defecation difficult for them unless the parent "practices" with the child. Even older children may need to practice defecating in the squatting position. Food for children can vary a great deal. The children of one trekking family soon became willing consumers of *daal bhaat,* the native rice-and-lentil dish. Those on treks organized by professional agencies have few problems if the cook prepares familiar foods. A great deal depends on the parents' attitude and their children's food fussiness. We strongly encourage you to try whatever is being served in the house, if you stay in local homes. This may not work with a fussy child, so bring some familiar foods in quantity to supplement the local fare if necessary.

Parents who have hiked with their children under various conditions should have no difficulties choosing clothing for them. Fleece (synthetic pile) garments, worn over a pajama suit, may be the best choice for infants on cold days. Such clothes are warm, light in weight, and quick drying.

Discuss each day's plans with the children, what the trail might be like, the kind of people they will meet, their fears, and how to interact with Nepalis. Rules for youngsters on the trail should include no running downhill, no getting out of sight, and no rock-throwing. Drink plenty of liquids, and put on extra clothing right away when stopping in the high, cold regions. Consider a sleep schedule that is close to the child's norm; this makes for happier kids. Usually they are pretty tired out, so it is not a problem.

Uphill portions become a challenge varying with the age and temperament of the child. Telling stories, singing songs, playing games, and focusing on the nearby surroundings may make a 2000-foot climb go by painlessly. They all take effort, the amount varying with the character and fatigue level of the parent, as well as that of the child. Try placing a bell on the parent's pack and have the child herd the "yak" up the hill with a long light stick. Give points to your daughter or son for gentle prods with the stick. Play hide-and-seek along the trail—there are many places to hide. Or guess the number of steps to the next tree, house, or *chautaaraa* (resting platform), and then have the child count them. Try using baby steps, giant steps, or animal steps. Count anything else— flowers, birds, porters, children. Count by twos, by fives.

Telling stories to their children along the trail can be natural to many parents but daunting to some. Do not think that you are unable—try. Choose the child's favorite characters and draw out the story—one tale can get you up several hills if related in chapters. Stories are best used before a child is whiny or cranky, as a preventive measure.

The longer flat trails along the way invite singing. Good songs include the old favorites, especially those with endless repetitions and cacophonous sounds. Rounds would be great for getting several kids along the stretch. As a last resort for the exhausted parent, consider a portable electronic device for stories and music.

It helps to choose daily destinations where there will be Nepali children to play with. So aim for villages, rather than lofty sites where there are only lodges for trekkers or lonely campsites. Make an effort to stay in a local home, rather than lodges or camping, for at least one night, and try this before the last day of the trek. This "night to remember" could be the highlight of the trek. You may want to continually put up in Nepali homes to share in the details of daily life: food preparation, family interaction, household tasks, use of water, and the open fire. In one such overnight stop, you may see many different kinds of food being prepared in ways unheard of back home, with hauled water and use of a dung fire. Your family will experience the novel sleeping arrangement of staying in a one-room upper-story over the stable, along with spinning of yarn from yak wool, planting food, and using the compost toilet. It is especially rewarding if the host family has children of similar ages, but even without this Nepalese are very family-oriented and will delight in the presence of children. There may be Nepali children in lodges with their innkeeper parents, and this could dictate your choice of a lodge. To get the children playing together and over the language barrier, use a simple play item such as a doll, small ball, jump rope, badminton set, or coloring book to facilitate the process. You the parent might play together with both sets of kids to get things going.

Most young kids will enjoy playing with Nepali children; you will be astonished to discover few language barriers among preteens. Your children may be surprised to see that Nepali children have few toys. It is wise to bring a few items to keep your children amused, because they will not be as inspired by the beauty of the countryside or the spectacular mountains as you. Playing with toys with the Nepali children could be fascinating for your children, but avoid setting an unfortunate precedent by indiscriminately giving out toys to local children. Nepali children are quite happy with the limited toys they have, and they could become quite envious if they knew about the toys they do not have. Getting your children to play with the simple toys that Nepali children use could be an important formative experience.

Most children, like many adults, find it difficult to be stared at. This may happen when staying in a Nepali home that is not set up as a hotel, with separate rooms for trekkers. To avoid this problem, take a tent or choose one of the popular treks with lodges or hotels along the way. A tent gives your children a familiar place to go, away from the prying eyes of the crowds that always assemble to stare at the funny little foreign kids. Some children may find it reassuring to sleep between their parents when staying in unfamiliar surroundings.

Consider getting your child to wear local dress. It is often easy to have clothes tailor-made in rural areas or in Kathmandu before you leave.

Hygiene can be a problem along the trail. Do the best you can, but you will not be able to attain the standards you left behind at home. Aim for a daily wet-washcloth wash. Focus on cleaning the child's hands before eating, and keeping everything out of their mouths except food and water.

School work should probably be carried out for long trips, and the child's teacher may request this and provide lesson materials. Build in time each day for this, preferably earlier before there is much fatigue. Be sure to bring adequate supplies of pencils, paper, and erasers. Keep all the materials and lessons in one special bag. Plan the approximate amount of material to be covered with the child each day, but be flexible with long days, illness, and so forth. Like the trail, go at it one step at a time. Make visits to local schools, and consider having your child sit in on the classes, which are usually quite informal anyway.

Be aware of the physical hazards in Nepal. There are plenty of places inside homes, along the trails, and in the fields where a slip or fall could be disastrous for a child. Dogs (particularly rabid ones) represent an occupational hazard for trekkers in Nepal, and even more so for children. Exercise extreme caution around all dogs and villages, as options after being bitten are few and unpleasant. Children should avoid petting stray dogs. Although they are not known to be carriers of rabies, water buffalo frequently have surly dispositions and delight in charging small children. We advise getting the pre-exposure rabies vaccine for your children.

Altitude may affect children more than adults. Also, it may be difficult to ascertain whether it is altitude or some other illness that is causing symptoms in infants and young children. (See the discussion of altitude illness in Chapter 5.)

Like most aspects of trekking in Nepal, the experience of going as a family can be rewarding and enlightening if you prepare yourself adequately.

ENVIRONMENTAL HAZARDS

Nepal, a mountain environment, has its share of dangers from rock fall, avalanches, and other acts of nature. Such incidents, along with slips on the trail, are now the leading cause of death in trekkers. In November 1995, a huge aberrant snowfall created extremely hazardous conditions for trekkers in the high country. Avalanches and landslides resulted in loss of life and in people being stranded for days. Huge rescue operations were mounted. In October 1996, snowstorms dumped many feet of snow on encamped trekkers who didn't continue digging out and succumbed. The worst tragedies have occured to trekkers on organized agency treks, partly because they gave up responsibility to the guides. In the third week of October 2005 a snowstorm hit the Manang region, resulting in an avalanche that killed over a dozen members of a Kang Guru Peak expedition. The heavy snow continued for three days and left many people stranded at tea houses and lodges in the area.

Bad weather happens, and is likely to increase with predicted shifts in worldwide climate. Some studies have shown that the Himalayan region's rate of solar warming is more accelerated than the global average. Snowfalls bury tents and cause avalanche-prone slopes to release. Steep faces are exposed to rock fall. Rocks frozen in place on glaciers release when warmed; scree slopes slide. Trekkers misstep and fall. Weather forecasts in Nepal can't warn of increased risk, even if they could predict the weather. Other hazards include getting lost and being stormed in. One man split from his companion near Gosainkund Pass in a storm and descended into a cul-de-sac where he survived without food for forty-three days before being rescued. While this was a remarkable survival story, the lessons are clear.

Stay away from potential avalanche slopes when snow is falling or when warming trends could cause depth hoar to release loaded inclines. Like having serious symptoms of altitude illness, evacuation from these areas cannot be delayed. If you are in an organized trek, be as vigilant as possible, recognizing that those who are looking after your welfare are only human, and may have a more fatalistic outlook than yours based on their sense of karma. You may have to take charge in such circumstances. Be prepared for difficult conditions up high, and keep the party together. There is strength in numbers. The Himalayan Rescue Association (tel.1- 4440292, 4440293, hra@mail.com.np, www.himalayanrescue.org) can help coordinate rescue parties.

Mountain travel requires judgment about dangers, something that can't be assumed, nor learned from books, nor necessarily expected of guides and certainly not of porters. Prepare yourself beforehand by gaining as much mountain experience as you can. Read also "Emergency Care and Rescue Facilities" in Chapter 5.

CONSERVATION

In addition to the effect trekkers have on the people of Nepal, they may have a profound impact on the countryside. During your visit to Nepal's protected areas, there are many ways in which you can help to ensure that you do not damage the environment.

FUEL

Nepal's limited supply of firewood is being consumed for tourism. Trekkers increase the demand for firewood, especially in alpine areas where forests are being cut down near tree line to provide it. This use of wood, especially in the high-altitude areas, must stop if trekking is to be a resource-conserving activity. Some may argue that wood is a renewable resource, while the alternative, kerosene, is a nonrenewable fossil fuel. True, but in Nepal the deforestation problem is too severe to be further worsened by trekkers. For those on agency treks, choose an agency that uses only kerosene as a fuel for all members and staff including the porters.

Independent trekkers who are camping should use butane/propane, mixed-fuel or kerosene stoves. Trekker pressure can exert a significant effect on innkeepers: if they cook food on kerosene, patronize them. Suggest to other hoteliers who do not use kerosene how important it might be to their business to do so. Porters will build fires with increases in elevation to keep warm unless you provide them with enough warm clothes and shelter, and even then they will make fires, but such acts may lessen the use of wood.

Eating the simpler Nepali staple dish, *daal bhaat* (described under "Food" above), rather than the less fuel-efficient foreign menus that hotels try to prepare, *will* help conserve Nepal's fuel supply. Some hotels offer hot showers for trekkers, and where the water is heated by a wood fire consider showering less often to conserve fuel wood. Patronize hotels that use solar water heaters for showers or have a heat exchange device (back boiler) to utilize the hot exhaust gases of a wood stove to heat water. Consider lowering your standards of personal hygiene to use less fuel in marginal areas. Hotels burn considerable quantities of wood in heaters to keep trekkers warm. Put on more clothing to keep warm and lessen the need for fuel.

ALPINE PRESERVATION

Much of the forest and shrubbery being depleted lies in the subalpine zone, the territory just below and up to timberline, and is especially sensitive because flora in this belt grows extremely slowly. When camping, especially in the frail alpine meadows, be careful not to add to erosion problems. It takes many decades to produce the vegetation that can be carelessly torn away by a boot or crushed by a tent. Similarly, when following trails, stay on the path and do not cut switchbacks. If the vegetation surrounding the trail erodes, it is much more likely that the trail will wash out during the torrential monsoon.

THREATS TO NEPAL'S NATURAL RESOURCES: HABITAT LOSS

The major threats facing wildlife in Nepal are the loss and deterioration of the country's forests. Nepalis depend on forests for fuel, animal fodder, medicinal herbs, bamboo for making baskets, and a host of other basic materials. As the population continues to increase, the forests can no longer meet the requirements of the people. In recent times this has been most pronounced in the Tarai, but loss has also occurred in the hills, as people clear land for agriculture to support the food needs of the increasing population.

In some places, however, and mainly in Nepal's well-visited protected areas, such as Sagarmatha and Langtang national parks and the Annapurna Conservation Area, trekkers and mountaineering expeditions are making the problems worse. Dr. Hemanta Mishra of the National Trust for Nature Conservation discovered that a tourist trekker uses nearly five times more fuel than a local Sherpa in Khumbu. The forests that are suffering are some of the best for wildlife in Nepal. An example is the forests along the trail between GhoRepani and Ghandruk in the Annapurna Conservation Area, a route once almost never used by local people. A huge, unbroken oak and rhododendron forest covered the surrounding ridges, supporting such rare species as the lesser panda and the orange-rumped honeyguide. In recent years, the trail has become a popular trekking route, and an increasing number of large forest clearings have been created by tourist lodges. ❖

WASTE DISPOSAL

The difference in waste along trekker-frequented and unfrequented trails is startling, especially today with consumer goods more widely available. Along the trekker trails, there are all types of detritus, including food packaging, tampons, condoms, toilet paper, and feces left behind by both trekkers and Nepalis catering to them. Trekkers often discard litter in Nepal in a way they would never do at home.

Carry your wrappers and other items throughout the day; burn non-plastic refuse in the evening, and carry out nonburnables for disposal in Kathmandu. Remember, however, not to throw any items into your host's hearth fire, at least not without asking first, and even then, it is not considered polite. Giving metal and glass containers to villagers is no longer as appreciated as it once was because of the abundance of containers that have accumulated over the years of trekkers offering them. Consolidate and carry out noncombustible items (metal, glass, and plastic). Burial is not an option. Spent batteries should be taken home out of Nepal and disposed of appropriately there.

Along popular trekking trails you may see garbage containers outside lodges and shops. Usually their contents, including noxious plastics, are burned and the metal discarded; otherwise the litter is just pitched off the back of the lodge or shop or piled in a site nearby. Talk to the lodge owners and operators about this, and give your preference for disposal. You can influence them, because they want to do the "right thing" to get your business. Those with guides and porters should not leave them in charge of garbage disposal—there is no way for you to ensure that the garbage is being properly sorted and incinerated or simply being discarded. If you suspect the latter and make a fuss, chances are it will just be done out of your sight.

The consumption of bottled mineral water that is now available along the popular trekker routes is not ecologically sound, unless you can carry all the empty bottles back home or at least to Kathmandu. Empty plastic bottles in various stages of destruction create a new category of despicable litter. Moreover, samples of popular brands have been tested and found contaminated. Use the ACAP Safe Drinking Water stations on the Annapurna Circuit. Otherwise, many lodges along the popular routes offer boiled water. Iodizing water makes sense and is far less costly while minimizing the amount of waste to carry out. Add vitamin C powder after the treatment period elapses if the taste bothers you. You will save a lot of money on the water; prices increase the farther away you get from populated areas. A liter of bottled water costs more than a night in a lodge in some places. Try not to consume bottled beverages, beer, and the like. Seeing the used bottles stockpiled or scattered in trekker-traveled areas will convince you this is appropriate advice. Glass bottles are recyclable, but they are being abandoned in remote areas as the deposit isn't enough to make it worthwhile to porter them out. Similarly, avoid packaged moistened towelettes for hygiene; instead, carry a reusable washcloth.

By not spending money for imported goods, you have money to spend on locally produced foods, services, and crafts, which benefits the local economy. Imported goods come from Kathmandu or abroad and do not help the local economy nearly as much while adding significantly to garbage and disposal problems.

Trekkers and mountaineers sometimes bring environmental pollution in the form of advertising, especially in areas such as the Khumbu, with expeditions passing through bound for the heights. Often they carry along stickers with an expedition logo that they affix to walls, counters, and windows in hotels. Especially in dwellings with few windows, the plastering of stickers results in less light getting inside. There is considerable wallpaper of unconventional sorts in these places, which seems a part of their decorative scheme. Help keep it off the glass windows.

Disposable plates in Nepal are assembled from leaves held together with wooden picks.
(Photo by Mary Anne Mercer)

Stephen sipping tea in Manang in 1978 (Photo by Peter Banys)

Disposing of body wastes is another problem facing trekkers. Trekkers staying in lodges should locate the latrine or toilet and use that. Without a "throne," it is sometimes difficult to squat comfortably, aim correctly, and avoid splattering. Make sure there is a good supply of water in the latrine before you use it, and bring a headlamp, as lighting is often minimal.

Those on large organized treks erect enclosed latrines at campsites. The feces and other material are then buried. This commendable practice avoids the unsightliness and potential for disease of mounds of exposed feces, each with a topping of toilet paper. In many areas, the pits are dug too shallowly, so the concentrated waste material easily contaminates the region. Ask for a deep hole to be dug.

Travelers who are staying in someone's home should ask whether there are communal latrines (*chaarpi* or *toylat*) in the villages or if a family has one. One of the many positive changes over the past decade has been the establishment of latrines in trekking areas. In addition, public health campaigns have resulted in the erection of latrine structures by many individuals near their homes. There are latrines in many of the villages of Langtang, Manang, Thak Khola, Solu–Khumbu, and other areas. Some have a container for used toilet paper so it won't clog the mechanism. Most homes in Khumbu and others in Helambu have traditionally had a convenient latrine arrangement on top of the hay pile situated in an alcove off the second floor, or more recently, a separate latrine near the house.

In much of Nepal, where there are no latrines whatsoever, you will have to do as the Nepalis do and find a place outdoors. Usually, they perform their eliminations before dawn or after sunset in obvious places near the village, bringing a *loTaa,* or container of water, to wash themselves and their hands afterwards. Find a corner of a field or other sheltered spot away from running water and bury your feces at least 6 inches (15 cm), or at least cover them with stones. You could carry a little plastic trowel for this. If you are using toilet paper (or sanitary supplies), carry a cigarette lighter or matches and burn the used paper (or tampon) at once. Some trekkers (including those with weary knees) unable to defecate squatting have taken small portable toilets for their personal use. At high altitude where there is no soil, overlaying the feces on an out-of-sight rock is best for the environment.

Whatever you do, be sure to exercise appropriate modesty and get out of sight of others. You rarely see an adult Nepali in an act of defecation. Nepali women often urinate discreetly by hunkering in their skirts. Some women trekkers find this quite appropriate if wearing long skirts with no underpants. If women separate their labia before urinating, it does away with the need for toilet paper and gives women more excretory freedom. The Shewee, a portable urinating device for women, offers another method.

Another way to use less toilet tissue is to use a handkerchief for nose blowing, or do it Nepali style, covering each nostril in turn and blowing out the other.

ENDANGERED SPECIES

Many wild animals and plants are being threatened by loss of habitat and even illegal commercial trade. To combat the threat of illicit activities, many countries, including Nepal, have become signatories to CITES (Convention on International Trade in Endangered Species of Wild Fauna and Flora). Do not be tempted to buy animal or plant parts, such as the fur of a spotted cat, a tortoise shell, or an orchid. To do so not only undermines Nepal's natural heritage, but breaks international laws. Let store or hotel owners know your feelings if you see illegal items for sale.

LEAVE ONLY FOOTPRINTS

Finally, in whatever you do, realize that you are not alone. If you carry off one *mani* stone from a prayer wall, saying that one less will make no difference, realize what would happen if everyone did so. Think of how you would like this country to be when you come to visit again, or when your children or grandchildren do. If we who travel in this exotic country respect its culture and customs, then by "leaving no trace," perhaps its spectacular countryside and the experience that we have found so worthwhile can be preserved for the benefit of Nepal and the enjoyment of future trekkers.

KEEP (KATHMANDU ENVIRONMENTAL EDUCATION PROJECT)

Pay a visit to KEEP in Jyatha, Thamel, and register with your embassy for free. KEEP strives to provide unbiased information on tourism and trekking. Their goal is to maximize the benefits of tourism while minimizing the negative impact. Maps are on hand, along with logbooks in which trekkers record up-to-date experiences along the trails. These logbooks are invaluable sources of current information on trail conditions and facilities. There are also notice boards announcing the latest news and regulations, with postings by travelers looking for trekking partners. KEEP has an in-house Green Café and store that sells eco-friendly trekking products such as biodegradable soap, anti-leech oil, and water purifiers. There is a convenient library as well with free videos, such as the BBC's documentary on porters *Carrying the Burden*, and a viewing room, too.

KEEP runs a Porter Clothing Bank—established by D. B. Gurung of KEEP and Ian Wall of Community Action Nepal (CAN), and financed and stocked by the IPPG, Porters Progress UK, Mountain Fund, and International Mountain Explorers Club—where you may get clothing for your porters (a deposit is required) and donate garments and gear as well. KEEP will also arrange collection of donations from your hotel (contact information below). The clothing bank is managed by a former porter who lost part of his feet to frostbite.

KEEP is always looking for volunteers to conduct English language courses (and sometimes German and other languages), mostly for porters and guides. They also provide training for these and other tourism professionals in trekking responsibly, first aid, mountain safety, flora and fauna, and cultural heritage, and conduct Environmental Awareness Programs for all comers. Financial donations are accepted directly at their office where you can also become a member of this exemplary organization. All funds will go toward running the organization and the aforementioned activities as well as ongoing outreach projects. KEEP also helps place travelers who wish to volunteer in some capacity in Nepal. Contact KEEP at tel. 01-4216775, 4216776; (email) info@kekep.org; and www.keepnepal.org. ❖

OTHER SOURCES OF INFORMATION ON TREKKING

Traditionally, trekkers read guidebooks, travel brochures, and stories of other's experiences, and converse with returned travelers. The Internet has changed that process immensely, allowing anyone to publish information that is of varying quality and accuracy. Search engines can uncover vast amounts of information that can overwhelm prospective travelers. The following sites may be useful: www.welcomenepal .com, www.trekinfo.com, www.info-nepal.com, www.nepal.panda.org, www.yetizone .com, www.nepalmountaineering.org, and www.taan.org.np. Another up-and-coming site that has community-driven content, www.exoticbuddha.com, is aiming to be a platform for connecting travelers and local people.

Himalayanists may find much of interest at the website of *Himalaya, the Journal of the Association for Nepal and Himalayan Studies,* at http://digitalcommons .macalester.edu/himalaya/. Additionally, an interesting aerial view of the Himalayan Range has been mapped out as a *Himalaya Atlas of Aerial Panoramas, Volume I,* available at http://130.166.124.2/himalaya_atlas1/.

ESSENTIAL TREKKING CHECKLIST FOR SAFETY AND "LEAVING NO TRACE"

- Plan enough time and limit your itinerary so you can enjoy your trek
- Register at your embassy (this can be done at the KEEP office in Jyatha, Thamel, as well as HRA in Thamel); let the embassy know your itinerary, even if traveling through an agency
- Verify the phone numbers for rescue in Chapter 5
- Keep to the trails to prevent erosion, and do not alter the natural surroundings
- Respect religious sites
- Dress modestly and appropriately
- Take responsibility for your employees
- Pay the standard price for food and other goods
- Burn combustible garbage
- Carry out plastic wrappers and other unburnable garbage; "pack it in, pack it out"
- Carry spent batteries back to your own country
- Bury your feces and burn all toilet paper used
- Use butane, propane, or kerosene stoves whenever you can rather than wood
- Patronize hotels and eating establishments that cook on kerosene; encourage others to do so
- Patronize hotels that have solar-heated showers
- Support local handicrafts that result from traditional cultural elements
- Eat local Nepali food for the most part
- Limit consumption of bottled beer and other bottled drinks and packaged items to avoid disposal problems
- Compliment lodge, *bhaTTi,* restaurant, and tea shop owners for the good aspects of their facilities

The following website has the Minimum Impact Code of conduct for model trekkers as suggested by ACAP and KEEP: www.lirung.com/en/info_file/file015acap_e.html.

5

HEALTH AND HEALTH CARE

I suffered increasingly from mountaineer's foot—reluctance to put one in front of the other.

—H. W. Tilman, *Nepal Himalaya*

Trekking in Nepal is beneficial to your health. Two questions usually asked of returning Nepal trekkers are, "Did you have fun?" and, "Did you get sick?" The answer is usually yes to both. (It is likely that you will have a bout of diarrhea and get a cold.) Field treatments and procedures are given for the medical problems commonly encountered in the hills. These are based on Stephen's experiences as a physician who has worked and trekked in Nepal, as a specialist in travel medicine who has written a lay book on the subject and on altitude illness (see Appendix B), and on discussions with other trekkers.

What follows may seem frightening to would-be trekkers who are used to the professional medical care available at a moment's notice in modern society. In Nepal you can be a week's walk or more from a doctor, though on popular treks you may find yourself surrounded by doctors! Hundreds of thousands of trekkers have followed precautions similar to those outlined here and have led a most enjoyable and healthy journey. For most people, trekking is not dangerous; it is the beginning of a new vitality.

PREPARATIONS AND POST-TREK PRECAUTIONS

Many people come to Nepal with no hiking experience and, though in poor condition, set out on their first trek, walk 100 miles (160 km) or more, and thoroughly enjoy themselves. Some treks are more conducive to doing this successfully than are others. Those over forty who are not regular backpackers or hikers and are out of condition will encounter considerable physical difficulty on strenuous treks. Jogging several miles a day is a great conditioner. Hiking uphill with an increasingly heavier pack is a good way to put variety into the regimen. Carrying bags of water that can be dumped on the summit is better on the joints during descent. Bicycling, cross-country skiing, swimming, and other aerobic activities are also excellent. But all of them must be started months ahead of time and carried on regularly with increases in the amount of exercise each week. Toughen your feet and break in your footwear through progressively longer hikes. Applying tincture of benzoin (also called Friar's Balsam) to your feet over pressure points where blisters may occur can toughen the skin.

Before you leave for Nepal, visit your physician or a travel clinic at least four to six weeks before traveling, and get necessary inoculations. The following immunizations are recommended: hepatitis A, hepatitis B, polio, typhoid, tetanus-diphtheria (possibly pertussis), seasonal influenza, and possibly MMR (measles, mumps, rubella) if you are not already up-to-date (or previously infected). Hepatitis A vaccine replaces gamma-globulin (immune globulin), long advised to protect against hepatitis. The only reason to use the less expensive but more difficult to obtain gamma-globulin would be if you are a once-in-a-lifetime trekker who will never again visit an area with poor hygiene, or will have less than two weeks before arrival in Nepal. Neither inoculation is needed if you have had hepatitis A before. Rabies exists in Nepal, and you may wish to get the expensive human diploid cell vaccine. Only one visitor to Nepal has been known to get rabies, but animal bites commonly occur and the risk is there. If you are bitten when you are far from anyplace where you could get the rabies shots, you face a dilemma: Should you abandon your trek and get to Kathmandu for the series of injections that take a month, including the very expensive agent rabies immune globulin, which may be in short supply? It is a matter of time, inconvenience, and money. If you have had the pre-immunization prophylaxis, then you need only get two doses of the human diploid cell vaccine, three days apart. It all depends on your level of risk assumption. Dr. David Shlim once estimated that a foreigner in Nepal had a 1-in-6000 risk of acquiring a bite requiring rabies vaccine protection. If this risk seems high to you, then Stephen suggests considering the vaccine, especially for your trekking children. If you have had it before, it is unlikely that you need a booster dose. The intradermal dosage scheme (0.1 ml on days 1, 7, and 21 or 28) is cheapest.

The old cholera inoculation was required in the past, but not now. Decline it if offered; the risk of getting cholera for someone with the socioeconomic background to travel to Nepal is negligible. Other vaccinations that might be appropriate for specific groups include pneumococcus (recommended for children, younger people with underlying medical conditions predisposing them to complications of influenza, and those over age sixty-five), as well as hemophilus B (routine now for young children). Several cases of meningococcal meningitis occurred in Westerners in Kathmandu during the mid-1980s, but it is not now considered a risk requiring vaccination, although one could choose that precaution. Another risk is Japanese encephalitis, a potentially fatal viral infection spread by certain species of mosquitoes. Many cases have recently been reported in Nepal, mostly occurring in the Tarai, during August and September, and it occurs in Kathmandu valley as well. It is rare among world travelers from the United States; most cases occur in students, aid workers, or soldiers, not in casual tourists. There is an effective, low-risk, expensive vaccine available, which is recommended to those who will be long-term visitors in the Tarai during the monsoon, and long-term visitors to Kathmandu from August to October. All vaccines have some risk of adverse reactions and should not be used indiscriminately. Plague vaccine is not recommended in spite of the plague epidemic in South Asia in 1994. In the interests of full disclosure, Stephen has had the rabies immunizations, but not the Japanese encephalitis one, and Alonzo has not taken these vaccines.

A knowledgeable physician can time all of these inoculations properly. They should begin several months before departure. State and local public health departments usually have knowledgeable people with whom you can consult. You can also pay a visit to the Center for Disease Control's country-specific website. If you are not up to date by the time you arrive, vaccinations are available in Kathmandu at the modern CIWEC clinic across from the British Embassy and the Nepal International Clinic (NIC) near the former royal palace, now Narayanhiti National Museum, in central Kathmandu as well as at other less modern facilities including the crowded Teaching Hospital near the U.S. Embassy in Maharajganj.

Shamans are sometimes called on to facilitate healing. (Photo by R.C. Sedai)

Before you depart, visit a dentist to have potentially disabling dental problems cared for. Good dental care in Nepal is not available outside of Kathmandu or Namche Bazaar (in the Everest region). Also, refill any prescription medications you currently take. Women taking hormonal contraceptive products should not stop them while trekking in Nepal.

Those with active chest and heart diseases that limit physical activity should avoid going to high altitudes. Individuals with the following conditions definitely should *not* go to high altitudes: primary pulmonary hypertension, cyanotic congenital heart disease, absence of the right pulmonary artery, chronic pulmonary disease with arterial unsaturation, coronary artery disease with severe angina or cardiac failure, congestive heart failure with arterial unsaturation, and disablingly symptomatic cardiac arrhythmias. These conditions are described in specific medical terms so the risks can be accurately assessed by your physician. Show this list to your doctor if you believe you have one of these conditions.

Some people with serious pre-existing diseases have died while trekking. Those with sickle cell disease or sickle cell trait greatly increase their risk at high altitudes. People with recurrent deep-vein thromboses and pulmonary emboli should also avoid high altitudes, but those with essential hypertension tolerate high altitudes well. Medical knowledge of the effect of high altitudes on people with mild or moderate chronic disease, as well as on the elderly, is limited. Information on drug effects at high altitudes is similarly lacking. Certainly many people in their sixties and seventies have trekked at high altitudes in Nepal with no problems. If you are in that age range or older and enjoy good health and physical conditioning, by all means consider trekking in Nepal, at least at moderate altitudes. You could later consider trying the high passes. Anyone with chronic diseases not discussed here should seek the advice of a knowledgeable physician and, if given the go-ahead, should first make supervised visits to high altitudes in his or her home country. Stephen's book *Altitude Illness: Prevention and Treatment* describes our understanding of people with various chronic diseases going to altitude. Similarly, those who wonder whether they have the physical stamina for trekking should first take backpacking trips in hilly areas before planning a trek in Nepal.

Pregnant women have trekked and ascended to high altitude. There are no data on hazards for pregnant trekkers who venture to altitude for a short time. Experiences early in life tend to program much of our health as adults; however, there is little understanding about possible adverse effects of altitude on that process. For lowlander women who are pregnant and ascend to significant altitudes, there may be untoward effects on the child or adult later on that are currently unknown.

Those with stable chronic diseases who can undertake strenuous exercise can certainly trek. Such people may wish the security provided by an organized trek with a doctor along. Others may have enough self-confidence to trek in small groups without a physician. To our knowledge, people with diabetes, recurrent cancer, amputations, arthritis, a history of coronary bypass surgery, and even blindness have enjoyed trekking. Those with chronic medical conditions would best bring a clinical summary with them including pertinent findings and medicines they take with dosage schedules.

Diabetics who are insulin-dependent should be adept at regulating their own insulin dose based on blood glucose determinations. The exercise involved in trekking will usually result in lower insulin requirements, and this must be monitored en route. It is wise to carry snacks, as well as glucagon for insulin reactions. Companions should be well versed in dealing with these situations. An informative website run by diabetics involving mountain activities is www.diabetic.friendsinhighplaces.org. Two useful journal citations are Brubaker, P. L. (2005), "Adventure Travel and Type 1 Diabetes," *Diabetes Care* 28(10): 2563–2572, and Leal, C. (2005), "Going High with Type 1 Diabetes," *High Altitude Medicine & Biology*, 6(1): 14–21.

Ask your physician about taking malaria suppressants. Malaria was once endemic in the Tarai, but today it has been controlled and in most areas your risk is low. Nevertheless, incidents of malaria continue to occur. We do not consider malaria to be a threat to trekkers on the popular routes and do not advise taking prophylaxis, but the situation could change in the future, so get the latest advice before you depart. Whereas chloroquine is no longer viable in Nepal, the current means of protection is to take one of the following antimalarial suppressants: atovaquone/proguanil, doxycycline, or mefloquine. Except during the monsoon, the chances of contracting malaria while trekking in the hills and mountains is slight, especially above 4000 feet (1200 m). Malaria transmission is thought to occur sporadically in Nepal at altitudes above 4000 feet (1200 m), perhaps up to 6500 feet (2000 m), but we are not aware of trekkers who have contracted malaria at these heights. We do not take malaria prophylaxis while trekking. But you may wish to as an additional protection, especially if trekking in the monsoon (pregnant women should consult with a physician before starting malaria prophylaxis). If so, start taking the pills one week, for mefloquine (or one day, for atovaquone/proguanil and doxycycline), before you reach the first area where there is a chance of getting malaria. Do not discontinue them until one month, for doxycycline or mefloquine (or one week, for atovaquone/proguanil), after you have left all infected areas. Rather than take it for prophylaxis, we would advise the concerned trekker to carry medicine for treatment of suspected attacks of malaria if his or her travels will involve a considerable stay below 4000 feet (1200 m).

In summary, every trekker should have current immunization status for polio, typhoid fever, seasonal influenza, tetanus, diphtheria (consider pertussis), measles, mumps, rubella, hepatitis B, and especially hepatitis A. Consider rabies vaccine and Japanese encephalitis vaccine. We suggest that malaria prophylaxis not be taken, except possibly for lowland treks during the monsoon.

Discuss the medical supplies mentioned here with your physician. Drugs and most supplies can be bought cheaply in Kathmandu.

Consider obtaining travel and evacuation insurance (see "Helicopter Rescue" later in this chapter) in addition to standard medical insurance. This will not prevent you from having to arrange payment for a helicopter rescue should it be necessary, but it can help recover the substantial costs involved. Travel agents and insurance brokers can provide policies. Make sure the policy you obtain covers trekking travel in Nepal. Some policies do not cover natural disasters (avalanches, earthquakes). Finally, do not neglect health-promoting practices that are part of your usual routine back home. This can include meditation, yoga, tai chi, and more. Similarly, if you are accustomed to using various herbal, naturopathic, homeopathic, ayurvedic, or other preparations for illnesses, bring these with you. What follows is based on the allopathic or biomedical model for disease.

HEALTH CARE OF CHILDREN

For those trekking with children, it is essential that a knowledgeable physician or other health professional be consulted before you leave home in order to get specific information appropriate to your children and their needs. See this person well in advance—several months may be necessary—to ensure that the required immunizations can be obtained in time.

The greatest health risk for children trekking in Nepal is the hazard of fecal–oral contamination due to of a lack of proper disposal. Children at oral stages tend to put everything into their mouths. Human and other animal feces pervade and tend to get into the hands and mouths of children. The problem is compounded because children with diarrhea and vomiting can get dehydrated quickly. Because there are essentially no medical care facilities in the hills, each family is on its own. Take solace in knowing that most trekking families have no problems.

Prevention is the key. Watch what your child puts in his or her mouth. Iodize or boil all water for drinking and feed your child only cooked food. Keep materials for making oral rehydration solution (outlined below) on hand in case diarrhea or vomiting develops. If the liquid losses in stool or vomitus are replaced gradually, no serious problems should result. Oral rehydration powder, Jeevan Jal in Nepal, can be purchased in drug shops, health posts, and stores in most parts of the country. Mix one packet with 4 cups (1 liter) of boiled or iodized water, and feed it to the child a little at a time by spoon or cup. Try to get the child to drink at least as much liquid as he has lost. Check for signs of adequate hydration, such as normal frequency and amount of urination, moisture on the lips and mouth, and fairly normal behavior. If in doubt, get the child to take more fluids. Do not use opiates or other similar drugs to "plug up" diarrhea in children. Do not use tetracycline drugs in children under age eight. If you lack a commercial oral rehydration powder such as Jeevan Jal, a substitute can be made up almost anywhere. Add one three-finger pinch of salt and a three-finger scoop of sugar to one *maanaa* (2½ cups, or 590 ml) of boiled or iodized water. Add orange or lime juice if available.

Colds and other upper-respiratory infections are very common in Nepal, and your children may get their share. A bulb syringe can be handy for clearing a young child's clogged nose. Your child could get scabies while in Nepal, so consider this if an itchy rash persists.

Children's doses for drugs are not given here. They vary, of course, with the age and weight of the child. They are listed in Stephen's book *The Pocket Doctor*. Be sure to discuss which drugs to take, and confirm their doses with your doctor. Liquid doses are best for young children.

The hazards of high altitudes are no less for children than for adults, and it may be even more difficult to determine whether a particular child's health problem is due to altitude or to some other cause. One family took their twenty-one-month-old child to 16,500 feet (5000 m) without difficulty, after appropriate acclimatization. An infant has been to 18,450-foot (5623 m) Kala Pattar. We have seen Sherpa mothers carry their one- or two-month-old babies over 19,000-ft (5800-m) passes. A woman who was six months pregnant ascended to 24,000 feet (7300 m). Such extremes are not recommended. Families should limit their treks to 13,000 feet (4000 m). With infants, 10,000 feet (3050 m) might be a safe limit. Unless born at high altitude, children tolerate ascent to heights less well than do adults.

All people with children who venture to high altitudes should descend immediately if there is any difficulty with acclimatization. It may be difficult to determine whether a newly acquired unnatural behavior in a child represents altitude illness. Stephen's three-month-old son became lethargic above 12,000 feet (3650 m) and improved dramatically with descent. Similarly, incontinence in a toilet-trained child at altitude could be a symptom of altitude illness. Descend in such circumstances to determine if it was the cause. The safety margin in waiting out the minor symptoms of altitude illness is significantly less in children than in adults.

THE MEDICAL KIT

A basic medical kit proposed here that can be purchased relatively inexpensively in Kathmandu will help trekkers be reasonably prepared for most problems and can be considered a kind of insurance. In most developed countries, prescriptions are required for some of the drugs. An understanding physician should give you these if you carefully explain why you need them. Do not use these medications when medical assistance is available nearby. When you are sick and there are appropriate treatments, it makes sense to use them. By following the suggestions in this chapter, the chances are excellent that you will recover, and the benefits of treatment far outweigh the risks. If you are not getting better in spite of self-treatment, then consider other alternatives, especially if the situation seems grave.

Names of drugs are always a dilemma. While the official or generic names are generally the same throughout the world, the advertising or brand names vary greatly from place to place. The generic names are used here whenever possible.

Our recommended medical kit—enough for a party of two—includes the following:

Moleskin. Felt or foam (molefoam) padding (about 1 mm thick for felt, 2 or 3 mm for foam) with adhesive backing, used for the prevention of blisters. About half a square foot per person should be enough. You are unlikely to find it in Kathmandu, but adhesive tape or zinc oxide strapping can be used as a substitute. See the "Foot Care" section for other alternatives.

Bandages. One roll of 2-inch adhesive tape, and five to ten adhesive bandages per person for small wounds.

Elastic Bandage. One 3-inch roll for relief of strains and sprains.

Thermometer. One that reads below normal temperatures (for diagnosis of hypothermia) as well as above (for fever).

Materials for a Dental Emergency. Temporary filling material or dental wax, crown or bridge cement, eugenol (oil of cloves, used as a topical analgesic and antiseptic), cotton swabs.

Instruments. Scissors, needle, or safety pin, and forceps or tweezers.

Plastic Dropper Bottles. One-ounce (30 ml) size for holding iodine. This is best brought from home. If your pharmacy no longer carries empty plastic dropper bottles for dispensing compounded ear, eye, or nose drops, buy a plastic dropper bottle of nose drops and dump the contents.

Water Purification Chemicals. Tetraglycine hydroperiodide or iodine in various forms (see next section) or chlorine dioxide (with activator). Vitamin C powder helps to mask the taste of iodine, as do electrolyte powders (added after appropriate treatment period).

Nose Spray or Drops (optional). Phenylephrine HCL (0.25 percent) for stuffed noses and sinuses. Put two drops in each nostril two or three times a day when symptomatic and when changing altitude. An alternative is oxymetazoline, used no more than twice a day.

Nasal Decongestant (optional). For those accustomed to taking these tablets for colds.

Antihistamine (optional). For treating symptoms of colds and hay fever. If you do not have a favorite, try chlorpheniramine maleate tablets (4 mg). Fexofenadine and astemizole are expensive, nonsedating antihistamines you could try.

Aspirin or Similar Drug. Twenty-five tablets (5 grain, 325 mg) of aspirin for relief of minor pain, for lowering temperatures, and for symptomatic relief of colds and respiratory infections. Ibuprofen (200 mg) which is also an anti-inflammatory or acetaminophen (paracetamol) are appropriate substitutes for those who can't tolerate aspirin.

Codeine. Fifteen tablets (30 mg) for relief of pain, cough, and diarrhea. A good multipurpose drug. It is customarily compounded with acetaminophen tablets in the United States.

Anti-motility Agent. Codeine, as already mentioned, or loperamide (2 mg), or diphenoxylate compound tablets. Bring twenty pills. Useful for necessary vehicle travel while struck with diarrhea.

Antibiotic. The current trekkers' wonder drug is probably ciprofloxacin, in 500-mg tablets; this should be adequate for most of the infectious bacterial causes of illnesses that might befall the trekker. Bring twenty capsules at least; the dose is one capsule every twelve hours. An alternative is norfloxacin, 400-mg tablets, one capsule taken every twelve hours. A related cheaper drug, nalidixic acid, has been used successfully in Nepal and is the drug of choice for children for diarrhea. Azithromycin would be a good choice for children and adults too. Other choices would best require that two different ones should be carried, a cephalosporin (cefaclor, cefuroxime, and cefadroxil are choices in the United States) and co-trimoxazole. Carry a ten-day supply of a 250-mg cephalosporin. The dose for the cephalosporin is either one or two every eight hours (cefaclor) or twelve hours (cefuroxime or cefadroxil). If allergic to penicillin, you might also be allergic to a cephalosporin, but this is relatively rare. Erythromycin (250-mg capsule) would be an alternative for allergic individuals, although it is not recommended for pregnant women and can also cause side effects of gastrointestinal disturbances including diarrhea and vomiting and might also alter the effectiveness of oral contraceptives. Bring co-trimoxazole (a combination of trimethoprim 160 mg and sulfamethoxazole 800 mg) in so-called double-strength tablets (abbreviated TMP/SMX later in this chapter) if not allergic to sulfa drugs. Bring twenty of these tablets. Be aware that there may be resistance to this drug in Nepal. For other choices, especially for diarrhea, read the section later in this chapter.

Antiprotozoan. Tinidazole is the best drug to self-treat presumed *Giardia* or rare *Amoeba* infections while trekking. Bring twelve to twenty 500-mg tablets.

Antihelminth (worm medicine). Three 500-mg tablets of mebendazole. A single 500-mg dose taken in the evening will take care of most worm infestations in porters. You won't be there long enough to require treatment in Nepal.

Oral Rehydration Solution (ORS, Jeevan Jal). A mixture of salts and glucose, this powder is added to a liter of water to provide the appropriate drink to rehydrate in almost any situation, but especially from diarrhea. Not easily available in the United States—buy it in Nepal in one serving packets or buy a larger pack of a powdered alternative.

Altitude Medicines. Acetazolamide (Diamox), 250-mg tablets, bring twenty; and also dexamethasone, 4-mg tablets, bring five. The first is to treat symptoms of mild altitude illness, and the second is to take if someone has serious, cerebral symptoms. The first drug is appropriate to use for prevention in suitable situations, at a half dose (125 mg). Read the later section on altitude illness, and consider carrying nifedipine in 10-mg capsules.

Altitude Chamber (Gamow Bag). A hyperbaric chamber for treatment of serious altitude illness. Recommended for parties in a group trek to significant altitudes (see "Trekking with an Agency" in Chapter 1).

Anti-inflammatory Agent. To be considered if you are prone to arthritic conditions or tendonitis. Aspirin or ibuprofen are good choices; acetaminophen is not as effective. If you've had such problems before, ask your doctor about indomethacin or meclofenamate. The latter is a good all-purpose pain medicine.

Sunscreen Preparation. You'll need sunblock with a sun protection factor (SPF) of at least 15 in order to get adequate protection from the sun at high altitude where the thin air provides less protection and especially on snow slopes. Sunscreens are best applied one or two hours before exposure and reapplied after heavy sweating. Be sure to apply them over all areas that can receive direct or reflected sunlight, especially under the nose, chin, and eyebrows. Lip balms containing effective sunscreens should also be used.

Topical Ophthalmic Antibiotic. Good choices of ophthalmic antibiotics are those that contain bacitracin, gentamicin, polymyxin, or tobramycin. Avoid any that contain steroids such as betamethasone, cortisone, dexamethasone, hydrocortisone, prednisolone, or others. If you wear contact lenses trekking, be sure to bring antibiotic eye drops.

Malaria Suppressant (optional). Bring atovaquone/proguanil, doxycycline, or mefloquine, if you and your doctor think it is necessary.

These items are considered a bare minimum by some, and too much by others; they are clearly adequate for most situations. It is not advisable to go into the hills without aspirin, iodine, sunscreen, moleskin, and an antibiotic. Other items are mentioned in the next section and can be added if desired.

Pregnant women should consult a physician regarding medical problems they might encounter and the use of aforementioned or other drugs.

A zippered nylon bag is handy for carrying the kit, or you can use a plastic container with a sealable lid. First, put the pills into small labeled plastic bags (such as the tiny bags that your airline cutlery is packed in cut short), and then assemble all these together inside a small plastic bottle. The whole kit never weighs more than a pound (½ kg).

Nepalis have their own remedies for many illnesses; if you don't seem to be getting better, in spite of these recommendations, you might consider their suggestions. While working as a doctor in Nepal, Stephen has sometimes been frustrated by an inability to help some unfortunate sick person, only to discover later that the individual was cured by a folk remedy or by a shaman!

PREVENTING HEALTH PROBLEMS

The vast majority of diseases that plague the trekker in Nepal are transmitted by food or water contaminated by infected human or animal feces. You should assume that all water and uncooked foods in Nepal are contaminated; this holds true in Kathmandu as well as along the trails.

WATER PURIFICATION

Boiling. The safest procedure is to bring drinking water to the boil and let it cool before drinking. Boiling water on a trek, especially if wood is used, wastes scarce resources. Better to use a chemical disinfectant.

Filtering. Water filters containing iodine-exchange resins are effective for purposes claimed and produce potable water rapidly, but they are bulky, heavy, and expensive. Other filters only remove parasites and bacteria but not viruses. If stuck without other options, filter water through several layers of cotton cloth.

UV Light (SteriPEN). The SteriPEN is a small handheld device with reputed ability to purify a liter of clear water in under 2 minutes. It requires expensive batteries. Devices are available in Kathmandu at KEEP and in some trekking supply shops. Don't depend on it without a backup system.

Bottled Water. Bottled water is available on the popular treks. It comes in sealed plastic bottles and is claimed to be treated, although studies have often found contaminated samples. Expensive, its use results in the profusion of empty plastic bottles littered about. Be advised that throughout the subcontinent unscrupulous people occasionally refill used bottles with untreated water to be recapped and sold as new. We advise using iodine or another method instead.

Chemical Disinfection. Elemental iodine is the best agent, added by one of several means. The dose stated here is for clear water; double it for cloudy water. Once the chemical is added, the waiting time depends on the temperature of the water. Ten minutes is adequate for warm water; twenty to thirty minutes should suffice for cold water. For very questionable, very cold water, double the dose and wait up to an hour, before consumption. Bottled soft drinks and beer of well-known brands are considered safe.

Chlorine Dioxide droplets or tablets, though not easily found in Kathmandu, are better than other chorine-based options available in Kathmandu, which do not offer full protection in Nepal.

Iodine Tablets (tetraglycine hydroperiodide). These tablets are most useful for water bottles. Use one tablet per quart (liter) of water. Available in Kathmandu at KEEP and elsewhere.

Tincture of Iodine (USP). This has several uses. Add five drops per quart (liter) or, conveniently, two drops per glass (250 ml). Stephen carries this in an opaque plastic dropper bottle and has used this technique exclusively for forty years. He tells Nepali people that it is medicine for the water if they ask, and explains why. If water doesn't taste like iodine, it isn't water (unless it has been boiled). In the United States, or elsewhere, look for the USP designation (United States Pharmacopeia), which indicates that the product is compounded to the correct standard, with 2 percent free iodine. This material can be useful to disinfect the skin around a leech bite (do not put it directly into a wound). The iodine taste can be removed by adding ascorbic acid (vitamin C): 50 mg of powder (a minimal two-finger pinch) in a liter of water after contact time has elapsed.

Strong Iodine Solution (British Pharmacopeia, BP) can be used in one-fifth the dose, that is, one drop per quart of clear water. It contains 10 percent free iodine. The Indian Pharmacopeia (IP) formulation is the same.

Weak Iodine Solution (BP) is used in the same dose as Tincture of Iodine (USP). The Indian Pharmacopeia (IP) formulation that is available in Kathmandu is used in the same dose as the BP.

Lugol's Solution, if labeled Aqueous Iodine Solution BP (or IP), can be used, adding two drops to a quart (liter) of water. Lugol's is available in some pharmacies in Kathmandu as well as the larger stores that cater to foreigners.

Iodine Solution. This solution is made by adding the supernatant of crystalline iodine carried in a glass bottle. This method is potentially lethal if crystals are ingested, and there are now commercial preparations (Polar Pure) available to make this unlikely.

Povidone Iodine Solution. This is used for surgical disinfection and usually comes as a 10 percent solution (do not get the scrub, which has a detergent added). It should probably be effective in a dose of eight to sixteen drops per quart (liter) of water, the higher amounts used in cold or cloudy water. The major advantage of this form of iodine is that it is less irritating than tincture of iodine when used around and in wounds.

Rare individuals may be allergic to iodine. These people would usually have a long-standing skin rash when taking iodine, and should not use this chemical for water purification. Pregnant women should have no problem with these chemical methods of water treatment, although there is a theoretical hazard. Persons with thyroid disease might have problems with the iodine. Discuss this with your doctor. Experiment at home before you leave.

Vitamin C and powdered drink mixes to flavor the water can be added after the proper time has elapsed to render the water potable. Assume that water touted to have been boiled has not been unless personally witnessed. All water should be purified, including that used for brushing your teeth and that used for making ice. If water is cloudy or murky, let it stand to clarify. Water used for cleaning open wounds is best boiled first and left to cool. However, we will use any water available if a wound needs cleansing.

FOOD PREPARATION AND HANDLING

Thoroughly cooked foods can be considered safe, but only if they are eaten soon after cooking. Fruits and vegetables that are eaten uncooked must first be washed and peeled under sanitary conditions. Leafy vegetables must be cooked, though it may be effective to wash them in a strong iodine solution and rinse with potable water though it is unlikely that this is done carefully. Best to peel it, cook it, or forget it.

Food prepared by Nepalis can be assumed to be safe if it has just been cooked and not left out to be contaminated by flies or widespread airborne contaminants. Be wary of foods prepared in the morning in hotels and heated up later in the day. Contamination is also possible from the plates the food is served on, but this is very difficult to control.

Milk should always be heated just to the boiling point and allowed to cool before drinking, unless it is known to be already pasteurized. Curds are made from boiled milk and can be assumed to be safe unless recontaminated after preparation. Scraping off the top layer of curd should be sufficient. If milk has been diluted with water, it is necessary to bring the mixture to a boil. Buttermilk and cottage cheese, especially when prepared by herdsmen in their alpine huts, can be considered fairly safe.

It is difficult to follow rigorous advice concerning homemade alcoholic drinks. To be safe, avoid them all. *Rakshi,* distilled from a fermented mash, is perhaps the safest because it has been boiled, but is sometimes diluted with untreated water by sellers wishing to increase volume and profit. The common fermented drink is called *chang* by the Sherpas and Tibetans and *jAAR* by other Nepalis. Unless the water from which it is made is known to be pure, it is possible to get sick from it (a hangover notwithstanding). Finally, in the east, there is *tumbaa,* a fermented millet mash that is served in a bamboo canister with a straw. Hot, hopefully boiled, water is poured over it and the leach sucked up with the straw—partly safe, except for the mash, container, and straw.

Recognize that if you follow these rules and those for water religiously, you may still get diarrhea. Most likely it results from contamination of the plates the food is served on, the touching of the food by unclean hands (hand soap is not widely used in Nepal), or by flies.

COPING WITH HEALTH PROBLEMS

Trekking in Nepal is not risk-free. Many challenges, both mental and physical, await. In general, by following the guidelines outlined in this chapter, you can minimize the probability of encountering serious problems and will be prepared for dealing with relatively minor isssues. For further information, *The Pocket Doctor* and *Wilderness 911,* listed in the appendix, are useful references. If something life threatening does occur, information on "Emergency Care and Rescue Facilities" is listed at the end of this chapter.

GASTROINTESTINAL AND ABDOMINAL DISTRESS

Along with colds and other upper-respiratory infections, gastrointestinal ailments are the most common health problems among trekkers, particularly diarrhea. Fortunately, the diarrhea affecting tourists in Nepal is not the scourge that kills millions a year worldwide; only one tourist is known to have died from diarrhea in Nepal.

Diarrhea and Dysentery

It is safe to say that almost every trekker will have a bout of diarrhea during his or her stay in Nepal. Diarrhea, frequent passage of loose stools, is not worth distinguishing from dysentery. You will know it when you have it. Back in the 1970s Stephen wrote about self-treatment of diarrhea with antibiotics, and Dr. David Shlim has further perfected the regimen.

Note the number and nature of the stools and whether the diarrhea came on suddenly or gradually. Begin taking clear fluids such as water, weak tea with sugar, juice, clear soup, or soda pop that has been left to stand until the carbonation is gone. Avoid dairy products. Drinking a lot of fluids is necessary to avoid dehydration, but few trekkers get severely dehydrated in Nepal. Perhaps the best liquid to take is an oral rehydration solution. Jeevan Jal, a powder manufactured in Nepal, contains the needed salts. Mix one bag with a quart (liter) of water and drink it in small sips.

Most cases of **traveler's diarrhea** are caused by infection with bacterial strains unfamiliar to the newcomer. Although the infection may be debilitating, the body can resolve it on its own; however, it might last up to two weeks if untreated. If you would prefer to use medical intervention, then for watery or loose diarrhea of *sudden* onset (you can recall when you first had the urge), and possibly vomiting and fever, take a tablet of ciprofloxacin, nalidixic acid, or norfloxacin soon after the diarrhea begins and continue at the proper dosage regimen until the movements stop. (TMP/SMX was formerly used, but there is increased resistance to this drug in Nepal.) If the diarrhea is particularly bothersome, take an anti-diarrheal, loperamide, codeine, or diphenoxylate. The one time we would be sure to use anti-motility agents in diarrhea is before a long bus or plane ride. Norfloxacin and ciprofloxacin should be avoided by children and pregnant women; nalidixic acid can be used in children. Return to solid foods gradually.

If your diarrhea comes on *gradually* over a few days, and perhaps you feel lethargic, then a **protozoan parasite** such as *Giardia lamblia* could be the cause, but it is overdiagnosed by visitors on no certain diagnostic grounds . The CIWEC clinic finds *Giardia* as the cause in roughly only one in ten cases of travelers presenting with diarrhea. It generally takes a longer time to acquire this infection than the bacterial ones, usually two weeks and sometimes longer, after ingesting the cysts. Stools will often contain mucus and, as with some bacterial cases, sometimes smell like rotten eggs or sulfur, as will expelled gas. A churning stomach, cramping, and bloating are common, although vomiting and fever are rare. If left untreated, *Giardia* might resolve within six weeks or less. However, if your symptoms persist for a long time far from help, it makes sense to treat yourself presumptively for giardiasis. Take 2 grams of tinidazole (now available in North America, and for sale in medical halls in Kathmandu) as a single dose and repeat in twenty-four hours. Some trekkers have developed *Giardia* neuroses, thinking that each loose stool has been caused by this flagellate germ. There are other causes of loose stools and foul-smelling burps. For these people, frequently taking tinidazole could be risky.

Cyclospora is a protozoan parasite aquired through contaminated food or drink. Risk of infection is mainly in the monsoon season of June through September. Common symptoms include watery diarrhea, bloating, gas, loss of appetite, and prolonged fatigue. Vomiting, fever, and other flu-like symptoms may be present, although some infected people may be asymptomatic. Without medical intervention, the illness may self-limit within a few days to a month or longer, and relapses can occur. Treatment is co-trimoxazole (TMP/SMX) every twelve hours for seven days. *Cyclospora* cysts are resistant to disinfectants and can survive chlorine and iodine, which then leaves boiling as the surest means of purifying water.

If you are really sick, then rest, and if getting worse, seek attention. Stool exams are not particularly helpful, as the labs in Kathmandu overdiagnose *Amoeba* and *Giardia*. If you had diarrhea before, treated yourself, and were better for a few days, and now are sick again, it is likely you have been reinfected and should treat yourself again.

Our recommended regimen for treating diarrhea is to (1) rehydrate if necessary, (2) decide *(very difficult)* if it might be *Giardia,* (3) if not, take a single dose of an antibiotic, currently ciprofloxacin, and (4) resume solid foods in a few hours. We do not recommend taking antibiotics to prevent getting diarrhea because the bacterial form is easily treated, and antibiotics don't prevent the other types.

Vomiting

Nausea and vomiting, if unaccompanied by diarrhea at altitude, suggest moderate altitude illness. If there is no ataxia (see below), treat altitude illness as below. Don't ascend. Otherwise it is probably associated with a viral or food-borne infection and can be treated by hydrating with liquids in small amounts as well as rest.

Constipation

This is not uncommon in the first few days of a trek, as you get used to the routine. A bulky Nepali diet usually prevents significant difficulties. If constipation does occur, drink plenty of fluids. Try a cup or two of hot water, tea, or coffee upon waking in the morning. In rare cases, mild laxatives may be needed, including psyllium seed husks dissolved in water. Better to just wait until the problem works itself out.

Hemorrhoids

These irritable dilated veins around the anus are usually a result of constipation. They may become larger while trekking, sometimes becoming hard with blood clots (thrombosed)—not a threat to life, but a nuisance. There are various creams, ointments, and suppositories that may provide some symptomatic relief for uncomfortable hemorrhoids. When they become thrombosed, however, frequent warm "sitz" baths (sitting with the affected part in the water) are the answer.

Worms

You probably won't be bothered by a worm infection while in Nepal. But your porters may tell you they have passed worms. If so, there are likely more inside. A broad-spectrum worm medicine such as mebendazole (mentioned in the medical kit list) may be of some benefit. The porters will, however, most likely get reinfected. Mebendazole is also a good drug to try if your porter complains of abdominal pain. Do not pass it out to villagers, for reasons explained in the previous chapter (see "Medical Treatment of

This man stands at the head of the 32-foot (9.75 m) tape worm he just passed. (Photo by Stephen Bezruchka)

Local People"). And be sure to get your own stool examined when you return home if you have symptoms (including stomach bloating and discomfort, constipation, anemia, diarrhea, disturbed sleep, digestive disorders). Trekkers do pick up worm infections. Although the common roundworm will die of old age and you will be rid of it if you avoid re-infection, this is not necessarily true of other intestinal parasites.

Appendicitis

Trekkers out in the remote hills may worry about appendicitis. The chances of it occurring are very slight, so this information is for your peace of mind. The pain usually starts in the mid-abdomen, soon shifts to the right lower quadrant, and becomes accompanied by nausea. The victim rarely has an appetite; vomiting or diarrhea is rarely persistent. In a case where appendicitis is suspected, give fluids and an antibiotic, and evacuate the patient. Cases of acute appendicitis may respond to antibiotics and even improve without treatment.

Heartburn

This is fairly common among those prone to it, especially if they try to eat a Nepali diet in Himalayan porter quantities. The burning is most likely to occur when on the trail soon after a meal. Better to eat smaller amounts. Don't fasten your pack waistband right after meals. Antacids may help, too. The liquid preparations are best in doses of two tablespoons every hour for symptomatic relief. Preparations are available in Kathmandu. The pain of heartburn could signify a heart attack. Such a person will usually look and act very sick, perhaps perspire profusely, and need gentle care and evacuation.

GENITOURINARY INFECTIONS AND DISORDERS

Many problems can be avoided simply by being prepared. Women plagued with vaginal yeast infections when taking antibiotics might bring along appropriate vaginal suppositories. Those prone to urinary infections (see below) could consider carrying extra medicine for this problem. These individuals should make sure to urinate right after sexual intercourse, a preventive measure for recurrent infection.

As mentioned earlier, tampons and other feminine hygiene products are not readily available in the hills, although health posts might have them. Instead, women might consider the reusable menstrual cup (Mooncup) that collects menstrual fluid and lasts for years.

Gynecologic Problems

Trekking is very strenuous and women who have been on the trail for a time may find that their menstrual periods stop. This is not serious; providing that a woman is not pregnant, menses should resume again with lessened activity. Vaginal bleeding may be profuse after one or two **missed periods** and will necessitate resting until the bleeding stops.

Heavy bleeding in a pregnant woman demands prompt medical attention, as does modest bleeding if accompanied by fever, light-headedness, pelvic cramps, or pain. If you are having profuse vaginal bleeding and there is not even the remotest chance that you could be pregnant, and you are far from any medical facility, you could try the following treatment (*Caution: If you are pregnant, this treatment will likely harm the fetus*): Take a birth control pill, if you have them, four times a day for five days. Bleeding should stop in a day or so. After stopping the pills, you should have a menstrual period within a week. If bleeding doesn't stop, then prompt attention is warranted. An alternative to taking birth control pills to control heavy bleeding is to take meclofenamate, the anti-inflammatory medicine suggested. The effect on a fetus is unknown.

Pelvic pain can have serious consequences if accompanied by fever (possibly due to an infection in the fallopian tubes) or associated with pregnancy (possibly a tubal gestation). This could be associated with vaginal bleeding. A leaking tubal pregnancy is a distinct possibility if defecation is also very painful. The treatment for a ruptured tubal pregnancy is surgical. Seek help immediately. If pain accompanied by fever is the predominant symptom, and you have had PID (pelvic inflammatory disease) or an infection in your tubes before, this could have recurred. If there are no medical facilities, you could take an antibiotic. Tetracycline, doxycycline, or ciprofloxacin would be the best choices from the drug list. If pelvic discomfort is accompanied by frequent and burning urination, sometimes with associated back pain, a urinary tract infection could be the cause (see treatment below).

Urinary Tract Infections

Bladder infections are common in some women, especially after vigorous sexual activity. If you experience burning, frequent urination, passing small amounts of urine, without a fever or back pain, and are not pregnant, take co-trimoxazole (TMP/SMX), ciprofloxacin, a cephalosporin, or tetracycline for three days. If you have a fever, or back pain, or are pregnant, in addition to the preceding symptoms, take an antibiotic in its appropriate dose for a week.

FEVER

Fever may be present as a symptom of infection or one of several insect-borne infectious diseases.

When there is no apparent cause, fever may be due to pneumonia, abscess, or other internal infection. When associated with joint aches, perhaps nausea and vomiting as well as diarrhea, a fever is likely due to a **flu** illness. Aspirin and fluid replacement are appropriate.

When the fever is severe, and the person very ill, sometimes delirious, **enteric or typhoid fever** may be the cause. Usually there is no diarrhea. Treat presumptively with ciprofloxacin, norfloxacin, azithromycin or co-trimoxazole (TMP/SMX) if medical help is not available.

If traveling in the Tarai, especially before and during the monsoon, and not taking malaria prophylaxis, periodic fevers might be due to **malaria**. In that case, seek medical evaluation immediately. Although there is no **dengue fever** in Nepal, travelers from other Asian countries, especially India and Thailand, might come down with it on the first few days of a trek if they set out soon after arriving in Nepal. The incubation period is around a week; the viral infection is transmitted by urban and jungle mosquitoes that bite during the day. Abrupt onset with high fever accompanied by severe muscle aches, headaches, and blanching rashes are common in milder cases, which are the norm among travelers who have not been previously infected. The fever subsides quickly after four or five days. Treat with aspirin, acetaminophen, or ibuprofen. Fatigue and fevers after getting over the initial attack are seen as well.

RESPIRATORY INFECTIONS

Upper-respiratory infections, including the common cold, are very common in Nepal. Physicians in the high-altitude Khumbu region have noted that the three most common ailments seen there are bronchitis (the so-called "Khumbu cough," brought on by cold, arid conditions), gastroenteritis, and viral upper-respiratory infections.

Colds

Now that we have a good sense of how to treat diarrheas, respiratory infections are turning out to be very disabling to trekkers. Medical science does not offer any widely agreed-upon remedies. Zinc gluconate 15 mg. tablets taken every 2 hours while awake when symptoms of a cold come on may decrease the days of symptoms. Stephen used to take large doses of vitamin C for colds but doesn't anymore.

Other ways of dealing with a common cold include rest, drinking plenty of fluids, and taking zinc. Do not smoke. Gargle with warm, salty water for a sore throat. Decongestants have been used for years by many people. You might want to try the antihistamine chlorpheniramine maleate, suggested in the medical kit, at a dose of 4 mg four times a day. Avoid decongestants containing many different drugs. People with high temperatures should not continue trekking. Investigate the cause for the fever (see above). Normal body temperature is 98.6°F (37°C), but there is little reason to be concerned if temperatures measured orally remain below 100°F (39°C) and the person feels pretty strong.

Coughing

Coughing normally brings up sputum and is beneficial in ridding the body of it. Sometimes, however, an annoying cough occurs that does not produce sputum, even after a few days. Smoky interiors may be the cause, otherwise a respiratory virus. Read the section below on altitude illness to make sure you are not dealing with HAPE.

Commonly encountered causes of coughs are colds, asthma, and bronchitis. **Bronchitis** features inflammation of the airways in the lungs, the hallmark of which is the production of plenty of sputum through coughing. The sputum is usually yellow, or green, but in **asthma** it is usually clear. Sufferers are less sick than those with pneumonia, rarely have fevers, and if they have chest discomfort it is more likely to be central, resulting from the prolonged coughing. Try a week's course of antibiotics.

Serious coughing could be due to **pneumonia**. An affected individual would have high fevers, sputum thick with pus and possibly streaked with blood (but not frothy), and often localized chest pain that is most severe with a deep breath. The sick person is usually too ill to travel. Treatment consists of an antibiotic, aspirin for high fever and pain, and plenty of fluids.

For a persistent virus-related cough, take one or two tablets of codeine (30 mg) every six hours for a day or two. General measures in treating an annoying cough include drinking plenty of fluids and breathing moist air. The latter is difficult in dry mountain areas. Steam inhalation—that is, getting a kettle of boiling water and putting it inside a tent or under a blanket or towel and breathing the water vapor—helps. Hard candy or throat lozenges provide some relief.

Sinusitis

Sinusitis, an inflammation of the sinuses often following a cold, can be characterized by headaches of a dull nature, pain in the sinuses, fever, chills, weakness, swelling of the facial area, and discomfort in the upper teeth if the maxillary sinus is involved. For severe symptoms, rest, drink plenty of fluids, take two aspirin every four hours for the fever, and use phenylephrine nose drops three times a day. Start an antibiotic if the temperature extremes are significant. This course should be continued for seven days, no matter when the symptoms subside. The best antibiotics are co-trimoxazole (TMP/SMX), amoxicillin, azithromycin, a cephalosporin, or ciprofloxacin.

EYE PROBLEMS

Conjunctivitis is an inflammation of the delicate membrane that covers the surface of the eye and the undersurface of the eyelid. The eye appears red and the blood vessels on its surface are engorged. The flow of tears is increased, and material may be crusted in the margins of the eyelids and eyelashes. Irritation from the ubiquitous smoke in rural Nepali homes is a common cause, especially among the Nepalis. Apply ophthalmic antibiotic solution beneath the lower eyelid next to the eye every four hours until the symptoms disappear.

If you wear **contact lenses**, at the first sign of any eye irritation that is distinct from the irritation caused by dirty lenses, you should remove them and apply the antibiotic solution. In cases of problems persisting, especially if the eye is very sensitive to the light, patch it for twenty-four hours.

Do not neglect regular cleaning. Use water that has been boiled when water is called for. If you do not want to bother with cleaning at all, disposable contact lenses may be the solution in Nepal with less risk of infection, although the packaging can be burdensome to carry out. Once, while getting up in the night to answer the call up in the high dry air,

Stephen's lens dried out, and he had to remove it. He used iodized water to rehydrate it and replaced it in his eye. Some irritation persisted for an hour or so, presumably caused by the iodine residue. Better to carry some commercial normal saline for this purpose.

Some people might use Nepal's trails as an opportunity to perhaps strengthen the eyes naturally by going without glasses and contacts more often, and training the eyes to focus alternately on things far and near and in differing light conditions. However, keep in mind that of the injuries and infrequent deaths of trekkers, falling off the trail is a leading cause.

DENTAL PROBLEMS

Most dental problems are unlikely among trekkers if they see a dentist before going to Nepal. For simple toothache, a small wad of cotton, soaked in oil of cloves and inserted in the appropriate cavity, often relieves pain. Temporary fillings might be used if you have them in your medical kit. Codeine and aspirin, two tablets each every four to six hours, help relieve severe pain. Abscesses, characterized by swelling of the gums and jaw near the site of the toothache, and often accompanied by fever and chills as well as persistent hot and cold sensitivity, call for the care of a dentist. In the interim, take an antibiotic.

One possible hazard is breaking a tooth while eating because of the possible presence of small stones in the rice or *daal*. Take pain medicine and avoid foods of extreme temperature.

Although good dental care is rare in Nepal outside of Kathmandu, there is an excellent dental clinic in Namche Bazaar in the Solu–Khumbu (Everest region).

ABRASIONS, WOUNDS, AND MUSCULOSKELETAL PROBLEMS
Blisters

Tape, moleskin, or molefoam (foam with adhesive backing) tends to spread friction over a larger area and reduce local shear stress between layers of the skin. When you feel a tender or hot spot on the skin while walking, stop and investigate. Put a generous piece of moleskin, foam, or adhesive tape over the area. The best method is to place moleskin and cover that material with a piece of smooth (slippery) adhesive tape; the sock then slides over this spot and less friction is generated. Don't remove the moleskin for a few days; otherwise, you may pull some skin off with it.

Well-fitting and worn-in boots or shoes and proper socks are a must (see Chapter 2) to prevent foot problems. Begin your trek with padding applied to potential trouble areas. Other products used by trekkers to prevent blisters include Spenco Second Skin and plain open-cell foam that is used for packing and cushioning. The latter is cut in pieces about one-half inch to an inch thick and applied next to the skin, held in place over the friction point by the lightweight sock. This is especially useful for toes and irregular areas of the foot where blisters might form. If you are developing blisters, and have other footwear, change to it and see if this eliminates hot spots.

Keep the feet dry, as moist feet are more prone to blisters. Change socks frequently in hot weather, and do not wash or soak your feet too often. By keeping feet dry, you develop calluses over pressure points, and this protects your feet against blisters. Don't soak your feet in streams or hot springs if blister prone.

Once a blister has formed, there are two schools of thought on what to do. Some advocate leaving an intact blister alone, in fact protecting it by cutting a hole the same diameter as the blister in a piece of moleskin or foam and applying that around the blister. Others prefer to drain the blister with a needle. Sterilize the needle in a flame until it turns red hot and allow it to cool. The needle should be inserted at the edge of the blister right next to the good skin. Then apply a sterile dressing or some moleskin or foam over it. Finally, if you have any of the biologic dressings that doctors use for wounds, they would be ideal for putting on broken blisters.

Strains, Sprains, and Sore Knees

As muscles flex, they shorten and move joints by means of tendons that attach to bones. Ligaments are fibrous tissue straps that cross joints and hold them together. Sprains are tears or stretching of ligaments; strains are tears in muscles. The tendons may get stretched, torn, or inflamed, too.

For most trekkers, the prolonged, continual walking necessary to reach a distant point places more demand on their musculoskeletal systems than they are used to. If you gradually increase the amount of activity, your body will toughen up and adjust. People who push themselves to walk long distances every day, especially with heavy packs, will find their poorly prepared body protesting. Leg strains, especially in the thigh and calf muscles, make climbing and descending painful. Everyone should pay attention to reducing the impact on the descent. Absorb the shock by bending the knee when the lower foot contacts the ground. Take short, choppy strides and don't keep your knees straight. Turn your feet sideways on steep descents. Watch how Nepali porters descend. Be sure to keep your shoes or boots laced tightly over the ankle during descents to avoid toe blisters.When tired, or not paying attention to the trail, anyone can twist and sprain a joint, most commonly the ankle. Ankle sprains are common when the foot turns inward momentarily with severe pain that can make walking difficult. Check for the points of maximum tenderness immediately after the injury. If they are just in front of the outside base of the ankle (lateral malleolus or distal fibula), and just below it, then you probably have the common variety of ankle sprain.

Treatment for strains and sprains is similar. Ice or cool the affected part, and elevate and compress the injured area. Compress with adhesive tape or an elastic bandage. Severe injuries will require rest for a few days. For strains in the bulky muscles of the thigh, there may be little you can do except to lighten the load and ease up on the amount of ground to be covered. This advice applies to sprains as well. Take anti-inflammatory and pain medicine.

Knees will rebel, especially on the downhill portions, if the cartilage (the shock-absorbing pads in the joint) gets too much pounding. Those with weak cartilage lining the kneecap (chondromalacia patellae), women being more commonly afflicted, will especially have pain climbing and descending. Those with knee problems will be better off wearing footwear with shock absorbency in the heel. Consider using a walking stick or ski poles to lessen the impact on knees and hips (see Chapter 2). Individuals with pre-existing knee or ankle problems should strengthen the muscles that pull across the joint by doing isometric exercises before they trek. Those with a tendency to ankle sprains should wear sturdy, over-the-ankle boots and do exercises to strengthen their peroneal muscles (those on the outside of the lower leg) by pushing outward with the foot against an immovable object. Others prone to knee injuries should work on their quadriceps muscles (those on the front of the thigh) by keeping the knee straight and pushing up on a fixed object with the top of the foot—an isometric exercise.

Small Wounds and Infections

Clean *any* wound that breaks the skin with soap and copious amounts of water, potable or not, to flush the wound and remove debris. Avoid using the common antiseptics, as they may damage healthy tissue. If you are using tincture of iodine or povidone io-dine for water purification, you might cleanse the skin around (not in) the wound with this material. A large wound should be covered with a sterile dressing, which should be changed periodically until a good clot has formed and healing is well under way.

A wound infection is often the result of contamination and is evident by signs of in-flammation (redness, swelling, tenderness, warmth) and pain several days after it occurs. These infections are more common at high altitudes, perhaps because the "resistance" of the body is less there. In this case, soak the wound in hot water for at least fifteen minutes. Afterward, cover it with a sterile dressing. With severe, spreading infections, antibiotics should be taken, preferably cephalosporin or azithromycin.

For abscesses such as boils, the treatment is similar to that for wound infections, ex-cept that antibiotics probably do little to help unless the boils are a recurring problem. Drain the abscesses by soaking them in hot water for fifteen minutes five or six times a day. They will usually spontaneously open, but you may have to assist the process with a sharp sterilized knife.

Animal and Insect Bites

Prevent getting bitten by being vigilant on your travels. Avoid making sudden move-ments toward animals on first encounter. When dogs threaten you, especially in herding sites at altitude, approach with stones or a stick. Most dogs and beasts of burden in Asia have been hit enough times with stones that the mere hint of throwing a stone or stick sends them away.

In case of an **animal bite**, treat by washing the site immediately with soap and water as well as a dilute solution of salt and water. Wash and irrigate the wound for thirty min-utes or more. In animal experiments, inoculating of a wound with rabies virus has shown washing alone to be effective in preventing clinical rabies. Irrigation with a quaternary ammonium solution (cetrimide or benzalkonium chloride, also found in the antiseptic Savlon) within twelve hours is also effective. Those who have had rabies vaccine before coming to Nepal face less risk than others but should get post-exposure inoculation as well, although they do not need rabies immune globulin.

If rabies is suspected, evacuate quickly so that the vaccine can be administered as soon as possible. The decision to seek help may be difficult if the animal bite is unpro-voked and the animal appears healthy. If other animals in the area have been acting strangely recently, there may be an epidemic. Rabies is spread by the saliva of infected animals penetrating the skin, usually through a bite or on a previous wound. Contact with rabid bats in caves has also caused the disease.

Ticks are best removed quickly, by grasping with a tweezer near the head, or with a gloved finger, as near to the skin as possible and pulling straight out with increasing force. Lyme disease is not known to occur in Nepal.

Leeches, abundant during the monsoon in the forests above 4000 feet (1200 m), are attracted to movement, warmth, and by-products of respiration, and can drop onto you from vegetation as you pass under them, or crawl up from the ground, or attach as you brush by leaves or rocks. When you feel a very localized cool sensation anywhere on your skin, stop immediately and investigate. It may be around your ears or neck, or just above your ankle. In leech-prone forests, stop periodically and search. Leeches can be quite responsive to movement by the prey. You may find it amusing to lure the critters with your finger as they scan with head and body waving while attached to a leaf or rock, trying to home in with their suckers. (For more on the natural history of leeches, see the sidebar on Leeches, Chapter 6.)

Leeches abound at middle elevations in the monsoon. (Photo by Stephen Bezruchka)

Once a leech is attached to your skin, use the leading edge of a fingernail scraped along the skin to dislodge the thinner, anterior end at the attachment site. Keep the wound clean. Other means of removal—such as pulling or using heat, salt, alcohol, or insect repellent—can cause the leech to release the contents of its stomach which might infect the bite wound. Jawed leeches are not known to be transmitters of disease, however, the resulting wound may bleed considerably. Control this with pressure, and watch for signs of infection later. Some people might have an anaphylactic or other allergic reaction to leech bites, and serious medical attention would then be required.

The best preventive to leech bites is to cover the skin. However, leeches often still find a way through to the skin. For preventive use, the usual insect repellents such as DEET will work for leeches. The KEEP office in Jyatha, Thamel, as well as some pharmacies sell "Anti-Leech Oil," which may be good to bring along on a monsoon trek. Otherwise, you might try eucalyptus oil, lemon juice, or smearing bath soap over dry skin. You might also consider wearing leech-proof socks over your regular socks.

ENVIRONMENT-INDUCED HEALTH PROBLEMS

While trekking in the lap of the highest mountains on Earth, precautions are necessary. Visitors must pay attention to the environment and to messages that their own bodies may be giving them as well as signs that fellow travelers might be in need of assistance.

Altitude Illness

Problems with altitude can strike anyone, even at relatively low altitudes such as 8000 feet (2450 m), where it has been fatal. But in general, trekkers going to higher altitudes quickly are more severely affected. People who fly to a high altitude and then proceed to an even higher area or cross a pass should be especially wary. Examples include flying to Lukla and going to the Everest Base Camp, or flying to Jomosom or Ongre (Manang) and crossing Thorung La. Some symptoms will be felt by most of those going to high altitudes. Those hiking up will ascend more gradually and acclimatize better and have fewer problems than those flying up. Serious illness occurs in less than 2 percent of people who go to high altitudes. The fatality rate for trekkers in Nepal has fallen significantly from the early days of trekking as people have become more aware and acclimatized. Every altitude illness death in trekkers is preventable. Learn about this condition from the Himlayan Rescue Association's informational sessions in Kathmandu and at aid posts in the Khumbu at Pheriche and Maccherma (run by IPPG) and in Manang.

Altitude illness can be prevented by acclimatization; that is, by a gradual rate of ascent, allowing sufficient rest at various intermediate altitudes. The proper amount of rest and rate of ascent vary greatly from individual to individual and even over time in the same individual. For example, a person who previously had climbed Mount Everest later had difficulties at modest altitudes from ascending too rapidly. One protocol would be to spend the first night below 10,000 feet (3000 m), and not raise the sleeping altitude more than 1000 feet (300 m) a day while building in one day of acclimatization (rest) for every 3000 feet (900 m) gained between sleeping sites above 10,000 feet (3000 m). This is feasible only if everyone is on the lookout for the signs and symptoms of maladaptation to high altitudes. If the party acts appropriately should anyone develop altitude illness, serious problems can usually be avoided.

For example, in ascending to the Everest Base Camp, Kala Pattar, Gokyo, or anywhere above 15,000 feet (4500 m), allow at least two rest and acclimatization days; three are preferable. One stop could be at 11,000 feet (3350 m) and the other at 14,000 feet (4250 m). On these days, people who feel good could take an excursion to a higher point, but return to sleep at the same altitude as the night before. In Khumbu, a rest day at Namche Bazaar, Khunde, Khumjung or Pangboche, followed by another at Pheriche, would be the minimum requirement. Then spend a night at Lobuje, and ascend to Kala Pattar the next day, returning to Lobuje for the night. However, this may be too fast for many people.

If you are on a group trek going to high altitudes, ask how many rest days are built into the schedule and how flexible it is. Find out whether the leader has had significant problems with members getting serious altitude illness on previous treks. Individuals on group treks are at greater risk of bad outcomes from altitude illness compared to individual trekkers.

Trekking leaders should be aware that group members often withhold symptoms of altitude illness when asked. The leader must be a detective and look for clues. The most significant blunder likely to be made by a leader is to deny that a member's symptoms represent altitude illness. Take this seriously; clients are in a more litigious mood these days (as if that should be the reason to be careful)!

There are other factors besides a slow rate of ascent that help in acclimatization. A large fluid intake to ensure good hydration is key. Four quarts (liters) or more per day of liquid are usually necessary. Urine volume should always exceed one pint (half a liter) daily, preferably one quart (one liter). The urine color should be almost clear. A strong yellow color indicates that more fluids should be drunk. Some trekkers and Himalayan climbers find that measuring urine output daily with a small plastic bottle helps ensure adequate hydration. A simple way to measure urine output is to wait until you are absolutely bursting before urinating. The volume is then close to one pint (half a liter). Empty a full bladder at least twice a day. One sign of adaptation to altitude is a good natural diuresis (passage of lots of urine). If this is not found, be extra cautious.

An easy way to judge the presence of dehydration is to compare heart rates standing and lying down, with a thirty-second interval in between. If the rate is 20 percent greater in the standing position, the individual may be significantly dehydrated and should consume more fluids. This can be water, tea, soup, or broth. Alcoholic drinks should be avoided by dehydrated individuals and at high altitudes by everyone until well acclimatized. Besides being detrimental to acclimatization, the effects of alcohol at high altitude may be impossible to distinguish from symptoms of altitude illness.

Caloric intake should be maintained with a diet high in carbohydrates. The tasty potatoes found at high altitudes in Nepal are an excellent source of carbohydrates. A good appetite is a sign of acclimatization. Avoid excessive salt intake at high altitudes. Don't take salt tablets.

Rest is also important. Overexertion does not help acclimatization. Give up part of your load to high-altitude porters who are already well acclimatized and can carry loads with ease (while keeping an eye on the lowland porters for possible altitude sickness). Avoid going so fast that you are always stopping short of breath with your heart pounding. Use the rest step and techniques for pacing yourself by checking your heart rate as described in the introduction to Section II. Plan modest objectives for each day so that you will at least enjoy your altitude amble.

Many people who frequent the mountains and often make rapid changes in altitude find that forced deep breathing helps reduce the mild symptoms of altitude illness. However, if done to excess, it can produce the hyperventilation syndrome, in which shortness of breath, dizziness, and numbness are present. Breathing in and out of a large paper or plastic bag for a few minutes (sometimes thirty minutes) will relieve these symptoms.

Taking acetazolamide (Diamox) has been shown to be beneficial in helping the acclimatization process, especially if flying to altitudes. The dose is 125 mg by mouth two or three times a day, begun two days before the flight and continued for three days after ascent, and can be increased to 250 mg when symptoms present. Acetazolamide can also help when begun upon arrival at high altitude by plane and by those walking beginning at, say, 9000 feet. Trekkers flying into a high-altitude area such as Lukla, Jomosom, or Manang should consider taking acetazolamide. Even one dose taken at supper may be beneficial. Common side effects are an increased urine output, some numbness and tingling in the extremities, and an unusual, perhaps unpalatable taste when drinking carbonated beverages, including beer. These are not reasons to stop taking the drug; they do not represent allergic reactions.

Dexamethasone, a powerful cortisone-like drug, also prevents the symptoms of acute mountain sickness upon exposure to altitude. Unlike acetazolamide, it has no effect on the acclimatization process, and we do *not* recommend that trekkers take it for prevention. However, it may have a place in treating severe symptoms of altitude illness. Other drugs for prevention of altitude illness that have been tried include furosemide (also called frusemide, or Lasix), and antacids. They are not helpful.

Personally, we do not use medicines to help to adapt to the altitude. On the other hand, we usually have few problems. If we had repeated, predictable difficulties in Nepal at altitude, we would try acetazolamide. If you have had HAPE before, discuss with your doctor using nifedipine or sildenafil as a preventive before ascent.

As for symptoms, it is best to assume that if you are not feeling well at altitude, it's altitude illness until proven otherwise. Most people trekking to high altitudes experience one or more *mild symptoms of altitude illness*. These include:

- headache
- nausea
- loss of appetite
- mild shortness of breath with minimal exertion
- sleep disturbance (difficulty sleeping)

- dizziness or light-headedness
- mild weakness
- slight swelling of hands and face

As long as the symptoms remain mild and are only a nuisance, rest at that altitude until better. As the HRA lecture states, "Do not take a headache higher!" Never ascend to and sleep at a higher elevation if you have mild symptoms. Symptomatic treatment with medicines may be helpful. If there is no improvement after a few hours, or after a night's rest, or there is worsening, descend on foot to below the altitude where symptoms first occurred. Only after getting better can an ascent at a more gradual rate be considered.

Serious symptoms of altitude illness are a grave matter, especially cerebral symptoms (starred with an asterisk). They include:

- inability to recover from shortness of breath with rest
- delirium, confusion, and coma*
- loss of coordination, staggering*
- severe, persistent headache*
- rapid heart rate after resting—110 or more beats per minute
- wet, bubbly breathing
- severe coughing spasms that limit activity
- coughing up pinkish or rust-colored sputum
- blueness of face and lips
- low urine output—less than a pint (500 ml) daily
- persistent vomiting*
- gross fatigue or extreme lassitude*

If anyone in your party develops any of these symptoms, he or she should descend *immediately* on the back of a porter or pack animal to avoid undue exertion. Descend to below the altitude at which any symptoms of altitude illness first occurred. This treatment should not be delayed until morning when you may have a corpse to transport. The victim should be kept warm and given oxygen if available. Give acetazolamide, 250 mg every eight hours. If dexamethasone is available, and cerebral symptoms are present as noted above (*), give 4 mg every six hours. After a descent of only a few thousand feet, relief may be dramatic. At the point where relief occurs, or lower, rest a few days. Then consider ascending cautiously again, only if none of the cerebral symptoms were present and you have not taken dexamethasone. For further information, refer to the information below on specific types of altitude illness.

Judgment is affected by altitude. Hence, possible altitude illness may be denied by the victim and his companions. To guide you, the clearest symptoms of significant altitude illness to watch for in *yourself* are:

- breathlessness at rest
- resting pulse over 110 per minute
- loss of appetite
- unusual fatigue while walking

The clearest ones to watch for in *others* are:

- skipping meals
- antisocial behavior
- difficulty keeping up (arriving last at the destination)

It cannot be stressed too strongly that you *must* descend at the onset of serious symptoms. If in Khumbu, go to the hospital at Kunde, the Himalayan Rescue Association's clinic in Pheriche, or IPPG's rescue station at Maccherma (with an outpost at Gokyo) if that is on your descent route. Oxygen and a hyperbaric pressure chamber to simulate the effects of descent are available there, along with other resources. But don't stop descending in Pheriche or elsewhere unless the victim is considerably better. Trekkers have died in Pheriche from not heeding this guideline. Don't wait up high for a helicopter rescue. Many trekkers, including Olympic athletes, doctors, and experienced climbers, have died in Nepal from altitude illness because they failed to heed symptoms. A disproportionate number of physicians, who should know better, have died from altitude illness in Nepal. Finally, it appears that those trekking individually rarely die from altitude illness. It is peer pressure in groups that contributes to deaths among trekkers. Those alone descend early, while in groups there seems to be a tendency to not hold the party back.

The Gamow Bag, the first portable hyperbaric chamber, has had an impact in treating serious, potentially fatal, altitude illness. Several other designs of pressurization bags, all similar, are now available. The victim is placed inside, and then the pressure inside is increased via an air pump to simulate descent of 3000 to 5000 feet (900 to 1500 meters). It can be useful for diagnosis, too. If you wonder if someone's symptoms might be due to altitude, put them into the bag and "descend" them 3000 feet or more and see if the symptoms improve. Treatment in the bag for an hour may produce temporary improvement in someone suffering from mild symptoms. For serious symptoms a minimum of two to four hours is required. The symptoms may recur once the victim leaves the bag, necessitating retreatment. Refer to the protocols provided with the bag. The bag requires continuous pumping to maintain air pressure, a tiring prospect if done manually. Use of the bag does not substitute for descent—so, after initial treatment, get the person down. Individuals successfully treated in the bag and then separated from it (as when another party took it on up), who didn't descend, have had symptoms recur and died.

The device is lightweight and expensive, but cheaper than the cost of a coffin. A large trekking group that will spend considerable time up high, where the way down is long and difficult, should carry one. It should be standard equipment for any group trek to altitude, especially away from popular areas, but to save costs many group treks do not carry one. If you are going on an expensive group trek, ask if they carry an altitude chamber, and if not, why not. Your money should be going to buy life-saving items such as this. The chamber should be standard insurance for all parties to altitude.

With the essentials now covered, what follows is advice for trekkers suffering from specific types of altitude illness observed in Nepal. These include acute mountain sickness (AMS), high-altitude pulmonary edema (HAPE), peripheral edema (PE), high-altitude cerebral edema (HACE), and high-altitude retinal hemorrhage (HARH). We'll discuss symptoms and treatment for each condition.

AMS commonly comes on after being at high altitudes for one to two days. A variety of symptoms are experienced, most often a persistent headache, usually present on awakening. The other mild symptoms listed above also occur. It is like an altitude hangover. Irregular or periodic breathing during sleep is common in most people at altitude, as is sleeplessness. The rate and depth of respirations increase to a peak, then diminish, stopping altogether for a fraction of a minute, then increasing again. If none of the serious symptoms are present, there is no cause for concern. Physical fitness *per se* is of no benefit. This is true for most altitude illness. The treatment is to deal with each symptom with whatever means you have and to not ascend until better. Acetazolamide is useful in treating the symptoms of AMS. Try a 125-mg tablet at suppertime and perhaps upon arising to see whether it helps the headache and malaise and sleeplessness. The dose can be doubled to 250 mg as well. Don't leave such a person alone, for the mild condition may progress and the victim can become helpless. Taking acetazolamide for AMS does not preclude your getting any of the more serious forms of altitude illness below. Pills to help sleep that may be taken at altitude include acetazolamide, zolpidem, and zaleplon. Studies suggest the latter two don't compromise breathing and performance if no more than 10 mg of either (not both) are taken once a night.

Tests for coordination (such as tandem walking) should be given. See if, after resting, the person can walk a straight line by putting the heel of the advancing foot directly in front of the toe of the back foot. Slight difficulty is tolerable if 12 feet (4 m) can be covered in a straight line. If in doubt, compare the individual with someone who is having no difficulty. Often the rugged terrain will make it harder for both to accomplish the maneuver. In exhaustion, hypothermia, or intoxication, mild degrees of loss of coordination (ataxia) can be seen, but there should be no staggering or falling. Ataxia is a sign of serious illness, probably HACE, and the person should descend while he is still able to do so under his own power, but always with someone else who is well. Even if this condition is diagnosed at night, descent should begin immediately. Give dexamethasone. If a hyperbaric chamber is available, place the person in it and descend him when better.

HAPE, the presence of fluid in the lungs, is a grave illness and is likely present if the respiratory problems on the above serious symptoms list are noted. The heart and breathing rates are useful clues. Do not delay in descending these individuals, as death can be only a few hours away. Get them down while they can still walk on their own. There are usually some signs of AMS. Trained people using stethoscopes may hear sounds called "rales" in the lungs of trekkers with no symptoms. This is common and no cause for alarm. The presence of the above symptoms are grounds for descent. If an altitude chamber and/or oxygen are available, use them.

Individuals with chest disease are more susceptible to HAPE, as are people who have previously suffered from it. Those with upper-respiratory infections or common colds may be at an increased risk.

Oxygen is beneficial and morphine may be, but other drugs used to treat pulmonary edema at sea level are probably not effective. Give acetazolamide and dexamethasone as well. Medical personnel who are carrying nifedipine could administer a 10-mg capsule to the stricken individual, asking him to chew it. Trekkers ascending to significant altitudes can consider carrying it. Blood pressure may drop sufficiently, making it difficult for the victim to climb down, and thus he becomes an evacuation problem. If this artery vasodilator helps, it can be taken perhaps hourly for relief or the long-acting preparation can be used in a dose of 30 mg three times a day. The other class of drugs that may be beneficial in treating and preventing HAPE are the erection drugs such as sildenafil or tadalafil. There are no direct clinical studies of these drugs for treatment, but they have been used along with other modalities and seem to help. Since they may be present in situations where HAPE occurs, consider using them but don't forget the proven treatments of descent, oxygen and a pressurization bag. Treatment doses of sildenafil (Viagra) have been 25 to 50 mg every 4–8 hours.

Descent for the seriously ill is best done without exertion, say on the back of a porter or a yak. Those with HAPE that has completely resolved with descent can consider re-ascending slowly.

PE—swelling around the eyes, face, hands, feet, or ankles—is present in some degree in many visitors to high altitudes. Women seem to be affected more than men. The hands are most often affected. Carrying a heavy pack with tight shoulder straps that affect venous return can be a cause. Remove or loosen rings on the fingers and constricting clothing or pack straps. Swelling of the feet and ankles should be treated by rest and elevation of the legs. Facial swelling, especially if severe enough to shut the eyes, requires descent. In general, check for other symptoms, and if any of the serious ones are present, descend. Otherwise, if the swelling is not especially uncomfortable or disabling and no other symptoms are present, continue cautious ascent. Such swelling can be an early indication of failure of the body to adapt to high altitudes. A diuretic to increase urination can be administered if swelling is an isolated problem; watch for serious symptoms. Others have used elastic compression bandages to the legs with good results.

HACE, or swelling of the brain, is a serious disorder that has killed many in Nepal. It usually occurs after a week or more at high altitudes and begins with mild symptoms that progress to the serious ones. Typically the heart and lung symptoms are not prominent. Characteristic features are a severe headache (usually but not always present), lack of coordination (tandem walking test already described is abnormal—this is the most reliable sign) progressing to severe lassitude, and total apathy, leading to coma and death. Do not leave such a person alone, assuming that he is tired. A good night's sleep is not the answer; you may find a corpse in the morning. Descend. If you have an altitude chamber, use it. Give acetazolamide and dexamethasone, 4 mg every six hours for the latter as well as oxygen. Do not consider reascending after the symptoms of HACE have resolved.

HARH, or bleeding in the retina of the eye, is more common at extreme altitudes. But it does happen to trekkers occasionally and usually is symptomless unless the vision clouds somewhat or the bleeding is near the macula (center of visual acuity) in the eye. Double vision or noticeable blind spots are sufficient cause for descent. Vision clears and bleeding resolves at lower altitudes.

For more details, see Stephen's book, *Altitude Illness: Prevention and Treatment*. This information may seem frightening to the trekker bound for the heights, but it has to be put in perspective. If you have previous high-altitude experience, you have some idea of what to expect. If you have not been to high altitudes, don't be scared away from enjoying the mountains of Nepal. Ascend at a rate appropriate for the entire party—that is, at the rate appropriate for the individual having the greatest difficulty. Know the symptoms of altitude illness and what to do about them. If descent becomes necessary for some members of the party, make sure they are not sent down alone but are cared for by responsible, informed people. Don't always assume that your employees understand altitude illness. A PDF file in Nepali that you can download for their use can be found at www.medex.org.uk. Give yourself permission to not be the high-altitude wanderer, summiter, and pass crosser, should you be one of the many who cannot tolerate high altitudes well. This does not reflect a lack of character or endurance.

Hypothermia

This condition, often termed "exposure," occurs when loss of body heat exceeds gain and body core temperature drops. The body gains heat by digesting food and consuming hot drinks, from an external source such as a fire, and through muscular activity, including shivering. Loss occurs through respiration, evaporation, conduction, radiation, and convection. The combination of physical exhaustion and wet or insufficient clothing, compounded by failure to eat, dehydration, and high altitude, can result in death in a very short time, even at temperatures above freezing. People venturing into cold, high regions must take adequate steps to prevent hypothermia and should be able to recognize its signs and symptoms. Be especially alert to its development in lowland porters, who may be inadequately clothed and prepared for cold. Obese people are better able to insulate their bodies against the cold than are slim individuals—a rare advantage to being overweight. Small adults and children are especially prone to hypothermia. Wear a well-insulated hat.

Initial symptoms of hypothermia are marked shivering and pale skin, followed by poor coordination, apathy, confusion, and fatigue. As temperature drops further, speech becomes slurred, and the victim has difficulty walking. Even at this stage, an external source of heat is needed to warm the victim. Further lowering of core temperature results in cessation of shivering, irrationality, memory lapses, and hallucinations. This is followed by increased muscular rigidity, stupor, and decreased pulse and respiration. Unconsciousness and death soon follow. Symptoms can appear in a few hours after the onset of bad weather, and the situation can quickly progress to the point where the victim cannot perform the functions necessary for survival. Hypothermia is easily diagnosed with a low-reading thermometer. Mild degrees of hypothermia are present when body temperature is below 94°F (34.4°C), most accurately measured rectally. But suspect it clinically whether you have a low-reading thermometer or not.

Treat by stopping further heat loss, and for mild hypothermia, applying heat to the person's body core. Remove all wet clothing and put the person in a sleeping bag together with a source of heat—a warm naked person, rocks warmed by a fire and wrapped in cloth, or similarly wrapped hot water bottles. Place these under the armpits, and around the groin. Cover the person's head. Feed the victim warm drinks and sweets if he is conscious and able to swallow. Seek shelter. For body temperatures below 88°F (31.1°C), evacuate gently and quickly.

Frostbite

Frostbite (frozen body tissues), most commonly affecting fingers, toes, ears, noses, and chins, is rare in trekkers because the temperature extremes necessary are not usually encountered for long periods of time. But it happens, especially on high passes and trekking summits. Inadequate boots, skimpy gloves or mitts, and lack of experience are common causes. So-called easy passes can become frostbite zones after unseasonable snowfall, especially if not wearing adequate footwear. Beware of someone developing frostbite or hypothermia if your party is moving slowly over easy ground due to fatigue or is being delayed by routefinding difficulties or by having to help another member. Prevent cold injuries with adequate clothing and equipment, by eating enough food, and by avoiding dehydration and exhaustion. Extreme altitudes increase the potential for the problem, as does a previous history of frostbite. Frostbite can occur at relatively warm temperatures if there is significant wind, if the victims are inadequately equipped, and if they suffer from dehydration and exhaustion, or if clothing or boots are too tight, restricting blood flow. Affected tissues initially become cold, painful, and pale. Then they become numb, which results in the trekker forgetting about the problem, with serious consequences.

An earlier, reversible stage is **frostnip**. At this stage, the affected area becomes numb and white. Treatment consists of rapid rewarming by placing the part against a warm area of the body—an armpit, a hand, the stomach of the victim, or another trekker. Once normal color, feeling, and consistency are restored, the part can be used, providing it is not allowed to freeze again. A part of the body that has suffered frostnip before is more likely to get frostnip again. It may be difficult, especially when at altitude and dehydrated, to decide whether the injury is reversible or not. If you have a prostaglandin inhibitor pain medicine, preferably ibuprofen (aspirin and meclofenamate are others, but acetaminophen is not), take it.

Once an extremity has become frozen, it is best to keep it that way until help and safety can be reached. A frozen foot can be walked on to leave the cold area. Do not rub snow on the frozen area, or rub it with your hands. Once feasible, the treatment is rapid rewarming in a water bath between 100°F (37.7°C) and 108°F (42.2°C). Thereafter, the victim requires expert care in a hospital and is not able to walk until treatment is completed. Trekkers are more apt to discover a dark toe or finger after an exhausting day crossing a high snowy pass. At this point, the part has already been rewarmed. Treatment consists of adequate hydration, elevation of the affected part, prevention of further injury, and evacuation.

Heat Injury

Not only does travel in Nepal pose problems in coping with extreme cold, but also in dealing with extreme heat. Both can happen during the same trek, if it is from the hot lowlands to the cold, windy, snowy heights. Heat produced by the body is eliminated mostly by the skin through evaporation of perspiration. Acclimatization to heat takes around a week. When the body becomes able to sweat more without losing more salt, the ability to exercise in a hot environment improves. Maladaptation to heat can be prevented by an adequate intake of fluids and salt. Thirst mechanisms and salt hunger may not work adequately, so extra salt and water should be consumed in hot weather. In humid regions where evaporation is limited, it is a good idea to rest in the shade during the hottest part of the day. Cover the head and wear light-colored clothing to reflect sunlight. Soaking bandannas, hats, and shirts in water to cool the body in hot valleys is helpful, too.

Suspect **heat exhaustion** when someone has a rapid heart rate, faintness, and perhaps nausea, vomiting, and headache. Blood supply to the brain and other organs is inadequate because of shunting of blood to the skin. The patient's temperature is normal. If the victim is treated with shaded rest, fluids, and salt, recovery is usually rapid.

Heat stroke is a failure of the swelling and heat regulation process, usually because of fatigue of the sweat glands themselves. The victim rapidly becomes aware of extreme heat and then becomes confused, uncoordinated (ataxic), delirious, or unconscious. Characteristically, the body temperature is very high, 105°F (40.6°C) or higher. The skin feels hot and dry and does not sweat. Treat immediately by undressing the victim and cooling him or her by any means available. Immersion in cool water, soaking with wet cloths, and fanning are all appropriate. Massage the limbs vigorously to promote circulation. Continue cooling the body until the temperature is below 102°F (38.9°C). Start cooling again if the temperature rises. The victim should be watched closely for the next few days, and strenuous exercise should be avoided.

Burns, Sunburns, and Snow Blindness

The severity of a **burn** depends on its area, its depth, and its location on the body. So-called first-degree burns are superficial—they do not kill any of the tissue but produce redness of the skin. Mild sunburn is a typical example. Second-degree burns kill only the upper portion of the skin and cause blisters. In third-degree burns, damage extends through the skin into the underlying tissues. First-degree burns require no treatment, but for the others, wash the area gently with iced or cold water, and cover with a sterile dressing. Antibiotic ointments may relieve pain and make it easier to remove the dressing.

Burns that cover more than 20 percent of the body surface are usually accompanied by shock, a serious threat to life. Attempt to get the injured person to drink plenty of fluids; the oral rehydration solution made from Jeevan Jal is best. Aspirin and codeine, two tablets of each every six hours, may help relieve pain. Evacuate the person to medical help.

Sunburn is common among trekkers visiting high altitudes, where there is less atmosphere to filter solar radiation, and where snow and ice can reflect additional radiation.

You may not want to take such hero poses with Ama Dablam in the background.
(Photo by Pat Morrow)

Effective sun screening agents are listed as contents of the medical kit, and ayurvedic sun creams are widely available in Kathmandu. Be sure to protect the lips and under the chin and nose when on snow. Treat sunburn as any other burn.

Eye protection in the form of dark, UV-protective glasses is needed on snow and generally at high altitudes. In an emergency, lenses made of cardboard with thin slits to see through can be used, or a coarse cloth with small slits cut out can be tied over the eyes. Hair combed over the face, a method favored by Sherpas and Tibetans, is effective. Otherwise, snow blindness, a painful temporary condition, can result. The condition gets better in a day or two. Darkness and cold compresses over the eyes may help relieve pain. A poultice of tea leaves can provide some relief. Patch the eyes tightly so the lids don't move. Use antibiotic eye drops if you have them. For severe pain, take aspirin and codeine, two tablets each, every six hours.

ACROPHOBIA, VERTIGO, BRIDGE, AND TRAIL PHOBIAS

These problems are common among those who trek in Nepal without previous mountain climbing and hiking experience. People with these fears usually choose environments and activities not requiring adjusting to exposure, and individuals living in the flatlands may be unaware that they have this problem. The trails of Nepal may present challenges not faced before.

Nevertheless, if you've come to Nepal and find yourself on a wobbly bamboo bridge, or on a ledge with a few hundred feet of drop-off, a few principles help. Obviously, don't look at the big drop-off, be it the river a hundred feet below your feet or the bottom of the cliff you are traversing. Instead, focus on a stationary object, say the end of the bridge. If you feel dizzy on a particularly exposed part of the trail, stopping and staring at a fixed object, even your thumb, can help. Don't hesitate for what seems an interminable time before you venture forth. As you walk the difficult portion, say a few verses of a familiar tune, or a prayer or mantra, to give you an aural focus, and do not let your eyes wander. Breathe slowly, using your diaphragm—that is, pushing your stomach out as you inhale in. Don't stop in the middle and wonder what you are doing, or whether you will make it. For some, holding another's hand helps. A positive mental attitude is best. Just believing you can do it will result in it being so.

If you know that there will be a particularly difficult stretch coming up, plan to do it when you are not exhausted. Vertigo is worse when you are tired. Wear shoes that have good traction. This will give sufferers some added confidence. Find companions who are sympathetic. Nepali guides, once they understand the magnitude of the problem, will likely be more helpful than macho-minded Westerners.

PSYCHOLOGICAL AND EMOTIONAL PROBLEMS

Trekkers and travelers to exotic countries can have emotional problems adjusting. Stephen can well remember squatting in the bush with diarrhea on the first few days of his first trek in Nepal on his first journey away from North America and pondering whether this was his reaction to being separated from his familiar environment and whether trekking was all it was cracked up to be.

While trekking, you may have to deal with more physical closeness with others than you are used to, being in a small tent with someone you only just met in Kathmandu two days ago or not having accustomed privacy in toilet or other personal matters. Some married couples at home have developed ways of living apart, but on a trek are suddenly cast together with no easy escape, and this can lead to serious difficulties. You may be an individualistic leader, who now has to cooperate in a group and agree to what the trip leader or guide decides. Giving up such control can be very difficult.

You may be separated from friends and familiar places, realizing that you are essentially alone a week or two from "civilization" and 15,000 miles (24,000 km) from home. Unexpected environmental stimuli—including new sounds such as the incessant barking of dogs, the flap of the tent in a wind, exotic smells including the ever-present stench of filth in some places, or the sights of abject poverty set in cultural wealth—all may be difficult to cope with and can overwhelm some individuals.

Prior expectations of one's performance in a new environment and a feeling of lack of control in unfamiliar surroundings must be dealt with. Accomplishing simple tasks such as finding a place to stay for the night or a place to eat can be very trying. The heroes of screen and stage are not flustered by unexpected obstacles. Most of us try to emulate this in our lives. Yet here on a trek, you get ill despite all your efforts at being careful, you are dirty and unkempt, unable to wash in the cold, you can't eat the food, you are too tired to enjoy the view, or bad weather has prevented you from seeing Mount Marvelous or has delayed your flight for four days. You want to cry, yet think you should appear in control.

As trek leader, you may have to deal with your reactions to the client's moods. Other travel-related factors can compound the difficulties (disturbed sleep, jet lag, fatigue, altitude, alcohol or other recreational drugs, prescription medicines, and the stresses of the life left on hold back home). Studies demonstrate an increase in seeking help for psychiatric problems among visitors to Nepal.

Preventing emotional stress is the key to not getting "burned out." Steps depend on the individual and the situation. Deciding on a reasonable goal for the trek before starting out can be helpful in limiting expectations. Make the journey itself a goal; it is the adventure itself, not standing on some patch of ground you have read about. If you have a spiritual agenda, it may be necessary to keep it in proportion to the realities of the trek. For some who never undertake new paths alone, emotional survival may be ensuring that you are with friends, with whom you can share the experience. For those who are fastidious in their personal habits, a daily bath, shaving every day, keeping hair combed, and putting on a clean change of clothes every few days may be necessary. Use ear plugs or short-acting sleeping pills (when not at altitude) to deal with sleep-disturbing noises at night. Sometimes the daily routine of constant walking, eating, and sleeping is too much. Take rest days every now and then and pamper yourself. Some trekkers may have to be flexible enough to accept that the schedule they have set is too ambitious or that difficulties in adjusting to altitude will prevent them from getting to that famous viewpoint or crossing that pass. Some people should not go trekking. Those with significant psychiatric diagnoses, such as bipolar disorder, might be better off on a private trek than a group trek.

Panic attacks are becoming more commonly recognized among travelers, perhaps because of increased awareness among clinicians or because less experienced adventurers are taking to the trails. Symptoms of these can be chest pains, palpitations, difficulty breathing, trembling, sensation of choking, nausea, tingling, weakness, dizziness, cramps, or a sense of impending doom. They peak in intensity in ten minutes and typically subside spontaneously in half an hour. Those afflicted feel they are dying. Often there is no apparent cause; everything had been going well up to that point. Others may not have been aware of the stresses they were under. There may be a history of these attacks occurring back home. Make certain there is no physical disorder that is causing the symptoms, then reassure the sufferer, and provide support. Various medicines can help prevent these attacks. Sometimes an evacuation may be necessary.

What if you are getting quite **depressed** or close to a "nervous breakdown"? First do some familiar, relaxing, comforting routines, such as bathing, shaving, washing your clothes, or putting on clean ones. If alone, find other trekkers to join. If carrying a heavy

RITUAL HEALING

Healing in Nepal is pluralistic; the afflicted try many remedies, including seeking a spirit medium. Western attention has focused on a variety of shamanic traditions in Nepal that are widely dispersed and highly developed, especially among the hill ethnic groups including the Thami in Ramechap and Dolakha Districts. Some, such as that of the Kham-Magar, are related to the classic Inner-Siberan legacy. Shamans are vehicles by which normal individuals communicate with divinities. Causes of illness are thought to be naturalistic, in that spirits for various reasons have conspired to cause sickness. The shaman drums and shakes rattles, enters into a trance, and can make spirit flights or become possessed. In the séance, the spirit speaks through him (usually), describing the reason for the sickness and what needs to be done. This community-approved practice can allow for the resolution of inner conflicts in the face of cultural norms. Shamans are often low-status individuals, who exemplify the ability to communicate with the spirit world early in life. Through training, they gain status and prestige, especially after an elaborate initiation ceremony where they demonstrate magical powers. Trekkers may encounter shamans in distinctive symbolic dress, drumming and performing healing rites, as well as those leading the dead to their proper dwelling places. ❖

load, hire a porter. If sick and weak, rest and eat better foods frequently during the day. If consuming marijuana and other mood-altering substances, stop them. If appalled by the conditions in Nepal, take comfort in the fact that you can leave if you choose. Ask yourself whether the local people are actually suffering or unhappy (or is it only your interpretation?). If your mood does not improve, head back to Kathmandu or Pokhara by plane, if possible. But be careful not to end up waiting a week for a plane when you could have walked in three days. If you have trouble adjusting to conditions in Nepal, don't go to India, which can be even more provocative and overwhelming.

If you are a trip doctor, and may have to deal with the sequelae of such problems, consider including an injectable anti-psychotic drug such as haloperidol in your kit. Stabilize a patient as quickly as possible and try to repatriate the individual accompanied by a reliable person. Many episodes occur in people without prior psychiatric history and may represent an acute situational psychosis or the first manifestations of further problems. Other victims may be those with a history of mental illness, some of whom have stopped their medicines or who are sliding into psychosis.

Few people end up having to curtail their treks in Nepal for these reasons. Rather, many will undergo a reverse "culture shock" upon returning home. Based on their experience in Nepal, they question the values of the environment in which they have grown up. In the end, trekking in Nepal is not for everyone. Don't despair if this includes you. There are many other superb activities elsewhere that await.

EMERGENCY CARE AND RESCUE FACILITIES

Nepal aims to have hospitals staffed by physicians to provide secondary health care in each of the seventy-five districts. Primary health care is provided by health posts staffed by paramedical personnel and community health volunteers scattered throughout each

district. The standard of care may not be that of your home country.

If an emergency occurs, try to enlist the help of Nepalis. If in a district center, contact the CDO (Chief District Officer), who will usually speak English. Otherwise, seek out elected officials. Schoolteachers may be especially helpful. If the problem is not life-threatening, but requires evacuation, you or your fellow trekkers may be able to assist the person out. For a seriously ill person, consider using a porter, a pony or a yak, or commercial air services. Amazing resources can be mustered in desperate circumstances.

The usual form of medical evacuation available to Nepalis
(Photo by Stephen Bezruchka)

If faced with a life-threatening emergency involving you or your staff in the hills, you should try to get word to Kathmandu to effect a rescue. Telephones, now rather widely available, are the best means of communication. If an air rescue is necessary, send a message to Kathmandu for a helicopter (see below). These days, there is widespread availability of helicopters.

HOSPITALS, AID POSTS, AND SOURCES OF HELP

The following provides an overview of Nepal's health care and rescue facilities, summarized by region.

Kathmandu

There are several choices for trekkers seeking health care services. Check with your embassy for advice. Many travelers use the CIWEC international clinic across from the British Embassy (tel. 01-4424111, fax 4412590, www.ciwec-clinic.com). The Nepal International Clinic (NIC), between Durbar Marg and Naxal (tel. 01-4434642, fax 4434713, www.nepalinternationalclinic.com), near the former palace, has Western-trained Nepali doctors. The Patan Hospital in Lagankhel (Patan) offers good care. There is the Tribhuvan University Teaching Hospital, in Maharajganj, close to the U.S. Embassy, which is affiliated with Nepal's first medical school. Private surgical clinics abound. The Himalayan Rescue Association has an information center in Thamel at the Sagarmatha Bazaar complex.

Annapurna

Pokhara has a regional government hospital, and an airport. Airfields are found in Jomosom, Hongde, and Balewa (south of Baglung, across the river from Kusma). There are district hospitals in Baglung, Besisahar, and Jomosom. An HRA Trekker's Aid Post at Manang is staffed by a doctor during much of the popular trekking season.

Solu–Khumbu and Rolwaling

There are government health facilities in Jiri, Namche Bazaar, Phaphlu, and Chaurikot. Private facilities are springing up; ask around. A hospital in Kunde is staffed by Western-trained physicians. There is an HRA Trekker's Aid Post, staffed by a doctor during most of the trekking season, at Pheriche and another similar rescue post set up by IPPG in Maccherma (with an outpost at Gokyo). In Namche Bazaar, there is a modern dental clinic.

Langtang, Gosainkund, and Helambu

There is a government hospital in Trishuli and Dhunche, and a private dispensary at a hotel in Kyangin Gomba with a Gamow Bag for acute altitude sickness.

Eastern Nepal

There are STOL airstrips at Tumlingtar, Lamidanda, Bhojpur, Chandragari, and Taplejung. There are government hospitals in Chainpur, Taplejung, Bhojpur, and Dhankuta.

Western Nepal

In addition to the facilities in Baglung and Beni, airstrips are found at Jumla, Jufal, and Chhaaujhari. There is a government hospital in Jumla.

COMMUNICATION

Public telephone access and mobile networks, run by private business, are rapidly changing the communication pattern in Nepal. Previously, emergency communication links were limited to various radio stations and telegraph links at police and army posts, national park check posts, and well-equipped aid stations. Telephone communication centers, operated by satellite or VHF relay, and solar or electricity powered, are cropping up in towns all over the country. Some have fax machines. You can call home from these places (expensive) and receive calls for a lesser charge. These phones along with mobile phones are becoming the most appropriate way to send an emergency message (information to include in your message is covered below). No comprehensive listing of communication centers can be given, as new ones are added frequently; you can ask, and many people will be able to direct you to the closest one. Like anything in developing nations, they may be broken when you try to use them.

The country telephone code is 977, with city area codes of 01 for Kathmandu and 061 for Pokhara (omit the zero if calling from outside these cities).

HELICOPTER RESCUE

The cost of a helicopter rescue is high—an hour of helicopter time costs over $1000 USD (according to HRA, average rescue flights total $2500 to $3000). This has to be borne by the party involved, unless rescue insurance has been taken out previously, which alpine clubs in your home country can sometimes provide and even some organizations in Kathmandu. Some trekkers might wish to obtain a comprehensive travel, accident, and rescue insurance policy before they leave home.

Register at your country's embassy in Kathmandu, in case they receive a rescue message. Approximately seventy-five people were helicopter-rescued for every hundred thousand trekking permits issued in the past. Helicopter rescues are more common now, in some part because more choppers are available and trekkers are more eager to avail themselves of this service.

If not previously set up, it may be possible to arrange rescue insurance in Kathmandu. The Himalayan Rescue Association (tel. 01-4440292, 4440293, hra@ mail.com.np, www.himalayanrescue.org) in Dhobichaur, Lazimpat (along the road to the north of the former palace), or the Nepal Mountaineering Association (tel. 01-4434525, www.nepalmountaineering.org) in Naxal, both in Kathmandu, can provide more information.

Emergency Messages

In organizing a rescue requiring a helicopter, it is important to provide the proper information and make sure it reaches the proper place. It is wise to send several messages to different organizations to ensure that at least one is delivered. Write them up beforehand, and take extra time to make sure they are comprehensible by nonnative English speakers. Addresses should be as specific as possible to speed delivery. The phone numbers of the agencies and rescue facilities should be rechecked once you reach Kathmandu. Phone numbers change all the time. There is no 911 emergency network as in much of the United States; however, you can try the police emergency numbers 100, 110, and 122. Rescue messages should be sent to one or more of these (redundancy helps ensure that one message will arrive) in order of preference:

- The embassy or consulate of the victim (for U.S., tel. 01-4007200, 01-4007266, 01-4007269, fax 01-400-7281, http://kathmandu.usembassy.gov or http://nepal.usembassy.gov; for Canada, tel. 01-4415193; for U.K., tel. 01-4410583; for Australia, tel. 01-4371678)

- The trekking agency that organized the trek, if applicable; (get the home phone number of the managing director before you leave Kathmandu)
- Helicopter services
- Nepalese Army (tel. 01-4246140, 01-4246932, 01-4241731, fax 977-1-4269624)
- Asian Airlines (tel. 01-4410086, 01-4423273, fax 01-423315, 01-411878)
- Air Dynasty Heli Services (tel. 01-4497418, 01-4497464)
- Cosmic Air (tel. 01-427150, 01-4467629, 01-416881, 01-427358, fax 01-427084)
- Gorkha Airlines (tel. 01-4435122, 01-4424012, fax 01-471136)
- Karnali Air (tel. 01-4473141, 01-4493302)
- Manang Air (tel. 01-4496253)

The message should contain the following information:

- **Degree of urgency.** "**Most Immediate**" means death is likely within twenty-four hours. "**As Soon as Possible**" is used for all other cases in which helicopter rescue is justified.
- **The location**, including whether the victim will remain in one place or be moved down along a particular route. Give the altitude of the pickup place. Generally, 17,000 feet (5000 m) is the limit for helicopter pickups. Describe the route of evacuation, if you will be moving the victim. Describe the pickup point in relation to other nameable features, and if you can, give the town, ward number, village development committee (*gAU bikaas sammitti*), and district.
- **The name, age, sex, and nationality of the victim**, passport, visa, and trekking permit numbers, national park, conservation area or TIMS number, trekking agency if any, and information as to other destinations to which the same message will be sent (embassy, trekking agency, airline, and so on).
- **Medical information**, including the type of sickness or injury, and whether oxygen or stretcher immobilization (as for back injuries) is needed.
- **Whether a doctor is at the scene**, and whether one might be required from Kathmandu. It may be difficult to send a physician along, and usually is not necessary, since the evacuation will bring the victim to medical attention.
- **The name, nationality, age, and sex of all people to be evacuated**.
- **The sender's name and organization**, along with information on the method and source of payment for the rescue. Include any local contacts and phone numbers, especially where you are calling from. Generally, airlines will not fly rescues without written assurance of payment, so include this in the message. This can sometimes be provided by the embassy of the victim. A credit card number may sometimes be accepted for payment.

When sending a message, you will not always be able to verify that it has been actually transmitted unless you can phone when there is a better chance to judge reception.

Signaling and Evacuation

A rescue can take several days, especially if a runner has to be sent with the message, to a site for transmission, or if there is flight trouble or bad weather. If notification to a helicopter company is received after 12 noon, there may be little chance of a flight that day. It is wise to move the person along the route, waiting each day until 10AM to start. In each sleeping place, a large, smoky fire should be built each morning, and a landing site cleared and marked with a large X, preferably using orange garments or a colorful sleeping bag or tent. Improvising a secure, colorful wind sock would be helpful. If you have a mirror to signal with, use it. If you are directing a helicopter to land, stand at the end of the "pad" with your back to the wind, and wear brightly colored clothing so that you are easily seen.

Once the helicopter is preparing to land, remove the signal garment or sleeping bag and any other material that may be blown around by the rotor down-draft while the helicopter is approaching or leaving. Do not signal a helicopter unless you can direct it to the victim. Locating the stricken party from the air can be quite difficult, and point-less waving has resulted in dangerous landings, increased costs, and delay in evacuating severely ill patients. Approach and leave the helicopter in a crouched position, always in view of the pilot and never toward the rear of the helicopter, and only after the pilot has signaled you to move. You will rarely have a flat landing site, and on uneven ground, always approach and leave on the downhill side. When boarding, carry any material horizontally, below waist level, and never on your shoulder. Secure any loose articles of clothing before you approach.

IN THE EVENT OF A DEATH

In the tragic event that a porter or trekker dies, be aware that airlines will not trans-port corpses on their scheduled flights. You might be able to charter a helicopter or carry the body out, though you may find it very difficult to hire porters to do this.

It is best to cremate the body and have this witnessed, preferably by a local police-man, village headman, or person not associated with your trek. Record the victim's name and address, as well as those of any witnesses, remove all valuables, and keep the ashes for relatives. If Westerners die, realize that even in Kathmandu there are no public cem-eteries, or mortuaries, or even a morgue. If you do get the body to Kathmandu, further difficulties in transporting it to your homeland ensue. The body must be embalmed. Enquire at the Department of Pathology, in the Teaching Hospital in Kathmandu or at other medical schools in the valley.

The risk of death while trekking in Nepal was estimated at fifteen deaths per hun-dred thousand trekking permits issued in the past. More recent studies have shown an increase in altitude illness deaths, with proportionately greater increases in the Everest and Langtang areas. There are increases in deaths of older people, likely because the age spectrum of trekkers has grayed and more trekkers have ongoing chronic conditions. Common causes of death are injuries, usually from falling off the trail, altitude illness, and the afflictions of older age.

Opposite: Near Manaslu (Photo by Pat Morrow)

section two

THE ROUTES

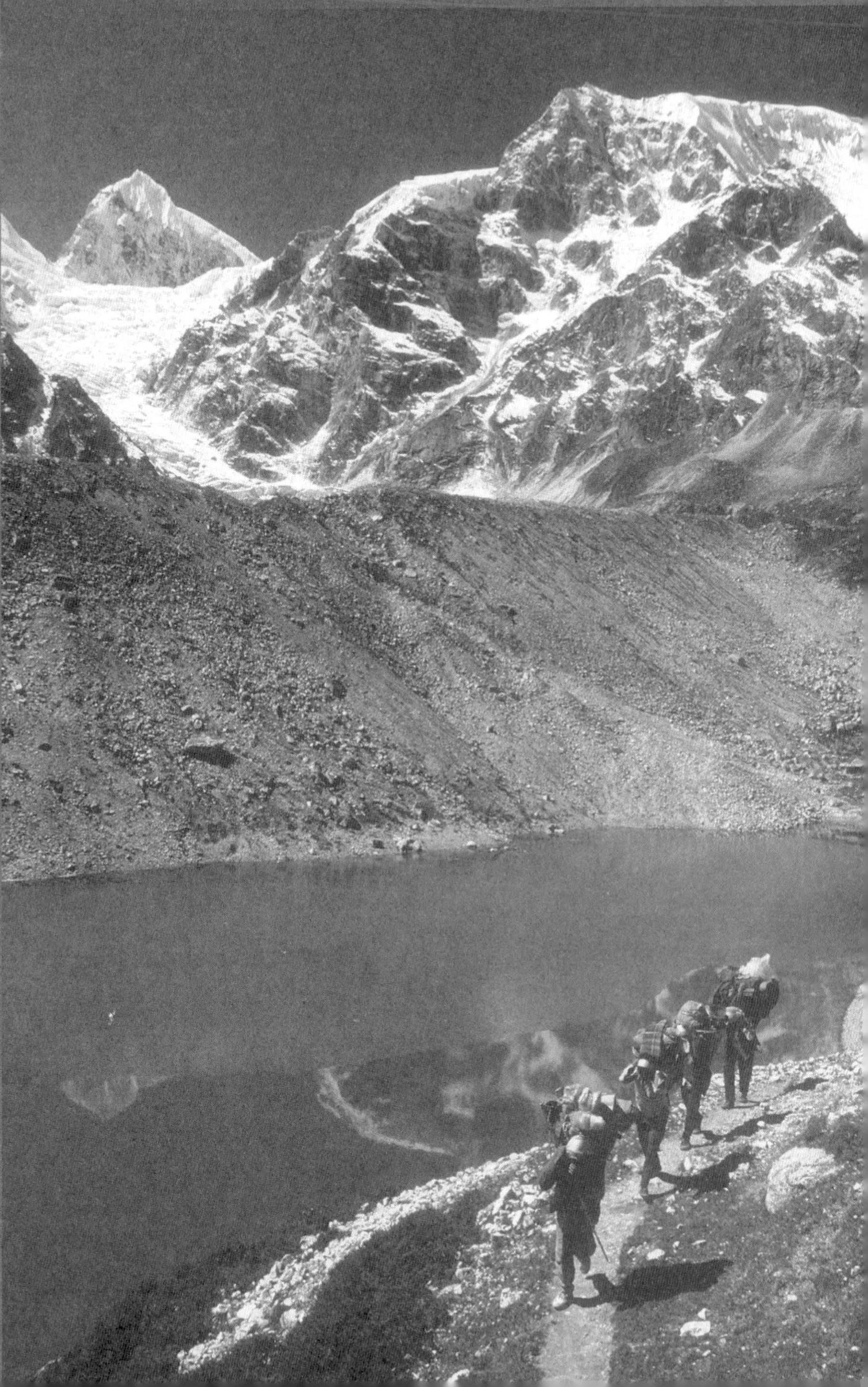

FOLLOWING THE ROUTE DESCRIPTIONS

INTERPRETING THE TREK INFORMATION

The following are guidelines and general information regarding life on the trail. These suggestions will help in interpreting route descriptions and formulating a daily schedule as well as providing hints for making the journey more enjoyable.

WALKING TIMES BETWEEN POINTS

In the route descriptions that follow, the times listed between points represent the actual time spent walking, based on our own experience. These times *do not* include any rests; we adhered to actual walking time using a chronograph. Over most of the trails we carried a moderately heavy pack. Like everyone else along the trekking routes, we rested, photographed, talked with the people, and so forth between trail segments, therefore our overall trekking times were longer.

We have included a few trail descriptions where time duration between waypoints is not supplied. In such cases, we did not survey these specific segments and are unable to provide time measurements, while the route information is still included for reference.

Planning Your Itinerary

The times are fairly uniform in that, if a person takes ninety minutes to cover a stretch listed as taking an hour, then it will take that same person one-and-a-half times as long as the time listed to cover any other stretch—providing the same pace is maintained. Some people have commented that they find the times too long, but most find them too short. The latter is usually because they do not add rest times to the estimates. The times and key waypoints (settlements bracketing a section of the route) are boldfaced in route descriptions to make it easier to total the time for a particular stretch. Times not in boldface are noted for additional information. These estimations help trekkers know what to expect and thus find the way more easily, and they make it easier to plan where to eat and to spend nights. These times are not meant as a challenge but, rather, as a guide. Trail conditions change for a variety of reasons, including a rise or fall in popularity (see "The Trails" below). As trails evolve and improve through use, trekking times change, usually decreasing.

At the end of each description of a major route, we have added a graph of cumulative walking times (excluding stops and rests) and altitudes from the start of the trek to significant points along the way. These do not include trail variations or side trips. Each graph tries to depict the high and low points along a trek, to give you an estimate of the effort required. Note that the abscissa (horizontal scale) is *not* horizontal distance (miles or kilometers) but, rather, hours of walking per the text. Until someone runs an odometer over the trails in Nepal (it will not be us), you will have to judge for yourself how far the trails go. By reading off altitudes and duration between points, you can estimate your night stopping points.

Treks are not set out on a day-to-day basis. Instead of adhering to a daily schedule, each party can adjust for long rests or interesting diversions. Those committed to

Gauri Shankar was once considered the world's highest mountain because it is so visible from the plains of India. (Photo by Pat Morrow)

straight traveling can count on covering about five to seven hours of the given route times in a day, allowing a two-hour food stop. In winter there is less daylight than at other times, but regardless of season, most people stop for the night before 5 PM and depart mid- to late morning, after breakfast. If you have many porters, expect to cover shorter distances. For those wishing a day-to-day itinerary, start with about five hours of trekking time per day, and use the trail profiles and route descriptions to select destinations. If necessary, you can adjust your itinerary as you progress.

For many trekking routes, the distance has traditionally been measured in number of camps (or days) necessary for large parties of trekkers accompanied by numerous porters to complete the route. Camp days make sense for large groups who need space for tents and allowance made for the porters to carry the loads the required distance. We do not follow this convention here, to allow trekkers to plan the days as they wish.

ASCENTS AND DESCENTS

Experienced trekkers find that often the first day on the trail seems fast. The next two or three days can be slow and painful. As the body strengthens and adjusts to the pace, the miles and hills seem to go by more effortlessly.

The altitudes listed in the descriptions are taken from several sources, including recent maps whose accuracy can be trusted and our own altimeter and GPS. The altimeter readings have not been corrected for temperature changes, but they are adequate to indicate the order of climbing or descending.

Ascent rates of 2000 feet (600 m) per hour are difficult to maintain for any length of time. Most trekkers find 1000 feet (300 m) per hour a reasonable rate if the trail is good and the climb easy. Similarly, a descent rate of 1500 feet (450 m) per hour is reasonable. Altitudes are usually converted from feet into meters and are not rounded off; they are only approximations at best and can be in error by a few hundred feet. Altitudes of most villages in the hills are difficult to interpret accurately because several hundred feet of elevation may separate the highest and lowest parts of a settlement.

Routes are described in one direction only. They can easily be followed in the opposite direction. The time for the trip in the reverse direction can be figured approximately if altitude to be gained or lost and the rate of ascent or descent is taken into consideration.

THE TRAILS

Directions in the trail descriptions are given with reference to the compass. In addition, right- and left-hand sides of rivers are indicated to avoid confusion. Right and left refer to the (true) right and (true) left banks when *facing downstream*. Sometimes they are abbreviated TR and TL, respectively, to designate true right and true left.

Often there are branches off the main trails that lead to houses. You'll quickly discover if you've taken one of these. If you follow large trekking groups, you may find direction arrows scratched in the ground or on rocks to help indicate the way. Nepalis do not do this for themselves.

Trail Conditions

Trekkers, even experienced backpackers, are sometimes surprised to find the trails more difficult and rugged than the ones they are used to back home. Trails in Nepal are maintained by local governments and other managing bodies, who are improving trails because of the increasing popularity of trekking. However, they don't have the machinery and resources to produce the quality of trail found in national parks and forests back home. Nor is the trail wear anything like what it is in Nepal, with countless animals and monsoon rain eroding the trails.

Improved trails may take different routes from those described here, and routes can shift in popularity for a variety of reasons. We have walked most of the trails described in this book several times. Notable changes range from improvements in some trails, to erosion and damage on others, to finding more villages and settlements catering to trekkers along the popular routes, to evading the roadbuilding and vehicle traffic in others. Landslides on steep valley-floor trails result in almost cyclical rerouting over a period of years to decades.

Seasonality

Travel is seasonal along trails in the high country where there are no settlements. Most Nepalis are there only during the pasturing times of the monsoon when few trekkers are afoot. Animal trails may be confused with human trails. Forest, fog, or whiteout may make finding the route difficult or impossible. Trekkers have become lost in such circumstances, and it is easy to remain lost for several days, especially if trying to bushwhack a return to an unfamiliar trail. If lost, backtrack to a point you know, rather than trying to push onward. It is prudent to travel with a guide in such country. Often a guide can be hired locally for a few days.

Trails vary considerably with the seasons. During and soon after the monsoon, when the rivers are still swollen, travelers take ridge trails rather than those following the valley floors. But in the dry season, November through May, many trails on ridges are abandoned in favor of more direct river routes. In addition, shortcuts across dry paddy fields are often favored over the well-worn trails. These shortcuts can be numerous and at times misleading, but they are still preferable in most cases. Other times, you may precariously balance on walls of irrigated terraces or end up sloshing on muddy trails. Appropriate trail etiquette is to let the uphill-going traveler have the right-of-way.

PLACES ALONG THE WAY

Along the popular trekking trails, it is likely that you will find many more hotels, tea shops, lodges, and so forth in places where we haven't reported them. Local people are responding to the increased demands of tourism. It is hard to know what to call a hotel, tea shop, inn, or lodge. We have tried to use the term *bhaTTi* to refer to a traditional Nepali inn, one used by local people, but as an area becomes popular with trekkers, these are often the first to cater to outsiders. Consider all the terms to be used interchangeably. Please note down any changes or new information and send it to us in care of the publisher.

Place Names

Names of towns and villages are taken from maps and other documents and our phonetic rendering of the names we hear. When possible, we spell the names according to the principles in Appendix B, so you may occasionally find that our spellings differ from those found on signboards, though we will also list some local English spellings.

In the route descriptions, the names of some settlements appear in boldface, as waypoints along the route in estimating walking times. They are usually large, well-known places whose names the trekker should use when asking the way. Food and accommodations are usually available in these places. This may help you plan your journey. No recommendations for where to stay are given. In addition to a wide variance in travelers' preferences, facilities change constantly, and there is no way we can evaluate them or describe them in Travlish, that evanescent dialect found in traditional guidebooks. Ask other trekkers about the latest finds, which, depending on your point of view, might be places to avoid. Stay in people's homes where you can, and discover an entirely different Nepal.

Place names in Nepal are not unique. There are many Bhote Kosis (rivers from Tibet), Benis (junctions of two rivers), Phedis (foot of hill), and Deoralis (passes). In addition, some villages may be called by two different names, but this should not cause much confusion in actual practice. Finally, as facilities that cater to trekkers are built in remote mountain regions, they may take on English names, such as Bamboo, albeit pronounced in an oft-confusing Nepali fashion.

The pronunciation and transliteration guide in Appendix B indicates the correct way to pronounce the place names. It is important to place the stress on the first syllable of most words—for instance, Kathmandu, Pokhara, and Tengboche. The meaning

Fresh yogurt is a seasonal delight. (Photo by Tokozile Robbins)

of capital letters occurring within words is explained in Appendix B. Place names and other proper nouns are capitalized in spite of the transliteration system. A correct spelling of Kathmandu in this transliteration system is *kaaThmaanDu,* but for the sake of convenience, the common spelling is used.

Wayside Structures

A *chautaaraa,* referred to in the trail descriptions, is a rectangular rock platform with a ledge for resting your load. Sometimes a *pipal* and a banyan tree, both of the fig family, are planted side by side in the center. In the east, you are as likely to find wooden benches. You can look forward to these welcome structures, found on many of the well-traveled routes. A *chorten* is a Buddhist religious structure, often cubical or conical, with carved tablets. The term *kani* or entrance *chorten* refers to a covered gateway or arch decorated with Buddhist motifs. A *stupa* is a large *chorten. Mani* walls are rectangular and made of stone tablets carved with *mantras* and prayers.

ON THE TRAIL

HINTS FOR WALKING

Everyone should learn the rest step for ascents. As you advance your uphill foot, plant it and then, before transferring your weight to it, consciously rest briefly with your weight on your downhill foot. Do this continuously, and the steep hills come easier. Try to coordinate your breathing with your steps. That is, breathe in on raising the left foot and out on raising the right. Or breathe in on raising each foot, if the ascent is very steep. This will also make the ascent less tiring. It is better to take several short steps up, rather than one long one, just as for going down.

On descents, tighten your shoe- or bootlaces so that your toes are not crammed into the front of the shoe with each step. Take short steps, bending your knees and hips to absorb the energy of the descent. Be limber. Watch the porters to see how they walk. People can easily get knee problems by not descending with bent knees. Knee injuries (see Chapter 5) take a long time to heal and can be quite disabling if they occur many days away from the road.

Staying Comfortable

Arrange your clothing in easy-to-doff and -don layers so you can adjust to temperature changes due to the environment and your own heat production. It is pointless to sweat profusely, only to get freezing cold as a blast of icy wind hits your wet body. Anticipate your increased heat production going uphill, and doff clothing soon into the climb, yet put some on just before a rest stop, so you don't chill. Garments with underarm zippers or vents allow removal of the arms from the sleeves to adjust to different temperatures easily.

At rest stops, drink fluids and elevate your feet. Take off your shoes, remove the insoles, and let the sweat dry from your feet, socks, insoles, and shoes. However, be aware that feet, as the lowest part of the body, are considered by Nepalis to be impure. Do not point your feet at any Nepali, and be considerate about where you rest them.

Trail Hazards and Mindfulness

During a walk of many weeks in such spectacular country, it is easy to let your mind wander from the task at hand, to daydream or gaze at people, mountains, or scenes. You must *always* pay attention to the trail in front of you and where you put your feet. This may sound obvious, but too many careless trekkers have had serious accidents or falls, and some have even lost their lives. As the late veteran trekker Hugh Swift stated, "Look when you look, walk when you walk."

If traveling with children, do not allow them to roll rocks off trails to see how far they go. This is an important matter not just of trail etiquette but safety—almost always there will be people, animals, and villages downhill.

When passing animals on the trail, keep to the uphill side, where the fall is much shorter should you be nudged by a yak or buffalo. Drivers of yak trains want you to pass on the downhill side of yaks. They feel the yaks are spooked less by this. However, stay on the uphill side unless the downhill side is perfectly safe. In the mountainous regions, you may be threatened by an ornery yak. If a yak makes an aggressive move, stand your ground, raise your hand or stick as to feign a blow, and shout.

Loud, threatening dogs are sometimes met along the trail. They rarely attack, but, just to be sure, carry a long stick and pass them assertively—or, if they are a safe distance away, feign as if to pick up a rock, which usually drives them a distance away to leave more room to pass. Often you meet large Tibetan mastiffs, but they are usually chained, except possibly at night and near herders' camps. If you suspect that there might be an unchained mastiff about, call and get the attention of people at the camps and ask them to chain the dog. Do not approach chained dogs.

INTERACTIONS ALONG THE TRAIL

During the day, especially along less trekker-frequented trails, you may pass many Nepalis who greet you and ask where you are coming from and where you are going. The accepted form of greeting or taking leave of a person is to place the palms of your hands together in front of your face as if to pray and say *namaste* or *namaskaar*. The latter is more respectful and formal. Both have the connotation of "I salute the god within you." Children will often badger you with endless such greetings. Always use the less formal greeting with children, and don't overdo it. To set yourself apart, use *namaste* followed by an appropriate kinship term such as *didi* (elder sister) or *bahini* (younger sister), *daaju/daai* (elder brother), or *bhaai* (younger brother).

Asking the Way

During the day's walk, you may pass through several villages and farming areas, cross major rivers, climb to the crest of one or more ridges, and descend down into the valleys again. When trekking without a guide, it is necessary to frequently ask the name of the current village and the way to the next village. Except along the most popular trekker routes, there are few trail signs in Nepal, and finding the route is a matter of asking the way as the Nepalis do. Nepali people traveling in unknown areas are constantly asking the way and exchanging news.

Often you may be confused by the answers Nepalis give to your questions about trails or times. If so, repeat the question or phrase it differently until you are satisfied with the response. The problem may be your pronunciation (retroflex D or T consonants can be particularly challenging). Ask the next person on the trail, too. It's all part of the fun of trekking and finding your way in Nepal. Along the more popular routes local people make a commotion when they think you are on the wrong trail. This can create confusion when you deliberately wish to take a side trip. When asking the way, keep in mind both the next town's name as well as a larger, well-known town farther along. Often the names of small hamlets may not be known, but nearly everyone knows the names of big settlements, even though they may be a few days' walk away. Keep in mind that because of the lack of standardized spelling, names on many maps may lead to improper pronunciation.

Nepalis are eager to be hospitable and to please visitors and, in their enthusiasm to do so, often give incorrect yet positive answers to questions. For example, a Nepali might say that a particular destination you ask about is close when it is actually a long way off. Or he might say that the trail you are on goes to the place you are asking for, rather than risk upsetting you by telling you the truth. And people who don't understand your questions sometimes answer nevertheless. Learning to get around these problems is all part of the experience. It isn't insurmountable or fraught with hazard.

Even if you ask the way, there are times when you might get lost, especially along the trails less traveled. If this happens, it is preferable to backtrack to a place that you know rather than forge ahead. If faced with an unknown trail junction, refer to the general route description, and apply it to the topography in your situation to arrive at a decision. Go off and see if the trail seems to be going where you expect.

Dealing with Officials

Register at police posts along the way, should you need to be traced in an emergency. Getting a small group processed at a police check post may take up to thirty minutes, and check posts along the popular trails have become much more efficient. The official will usually make a note in your permit. Do not produce your passport or photocopy of it unless necessary, or there may be further delays. If you are carrying binoculars, keep them discreetly out of sight, or the officials may suspect you have motives other than bird-watching. The same discretion is advised for other belongings. Be patient and courteous in dealing with officials; bureaucracy can be similar and yet quite different than back at home.

ENJOY YOUR TREK

Don't always be in a hurry, eager to cover as much ground as possible. Sometimes, stop at noon and watch village life or explore the surroundings. Consider spending an entire day in some place that is *not* the highest, the most spectacular, the most beautiful, and just let things happen.

Many trekkers have found their greatest enjoyment from finding new trails little used by foreigners. After you get the hang of it, don't be afraid to venture forth on undescribed terrain, especially if you are trekking independently. Encouraging you to explore on your own, without route descriptions at hand, may be the best advice we can provide to find the heart of Nepal.

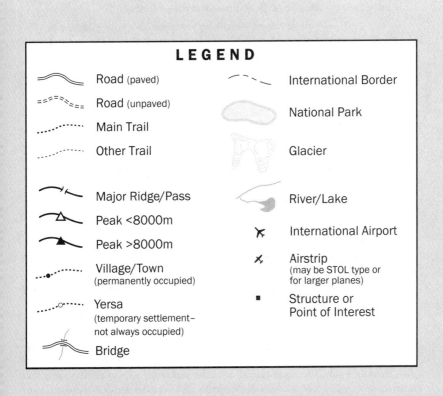

L E G E N D

Road (paved)

Road (unpaved)

Main Trail

Other Trail

Major Ridge/Pass

Peak <8000m

Peak >8000m

Village/Town
(permanently occupied)

Yersa
(temporary settlement–
not always occupied)

Bridge

International Border

National Park

Glacier

River/Lake

International Airport

Airstrip
(may be STOL type or
for larger planes)

Structure or
Point of Interest

6

THE ANNAPURNA REGION

If there be a Paradise on earth, it is now, it is now, it is now!
    —Wilfred Noyce, describing the area above NagDAADa in
        Climbing the Fish's Tail (Machhapuchhre)

Scenic Pokhara is the usual starting point for a visit to the Annapurna Conservation Area Project (ACAP). A circuit of the Annapurna massif combines superlative mountain scenery with incredible ethnic and cultural diversity and traverses through very different ecological life zones. Despite encroachment by motor roads, this classic trek is among the world's best and receives the most visitors of Nepal's trekking areas, over 75,000 in 2009.

The government decided in 2005 to construct roads to both Jomosom and Manang, headquarters of their respective districts. The Annapurna Circuit was formerly over 135 miles (215 km) long, and the roads, when completed, could potentially reduce the Annapurna Circuit to around 19 miles (30 km), although variations abound and will be covered below. The road to Jomosom is already complete, barring seasonal monsoon washouts, while construction work remains on the Manang side. (An unpaved road from the Tibet Autonomous Region has also been constructed into Upper Mustang and will soon link to Jomosom as well.)

Ostensibly, the road construction was to alleviate poverty by facilitating development. However, politics played a role, and the construction has been controversial among Nepalis and foreign visitors. ACAP is under a lot of change because of these new roads, and nobody knows how it will settle out. Alternate routes are being explored away from the roads. There is genuine fear on the part of some lodge owners along the main routes of losing their livelihood. New paths have yet to be decided or prepared for tourist arrivals. Even still, it is possible to trek the circuit while avoiding the current vehicular traffic for much of the way, as will be outlined below. Often where there is a road, there are two options to follow: (1) more adventurous routes where you might have to arrange your own lodging and food in homes, or (2) the well-trodden, often jeepable routes. If you get off the main routes, be prepared for more of an adventure and to take it how it comes; be prepared for a lack of facilities and comforts, and to ask for the generosity of the local people if caught short in a village without a lodge or restaurant.

Traditionally, the Annapurna Circuit is completed in a counterclockwise direction. That is, most people start at Besisahar and follow the Marsyangdi valley to Manang before crossing to the high Thorung La over to Muktinath and the Thak Khola/Kali Gandaki valley.

The Annapurnas viewed from Ghorepani (Photo by Tokozile Robbins)

The circuit route and facilities make the counterclockwise direction more feasible for crossing the Thorung La, as the only lodges between Muktinath and the pass (clockwise) are at Chaharu (also known as Phedi) at 13,690 feet (4172 m), whereas there are lodges up to 15,995 feet (4875 m), over 2300 feet (700 m) higher, on the Manang side and seasonal tea shops beyond. Trekkers who do not have the inclination or time to

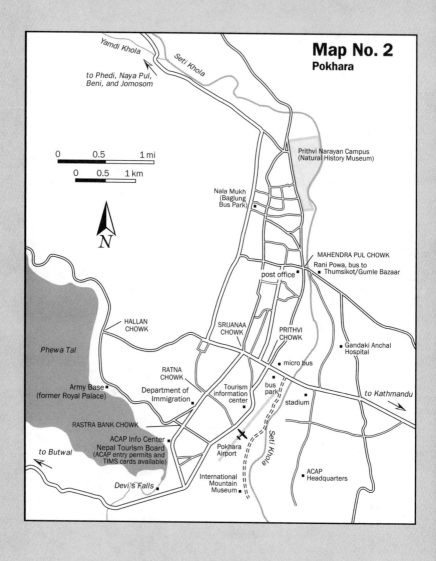

Map No. 2
Pokhara

Yamdi Khola

Seti Khola

to Phedi, Naya Pul,
Beni, and Jomosom

0   0.5   1 mi

0   0.5   1 km

N

Prithvi Narayan Campus
(Natural History Museum)

Nala Mukh
(Baglung
Bus Park)

MAHENDRA PUL CHOWK
Rani Powa, bus to
Thumsikot/Gumle Bazaar

post office

HALLAN
CHOWK

SRIJANAA
CHOWK

PRITHVI
CHOWK

Phewa Tal

Gandaki Anchal
Hospital

micro bus

RATNA
CHOWK

Army Base
(former Royal Palace)

Department of
Immigration

Tourism
information
center

bus
park

to Kathmandu

stadium

RASTRA BANK CHOWK

ACAP Info Center
Nepal Tourism Board
(ACAP entry permits and
TIMS cards available)

to Butwal

Pokhara
Airport

Seti Khola

ACAP
Headquarters

Devi's Falls

International
Mountain
Museum

complete the whole circuit and cross Thorung La may opt for visiting one or the other of the major river valleys of the circuit, the Kali Gandaki/Thak Khola (west) and the Marsyangdi (east).

The term **Annapurna Sanctuary**, coined by outsiders, denotes the high basin southwest of Annapurna and the headwaters of the Modi Khola. This vast amphitheater, surrounded by Himalayan giants, can be visited as a circuit from Pokhara in less than 10 days. However, to enjoy the route and the sanctuary itself without feeling rushed, plan a few more days. This area can be easily combined with the entire Annapurna Circuit or with a trek to Jomosom that offers various link-up possibilities.

Many people take shorter journeys from Pokhara. Popular options are below; the relevant trail portions can be picked out from the descriptions that follow.

- Naya Pul to Tatopani via GhoRepani and Poon Hill, down to the Kali Gandaki and the developed hot springs at Tatopani where transportation is available to Beni and on to Pokhara (4–5 days);
- A circuit from Phedi through Landruk and Ghandruk, beautifully placed villages, and then out to Naya Pul (3 days) or on to GhoRepani and out to the road at Naya Pul or Tatopani (5 days);
- The less-traveled Gurung Heritage Trail, Thumsikot to Khudi, see Chapter 9 (4 days).

A short trek, almost all downhill, is to fly to Jomosom, perhaps paying a visit to Kagbeni and Muktinath if you first acclimatize, then walking south to Tatopani in 4 days, and then taking a vehicle to Pokhara. Those wishing to get a taste of a climb and viewpoint could visit GhoRepani and pick up the bus at Naya Pul. The section from Jomosom to Tatopani is one of the most westernized rural areas in Nepal. It has been very popular with trekkers. Well-furnished lodges and restaurants provide many tourist facilities unheard of elsewhere in Nepal. For this reason, some trekkers prefer to avoid this area, but it is very attractive to others.

Many of these treks begin at low elevations and follow valley floors. It can get very warm in late spring, so dress appropriately and try not to push yourself, especially in the first few days. Relax during the midday, try to be in the shady side of the valley in the afternoon, or carry an umbrella against sunlight.

A visit inside anywhere in the ACAP area requires an ACAP permit and TIMS card. The ACAP entry permit is available at the conservation area's counter in Bhrikutimandap, Kathmandu, on Exhibition Marg Road, just up from Ratna Bus Park, or at the ACAP offices in Pokhara. The permit fee is 2000 NRS; that amount is doubled if the permit is purchased at a park entry point rather than beforehand. TIMS cards, $20 USD, are also available at Bhrikutimandap at a separate TIMS counter as well as at the combined ACAP/NTB office in Pokhara and at the TAAN offices (difficult to locate) in both Kathmandu and Pokhara.

THE KALI GANDAKI/THAK KHOLA AND MUKTINATH

(The Western Valley of the Annapurna Circuit)
(Map No. 3, Page 189)

Although now there is a road route, the trek from Pokhara to Jomosom on the Kali Gandaki, or the Thak Khola, as the river is called in its northern portions, is one of the easiest and most comfortable treks, in addition to being one of the most popular, in Nepal. ACAP is considering alternative routes away from the road, and we have described what is currently available, although more is to come. There is relatively little climbing, cooked food and lodging are easily available along the entire route, and the terrain is more varied than on any other trek of comparable length. Although the route passes among some of the highest mountains in the world, the scenery may not be as exciting as in, say, Khumbu. Despite the road, on this route you are still likely to encounter colorful mule caravans made musical by the tinkling of neck bells. There are several side trips out of the Kali Gandaki valley less frequented by trekkers. Though strenuous, they reward tired hikers with spectacular views and give them a glimpse of the immense scale of the valley. Muktinath, a Hindu and Buddhist pilgrimage site, is a day's walk north of Jomosom.

FORESTS OF THE TEMPERATE ZONE

The temperate zone can be divided into the lower temperate zone (approximately 6500–9000 feet/2000–2700 m in the west and 5500–8000 feet/1700–2400 m in the east) and upper temperate zone (9000–10,200 feet/2700–3100 m in the west and center and 7800–9200 feet/2400–2800 m in the east). Oak, rhododendron, and fir forests dominate the zone. Upper temperate forests are much less disturbed than those lower down, especially those in the west, because they mainly lie above the limit of cultivation.

In wetter parts of the lower temperate region, there are mixed broad-leaves with abundant laurels (*Lauracea*) and oaks (broad-leaved evergreens with acorns): *Quercus lamellosa* (*bAshi, shaalsi, gogane*), a very large tree with a massive spreading crown, and alternate, toothed, oval leaves with dark green uppersides and bluish green undersides, in the east; and Q. *floribunda* (*bele kharmendo*), with small, leathery, spiny-margined leaves, in the west. Drier, lower temperate forests consist of Q. *lanata* (*bAAjh*), with leaves dark shiny green above and rust-colored below; Q. *leucotrichophora*, with undersides of leaves covered in dense, white, woolly hairs; and Himalayan blue pine, *Pinus wallichiana* (*gobre sallo*), a conifer with clusters of long, cylindrical cones and drooping, gray-green needles in clusters of five.

Rhododendrons (*lali gurAAs*) are common in the upper temperate zone in the center and east, either as the dominant tree or scattered among other forest types. They grow as shrubs or trees and are broad-leaved evergreens with shiny, leathery leaves. The rhododendron is the national flower. The gorgeous flowers, colored red, pink, and white, are the most conspicuous Himalayan feature in the springtime in this and the subalpine zone, the region between the upper temperate zone and the treeline.

Forests of Q. *semecarpifolia* (*khasru*), with leathery, sometimes prickly leaves and globular fruits that have concave cups, occur throughout the upper temperate region, especially on south-facing slopes. Mixed broad-leaved forests grow in wetter places, while coniferous forests occur in the west. ➝

Unless you plan a side trip to one of the uninhabited areas, there is no need to carry food or shelter. Lodges or hotels in most villages offer food and accommodations that are Western in style. These places are run by the Newar, Thakali, Gurung, and Magar ethnic groups.

Transportation from Kathmandu to Pokhara is available daily via several airlines or by road. To avoid backtracking, you could take a plane to or from Jomosom, although flying in is not recommended because of rapid altitude gain (Jomosom is at 9120 feet, 2780 m). It may be difficult to get a seat on a scheduled flight, as flights are often canceled due to bad weather and high winds.

Frequent buses ply the road from Pokhara all the way to Beni, a starting point that avoids the steep uphill and subsequent downhill through GhoRepani. Otherwise, you can start from the road at Naya Pul or Phedi and then pass through GhoRepani and meet the route from Beni near Tatopani with sensational views along the way. See the alternate approach in the Annapurna Sanctuary section for the route from GhoRepani to Ghandruk. Stephen's first trek in 1969 began from the airstrip in Pokhara because there was no road, and beginning at Pokhara can still be done by first ascending to Sarangkot

← (CONTINUED)

Look for Himalayan blue pine; Himalayan hemlock, *Tsuga dumosa* (*thinge salla*), a conifer with distinctive small, egg-shaped cones and flat needles that are dark green on the top and silvery white underneath, in two rows; and others, including Himalayan silver fir, *Abies spectabilis* (*talis patra*), which has flat needles with two whitish lines on their undersides spread around the branchlets; and west Himalayan spruce, *Picea smithiana* (*jhule sallo*), a floppy-looking tree with vaguely four-sided, pendulous branches, and needles arranged in a spiral, leaving scars where they have fallen off. In the drainage of the Thulo Bheri and Karnali, look for the Himalayan cedar or deodar, *Cedrus deodara* (*devdaar*), with its pyramidal crown and three-sided needles mostly scattered in tufts on the branches, and cones that have fan-shaped scales. Also limited to the west is Himalayan cypress, *Cupressus torulosa* (*raaj sallo*), a large tree with pyramidal crown, horizontal to up-sloping branches, small, flat, triangular leaves that overlap each other closely, tiny cones, and gray-brown bark that peels off in strips. The larch, *Larix griffithiana* (*lekh sallo*), a deciduous tree, golden in autumn, is found in dry inner valleys of the northeast corner as well as in north central Nepal.

Bamboo (*Bambusa* spp. and *Arundinaria* spp.) flourishes in high rainfall areas. In a few places, such as in the Modi Khola valley on the Annapurna Sanctuary trek, it forms dense stands up to 23 feet (7 m) high. Elsewhere, bamboo occurs in the forest understory. The damper forests of the center and east are draped in mosses and lichens. In spring, beautiful epiphytic orchids, such as the white coelogyne, bloom on the tree trunks. Ferns and numerous wildflowers, including fritillaries, primulas, and many orchids (*sunaakhari*), grow in damp ravines and along streams.

Note the following associations: Himalayan fir in rhododendron and oak forests on northern slopes, and with Q. *semecarpifolia* on southern aspects; west Himalayan spruce in the drier region around Jumla but as far east as Ganesh Himal; and Himalayan hemlock, found almost exclusively on northern aspects. ❖

on the ridgeline above Pokhara, and then following the ridge to Naundanda and from there the road down to Phedi (or on to Lumle and beyond).

The Annapurna Conservation Area Project (ACAP) has sought to standardize facilities for trekkers and to facilitate travel north of Pokhara. Trekkers will find signboards at the entrance to many villages in this area. Developed by the ACAP, they indicate the route through the village as well as the registered establishments. There is an ACAP trekker's information center a five- to ten-minute walk south of the Immigration Department in Pokhara, near an intersection that is known as Rastra Bank Chowk (see the map of Pokhara in chapter introduction). Trekking permits are arranged here, as well as Trekkers' Information Management System (TIMS) cards at the Nepal Tourism Board desk in the same building. The separate, large compound of the ACAP headquarters is in a different location of Pokhara and is also a source of information for the visitor. To get there, follow the road toward Kathmandu on the way out of town. After the bridge over the Seti Gandaki River, pass a stadium on the right, and take the first avenue to the right. Follow the street for about a half hour's walk, and the ACAP headquarter offices will be a large compound on the left-hand side of the road.

POKHARA TO TATOPANI

From **Pokhara** (2713 feet, 827 m) you can either walk, or board a bus or taxi to to the Baglung bus station (Nala Mukh or Besi Parak, different from the Bas Parak, near Mahendra Pul), at the northern end of Pokhara. Buses leave regularly.

The first place trekkers leave the road is at Phedi to travel either into the sanctuary or up to Ghandruk and over to GhoRepani and then down to Birethanti/Naya Pul for a short circuit loop, or down to Tatopani.

Another place to leave the road is near Lumle, the site of a British agricultural development project where former Gurkha soldiers are trained in farming. It has one of the highest rainfalls in Nepal. Walk from **Lumle** (5300 feet, 1615 m) to **Chandrakot** (5250 feet, 1600 m) at the west end of the ridge in **30 minutes.** The views from Chandrakot are unforgettable. You will cross the Modi Khola, flowing south from between the peaks Annapurna South and Machhapuchhre, which stand before you. (The Annapurna Sanctuary, which lies upriver inside the gate formed by Machhapuchhre and Hiunchuli, the peak east of Annapurna South, is described later.) The trail descends to the Modi Khola, follows its east (left) bank southward a short distance to a suspension bridge, and crosses to the prosperous town of **Birethanti** (3600 feet, 1097 m), 1¼ **hours** from Chandrakot.

Usually, trekkers come to Birethanti by taking the bus going to Beni and getting off at **Naya Pul,** 30 minutes south of Birethanti. If coming from the road at Naya Pul, cross the Lumle Khola (3315 feet, 1010 m) from the bus drop-off point and walk north to the suspension bridge (3430 feet, 1045 m) just east of Birethanti. There is an ACAP check post where you register. From here, one trail heads up the Modi Khola on its west (right) bank toward the Annapurna Sanctuary. The trail to GhoRepani and on to the Kali Gandaki/Thak Khola heads west up the Bhurungdi Khola. Just up from the town by a picturesque waterfall is a cool pool on the Bhurungdi Khola. If you swim here, be sure to wear adequate clothing in order not to offend the Nepalis.

Follow the Bhurungdi Khola westward, at first through forests. Stay on its northeast (left) bank, crossing a suspension bridge (3707 feet, 1130 m) over a tributary to reach **Malathanti** (3793 feet, 1156 m) in **45 minutes** while avoiding suspension bridges across the Bhurungdi Khola. Pass through the settlements of Lamthali, Rangai, and Sudame. **Hille** (5000 feet, 1485 m) is reached in 1¼ **hours from Malathanti,** and 10 minutes beyond is **TirkheDUgaa** (5175 feet, 1530 m). Farther on, the branches of the Bhurungdi Khola are crossed on several bridges (the last bridge is at 5075 feet, 1500 m). The steepest climb so far, up to picturesque **Ulleri** (6800 feet, 2025 m), a Magar village, takes **2 hours** from Hille.

If you want to pace the climb, there are 3767 steps to ascend to Ulleri; trekker Lance Hart counted them! Note the handsome slate roofs on the village houses. Higher up, at a *chautaaraa*, you may still see a worn rock tablet faintly inscribed as follows: "Once, sweet, bright joy, like their lost children, an Ulleri child." It is a memorial to eighteen-month-old Ben, the son of anthropologist John Hitchcock. Ben died here in 1961 while his father was doing fieldwork.

From Ulleri, the trail climbs steadily, enters lush oak forest, and crosses numerous small streams. It is a great place for bird-watching; however, lone trekkers have been attacked by bandits in this forest. If by yourself, hire a porter or join up with others. This caution applies all the way to Chitre on the other side of GhoRepani.

Above Ulleri you pass through Banthanti (7775 feet, 2240 m), and then Nayathanti (8550 feet, 2535 m), both with lodges and small shops. The trail emerges at **GhoRepani** (9250 feet, 2790 m), with a cluster of hotels and an ACAP office, below the pass some

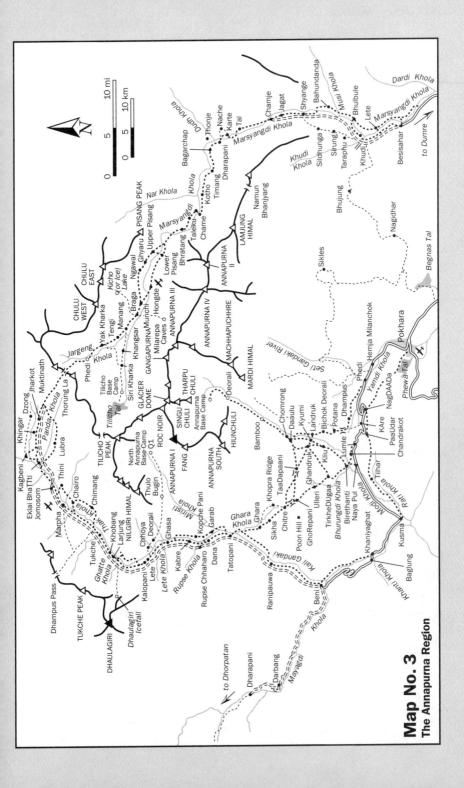

Map No. 3
The Annapurna Region

3 hours from Ulleri. GhoRepani, meaning "horse water," is now a far cry from the one building Stephen saw on his first trek in Nepal in 1969. Then it truly was a watering hole for the horse caravans that traveled between Pokhara and Mustang. There is public telephone service here. There are more hotels at the pass, GhoRepani Deorali (9450 feet, 2880 m). Trekkers should make certain they catch the views, either from the pass itself, which is now a swarm of lodges, or from east or west of the pass. On Stephen's first trek here, there were no views from the pass, as it was in a dense rhododendron forest.

Poon Hill (named for the Pun clan of the Magar ethnic group), on the ridge to the west, is a popular viewpoint (10,478 feet, 3194 m). Reach the lookout in less than **1 hour**. Signs point the way to Poon/Pun Hill from GhoRepani and from the pass. Views from Poon Hill of Dhaulagiri and the Kali Gandaki gorge are best in the early morning, when it can get pretty crowded. Some people enjoy the view best an hour after sunrise, when most trekkers have left. The south face of Dhaulagiri, the most impressive feature seen, was climbed first by a Japanese party in 1978 via the left buttress and by a Yugoslav team in 1981 via the eastern. The most challenging central section awaits an ascent, although a large portion of it was climbed solo in 1999 by the late Tomaž Humar, a prodigious climber from Slovenia; however, the summit of Dhaulagiri was not reached.

From the pass, a trail follows the ridge to the east to link with the trail from Ghandruk. The views to the east along the ridge are impressive as well. This route, which will be described later, offers a different return to Pokhara for those who have traveled north from Ulleri.

A guest house balcony offers a sensational viewpoint of the Dhaulagiri Range as well as a place to dry laundry. (Photo by Tokozile Robbins)

PEOPLES OF CENTRAL NEPAL: MAGAR

The Magar are farmers and herdsmen who live along the tributaries of the Kali Gandaki river in the Myagdi District both north, west, and southwest of Beni. Magar villages situated under the Dhaulagiri Himal seem to cling like postage stamps to the high cliffs. In some regions, indigenous Magar call themselves by clan names, such as Pun, Chantel, Kaiki, and Tarali. Pun Magar are renowned for rock-cutting skills, which are sometimes visible along the Kali Gandaki river trail. Some of the more northerly trails were cut out of the cliffs in the 1950s by Tibetan refugees. Chantel Magar, who also dwell below the south face of the Dhaulagiri massif, are herdsmen and farmers who are noted also for their skills in local copper mining. The culture of the northernmost Magar, the Tarali of the Dolpo District, blends into that of the BhoTiya. ◈

To continue to Thak Khola, descend through rhododendron forest, then prickly-leafed oak, to cultivated areas. Reach the right fork (7900 feet, 2407 m) of the trail to Ghandruk, with **Chitre** (7875 feet, 2400 m) below, and cross landslides to **PhalaTe** (7400 feet, 2256 m) and an ACAP checkpost, before reaching **Sikha** (6820 feet, 2020 m) in a notch that is **2 hours** from the pass. This unforgettable descent offers views of the immense south face of Dhaulagiri to the north. There are plenty of facilities all along here. Reach **Ghara** (6000 feet, 1828 m), a sprawling settlement, less than **1 hour** from Sikha.

🐾 *Side Trip from Chitre to Khopra Ridge. There are now facilities to make a side tour to the high ridge north of Chitre that offers sensational, close-up views of Annapurna South (23,684 feet, 7219 m), Fang Peak (25,089 feet, 7647 m), as well as Nilgiri and Dhaulagiri. Trekkers rarely make this steep detour, and there is a real danger of altitude illness, as the lodging at Khopra Ridge is at 11,975 feet (3650 m).*

The route from Chitre first traverses to Swanta and follows the ridgeline to Chistibang (10,170 feet, 3100 m) to rise above the treeline, reaching the sensational lookout point of Khopra Ridge. There is a community lodge in Khopra as well as wireless Internet, thanks to the efforts of Mahabir Pun, a local resident who has provided communication service to villagers in the area with side-benefits for tourists as well. A day's trip toward Annapurna South reveals two small glacial lakes, Kalibaraha and Khairbaraha, which are tremendously scenic pilgrimage sites. Return to the main route by retracing your steps to Chitre, or follow the ridgeline to the west and then south down to Paudar and on to the main route near Ghara. It may be possible to travel to Narchyung to the north of Tatopani and meet the route to Jomosom on the east side of the Kali Gandaki near the Miristi Khola, but it would be useful to hire a local guide.

Continue through a notch now called Durbin Danda ("binocular ridge"), and descend steeply to the south (left) bank of the Ghara Khola. Cross it on a wooden bridge (3850 feet, 1173 m) and reach the few houses called Ghara Khola above the junction of the Ghara Khola and the Kali Gandaki. As the junction of two rivers, this area is sacred and has a little temple below. The trail to Beni continues south following the Kali Gandaki downstream, but you should head upstream, cross the Kali Gandaki on a suspension bridge (3970 feet, 1210 m), and go on to **Tatopani** (3900 feet, 1189 m), **1½ hours** from Ghara. Nilgiri is the summit in the valley floor, and the photograph of it silhouetted by porters crossing the old suspension bridge here graced the covers of the first and only coffee-table book on Nepal for decades. If you head up to Kagbeni, you will go around Nilgiri to the north side.

In September 1998, a large landslide dammed the Kali Gandaki south of Tatopani for 7 hours. Water levels rose, flooding several homes before the Kali Gandaki cut a passage through the western end and waters receded.

Tatopani, a prosperous Thakali town, takes its name (*taato paani,* literally "hot water") from the hot springs located along the banks of the river, near the middle of town, just below the motor road. There are currently two pools, and a usage fee is required. Don't foul the water with soap, even though some locals may. Wash in the effluent below the pools or in the river, rinse, and then soak in the hot water. Be discreet and modest, as the Nepalis are.

There is another hot springs located on the other, east side of the river. The built-up pool area can be seen across the river from the upper, north end of Tatopani. Reach a bridge to the other side by traveling upstream along the road for 20 minutes. Cross the suspension bridge (4200 feet, 1280 m) and return downstream on the other side for 20 minutes to the bathing area, used mainly by locals.

TATOPANI TO MUKTINATH

To escape a section of the road, after 20 minutes of following the road north from **Tatopani,** cross a suspension bridge (4200 feet, 1280 m) to the east side of the Kali Gandaki. Pass by a few teahouses and contour up the river, staying to the left before passing just above a school. Stay left again to cross to the north side of the Miristi Khola on a suspension bridge (4373 feet, 1333 m) about 40 minutes after crossing the Kali Gandaki. Ascend to a small plateau before descending to Patar (4396 feet, 1340 m) in 15 minutes. There are no facilities in Patar.

Beyond Patar, the trail passes through a bluff and descends to a suspension bridge in 15 minutes. Do not cross the bridge here but stay on the east bank of the Kali Gandaki and contour past a hydropower project to reach **Garab** (4478 feet, 1365 m) in 5 minutes,

THE KALI GANDAKI VALLEY—A GREAT BIOGEOGRAPHIC DIVIDE

When trekking up the Kali Gandaki valley to the Thak Khola, you experience changes in flora and fauna that are more dramatic than anywhere else in Nepal. For example, in one day you can descend from the arid Tibetan steppe flora at Tukche through temperate coniferous forests to reach the humid subtropical zone around Tatopani. The Kali Gandaki has cut the world's deepest river gorge right through the Himalaya. The river runs from the Tibetan plateau to the north, through almost the center of Nepal and the middle of the Himalaya.

The valley is a biogeographic divide for Himalayan flora and fauna. Forests to the west of the valley are generally drier and have fewer plant species than eastern forests. In their field guide *Birds of Nepal,* the Flemings point out that the Kali Gandaki is a very distinctive break in bird distribution. Some species, such as the fire-tailed myzornis and the brown parrotbill, are restricted to the valley and farther east, while others, the cheer pheasant for instance, only breed in the valley and westward. Forests to the east of the valley are significantly richer in bird species than western forests, even taking into account that western forests are relatively poorly recorded. ❖

The view north from Tatopani up the Thak Khola valley includes Nilgiri as well as a road plied by buses and other vehicles. (Photo by Tokozile Robbins)

1 hour 35 minutes from Tatopani. There are shops, and simple lodging may be available here, too. Continue contouring along the river, eventually passing another suspension bridge before ascending up to Gadpar (4823 feet, 1470 m) in 40 minutes. Ascend to the few houses of Bhalebas (5633 feet, 1717 m) in **40–45 minutes**, with a grand vantage point of the waterfall across the river. There are no facilities in Bhalebas or Gadpar. Descend to reach **Kopche Pani** in 20–25 minutes, **1¾ hours** from Garab, across the river from Rupse Chhaharo and along the east-side route described below.

Alternatively, from **Tatopani**, you can simply follow the motor road on the west (right) bank of the Kali Gandaki and pass through Sukebagar to **Dana** (4600 feet, 1402 m) by the Ghatte Khola. This wealthy, stretched-out former customs post is reached in about **1½ hours** from Tatopani. In the lower end of Dana you can see the spectacular west face of Annapurna. It took Stephen five trips before the clouds cleared enough to see it. Continue on the west (right) bank to Titar, and then climb to the few houses of **Rupse Chhaharo** (5350 feet, 1631 m), named after the waterfall above the bridge. Rupse Chhaharo is reached in **1¼ hours** from Dana. Note the appropriate-technology water mills here.

There are two route choices here: the east (left) or the west (right) bank. The east-side trail is currently the more used and is probably safer in the monsoon, but inquire locally about conditions. Trekkers have perished, slipping on this path. The west-side route follows the road.

ALTERNATE
ROUTE

East-Side Route

To follow the east-side trail between **Rupse Chhaharo** and Ghasa, fork right just after the bridge at the waterfall. Descend to cross the Kali Gandaki on a bridge (5360 feet, 1634 m) at a narrow point in the gorge. Head upstream, keeping close to the powerful torrent, now chocolate brown carrying sand and soil south. Reach **Kopche Pani**, with several small clusters of teahouses (5500 feet, 1676 m), in **30 minutes.** A further **1 hour's** steep climb from Kopche Pani brings you to **Pahiro Tabla** (meaning "landslide place," 6400 feet, 1897 m). As you go along, look for the old trail on the west side and the ancient pilgrim trails above it. Pilgrims traveled this dangerous route to Muktinath as long ago as 300 BCE. Along the way, you may see monkeys in the forests. In another **45 minutes,** reach the suspension bridge and trail junction (6400 feet, 1910 m) **15 minutes** below **Ghasa.** ❖

ALTERNATE
ROUTE

West-Side Route

On the west-side route along the road, climb above the teahouses of **Rupse Chhaharo** to reach **Kabre** (5600 feet, 1750 m) in less than **30 minutes**. Kabre is the northernmost village inhabited by hill castes in the Kali Gandaki valley. From Kabre, continue north along the steep cliff side to where the valley narrows spectacularly and the cascading river torrent resounds across the canyon walls. Probably the world's steepest and deepest large gorge, the gradient to the summit of Dhaulagiri is more than 1 mile (1.6 km) vertical to 1 mile (1.6 km) horizontal (1:1.05 to be exact). The steepest part, however, is south of the line between the two summits. The east-side trail rejoins the road **2 hours** from Kabre and 15 minutes south of Ghasa. ❖

AMPHIBIANS AND REPTILES OF THE SUBTROPICAL ZONE

Nepali amphibians and reptiles are primarily found in the warmer tropical and subtropical zones (3300–6500 feet/1000–2000 m in the west, to 5500 feet/1700 m in the east). Over thirty-six species of amphibians, including frogs (*bhyaguto*), toads, newts, and a caecilian, have been recorded so far. One of the commonest is the aptly named skittering frog (*Rana cyanophlyctis*), which can float and skip over the water surface. The six-fingered frog (*Rana hexadactyla*) is the largest Nepali amphibian. Not aquatic, it is reported to feed on mice, shrews, birds, and lizards. In the breeding season it calls deep "oong-awang" throughout the night. Reptile species include crocodiles, turtles, lizards, skinks, and geckos. Snakes (*sAАp, sarpa*) are elusive; most are nonpoisonous. One of the commonest is the buff-striped keelback (*Amphiesma stolata*), which occurs in grassy areas near cultivation. It is olive-green or brown above with black spots or bars intersected with buff stripes. Lizards (*chhepaaro*) are more obvious and can often be seen basking in the sun on stone walls or rocks. A familiar lizard is the Himalayan rock lizard (*Agama tuberculata*). It is coarsely scaled, has a long tail, and is generally colored brown with black spots; breeding males have blue throats. ❖

It takes **30 minutes** to get through **Ghasa** (6700 feet, 2040 m), a sprawling, flat-roofed Thakali village with an ACAP Safe Drinking Water Station. (In reverse, traveling from Ghasa to Dana, avoid the trail that heads left immediately after leaving lower Ghasa. It leads to an unused bridge and path. Instead follow the road for 15 minutes and then cross to the east bank on a suspension bridge.)

Note how remarkably the land has changed over this short stretch, as the climate becomes colder and drier. To the south, you may see lizards throughout the year, but from here northward none are seen in the cold season. Similarly, as you head north, you will encounter more pine forests and fewer broad-leaved trees. Most houses beyond here have flat roofs because there is less rainfall. The changes will be even more dramatic farther along. Be careful not to twist your ankle on the river-worn trail boulders.

To continue north from Ghasa, cross a tributary, and pass through Kaiku and the few houses of Gumaaune (literally "walking around"). There is a huge landslide scar on the east side. Reach a bridge over the Lete Khola (8000 feet, 2438 m), a tributary from the west, and cross it to a lodge. **Lete** (8100 feet, 2469 m), some 30 minutes beyond, is **2 hours** from Ghasa. Annapurna I, the first 8000-meter peak ever climbed, can be seen to the east from Lete. Again, note the change in ecology; Lete gets 49 inches (124 mm) of rain a year, whereas a mere half day to the north, Tukche gets only 8 inches (20 mm).

A trip is described below from Lete east to the original Annapurna Base Camp. This hard-found camp was the base for the French expedition that accomplished the first ascent of an 8000-meter peak, Annapurna (26,545 feet, 8091 m), in 1950. From Lete, the route is a strenuous 5-day camping trip to substantial altitudes where food, fuel, and shelter must be carried. See "Explore: North Annapurna Base Camp" later in this chapter for more details.

Heading north, pass the police check post in the spread-out village of Lete, which then blends into **Kalopani** (8300 feet, 2530 m). Sunsets from Kalopani and Lete are memorable. The Cultural Thakali Museum is in Kalopani next door to the ACAP Safe Drinking Water Station.

A few minutes north of Kalopani, take the suspension bridge (8251 feet, 2515 m) over the Kali Gandaki/Thak Khola to the east side. The trail passes through Dhampu to reach Dada (8383 feet, 2555 m) in 30 minutes. A trail up to Titi village with a nearby small lake leads off from here. Continue on to KokheThAATi (8300 feet, 2530 m) in less than 10 minutes before crossing back to the west (right) bank in another 20 minutes. In less than 15 minutes more, reach the broad Ghatte/Boxe River delta. In the dry season, you can head straight across the delta with minimal wading to meet the road on the other side and follow it to reach **Larjung** (8400 feet, 2570 m) in 30 minutes or **1¾ hours** from Kalopani. (If wading is not possible, then head up the tributary valley to a suspension bridge [8317 feet, 2535 m] over the Boxe Khola.) There is an ACAP Safe Drinking Water Station in Larjung and many walnut trees in both Larjung and Khobang.

To the west is the incredibly foreshortened summit of Dhaulagiri, almost 3.5 miles (5.5 km) higher. The temples above Larjung are where the local deities are kept for Thakali clans residing here. There is a festival honoring them every twelve years. Bhurjungkot lies to the west above Khobang and Larjung. A trail to the village heads west from the lower, southern end of Larjung, reaching Bhurjungkot in 30 minutes. A cave said to be used by Padmasambava lies a few hours north of this village.

Side Trip from Larjung to Dhaulagiri Icefall. *This can be made in a long, full day trip involving 3940 feet (1200 m) of ascent with no facilities en route. To get to the trailhead, retrace your steps from Larjung, heading down the Kali Gandaki, and after 30 minutes reach the broad Ghatte/Boxe River delta. Rather than wade across the delta, head up the valley to a suspension bridge (8317 feet, 2535 m) over the Ghatte/Boxe Khola. Cross the bridge and, after a few minutes following the road downriver, you will see a trail (indicated by an ACAP sign) on the right that leads to Bhuturcho Lake, a small body of water 30 minutes above the road. However, continue following the road and just after crossing a tributary, there is an ACAP sign indicating the trail to the right leading up to Sekong Lake and on to Dhaulagiri Icefall. It may be best to hire a local guide. The area below the icefall (12,400 feet, 3780 m) can be visited in a very long day, but it's better to camp and enjoy the sunrise and sunset. The area below the east Dhaulagiri Icefall abounds with yak pastures and was the location of the 1969 American Base Camp. At a lower altitude than Dhampus Pass, it has correspondingly less severe conditions. The views of the mountains are excellent, possibly better than at Dhampus Pass. Beware of avalanches in the vicinity of the icefall.*

From Larjung, head north, cross a tributary, and in a few minutes enter the fascinating town of **Khobang** (8400 feet, 2580 m). The trail used to pass through a tunnel, and doors to the houses opened off it. The village was thus protected from the strong winds that blow up the valley almost every afternoon. The northern, open segment of the series of settlements is called Kanti. The dry-season path keeps closer to the river. Cross another tributary, either on a temporary bridge or upstream on a more substantial one. **Tukche** (8500 feet, 2591 m), an historically important town, is **1 hour** beyond Khobang. There is an ACAP Safe Drinking Water Station here.

Tukche was once an important center for the trade of Nepali grain for Tibetan salt through the valley of the Thak Khola. Thakali Subbha, or customs contractors, controlled it and exacted taxes at Tukche in the summer and at Dana in the winter. The

PHEASANTS OF THE TEMPERATE ZONE

Nepal is famous for its variety of Himalayan pheasants. There are six species, all of which can be seen in the Annapurna Conservation Area. Most are shy and difficult to see unless you flush them from the forest. They call frequently in spring. The Kalij pheasant (*Lophura leucomelana*), or *kaali* (length 24–27 inches, 60–68 cm), inhabits all types of forest with dense undergrowth, especially near water, and also occurs in subtropical and tropical zones. The male is mainly black with a long tail and red on the face; the female is reddish brown with a shorter tail. The Koklass pheasant (*Pucrasia macrolopha*, or *phokraas* (length 20–24 inches, 52–61 cm), inhabits oak and conifer forests from the Modi Khola valley westward. The male is dark, with a long crest and tail, black head, and white ear patch. The female is brownish, with a shorter crest and tail. It crows loudly at dawn. The satyr tragopan, or crimson-horned pheasant (*Tragopan satyr*), or *munaal* (length 23–27 inches, 59–68 cm), is found in damp oak and rhododendron forests with dense undergrowth. The male is bright red, spotted with white and with a blue wattle; the female is mottled brown. In spring, it makes a strange, mammalian "waaa" noise at dawn and dusk.

handsome architecture and great woodcarving in Tukche attests to the importance of this town. By the middle of this century competition had reduced this trade, and the enterprising Thakali turned their attention south and became more involved in business ventures around Pokhara and in the Tarai. Their spread throughout many of the trade routes in Nepal resulted in the establishment of many *bhaTTi*, even before trekking became popular. With the coming of foreigners, the Thakali developed hotel facilities for them, and many of their family homes have been developed into lodges. Try to find a traditional *bhaTTi* and sample a good Nepali meal of *daal bhaat tarkaari* (lentils, rice, and vegetables) or at least have such a meal in a tourist restaurant.

The Thakali seem to prosper in whatever they turn to. In comparing his visits to this region twenty years apart, Stephen found the improvements impressive—water systems, latrines, more schools (indeed, *functioning* schools), better trails, more varieties of crops, and cleaner homes. The Thakali have always exhibited a strong ethnic group consciousness, and Thak Khola is their homeland. Many of the towns have been electrified through the installation of a mini-hydroelectric generator across and up from Khobang on the Chhokopani Khola, which produces 260 kilowatts. Visit the active *gomba* at the northeast end of town and tour the distillery (the first of many to the north).

A strong wind blows from the south up the valley, beginning in the late morning and lasting most of the day. This is caused when the air mass over the plateau to the north warms, rises, and creates a pressure difference. The best time to head south is in the early morning when the wind may be from the north. As you go up the valley from Tukche, notice that there is relatively little vegetation on the valley floor itself, but there are trees and forests on the walls. The valley floor is in a rain shadow due to the strong winds. When the wind is blowing, you may notice that there are no clouds over the center of the valley, but clouds do hang on the sides.

Side Trip to Dhampus Pass and Hidden Valley (*visitors must be acclimatized and self-sufficient to travel into the Hidden Valley). A trail to Dhampus Pass goes up the hill to the west of the* gomba (*monastery*) *at Tukche (another trail departs from Marpha). Dhampus Pass (17,000 feet, 5182 m) connects the valley of the Thak Khola with Hidden Valley. Semiwild yak herds, snow leopards, and blue sheep might be encountered in Hidden Valley. It lies beyond the treeline and is often snowed in. Huts used for pasturing yaks can be used for shelter and cooking en route to the pass. There are no facilities at the pass. Carry food, fuel, and shelter. Temperatures below freezing can always be expected, and in the winter months the temperature drops below 0°F (−18°C). A trip to the pass is ideal for those who want a more vivid experience of being in the mountains.*

Reach the pass from Tukche or Marpha by going to some yak huts (13,000 feet, 3962 m) the first day and to the pass the second. This may be too rapid an ascent for many people. If you are unprepared to spend a night at the pass, you could go up and return to the yak huts in a day. Yak yogurt is delicious—during the warm season you should try to buy some at the herders. If there is any possibility of cloudy weather, hire a local person from Tukche (or Marpha) as a guide. Once clouds settle in, it is very easy to get lost.

ALTERNATE ROUTE

Tukche to Jomosom via Thini

A recommended alternate route exists from **Tukche** to Thini, the village that overlooks Jomosom. This route avoids much of the road while passing through the magnificently set village of Chimang and the Tibetan refugee camp of Chairo. To take this route, about 40 minutes from Tukche cross a suspension bridge (8573 feet, 2613 m) over the Thak Khola (which is the name of the Kali Gandaki north of Ghasa). To the right, across a broad alluvial fan, is the small village of Chhokopani, believed to be a source of holy waters and religiously important to Thakalis. Instead, head left and in 25 minutes cross the Chimang Khola just upstream on a variable bridge. Ascend to the village of **Chimang** (9131 feet, 2783 m), surrounded by orchards, in another 20 minutes, less than **1½ hours** from Tukche. There are no lodges here.

Continue on 15 minutes to where the trails from upper and lower Chimang meet. After 15–20 minutes you reach another trail junction; stay with the middle path to reach **Chairo**, set among tall juniper trees **45–50 minutes** from Chimang. It is a Tibetan refugee camp and no boarding is available unless permission is first taken from ACAP.

To reach Marpha from Chairo, cross a bridge over the Thak Khola and head upriver for 20 minutes to Marpha (8825 feet, 2690 m) on the west bank. Otherwise, to continue avoiding the motor road, stay on the east bank from Chairo and contour before ascending steeply to pass above bluffs. Descend steeply to reach a tributary riverbed (9186 feet, 2800 m) and cross this delta in 2 hours from Chairo. Ascend past the village of Dhumbra to a ridgecrest (9498 feet, 2895 m) in 15 minutes. There is an oft-closed *gomba* nearby. Descend to Dhumbra Lake (9297 feet, 2834 m) in 15 more minutes. This lake is considered to be sacred, and a local *lama* prohibits access to its waters. Descend through the village of Samle to reach a bridge (9071 feet, 2765 m) over a tributary in 20 minutes. Ascend to the village of **Thini** (9383 feet, 2860 m) in 20 more minutes, some **3 hours 10 minutes** from Chairo. There are no lodges here. Jomosom lies 20–25 minutes below. ❖

Ammonite fossils or shaligram can be found in the area north of Jomosom and are highly prized by pilgrims as a symbol of the Hindu deity Vishnu. (Photo by Tokozile Robbins)

PEOPLES OF CENTRAL NEPAL: THAKALI AND OTHER PEOPLES OF THE THAK KHOLA

Above the dramatic gorge of the Kali Gandaki, north from the town of Ghasa, is the region known as Thak Khola, from which the Thakali take their name. They consider this their ancestral homeland. Thakali villages line the route north along the high Kali Gandaki valley. Their language is very close to Gurung and Tamang, but their cultural history has been more influenced by Tibet. The Thakali are noted for their strong trading spirit, which they developed as middlemen in the formerly active Nepal–Tibet rice and salt trade through their region. The largest town until recently was Tukche, the center of the Thakali ethnic culture and, for many decades earlier in this century, the regional center of the Tibetan salt trade. Since 1959, when the Tibetan border trade diminished, the Tibetan salt business has come to a virtual standstill in Thak Khola, and many Thakali have turned southward for other economic opportunities. Today, Jomosom, the district center north of Tukche, is much larger and at times Tukche appears almost abandoned. Some Thakali have dropped their Tibetan and Buddhist predilections and have adopted Nepali culture and Hinduism. Some have moved permanently out of Thak Khola to take advantage of business ventures in the larger bazaars and trade centers of Nepal.

Despite their uniform appearances, Thak Khola is actually the home of two similar ethnic groups and one quite distinct group. The Thakali proper live between Ghasa and Tukche. North of them, and virtually indistinguishable, are a people known as PaunchgaaUle (which literally means "people of the five villages"— Marpha, Syang, Chiwong, Cherok, and Jomosom-Thini). The PaunchgaaUle sometimes call themselves Thakali, but intermarriage between them and their "true" Thakali neighbors is not condoned. The third group are a BhoTiya people who inhabit the valley of Muktinath, from Kagbeni east to the Muktinath shrine at the base of Thorung La. They are also sometimes called the BaragaaUle, or "people of the twelve villages." Muktinath is a special place to these BhoTiya people, as it is a Hindu–Buddhist shrine of great significance. There are many religious observances throughout the year that attract Hindu and Buddhist pilgrims. The most important event to local Buddhists is the celebration of the Yartung festival in the fall, when the animals have been brought down from the high pastures for the winter. Yartung is highlighted by horse racing and great revelry. For Hindus, one of the largest events of the year falls on the occasion of Janai Purnima, the "full moon day (*purnima*) of the sacred cord (*janai*)." The sacred cord is worn by men of the highest twice-born Hindu castes, as a sign of their privileged social status and religious sanctity. More about Muktinath as a sacred center is given later in this section. ❖

Tukche to Jomosom via Marpha

Rather than the alternate route outlined above, most people will stay on the west bank from **Tukche** all the way to reach **Marpha** (8825 feet, 2690 m) in **1½ hours**. About 15 minutes before Marpha, pass by the Marpha Agricultural Farm, which has introduced many of the new crops you see around. Marpha, a charming town, has a fine sewer system—a series of canals flowing down the streets. There are plenty of choices for accommodation and food here, especially given the variety of fruits and vegetables available. Some of the hotels here, and also in Jomosom, advertise pony rides as far as Muktinath. Visit the new large *gomba* in the center of town. There is an ACAP Safe Drinking Water Station here, too. Dhampus Pass can also be reached from Marpha.

To continue upstream, leave the town through the *chorten* and cross first a tributary and then the Pongkyu Khola, another alluvial fan, with a water mill, that flows from the west. Along the trail you will see willow plantations, part of a reforestation project. The town of Syang is beyond, and its monastery is up the hill a bit farther. On certain days during late October to early December, monks stage dance festivals in the *gomba* of Marpha, Syang, and Tukche that are somewhat similar to the *Mani-rimdu* festivals of Solu–Khumbu. Consider a side trip east across the river to the *gomba* on the hillock with its commanding views of the valley.

Cross a tributary farther up the valley, and reach **Jomosom** (8900 feet, 2780 m), the capital for the Mustang District, **1½ hours** from Marpha. There are many facilities here and an ACAP Safe Drinking Water Station and ACAP Information Center. There is an airfield here with scheduled service to Kathmandu, but because of the erratic winds service can be unreliable. Winter winds regularly reach 30 to 40 knots, with gusts to 70! If you fly in and head upvalley to rarefied air, beware of altitude illness. Other attractions include banks, a hospital, rather luxurious accommodations and food, climbing cliffs with a welcome sign, and, of course, a police check post. An ecomuseum has opened at the southern end of town and has informative displays. This town has prospered immensely over the years and has expanded to both sides of the river to provide space for the many government employees and offices. Pony caravans used to bring food to Jomosom to feed the bureaucracy but are being replaced by vehicular transport.

The countryside to the north is very arid, not unlike the Tibetan plateau farther north. To the south, Dhaulagiri impressively guards the Thak Khola valley. It is much less foreshortened than at Larjung. To the east, across the river on a shelf of land, is the traditional town of **Thini** (9500 feet, 2897 m), reached in **30 minutes** from Jomosom. The inhabitants are technically not Buddhists (though they may say otherwise) but followers of Bon-po, the ancient religion that antedated Tibetan Buddhism.

Up the valley east of **Thini** is Tilicho Pass and Tilicho Tal. The latter, at 16,140 feet (4919 m), is a high, spectacular lake. It is better to access this area from the west not only because the trail is clearer and there are facilites en route on that side but because you start higher and are more likely to be acclimatized. Additionally, a Nepali army camp on this side of the pass, used for mountain warfare training, might restrict some of the route. You might have noticed their "R&R" facilities in Jomosom.

To continue on to Kagbeni and Muktinath, travel on the east (true left) side of the river. The perennial high wind gusts strongly down the riverbed, which can be half a mile wide here; sunglasses or other eyewear and a mask or bandanna to cover the nose and mouth can be useful to protect against airborne dust particles. In **1½ hours** reach the trail junction of Eklai BhaTTi (also known as Chyancha-Lhrenba) at 9186 feet (2800 m). **Eklai BhaTTi** means "lonely inn," which bespeaks a former time as there are now several lodges. If traveling to Kagbeni, the suspension bridge just south of Eklai BhaTTi leads to a west bank route that avoids a section of the road. Another alternative to following the road is to head east up the Panda Khola valley (15 minutes south of Eklai BhaTTi) to Lubra. The route from Lubra to Muktinath is described below in reverse.

From Eklai BhaTTi, the route to the left continues up the river to the captivating village of **Kagbeni** (9383 feet, 2860 m) in just over **30 minutes**, while the right ascends out of the valley and heads more directly to Muktinath. The right branch reaches the junction (10,350 feet, 3155 m) of the trail from Kagbeni to Muktinath in **1¼–1½ hours**.

MUKTINATH PILGRIMAGE

Muktinath, located in a poplar grove, is a sacred shrine and pilgrimage site for Hindus and Buddhists. The *Mahabharata*, the ancient Hindu epic written about 300 BCE, mentions Muktinath as Shaligrama because of its ammonite fossils called *shaligram*. Brahma, the creator, made an offering here by lighting a fire on water. You can see this miracle (burning natural gas) in a small Buddhist shrine (*gomba*) below the main Hindu temple (*mandir*). Many people from Mustang and other areas come to sell handicrafts to the pilgrims. Some sell the *shaligram*, the mollusk fossil dating from a period roughly 140 to 165 million years ago before the uplifting of the Himalaya. These objects, treasured for worship by Hindus, are said to represent several deities, principally those associated with Vishnu, the Lord of Salvation. You are apt to find them along the flats north of Jomosom and for sale in Baudha, Kathmandu. You are not allowed to export them, however.

Hindus named the site Muktichhetra, meaning "place of salvation (*mukti*)," because they believed that bathing there gives salvation after death. Springs are piped into 108 brass water spouts in the shape of boars' heads near the temple dedicated to Vishnu, the focal point for Hindus. The boar was the third incarnation of Vishnu. Because Buddha was the ninth avatar, the Hindus tolerate the Buddhists here. The Buddhists consider the image of Vishnu in this typically Newar-style temple as the Bodhisattva Avalokiteshwara. Vishnu is in the shape of an icon as well as a large ammonite fossil. The same fossil image is worshiped by Buddhists as Gawa Jogpa, the "serpent deity."

The miraculous fire revered by Buddhists and Hindus burns on water, stones, and earth, and is inside the Jwala Mai Temple (also called the *Salamebar Dolamebar Gomba* or *Mebar Lhakang Gomba*), south of the police check post. Natural gas jets burn in small recesses curtained under the altar to Avalokiteshwara. On the left burns the earth, in the middle water, and on the right the stone. One flame has died out; only two remain lighted. Sherpas and Buddhist porters with you may ask you for a bottle to take some of the "water that burns" with them. It is traditional to leave a small offering of money.

Padmasambhava, who brought Buddhism to Tibet in the eighth century, is believed to have meditated here. His "footprints" are on a rock in the northwest corner of this sacred place. On their way to Tibet, the eighty-four *siddha* ("great magicians") left their pilgrim staffs, which grew into the poplars at the site. You will find many old *chorten* and temples cared for by Nyingmapa nuns or old women from the nearby villages. A full moon is an especially auspicious time to visit Muktinath. In the full moon of August–September, thousands of pilgrims arrive. ❖

The name Kagbeni aptly reflects the town's character—*kak* means "blockade" in the local dialect and *beni* means "junction of two rivers"—and this citadel does effectively block the valley. River junctions are often considered especially sacred to the people living nearby. Since the town is at the confluence of trails from the north, south, east, and west, the ancient king who sat here could control and tax the exchange of grain from the south and wool and salt from the north. The ruins of his palace, which can still be seen, are a reminder of the ancient kingdoms that predated the unification of Nepal. Some scholars believe the family that ruled here was related to the ancient kings of Jumla. The

A mendicant fakir's *offerings* (Photo by Tokozile Robbins)

Sakyapa monastery here charges an entry fee for a visit. You may see two large terra-cotta images of the protector deities of the town—a male at the north end and the remains of a female at the south. This mingling of old animistic beliefs with those of the more developed religions is common in Nepal.

People here call themselves Gurung but are clearly not the same as the Gurung to the south. People from Tibet who have settled in Nepal often call themselves Gurung to facilitate assimilation.

The impressive folding of the cliffs west of town illustrates the powerful forces of orogeny (discussed in Chapter 1's geology section). There is a viewpoint called Sher Dhak several hundred meters above on the opposite side of the river. It involves a steep scramble up loose rock. From Kagbeni, you can just make out the crest of Thorung La up the valley to the east of town, with Kagbeni visible from the pass, too. There is an ACAP Safe Drinking Water Station as well as a police check post in Kagbeni, at the northern limit for trekkers.

North of Kagbeni is the Upper Mustang restricted area and the kingdom of Lo. Permits to enter can be obtained at the Immigration Office in Pokhara or Kathmandu; the cost is $500 USD per person for the first 10 days and $50 USD per day thereafter. Additionally, the trip must be guided and arranged through a registered trekking company. However, it is possible, without a restricted area permit, to visit the fascinating village of **Tiri** a short distance north on the opposite (west) bank of the Kali Gandaki. A road is being built to Tiri (and beyond); to hike there, from the lower end of Kagbeni, cross the bridge (9334 feet, 2845 m) to the true right/west bank of the Thak Khola and traverse north. Reach Tiri (9439 feet, 2877 m), a village surrounded by walled orchards, in **25 minutes**. A *gomba* is perched above town. Continuing north of Tiri is restricted.

To travel to Muktinath from Kagbeni, head up from the Jhong Khola, the tributary from the east, following the road for the most part, with some sections of trail away from the road.

Continue east, noting the caves on the north side of the valley. So ancient are these caves that no one remembers if they were used by hermits or troglodytes. On a clear day, the walk can be ethereal, as the dry valley sparkles and the north wall seems suspended close to you. Climb to **Khingar** (11,190 feet, 3410 m) in **2 hours;** the old part of town is north of the trail. Continue to **Jharkot** (11,715 feet, 3570 m) in **40–45 minutes** more, a crumbling but still impressive fortress perched on a ridge. Jharkot, called Dzar by Tibetans, is believed to have been the home of the ruling house of this valley. Note how some houses around the ruins of the fort are made of blocks of earth.

Go on to what is now called **Muktinath**, also known as Ranipawa (12,047 feet, 3672 m), with a large rest house for pilgrims, many hotels, a police check post, and an ACAP visitor center office you should visit to register your name. The office is **30–40 minutes** from Jharkot. If your intention is to cross the Thorung La from this side, then check with the ACAP information center here, as they may advise you against proceeding in marginal conditions.

Across the valley you can see the extensive ruins of Dzong ("castle" in Tibetan) and the town built around it, the original seat of the king of this valley. Consider a side trip to that side of the valley, outlined below.

The wall-ensconced compound of the holy shrine of Muktinath is less than 15 minutes from the ACAP center. Dhaulagiri (26,795 feet, 8167 m) looms impressively to the south. It was first climbed from the north, the view you see here, by a German expedition in 1960. The Muktinath Foundation International supports the interfaith aspect of the region and has a website, www.muktinath.org.

To the east is Thorung La (17,700 feet, 5416 m), which leads to Manang and the eastern half of the Annapurna Circuit.

Crossing the pass from Muktinath to Manang is more difficult than crossing in the other direction. The only lodges between Muktinath and the pass (clockwise) are at Chaharu (also known as Phedi) at 13,687 feet (4172 m), whereas there are lodges up to 15,990 feet (4875 m) on the Manang side and seasonal tea shops beyond. It is a very long day to ascend from Chaharu to the pass and then to descend to facilities on the

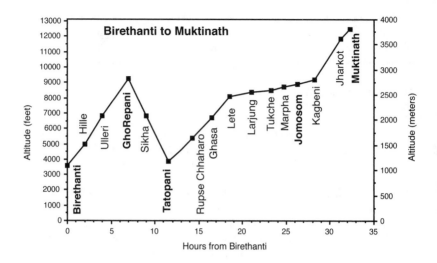

other side. Additionally, in the dry season there are few if any suitable campsites with water on this side of the pass.

Altitude illness may jeopardize those who are unacclimatized. Crossing from Manang, on the other hand, is easier because of the comparatively long time spent at high altitudes before approaching the pass. Most people start at Besisahar and follow the Marsyangdi valley to Manang before crossing to the high Thorung La over to Muktinath and the Kali Gandaki/Thak Khola valley. The pass is often crossed from Muktinath, but it certainly is more difficult and hazardous. Under no condition should you ascend from either direction unless the entire party, including porters, is well equipped to camp in snow should a storm arise. The trail descriptions for the Manang to Muktinath crossing are given with the Manang section later in this chapter.

Side Trip from Muktinath to Chaungar, Dzong, and Beyond. *A short excursion from* **Muktinath** *across the valley to the beautiful villages of* **Chaungar** *and* **Dzong** *(Jhong) provides a glimpse of life outside the tourist areas. This trip can be made out and back on the same path,* **less than 30 minutes** *each way. Alternatively, it can be made into longer excursions as the following three circuit routes: crossing the valley from* **Dzong** *to* **Jharkot** *and back to* **Muktinath** *(2½-hour loop), crossing the valley from* **Puthak** *to* **Khingar** *and returning to* **Muktinath** *(3½–4 hours), or continuing all the way to* **Kagbeni** *on that side of the valley* **(3½ hours)** *and returning along the road. All of the above will be described.*

From the upper end of Muktinath/Ranipawa, proceed north to Chaungar (12,110 feet, 3692 m), reached in an easy 25 minutes. There are no facilities in Chaungar, but there is lodging in Dzong, which lies down the valley from Chaungar. Descend from Chaungar to cross a suspension bridge (11,920 feet, 3632 m) to the west bank of a tributary and reach Dzong (11,750 feet, 3580 m) in under 30 minutes. This village was the seat of an ancient regime, and the remains of the old castle can be seen along the crest along with a gomba above which can be visited for a fee.

From Dzong you can retrace your steps to Muktinath, or complete a loop back to Muktinath by way of Jharkot across the valley. For the latter, descend through a grove of pipal trees to cross the Jhong Khola on a steel bridge (11,290 feet, 3440 m)

*in 20 minutes. Ascend through more pipal trees on the other side to the circuit trail
just below Jharkot in 30 more minutes.*

*Otherwise, to continue down the valley, reach the village of Puthak (11,290 feet,
3440 m) in 20 minutes from Dzong. From Puthak, there is a route to link with Khingar
(11,190 feet, 3410 m), across the valley to the southwest, in under an hour. This involves a steep descent to the Jhong Khola (10,780 feet, 3285 m) and then a steep ascent.
However, check first locally to see if the bridge is operational.*

*If you would like to continue on down the valley, it is also possible to reach Kagbeni
from Puthak along the motor road on this north side of the valley. It is a long and desolate stretch on what locals refer to as The Muktinath Ring Road; however, this road
receives less traffic than the road on the opposite side of the valley. To head to Kagbeni
on this side, 15 minutes below Puthak cross a suspension bridge (11,100 feet, 3382 m).
Kagbeni is 2 hours from this bridge, with no facilities or water available along the way.*

ALTERNATE
ROUTE

Return Journey Variation:
Muktinath to Jomosom via Lubra Village

To return, follow the reverse of the trail descriptions for the trek from Pokhara to
Muktinath, or follow the alternate route from Muktinath to Jomosom via pleasant Lubra
village. This latter route avoids a large section of the motor road by heading over the high
ridge to the southwest of Muktinath and descending to the Panda Khola valley, with a
visit to the picturesque hamlet of Lubra. It involves a steep climb and steep descent but
avoids the annoyance of vehicles for at least part of the way to Jomosom and meets the
usual route south of Eklai Bhat'TTi. Check first with the ACAP information Center on
the availability of bridges over the Panda Khola and fill up water in **Muktinath**, as there
may not be another chance until **Lubra, 3¼ hours** away.

*Buckwheat fields in the hamlet of Lubra along an alternate route between Jomosom and
Muktinath* (Photo by Tokozile Robbins)

Find the trail as it branches to the left from the road as you head out of the lower (western) end of Muktinath. In 20 minutes stay right at a trail junction. Stay right again 25 minutes beyond and ascend to reach a saddle (12,530 feet, 3820 m) in 30 more minutes, **1¼ hours** from Muktinath. Contour shortly before descending steeply into the Panda Khola valley. Reach the riverbed (10,040 feet, 3060 m) in **1½ hours** from the saddle.

The trail through the riverbed at the valley floor may be faint and is of variable condition; wading might be necessary depending on the season. Either cross a bridge that ACAP has planned to build to meet a trail on the other side of the valley from where you descended, or travel downstream along the valley floor to a seasonal bridge. Reach Lubra (9859 feet, 3005 m) in **30 more minutes**. There are no tourist facilities here, but there are two (rarely encountered) monasteries of the Bon religion as well as a boarding school situated above the village. Across the Panda Khola from the village, meditation caves can be seen.

To continue on to **Jomosom** from Lubra, head down the valley. Reach a suspension bridge (9711 feet, 2960 m) in 15 minutes. Do not cross here but stay on the south side and traverse down to the valley floor (9547 feet, 2910) in another 15 minutes. Reach the Kali Gandaki valley (12,450 feet, 3795 m) in 40 minutes. Head left/south here to Jomosom, a further 1¼ hours away (**2¼–2½ hours** from Lubra). ❖

EXPLORE: NORTH ANNAPURNA BASE CAMP

This route from the Kali Gandaki valley to the original Annapurna Base Camp was discovered by the 1950 French Expedition that summited Annapurna led by Maurice Herzog. The French first tried to climb Dhaulagiri but found it beyond their capabilities and instead tried to find a way to the base of Annapurna. They had difficulty getting there from the Kali Gandaki, and the route still has a bad reputation. It is seldom used except by shepherds and mountaineering expeditions. However, in the relatively snow-free early fall and late spring, the route is neither very difficult nor dangerous. However,

YARTUNG FESTIVAL

At about the same time as the major pilgrimage *(Janai Purnimaa)* to Muktinath in the full moon of August–September, local Tibetan villagers of the valley hold a great end of summer festival called Yartung—a time of horse racing, dancing, gambling, and general merriment. This is held on the race grounds of Ranipauwa, adjacent to the Muktinath pilgrimage site in the Mustang District. BhoTiya people from all over Bargee (the Muktinath or Dzong river valley) and Lo-Manthang (upper Mustang), and some from Manang (east of Mustang), Lamjung (southeast), and Dolpo (west), attend. The men of BaragaaU region compete in a day of horse racing, and other games. It is a raucous occasion spiced by drinking and gambling in tents set up on the hills around the small community below Muktinath. The day begins with processions of laymen and monks in colorful attire, some riding equally decorated horses, from each of the surrounding villages. The monks lead the processions to circle the Muktinath shrine, and women perform purification rites at the temple's 108 water spouts. Yartung signals the return from the highlands of the animals, which are pastured in the lower valleys during the coming winter. Yartung annually attracts the majority of BhoTiya people from throughout upper Thak Khola, northern Mustang, and neighboring Manang District (over Thorung La). The participants wear their traditional ethnic dress. ❖

the trail is often indistinct and traverses steep grassy slopes. From **Lete**, it is a strenuous 5-day camping trip to substantial altitudes where food, fuel, and shelter must be carried. At certain times of the year, snow can make the trip almost impossible. Parties should be prepared for cold at any time of the year. It is always best to have someone along who is familiar with the route. Porters do not like this trail, but it is certainly no worse than little-used trails in many other areas of mountain wilderness.

The views along the way are supreme. As the trail climbs steeply out of the Kali Gandaki valley, the incredible gorge becomes more and more impressive. The views of Dhaulagiri and Annapurna from the crest of the ridge separating the Kali Gandaki from the Miristi Khola are breathtaking. From this perch (14,000 feet, 4267 m), some 7000 feet (2134 m) above the valley floor, you can appreciate just how high these mountains are. From the foreshortened view from **Kalopani**, it is hard to believe that Dhaulagiri is the sixth highest mountain in the world. If you venture beyond the base camp toward Camp One, on the north side of Annapurna, you can appreciate the impressive features of that side of the mountain.

You will want to get provisions in **Lete** for onward travel. There is a tea shop in Chhoya, but it is best to stock up in Lete for at least 5 days of self-sufficient travel. You might be able to hire someone from Chhoya to show the way. In times of high water, it may not be possible to cross the Miristi Khola and reach the base camp without building a bridge, an undertaking most trekkers prefer to avoid. If a recent expedition has been on Annapurna, the chance of finding a usable bridge is good. Check beforehand to find out if there has been a recent expedition. In low water, the river can be forded with some difficulty downstream.

If you are coming from the south, turn right off the road **20 minutes** after crossing the Lete Khola on a suspension bridge. In **10 minutes** more cross the tumultuous Kali Gandaki on a suspension bridge (7890 feet, 2405 m) to reach **Chhoya** (8000 feet, 2415 m). If you are coming from the north, across from the Primary Health Center in upper Lete, take a left fork. This left fork takes you through a beautiful pine forest before you descend slightly in 20 minutes to the same suspension bridge to Chhoya.

From Chhoya the right (east) fork heads to North Annapurna Base Camp via Jhipra Deorali. The left fork heads to Taglung, Kunjo, and on to Titi village/lake. To head to North Annapurna Base Camp, cross the delta of the Polje Khola and ascend to the few houses of Poljedanda (8175 feet, 2492 m). Then turn right and head southeast to a few more houses of Jhipra Deorali (8275 feet, 2522 m) **30 minutes** from Chhoya. This is the last village on the route. Here the trail forks left and you contour above fields to enter the valley of the Tangdung or Bhutra Khola, a little more than 30 minutes later. Contour below a small waterfall of a tributary to the main river (8075 feet, 2461 m) after a short, steep descent through forest, 1¼ **hours** from **Deorali**. There should be a bridge here unless it has been washed out during the monsoon. Fill up all your water containers, as you may not get another chance during the next day.

The next section of the trail is exceptionally steep. There are few suitable campsites until near the end of the climb. There are occasional vistas to inspire the weary. In 2–2½ **hours**, reach a saddle called **Kal Ghiu** (11,000 feet, 3383 m), although some trekking groups call this place Jungle Camp. Camping is possible here if you can find water down the other side of the saddle. Keep close to the crest of the ridge as you pass several notches. Enjoy the rhododendrons in bloom in the spring. After keeping to the southeast side of the ridge and leaving the forest, the trail becomes fainter, reaches a minor ridge crest (12,600 feet, 3840 m), and crosses over to the northwest side. Keep climbing to a prominent notch with a *chorten* (13,350 feet, 4069 m), some **2 hours** from Kal Ghiu. The views of Dhaulagiri are unforgettable.

The slope eases off now and continues over more moderate grazing slopes to a place near a ridge crest called **Sano Bugin** (13,950 feet, 4252 m), where herders stay during the monsoon. There are rock walls here that the herders convert to shelters with the use of bamboo mats. If there is no snow to melt, water may be difficult to obtain. The gigantic west face of Annapurna, first climbed by Reinhold Messner in 1985, is before you. Head north along the ridge crest, or on the west side. The trail is marked with slabs of rock standing on end. In **1 hour**, reach another ridge crest (14,375 feet, 4382 m) and cross to the southeast side of the ridge. This may be the *"passage du avril 27"* that Herzog's expedition discovered in order to get to the base of Annapurna. You are now in the drainage area of the Miristi Khola, the river that enters the Kali Gandaki above Tatopani.

Continue contouring for a few minutes to **Thulo Bugin** (14,300 feet, 4359 m), where seasonal herders stay. There is a small shrine here. Contour, crossing several tributaries of the Hum Khola, a tributary of the Miristi. The last stream (13,375 feet, 4077 m), reached in **30 minutes**, is a little tricky to cross. Climb on, at first gradually, then more steeply, to reach a flat area sometimes called **Bal Khola** (14,650 feet, 4465 m) in 1¾ **hours**. Camp here, for there are few other suitable places until the river is reached. The west face of Annapurna looms before you. Local people do not venture much beyond here in their tending of sheep and goats.

Descend and round a ridge crest to the canyon of the Miristi Khola proper. The river is almost a mile below you, yet its roar can be heard. Continue on steep grassy slopes and pass an overhanging rock (14,075 feet, 4290 m) suitable for camping, **45 minutes** from the high point. Descend more steeply on grass, cross a stream, and go down into shrubbery until it appears that a 1000-foot (300-m) cliff will block the way to the valley floor. The trail heads west to a break in the rock wall and descends through the break to the river (11,500 feet, 3505 m) **1½ hours** from the overhanging rock. The impressive gorge at the bottom gives a feeling of isolation. Head upstream on the northwest (right) bank. The dense shrubs may make travel difficult. There are campsites by some sand near a widening in the river (11,575 feet, 3528 m), where it may be possible to ford in low water. Otherwise, head upstream for 10 minutes to a narrowing where there may be a bridge. Cross the river, if possible, and camp on the other side if it is late.

Once on the southeast (left) bank of the Miristi Khola, follow the trail upstream. The vegetation soon disappears as altitude and erosion increase. The trail becomes indistinct in the moraine. As the valley opens up, bear right to the east and leave the river bottom to climb the moraine to a vague shelf. Continue beyond to a small glacial lake in the terminal moraine of the North Annapurna Glacier. Cross its outflow to the right and climb the lateral moraine to the left. There are views of the Nilgiri to the west. The base camp for the various attempts to climb Annapurna from the north is on a flat shelf of land (14,300 feet, 4359 m) to the north of the glacier. There is a steep drop-off to the glacier valley to the south and east. The base camp is reached in **3–4 hours** from the crossing of the Miristi Khola. Annapurna (26,545 feet, 8091 m) was the first 8000-m peak to be climbed, in 1950, by the French from this side.

The view of Annapurna I from the base camp is minimal. Better views can be obtained by contouring and climbing to the east to a grassy knoll from which much of the north face can be seen. You could also proceed toward Camp I by dropping from the shelf and climbing along the lateral moraine of the glacier to 16,000 feet (4877 m). Exploratory and climbing journeys will suggest themselves to those with experience. The Great Barrier, an impressive wall of mountains to the north, separates you from Tilicho Tal. Be sure to take enough food to stay awhile and enjoy this unforgettable area.

BIRDS OF THE SUBTROPICAL ZONE

The subtropical zone is considered to be (3300–6500 feet/1000–2000 m in the west, to 5500 feet/1700 m in the east).

Birds of prey either kill other animals or feed on their carcasses. Nepal has over seventy species, including twenty-one owls. The Egyptian vulture (*Neophron percnopterus*, length 24 inches, 60 cm) is a familiar small vulture around villages. It has a wedge-shaped tail. The adult is white with black flight feathers and yellow head (immature is brownish). It also occurs in tropical and temperate zones. The steppe eagle (*Aquila nipalensis*, length 29–32 inches, 74 to 81 cm) is a large eagle with long, broad wings and medium-long tail. From below, while in flight, it looks dark brown with one or two white wing bars across the undersides of its wings. It is a common winter visitor between September and April and occurs from tropical to alpine zones.

Its call monotonously repeated all day in spring and summer, the barbet usually remains hidden in tree tops. The blue-throated barbet (*Megalaima asiatica*, length 9 inches, 22 cm), green with a blue throat and face and red forehead, makes a loud "chuperup." It also occurs in tropical and temperate zones. The coppersmith (or crimson-breasted) barbet (*Megalaima haemacephala*, length 5½ inches, 14 cm), greenish with yellow throat and reddish breast, makes a metallic note said to resemble a coppersmith beating on metal. It also occurs in the tropical zone. The Indian cuckoo, or *kaphal pakyo* (*Cuculus micropterus,* length 13 inches, 33 cm), like several other cuckoo species, is grayish above and on the throat, with the rest of the underparts barred black and white. It occurs in tropical and temperate zones. Its bubbling call sounds like "one more bottle." It calls all night, as does the common hawk cuckoo or brain-fever bird (*Hierococcyx varius*, length 13 ½ inches, 34 cm), which is gray above and mottled or barred brown below. It occurs in the tropical zone. Calls start slowly and accelerate to a high pitch.

Nepal has six species of minivets. These are long-tailed, brightly colored arboreal birds. Long-tailed minivet, or *Ranichara* (*Pericrocotus ethologus*, length 7 inches, 18 cm) males are red and black, females yellow and black. Flocks often perch on treetops and twitter to each other as they fly from tree to tree. They occur in the temperate zone.

The Asian magpie robin (*Copsychus saularis*, length 7½ inches, 19 cm) is a long-tailed, black-and-white robin. The male is black above, on throat and breast, and rest of underparts; the wing bar and outer tail coverts are white. In the female, black is replaced by gray. Common in gardens, it has a sweet song of short, repeated phrases.

The spiny babbler (*Turdoides nipalensis*, length 11 ½ inches, 24 cm) is Nepal's only endemic bird. It is very secretive and rarely seen but fairly common in thick scrub. Grayish brown and streaked, with a long tail, it also occurs in the temperate zone. ❖

THE ANNAPURNA SANCTUARY

The term Annapurna Sanctuary, coined by outsiders, denotes the high basin southwest of Annapurna and the headwaters of the Modi Khola. This vast amphitheater, surrounded by Himalayan giants, was explored by Jimmy Roberts in 1956 and brought to the attention of the Western world by the British Expedition to Machhapuchhre in 1957. The presence of the gigantic mountains named for the goddesses Anna-purna and Gangapurna, important figures in Hindu myth and folklore, justify calling it a sanctuary. Its gate, the deep gorge between the peaks Hiunchuli and Machhapuchhre, marks a natural division between the dense rain forest and bamboo jungle of the narrow Modi Khola valley and the scattered summits and immense walls of the mountain fortress inside. This sanctuary area is also referred to as the Annapurna Base Camp and the Machhapuchhre Base Camp.

Trekking possibilities are varied. Those without time to head up the Kali Gandaki river, also known as Thak Khola, can make a circuit from Pokhara into the Annapurna Sanctuary in less than 10 days, with little backtracking. However, to enjoy the route and the sanctuary itself without feeling rushed, plan a few more days. This area can be easily combined with the entire Annapurna circuit or with a trek to Jomosom that offers various link-up possibilities.

The route up the Modi Khola has always had a reputation among porters for being slippery and difficult. While lodges and inns that cater to the trekker now exist outside

Extracting lokta *or bark from the* Daphne bholua *shrub for papermaking*
(Photo by R.C. Sedai)

TRADITIONAL PAPERMAKING

The centuries-old technique of making paper in Nepal has been revived by outsider interest in handmade paper. In addition to the manufacturing along the Kali Gandaki, you will find it made along tributaries of the Arun and parts in between. The *Daphne bholua* shrub grows at elevations of 7000 to 11,000 feet (2100 to 3300 m), and the barks used for making paper are called *lokta* or *baruwa* locally. The outer barks are stripped off, cleaned, then soaked in water and dried and carried down to the processing area. The alkali leachate of wood ashes is used for digesting the barks by boiling the mixture in copper vessels, cutting them, and continuing the process until they are soft and breakable. The bark material is then pounded into a pulpy mass and mixed into a dense emulsion with water. The casting of the pulp into paper is done by a stream or pond by mixing the concentrate in a tank of water, and swirling just the right amount on a mesh frame. The slurry on the frames is left to dry in the sun, when the paper is removed. ❖

the inhabited areas, the trail has not changed much. It is often wet, and in the steep and slippery places a fall could be disastrous. But the trail doesn't quite live up to its old reputation; the route to the North Annapurna Base Camp (covered in the previous section) is a much more serious undertaking.

You can find cooked food and lodging along the entire route in season (ask at Chomrong before venturing forth at other times). During winter months, snowfall may make the trip difficult or impossible, and avalanche hazard can increase the risk.

This is the homeland of the Gurung people, an ethnic group renowned for bravery in the Gurkha regiments. They speak their own unwritten language, a member of the Sino-Tibetan family, and names of villages don't transliterate accurately into Nepali. Hence the variations in spelling that you will see on signboards here. Is it Ghandrung or Ghandruk? Landrung or Landruk? Chomro or Chomrong? Kyumunu, Kimrong, Kymnu, Kyumnu, or Kimnu? We try to use the ACAP spellings.

For those traveling from Pokhara, one access route to the sanctuary leaves the road at Lumle to pass through Chandrakot. This is not a popular approach, as more people prefer beginning from Phedi or Naya Pul. If coming from the Kali Gandaki/Thak Khola, you could leave the standard trail at GhoRepani or Chitre.

NAYA PUL/BIRETHANTI TO THE ANNAPURNA SANCTUARY

Accommodations are available in almost all villages en route with opportunities to stay in traditional *bhaTTi* lower down.

From **Pokhara** (2713 feet, 827 m) you can either walk, or board a bus or taxi to get to the Baglung bus station (Nala Mukh or Besi Parak different from the Bas Parak, near Mahendra Pul), in the northern section of the city. Buses leave regularly. The first place trekkers leave the road is Phedi to either travel into the sanctuary via Landruk or to travel on the east side of the Modi Khola until reaching Himalpani.

Another place to leave the road is near Lumle, the site of a British agricultural development project where former Gurkha soldiers and others are trained in farming. It has one of the highest rainfalls in Nepal. Walk from **Lumle** (5300 feet, 1615 m) to **Chandrakot** (5250 feet, 1600 m) at the west end of the ridge in **30 minutes.** The views from Chandrakot are unforgettable. You will cross the Modi Khola, which flows south from between the peaks Annapurna South and Machhapuchhre, which stand before you. The Annapurna Sanctuary lies upriver inside the gate formed by Machhapuchhre and Hiunchuli, the peak east of Annapurna South. The trail descends to the Modi Khola, follows its east (left) bank southward a short distance to a suspension bridge, and crosses to the prosperous town of **Birethanti** (3600 feet, 1097 m) 1¼ **hours** from Chandrakot.

Trekkers usually arrive in Birethanti by getting off the bus at **Naya Pul**, a **30-minute** hike south of Birethanti. Those who are camping must be self-sufficient in fuel; there is a kerosene depot in Naya Pul. From Naya Pul, cross the Lumle Khola (3314 feet, 1010 m) from the bus drop-off point and walk to the suspension bridge (3428 feet, 1045 m) just east of Birethanti. There is an ACAP check post where you register. From here, the trail heads up the Modi Khola on its west (true right) bank toward the Annapurna Sanctuary. (The trail to the GhoRepani and on to the Kali Gandaki/Thak Khola heads west up the Bhurungdi Khola.)

Head east past the school, keeping close to the river, and passing fields and forests, to **Chimrong** (3707 feet, 1130 m) in **35 minutes.** Keep alongside the river to Syauli Bazaar and then ascend to the village of Kliu (4593 feet, 1400 m) with lodges in 40 minutes. From here, the trail divides, providing two options.

The more direct route to Chomrong and the sanctuary, bypassing Ghandruk, is to proceed right and keep along the valley to reach **Kyumi** with a pair of lodges in **40–50 minutes.** Kyumi (4380 feet, 1335 m) lies at a junction near the river between Ghandruk, 1970 feet (600 m) above to the west, and Landruk, across the river on a steel bridge and 820 feet (250 m) above. From Kyumi, continue following upriver to **Himal Kyu** (also, Naya Pul or New Bridge) with more lodges in **1½ hours**, passing through Jhinu Danda (with a developed hot springs 15 minutes below the lodge area) and up to **Daaulu** (also Taulung; signs here might refer to this area as part of Chomrong) and **Chomrong** in **2¼–2½ hours** from Himal Kyu.

Most people opt to ascend to Ghandruk from Kliu. Stay to the left and ascend along stone steps to Kimche (5381 feet, 1640 m), which has lodging, and on to teashops of **Chane** (5600 feet, 1707 m) at the entrance to Gurung country in **30–40 minutes** from Kliu.

PEOPLES OF CENTRAL NEPAL: GURUNG

The Gurung are most prominent on high ridges and upper valleys below the Annapurna and Himal Chuli massifs north and east of Pokhara, eastward beyond Gorkha. They are an enterprising upland farming and herding people; their sheep herds are often seen along the Manang trail on the Marsyangdi river route. They are subdivided into many clans, but except for the Ghale (pronounced like "golly"), who prefer to use the clan name, most call themselves, simply, Gurung. They, like their Magar counterparts, occupy some of the most inaccessible villages, high on the mountainsides above the trekking routes. Young Gurung men are often encountered as porters; older Gurung of distinction may have served in the Gurkha regiments, and many have interesting tales. If you happen to stop at a Gurung village for the night, you might see their colorful dances, or other ritual or festival activities, some of which display very ancient characteristics. Especially interesting are Gurung funerary rituals (called *arghun*), which are described later. ❖

Machhapuchhre (Fishtail Peak) lit by the setting sun with accompanying moonrise
(Photo by R.C. Sedai)

From Chane, a trail forks left to TirkheDUgaa in the headwaters of the Bhurungdi Khola, on the way to GhoRepani.

Stay right and ascend and cross a tributary a few minutes later, and continue uphill on a stone-laid path. Those coming from Landruk will join this trail near a *chautaaraa* and just beyond is a large, cement entranceway. Reach **Ghandruk** (6600 feet, 2012 m) in **40 minutes** from **Chane**. Ghandruk is a large, affluent Gurung village. Much of the wealth comes from handsome pensions provided to Gurungs who have served in the British Army. This income was one of several factors that changed their primary livelihood from herding and hunting to sedentary farming. Tourism has further increased their wealth.

At the top end of Ghandruk, the trail leads to Banthanti and GhoRepani, at least a day's walk. It takes **15–20 minutes** to pass through Ghandruk, and the mountain views are spectacular. Do pay a visit to the ACAP complex on a spur near the lower end of town to see the energy conservation technology they espouse and more. There are two locally run Gurung museums as well as a medical post. Sometimes, Gurung dancing and singing can be staged for trekkers willing to pay for the show. A Local Youth Eco-Trekking Centre has been set up where local guides might be hired and tours arranged.

Leave the town to the northwest, and in 10 minutes cross a tributary. (The trail branching left here heads to TaaDapaani and on to GhoRepani.) Stay with the right branch and ascend through fields and oak forest in a side draw to reach Komrong Danda (also Kimrong Danda), a prominent notch (7400 feet, 2255 m) with lodges and magnificent mountain views, **50 minutes** beyond Ghandruk. Descend steeply into the valley of the **Kimrong Khola** (also called Kyumnu and Kimnu) on a trail much improved over the one where Stephen got lost in 1969, to reach the river in **45 minutes** (5940 feet, 1810 m). Cross here and head up to the few simple lodges of Kimrong Khola just beyond (where another trail ties in from TaaDapaani). Now climb steeply up the hillside and come to a junction near a hotel. The left branch heads to TaaDapaani. Stay with the right branch and enter the Modi Khola valley at **Daaulu** (also Taulung; signs here might refer to this area as part of Chomrong), **70 minutes** from the Kimrong Khola crossing.

At this junction of the two valleys (7160 feet, 2182 m), there are signs pointing out the routes. On the return you can take the right fork here and descend the spur below, and then either cross the river beyond, and reach Landruk or stay on the west side of the river to Syauli Bazaar on a direct route to Birethanti. But to head to Chomrong, enter the tributary valley draining the south side of Annapurna South (left) and Hiunchuli (right), the major peaks before you. On the way is ACAP with a Safe Drinking Water Station as you reach **Chomrong**, a prosperous Gurung village (7054 feet, 2150 m), in **15 minutes** from Daaulu. Pass the school 400 feet (122 m) above the center of town. There are many large hotels for trekkers here and shops, some of which rent out warm clothing and equipment. Chomrong had one of the first hyrodropower projects in the ACAP region, built in 1982, and the area now boasts a newer 30-kw plant.

From Chomrong, descend northward to cross the main tributary, the **Chomrong Khola**, on a suspension bridge (6200 feet, 1890 m) **20–25 minutes** beyond. Climb through terraces and the few houses and tea shops of Kilche (6700 feet, 2042 m) and Banuwa with lodges and enter the main Modi Khola valley, which you will follow for the next 2 days. The trail was previously used only by shepherds, who drove their flocks of sheep and goats up during the monsoon to browse in the forests and the shrubbery above tree line.

Continue uphill to **Sinuwa** (7625 feet, 2324 m) in **1–1¼ hours** from the suspension bridge. This last permanent settlement with lodges resulted from the trekker traffic. ACAP strictly regulates the area beyond Sinuwa with rules regarding fuel use as well as lodge location and size. Contour along a reasonable trail in a rhododendron-and-oak forest, reaching growths of bamboo as you go farther up the valley. Pass an abandoned shack that was a former ACAP post at a place currently without facilities known as **Kuldhighar** (8200 feet, 2499 m) in **60–70 minutes** as you go through increasingly dense forest. The trail drops slightly from here and then appears transformed into the stone staircases similar to those of the Gurung villages to the south, but with the addition of drainage ditches.

The main mountain visible at the head of the valley is Annapurna III; Machhapuchhre, the "fish-tail" mountain whose name has been obvious for some time now, is off to the right. Enter a dense bamboo rain forest. The area around Pokhara and south of the main Himalaya receives considerably more rainfall than almost any place in Nepal. South of Pokhara, the Mahabharat Lekh, the range of hills above the Tarai, is lower than in other parts and does not obstruct the northerly flow of moisture. The trail is usually wet, and do not be surprised if leeches are lurking in this jungle except during the cold season. (For more about leeches, including tips for prevention and first aid, see Chapter 5 and

USES OF BAMBOO

Bamboos are prolific, especially in the high-rainfall areas around Pokhara and the eastern hills. Bamboo (a type of woody grass) can be found at altitudes up to 13,000 feet (4000 m) in the east. It is a multipurpose raw material with an incredible variety of uses. Some species are very hard and can withstand great compressive forces as pillars. Bamboos don't last long, and thus need to be replaced regularly. The softer ones are flexible, and thin strips can be woven into baskets and trays. They provide good protection against erosion because of their dense surface roots. This rhizome root system can hold up terraces and road banks. Villagers cultivate many species and harvest them in controlled fashion by thinning older poles, preserving the clump to protect the soil. Because they grow so rapidly, new shoots are soon out of the reach of grazing animals. Species take long periods to flower, sometimes up to 150 years. Some can be a foot (30 cm) in diameter and used as pillars or storage containers but are too large for most purposes. Smaller culmed species are used as fodder, while shoots are eaten by people. There are well over twenty species found, usually with specific Nepali names. Broad categories include *bAAs*, the large-stature species, at moderate altitudes; *nigaalo*, the smaller species; and *maalingo*, at higher altitudes, which produce the best weaving materials. Human torpedoes may be met catapulting down steep trails headed for home as they clutch their bamboo charges under their arms. You will often see people in villages stripping bamboo and weaving articles of it. Bamboos are used as building materials for bridges, roofs, floors, ceilings, and walls. Sitting mats (*gundri*), winnowing trays (*naanglo*), twine, sieves, pipes, water carriers, containers, straws, and a large variety of baskets are other uses of this versatile grass. ❖

the sidebar on Leeches in Chapter 6.)

Reach a clearing and several lodges of **Bamboo** (7700 feet, 2347 m), in **30 minutes.** Cross several substantial streams. The third has an overhanging rock upstream that could serve as a shelter in a pinch. Eventually, you reach **Dovan** (8366 feet, 2550 m), with three inns, in **40–50 minutes.** The rhododendrons festooned with moss in the forest beyond are gigantic; sometimes orchids can be spotted. This region has over 100 varieties of orchids. There are hemlocks too, but, due to excessive rainfall, not as many as elsewhere at this elevation.

Onward from Dovan the trail is subject to avalanches, passing several channels on the way to Annapurna Base Camp. You may find the remains of some near the trail. After heavy snowfall above, which may be rain along the trail, the safest course may be to wait a few days for the slopes to clear. Because none of the avalanche slopes can be easily seen from the valley floor, it is difficult to be sure when it is safe to proceed. Be aware that trekkers have been buried by avalanches along here. If up in the sanctuary, wait a few days if food supplies allow. If you need to cross this portion, especially between Hinku and Machhapuchhare Base Camp, you could cross to the east bank of the Modi Khola.

As you wend your way through the forest and cross several streams, at a slight rise you will find a small shrine (Panchenin Baraha or Barahathan). Local custom prohibits meat and eggs north of here, so as not to arouse the ire of the mountain gods, resulting in sickness and even death in your party. Although the custom is widely broken nowadays, Nepalis might explain the misfortune that has befallen some trekking groups

A typical guest house sign near the Annapurna Sanctuary (Photo by Mark Jackson and Susan Bergin/SAFA Himalaya Collection/Nepal)

and mountaineering expeditions in the sanctuary by its breach. Notice the weeping wall across the valley coming down from Machhapuchhre, a gift from the god Baraha. Shortly beyond, the forest opens slightly and below you can see the rushing river torrent.

Come to a pair of lodges at a clearing, called **Himalaya** (9425 feet, 2890 m), in just over **1–1¼ hours** beyond Dovan. After another stretch of forest, the valley begins to open up. In **35–45 minutes** reach **Hinko** (10,300 feet, 3139 m), a large overhanging rock.

Cross streams and proceed through the boulders of an avalanche trough and reach **Deorali** (10,600 feet, 3231 m) **30 minutes** from Hinko, where there are several lodges. Notice the beautiful birches growing in this area. A route on the other side of the valley might be in use as a detour around the avalanche channel. It ties back in near the former lodges at the site named Bagar. Pass these former lodges, now abandoned, and cross streams. As you proceed along, you can admire before you the triangular snow-and-rock face of Gangapurna.

Suddenly, you cross through the imaginary mountain gates and are inside the sanctuary! A stream flows in from the west and a large grass-covered moraine is ahead of you, with more grassy slopes beyond. Reach a shelf with several inns, the so-called **Machhapuchhre Base Camp** (12,150 feet, 3703 m), in **1½–2 hours.** Nearby is a meteorological data collection station. The west face of Machhapuchhre looms above you. There has not been a legally sanctioned expedition to sacred Machhapuchhre since 1957, and that one stopped short of the summit. Be cognizant of the rapid gain in altitude and possible symptoms of AMS. As Annapurna Base Camp is more than 1300 feet (400 m) higher, some people use Machhapuchhre Base Camp as the base for trips higher.

The trail heads along a stream between the lateral moraine to the right and the north slopes of Hiunchuli on the left and ascends to pass seasonal *goTh* along the

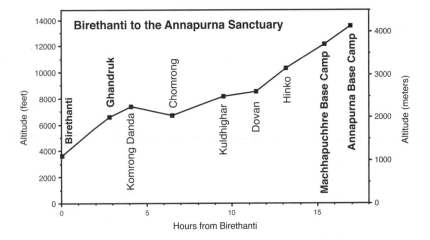

Birethanti to the Annapurna Sanctuary

way. In less than **1 hour**, the **halfway point** to the Annapurna Base Camp is reached (12,925 feet, 3939 m). The views are exceptional from here but are even more monumental farther on, at the **Annapurna Base Camp**, where several lodges provide food and shelter during peak season. This flat area (13,550 feet, 4130 m) was first used by the British in their successful first ascent of the South Face of Annapurna in 1970. It is the coldest and windiest of all places to stay, but is well worth it in views if you are acclimatized and suitably equipped. Wandering around here, it would be difficult to not feel at peace with nature. Venture beyond to the crest of the moraine to gaze upon the awesome mountain walls. From left to right they are Hiunchuli, Annapurna South, Fang, Annapurna, Annapurna III, and Machhapuchhre. Tent Peak and Fluted Peak, rising above the hills to the north, complete the unforgettable panorama. *Ghoral*, a type of goat-antelope, might be seen in this area as well. Consider emerging from the warmth of the lodge to view the majestic scene under moonlight as well.

ALTERNATE APPROACH: GHOREPANI TO GHANDRUK AND CHOMRONG

This route keeps high, traversing the ridge system to reach Ghandruk. Do not travel this route alone, as bandits sometimes work the forest. A viewpoint 40 minutes along the way from GhoRepani offers a grand panorama that rivals Poon Hill and could be a time- and energy-saving alternate to the early-morning jaunt in the opposite direction.

The trail begins from both upper or lower GhoRepani. Follow the signpost from the lower section to climb to the ridge above, or from the upper part, properly known as **GhoRepani Deorali** (9450 feet, 2880 m), head east through the forest, keeping close to the ridge. Reach a clearing (10,360 feet, 3158 m), in **40 minutes,** with an immense panoramic view of Machhapuchhre to beyond Gurja Himal. Climb a little more before descending to **Deorali Pass** (10,140 feet, 3090 m) in another **30 minutes.** (The trail mentioned earlier from Chitre joins here.) There are inns here and a viewpoint 30 minutes above. Head south to descend a steep gully that is treacherous when wet or icy. Pass another lodge, and continue in a moss-festooned rhododendron forest until you reach **Banthanti** ("place in the forest" with several inns) (8740 feet, 2664 m) beneath a steep cliff in **45 minutes–1 hour.** Himalayan black bear have been recorded here, but your chances of spotting one are slight, for it is nocturnal.

Cross the stream and begin climbing, pass a lodge and another at a viewpoint before heading downhill to cross a stream. From here it is uphill along a stone staircase through forest to **TaaDapaani** (meaning "far water," 8800 feet, 2682 m), beautifully situated in a notch, in **45 minutes–1 hour** from Banthanti. All of the facilities at these places where there is no farmland have been set up for trekkers. There was no sign of habitation here 30 years ago. Just below the pass, to the southeast, there is a trail fork, with the right branch going to Ghandruk, the left to Chomrong, the gateway to the Annapurna Sanctuary trek. Both options will be mentioned.

ALTERNATE ROUTE
- -

TaaDapaani to Ghandruk

To go to Ghandruk, take the right fork to head downhill through rhododendron to **BhAIsi Kharka** ("buffalo pasture," again with lodges, 8260 feet, 2518 m) in **35 minutes.** From here the trail diverges, offering two routes to Ghandruk. Take the branch to the right and then continue to descend. The path crosses a tributary along the way and reaches the upper flank of **Ghandruk** in another **1½ hours**. ◈

TaaDapaani to Chomrong via Gurjung

If taking the left fork at **TaaDapaani** to go to **Chomrong**, there are two choices, and both lead to the route to Chomrong. The first is considered less strenuous and descends steeply to the north, passing lodges along the way to Chiule and more lodges as you reach Siprong (6480 feet, 1975 m). Continue downhill to cross the Kimrong Khola (6266 feet, 1910 m) before ascending to the village **Gurjung** (6644 feet, 2025 m) with lodges in **1¾–2 hours** from TaaDapaani. Continue ascending to reach a trail junction in **30–40 minutes**. Here the trail meets the trail from Ghandruk (as well as the other, more strenuous alternate route from TaaDapaani which ties below with the trail from Ghandruk). ◈

TaaDapaani to Chomrong via MelAAje

To take the alternate route from **TaaDapaani** to the junction with the trail from Ghandruk, begin by descending less steeply to the northeast. Reach **MelAAje** (7260 feet, 2213 m) village in **50 minutes**. Descend steeply through terraced fields to the Kimrong (Kyumnu) Khola. Cross a suspension bridge to meet the trail from Ghandruk near the lodges of Kimrong Khola in **45 minutes** from MelAAje. ◈

RETURN JOURNEY VARIATION: CHOMRONG TO THE ROAD AT PHEDI

This route avoids some backtracking and could be followed in reverse as a direct route to the Annapurna Sanctuary.

From Chomrong, return to **Daaulu** (also Taulung), (7160 feet, 2182 m), above the spur of mostly terraced land that appears to jut out into the Modi Khola valley. Take the left fork that descends steeply through terraced fields of millet. Reach the lodges of **Jhinu** (also Chinu) **Danda** (5758 feet, 1755 m), **40–45 minutes** from the junction. This is a settlement of Jaishi Brahmans. There is a hot spring near the river about 15 minutes away, and a sign points the direction to the concrete pools.

Beyond, the main trail drops on the south side of the spur, to a bridge (5180 feet, 1579 m) at the Kimrong Khola some **15–20 minutes** from Jhinu. Cross and make a brief, steep climb to return to the Modi Khola valley and drop down through stands of bamboo to the lodges at **Himal Kyu/New Bridge** (also known as Naya Pul), (4642 feet, 1415 m), some **25–30 minutes** from the previous bridge. Himal Kyu has a Gurung meaning of "water from the snows."

Just down from Himal Kyu/New Bridge, cross the Modi Khola to the east (true left) bank to another lodge at Himalpani, and then climb and contour through thick forest before reaching cutivated terraces. About halfway to Landruk you cross a suspension bridge over a tributary (5175 feet, 1577 m) near a waterfall. About 10 minutes beyond, do not take the stone staircase that descends to a hydroelectric plant. Cross another stream on a suspension bridge and within 5 minutes reach the main trail from Landruk to Ghandruk. A brief climb brings you to **Landruk (5250 feet, 1600 m)**, a large Gurung settlement set on a hillside with many accomodations, **1½ hours** from Himal Kyu/New Bridge.

Take the upper trail that heads out of the valley, to climb into the Pokhara drainage beyond as you contour south through tributary valleys. Ascend to **Tolka** (5660 feet, 1725 m), with many lodges, in **45 minutes.** Pass through more lodging at Bheri Kharka and climb through the woodland out of the valley and a clearing with lodges at **Bhichok Deorali** (6923 feet, 2110 m) in **1¼–1½ hours.** Continue in the same direction you have been walking and cross to the opposite (east) side of the ridge to contour above the Indi Khola valley, staying to the left at branches. Descend slightly to the lodges and tea shops and ACAP check post at **Potana** (6460 feet, 1969 m) in **30 minutes.**

ALTERNATE ROUTE

Potana to KAre

To head directly from **Potana** to the road at KAre, bypassing Dhampus, fork right on the way out to reach lodging at ThulA Kharka in 15–20 minutes. Descend and eventually pass through the village of GolDAdA before reaching **KAre** and the road in **1–1¼ hours** from Potana. ❖

Most people will opt to return to the road via Dhampus. To do this, do not take the right fork from Potana but stay to the left at junctions and continue to descend through rhododendron to reach **Dhampus** (5560 feet, 1695 m) in **1 hour** from **Potana**. The main village is spread out farther along the north side of this ridge. The views of the snowclad giants from here are worth the wait if the weather has been bad. The road now reaches here and it might be possible to catch transport to avoid a steep descent to Phedi. Otherwise, descend along stone stairs. There are *chautaaraa* along the way as you descend through sala and *chilaune* trees.

As you drop down to the river valley floor, you'll be impressed with this uncut forest so close to Pokhara. The people of Dhampus have traditionally protected this forest, and governmental programs belatedly realized that this social forestry should be encouraged. The path will cross the road several times as you continue steeply downhill. Reach **Phedi** (3750 feet, 1143 m) and the road to Pokhara in less than **1 hour**.

TO MANANG AND OVER THORUNG LA

The Eastern Valley of the Annapurna Circuit

The Manang area offers many of the same attractions of a trek to Jomosom via the Kali Gandaki/Thak Khola. The Manangba, the people of Manang, are a most worldly ethnic group, and some of the men may have traveled farther on the globe than you. The mountain scenery is perhaps more breathtaking than on the other side, if only because the peaks in the open Manang valley are closer. It takes a week to reach the town of Manang if you walk the entire way from Khudi or Besisahar (add 4 days if you walk from Thumsikot via The Gurung Heritage Trail, Chapter 9). There are no Thakali here running the kind of hotels and lodges for tourists that you find on the trail to Jomosom, but the local people have set up comparable inns and hotels that cater to Western tastes. A motor road is well on its way to connect Besisahar with Manang; however, much of the classic trekking avoids the road, and there are alternative routes to escape sections of the road as well.

Enjoy it all. Cross Thorung La and circle the Annapurna massif. It is a walk of nearly 135 miles (215 km), but the rewards certainly compensate for the effort. The circuit takes at least two-and-a-half weeks, perhaps a week more than just walking to Manang and then retracing your steps, but this includes time for some diversions. There are now seasonal inns set up on both sides of the pass, so it is possible to cross without being self-sufficient, though storms that catch you up high may make it difficult to reach lodging. A number of trekkers have died because they pushed on in deteriorating conditions when not adequately prepared with food, clothing, and shelter. Bad weather can threaten the party at any time, and it is prudent to wait it out or turn back rather than risk lives. Serious frostbite is not uncommon among those who are inadequately prepared. Crossings can be difficult or impossible if there is deep, soft snow on the pass. Such conditions can be expected from January to March, and often longer. The check posts on either side of the pass will advise you when conditions prevent safer crossings; however, this is not a substitute for good mountain sense.

As a variation in returning from Manang (or as an alternate approach to Khudi), you might consider taking a trekking route from Khudi toward Pokhara, avoiding Besisahar and Dumre while experiencing the scenes and culture of mid-hill Gurung villages, which cannot be had on the more commericialized circuit. The Thumsikot to Khudi route is described under The Gurung Heritage Trail in Chapter 9 (follow the route description in reverse if you choose to walk out this way). This route takes 3–4 days, and there are traditional accommodations, nothing like the usual trekker lodges. Most of the villages passed are inhabited by Gurung, who farm the high hills and raise sheep. Trekkers wishing to meet few other foreigners should consider this route.

DUMRE TO MANANG

The route is described from Besisahar, reached from the town of Dumre on the Kathmandu–Pokhara highway. The basic route description is very simple. The entire trek is spent going up the Marsyangdi Khola to its headwaters and then crossing a pass to reach the Kali Gandaki drainage. The lower portions of the valley are broad, and then the modern trail passes through the bottom of the gorge where the river cuts through the main Himalayan system, until it finally opens into a broader alpine glacial valley. Like the next major valley to the west, the Kali Gandaki, the Marsyangdi Khola was once a major salt-for-rice trade route. We have occasionally borrowed shamelessly from Liesl Messerschmidt's booklet *Kings, Myths and Apple Pie*, on the local lore.

Dumre (1500 feet, 457 m) is reached in some 5 hours by bus from Kathmandu, or 2½ hours from Pokhara (depending on road conditions). From Pokhara, board the bus at the tourist bus station, Lakeside, or at the main bus staging area near the Prithvi/ Lakan Chowk intersection, on the road that heads from Pokhara to Kathmandu. The bus terminals are often called *bas parak* ("bus park"). Minivans ("micro") can be found 325 feet (100 m) north of Prithvi Chowk at the Micro Bus Stand.

Nepal's dramatic landscape flourishes during the rainy season. (Photo by Gail Robson)

From Kathmandu, there are direct buses to Dumre or Besisahar from Baleju Bus Park in Kathmandu, and tickets can be purchased a day in advance. Minivans are available near Baleju, along the Ring Road from the bus park. During tourist season, tourist buses line up in the early morning along Kantipath just down from Thamel's Tridevi Marg for transport to Pokhara and elsewhere. Additionally, you can find bus and minivans at Kalanki Chowk, the main intersection on the way out of Kathmandu before heading to the Thangkot escarpment. Be advised that those susceptible to motion sickness should choose to take a bus rather than a minivan.

The bus journey from Kathmandu follows the Prithvi Rajmarg, the highway between Kathmandu and Pokhara. This highway is the main artery out of Kathmandu for vehicles traveling to eastern and western Nepal as well as south to India. Just after leaving the Kathmandu valley, the road descends through the steep, twisting Thangkot escarpment. It is usually slow going up to Mugling, halfway to Pokhara, and the point of confluence of the Marsyangdi and Trishuli rivers, which become the Narayani River. Most vehicles turn south here to follow the Narayani 22 miles (36 km) to the highway that runs the length of Nepal, the Mahendra Rajmarg. Roads are planned for a direct route from Kathmandu to the Tarai to a possible new international airport in Bara District as well as to eastern Nepal. However, until completed, this current route is likely to remain clogged with buses and trucks.

Dumre, farther west along the Prithvi Rajmarg, is one of the many towns that have sprung up to serve the needs of travelers, traders, and villagers. It is a principal staging area for people arriving and departing for the hinterland of the Marsyangdi Khola. Keep a close eye to your belongings, as theft has been a problem in Dumre.

If you did not arrange transport all the way to Besisahar from Pokhara or Kathmandu, you can do so in Dumre. The feeder road is paved to Besisahar, reached in less than 2 hours from Dumre by bus, with occasional mountain views along the way.

Besisahar (2579 feet, 786 m) is a major town situated on a shelf of land above the Marsyangdi Khola, and is the Lamjung District headquarters and the site of a police check post. The town also has a district hospital, a prison, a high school, government offices, shops, a cinema, lodges, and electricity. It is a real "boomtown" in every sense. Above Besisahar on the ridge to the west is Lamjung Durbar, which was the summer palace of the sixteenth-century Ghale Gurung Rajas, who wintered down below. Climb up there for a view and a sense of the history of this region.

There are several choices from Besisahar onward to the circuit. The traditional route follows the road to Khudi. However, there are other options than following the road the entire way. We recommend taking the road as far as Belauti Bisauna and crossing the Marysyangdi to Lete, then continuing on to Bhulbule. The section from Lete to Bhulbule is described below, as is the way from Besisahar to Belauti Bisanna.

ALTERNATE ROUTE

Left Bank to Lete

Another route that entirely avoids the road and travels to Bhulbule from Besisahar follows the opposite, true left bank of the Marsyangdi, bypassing Khudi. For this route, from the main bazaar in **Besisahar** follow the road down toward the hospital. Just before the hospital, at the main post office, head north on the road that branches left, paralleling the main bazaar road. After 15 minutes, take a trail that branches right from the road just before a large boarding school. Descend to the Marsyangdi Khola, crossing over a suspension bridge (2228 feet, 679 m) in under 15 minutes. Pass the tea houses of the small hamlet of Botephanth, ascend steeply, then descend to a bridge over the Bacchoukhola in 45 minutes. Cross the bridge rather than continuing up to the village of Khasur Besi, then contour to **Lete**, a walk of 45 minutes or **1½ hours** from crossing the **Marsyangdi**. (A less obvious but shorter route from Botephanth forks to the left after climbing for approximately 25 minutes, then descends steeply to cross the Bacchoukhola on a makeshift bridge in under 10 minutes. From here, climb to a crest and then descend steeply to the Marsyangdi and follow the river to reach Lete in another 45 minutes.) The route from Lete to Bhulbule is described below. ❖

Right Bank to Lete

Otherwise, to proceed from **Besisahar** on the west (true right) bank of the Marsyangdi, continue north through town to the end of the wide roadbed. The peak up the valley is Gyahi Kang. Just where the tarmac ends and the road (now dirt) descends, fork to the right by *a chautaara* across from a forestry office. Descend from the shelf and cross the tributary PoDjo Khola **10 minutes** later. Follow the road from here. (For a short detour, reach a stone staircase in 5 minutes and climb steeply to the Magar village of Tanaute [2560 feet, 780 m].) Pass below Tanaute in **10 minutes.** Continue along the road above the Marsyangdi Khola and reach **Belauti Bisauna** in 35 minutes.

From Belauti Bisauna, take the trail to the right away from the road to cross the Marysyangdi on a suspension bridge across to **Lete** in **1 hour** from Besisahar. ❖

From **Lete**, contour through fields and pass through Badagau, and ascend to the settlement of **Batisemul/Mul Bazaar** (2795 feet, 852 m), with tea shops, in **45 minutes.** The trail forks from Batisemul, with the right branch leading on to Bhulbule (and the left to Khudi, crossing the Marsyangdi two times). Take the right branch and ascend through fields to the village of **Simulchaur** (3048 feet, 929 m) in **15 minutes.**

The "Model Tourism" village of Sirung (Photo by Tokozile Robbins)

WEAVING TRADITIONS: NETTLE

Trekkers commonly come across weavers during their travels. A variety of fibers are used, including the giant Himalayan nettle (*allo*) in the east for making clothing, casting fish nets, and tumplines; *raDi*, a rough, felted woolen cloth used as a hooded blanket; or cotton used for the dhaka cloth to make traditional Nepali hats for men (*Topi*).

With nettle as an example, the fiber is harvested after the monsoon before the plant flowers. Hands are protected by a bundle of cloth used to strip off thorns and leaves. The stems are cut, then the outer bark of a bundle of five is stripped off by incising the stem with the harvester's teeth and pulling with the hands supporting the end by the feet. The outer barks are stored in twisted bundles and then boiled in a water/ash mixture. The subsequent washed fibers are rubbed with clay to separate them and then dried. The fibers are teased apart by stretching between the upper arm and toes and then spun using a hand spindle. The tip fibers are kept for fine yarn, the coarser middle ones for making mats. Trekkers can sometimes see people spinning while walking along the trail or attending to other chores. Borrow the "works" and see if you can do it!

Nettle is woven on backstrap looms in the winter when there is little fieldwork to be done. First the warp yarns have to be prepared for the loom and assembled, often stretching them around stakes in the ground. The loom's warp beam is attached to the roof rafter or on a support beam and weaving begins. Items made from *allo* include sacks (*bhangra*) done in about five days, smaller bags (*jholaa*), tumplines (*naamlo*), jackets (*phenga*), often with cotton embroidery along the seams, and casting fish nets (*jal*) woven exclusively by men. ❖

Shortly beyond Simalchaur the trail forks; stay right. Ascend and pass above the villages of Bandre and Ambote to contour around the mountain before descending to **Bhulbule** (2723 feet, 830 m) in less than **1¼ hours** from Simalchaur. The trail ties in to the main Annapurna Circuit trail at Bhulbule. The route continues up the true left bank of the Marsyangdi. However, the ACAP check post is on the north or true right bank just beyond the suspension bridge across the Marsyangdi.

If staying on the road to Khudi rather than detouring through Lete to Bhulbule, continue to the Khudi Khola, a main tributary stream that drains the east end of the Lamjung Himal. Reach tea shops and a lodge near the old suspension bridge in **35 minutes** from Belauti Bisana. The mountains seen to the northeast are Ngadi Chuli and Baudha Himal. Either cross the old bridge (2600 feet, 792 m) to the older section of Khudi, or ascend and cross on a vehicle bridge (less than 10 minutes upstream) to the newer part of **Khudi**, on the east (left) bank of the Khudi Khola. There is a *gomba*, a Buddhist temple, on the ridge above the village. From Khudi north, the Marsyangdi valley turns, narrows, and changes character.

If traveling by way of Khudi, two trail options are available from Khudi onward. Both choices meet up in Shyange a few days up the Marysangdi Khola. The traditional route is to continue on to Bhulbule and follow the Marsyandi along its true left bank before crossing back at Shyange. The other infrequently chosen adventurous option is to stay high, traversing the hills to the northwest of the Marsyangdi before descending to Shyange.

West-Side Route from Khudi to Shyange

The lesser-used passage from Khudi to Shyange travels via villages high above the river's northwest (right) bank and will take a full day longer than the traditional route. There are currently only a few lodges with basic facilities, although more facilities are being developed. Home stay might be required, and the route is not always obvious— you might have to ask locals for directions.

Just above **Khudi**, to the left from the road ascend on concrete stairs to a *gomba* on a crest above the village (this high route bypasses the first ACAP check post at Bhulbhule). Pass to the left of the *gomba*. There are several paths that make a shortcut of the more circuitous, wider trail to the spread-out settlement of **Taraphu** (3018 feet, 920 m), which lies on a plateau **20 minutes** from leaving the road. From the upper houses at the northeast end of Taraphu, follow the wide track for 15 minutes before taking a narrower trail that branches to the left to contour and ascend to the east of a ridge. In under 1 hour the trail forks; the left/upper trail crosses a tributary and ascends steeply to pass a *chorten* on the way into **Dhangai** (5194 feet, 1583 m), a Gurung village, **1½ hours** from Taraphu. There are a few shops and plans to build lodging facilities. (If you take the right/lower path, you will cross the same tributary where there is a natural pool in the stream. This lower trail heads below the village of Dhangai, ascending steeply and then contouring up the Marsyangdi Khola valley before tying in later with the upper route that went through Dhangai.)

From the lower end of Dhangai village, the trail passes a *chorten* on the way out of town and contours to the northeast. (A lesser-used and more difficult trail to Sirung village heads from the upper end of Dhangai and ascends to cross the ridge to the northeast.) After 10 minutes, the trail divides. Take the right/lower path to head to Ghosing and on to Sirung. After 20 minutes from the fork the trail ties in with the lower trail to Ghosing that bypasses Dhangai. In another 2 hours the trail branches again. The right/lower fork bypasses Ghosing and heads directly to Sirung. Take the left/upper path which ascends to pass by a school and then reaches the Tamang village of **Ghosing** (5840 feet, 1780 m) in 30 minutes from the juncture or **3 hours** from Dhangai. Ghosing has a simple lodge and a few shops. Another 10 minutes beyond Ghosing is the hamlet of Nanamro (5794 feet, 1766 m). From the northwest end of Nanamro, the trail descends and meets the trail to Sirung that bypasses Ghosing and Nanamro. Just beyond is a suspension bridge (5463 feet, 1665 m) over the Gade Khola. Cross the bridge and ascend sharply to the "Model Tourism" village of **Sirung** (6115 feet, 1864 m) in just over **1 hour** from Ghosing. A small *gomba* lies above town. (To the left and below the *gomba* is the difficult, high trail link to Dhangai.) Another trail ascending to the right of the *gomba* leads to Dudh Pokhari, a high lake 2 days away requiring self-sufficiency in food, fuel, and shelter as there are no facilities.

The trail to Kalagiring heads from the northwest end of Sirung. Contour, keeping to the largest trail and reach **Kalagiring** (5961 feet, 1817 m) in **45 minutes**. Continuing on, the trail heads out from the northwest end of the village and after 15 minutes reaches a junction. Take the right/lower path to head to Sildhunga (the upper path leads to a village named Garigaun). After another 30 minutes, come to a rest area at a major junction. The left path ascends steeply to Garigaun; the right descends to Ghoptegaun. Continue straight. Be aware that this area is especially leech-infested during the rainy season. The path then crosses an area prone to landslides and arrives at the large village of **Sildhunga** (5164 feet, 1574 m) in **2 hours** from Kalagiring.

The trail heads out from the northeast of Sildhunga and descends to reach Atkhet (4741 feet, 1445 m), a Chhetri village, in 30 minutes. From here the trail branches.

Head left/north, rather than descend, and then contour, passing below a small *gomba*, to the Gurung village of Chapdanda (4757 feet, 1450 m) in 30 minutes. Head west out of Chapdanda, contour, and descend to cross a suspension bridge over a dazzling gorge of the Sangu Khola in 20 minutes. Shortly beyond the gorge, just past a *pipal* tree, the trail divides again. Take the left branch to reach the upper houses of Mipra (4350 feet, 1326 m) a few minutes beyond and then descend to the lower section of Mipra. From the bottom of the village the trail diverges. Rather than descending directly toward the river, take the path to the left and contour through fields for a few minutes before descending steeply along stone laid steps to meet the road in 30 minutes. Follow the road to the left for five minutes to cross a vehicle bridge below a giant waterfall and reach **Shyange** (3609 feet, 1100 m) in a little over **2 hours** from Sildhunga. ❖

ALTERNATE ROUTE

East-Side Route from Khudi to Shyange

To reach Manang from **Khudi** via the usual route along the east side of the Marsyangdi Khola, follow the road along the river for **30 minutes** to **Bhulbule** (2723 feet, 830 m), where there is an ACAP checkpoint. Cross to the south (left) bank on a long suspension bridge (2720 feet, 829 m). Bhulbule originally gets its name from the sound of a natural spring that bubbles up from cracks in the rocks nearby.

The route continues eastward out of Bhulbule along the south (left) bank of the Marsyangdi Khola. A vehicle road is being planned from Khudi to Ngadi on this side of the river but may not materialize for some time to come. Continue upstream from Bhulbule and pass the first beautiful, thin waterfall on your right. You discover the rest! Below it is a fine pool for bathing—much better than the main river, but keep in mind that this is a drinking water supply. Beyond, fork left, rather than climbing, except in the monsoon. Pass below rather than climbing above to the town of Taraanje.

In **1–1¼ hours** from Bhulbule, reach **Ngadi** (3000 feet, 914 m), on the banks of a small tributary stream. Lodges and shops strung out along the trail refer to themselves as part of Ngadi as well. The village of Tainchowk, above Ngadi, is worth exploring. There is more of Ngadi beyond a suspension bridge (3060 feet, 933 m) over the Ngadi

LEECHES

The terrestrial leeches of Nepal are sanguivorous ecto-parasites living off the blood of their hosts. They thrive during the wet conditions of the monsoon season and find hosts by detecting mechanical stimuli such as vibrations, heat, and chemicals (carbon dioxide) given off by their prey. These jawed leeches (*Gnatbobdellida*) attach themselves by means of tiny teeth or sharp cutting edges; however, a bite usually goes unnoticed because they are capable of dispersing a concomitant anesthetic. Leeches also use an anticoagulant to keep the blood flowing and eventually will drop off the host once sated. This may take upwards of twenty minutes, in which time the leech can swell several times in size. A single feeding is enough to sustain a leech for several months. Some burrow into the ground to survive long dry periods. Leeches are hermaphroditic and deposit eggs in a cocoon after copulation. They can exhibit advanced care of their young not regularly seen in the phylum *Annelida*. Leeches are still used medically during recovery in some plastic/reconstructive surgery cases. For information on removing leeches as well as preventing and treating leech bites, see Chapter 5. ❖

Khola. Cross it to the right bank of the Ngadi Khola, and take the left of the two trails, heading toward the Marsyangdi Khola.

Contour above the river to meet a road in 15 minutes. (This road was built for a hydroelectric plant and continues 10 km up the Ngadi Khola to the Gurung village of Naiche and beyond in an area famous for honey hunting.) Ascend on this road for 15–20 minutes to where the trail branches to the left/north from the road. Climb through Lampata to reach **Bahundanda** (literally, "Brahman hill"), on the right of a prominent brow at a saddle (4232 feet, 1290 m) **1 hour 20 minutes** from the crossing of the Ngadi Khola. There is a police post here and good views to the north if the weather is clear. On the high hills all around are Gurung settlements, and this used to be the northernmost settlement of Brahmans in this river system. There is a hot springs (*taato paani*) at the edge of the Marsyangdi Khola, below the knob of Bahundanda hill. A trail to the hot springs branches down from Lampata or from the lower end of Bahundanda and heads to the village of Dingding and then over the ridge to its west and down very steeply to the river. The pools can be excessively hot.

To continue onward, descend into another tributary valley, pass **Badalbisaunaa** (meaning "resting place in case of clouds") in **45 minutes**. (Shortly before reaching Badalbisaunaa, the trail divides. Avoid the left/lower fork, which descends to the river.) In another **25 minutes** cross a stream on a cantilever bridge and ascend up large stone stairs to Lili Bhir (3700 feet, 1127 m). The name Lili Bhir originates from the Gurung word for ladder, *li*, while *bhir* means "bluff." Formerly, ladders were used to cross the next section with sheer dropoffs and it is along here that prominent Nepali journalist Kanak Mani Dixit slipped from the trail and waited several days to be rescued. Follow the main river valley and trail, beautifully carved out of the rock wall of the valley. Pass the houses and lodges of **Khanigaon** (3900 feet, 1140 m) in **30 minutes,** and then Ghermu Phant (3789 feet, 1155 m), from which a large waterfall above the settlement of Shyange can be seen, along with a hydropower plant at its base. Arrive at the large suspension bridge over the Marsyangdi (3609 feet, 1100 m) in **30 more minutes** and cross it to the west (right) bank to **Shyange** in **2 hours 10 minutes** from Bahundanda. ❖

Shyange was named after the sound of its nearby waterfall. The village used to be higher up during the heydays of the salt trade but was relocated as the valley floor became the main route through here.

You are now in the gorge of the Marsyangdi Khola. The trail follows the road and is different from the salt trade trail that snaked up and down the cliffs on bamboo ladders high up the walls. Then there were no settlements in the floor of the gorge, but as the trail was improved, the ups and downs diminished; traffic and facilities followed.

From Shyange the trail continues to Shirchaur and in **1 ¼ hours** reaches the village of **Jagat** (4347 feet, 1325 m), meaning "toll station," situated in a saddle in the forest. This used to be an old customs post for the salt trade with Tibet until 1950, and is inhabited now mostly by BhoTiya. Thakali not from here were given the power to collect taxes and were resented by the Gurung residents. There is a hot spring below by the river. The trail to the spring branches down steeply from the main trail 15 minutes from Jagat on the way to Chamje.

In **1 hour** beyond Jagat, reach the small settlement of **Chamje** (4560 feet, 1390 m), which has a large overhanging rock that was a convenient sleeping spot for the porters carrying rice to trade for salt. There are many changes in the people, architecture, and vegetation as you head upstream. Structures are now built of stone, the vegetation is less tropical, and the culture more resembles that of Tibet.

FORESTS OF THE SUBTROPICAL ZONE

Extensive forests of chir pine (*Pinus roxburghii*), locally known as *khoTe sallo*, occur throughout the subtropical zone in western Nepal (3300–6500 feet/1000–2000 m in the west, to 5500 feet/1700 m in the east). The forests are typically open, with no understory, because of frequent fires. Chir pine is a conifer with needles arranged in clusters of three.

Broad-leaved, evergreen forests of *Schima wallichii* (*chilaaune*) and chestnut (*Castanopsis indica*), or *dhalne katus*, once covered much of subtropical central and eastern Nepal. Almost all of them have either been converted to agriculture or are much depleted, as they lie in regions of highest population density. Both species have oblong-elliptical, leathery leaves, alternately arranged on the twigs. The chestnut has silvery-gray fissured bark, while that of *Schima* is dark gray and rugged. The chestnut has a prickly fruit.

Riverine forests with *Toona* spp. (compound leaves divided into eight to thirty pairs of leaflets) and *Albizia* spp., or Nepali alder (*Alnus nipalensis*), called *utis*, often grow along streams. The alder has elliptical leaves alternately arranged on the twigs, and the fruits resemble miniature fir cones. Alder also frequently colonizes abandoned cultivation and landslides.

There are small areas of evergreen forest in far eastern Nepal. The showy, large, red flowers of the silk cotton tree (*Bombax malabaricum*, syn. *B. ceiba*, known as *simal*, are a characteristic feature of the subtropical zone in spring. The flowers are clustered toward the ends of bare horizontal branches and are alive with mynahs, sunbirds, drongos, bulbuls, and other birds that feed on nectar. This tall, deciduous tree has branches that grow out from the trunk in regular whorls. ◈

Just beyond the village of Chamje, the Marsyangdi Khola gorge is very impressive. Descend for less than **10 minutes** and cross to the east (left) bank of the river on a suspension bridge (4420 feet, 1347 m). The motor road stays on the right bank. The forests here are temperate broad-leaved with bamboo. Continue upstream to reach a few tea houses after 40 minutes and a lodge beyond.

Climb to emerge from the gorge with its torrent below. An ancient landslide from the mountain to the east filled the gorge here, creating a lake that has become silted in above (see sidebar below). Enter a broad, pleasant, flat valley with a somewhat quieter river; there is a nearby army post and a suspension bridge across the river that is not taken. During the monsoon, you might have to make a short steep ascent to the right before descending to the village. You have entered the Manang District, as indicated by a welcome archway. Continue ahead to the houses of **Tal** (named after the body of water beside this village) in the center of the flat valley (5460 feet, 1664 m) in **1¾–2 hours** from **Chamje**. There are many facilities here including a police check post, a health post, an ACAP Safe Drinking Water Station, and a small *gomba* northeast of town and even a Christian church mid-town. Try to spend a night here, for there is nowhere else along the trek quite like it.

The area of Manang to the north is called Gyasumdo, meaning "meeting place of the three highways," referring to the proximity of three rivers, Marsyangdi, Didh, and Nar Kholas, to the north of here. It is inhabited partly by BhoTiya, who are primarily agropastoralists. These people were the real trans-Himalayan traders of the region until 1959 or 1960, when the trade closed after the Chinese takeover of Tibet.

Prayer wheels (Photo by Gail Robson)

Make your way north up the valley. The trail forks in 30 minutes. Stay left to reach a suspension bridge (5610 feet, 1710 m) and cross to the right/west bank. If it is the monsoon season, you will have to ascend briefly and then descend to the bridge. Pass a few shops and a lodge as you proceed on a section that has been blasted out of the rock. In **1 hour** come to a long suspension bridge (5960 feet, 1817 m) and cross to the left/east bank of the Marsyangdi and the settlement of **Karte,** also known as Khotro.

A trail heads south to Nache village and on to Dona Lake at about 15,420 feet (4700 m), but you must be self-sufficient in food and shelter to go on to this high lake.

LEGEND OF THE FORMATION OF TAL VILLAGE

Tal, meaning "lake" in Nepali, refers to the feature created when a gigantic landslide, whose scar can be seen at the southeast end of the valley, blocked the outflow of the Marsyangdi. Eventually the lake became silted in and became this flat area.

Liesl Messerschmidt describes a Gurung legend about this lake. The mountains on either side of the valley are sacred deities. The east one is Akhe Kai Du, meaning "old grandfather rock," which looks to local people like a *torma*, the Buddhist ritual *tsampa* offering. The western one is Pakre, which is the entire eastern end of Lamjung Himal. These two deities, angry with one another, started to fight and threw boulders across the gorge, until Pakre won. The fight caused the slide on Akhe's side. Afterward, they made up and became blood relatives or *mit* (pronounced "meet"). In front of the falls, you may see a *chorten* built by the local *lamas* to appease the gods to not send more landslides. ❖

Karte to Dharapani via Nache Village

This alternate route to **Dharapani** provides an opportunity to get away from the main route to visit the serene village of **Nache** before descending to meet the main route near Dharapani. It is an arduous climb but worth the effort to visit a location unblemished by mass tourism. There are few facilities here, but home stay might be arranged if you would like to spend the night.

From **Karte,** head right after the bridge. Just out of the village, take a left fork and ascend steeply up a narrow gorge. Reach **Nache** (7441 feet, 2268 m) in **1 hour** from Karte. The trail to Dona Tal heads east from here past the school below the village; however, self-sufficiency is required in food and shelter along with vigilance for the signs of AMS. The trail to Dharapani heads down to the west from the *chorten* passed on the way up from Karte and just south of Nache. In **40 minutes** of steep, sometimes exposed downhill with sheer dropoffs, tie in to the lower, main trail from Karte to Dharapani. The bridge is a few minutes beyond. ❖

The direct, faster route from Karte to Dharapani is to head left/north; this route is prone to landslides. In **25 minutes** cross back to the west bank. Beyond is **Dharapani** (6180 feet, 1884 m). The lower portion is where traders used to graze their pack mules in the fields overnight. Continue to an ACAP and police check post in 10 minutes.

As you continue on from the check post in Dharapani, note the valley coming in from the northeast. It comes down from Larkya La and leads north of Manaslu to the Buri Gandaki. A trail from Dharapani leads to this pass and the Manaslu Conservation Area Project (MCAP). An MCAP entry permit is needed as well as a restricted area permit to enter the Manaslu Conservation Area near Bhimdang, and independent trekkers are currently not allowed to visit unless in a group of two or more that is led by an agency.

The general direction from Dharapani along the road is northwest, rather than north. The village of **Thonje**—in Gurung, "pine trees growing on a flat place"—lies to the right across the Marsyangdi at its confluence with the Dudh Khola. Such river junctions are considered to be sacred places in Nepal; there is a small shrine located there. Some Gurung along here practice shamanism with blood sacrifice, which is distinct from the Tantric Buddhism of the *lama* who migrated here from Kyirong to the north, which proscribes such practices. Such tolerance of different traditions is the norm in Nepal.

A pleasant **35-minute** walk along the road brings you around the corner to the fractured town of **Bagarchap** (6955 feet, 2120 m), meaning "butcher's place." This once picturesque town with a waterworks flowing through it was divided by a landslide in 1995. There are views of the Annapurnas and part of Lamjung Himal, and better views can be found from the village of Galangchowk, 10 minutes up on the ridge top south of Bagarchap (see below).

BIRDS OF PREY OF THE TEMPERATE ZONE

The Himalayan griffon vulture (*Gyps himalayensis*, length 4 feet, 122 cm), like most vulture species, has long, broad wings and a short, broad tail. It sails majestically on motionless wings over mountains and valleys searching for food. From below, adults show white underparts and forewing and a dark trailing edge to the wing; immatures are dark brown. Occurs from subtropical to alpine zones. ❖

Dharapani to Bagarchap via Thonje along the River

To visit Thonje and briefly avoid some of the motor road on the way to Bagarchap, the serene trail heads right/east out of the upper end of **Dharapani**. Cross to the right/east bank of the Marsyangdi on a suspension bridge (6289 feet, 1917 m). Just up from the bridge, the trail forks. The right fork heads to Bhimdang and on to the Manaslu Conservation Area Project area. Take the trail to the left/north and pass through Thonje in less than **10 minutes** from Dharapani, and continue up the east side of the Marsyangdi for **20–25 minutes** to another suspension bridge (6522 feet, 1988 m) back to the west side of the river. There is a difficult-to-reach, undeveloped hot springs below the west side of the bridge here. Ascend up to the road and follow it to **Bagarchap** in **20–25 minutes**, less than 1 hour from Dharapani. ❖

Dharapani to Bagarchap via Odar and Ghalangchowk

This scenic upper trail offers a detour that climbs high away from the road to pass through beautifully situated villages that receive little tourist attention. The trail branches to the left from the road some 10 minutes from Dharapani, and climbs to reach the cluster of houses of Odar (7201 feet, 2195 m) in 25 minutes. A further 10 minutes uphill brings you to a few more houses and then a gradual descent to the hamlet of Ghalangchowk (7218 feet, 2200m) in 10 more minutes. **Bagarchap** is a 10-minute descent from Ghalangchowk, a little more than **1 hour** from **Dharapani**. ❖

Landslides happen frequently beyond **Bagarchap**. From town, take the left fork and do not go down to a bridge crossing the Marsyangdi Khola which heads up to Tache village on the other side of the valley. **Danakyu** (7140 feet, 2190 m), a long village stretched along the trail, is **30 minutes** beyond with an ACAP Safe Drinking Water Station. There are apple, plum and peach trees around here. Continue in temperate mixed broad-leaved forest. The route now ascends to Timang rather than along the old valley bottom route. A few minutes from Danakyu, cross a bridge over a tributary and fork left to ascend to **Timang** (8642 feet, 2634 m) in **1–1¼ hours**. A high trail from Timang to Dudh Pokhari and on to the large Gurung settlement of Bhujung heads off to the southwest but crosses a high pass with no facilities and you must be self-sufficient in food and shelter for several days.

The trail to the northwest out of **Timang** gradually contours to several lodges (8900 feet, 2713 m) in 35 minutes.

Descend to cross a tributary on a suspension bridge (8660 feet, 2640 m) in under 15 minutes and then ascend to the village of Thanchowk (8822 feet, 2689 m) in less than 15 more minutes. From here, the trail proceeds west out of town. Just after leaving, avoid a fork that descends to a school. Contour above the river to **Kotho** (meaning "walnut" in Gurung), also known as Kyupar, 8300 feet, 2530 m) in less than 1 hour, **2 hours** from Timang.

The prominent tributary valley to the north is the Nar Khola, which drains the region called Nar Phu, whose inhabitants are traditionally pastoralists. Do not take the right fork heading there, just beyond the police check post in the upper part of Kotho, unless you have permits to enter this restricted area, obtained from the Immigration Office in Pokhara or Kathmandu. Permits cost between $75 and $90 USD a week per person depending on the season. The splendid valley walls around Kotho are reminescent of Yosemite National Park in California.

Wooden cantilever bridge spanning the Marsyangdi River (Photo by Tokozile Robbins)

To continue to Manang, enter **Chame** (8580 feet, 2615 m) in **25 minutes.** The name means "fields in the warm sunny corner under the cliffs," an all too brief daily occurrence. Above town is a *gomba* as well as a Hindu temple, the result of being a government town. Chame is the district center for Manang with many transplanted lowlanders and practicing Hindus subsequently living here along with the resident Buddhists. Chame has a bank, a health center, a local jail, and many supply shops and a few Internet cafes as well as an ACAP Safe Drinking Water Station.

At the far end of town, first cross a tributary from the south and then the main Marsyangdi Khola, on a cantilever bridge (8620 feet, 2682 m), to the north (left) bank, there are more houses here as well as some hot springs. The hot springs are at the river's edge about 650 feet (200 m) downstream from the bridge and beyond the last lodge.

Go up the valley past a *mani* wall of stones inscribed with prayers and through an elaborate *chorten*-topped gateway and more of Chame, to **Taleku** (8960 feet, 2791 m) in **30 minutes.** Continue in the unrelentingly narrow valley of pine, hemlock, and cypress forest, crossing a landslide area, and in 1¼ **hours** reach **Bhratang** (9340 feet, 2895 m).

There used to be a Khampa village situated across the valley from here. These Tibetan refugee warriors settled here after the Chinese occupation of Tibet in 1959 and subsequently made raids to the north. They built several bridges; on Stephen's first journey to this area, the bridge here was still in use and had remnants of a gate used to maintain control over travelers. The former village had a huge meeting hall for strategy sessions. The Khampa were all resettled in 1975, and the town was eventually demolished, with some structures rebuilt on the other side of the river to serve trekkers.

From Bhratang, head upstream on a trail carved out of the narrow canyon walls, through hemlock and pine forest. Cross again to the south (right) bank in **45 minutes** on a suspension bridge (10,010 feet, 3050 m), and then climb into a serene pine, hemlock, and fir forest. After the days in the gorge, you can appreciate the beauty and silence of these next **45 minutes** up to the facilities at Dhukur Pokhari Danda (10,470 feet, 3190 m), 1½ hours from Bhratang.

As you look east, behind you, the Great Wall of Pisang rises almost 5000 feet (1500 m) up from the valley floor. The names for the wall include *Oble* in Gurung, *Yunga Drag Thang* in Tibetan, and *Paungda Danda* in Nepali, all roughly equivalent to the "Mountain of Heaven." This arc of slate portrays the intense folding of lakebed sediments that were upturned in the creation of the Himalaya. At the top are two stone formations, locally known as either a temple with a dog-hitching post next to it, or the house of the wise old grandfather with himself standing beside it. Legends regarding the wall involve the Manang salt trade and Gurung death rituals. For the Gurung, traveling to this wall was an important life milestone. As they passed it, they would ask the grandfather up above the price of salt farther along the salt trail, and dance and drum before continuing on. For the Gurung of Gyasumdo below, this dome is the entrance to the land of the dead. The spirits of the dead must be led by a shaman's ritual, and the huge boulders at the top represent the temple of the dead. For details, see Mumford's book listed in Appendix A. Relatives of the dead travel to the wall to pay their respects; they build *chorten* and make offerings and shout their ancestor's names, which echo back to them.

As you proceed on from Dhukur Pokhari Danda, just beyond a *mani* wall the trail divides.

If you fork right, the trail goes directly to Upper Pisang by first crossing a wooden cantilever bridge over the Marsyangdi Khola to the north (left) bank (10,390 feet, 3167 m) in 10 minutes. Then in 10 more minutes the trail forks. Stay right, passing Tarkang GoTh, a seasonal pasture settlement, and pass through a gate in another 5 minutes. The trail passes above a large playing field (sometimes used for soccer matches) in 10 more minutes and then forks again in another 10 minutes. Stay left and reach **Upper Pisang** (10,600 feet, 3305 m), with lodges, in **45–50 minutes** from the cantilever bridge crossing or under **1 hour** from Dudh Pokhari Danda.

The left fork at the *mani* wall just out of Dhukur Pokhari Danda keeps to the valley floor and leads to Lower Pisang. Take this trail, and reach **Lower Pisang** (10,280 feet, 3207 m) in **45 minutes.** This town is now mostly a collection of well-furnished lodges and has an ACAP Safe Drinking Water Station as well. Its name is derived from a word in the Managi dialect meaning "to work together at something." Beyond the hill to the south of Lower Pisang are meditation huts at an overhanging rock. To visit on a day trip, the trail begins at the eastern end of town and climbs the ridge of the hill to the southeast.

For amazing views of Annapurna II, climb to Upper Pisang (10,600 feet, 3305 m) in 20 minutes, where there is a *gomba*. Like in many villages here, the roofs are flat. The roof of one house serves as the yard or open area of the house above it. In the middle of the village is a long, handsome wall of prayer wheels in an open space.

TO BRAGA AND MANANG

You are now in the wide, dry, arid region of Manang called Nyesyang, an abrupt change from the gorge. Because it is in the rain shadow of the Himalaya, which acts as a barrier to the wet monsoon clouds from the south, the area gets little rain in the summer. Snow falls here in the winter and remains on the ground much of the time. Unlike the people in the gorge to the south, the inhabitants here have been here for centuries. The men are traders and part-time farmers, and the women are full-time farmers. There is comparatively little animal husbandry. In the winter many leave for warmer places. You may meet many young men with considerable facility in English who have traveled far and wide in Asia. The people of Nyesyang were granted special trading privileges by the king in 1790. This included passports and import and export facilities. These privileges have been extended to all the people of the Manang District. Initially, they traded local items, mostly medicinal herbs, animal products, and semiprecious stones for manufactured goods, usually in India and Burma, but have also been using hard currency from the export of expensive items to import machines and other manufactured goods from South Asian countries. Seasonal migration means less practice of agriculture and animal husbandry, and you will not see many herds of yak, sheep, or goats at the higher elevations. These people are becoming dependent on foodstuff brought in from other areas.

From Lower Pisang there are two routes, which join up in the valley at Munchi, before the village of Braga (also known as Braka). The direct route keeps to the valley floor, staying mostly to the south. The other trail ascends on the north side of the valley to reach several villages on that side of the valley. The views of the mountains and the valley from this route are tremendous, and the villages are quite interesting, but it takes an additional 2½ hours to reach Braga with a steep climb. You will find fewer facilities here and as well fewer trekkers. We strongly advise you to take this higher route, and, if you can arrange it, to stay in local people's homes.

ALTERNATE ROUTE

Upper or Lower Pisang to Munchi via the High Route (Recommended)

The high, north-side route begins in either Lower or Upper Pisang. From Lower Pisang, cross the Marsyangdi Khola (10,510 feet, 3204 m) and immediately fork left to head upstream. Contour northwest in a pleasant pine and juniper forest. Pass by a small green lake, Mringcho Tal. (If you are coming from Upper Pisang, follow the long wall of prayer wheels to pass through a gateway. Contour and pass above this lake and meet the trail coming from Lower Pisang in 40 minutes.) Continue to contour, eventually reaching a long *mani* wall, then fork right to cross a tributary on a suspension bridge (10,890 feet, 3320 m) in **1 hour** from **Upper Pisang.** Take the upper fork and begin a steady, steep climb for **1–1¼ hours** to the hamlet of **Ghyaru,** meaning "goat pasture," at 12,140 feet (3700 m). There are lodges here. Lore has it that when Tibetans came here to see if this was a good place to farm, they planted some wheat seed inside a yak horn. If the seeds germinated, as they did, it would be a good place to settle. The surrounding fields of wheat and buckwheat attest to that prophesy. Spectacular views of Annapurnas II and III and Gangapurna are the main attractions, along with the tunnel-like passageways of the village.

Contour out of the town to the northwest, cross a tributary, and take the higher fork to follow a *mani* wall, then another higher fork to reach a ridge crest (12,380 feet, 3772 m) some 100 feet (30 m) above ruins of an old fort in **45 minutes** from Ghyaru. The fortress perched on this strategic site, Tiwol Danda ("red fort on the hill"), was the palace of the Manang Raja before the Gurkha conquest in the late eighteenth century. There are views of Gangapurna, Glacier Dome, and Tilicho Peak to the west. North of Tilicho Peak lies Tilicho Tal, the "great frozen lake," named by Herzog, although it is out of view from here. If you cross Thorung La, you will eventually return to Pokhara by heading well north and then west of this peak.

Continue to contour, cross a tributary, and in less than 5 minutes from the crest take the left/lower fork and contour; another less-used trail joins from below. Reach a ridge crest with a view of Hongde air strip down in the valley. Cross another tributary to **Ngawal** (11,980 feet, 3650 m) **50 minutes** from the ruins. A trail from the restricted Nar Phu valley reaches Ngawal from a high pass. If you ascend the hill to the northeast of the village, local folklore has it that a cave there, allegedly visited by Padmasambava, has underground channels that extend all the way to Mustang on the other side of the Annapurna range (a 3-day journey via the tunnel!).

Descend to the north to cross a tributary (11,950 feet, 3642 m), and then continue descending, avoiding a trail branching to the left 10 minutes beyond town just after passing a *mani* wall. Stay to the right and descend to the valley floor (11,270 feet, 3436 m), cross another tributary (11,320 feet, 3450 m), and pass above a school for Tibetan refugees. Reach the few houses of **Munchi** (11,425 feet, 3467 m) and lodge in **1¼ hours** from Ngawal, or some **5 hours** from **Upper Pisang**, and meet the main lower trail from Lower Pisang.

There is a large nunnery, Sher Gomba, above Munchi. It is of the Kagyupa sect and under the direction of Thrangu Rimpoche, and is associated with a nunnery at

"Om mani padme hum" mantra in Tibetan script, found carved in a rock along the High Route from Pisang to Braga (Photo by Tokozile Robbins)

Swayambunath Temple in Kathmandu. *Sher* means east; this *gomba* lies to the east of the renowned Braga Gomba, which predates it. ❖

Lower Pisang to Munchi via the Low Route

For the lower route, start from Lower Pisang, crossing a tributary from the south just beyond. Avoiding a left fork, regain the Marsyangdi River by a row of *mani* walls, and continue on its south (true right) bank. Climb to a ridge crest, **Ngoro Danda**, in **45 minutes** with a splendid view of the valley of Manang. Beyond, on the hill to the north is the "red fort on the hill," the Manang Raja's former fortress. **Hongde** (or Ongre, Omdhe, HumDe, or Hongre, 11,130 feet, 3392 m), a sprawling settlement with an air-field, is reached in another **45 minutes.** The name degenerated from the Tibetan word meaning milk, referring to what was available when many yaks were pastured here.

Continue along on a wide track to cross another tributary, the Sopje Khola, from the south in **25 minutes**. Some **25 minutes** later, cross the Marsyangdi Khola (11,220 feet, 3420 m). Ascend along the north (left) bank for 10 minutes to Munchi (11,370 feet, 3467 m), **2½ hours** from **Lower Pisang**, with a lodge and shops as well as a dilapidated series of houses where the high, north-side route from Upper Pisang joins the main valley route from Lower Pisang. ❖

From **Munchi**, stay on the north (left) bank of the Marsyangdi for **25–30 minutes** to **Braga**, also known as Braka (11,398 feet, 3474 m). There are several hotels below the village proper.

Braga (the name refers to the nearby white cliffs) is a large and interesting village, and the seat of the oldest monastery in the area. The *gomba* is perhaps 900 years old, and belongs to the Kagyupa sect of Tibetan Buddhism. Like most of the *gomba* in this region, it is not very active but is well worth a visit, for it contains some unique works of art and is spectacularly perched. The *konyer* ("custodian") will show you around, sometimes with varying amounts of patience. The main temple holds 108 terra-cotta statues, each about 2 feet (60 cm) high, arranged in rows along three of the four walls. They represent the Kagyupa lineage and much more. There is another three-story temple above this main building. The temple is described in detail in David Snellgrove's *Himalayan Pilgrimage*.

The village of **Manang** is **30 minutes** beyond Braga. Along the way, 15 minutes above on a ridge to the north, lies the Bodzo *gomba* (11,750 feet, 3581 m). Directly to the north of it, across a tributary, is a Kagyupa *gomba*. Before going to either of these, try to determine whether the key bearer is around.

There is ample lodging in Manang (11,480 feet, 3560 m). You can restock your provisions, and there is an ACAP Safe Drinking Water Station here. Attend one of the Himalayan Rescue Association post's lectures on altitude illness that are given daily in the high season. If you are planning to cross Thorung La and reach the Kali Gandaki to the west, it is important to spend a day or two acclimatizing here before proceeding. Do not go on to sleep higher if you have a headache. If you have flown to Manang, you should spend at least 3 or 4 days in this region before attempting to cross the pass. In addition, it is advisable to spend an additional night at Leder, before going on to Phedi.

Manang is spectacularly perched across from a glacial lake formed by water from Gangapurna and Annapurna III. To visit this lake, cross the Marsyangdi below town by an abandoned school and proceed to the right. Or, stay left and climb up the lateral moraine on its southeast side for good views of the Chulu peaks and Manang.

PEOPLES OF CENTRAL NEPAL: BHOTIYA

Tibetan BhoTiya groups of northern central Nepal come from Nupri (northern Gorkha District, upper Buri Gandaki), Manang (upper Marsyangdi), Lo–Manthang (upper Kali Gandaki), and from Dolpo and Tarap (north of the Dhaulagiri massif). During the winter months, large numbers of these high-mountain peoples trek south to the lower hills and are often encountered in and around bazaar towns, where they engage in trade and sometimes run inns and small shops. Many of the pony trains that are becoming rarer but still encountered along the Thak Khola trek route are operated by BhoTiya men from the Lo–Manthang region, northern Thak Khola, and the valley of Muktinath, all in the northern Mustang District.

Finally, north of the Muktinath valley, there are the Lopa, the BhoTiya people of the upper Mustang District, in what was once the pretty kingdom of Mustang. Their lives center around high, dry-land agriculture on oasislike farmland wherever nearby streams can be diverted for irrigation water, and they follow pastoral pursuits with sheep, goats, and yak. In winter, many of them migrate south as traders and pony drivers. These people are Tibetan Buddhists, and some practice the pre-Buddhist religion called Bon. There are a number of small monasteries of both religions throughout the Thak Khola and upper Mustang. In their northernmost walled town of Manthang lives the king of the Lopa, the Raja of Mustang, whose allegiance is firmly with the government in Kathmandu. ◈

Another shorter excursion above the town of Manang leads to a hermitage (10,040 feet, 3060 m) built into an overhang in the cliff. The trail leads up from above the village to a large *chorten* in 20 minutes; an hour farther is the hermitage. "Donations" are required for the *lama* to perform a blessing.

Acclimatization days are best spent being active and climbing to high elevations for views but returning to lower altitudes to sleep. There are many suitable hikes near Braga and Manang on both sides of the valley; along with the two hikes just mentioned, several "rest day" activities are suggested in the side trips that follow. You may even see an archery contest or a horse race! These extra acclimatization days may be unnecessary for some or not long enough for others; they are guidelines on how to proceed with less risk.

For people traveling without food or tents, it is possible to cross the pass relying on local facilities, except during the winter, when crossing the pass is a mountaineering endeavor. However, it is best to bring some extra food from Manang or Braga. Ask here if Phedi is set up to provide services outside of the usual trekking season. This has recently become the case, even in the monsoon!

⋎⋏ Side Trip to Ice Lake. *Ice Lake (also known as Kicho Tal) lies over 3500 feet (1100 m) higher to the north of Braga (this lake can also be accessed by a trail from behind Bodzo Gomba, between Manang and Braga; however, the route is difficult to follow). The breathtaking hike offers sweeping panoramas along the way and is highly recommended. The trail emerges from above the village of* **Braga,** *leading east, and is signed along the way by ACAP. Fill your water bottles, as there are no water sources after leaving Braga until the lake itself, which is 2¾–3* **hours** *away.*

Ascend to a point above the village on the ridge between Braga and Munchi and just above Sher nunnery in 30 minutes. The trail then switches back to the northwest (a route from Munchi ties in here) and zigzags up the hill. In another 1 hour 20 minutes, reach a **seasonal pasture area** (14272 feet, 4350 m). About 45 minutes farther is a small pond, and 10 minutes beyond are the striking waters of **Ice Lake** (15,144 feet, 4616 m, N 28°40.723' E084°03.603') with a nearby goTh reached in **2¾–3 hours** from **Braga**.

🏔 **Side Trip to Milarepa Caves.** These caves lie to the south of Braga across the Marsyangdi Khola and over 1800 feet (550 meters) up toward the base of Annapurna III. Jetsun Milarepa was an eleventh-century ascetic who lived an austere life in the high mountains between present-day Nepal and Tibet. He is revered by Tibetan Buddhists, especially of the Kagyupa lineage.

To reach the trailhead from **Braga**, head downstream (southeast) along the valley for a few minutes to cross the Marsyangdi on either a suspension bridge or nearby wooden cantilever bridge. There is more than one route up to the caves which lie **1 hour 40 minutes** from **Braga**. The easiest is to head directly south from the cantilever bridge toward the hills (and not along the left fork to the southeast, a steeper ascent). Pass through fields before climbing steeply up the hill on a zigzagging trail. Within **45 minutes** from Braga, reach a seasonal **goTh settlement** (12, 073 feet, 3680 m) with a possible camping area just below. Follow the trail to the southeast as it contours. In less than 10 minutes, cross a streambed. Water might be available from a small spring in the gully a minute below the trail here. A few more minutes beyond, the trail ties in with the steeper, more direct route. There is another goTh settlement just below the trail here. Another 10-minute ascent brings you to a **stupa** (12, 427 feet, 3788 m), **20–25 minutes from the goTh settlement,** with a camping area just to the east and a nearby cement tap that might have water.

Another **30-minute** climb up the glacial valley alongside the terminal moraine brings you to another large chorten, with a **shrine** and gomba (13,255 feet, 4040 m) just beyond. The caves are set in the cliff face to the west some 100 yards (meters) up and marked by prayer flags. The upper cave is inaccessible, whereas the lower involves a steep scramble from the gomba. A nearby, small chorten marks a place where footprints were allegedly imprinted in rock. The rock portion with these imprints is now housed below in the gomba. Devotees will tell you that a hunter's bow hangs in the bluffs near the caves. Indeed, a bow-like shape can be made out. This is believed to be the retired weapon of a legendary hunter who gave up the chasing of animals after a fortuitous encounter with Milarepa.

The central figure in the gomba is, of course, Milarepa, flanked by his guru Marpha and chief disciple Gampopa (also known as Dokpa Kagyu). Nearby are stone huts for meditators, as well as a camping area with water available. Annapurna III glacier can be viewed by climbing south from the gomba 45 minutes to 1 hour along the lateral moraine to an otherworldly vantage point (14,249 feet, 4343 m).

🏔 **Side Trip to Khangsar Village.** An enjoyable hike is a trip up to Khangsar, the last town before Tilicho Tal. A motor road is being built from Manang to Khangsar, and there are several starting points from Manang as well as from Braga. If you are starting from **Braga** (**2¼ hours to Khangsar**), the route passes below Manang. Begin by following the route toward Manang and take the left fork just after passing a stupa in less than 15 minutes. Travel below Manang village in another 15 minutes, not crossing the Marsyangdi on the bridge below Manang. Do not cross another bridge a further 10 minutes up where the trail from Manang ties in to the direct trail from Braga.

Starting from **Manang** (**1¾ hours to Khangsar**), one trail begins from a large

Prayer flags at the viewpoint overlooking Tilicho Lake (Photo by Tokozile Robbins)

stupa *with prayer wheels that is mid-town and located just after the newer part of town. Fork left and descend to the bridge by the river. Do not cross the river here. The trail from Braga meets the trail from Manang at this point.*

Keep heading upstream to the west, traversing on the true left/north bank of the Marsyangdi to another bridge (11,729 feet, 3575 m) above the confluence with the Khangsar Khola in 30 minutes. Cross to south bank of what is now known as the Thorang Khola (also Jargeng) and ascend to a plateau, then continue to **Khangsar** *(12,303 feet, 3750 m),* **1 hour** *from crossing the river.*

EXPLORE: TILICHO TAL

The trip to Tilicho Tal is an arduous, rewarding, several-day excursion through remote landscape away from the main circuit trail. On the return, rather than revisiting the main trail at Manang, a timesaving shortcut is introduced.

Tilicho Tal is a large, spectacularly set lake nestled at the foot of the north face of Tilicho Peak, part of the snowy wall that the 1950 French expedition team referred to as The Great Barrier. Hidden beyond this bulwark to the south was their objective, Annapurna (26,545 feet, 8091 m). The leader, Maurice Herzog, referred to Tilicho Tal as The Great Ice Lake, and it is often frozen in winter, and periods of thaw vary from year _ar. Hindus believe that this sacred lake features in the Ramayana holy text.

The lake can be reached from Khangsar in 2 days; however, parties must be acclimatized. The trail beyond Siri Kharka can be very difficult if not treacherous under snowy conditions. Check with ACAP in Manang and in Khangsar about current conditions as well as to see whether the Tilicho Base Camp lodge halfway up the valley is in operation. From there you could make a long day trip to see the lake and return, without having to camp.

To proceed from **Khangsar**, join the trail from the *stupa* at the upper (northwest) end of the village and head west. A few minutes from Khangsar is a juncture. Keep to the right and in 5 more minutes pass through a gate and then fork right again. Reach Thare Gomba (12,959 feet, 3950 m), an ancient *gomba* of the Sakya sect, in 45 minutes from Khangsar. The trail ascends from behind the *gomba* and diverges 15 minutes beyond. (The right fork heads to Yak Kharka, on the Annapurna Circuit; this route can be followed to avoid backtracking to Manang on the return from the lake. Be sure to check beforehand that a seasonal bridge is in place over the Thorang/Jargeng Khola before taking this shortcut. This route, from Siri Kharka to Yak Kharka, will be described below.) Keep left, cross a tributary, and reach a lodge at **Siri Kharka** (13,320 feet, 4060 m) in 10 more minutes, **1 hour 10 minutes** from **Khangsar.**

From **Siri Kharka**, reach a junction in the trail in 25 minutes and stay right rather than descend. Another 35 minutes beyond this junction the trail diverges again; stay left on the lower branch. This section from Siri Kharka to the lake was improved for a visit by a high-ranking *lama* of the Sakyka lineage in the spring of 2009. (The alternate high trail is not currently recommended, as it ascends over 2300 feet (700 m) and then descends precipitously through scree to Tilicho Base Camp.) Enter an area prone to landslides in 15 minutes, and for the next hour be wary of rocks tumbling from above as the trail passes through a steep incline of scree to a lodge at the so-called **Tilicho Base Camp** (13,583 feet, 4140 m) in **1¼–1½ hours** from the trail junction (**2¼ hours** from **Siri Kharka**).

Continue west from Tilicho Base Camp. *Bharal* (blue sheep) abound in this area, and likely there are a few prowling snow leopards, which prey on the sheep but are rarely sighted. Reach the base of a series of switchbacks (15,607 feet, 4757 m) in 1½ hours. In another 45 minutes to 1 hour, reach a crest (16,375 feet, 4991 m) and follow the stone-lined trail past a few tarns on the left to an ACAP sign and prayer flag-laden **lookout point** (16,467 feet, 5019 m, N 28° 40.660' E 083° 51.869') in under 20 minutes (**2½–2¾ hours** from Tilicho Base Camp). You can pick a route down through the moraine to reach the lake nearly 100 meters below. Be aware that storms can blow up quickly and unexpectedly from the south in this region. On one trip, it went from not a cloud in the sky to pelting-down snow in an hour—and an accumulation of several feet by the morning!

ALTERNATE ROUTE

- -

Siri Kharka to Yak Kharka

On returning from Tilicho Tal, this route from Siri Kharka to Yak Kharka, which lies on the main circuit trail, avoids backtracking to Khangsar and Manang. **Caution:** *Check with ACAP and locally to make sure a seasonal bridge is in place over the Thorang/Jargeng Khola before taking this shortcut.*

Descend from **Siri Kharka** *toward Thare Gomba and in 5 minutes from Siri Kharka reach a trail junction. Head to the left for Yak Kharka. Less than 15 minutes beyond is another trail junction. Again, stay left and in 20 minutes reach Old Khangsar (13,560 feet, 4133 m),* *which is uninhabited except for occasional herders and during festival times. Follow the rock wall north out of Old Khangsar and then contour along it to the east. In under 20 minutes the trail separates from the walled enclosure and begins rising. There are many grazing trails in this area. Keep to the widest path and ascend to a ridge crest (13,652 feet, 4161 m) in 25 minutes with a steep drop-off overlooking the Marsyangdi Khola valley. You might even make out the circuit trail across the valley to the northeast.*

From the crest, the trail leads north as it descends through birch into the Thorang/Jargeng Khola valley. Reach a seasonal bridge (12,648 feet, 3855 m) in 45 minutes just upriver from a feeder tributary, the Khenjang Khola, coming in on the other side of the valley. Cross to the east bank of the Thorang/Jargeng Khola and ascend along the feeder tributary's north bank, to a plateau. Just beyond the trail ties in to the circuit trail where there is a long mani *wall (13,058 feet, 3980 m), 40 minutes from the seasonal bridge. Reach the collection of lodges known as* **Yak Kharka** *(13,020 feet, 4040 m) in less than 1 hour (**3¾ hours** from Siri Kharka).* ❧

MANANG TO THORUNG LA AND MUKTINATH

A week (perhaps a year!) in Manang or Braga would not exhaust the interesting options available in this area, especially useful for acclimatizing. However, if you have walked in from Besisahar and have spent a day or two in Braga or Manang without symptoms and are feeling healthy, then you are likely ready to continue onward to Thorang La. Keep in mind that this pass is higher than most of the world's mountains (outside of central Asia) and the highest point that most people will likely ever reach in a lifetime. The pass is desolate and stunningly beautiful and will be a memorable experience. However, it is not for everybody. Be vigilant for signs of altitude sickness, and descend back to Manang or lower if necessary.

Additionally, do not attempt to cross Thorung La unless all of the party, including the porters, are equipped for cold and bad weather. If the weather is threatening, do not proceed. Lives of trekkers and porters have been needlessly lost on this pass because parties proceeded in bad weather. Many people have been crossing the pass wearing running shoes and other light footwear. If you do not carry proper boots, at least recognize that there is risk of frostbite should a storm occur. Trekkers have gotten serious frostbite on this pass. Losing fingers and toes is a big price to pay! If stuck with poor footwear, in bad conditions, and unwilling to turn back, wrap your feet in plastic socks as a vapor barrier. This may help, but there are no guarantees. There is safety in numbers, and it is best to travel in a group.

To proceed from **Manang** over Thorung La, cross a tributary below a falls northwest of Manang and climb up to **Tengi** (12,106 feet, 3690 m) in **30 minutes.** This last permanent settlement below the pass has few tourist facilities. Climb gradually and avoid a right fork after 45 minutes to reach some *goTh* and hotels at Ghunsang (12,874 feet, 3924 m) in **1 hour.** Another **30 minutes** farther is a higher settlement of *goTh* and a hotel at Khenjang Khola (13,002 feet, 3963 m) with a tea shop over the bridge on the other side of the river. The trail has now turned northwest up the valley of the Jargeng Khola. If you are here early in the morning or late in the afternoon, look for herds of blue sheep, which often descend for water at those times. Reach the collection of lodges known as **Yak Kharka** (13,020 feet, 4040 m) in **1 hour,** passing one lodge 10 minutes before as well and finding another lodge 15 minutes beyond the main lodge cluster.

In less than 20 minutes from the last Yak Kharka hotel, cross a tributary on a suspension bridge (13,806 feet, 4208 m). Within 5 minutes, reach the first lodges of Letar

(13,862 feet, 4225 m). There is an ACAP Safe Drinking Water Station in Letar. It is possible to hire a horse from here to the summit of the pass. Keep in mind that people have been put on a horse only to arrive higher up unconscious and moribund from altitude illness. Acclimatizing and walking is safer.

From **Letar**, climb, pass above a tarn, contour, and then descend to the river and a bridge (14,288 feet, 4355 m) in **50 minutes.** The current route is to cross to the true right/west bank and ascend to a tea shop within 10 minutes. Traverse through a slide area and scree to reach **Phedi** in another 35 minutes (**45 minutes** from the bridge and **1½–1¾ hours** from Letar). Phedi (14,846 feet, 4525 m), meaning "foot of mountain," has two large lodges and an ACAP Safe Drinking Water Station, and Internet access might even be available during the season. A lucky trekker has spotted a snow leopard near here at dusk!

Leave Phedi at daybreak. It takes a long day to cross the pass, but doing the first quarter in the dark is unnecessarily tiring, and stumbles and falls can result in injury, fatigue, and getting wet, which can lead to hypothermia and frostbite higher up.

The trail now leaves the river valley, which continues northwest and then ascends west. In dry weather, water can be scarce, and it is best to fill up where you can. There are no good campsites with water beyond the pass unless you camp on snow in the appropriate season. Some parties bring a stove to melt snow and rehydrate along the way. In early-season snow (November through December) or early-spring conditions (March through April), do not underestimate the difficulties of proceeding, especially if you do not have mountaineering experience. In deep snow, an ice ax, ski pole, or walking stick is helpful.

From Phedi, ascend to a notch (15,994 feet, 4875 m) with a large lodging complex known as **Thorung High Camp** in **1 hour.** From here to the pass, 10-foot (3m) poles frequently mark the trail (as well as from the pass, 1½–2 hours down along the other side). Head left/west, traversing to a bridge (16,339 feet, 4980 m) at the base of a prominent lateral moraine in under 30 minutes. Reach its crest (16,522 feet, 5036 m) less than 10 minutes later (40 minutes from High Camp), and continue west along less steep terrain to a seasonal tea house (16,699 feet, 5090 m) in less than 15 minutes beyond here and less than 1 hour from Thorung High Camp. After many false crests, reach **Thorung La** (17,769 feet, 5416 m) in 1½–1¾ hours (**2½–3 hours** from High

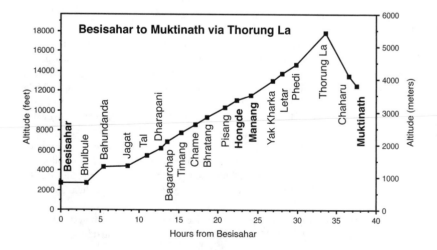

MAMMALS OF THE ALPINE ZONE

The snow leopard (*Panthera uncia*), or *hIU chituwaa* (length, 3–3½ feet, 100–110 cm), is one of the Himalaya's most elusive animals. It occurs above the treeline, mainly in the trans-Himalayan region near the Tibetan border. Well adapted for life at high altitudes, it has a long, thick coat. There have been sightings by trekkers near Thorung Phedi, north of Manang, as well as south of Ganja La in Langtang, and in the Kangchenjunga region. There are an estimated 3500–7000 snow leopards in the wild, with an estimated population in Nepal of 300–400.

The Himalayan marmot (*Marmota bobak*), or *himali marmot* (length, 2 feet, 60 cm), has a distinctive squat build, medium tail, and small ears. Large colonies live in deep burrows in the open country of the trans-Himalayan region.

The blue sheep, or *bharal* (*Pseudois nayaur*), locally known as *nyaaur* (shoulder height nearly 3 feet, 90 cm), is intermediate in appearance between sheep and goats. It has long backward-curving horns. Herds of ten to fifty graze on grass slopes between treeline and snowline, usually within cover of rock cliffs, rarely descending below 12,000 feet (3660 m) in winter. It can be seen in the Manang District of the Annapurna Circuit, near Kangchenjunga, and north of Dhorpatan. ❖

Camp) if you are adequately acclimatized. A large cairn marks the pass, and, amazingly, in season you may find a tea shop operating here. The pass is exhilarating to reach and is a transition from one major Himalayan valley to another, but views from the pass are probably less impressive than those on either side. Far below you to the west is the Kali Gandaki. Those with sharp eyes and binoculars can pick out below the green oasis of Kagbeni.

The descent from the pass is gradual at first and follows the middle of the valley for the first hour. It becomes considerably steeper and keeps to the south side of the valley on scree. The first campsites (14,450 feet, 4404 m) are some 1¾ **hours** down from the pass. In the dry season, after and just before the monsoon, when all the snow has melted, there is no water available. The nearest lodges are at **Chaharu** (also known as Phedi, 13,688 feet, 4172 m), 2¼–2½ **hours** from the pass. Just as at the other Phedi, there will be no one here in the middle of the winter—if you are coming up from Muktinath at that time, ask there first as to whether these lodges are operational.

About 10 minutes from Chaharu, fork left and in 20 more minutes cross a major tributary on a long suspension bridge (12,740 feet, 3883 m). The wall-ensconced temple of Muktinath lies 15 minutes beyond. The motor road reaches all the way to the temple, and from this point there will be motorcycles and jeeps.

Another 15 minutes beyond the temple (**1 hour** from Chaharu), reach the village of **Muktinath**/Ranipawa (12,047 feet, 3672 m), with an ACAP Safe Drinking Water Station. Muktinath and environs and the route down are described above in the Kali Gandadki/Thak Khola section.

7

SOLU–KHUMBU:
THE EVEREST REGION

Because it's there.

—George Mallory, one of the first climbers to attempt Everest, when asked why he wanted to climb it. (He disappeared into a cloud near the summit in 1924, where his body was found in 1999.)

There are several possible ways of reaching the Solu–Khumbu District of Nepal. The classic way to Khumbu, the northernmost part of the district, was to walk all the way from the Kathmandu valley. But because roads continue to be built ever closer to Khumbu, the route now begins at Jiri, Shivalaya, or even Bhandar, all reached in a day-long bus ride from the Old Bus Park (also known as Ratna Bus Park) in Kathmandu. Consider walking in (or out) for a contrast of culture and scenery.

Scheduled inexpensive plane service to Lukla and some helicopter service to Shyangboche have markedly changed access and egress to the Khumbu region. Rapid ascent to high altitudes can be dangerous, even fatal, so it is safest to walk to Khumbu and fly out, if you want to fly a segment. If you must fly in, choose Lukla as the destination, rather than Shyangboche, because it is sufficiently lower and therefore somewhat safer. Currently, helicopters are chartered for taking supplies, equipment, and passengers to or from Shyangboche, but fixed-wing services are unavailable at this airfield.

Days of acrimonious bottlenecks at Lukla occur when the weather deteriorates, with stranded trekkers desperately trying to get back to their hectic home schedules. Leave some margin of comfort between the scheduled day of your flight from Lukla and your departure date from Nepal. There is also air service to Phaphlu a few days' walk away.

Change in tourist access has significantly impacted the local economy, as lodges on the Jiri-to-Lukla route are relatively empty compared to those from Lukla and above. Projected increase in Khumbu trekker traffic has resulted in much lodge building there, and the benefits from tourism continue to contribute to regional economic inequality. Prices in Khumbu have soared; be sure to budget enough money, keeping in mind that "prices climb as you climb." Expect a minimum of $15–$25 USD per day (1100–1500 NRS) starting from Lukla, and half of that amount getting to Lukla. Prices are usually better away from the most popular stopping points. There are banking and money-changing facilities in Lukla and Namche, and some hotels will give a cash advance on credit cards, though for a large transaction fee.

First glimpse of Mount Everest and Ama Dablam from a chorten *near Namche Bazaar* (Photo by Mark Jackson and Susan Bergin//SAFA Himalaya Collection/Nepal)

Trekkers who walk from Jiri to Khumbu through Solu, the southwest part of Solu–Khumbu District, continuing the tradition of the past, often find that part of the journey the most enjoyable. Even if trekker traffic from Jiri were to decline, and the lodge situation described here (lodges available all the way) were to decline as a result, trekkers might then be more inclined to sleep in traditional inns or people's homes, and truly experience life in hill Nepal, in many ways unchanged for centuries!

If you are walking one or both ways, the journey from Kathmandu to Khumbu can be combined with the trek from Khumbu to the Arun valley in eastern Nepal, using air transportation from Tumlingtar to Kathmandu or a seasonal motor road from Tumlingtar to the bus service at Hille. You can also reach and leave the Khumbu region via Rolwaling to the east by crossing the Trashi Labsta. This route is hazardous and not recommended. Trashi Labsta is a high, glaciated pass to the west (18,947 feet, 5775 m), and goes through Rolwaling to the Kathmandu–Kodari Road or a rough dirt feeder road to Chaurikot along the highway to Jiri. This long crossing is dangerous and requires some mountaineering skills and equipment and considerable stamina. Sir Edmund Hillary once said it was one of the hardest passes he had ever crossed. This trek, best attempted in the early autumn or late spring, takes a minimum of 10 days (or a minimum of 7 days to a rough feeder road).

The Himalayan Rescue Association offers lectures on acclimitization and altitude sickness in Pheriche (and sometimes in Dingboche). Pheriche also has an HRA clinic where consultations can be arranged for the equivalent of $50 USD, credit cards accepted, with free follow-up as well. There are also lectures in Machherma at a rescue post set up by the International Porter Protection Group and staffed by international volunteers. Keep in mind that there are casualties in the Khumbu every year due to altitude sickness. It is important to take your time at altitude and above all, listen to your own body's signals.

There is mobile phone network service, granted the right provider, to Namche Bazaar and even beyond, and batteries can be charged in most places, given the right adapter (bring a universal adapter, or adapters can be found in Kathmandu). Lodge owners do still use firewood as well as yak dung, and although boiled water is available in the Khumbu, it is better to purify your own, perhaps with iodine. Plastic water bottles as well as toilet paper are two of the most common items left behind by trekkers that despoil the trail. Nepalis, for their part, leave an abundance of packets for tobacco and instant noodles as well as cookie wrappers along the way. As a trekker once lamented, if you are ever in doubt of the main route, then follow the trail of refuse.

Higher up, trekking in December and January can offer the advantages of good (albeit cold) viewing weather, and relatively fewer trekkers than at peak times. However, not all lodges and facilities are open (check before continuing upward), and snow and ice on the trails and rocks can be treacherous (as can ice around toilet areas).

JIRI TO SOLU–KHUMBU
(Map No. 4, Page 247)

The walk from Jiri to Khumbu is a fine introduction to the hills of Nepal, with a few pleasant diversions along the way. Average walking time to Namche Bazaar is 7–9 days from Jiri, though athletes can do it in 4 or 5. The climb is more than the height of Everest along the way if you total all the ascents, but it is well worth it. The main rivers run south and are separated by high ridges, so the west–east travel to Lukla is a succession of ups and downs. The ridges and valleys are high and the climbs and descents are strenuous. There are lodges along the way, and not much trekker traffic. The route is strongly recommended.

From Kathmandu, take one of the buses heading to Jiri or Shivalaya (or even possibly Bhandar, depending on the season/road condition), which leave from the Old Bus Park (also known as Ratna Park) east of Tundikhel Parade Ground in the center of the city. The ride of nearly 120 miles (190 km) takes a full day and can be exhausting; however, the last half of the road to Jiri is relatively decent and was constructed with aid from the Swiss. Buses leave as early as 5:30 AM. Buy a ticket on the morning you leave, or the

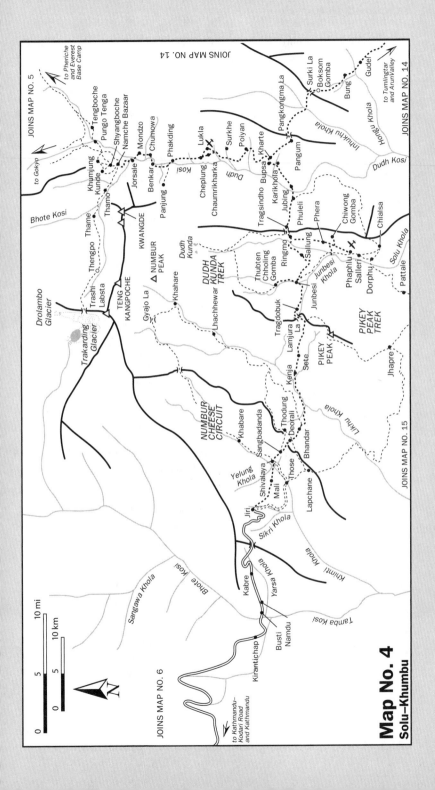

Map No. 4
Solu–Khumbu

afternoon before. More buses go to Charikot and Tama Kosi, which can give trekkers a different starting point and a walk to get to Jiri.

Be aware that there have been incidents of theft on the public buses that take trekkers to Jiri. Luggage is broken into and pickpocketing occurs. Keep your pack inside the bus if possible, but likely it will go on top of the bus. Be watchful, and consider getting on the rooftop once outside of the Kathmandu valley if others are up there. Or hire a private vehicle (and still be watchful!). It can be difficult to arrange a private vehicle back from Jiri or Shivalaya.

Jiri (6250 feet, 1905 m) was the site of a Swiss hill development project that built a hospital and technical school and focused on agricultural inputs. A police check post is located near the market site, before the trail descends to the valley floor. There are tourist lodges in Jiri where you can arrange porters and buy last-minute items. There are many trails around Jiri; when in doubt, ask and observe the direction of porters.

JIRI TO CHEPLUNG/LUKLA

From the south end of the bus park in **Jiri**, take the Those road briefly, forking left at a bend in the road to climb the east side of the Jiri valley in a rhododendron forest. Continue east through Chitre, with tea shops, to reach a pass with more tea shops (7875 feet, 2400 m) **1 hour 40 minutes** from Jiri. Then descend through Mali to a bridge over the Yelung Khola. Along the way are simple tea shops and lodges. As you drop down, notice the cliffs on the north side, and look for beehives. In late spring, villagers will dangle on rope ladders to harvest honey from them. Cross the bridge to the northeast (left) bank and cross a suspension bridge over the Khimti Khola. **Shivalaya** (5873 feet, 1790 m), "the home of Shiva," where there are lodges, is the village on the other side, **1½ hours** from the pass. The trail to the Numbur Cheese Circuit (see Chapter 9) begins here and follows north up the Khimti Khola.

From Shivalaya the trail climbs steeply up the ridge to the scattered village of **Sangbadanda** with its schoolhouse (7350 feet, 2240 m) in **1½–1¾ hours.** Just up from the schoolhouse, the trail branches. The right fork leads to Kasourbas, another Sherpa settlement, reaching Deorali in another **1¾ –2 hours**. Alternatively, the left branch heads up to the Swiss-designed cheese factory at **Thodung** (10,140 feet, 3091 m), about **2½ hours** from Sangbadanda. Besides buying cheese here, you can get a good view of Gaurishankar (Chomo Tseringma) to the north. This peak (23,458 feet, 7150 m) was once thought to be the highest in the world because it was visible from far away. Thodung is a worthwhile detour not taken by many trekkers. There is a monastery 30 minutes south of the cheese factory.

To rejoin the regular route, from Thodung head south along the ridge to a pass at **Deorali** (8900 feet, 2713 m), reaching it in less than **1 hour**. The *mani*-walled pass originally had no name (being insignificant in the Nepali perspective, so as settlement occurred and trekkers asked the name, Deorali, or "pass," was the obvious choice. There are now tea shops and lodges run by Sherpas at the pass.

From the Deorali pass, keep to the left to descend into the beautiful, lush valley to the east and toward the large *stupas* by a small *gomba* at the town of **Bhandar**, called Chyangma by Sherpas (7200 feet, 2194 m) in **1 hour**. Depending on the season and thus the condition of the road, it is possible to reach Bhandar by vehicle.

From the scattered village of Bhandar, descend the fertile plateau toward a notch to cross a river (6600 feet, 2012 m) on a bridge. Just beyond, take the far left fork. (There is a new trail to Kenja favored by porters, above the old one, that could be taken, shortening the journey by 45 minutes. It mainly follows a dirt road being built to Kenja; as of yet it has few facilities.) Go on through forests and terraces, asking villagers the way to Kenja, as there are numerous trail junctions, and cross the Surma Khola (5100 feet, 1555 m) to its north (left) bank. Continue to the Likhu Khola and do not cross on the first suspension bridge which heads toward Pikey Peak, but cross it on the second suspension bridge (5060 feet, 1543 m) to its east (left) bank. It takes **2 hours** to reach the river from Bhandar and then less than 1 hour of walking upstream along its east bank through forest to reach the Kenja Khola, which is crossed to **Kenja** (5360 feet, 1634 m) with its numerous lodges, **3 hours** from Bhandar.

The biggest climb of the journey so far, up to Lamjura La (11,580 feet, 3530 m), begins behind the town and follows a ridge more or less on its south side through forest passing through Chimbu (7168 feet, 2185m) with lodges to the settlement of **Sete** (8450 feet, 2575 m), which also has lodges. Be sure to obtain water here, as there is little until you have descended the other side of the pass. It takes **2¾–3 hours** to reach Sete from Kenja. Beyond, the trail continues along the ridge in a prickly-leaved oak forest. Reach the few houses and lodges of Dakchu (9350 feet, 2850 m) 1 hour beyond. In 45 more minutes reach Goyem (10,350 feet, 3155 m), which has a spread-out selection of tea shops and lodges in clusters a few minutes apart. Stay to the left out of Goyem. The ridge you have been following meets the main ridge, striking north–south. There are now tea shops and lodges along the way to the pass. During the monsoon, people use makeshift shelters to churn milk into butter or *ghiu*. **Lamjura La** (11,582 feet, 3530 m) is **3¼–3¾ hours** from Sete with lodges before it. People with time and energy can take a half-day side trip to climb to the peak north of the pass (13,156 feet, 4010 m) for views in good weather. (Additionally, a trail to Pikey Peak branches south near the pass; for information on the Pikey Peak Trek, see Chapter 9).

From Lamjura La, the trail descends through a fir and rhododendron forest past lodges and emerges at **Tragdobuk,** also called Taktor, with several lodges (9380 feet, 2860 m), in **1½ hours.** Continue on the north side of the valley, avoiding right forks leading down over a notch, and drop down to the town of **Junbesi** (8775 feet, 2675 m) in **1 hour.** There are several active monasteries in this area that are worth a visit, including Serlo, reached from a branch to the left of the trail on the way into Junbesi.

Junbesi, with its many lodges, has prospered from trekkers, Hillary's Himalayan Trust development efforts, and the dedication of western Buddhist seekers. *Rhythms of a Himalayan Village* by Hugh Downs is an informative book about this area's past. Amenities now include television, phone service, well-stocked shops, and a visitor information center near the school.

THUBTEN CHHOLING GOMBA

A 1¼-**hour** walk away from the main trail to the north of Junbesi brings you to Thubten Chholing Gomba, a large, active monastery with several hundred monks and nuns. The founder, Trulshik Rimpoche, arrived here from Rongbuk Monastery in exile following the Chinese occupation of Tibet. Rimpoche was the subject of a 1986 British documentary film entitled *Lord of the Dance, Destroyer of Illusion.* There is a high route that continues on to a lake, Dudh Kunda, in the lap of the mountains; however, self-sufficiency is required. See Chapter 9, the Dudh Kunda Trek, for this route. From Junbesi you can also head south to the mid-hills Pikey Peak Trek, also in Chapter 9. ❖

To continue to Namche Bazaar from Junbesi, cross the Junbesi Khola on a bridge below the *stupa* (8700 feet, 2552 m). Stay to the left (to the right heads to Phaphlu where there is an airstrip and Salleri, headquarters of Solu–Khumbu District). The trail passes through blue pine forest to rhododendron and prickly-leaved oak forest typical of western midland forest. Such forests are often found on south-facing slopes in this region. Enter open country, round the crest of the Sallung ridge to Phurtyang (9975 feet, 3040 m), and look for Mount Everest on a clear morning. There are lodges here. You can climb up the ridge to the north for better views. Head north up the valley of the Dudhkunda/Ringmo Khola to the town of **Sallung** (9688 feet, 2953 m), with more lodges, in **2 hours** from Junbesi.

From here, the trail descends through oak forests to cross tributaries, and then the main river of the Dudhkunda/Ringmo Khola (8300 feet, 2530 m). The trail then ascends to the orchard-surrounded houses of **Ringmo** (8924 feet, 2720 m), a Sherpa settlement, **1½ hours** from Sallung. The right branch from Ringmo heads south to Phaphlu. You could also head north to yak pastures and reach the high lake, Dudh Kunda, but this challenging route requires camping and self-sufficiency. From Ringmo, the trail ascends east through juniper woods past some rectangular *mani* walls to **Tragsindho La** (10,075 feet, 3071 m) with *chorten, mani* walls, prayer flags, and simple facilities reached in **1 hour**. To the east is the valley of the Dudh Kosi, and the region called Pharak (meaning "different" from Solu and Khumbu regions). You will follow the Dudh Kosi valley all the way north to Khumbu. Meanwhile, less than 10 minutes below you is **Tragsindho Monastery** with lodges nearby.

From Tragsindho, the trail descends to the southeast, passes through forests, and emerges at the prosperous Sherpa village and lodges of **Nuntale** (Manidingma, 7365 feet, 2245 m) in **1½ hours**. Beyond, descend past terraces into oak forests to emerge at a bridge over the Dudh Kosi (4898 feet, 1493 m) **1½ hours** from Nuntale.

From here, the trail crosses the river to the east (left) bank and heads north to reach Namche Bazaar in 3 days. Sometimes the trail is over a mile above the river, which falls through a steep gorge. There have been many improvements in agriculture in Pharak over the years. You may notice fruit trees and many varieties of vegetables. The main trail north of here is being continuously improved. Ask locally for the latest routes.

Follow the river through forests, and then climb through terraces to reach the Rai village and lodges of **Jubing** (5500 feet, 1676 m) in **40 minutes.** This is your only opportunity along this trek to see a settlement of these people who populate so much of eastern Nepal. The British found the Rai to be excellent soldiers and actively recruited them as Gurkhas. Rai are ethnically and linguistically diverse, speaking many different languages, with attendant different customs. Climb through the village and 10 minutes outside of Jubing, stay right to ascend. Round a ridge and reach Chokha, and either take the newer left fork or the older, steeper right fork, preferred by Nepalis, to the prominent notch in front of you.

Reach the village of **Karikhola** (6575 feet, 2004 m), inhabited by Sherpas, Rai, and Magar. Karikhola is **1½ hours** from Jubing. The Magar hail from western Nepal, settling here generations ago. The town has many lodges and shops and a newly built *gomba* perched above the village. Tuesday is market day. Across the river you may see papermaking. Locals advise not to walk alone to Surkhe and beyond for security reasons.

Cross the bridge over the Kari Khola, and ascend steeply to reach **Bupsa,** with lodges (7700 feet, 2347 m), in **1 hour**. A visit to the old, small *gomba* below the village is worthwhile. Contour north into the next valley (rather than along the ridge to the east, unless trekking toward the Arun valley and Tumlingtar, an arduous journey that crosses through several river valleys; see the end of this chapter for a descripton of this route), pass some lodges, and climb below the old trail. If coming from Pangkongma La, and the Arun valley, the trails meet here. The next tributary valley to the north has to be traversed followed by an ascent to the Khari La from where you can see Cho Oyu and Gyachung Kang. Continue on the north side of the valley before crossing the Poiyan Khola to ascend to **Poiyan** and its spread-out lodges (9173 feet, 2796 m) in **2¾–3 hours** from Bupsa.

Continue and pass through Cheubas with more lodges to Chutok/Paiya La (9098 feet, 2773 m) on the crest of a ridge with wonderful views. Almost due north is the sacred mountain Khumbiyula, at the head of the valley; standing above Namche, the mountain has never been climbed per the wishes of locals. Pass lodging facilities of Paakapaani and enter the valley of another tributary, the Surkhe Khola, while being aware of drop-offs. The village and lodges of **Surkhe** (7523 feet, 2293 m) on both sides of the tributary are **2 hours** from Poiyan.

MAMMALS OF THE TEMPERATE ZONE

The gray or hanuman langur (*Presbytis entellus*), known locally as *bAAdar*, head and body length 2–2½ feet (60–75 cm), is long-tailed and long-limbed, with silver-gray fur and a distinctive black face. Troops of these old-world monkeys inhabit forests and feed on leaves, flowers, and fruits. Often seen on the Thak Khola trek near Ghasa and GhoRepani, the gray langur occurs from tropical to alpine zones.

The lesser (or red) panda (*Ailurus fulgens*), or *haabre*, head and body length 2 feet (60 cm), is rich chestnut above with a white face, dark legs, and a long, ringed tail. A forest dweller, it is nocturnal, remaining in treetops during the day. It has been seen in Langtang National Park and between GhoRepani and Ghandruk in the Annapurna Conservation Area.

The yellow-throated marten (*Martes flavigula*), or *malsAApro*, length 18 inches to 2 feet (45–60 cm), a lithe, arboreal predator, has a yellow throat and a long tail that makes up over a third of its length. It also occurs in the subtropical zone.

The leopard (*Panthera pardus*), or *chituwaa*, length 6–7 feet (185–215 cm), is rarely seen but not uncommon; you may find tracks on the trail. Found in open country, scrub, dense forest, and near villages, it also occurs in tropical and subtropical zones.

The Himalayan musk deer (*Moschus chrysogaster*), or *kasturi mriga*, shoulder height 20 inches (50 cm), is a small deer with large, rounded ears. The male has long upper teeth that form tusks. Now rare because of persecution, it inhabits upper temperate and subalpine forests and shrubbery.

The Indian muntjac (*Muntiacus muntjak*), or *ratuwaa*, male shoulder height 20 inches to 2½ feet (50–75 cm), is also known as the barking deer after its distinctive barking alarm call, which sounds remarkably like a dog. It inhabits forests and forest edges, especially rocky ravines, and also occurs in tropical and subtropical zones.

The mainland serow (*Capricornis sumatraensis*), or *thar*, male shoulder height 3⅓–3⅔ feet (100–110 cm), is a thick-set, goatlike mammal. Chestnut or blackish, usually solitary, it occurs in thickly forested ravines and steep slopes. ❖

The trail to Namche now leaves this tributary valley and heads more directly north toward the town of Chaumrikharka, another scattered village. Along the way, 15 minutes beyond Surkhe, the trail forks right for Lukla. The airstrip of Lukla is 1 hour from here. The easier, more direct route to Khumbu continues straight. More likely, you will opt for the alternate route to the well-appointed town of Lukla for provisions and supplies.

ALTERNATE
ROUTE

To Cheplung via Chaumrikharka

To continue straight to Cheplung, stay left and pass through Mushe before ascending to reach **Chaumrikharka** (also known as Dungde, 8900 feet, 2713 m), with lodges, in **1½–1¾ hours** from Surkhe. The trail from Chaumrikharka (which means "pasture for yak-cow cross-breed," referring to days long past) traverses through pleasant fields to a small ridge where the trail from Lukla joins this main trail up the Dudh Kosi valley at **Cheplung** (8792 feet, 2680 m) in **20 minutes** from Chaumrikharka. There are several lodges here, and you can pay a visit to a small *gomba* built into the cliff above the village. ❖

ALTERNATE
ROUTE

To Cheplung via Lukla

Traveling on foot, take the right fork 15 minutes north of Surkhe, ascending along stone steps. Most people opt to fly into Lukla (9350 feet, 2850 m) rather than hike in

from Jiri or the Arun valley. Although arriving by plane saves walking time, it also necessitates time spent acclimatizing. Lukla has become a major trekking center over the years, with shops that sell and rent gear (as well as in Namche). The name Lukla means "place with many goats and sheep," but clearly things have changed. In addition to the airstrip nestled among spectacular mountains, there are many hotels featuring food and accommodations of varying standards, and banking, Internet services, and even billiards are available here.

Lukla is a major staging area for treks to Khumbu. The airfield (9350 feet, 2850 m) was constructed in 1964 primarily to bring in supplies for Hillary's school and hospital projects. There are regular flights here from Kathmandu, and it can be a fierce bottleneck in bad weather. If you plan to fly out,

Along the main routes, bakeries cater to tourists. (Photo by Tokozile Robbins)

reconfirm your ticket with the airline as soon as you reach the town. The high-elevation landing strip built at an incline is not immune to plane crashes. As recently as October 2008, a passenger plane crashed while landing and all eighteen people aboard perished.

If you are here on a Thursday, there is a weekly market on that day, with people coming from the surrounding areas to sell and trade goods. Additionally, there is a porter's clothing bank here (supported by Porters Progress UK) to which you could consider donating on your way out.

To proceed from Lukla toward Khumbu, head north past an entry/exit *kani*, a police post that may require you to register (although park entry permits are not required until passing through Mondzo, 3–4 hours ahead). Descend and within **40 minutes** join the main trail from Jiri/Shivalaya at **Cheplung** (8840 feet, 2680 m) where there are lodges and a small *gomba* built into the cliff above the village. ❖

CHEPLUNG/LUKLA TO NAMCHE BAZAAR

All trekkers heading to Khumbu, whether on foot from Jiri or by plane to Lukla, will end up at Cheplung. The route follows through temperate forest up the dramatic valley cut by the Dudh Kosi to the Sagarmatha National Park entry at Mondzo and beyond to the Khumbu region starting at Namche Bazaar. Snowy mountains will occasionally peek at you from all angles along the way. From the dramatically set town of Namche there are several options including a visit to the lofty doorstep of the mountaineering holy grail, Everest.

To proceed from **Cheplung**, head north, crossing the Thado Khola on a steel box bridge (8380 feet, 2554 m) with the awesome trekking peak Kusum Kanguru (20,898 feet, 6370 m) at its head and lodges at the bridge. Soon, come to a bridge over the Dudh Kosi, with the village of Ghat (8350 feet, 2545 m) in under 40 minutes. There are lodges here. To proceed, stay on the east (true left) bank to **Phakding** (8700 feet, 2652 m), now expanded to both sides of the river, in 35–40 minutes, **1 ¼ hours** from Cheplung. Phakding is a common overnighting spot for trekkers flying to Lukla and, if crowded, other lodging choices (there are many) along the way may be more attractive. Cross to the west (right) bank (8600 feet, 2621 m) of the Dudh Kosi. Above on the wooded hillside lies Pema Choling Gomba. To reach it, continue on and north for 10 minutes to Zanphute; a left fork here ascends for 25 minutes to the *gomba*.

🏕 *Side Trip to Panjung. For those without the time or inclination to enter the Sagarmatha National Park, this full-day hike to a viewpoint south of the park boundary offers outstanding views of Everest and more. It is best to take a local guide. The trail ascends from the west side of the river just to the north of* **Phakding** *at Zanphute and passes the village of Thulo Gomela (Rimjung is the Sherpa name) and seasonal herder's huts along the way to* **Panjung**. *The endeavor involves sensational views and a climb of over 3300 feet (1000 m). Allow at least* **3 hours each way**. *This less-traveled trail might be your best chance to see wildlife.*

Continue through blue pine and rhododendron forests, past the timber houses of a small settlement called Tok Tok, orginally named for the sound made in hammering out vessels by metal workers here. Continue with views of Thamserku on the way to the next village of **Benkar** (8875 feet, 2905 m) with lodges, reached in **1 hour** from Phakding. Watch for large, hanging, tonguelike beehives just beyond a waterfall on the east (left) bank cliffs opposite you in this steep-walled canyon.

PEOPLES OF EASTERN NEPAL: THE SHERPAS

Next to the Gurkha soldiers of Nepal, it is perhaps the Sherpas, famous as mountain guides and porters, who have attracted the most worldwide attention. Some Sherpas dwell in the remote Rolwaling valley, and as far west as the Helambu region north of Kathmandu, but the most renowned come from the villages of Shar–Khumbu (Solu–Khumbu), along the upper valley of the Dudh Kosi and its tributaries, in the Mount Everest region. Sherpas are relatively recent immigrants to Nepal. Pangboche, their oldest village and one of the highest in the world, is thought to have been built a little over 300 years ago. The Sherpas speak a Tibetan dialect, dress like their Tibetan neighbors—or often like Western trekkers—and live as traders and agropastoralists, farming their high fields (mostly potatoes, wheat, barley, and buckwheat) and herding yak and sheep in alpine pastures up to 17,000 feet (5175 m).

Their region is divided into three subregions: Solu, Pharak, and Khumbu. Solu, at the south, includes such villages as Junbesi and Phaphlu, and the monastery at Chiwong, in picturesque valleys at approximately 9000 feet (2700 m). Pharak is situated between Solu and Khumbu along the steep banks of the Dudh Kosi. Most Sherpa mountaineers hail from Khumbu, the highest and most northerly of the three regions, at elevations of 11,000 feet (3350 m) and up. Their villages include Namche Bazaar, Thami, Khumjung, Kunde, and Pangboche, as well as the famously beautiful Buddhist monastery of Tengboche. Among the Sherpas, the practice of Tibetan Lamaism remains strong.

People from other areas, including the upper Arun and upper Tamur, have adopted the name Sherpa; they include migrants from Solu–Khumbu, but also other peoples of Tibetan origin who live in the northern regions, or more Hindu-acculturated peoples on the interface between the mountain and hill cultures. Their Sherpa identification may be for status, but often because when such people were given citizenship papers, or asked about their ethnicity for a census, their responses were constrained into a few available categories. Recent census figures show the number of Sherpas increasing faster than birth rates and migration could allow. Some have avoided this dilemma by adopting the surname Lama. It is mostly our problem as Westerners trying to classify things.

Their religion gives Sherpas a concern for all living things and for their Western clients on treks and expeditions. Their warmth of character, shared by many Himalayan peoples, is perhaps best displayed in their sense of hospitality. Visitors to a Sherpa house are considered guests of honor, for whom nothing is spared (sometimes to the point of embarrassment for Westerners). The best response to an outpouring of generosity by a Sherpa, or any Nepali host, is reciprocity—your own generosity and care in their regard.

Sherpa names of men often reflect the day of the week on which the boy was born. Nima on Sunday, Dawa on Monday, Mingma on Tuesday, Lhakpa on Wednesday, Phurbu on Thursday, Pasang on Friday, and Pemba on Saturday. Like any tradition, this one is not strictly adhered to.

The Sherpas have received considerable attention from anthropologists, mountaineer-writers, and traveling journalists, so we need not go into detail here. One facet of Sherpa culture not often described in the literature is the Namche Bazaar Saturday market, which is interesting from a traveler's perspective because of the chance to see several ethnic groups and a wide variety of local handicrafts and trade goods on display. If traveling toward Namche Bazaar immediately before a Saturday, trekkers may see many groups of lowlanders, mostly Rai and a few Brahman and Chhetri, carrying baskets of produce such as →

← (CONTINUED)

rice, corn, and fruits to sell or trade for highland produce such as wheat, wool, potatoes, *ghiu* (clarified butter, or ghee), and other animal by-products. This is part of the natural economic exchange that keeps each community supplied with the produce of the other. The lowlanders are easily singled out by their style of dress (light, tie-across Nepali shirts and baggy trousers that fit snugly at the calves) from the Sherpas and Tibetans. Sherpa and Tibetan men, by comparison, prefer heavy woolen cloaks and trousers, with leather or woolen boots. And these days, some dress in down jackets as well. At the market itself, Tibetan boots and handicrafts of silver, wool, and leather are displayed. A market day is a lively occasion, a time when Tibetans, Sherpas, Rai, and others (including foreign visitors) intermingle to trade, gossip, eat, drink, and even dance and sing in a spirited, sharing atmosphere.

The BhoTiya people east of Makalu, out to Kangchenjunga, sometimes call themselves Sherpa, sometimes not. Generally their language is Tibetan, which is distinct from the Sherpa dialect of Solu–Khumbu. With the increasing numbers of trekkers flying to Lukla and quickly climbing to Namche, they miss the opportunities to appreciate the valley below the Bazaar and to get a sense of hill Nepal. Consider spending two nights in this region and making side trips up tributary valleys to the east or west. Visit small conventional villages and handsome *gomba* nestled in temperate forest with snow-clad peaks at the valley heads. Stay in Sherpa homes there rather than in lodges. Observe traditional lumber making. Benefits include a warmer climate, less risk of altitude illness later, and sylvan surroundings. ❖

In a short while, cross to the east (left) bank and climb up through the hamlet of Chumowa surrounded by pine. Drop down to cross another tributary, the Kyangshar Khola (9098 feet, 2773 m), before steeply climbing to the large village of **Mondzo** (9300 feet, 2835 m) about **45 minutes** from Benkar. As an acclimatization side trip, consider spending an extra night in Mondzo and ascending to the east to tranquil meadows above the village with the reward of outstanding views. At the north end of Mondzo, enter Sagarmatha (Everest) National Park and pay the entrance fee at the check post (which has a visitor center as well) if you have not already obtained your permit (a passport-sized photo will be requested). The trail then descends in a cleft to the left of a huge rock and crosses to the west (true right) bank of the Dudh Kosi on a suspension bridge to reach **Jorsale** (Thumbug) (9100 feet, 2774 m) in **45 minutes**. This is the last village before Namche Bazaar.

Continue briefly up the west bank from **Jorsale** through blue pine forests to a bridge that crosses again to the east (left) bank. This area has had the bridges rebuilt several times because of large floods. There will likely be more changes in the future, but you should have no difficulty finding the way. The trail follows along the river, crossing a feeder stream before climbing steeply above the confluence of the Bhote Kosi from the west and the Dudh Kosi from the east, whose gorge is crossed on a high, hanging bridge (9400 feet, 2865 m).

The climb of some 1900 feet (600 m) to Namche Bazaar ascends through pine. A little less than halfway up at the crest of the prow, you have views of Everest behind the Lhotse–Nuptse ridge! Continue through pine, to a police post and junction. Both tracks lead on to Namche; the lower honors you with a traditional entry *kani*. **Namche Bazaar** (11,306 feet, 3446 m), the gateway to Khumbu, is **1½–2½ hours** from Jorsale. The village is expanding down the hill and everywhere else. *NAUje*, the preferred Sherpa pronunciation for Namche, refers to a big forest, which may again be realistic with the fenced-in reforestation projects above town.

Namche Bazaar is a remarkably entrepreneurial town. The electricity here and in surrounding villages comes from a generating plant in the Thami valley that became operative in 1995. As the administrative center for Khumbu, Namche Bazaar has many officials and offices, including an army base, police post, government-run health post, a small post office, a bank, and even ATM access (often out of service). Be aware that most government offices are closed Saturdays, the weekly day of rest for Nepal, and otherwise are supposed to operate from 10 AM to 4 PM. Namche Bazaar used to be a trading center, where grain from the south was exchanged for salt from Tibet, and it remains a trading center, even though the salt trade has ended. Sherpas own and run the stores, hotels, and restaurants, and an increasing amount of staff come from the lowlands. Bars, billiard halls, bakeries, laundry service, and Internet providers reflect recent changes. Prices are high, but a wide variety of goods are available and many curios as well. Supplies and equipment from previous expeditions can be found in the shops. If you find Namche too commercial, stay in Kunde, Khumjung, or even Phortse.

There is a modern dental clinic to the east side of town, helping to stem the decay wrought on Sherpa children partially by well-meaning trekkers dispensing candy. Trekkers can also use the clinic's excellent facilities with reasonable prices. Visit the national park headquarters and information center with nearby Sherpa cultural museum above town to the east (this area is called Choi Gang), with impressive mountain views as well. The famous weekly market, held on Saturday at the southern end of town, is a colorful gathering and well worth seeing. There is another daily market near the large *chorten* at the south end.

Although a well-equipped high-elevation town, especially by Nepal standards, always keep in mind the remoteness and elevation

A vast accumulation of empty bottles littered an area near the Shyangboche airstrip for years. Consider doing without bottled goods on your trek. (Photo by Stephen Bezruchka)

CHANGES IN KHUMBU OVER FORTY YEARS

Much has changed in this area since Stephen's first visit in 1969. Immediately noticeable are the new houses with Western-style windows, painting of trim on houses, electric lights and hot plates, corrugated tin roofs, and more efficient mudded stoves. People are more cautious with their use of firewood because it is time-consuming to search for it.

Families have a greater variety of Western goods. With the availability of electricity, satellite TV and video are making an impact. Modern clothes are usually worn rather than traditional apparel. Some Sherpani women dress in pants. Wealth is more often measured in terms of equipment and money rather than traditionally in the size of yak and sheep herds. The general level of education has improved greatly, but relatively few Sherpa have gone beyond high school, often preferring to work in the tourist industry, which provides great monetary rewards. Sweet tea is replacing the salt-butter variety (solja). Affluent Sherpa families now prefer to live in Kathmandu and can afford to send their children to private schools there and abroad. Many such Sherpa do not speak their mother tongue.

A major change in Sherpa society is the breakdown in the extended family, with elders alone in their senescence and families away in Kathmandu. It was traditional for a family to send the youngest child to the monastery, but now such practices are less common. Nowadays, it is not unusual to find women alone caring for children and looking after homes.

Mountaineering expeditions take their toll, and the Sherpa as an ethnic group were never large in number. The recent increase in the helicopter access has disrupted the local porter economy, and the overall net gain in the economy may be negative.

Some of the changes are for the good, and some are questionable. No matter how we perceive it, the Sherpa feel their lot is better now. ❖

of the Khumbu. Although at a relatively low altitude, acute mountain sickness (AMS) has struck in Namche. Make sure you are adequately acclimatized before trekking onward and upward. An excellent day hike for acclimatization is to explore the crest of the ridge above Shyangboche before descending to the prosperous villages of Khumjung and Kunde (described below). Another would be to head up the Thame valley as far as **Thamo**, **1½ hours** away, or go all the way to Thame in **3 hours** and spend a night there (see the Namche to Thame route description below).

ACCLIMATIZATION IN NAMCHE: SHYANGBOCHE, KHUMJUNG, AND KUNDE

The infrequently used airfield of **Shyangboche** (12,205 feet, 3720 m), with nearby lodges, is reached in less than **1 hour** from **Namche Bazaar**, by taking the trail that climbs up from the *gomba*. This is a helicopter landing site, as fixed-winged craft no longer operate here. In the unlikely event that you you flew in here from Kathmandu, descend to Namche Bazaar for the next 2 nights to acclimatize.

Beyond the airstrip the trail diverges, with signs pointing the way. To head to Kunde, stay left, proceeding past the yak preserve, and climb to a crest (12,700 feet, 3871 m) in peaceful juniper forest, then descend stairs to **Kunde** (12,602 feet, 3841 m) with

BUDDHIST FESTIVALS: MANI-RIMDU

Mani-rimdu is a Sherpa dance drama performed in the Khumbu region. It is held annually at Tengboche and Chiwong monasteries during November or early December and at Thame each May. Although usually held during the full moon, this is sometimes scheduled at a more auspicious time, so inquire in Kathmandu and along the way to learn when it will take place. This colorful, uniquely Sherpa festival has its origins in ancient Tibetan theatrical genres. The performers are monks, but the occasion is highlighted by much merriment and feasting by monks and lay spectators alike. ❖

a welcome gateway and many lodges in **30 minutes** from **Shyangboche**. The north end of this town is the site of locally staffed, well-equipped Kunde Hospital, built by the Himalayan Trust. If you want a tour, be prepared to wait until patients are seen. Consider a side trip to the *gomba* and crest of the ridge above Kunde.

To reach Khumjung, the "sister city" of Kunde, you can either traverse east from Kunde for **10 minutes** or go directly from Shyangboche. From Shyangboche, take the trail heading right from a sign-posted junction near the airstrip, pass a large *chorten* and *mani* wall in a blue pine forest with fine mountain views. Descend past the Himalayan Trust school buildings to the lodges of **Khumjung** (12,400 feet, 3780 m) in **30–40 minutes** from Shyangboche. The village *gomba* is situated in a grove of trees to the north.

To head to Pangboche or Gokyo, follow the trail out of the eastern end of Khumjung village past several *chorten*; just beyond, a path branches to the left toward Mong, or head straight to continue down to Sangnasa.

If heading back to Namche from Khumjung, an option is to climb up the Everest View Hotel from the eastern end of Khumjung. This high-end hotel was built in 1974 and is beautifully situated on a shelf (12,700 feet, 3870 m) with views of Everest and more. Descend past another fancy hotel to the Shyangboche airstrip to return to Namche.

ACCLIMATIZATION IN NAMCHE: NAMCHE TO THAME

Most tourists who visit Thame do not stay the night, which may make it all the more attractive for those who do overnight here. Additionally, at over 1000 feet (300 m) higher than Namche, it can be a part of an acclimatization regimen. The trail from **Namche** heads west from the *gomba* to round a ridge and travel up the Bhote Kosi river valley. Contour through juniper and fir forest, and soon the direct trail from Shyangboche comes in from the right. Reach **Phurte** (11,155 feet, 3400 m), with tea shops, a lodge, as well as a nursery, in **30 minutes** from Namche. Cross a tributary from the north at the small settlement of Kyajo.

Continue on to **Thamo**, with lodges (11,319 feet, 3450 m), in **45 minutes–1 hour** from Phurte. Above to the north lies the small village of Mende, and above that is a monastery (Laudo Gomba) where Westerners affiliated with Kopan Monastery in Kathmandu sometimes take retreat. Thamo is the office headquarters for the 630-kilowatt power project built below Thame with Austrian assistance. It began functioning in 1995 and electrifies the western end of Khumbu. In towns, the distribution wires are buried. The predecessor of this project was flooded when a glacial lake burst, and the remnants of this project can be seen across the valley to the south.

Leaving Thamo from the *kani* gateway, do not descend to the left to the river but climb past the monastery, mostly inhabited by nuns. Proceed to **Samde** (11,844 feet,

Chorten *framed by Thamserku* (Photo by Matt Freedman)

3610 m), with tea shops and fine vantage of the Kwangde peaks. The trail continues above the river before descending sharply to a narrow crossing near a cliff wall with large portraits of Buddhist saints. Cross the Bhote Kosi and ascend steeply to **Thame** (12,400 feet, 3780 m), with several lodges, in **1¼–1½ hours** from Thamo.

Above the village, a dramatically set monastery (12,925 feet, 3940 m) sits in a cliff. The May occurrence of the Mani-rimdu festival takes place here. To the north up the Bhote Kosi lies Nangpa La (18,753 feet, 5716 m), an important pass into Tibet that was once the popular trading route. A route to Gokyo follows this old route before branching east to cross the Renjo La. However, for acclimatization purposes it is better to cross from the Gokyo side (described below in the section on Gokyo).

The Thame/Thengpo Khola comes in from the west from the head of the valley where lies the Trashi Labsta, a high pass (18,882 feet, 5755 m) leading to the Rolwaling valley. This challenging route requires ropes and an ice ax as well as technical know-how, or an experienced guide and camping gear.

Return to Namche Bazaar along the same way that you arrived, or follow a trail from the southwest end of the village near the school. This trail passes the hydropower collection reservoir before reaching the powerhouse itself. From here a bridge over the Bhote Kosi leads to Thomde before ascending to Thamo where you meet the earlier route that was used on the way to Thame.

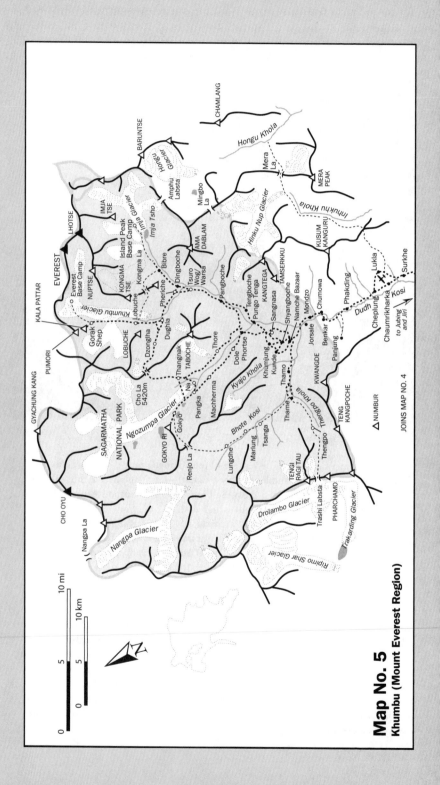

Map No. 5
Khumbu (Mount Everest Region)

KHUMBU
(Map No. 5, Page 260)

There are enough things to do in Khumbu to occupy two or three weeks. Four main river valleys can be explored, each with differences and all with spectacular mountain scenery. From east to west they are the Imja Khola valley (Chukhung), the Khumbu Khola valley (Everest), the Dudh Kosi valley (Gokyo), and the Bhote Kosi valley (north of Thame). Facilities exist along the way in each valley, and all are connected via high passes that can be crossed under good weather conditions if you are acclimatized. Of these four different valleys, the Gokyo trek, with its exceptional views and scenery with different-colored lakes, is rivaling the Everest trek in popularity, whereas Chukhung and north of Thame see less traffic.

If you have employed a Sherpa whose home is in Khumbu, you may likely be given the hospitality of his or her home. Those fortunate enough to be in Khumbu during the full moon in May or November may see Mani-rimdu, the Sherpa drama festival depicting the victory of Buddhism over Bon. The May production is usually at the Thame Monastery, and the November event at the Tengboche Monastery. Usually, trekkers want to head to the foot of Everest, and bottlenecks can exist in competition for space and facilities—do not be surprised if tour groups are given priority. If you will be satisfied by breathtaking mountain scenery that doesn't include the closest possible view of Everest, follow some of the alternative routes described here.

A reasonable itinerary for a grand tour of Khumbu for those with at least three weeks available would be to proceed to Namche, then to Dingboche, Chukhung, and beyond, and then to Kala Pattar and the Everest Base Camp. If conditions permit, cross Cho La to Gokyo; otherwise, backtrack to Pheriche, then go on to Pangboche, and take the high-level traverse to Phortse. Follow the Dudh Kosi up the Gokyo valley. Explore around Gokyo, then ascend the pass to the west of Gokyo, the Renjo La, and descend to Thame, and return to Namche. Those with less time must decide how important a close-up view of Everest is to them and whether they want to spend more time in permanently settled areas or proceed to high-altitude areas.

TOWARD EVEREST: NAMCHE BAZAAR TO DINGBOCHE

The times given for the journey beyond Namche Bazaar are quite variable. They depend on the weather conditions as well as the fitness and acclimatization of the party. Allow at least 5 days to reach Gorak Shep from Tengboche, the absolute minimum time. Hire porters to carry your loads, because they can handle the altitude much better than you. If you are going to high altitudes, be prepared for cold winds and snow, and temperatures below freezing, especially at night. It is critical to heed the warning signs of altitude sickness described in Chapter 5. Many trekkers have died in this region because they did not do so, and each year more people are added to that unfortunate and unnecessary statistic.

Wildlife is often seen on the way to Tengboche, and the forest of pine, fir, black juniper, and rhododendron en route is remarkable. Early in the morning or late in the afternoon, if you are quiet, you may be able to spot a musk deer.

From **Namche Bazaar** the usual trail to Tengboche rises to the saddle to the east, Choi Gang, where the Sagarmatha National Park headquarters and a museum (11,550 feet, 3520 m) sit. (Another option is to head to the airfield of Shyangboche. Beyond the airstrip the trail divides; head right for Khumjung and then on to Sangnasa where the trail meets the main trail.) Catch the trail onward from the boulder with *mani* inscriptions and contour high above the Dudh Kosi on a wide track, past lodges of Kyangsuma, in 1 hour from Choi Gang. Just beyond is a trail junction with a sign pointing the way to Khumjung and then more lodges in nearby **Sangnasa** (11,800 feet, 3597 m), **1¼ hours** from Namche. From Sangnasa a trail ascends to the trail from Khumjung to Mong, the entrance to the Gokyo valley.

To go on to Tengboche, continue through forests of blue pine and rhododendron, passing the village of Trashinga and the tea shops of Labisyasa, and drop steeply to reach the Dudh Kosi and a small settlement called **Pungo Tenga** (10,650 feet, 3247 m), with some hotels, on both banks, **1–1¼ hours** from Sangnasa (**2–2½ hours** from Namche Bazaar). Consider spending a night at this lower altitude, especially if you flew to Lukla and spent only one night in Namche or if you made the mistake of leaving Namche with a headache. After crossing the Dudh Kosi to the true left at a narrowing, the trail climbs past the prayer wheels and then steeply through pleasant rhododendron and juniper, with *chautaaraa* rest areas and impressive views of Kangtega, a peak named for its shape of a saddle made of snow. Pass a *kani* gateway into **Tengboche** (12,887 feet, 3867 m) some **1¾ hours** from the river crossing at Pungo Tenga.

There is lodging at Tengboche, and even intermittent Internet access; however, the limited facilities do not begin to accommodate everyone during popular times. Camping parties often dig minimal latrines, so the waste is easily unearthed. Effluent sometimes taints the water supply, resulting in trekkers getting sick here. Better to spend the evening at Pungo Tenga, or closer to Khumjung, and then visit Tengboche, and continue on for 15 minutes and spend the night east at Deboche or beyond. Although most of this area is controlled by the monastery with the accompanying monetary benefit, the trekker traffic also disrupts the functions of the monastery. There are plans for separating the touristic activities from those of the monastery in some way, possibly rerouting the main trail to bypass this place. Moral dilemmas here.

Across the valley to the south, there are silver birch forests, which grow well on the colder north slopes. Look for blood and Impeyan pheasants feeding near Tengboche in the morning. There are many places to explore around the monastery; those feeling strong can climb the ridge to the south for more views.

TENGBOCHE MONASTERY

The Tengboche Monastery was founded in 1916 by Lama Gulu, and the building was completed three years later, but the main temple was destroyed in a 1934 earthquake and rebuilt. The monastery was electrified in 1988, and on January 19, 1989 the *gomba* burned to the ground. It has been again rebuilt with foreign and local funding. The monks follow the Nyingmapa tradition of Buddhism. Currently there are some forty monks and thirty students, all of them Sherpas. Sometimes respects can be paid to the venerable abbot, believed to be an incarnation of Lama Gulu. When visiting the abbot, it is traditional to offer a ceremonial scarf, *kata*, which usually can be obtained from another monk, if not from the nearby visitor center. Information and souvenirs are also available from the visitor center. Donations for the monastery are appropriate.

Be aware that the heavy use of this area for tourist purposes is disrupting the religious life here. A wall to seclude the large monastery has been erected. Be sensitive to these issues. That being said, it may be possible to politely observe the early-morning or late-afternoon prayer ceremonies in the main hall, which has a large figure of Buddha, and tours of the monastery are often available. ❖

Yak caravan at Tengboche (Photo by Matt Freedman)

From **Tengboche** the trail heads east and descends slightly, past several lodges some 15 minutes beyond and 400 feet (122 m) lower, at Deboche where there is a nearby nunnery (Ani Gomba) that is worth a visit. In the formal Buddhist tradition, monks and nuns should be considered equal, although the reality is different, with nuns receiving lower status in a male-dominated system. Families usually give less support to daughters in religious pursuit.

Shortly beyond Deboche, you pass more lodging and tea shops, all the while traveling in a fine forest. Where you have a choice, take the lower trail. These trees are festooned with moss lower down. Continue to the river, the Imja Khola, and cross it at a narrowing on a steel bridge (12,400 feet, 3780 m), from which you get a spectacular view of Ama Dablang. This is 40 minutes from Tengboche. Just beyond a trail to the left heads toward Phortse; stay right to ascend. Pass a sacred site near a *stupa* marked with flags and believed to have a foot imprint set in rock of the seventeenth-century Lama Sangwa Dorje. Just beyond is a *kani* gateway where the trail diverges. The left (higher) fork ascends to the Pangboche Gomba (13,075 feet, 3985 m) and upper Pangboche, while the right goes directly to the village of lower **Pangboche** (12,800 feet, 3901 m), some 1¼ **hours** from Tengboche. There are lodges in both areas.

The Pangboche Gomba, the oldest in Khumbu, was built nearly 350 years ago at the time that Buddhism is said to have been introduced into Khumbu. According to legend, Lama Sangwa Dorje tore out his hair and cast it around the *gomba;* the black juniper trees surrounding it sprouted from those hairs. The trees are so large because it is forbidden to cut them.

Upper Pangboche appears to maintain more traditions than the lower villages. Residents here may be especially sensitive to intrusions by camera-wielding trekkers. For the trekker willing to seek out staying in a family's home as a guest, here is a chance to glimpse typical Sherpa life. For side trips, explore the slopes to the north. The National Geographic's *Mount Everest* map shows the area beyond Pangboche in great detail.

Continue northeast from either the village itself or from the *gomba,* with the last views of Everest for some time, to reach the junction above a cantilever bridge over the Imja Khola (which is not crossed). You are rising above the tree line. Continue following along the river to Shomare (13,287 feet, 4050m), with lodges, and the landscape becomes more arid as you reach more lodging at Orsho. In 5 more minutes, or **1¼–1½ hours** beyond Pangboche, the trail forks above **Tsuro Wog/Warsa**, a small summer yak-herding pasture with seasonal stone dwellings (13,725 feet, 4183 m). The right fork goes toward Dingboche, while the left fork leads to Pheriche; both are reached in the same time, and from both one can continue on to Kala Pattar and Everest Base Camp (additionally, there is a side trip from Dingboche along the Imja Khola to Chukhung and nearby viewpoint; see below).

Every party should spend 2 nights, or at least a complete day and night, at Pheriche or Dingboche. During the day spent here, an ascent or hike is an especially good idea. From Pheriche, you could spend this day going to Dingboche and farther east up the Imja Khola, as described later, or you could climb the ridge to the northeast to as high as 17,000 feet (5180 m) (and even higher to Nagatsang Peak at 18,208 feet (5550 m) for magnificent views of Makalu to the east and of nearby summits. There is a hermitage on the way. You could also recross the Khumbu Khola and climb up on the shoulders of Taboche to the west, or simply do the next day's walk, but return to Pheriche for the night. If you are already bothered by the altitude, it may be best to walk along the valley floor or just rest. Check the section on altitude illness in Chapter 5. If going beyond out of the popular season and dependent on facilities, find out whether they are open.

Dingboche is preferred over Pheriche as a stopover en route to Kala Pattar; it is less windy and sunnier, and more local activities can be observed. Many lodges abound; phone service is available, as well as Internet, and batteries can be charged. Dingboche is seasonally settled by Sherpas and fields can be irrigated for growing revered barley for *tsampa.*

There are several ways to reach Dingboche, depending on where you happen to be. If coming from Pangboche, and heading directly to Dingboche, it is best to avoid going to Pheriche, which is generally more windy and colder. Both routes are described below.

ALTERNATE ROUTE

- -

Tsuro Wog/Warsa to Dingboche

At the trail junction 5 minutes beyond Orsho, and **1¼–1½ hours** from **Pangboche**, take the right-hand branch (the left goes to Pheriche, as previously described). Descend to a bridge just above the confluence of the Khumbu and Imja Kholas, and cross the Khumbu (also known as Lobuche) Khola. Continue heading east along the true right side of the Imja Khola into the Imja valley, climbing gently to reach **Dingboche** (14,304 feet, 4360 m) in **45 minutes** or about **2–3 hours** from Pangboche, depending on acclimitization. ❖

Tsuro Wog/Warsa to Dingboche via Pheriche

From the trail junction 5 minutes beyond Orsho, **1¼–1½ hours** from **Pangboche**, the trail to Pheriche climbs to the crest of a small ridge (14,050 feet, 4282 m) marked by a cairn. From this crest, one can climb up to the north on the ridge to get great views including the west face of Makalu. To proceed on, descend a short distance to the bridge over the Khumbu (or Lobuche) Khola (13,875 feet, 4229 m) and cross it to the west (left) bank to reach **Pheriche** (13,950 feet, 4252 m) in **35–40 minutes**, some **2–3 hours** from Pangboche, depending on acclimatization.

Pheriche, once a *yersa* or temporary yak-herding area, is now settled entirely because of the trekking traffic, and is a very different place from the one Stephen encountered on his first visit in 1969. There are hotels built from blocks of sod, exhumed from the topsoil en route, a garbage dump, and some latrines. Pheriche is usually crowded with people. Nearby Dingboche is less windy and has nicer lodges and traditional agriculture. There is a Trekker's Aid Post in Pheriche, which was set up by the Himalayan Rescue Association in 1973 and is staffed by volunteer physicians during the tourist season to provide medical care to trekkers and porters. There are also daily lectures during the peak season regarding acclimitization safety that take place at 3 PM; these lectures are also frequently given in Dingboche, too.

To continue on to Dingboche, climb up and over the ridge (14,250 feet, 4343 m) behind HRA's trekker's aid post at Pheriche and descend to **Dingboche** in **35–45 minutes**. ◈

▼ *Side Trip from Dingboche to Nangkartshang. An acclimatization side trip from* **Dingboche** *would be to climb up to* **Nangkartshang** *hermitage on the ridge to the north of the village in 1½ hours for impressive views of the surrounding peaks (and the ambitious can go even higher to Nagatsang Peak at 18,208 feet (5550 m). This is a detour if you are going to Chukhung, but you could then head east to join the trail coming from Dingboche at Bibre (15,000 feet, 4571 m) with its tea shop.*

EXPLORE: DINGBOCHE TO CHUKHUNG

Advancing to Chukhung by the direct valley route that follows the Imja Khola, **Bibre** is reached in **1¼–1½ hours** from **Dingboche**. A high route exists from Bibre to Lobuche that crosses a pass to the northwest, the Kongma La (18,135 feet, 5527 m). There are no facilities along this route, and the trip makes for a very long, strenuous day and requires confidence on rock. Pokalde Peak (19,048 feet, 5806m), south of the pass, could also be climbed.

The trail to Chukhung continues toward the east, with Imja Tse (Island Peak, 20,253 feet, 6173 m) vibrant before you, crossing numerous streams that flow from the Nuptse and Lhotse Glaciers, to luxurious lodges at **Chukhung** (15,535 feet, 4734 m) in less than **30 minutes** from Bibre. This area is less crowded and perhaps more spectacular than the way to Kala Pattar; consider it for an acclimatization stage.

Chukhung Ri (18,238 feet, 5559 m), to the north of Chukhung, is inexplicably considered a "Group A Trekking Peak" and as such requires special fees to reach its summit (which involves a rock scramble) until it is reclassified. Alternatively, you can reach a slightly lesser crest. Check with the local lodge owners to see what is allowed. Both the peak itself and the lesser summit are destinations that provide viewpoints of the remarkable amphitheater you are in as well as of the west face of Makalu. Another option is Chukhung Tse (Peak) (19,160 feet, 5840 m), immediately north of Chukhung Ri, but

GLACIAL LAKES AND GLOBAL WARMING

Imja Glacier is considered to be one of the fastest-retreating Himalayan glaciers at approximately 243 feet (74 m) per year. The retreat is attributed to solar warming. Imja Tsho has increased in size alarmingly over the last half century from mere melt ponds in the 1950s to a lake of nearly 0.38 square mile (1 km²), or 247.11 acres, with an estimated volume of 47 million cubic yards (35 million m³) of water and growing. Its moraine is considered to be unstable, and a bursting of its fragile banks of rock and ice is termed a glacial lake outburst flood (GLOF). If extensive, a GLOF could result in severe flooding and devastation downstream.

A 2002 report by the International Centre for Integrated Mountain Development (ICIMOD) and the UN Environment Program puts twenty of Nepal's glacial lakes at risk for a GLOF, and Imja Tsho is considered the worst threat. According to Nepal's Department of Hydrology and Meteorology (DHM), there have been more than fifteen GLOFs in Nepal, occurring at a frequency of one every two to five years. The most recent in the Khumbu was recorded in September 1998, which caused flooding on the Inkhu Khola.

There are over 3200 glaciers and 2300 glacial lakes in Nepal above 11,480 feet, (3500 m). It is predicted that a 4°C rise in the global average temperature, which is within some projections for the end of this century, would eliminate these glaciers. According to the DHM, the temperature in the Nepal's Himalaya may be increasing by an average of 0.04° Celsius per year, more rapidly than the worldwide average. ◈

a direct route is not safe. This peak is best attempted by heading up the draw northeast from Chukhung and then ascending from the east. Each of these climbs would be a full day's journey, out and back.

Even if you do not scale this peak, it is worthwhile to spend a day or two traveling around to this area for close views of the incredible Lhotse–Nuptse Wall. Lhotse (27,923 feet, 8511 m), the stupendous summit above the 2-mile-high rock wall, was reputedly scaled from this side in 1990 by Tomo Cesen, a Slovenian. It was first climbed by the Swiss in 1956 from the Western Cwm, beyond the Khumbu Icefall.

Imja Tse (Island Peak), also a "Trekking Peak," is east of Chukhung, and a popular day trip is out and back to the base camp south of the peak. Along the way you will pass Imja Tsho with views of nearby glaciers, including Imja Glacier (see sidebar above).

DINGBOCHE TO KALA PATTAR AND EVEREST BASE CAMP

If continuing toward Everest from **Dingboche**, ascend to the ridge above the lodges and past a *chautaaraa*. This high route is more direct than the route through Pheriche and spans the broad plain above the Khumbu Khola valley. Enjoy brilliant views of the surrounding peaks along the way, including Ama Dablam, Thamserkku, Cholatse, Taboche, Lobuche, and even a glimpse of Pumori. The seasonal dwellings of Dusa (14,780 feet, 4505 m) and Chola Cho (Chola Lake) come into view before descending to cross the stream that emanates from the snout of the Khumbu Glacier, to then ascend to Dughla in **1½–2 hours** from Dingboche.

Pheriche to Dughla

If heading on from **Pheriche** to the foot of Everest, continue north along the flats past the *yersa* of Phuling Karpo, and then follow the grassy lateral moraine of the Khumbu Glacier. The route from Pheriche crosses the moraine's crest, descends to cross a glacial stream emerging from the snout of the glacier, which is covered by the moraine (15,025 feet, 4579 m), and ascends to the lodges at **Dughla** (also called Tughla, 15,075 feet, 4593 m). It takes **1½–1¾ hours** to reach Dughla from Pheriche. ◈

If you have a headache, stop at Dughla for the night rather than pushing on. Accommodations may be limited in peak season for trekkers who want to stay in lodges in Dughla or beyond, so early starts are advised. Those prepared to camp should have an easier time. Proceed by climbing to a ridge crest (15,879 feet, 4840 m) with stone memorials. These are built for climbers killed on expeditions to nearby summits, mostly Everest—there were none here when Stephen first walked up this valley in 1969. The trail then contours on the west side of the glacier. After crossing another stream of meltwater, the trail heads northeast, gradually rising to the variable lodges of **Lobuche** (16,175 feet, 4930 m), situated below the terminal moraine of a tributary glacier. Lobuche is about **1½ hours** from Dughla. Lobuche has had a bad reputation for sewage management, and sanitation facilities are limited here and higher up. A climb to the ridge crest to the west provides fine views, especially at sunset.

Just north of Lobuche is The Pyramid Laboratory, an Italian-built compound that includes a pyramid made of glass. Researchers arrive in spring and autumn to conduct projects in glaciology and sedimentology in the surrounding areas, as well as physiology and medicine. The center houses a meteorological station that collects data on monsoon development and other phenomena such as pollution levels, and houses a seismological station as well. Additionally, the lab is fitted with a GPS to measure long-term tectonic movements versus other regional GPS stations. Raw data from the laboratory and further information can be found on the web at http://evk2.isac.cnr.it/ and www.evk2cnr .org/cms/en (if you are fluent in Italian, visit www2.units.it/telegeom/). The laboratory also has rescue equipment and is less than **15 minutes** north of Lobuche (to the left from the trail to Gorak Shep). ◈

It is possible to use Lobuche or Dughla as a base to climb to Kala Pattar for views and to return the same day. This is advisable to avoid altitude problems.

Beyond **Lobuche** the trail contours a trough beside the Khumbu Glacier before climbing up the side of Changri Glacier's lateral moraine and working through it. **Gorak Shep** (17,008 feet, 5184 m) is reached in **2¼–2¾ hours** from Lobuche with lodges that can be crowded during busy times and Internet might even be available at an elevated price. Gorak Shep has porter shelter built through the efforts of Community Action Nepal (CAN) and the International Porter Protection Group (IPPG). There may be Tibetan snow cocks in this area that can be approached quite closely.

Gorak Shep is the starting point for one of the world's highest marathon races, the biennial Everest Marathon to Namche Bazaar (including a journey to Thame and back), which began in 1987 as a charitable event (www.everestmarathon.org.uk). Another marathon, the annual Tenzing Norgay Marathon, was begun in 2003 and is held on May 29th to commemorate the first ascent of Everest (www.everestmarathon.com). It begins at Everest Base Camp and finishes at Namche Bazaar. (See also www.trailrunningnepal.org/ for other running activities in Nepal.)

BIRDS OF THE ALPINE ZONE

Snow cocks (*Tetraogallus* spp.) are represented by two Nepali species. Large, mainly gray gamebirds, they frequent steep grassy slopes and stony ridges up to 18,000–19,700 feet (5500–6000 m) in summer, then descend to the subalpine zone in winter. They escape from people by running uphill. These birds can be seen on the Muktinath side of the Thorung La on the Annapurna Circuit, and in Sagarmatha National Park.

The snow pigeon (*Columba leuconota*), length 1 foot (34 cm), a pale gray and white pigeon with a black head, occurs in flocks on rocky cliffs. It may descend to 5000 feet (1500 m) in severe winter conditions.

Most of the nine Nepali species of pipits (*Anthus* spp.), length 5½–9 inches (14–23 cm), inhabit grasslands. Slim, brown, and streaked, they run or walk quickly and have both an undulating flight and song flight.

Accentors (*Prunellidae*), length 6 inches (15–16 cm), of which Nepal has seven species, resemble sparrows but have sharp, pointed bills. Most are drab gray or brown and heavily streaked above. They feed quietly on the ground, often in small groups in winter. Look for them on grassy and rocky slopes or, in winter, in open forest.

The grandala (*Grandala coelicolor*), length 9 inches (23 cm), belongs to the thrush family. The male is deep, brilliant purple-blue; the female is brown with a white wing patch. It forms flocks of several hundred birds in winter, and inhabits rocky slopes and stony alpine meadows. It can be seen on Laurebina Pass on the Gosainkund trek and between Dole and Gokyo in Sagarmatha National Park.

Choughs in Nepal include the red-billed chough (*Pyrrhocorax pyrrhocorax*), length 18 inches (46 cm), and the alpine, or yellow-billed, chough (*Pyrrhocorax graculus*), length 15.5 inches (40 cm). Both are all black, except that the former has a red bill and legs, and the latter yellow. Behavior and appearance are crowlike: sociable and noisy. They engage in fantastic aerial acrobatics. ❖

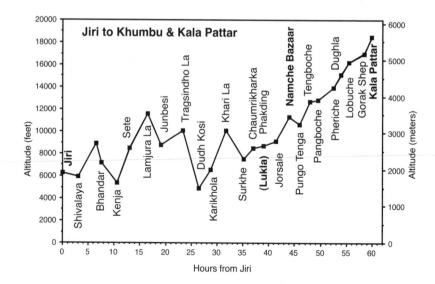

"Everest is a jewel, and the earth is a garland around it." —Tom Hornbein
(Photo by Mark Jackson and Susan Bergin/SAFA Himalaya Collection/Nepal)

The cairn of upper **Kala Pattar** (the name translates to "black rock" in Hindi) (18,208 feet, 5550 m), to the north of the rounded hill that is the surveyed point of Kala Pattar, can be reached in **1½ hours** from Gorak Shep by ascending directly and keeping slightly to the northeast. You can see the South Col of Everest from here, as well as the immense west and south faces. This is certainly one of the most majestic mountain viewpoints in the world. You might notice instruments set up nearby for data collection by the Pyramid research group (mentioned above). The Nepalese government held a cabinet meeting on the plateau on December 4, 2009, a week ahead of the world summit on climate change in Copenhagen, to draw attention to ramifications in the Himalaya of increased weather imbalances due to the modifications in climate. Many people make an early start to get here at sunrise, and the weather is generally clearer in the morning. However, the positioning of the sun in relation to the peaks makes the light more favorable later rather than earlier, and dusk provides an unforgettable light show. As Tom Hornbein remarked, "Everest is a jewel, and the earth is a garland around it!"

The world's highest mountain was named after Sir George Everest, the head of the Survey of India from 1823 to 1843. Sherpas use its Tibetan name, Chomolongma, which means "Goddess of the Wind." Sagarmatha, its Nepali name, means "the Forehead of the Sky" or "Churning Stick of the Ocean of Existence," from a Sanskrit interpretation. Current estimates of its height above sea level are 29,022.6 feet (8846.1 m), plus 8.4 feet (2.55 m) of snow, making it 29,031 feet (8848.65 m) high!

The mountain was first explored by outsiders from the Tibetan side beginning in 1920, with the last early expedition there in 1933. A joint British–U.S. group visited the south side in 1950, and climbing attention shifted to Nepal. It was first climbed in 1953 by Sir Edmund Hillary and Tenzing Norgay. The Swiss reached the summit the following year, and the mountain rested until 1963, when the Americans climbed it by the West Ridge and came down the original route, the first traverse of the mountain. Activities resumed in earnest in the 1970s, mostly nationalistic endeavors. By 1990 it was being exploited by commercial expeditions who tantalized aspiring, inexperienced mountaineers with bulging wallets. Recent carnage there reminds us of the powerful forces residing on the big summits. A fatality rate of almost 3 percent accompanies those who try to climb and those who are paid to climb it, especially guides and high-altitude porters. In May 2010, Jordan Romero, a thirteen-year-old, became the mountain's youngest summiter. The oldest was over 75. (For more information on Everest, including climbing statistics, visit www.everestnews.com, and www.himalayandatabase.com. An extensive, valuable database of information on climbing in Everest and Nepal and its border peaks is available primarily because of longtime chronicler of Everest expeditions Elizabeth Hawley, who began archiving expedition data in 1963.)

The sites of the various **base camps** used for climbing **Everest** are close to the foot of the Khumbu Icefall (17,575 feet, 5357 m) and can be reached from **Gorak Shep** in **1¾–2¾ hours.** Start at the flat, sandy area to the northeast; pass memorials and work through boulders to follow the lateral moraine before venturing over the rubble-covered surface of the Khumbu Glacier. Many trekkers find the serac formations along the glacier a fascinating change from the majestic mountain walls, and this is the prime attraction for the journey toward base camp. There are no views of Everest from the base camp area, although there are plenty of other soaring peaks and Everest is seen en route. If you are here when no expedition is climbing Everest, it may be tedious and time-consuming to find the exact location of recent base camps. Even if there is an expedition there and you are not following a supply team, it is easy to get lost and wander about.

It is possible to visit the base camp from Lobuche and return the same long day if you are well acclimatized. There is no accommodation for trekkers at base camp, although during the season enterprising Sherpas may be selling food items. An outpost of HRA's Pheriche operation runs a medical station there during the high climbing season of April and May.

You can vary your return trip from Gorak Shep by heading back down the valley to Pheriche and Pangboche or climbing the Cho La, a high pass that links up with the Gokyo valley.

RETURN JOURNEY VARIATION: LOBUCHE TO GOKYO VIA CHO LA PASS

Crossing Cho La offers a high, scenic route to Gokyo for people who want to combine the visit to the Everest Base Camp region without extensive backtracking. In the process, you circumnavigate Cholatse (20,784 feet, 6335 m) and Taboche (20,889 feet, 6367 m). It involves a short glacier crossing, and most people cross without a rope and ice ax; however, these items would provide added safety. Although there are no serious dangers or technical difficulties under good weather conditions, be aware that fresh snowfall on the pass seriously increases the difficulty and exacerbates steep, slippery sections near the top.

If you do not have enough experience to be sure that the new snow will not cause problems, consider skipping the pass. In the autumn of 1982, snowfall resulted in at least five trip-ending cases of frostbite, and some trekkers suffered permanent damage.

At that time, renowned mountaineer Reinhold Messner assessed the conditions and elected to avoid the pass and go around via Phortse. Deaths from rockfall and other hazards have also occurred. If you are depending on the lodges for accommodation, verify in Lobuche or Dughla that they are open. Lodging facilities are available at Dzonglha (Everest side) and Thangnak (Gokyo side).

Begin by retracing your steps on the trail down from **Lobuche** following a stream. Continue along the lateral moraine as far as the stream crossing. Instead of crossing here (which then descends to Dughla), the trail to Dzonglha and the pass branches to the right to continue along on the side of the valley. Eventually the route reaches a ridge and turns northwest into the valley of the pass to contour high above a lake (Chola Tsho). You will have not only arresting views of the lake below, but the surrounding peaks of Taboche and Cholatse to the south, and Lobuche to the north. Cross through a dip in the valley before ascending to **Dzonglha** (15,869 feet, 4843 m) in **2½–3 hours** from Lobuche. The lodges here may be overcrowded with tourists. Nevertheless, the site is situated on a shelf of land where the feeling of being under the north face of Cholatse is unforgettable.

ALTERNATE
ROUTE

Dughla to Dzonglha

Alternatively, if you happen to be coming from **Dughla,** a lower trail approaches Dzonglha from the south. Follow the trail slightly below Dughla before bearing west to the small trail that skirts the end of the Chola Glacier moraine, which has almost blocked the valley and formed Chola Tsho (lake) above it. Reach the end of the lake (14,803 feet, 4512 m)—it is ice-covered later in the season—in **30 minutes.** The best camping spot for spectacular views is near here. The trail follows the north shore of the lake and rises gradually until it reaches Chola Og (15,305 feet, 4665 m), a *yersa* of seasonal stone huts, in **45 minutes.** Above this *yersa* the trail is less distinct. **Dzonglha** (15,889 feet, 4843 m) with lodges, is another **hour** up the faint trail. ❖

Cross over a small crest from Dzonglha and descend slightly into the gentle, wide valley coming down from the glacier and the pass. Cross streams to work your way up to the head of the valley in 1 hour from Dzonglha. Climb through loose rock and then steeply up through boulders, sometimes over the large slabs with handsome grain, alongside a granite wall. Look for cairns to indicate the ascent route. Eventually, gain the glacier and keep to its south side on the snow-covered surface. Try to follow whatever path may have been previously made. The surface may be bare ice and thus slippery, in which case crampons would be useful. Porters sometimes make do with cord lashed around the soles of their footwear for traction. Be aware that crevasses may be covered by snow and also may be near the bergschrund where the glacier pulls away from the rock. The pass (17,783 feet, 5420 m), marked by cairns strung with prayer flags, is reached in at least **2½–3 hours** from Dzonglha. A valley and new vistas open up before you, and the trail that goes on to Thangnak can be made out below.

The descent to the trail from the pass can be hazardously steep over hard snow and variegated talus. Be aware of loose rocks as well as rockfall, and look for cairns to mark the way. Eventually you pass through scree to reach the valley floor, with its boulders and hummocks. You then bear west to a saddle, crossing minor ridges, and descend steeply to reach **Thangnak** (15,387 feet, 4690 m), with three substantial lodges and a few stone-built homes. It takes **2–2½ hours** from the pass to here in good conditions (**4½–5½ hours** or more from Dzonglha).

Proceed up the lateral moraine to a cairned notch, and then cross the dry (that is, the crevasses are not hidden under snow) Ngozumpa Glacier. This path changes with the seasons as more and more meltwater begins to intersect and redirect the route. Ascend the moraine's western wall and come out to join the trail below Gokyo. Head right/ north to reach **Gokyo** in less than **2 hours** from Thangnak. (See the section on the Gokyo trek for further description of this area.)

RETURN JOURNEY VARIATION: PANGBOCHE TO PHORTSE

An excellent route back from upper Pangboche, where the *gomba* sits, is to traverse the trail over to Phortse, then either head up to Gokyo, or cross the Dudh Kosi and climb up to Khumjung or Namche. The high-level traverse, sometimes with precipitous drop-offs, from **Pangboche** to Phortse is exhilarating for mountain panoramas. It takes **2–3 hours** to reach **Phortse**, and tahr and other wildlife may be seen en route as well as around the village. Phortse (12,500 feet, 3810m) is a traditional Sherpa village that appears to be least affected by trekker tourism and lies between the routes up the valleys to Everest Base Camp and Gokyo. Silver birch and rhododendron forests surround it. It has its own hydropower station, and use of firewood is prohibited. Phortse has some eighty households, and locals report that over thirty-five people from the village have scaled Everest. Lodging is available, and it is a good chance to arrange a home stay.

From Phortse you can follow a trail that stays above and to the east of the Dudh Kosi to reach Na on the way to Gokyo, described below in reverse in the section on return options from Gokyo. Alternatively, descend to cross the Dudh Kosi to Phortse Tenga and reach the usual route that heads right on the west side of the Dudh Kosi to ascend to Dole and on to Gokyo, or head south to descend to Namche Bazaar. The east and west routes meet up on the west side at Pangka. (See the Gokyo section for further information on these routes.)

EXPLORE: NAMCHE BAZAAR TO GOKYO

This valley has become a justifiably popular destination, as the trail takes you to summer yak-grazing country, to beautiful small lakes, and to the foot of Cho Oyu and Gyachung Kang peaks. Lodges now abound everywhere. The route rapidly gains elevation, and if you are not already acclimatized your days will be necessarily short in order to ascend at a safe rate. Watch for signs of altitude sickness. If doing both the Everest route and this route, then consider doing this route after Everest for acclimatization reasons. Some trekking parties, when faced with a choice, avoid the trek to the foot of Everest and visit the Gokyo region instead. However, there is disproportionately more serious altitude illness among trekkers who venture up here from the lowlands, because elevation gains can be great, given the short horizontal distances. Spend several nights at Namche, and then take at least 3 more days to get to Gokyo. This may not be slow enough for some trekkers, as people acclimatize at different rates.

There are four choices to reach this valley. The more direct route from Namche is through Kyangsuma to the junction near Sangnasa. Alternatively, if you are not acclimatized, it is better to first spend a night in Kunde or Khumjung (described above). The trail heads north from just below Khumjung, meeting up with the trail just north of Sangnasa to travel to Gokyo along the west side of the Dudh Kosi valley.

Another way to Gokyo is from Phortse, reached from upper Pangboche on the return from Everest (mentioned above and described below in reverse). The trail from Phortse travels up the east side of the Dudh Kosi valley, passing teahouses with basic lodging en route.

Alternatively, after visiting Kala Pattar/Everest, you could cross the challenging pass,

World view from Gokyo Ri (Photo by Mark Jackson and Susan Bergin)

the Cho La to Gokyo. And finally, you could head north from Thame up the Bhote Kosi and over the Renjo La; however, most people do this pass in the other direction and only those previously acclimatized should follow this route, as the increase in altitude is otherwise too swift.

ALTERNATE ROUTE

Namche to Mong via Kyangsuma

To follow the usual trail up the west side of the Gokyo valley, first climb from **Namche Bazaar** to the saddle to the east, Choi Gang, where the Sagarmatha National Park headquarters and a museum (11,550 feet, 3520 m) sit. Catch the trail onward from the boulder with *mani* inscriptions and contour high above the Dudh Kosi on a wide track, past lodges of Kyangsuma, in an hour from Choi Gang. Just beyond find the trail junction near **Sangnasa** (11,800 feet, 3597 m). From here a trail ascends to the trail from Khumjung and on to **Mong La** (13,000 feet, 3962 m), the entrance to the Gokyo valley in **45–50 minutes** or **2 hours** from Namche. ❖

ALTERNATE ROUTE

Namche to Mong via Khumjung

Or, more favorably, spend a night in Kundhe or **Khumjung,** mentioned above as a day-hike option from Namche, for better acclimatization. The trail ascends from just below the east end of Khumjung and climbs along the side of the sacred Khumbiyula mountain. Cross a small ridge and just beyond there is the former, higher trail that is to be avoided. Stay to the right, and a little farther along, the trail from Sangnasa ties in with this trail. Continue on to ascend stone steps and after crossing a prominence, stay left at another fork. Reach **Mong La,** at a crest of a ridge (13,000 feet, 3962 m), where stands an old *stupa*, some lodges, and a panoramic view. This takes **1–1¼ hours** from Khumjung. ❖

Above you, on the slopes of Khumbiyula, watch for a herd of Himalayan tahr (called *ghoral* by locals). Phortse is seen across the river. The trail descends steeply to **Phortse Tenga** (11,950 feet, 3643 m) with lodges in **1 hour.** The right fork descends to a bridge to cross the river and climb to Phortse. The track to Gokyo heads north. You will pass an unused national park office and an old army post, apparently built to check poaching. Cross several tributaries on wooden or iron bridges (with nearby waterfalls) and climb through forest to **Dole** (13,400 feet, 4084 m), where there are many lodges. It takes **1½ hours** to walk from Phortse Tenga to Dole. A brook runs through Dole as well as both Luza and Machherma farther along the way.

The trail passes above the *kharka* of Gyele, with its seasonal stone dwellings, to Lhapharma (14,200 feet, 4328 m), with lodges. It then contours to **Luza** (14,304 feet, 4360 m), in a small tributary valley, with lodges. In the next tributary valley is **Machherma** (14,485 feet, 4415 m), with many lodges, reached in **1½ hours** from Dole. Similar to the HRA post in Pheriche, this rescue post offers lectures and information on acclimatization, altitude sickness, and porter safety. The clinic and porter shelter was set up and is run by IPPG with assistance from CAN, and is staffed by international volunteers. It has a portable altitude chamber, oxygen generator, stretcher, medication, and more. From here, continue **30–40 minutes** to **Pangka** (14,633 feet, 4460 m), with basic lodging, and where a huge snowstorm in November 1995 dumped over 6.5 feet (2 m) of snow and caused an avalanche that killed trekkers and porters nestled against the hillside in a lodge. There was an extensive rescue mission to recover those who were stranded. A trail drops down from Pangka to Na at the crossing to the east side of the valley and a possible return route to Phortse and then Namche (described below).

From Pangka, descend slightly, following one of the brackish melted glacial rivers that flow down the west side of the Ngozumpa Glacier. The trail steeply climbs to put you to the west of the lateral moraine to follow an outlet stream from the lakes. Cross it on a bridge and arrive at the first small, shallow lake (15,450 feet, 4709 m). Look for Brahminy ducks resting at these lakes. The trail continues gently now. Before reaching the second lake, the trail from Cho La and Thangnak that crosses the Ngozumpa Glacier ties in from the east. Continue to the third lake (sometimes called Dudh Pokhari), and the tourist enclave of **Gokyo** (15,666 feet, 4775 m) on its northeast shore, in less than **2 hours** from Pangka. An outpost to the Machherma rescue station is to be set up here

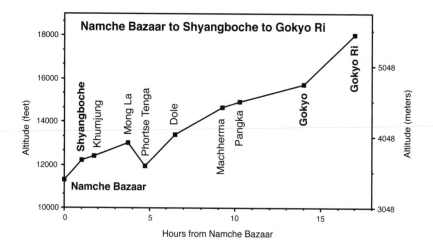

along with another porter shelter. The stunning beauty of the mesmerizing lake and lofty mountains speaks volumes for itself.

☟ Side Trip to Gokyo Ri. *From* **Gokyo,** *Cho Oyu (26,906 feet, 8201 m) looms to the north and straddles the border between Nepal and Tibet. It is the world's sixth highest peak and was first scaled in 1954 from the northwest by an Austrian expedition. The face you see has also been climbed. There are many places to go for views and excursions, which make this an attractive place to spend a few days.*

Currently, the most popular excursion is to ascend the ridge to the northwest to the summit lookout point of **Gokyo Ri** *(17,990 feet, 5483 m) some 2300 feet (700 m) above Gokyo. This continuous climb takes* **2 hours** *for those well acclimatized and provides an excellent panorama of the turquoise lake below, the swath of Ngozumba Glacier, and peaks from north working east from Cho Oyu (26,906 feet, 8201 m) to Everest (29,028 feet, 8848 m) to Lhotse (27,890 feet, 8501 m), and all the way to Makalu (27,765 feet, 8463 m)—four of the planet's six highest summits. Gyachung Kung (26,089 feet 7952 m), No. 15, is seen as well, and of course, much more. (The top ten highest mountains are, in the following order: Everest, K2, Kangchenjunga, Lhotse, Makalu, Cho Oyu, Dhaulagiri, Manaslu, Nanga Parbhat, Annapurna.) Consider being here at sunset, or sunrise, which is spectacular as well (and weather is usually better in the morning).*

☟ Side Trip to Northern Gokyo Lakes. *Heading north of* **Gokyo,** *there is relatively little elevation gain to reach more lakes. Follow the trail north between the lateral moraine of the Ngozumba Glacier and the hills to the west, or follow a more strenuous route along the moraine crest for better views until you reach the next, fourth lake,* **Thonak Tsho** *(15,912 feet, 4850 m) about* **1–1¼ hours** *from Gokyo. The next lake,* **Ngozumpa Tsho** *(16,355 feet, 4985 m), is reached in a further* **1¼–1½ hours.** *Hike up to the crest of the moraine for an astounding vista, informally known as "Scoundrel's Viewpoint," or climb a few hundred feet up the hill to the north of the lake for fine vistas. (Climbers can get much higher, to Ngozumpa Tse [18,208 feet, 5550 m],*

CREATURES OF THE AEOLIAN ZONE

This is the region where snow lies permanently, although much terrain is not covered because snow accumulates unevenly. A. F. R. Wollaston, writing in *Mount Everest, The Reconnaissance,* 1921, records the highest flowering plant species as a small, white-flowering sandwort (*Arenaria bryophylla*) at 20,277 feet (6180 m). Some invertebrates make their homes at even higher altitudes. Large populations of fairy shrimp have been reported in glacial pools at 19,000 feet (5790 m), for example. Insects, such as snow fleas (*Proistoma*) and some carabid beetles, feed on pollen grains, spores, seeds, dead spiders, and insects uplifted on air currents from the distant plains of India. Permanent life even exists at the highest point on Earth: samples of soil and snow collected on the summit of Everest were found to contain microorganisms. Birds and mammals are brief visitors to the high peaks and passes. Flocks of bar-headed geese (*Anser indicus*) have been seen flying over the summit of Everest at over 30,500 feet (9300 m). Mountaineering expeditions have reported alpine choughs scavenging from tents above 26,900 feet (8200 m). ❖

with the rewards of spectacular, unparalled views.) To continue on to the sixth lake, **Gyazumpa Tsho** *(16,896 feet, 5150 m), you need to be self-sufficient with camping gear to spend the night rather than making a long day's return to Gokyo. Gyazumpa Tsho is reached in* **1¼ –1½ more hours,** *and offers a supreme panorama in an other-worldly locale. Beyond are smaller lakes and even more sensational views.*

There are four options from **Gokyo**. You can retrace your steps all the way down, or for variation, you can retrace as far as Pangka and then cross to the east side of the valley and travel down to Phortse. Alternatively, to head to the foot of Everest you could follow in reverse the Cho La route described earlier to reach the Khumbu Glacier and the main trail to Lobuche. Finally, you can take the challenging, lesser followed option of crossing the Renjo/Lhenjo La (17,635 feet, 5375m) to the west and descend into the Bhote Kosi valley to Thame and on to Namche (this is described below following the route description on the east side of the valley via Phortse).

RETURN JOURNEY VARIATION: GOKYO TO NAMCHE (OR PANGBOCHE) VIA PHORTSE

To return to Namche by following the east side of the valley, retrace your steps from **Gokyo** to Phangka and then drop down to cross the headwaters of the Dudh Kosi at **Na** (14,435 feet, 4400 m), below the tongue of the glacier, in **1½–1¾ hours.** Continue south and cross a tributary to reach the valley floor and Kanasa with some huts (no lodges), potato fields, and yak pastures. Reach **Thare,** with a teahouse and basic lodging (14,250 feet, 4343 m) on the hillside, and go on to reach **Thore** with another teahouse and simple accomodation (14,435 feet, 4400 m) in **1 hour** from Na. After a couple of tributaries, and the tea shop at Genkewa (or Genjha), reach a high point with a *chorten,* then drop down to reach the *yersa* of **Konar** (13,425 feet, 4092 m), in an idyllic tributary valley, in **1½–1¾ hours.** Consider exploring the valley below the south face of Taboche. The ambrosia along here in the spring is intoxicating.

Continue into a handsome juniper and birch forest to a tributary and through rhododendrons to upper **Phortse** (12,500 feet, 3810 m), some **30–45 minutes** from

---

PHEASANTS OF THE SUBALPINE ZONE

The subalpine zone (the territory between the upper temperate zone and the treeline) of Nepal extends from 10,000–13,800 feet (3000–4200 m) in the west, to 12,500 feet (3800 m) in the east.

Himalayan monal, or Impeyan pheasant (*Lophophorus impejanus*), locally known as DAAphe (length 2 feet 4 inches, 72 cm), is Nepal's national bird. The male has nine iridescent colors but at a distance looks black; the female is dull, brown-mottled buff. Both sexes have white rumps and brown tails. It summers on grassy slopes above the treeline and winters in oak and rhododendron forests. It is easily seen on the Gosainkund trek and in Sagarmatha National Park.

The blood pheasant (*Ithaginis cruentus*), or *chilime* (length 1½ feet, 46 cm), a small short-tailed pheasant, is often tame and curious. The male is pale gray, green, and red; the female is reddish brown. Both sexes have red legs. It is found in rhododendron, juniper, or bamboo, and is most easily seen in Sagarmatha National Park. ❖

Konar. Phortse (also pronounced "Furtze") is perched on the flats you have probably seen from the west and south, and dominates the entrance to the valley you have descended. It lies between the routes up the valleys to Everest Base Camp and Gokyo. Phortse is a Khumbu village that may be the least affected by trekker tourism. Silver birch and rhododendron forests surround it, and more wildlife may be seen around Phortse than near any other village in Khumbu. Phortse has its own hydropower station, and use of firewood is prohibited. Lodging is available, and it is a good chance to arrange a home stay.

To leave Phortse, descend for **30 minutes** through the fine forest to the west to the Dudh Kosi (11,200 feet, 3414 m) to meet the main trail to Namche on the west side of the valley at Phortse Tenga; this route, which has already been described, will be quicker going downhill toward Namche than the 3 hours it takes going up. Another option is to continue east on the high traverse with occasional precipitous drop-offs to upper **Pangboche**, a **2–3-hour** traverse.

RETURN JOURNEY VARIATION: GOKYO TO THAME VIA RENJO LA

Renjo La is the pass (17,634 feet, 5375m) to the west of Gokyo that links the Gokyo valley to the Bhote Kosi valley and descends to Thame and on to Namche. It is a long, arduous day from Gokyo, and there are no facilities along the way until the lodges of Lungdhe some 5½–6½ hours away. Check in Gokyo that the facilities in Lungdhe are open before proceeding. The path becomes quite steep as you near the pass and, as with other high crossings, it should not be attempted under poor weather conditions or after recent snowfall and only by those well-acclimatized.

The trail from **Gokyo** branches left from the track to Gokyo Ri and follows along the north side of the lake. Views along the way and on the top are, as elsewhere in this region, astounding. The path gets very steep toward the top, traveling around snow and ice and through scree. Cairns lead the way, and **Renjo La** is reached in **2½–3½ hours** from Gokyo. Take a last look of the beautiful lake beside Gokyo, and descend the other side on stone-laid path to the south to a small lake.

Continue down on a wide path and pass by ponds on the descent into **Lungdhe** (14,370 feet, 4380 m) where there are lodges in **3 hours** from the pass. Descend shortly to where the trail meets the centuries-old trading route that heads north over the Nangpa La (18,750 feet, 5715 m) into Tibet. Follow downstream along the east side of the Bhote Kosi to reach **Marlung** (13,812 feet, 4210 m) with teahouse and basic lodging in **40 minutes**. Descend and cross the Bhote Kosi below Marlung and travel on the west bank of the river to the seasonal settlement of **Taranga** in **30–40 minutes**. Continue on the west bank, crossing the Langmoche Khola, and reach **Thame** in **1½ hours**, enjoying the greenery that may have been absent for some time. The route from Thame to Namche has been described previously in the section on side trips from Namche.

⚑ *Other Side Trips in Khumbu.* *Many places in Khumbu are worth a detour. Almost any ridge can be hiked up for views, and some are mentioned in the route descriptions. Climbing to base camps such as Ama Dablam, reached from Pangboche in a long day, provides a different Khumbu perspective. Hikes west of Lobuche provide different views than from Kala Pattar, as does the southeast ridge of Pumori. The Gokyo valley is full of numerous wonderful smaller valleys and ridges to explore.*

MAMMALS OF THE SUBALPINE ZONE

The subalpine zone (the territory between the upper temperate zone and the treeline) of Nepal extends from 10,000–13,800 feet (3000–4200 m) in the west, to 12,500 feet (3800 m) in the east.

The Asiatic black bear (*Selenarctos thibetanus*), or *himali kaalo bhaalu*, length 4½–5½ feet (140–170 cm), is all black with a creamy V on the chest. A powerful and potentially dangerous animal, it is seldom seen. Active between dusk and dawn, it inhabits subalpine forests in summer and descends to temperate or subtropical forests in winter.

The common ghoral (*Nemorhaedus goral*), or *ghoral*, shoulder height 2–2¹/₃ feet (65–70 cm), is one of the goat-antelopes. Found singly or in small groups on steep grass- and rock-covered slopes, it can be seen on the Gosainkund and Helambu treks.

The Himalayan tahr (*Hemitragus jemlahicus*), or *jhaaral*, male shoulder height 3–3¼ feet (90–100 cm), is a large goat with a black face. The male has a shaggy shoulder ruff. It grazes in herds at 12,000 feet (3660 m) and below, on precipitous slopes and in dense forests and scrub, and can be seen above Langtang village and around Phortse and Pungo Tenga in Sagarmatha National Park.

Royle's pika, also known as the mouse hare (*Ochotona roylei*), or *musa kharayo*, *pikaa*, length 6–8 inches (15–20 cm) is a delightful small mammal. It has a short muzzle, small ears, and no visible tail. It lives above the treeline in open country among rocks and can be seen on the Gosainkund trail, at Lobuche, and along the trail above Pheriche in Sagarmatha National Park. ❖

DUDH KOSI VALLEY TO ARUN VALLEY AND TUMLINGTAR VIA SALPA BHANJYANG

Some trekkers hike into or out of the Solu–Khumbu via Tumlingtar in the Arun River valley. It is an arduous journey, cutting across several tributary valleys with attendant strenuous ups and downs. Facilities along this route are less developed and the path is often unclear; travelers will need to ask locally for directions along the way. The journey from Solu–Khumbu and the Dudh Kosi valley to the Arun valley begins at Bupsa.

From **Bupsa**, climb up to Kharte, and leave the Dudh Kosi valley trail to ascend to the village and pair of lodges of Pangkongma, or **Pangum** (9338 feet, 2846 m), **2–2½ hours** from Bupsa. You could also reach this village up the valley to the east of Karikhola. Continue past the *gomba* up to Pangkongma La (10,410 feet, 3173 m), a pass in a rhododendron forest, **45 minutes** beyond.

Head east down the ridge crest and descend to the Sherpa village of **Shibuche** (9000 feet, 2743 m), with lodging, in **45 minutes**. Descend steeply to cross a high suspension bridge (6200 feet, 1890 m) over the Inhukhu (Inkhu) Khola to the east (left) bank. Ascend steeply on an exposed trail and pass through Gai Kharka and reach Najingdingma (8531 feet, 2600 m), with tea shops, in **3–3½ hours** from Shibuche. A steep, rocky ascent reaches **Surki (Sipki) La** (10,120 feet, 3085 m) in another **1–1¼ hours**.

Descend through rhododendron forests to a promontory with *chorten* and reach **Boksom/KhirAUle Gomba** (8399 feet, 2560 m) in **1–1¼ hours** from Surki La. The distinctive juniper trees surrounding the *gomba* were introduced from Darjeeling. Continue to Lenji Kharka and south down to **Bung** (5250 feet, 1600 m) with a Makalu–Barun National Park check post and lodges, in **2 hours**.

Descend through this large hillside village to cross the Hongu Khola to the southeast (left) bank on a suspension bridge (4318 feet, 1316 m) and stay to the left to ascend steeply to the Rai village of **Gudel** (6400 feet, 1950 m), with lodging, in **1¼–1½ hours**. Climb above to a ridge promontory and stay high, traversing above the river, to reach the Sherpa village of **Nimchola**, or Share (8100 feet, 2469 m), with a *gomba* and lodging, in **1¾ to 2 hours**. Reach another Sherpa village of **Sanam** (8770 feet, 2700 m), with lodging, in **¾–1 hour** from Nimchola. Descend and pass a pair of tea shops and cross the Lidung Khola to the south (left) side. Fill up on water here, as it may be scarce until after the pass. Ascend steeply through dense coniferous forest to **Salpa Bhanjyang** (11,018 feet, 3349 m) in **2–2¼ hours**, with a *stupa* and good views of Numbur and Katang to the north as well as more distant views to the east and west. A 30-minute walk northeast of the pass will bring you to a pond where festivals are held several times a year; from this pond you could follow a path down to the east to tie back in with the more direct trail at another small pond mentioned below.

Descend from the pass to the southeast by *chorten* and *mani* to **GurAAse**, with *bhaTTi*, and then a small pond before rounding the ridge and descending steeply in **2½ hours** from the pass to the spread-out hamlet of **Jaubari**, with basic lodging and a small *gomba* nearby. Descend steeply to the Rai village of **Phedi** (4900 feet, 1493 m) in 1¾ hours, where there is a *gomba* and lodges on the prow between the Irkhuwa Khola to the west and the Sabu Khola to the north. In this area, there is a significant *lokta* papermaking industry. Head east out of Phedi and cross a tributary, before descending slightly to cross the Irkhuwa Khola. Pass through the village of Tendor and cross a tributary to

THE YETI

It was in the autumn of 1951 near Menlung La that the famous yeti (abominable snowman) footprint photographs were taken. The footprints were found in the afternoon at around 16,000 feet (5000 m) on a snow-covered glacier among crevasses. They were about a foot long (0.3 m) and half as wide. Could it have been a person traveling several hours from the nearest habitation without shoes and with deformed feet? The authors have seen mountain people carry heavy loads barefoot in the snow. Others have documented unclothed individuals with seemingly superhuman abilities to adapt to extreme temperatures.

Sherpas and other mountain groups speak of a hairy man-bear creature, and scalp and hand bone relics have been on display at Khumjung and Pangboche (the former can still be seen, the latter has been stolen). Sir Edmund Hillary's 1960–61 expedition took the Khumjung relics on an around-the-world trek to authenticate them without success. The renowned mountaineer Reinhold Messner wrote a book on his search for the yeti. Other expeditions have tried to find this animal whose existence is based on anecdotal reports rather than scientific evidence.

Many years ago, when outsiders expressed disbelief in the creature, a Sherpa said, "You tell us of buildings as tall as our hills, with magic carpets in them that carry you to the top, and we can't believe this, so how can we expect you to believe in the yeti?" Although the yeti remains a figure of cryptozoology, it has become a pop-culture legend whose name surfaces not infrequently in the media and is used to promote services and products from bicycles to hotels and more, not only in Nepal but throughout the world. ❧

While passing a chorten, *keep it on your right.* (Photo by Tokozile Robbins)

reach **Dobhane** (3200 feet, 975 m), with tea shops and simple lodging, in **1¼ hours** from Phedi.

Trails exist on both sides of the Irkhuwa Khola; ask which is currently the best. Reach **Gothe**, with lodging, in **1¼–1½ hours**. Continue down and cross the Irkhuwa Khola to the south bank and follow along it before ascending to Chharlise and through the village of Marjhuwa up to a lodge on a ridge crest in **1½ hours**. Descend to the southeast into the Arun Khola valley. Cross the Chikhuwa Khola to its south (right) bank to **Balawa Besi**, with tea shops and *bhaTTi*, in another **1½ hours**. Continue downstream for **20–25 minutes** to the bazaar of **Kartikeghat/Kartikepul**. Cross the Arun Khola (1200 feet, 366 m). Head downriver on its left/east bank, passing Chewa Besi, and then ascend away from the banks steeply to the southeast to a *chautaaraa* and lodges of **Gidhe/Kumal** in **2 hours** from Kartikeghat. Head south for ¾–1 hour to **Tumlingtar** (1500 feet, 457 m), a broad, flat plateau on the east (left) bank of the Arun Khola, with an airport and overland transport as well (see the Makalu Base Camp trek in Chapter 9 for more details on Tumlingtar).

8

LANGTANG, GOSAINKUND, AND HELAMBU

(for the Tamang Heritage Trail, see Chapter 9)

The best journeys are the ones that answer questions that at the outset you never even thought to ask.

—Rick Ridgeway

Trekkers heading into this area may find accommodations for the entire journey in the popular season. Langtang, a Himalayan valley north of Helambu and Gosainkund, is inhabited by Tamang and Tibetan (Bhote) peoples and provides a glimpse of mountain life. Trails are straightforward, yet you can head east in the Langtang valley beyond the last habitation to spectacular remote mountain areas, taking various side trips. Food and lodging are available except for the highest areas. Link-ups with Gosainkund are reasonably simple, but to link with Helambu requires crossing a substantial pass, the Ganja La, for which you must be self-sufficient in food, fuel, and shelter.

The Gosainkund area is the site of several sacred lakes that lie south of a major ridge between Helambu and the Trishuli Khola to the west. The area is uninhabited for the most part, but every August as many as 50,000 pilgrims crowd into the area for a festival, Janai Purnima, by a lake that figures prominently in Hindu mythology (more below). Trekkers can visit this area from Dhunche or Syabrubensi, reached by road from Kathmandu, and, if conditions permit, cross a pass to link up with Helambu. It is spectacular in the spring when rhododendrons are in bloom. Most of Langtang and Gosainkund have been included in the boundary of Langtang National Park, and there has been an attempt to create uniform restaurant and lodging services as in the ACAP region north of Pokhara. This practice has become the standard from Langtang village and beyond.

Helambu, the region closest to Kathmandu, can be approached from the northeast rim of the Kathmandu valley. The name refers to a region at the north end of the Melamchi Khola. It is inhabited by Yolmo, also called Sherpas. This region south of the main Himalayan chain provides an example of typical hill life in Nepal. A circuit can be made through the area from Kathmandu. The route begins in areas of Hindu influence and goes through Buddhist villages. There are distant views of the Himalaya. Rather than backtrack to Kathmandu, you can make a circuit to reach the road: either at Melamchi Pul, if you head south from Shermathang; or at Chautaaraa, if you take the Panch Pokhari side trip, a challenging trek to some high-altitude lakes not visited by many trekkers.

The newer Tamang Heritage Trail (see Chapter 9) lies to the west of the Langtang area and takes you through mainly Tamang villages in the mid-hills that have received relatively fewer tourists. Although the mountain views are a bit farther away than in Langtang, follow this trail and stay in people's homes for a deeper cultural experience than can be had on the more touristic routes. A trek along the Tamang Heritage Trail can be combined with the Langtang trek. The routes coincide at Syabrubensi or along the high route from Syabrubensi to Rimche where the trails tie in at the village of Khangjim.

LANGTANG
(Map No. 6, Page 297)

Langtang is a spectacular valley nestled in the Himalaya and the third most visited trekking region after Annapurna and Everest. Lodges and food are available for most of the way, but it is best to arrange food and shelter to be able to explore the upper part of the valley; this can be organized at Kyangjin Gomba, the last area with lodges. First, we describe the trip from Dhunche (or Syabrubensi, a quicker valley-bottom option) to Langtang and then several side trips up the valley. A high pass, the Ganja La, links Langtang with Helambu; going with a guide is advised. Return routes to avoid back-tracking from Langtang and link up with Gosainkund complete the description.

Dhunche was the traditional starting point for the trek. However, with the construc-tion of a trail from Syabrubensi to Landslide/Pairo, it is possible to cut about a day off the usual trekking time. The price paid in starting from Syabrubensi rather than Dhunche is not passing through Syabru, missing views of Ganesh Himal and peaks to the north in Tibet, and opting for an entire valley-bottom route. However, if you are going on to Gosainkund, you will pass through Syabru anyway, so the valley-bottom option makes sense. You could also start (or vary your return) by traversing from Syabrubensi high on the north side of the Langtang valley and reaching Rimche (or if going the other direction, return this way to Syabrubensi). A start from Syabrubensi is described first, followed by that from Dhunche.

The first part, often the most difficult, consists of road travel. If you have the resources, consider hiring a jeep. Trekkers have occasionally chartered a helicopter to Kyangjin Gomba and descended from there. Altitude illness is more likely to strike such groups. Better to board a bus from Kathmandu to Dhunche or Syabrubensi. Some buses go di-rectly to Syabrubensi; others go only as far as Dhunche. Departure points for these tour-ist buses are from the Nayaa Bas Parak ("New Bus Park") near Baleju on the Kathmandu Ring Road. Purchase the tickets the day before, and specify which destination you want.

The road rises out of the Kathmandu valley to the northeast. Enjoy refreshing sights of fertile hills along the way and the occasional symphony of cicadas if they can be heard over the din of the bus. There are glimpses of Ganesh Himal and west to Himal Chuli and the Annapurna Range, but you will be closer to the mighty Himalaya soon enough. Trishuli, the administrative center of Nuwakot District, is less than 45 miles (70 km) by road from Kathmandu.

North of Trishuli the rough feeder road climbs up from the valley bottom. Views of the Langtang Range and Paldor Peak as well as the incredible gorge below you give a sense of the scale of the terrain. Pass through the village of Kalikhastan and eventu-ally enter the Langtang National Park area. Park entry permits are inspected along the road just before reaching Dhunche (6594 feet, 2010 m), the headquarters of Rasuwaa

Mani *wall with Kyangin Gomba and prayer flags* (Photo by Tokozile Robbins)

District, 30 miles (48 kms) from Trishuli. The check post and national park office and information center are just over ½ mile (1 km) before Dhunche or a 10-minute walk. The road continues 9 miles (14½ kms) on to Syabrubensi and farther west to Thaambuchet (road travel even farther west into the Ganesh Himal area to lead and zinc mines at SomdAng is by private vehicle) or north to the border.

SYABRUBENSI TO KYANGJIN GOMBA

Syabrubensi (4650 feet, 1417 m) is at the junction of the Langtang Khola with the Bhote Kosi, which join to form the Trishuli Khola. This large town has a settlement of Tibetan refugees, as well as BhoTiya, who call themselves Tamang. The newer part of town is to the south. Below here, on the true right (TR) bank of the Trishuli Khola, there are hot springs with five small pools that used to be clean enough for bathing but more recently have become too polluted and are in disrepair. There are attempts to clean them up, so inquire locally if they are usable.

Cross the Bhote Kosi and then the Langtang Khola on suspension bridges to begin on the south side of the Langtang Khola. The trail follows the Langtang Khola upstream on the true left (TL) bank, if facing downstream. Don't take the right-hand fork, reached in 20 minutes from the bridge, unless you would like to go to Syabru.

Syabrubensi to Syabru

If you are returning from the Tamang Heritage Trail or from a circuit of Langtang via **Syabrubensi** and walking out to Dhunche or Gosainkund, the route to Syabru (also known as Thulo Syabru) is described here. To climb up to the village of Syabru, take the right fork that leaves the valley floor 20 minutes from the **Langtang Khola** bridge in Syabrubensi. The trail ascends steeply following the powerlines most of the way. In about **1 ¼ hours** the trail forks. The lower trail heads to the lower end of Syabru along the powerlines, while the upper passes *mani* walls before arriving mid-town among lodges. Reach **Syabru** (7350 feet, 2240 m) in **1¾ hours** from the bridge. For options from Syabru, see below. ❧

In **1½ hours** from the bridge, cross the Ghopche Khola to reach the few tea houses of Domin (Dhoban, 5380 feet, 1640 m). Ascend to where a trail from Syabru joins in just west of a major landslide area (5800 feet, 1768 m) in 15 minutes. Turn left and head up the valley, crossing the landslide of 1987 near its terminus, to reach the lodges of **Landslide,** also known as Pairo (meaning "landslide") (5500 feet, 1676 m), in **20 minutes**. The first lodge has piped hot water from a small hot spring across the river; however, the spring itself is not accessible, as there is no bridge. Most lodges are operated by Tamang until well into the Langtang valley.

Continue upstream from Landslide/Pairo in a lush oak forest to reach **Bambu** (6480 feet, 1975 m), a collection of lodges in a cleared bamboo jungle with spaces for tents, in **1 hour.** Water cascades off the north side of the impressive canyon here. Climbing beyond, cross a tributary and a stand of birch trees and in **45 minutes** come to the bridge across the Langtang Khola (6972 feet, 2125 m). There is a simple lodge on the north side that receives little sunshine in this narrow gorge cut by the river tumbling down from above. As you climb upstream, be careful of the nettles that guard the sides of the trail in this wild jungle. Reach the first lodges of **Rimche** (7881 feet, 2402 m) in **45 minutes.** A further **20-minute** climb brings you to another lodge, misnamed for a view not possible from there (8169 feet, 2490 m), where the high north-side trail to Syabrubensi meets the valley-bottom trail. This higher trail is described below and can be taken to Syabrubensi on the return for variation. A few minutes beyond is another lodge, and all these are referred to as Rimche.

The forest here abounds with wildlife, marten, bear, langur monkey, and red panda, which one lucky trekker watched and photographed on his first trek in Nepal in the winter months.

Compare the forests on both sides of the valley; they go much higher on the north-facing aspect, even though it receives less sunlight, because there is more rainfall there. Descend slightly to reach **Changdam** (8140 feet, 2481 m) in 15 minutes, a group of lodges in a clearing with solar power and phone service. This location is more usually referred to as Lama Hotel, after the first structure built in 1973 that has since been replaced.

Relax your vigilance for nettles now, and climb into more lush forest with hanging moss, bamboo, birch, and oak, and be glad the huge landslide on the other side didn't catch you in this orogenically active area. Nevertheless, small parts of the trail slide away, so it is being constantly rerouted and rebuilt. Reach two lodges 10 minutes apart, known collectively as **Gumnachowk,** meaning "trekker's corner," as well as Riverside/Chunama (9101 feet, 2774 m), in **1–1¼ hours.** Look for troops of well-fed monkeys. Climb on through more resplendent forest to reach two lodges at **Ghora**

BUDDHIST FESTIVALS

Losar, the Tibetan New Year, is in mid-February. There are festive activities at Baudhnath and Swayambhunath temples in the Kathmandu valley and at the Tibetan refugee center near PaaTan. Festivals are also held in outlying Tibetan refugee communities, such as in the Pokhara valley, in the Langtang valley, and at Chialsa near Salleri in Solu–Khumbu. Buddhist pilgrims visit the big temples and monasteries at this time, and family reunions—with feasting, drinking, and dancing—highlight home life.

The birth of Siddhartha Gautama, which took place in Lumbini, Nepal, during the full moon, is celebrated as Buddha Purnima or Buddha Jayanti (also Saga Dawa). The commemoration occurs on the full moon, usually in May, but sometimes in April or as late as June. A solemn occasion, it is also considered to be the anniversary of his attainment of liberation which occurred in Bodh Gaya, India, as well as his death in Kushinagar, India. Foreign dignitaries are usually invited to observances during the day at Swayambhunath and Baudanath, where Tibetan and Newar Buddhist monks perform elaborate rituals. Observances are also held in other Buddhist temples and monasteries. Prayer flags fly overhead, and at night the Swayambhunath hilltop is brightly lit. The celebration of Buddha's Birthday is less elaborate in outlying Buddhist communities, where observances at the local *gomba* are common.

The current, 14th Dalai Lama's Birthday, on July 6, is a time for prayer, invocation of blessings, and feasting, especially by Tibetan refugees. For some refugees it is a time of patriotic expressions in remembrance of former times, when the Dalai Lama led Tibet. Prayer flags fly overhead, and within the monasteries, butter lamps are lit in the name of the Dalai Lama. Prayers are said for his long life and good health.

A weeklong festival at Kyangjin Gomba, Dukpa Chesyi, is celebrated toward the end of July or early August (the sixth month and fourth day according to the Tibetan calendar). This festival commemorates the Buddha's first teaching and includes singing, drinking, dancing, and archery, among other merrymaking activities. ❖

Tabela (9860 feet, 3005 m) in ¾–**1 hour** as the valley opens out. This was once a settlement of Tibetans, then a Khampa staging center, and now the army has taken over. Your national park permit will be checked **10 minutes** beyond the collection of lodges, and you will also be asked to sign the register when you leave. The altitude gain should make you cautious to look out for signs of mountain sickness.

Climb on, being wary of slippery sections of the trail when cold temperatures freeze the water in tributaries coming off the walls to the north. Pass through pasturing areas and ascend to the lodges of **Thang Shyap** (10,460 feet, 3188 m), in **45 minutes** where you leave the forest behind and reach **Tchamki** (10673 feet, 3253 m), with a tea shop and lodge, in a further 15 minutes. The village of Langtang is visible up the valley. A long suspension bridge crossses over a tributary to more tea shops of Tchamki.

As of July 2009, lodge owners from Tchamki and above have decided to reduce competition by allowing only selected lodges to be open for business, depending on the season, while fixing prices at higher rates.

In another **30–45 minutes** reach lodges below **Kangtangsa**, a village also known as **Gomba**, for the *gomba* nearest to Langtang village. This *gomba* and the one at Kyangjin operate with villagers performing the rites, and monks visiting occasionally to officiate,

There are now more than twenty hotels operating in Kyangin Gomba, a far cry from the yak pastures of yesteryear. (Photo by Tokozile Robbins)

in the Nyingmapa tradition. Pay a visit and leave a donation, asking at a lodge for the whereabouts of the *konyer* or key custodian. There is a smaller temple to the left of the main temple that is also worth a visit. A *lama's* quarters are next to this smaller temple.

Continue climbing in the widening valley, and approach Langtang village (11,220 feet, 3420 m), **30 minutes** up from Gomba/Kangtangsa. Lodges are concentrated on the newer lower part of town. Off to the north is a small hydroelectric power supply that powers a community-run bakery where fresh cookies and more are available! Except for joint community operations, electricity to the villagers is limited from early evening to early morning.

Kangtangsa and Langtang are the first opportunities you have in this valley bottom to stay in a village. Every other place up to here, if you came from Syabrubensi, has been built for tourists. Try to stay in the traditional upper part of Langtang to get a better sense of life in this valley. The people, although they call themselves Tamang, have a much different culture than the relative lowlanders, much more Tibetan, as is their language. If you later go to Helambu, compare the peoples there with those here.

Climb on, passing *mani* walls, and notice how there are few new carvings, reflecting the decline in this practice. The beautiful peak at the head of the valley is Gangchenpo. Pass tea shops and lodges as you go below Mundu in 30 minutes, a village off the trail where home stay might be arranged, and 10 minutes beyond is the village of Simdum. Look ahead at the U-shaped glacier-scoured valley, and contrast it with the V-shaped river-eroded valley behind you. In under 25 minutes pass a lodge sheltered behind a large boulder. Another 30 minutes farther, reach more tea shops in a pasture area known as Yamphu (12,160 feet, 3706 m), passing through an otherworldly landscape along the way, much different from the luxuriant flora passed while coming up the narrower valley from Syabrubensi.

Ahead is the moraine of the Ledrup Lirung Glacier; cross its outflow on a cement bridge. Just before crossing this bridge, a set of stone stairs leads a few minutes up to the quarters built by locals for monks of the Kagyupa lineage. Beyond the bridge, climb over the boulders of the moraine to drop down into **Kyangjin Gomba**, just below the eponymous *gomba* itself (12,795 feet, 3900 m), in 30 minutes, or **2 hours 10 minutes** from Langtang village. There are twenty-three lodges here (and eighteen in Langtang village), as well as a saloon and pool hall (the single pool table was brought in by helicopter). This destination resort is a far cry from the yak pastures Stephen found here almost thirty-five years ago. Additionally, there is a small medical shop at Yeti Guest House with medicines as well as an altitude chamber and even a stretcher for carrying a debilitated person down the mountain.

The large fenced-in area southeast of the lodges is an agricultural experimental area. There is no longer an army post in this locale. Remains of the former post can be seen

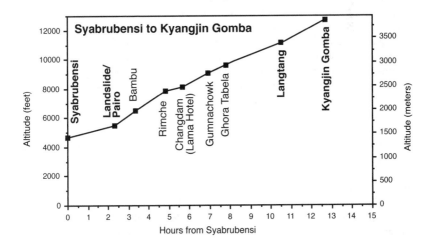

CUCKOOS AND BARBETS OF THE TEMPERATE ZONE

Cuckoos and barbets call repeatedly in spring and summer while concealing themselves in treetops. The great barbet (*Megalaima virens*), length 1 foot (33 cm), has a large yellow bill, dark head, and red vent. It sings a duet with its mate: he repeats "pir-ao," while she replies with a trilled "pur." It occurs in oak forests; it is also found in the subtropical zone. The common (or Eurasian) cuckoo (*Cuculus canorus*), length 1 foot (33 cm), is a familiar bird in Europe. It sings its English name. Found in open wooded country, it also occurs in tropical, subtropical, and subalpine zones. The oriental (or Himalayan) cuckoo (*Cuculus saturatus*), length 1 foot (33 cm), makes a monotonous "oop-oop" call. The appearance of both species is similar to the Indian cuckoo (see "Birds of the Subtropical Zone").

The large hawk cuckoo (*Cuculus sparverioides*), length 1 foot 3 inches (38 cm), has a call and appearance similar to the common hawk cuckoo but is larger and occurs at higher altitudes. The latter two species are found in oak and rhododendron forests. The orange-rumped (or Himalayan) honeyguide (*Indicator xanthonotus*), or *mauricharo*, length 6 inches (15 cm), is a drab, sparrowlike bird that is remarkable for its ability to digest beeswax. It will defend the nest of the giant honeybee from other honeyguides. It can be seen on cliffs north of Ghasa (on the Thak Khola trek) and near Syabru and Changdam (on the Langtang trek). ❖

in the lower pasture below the lodges; look for two large mounds of stones. According to lodge owners, too much wood was being used as fuel to support the twenty-five to thirty soldiers, and the army heeded the locals' requests to leave the ecologically sensitive area. Lodge owners prefer to use deadfall for fuel from the hillside across the valley. Details for side trips around Kyangjin Gomba are given below the section that describes starting this trek from Dhunche.

ALTERNATE APPROACH: DHUNCHE TO LANDSLIDE/PAIRO VIA SYABRU

If you disembark from the bus in **Dhunche** (6594 feet, 2010 m), the administrative center for the Rasuwaa District, you will find shops, comfortable lodges, and an army check post. Register and pay the park entrance fee at the Langtang National Park headquarters and information center just over half a mile (1 km) before reaching the town (a 10-minute walk), if you didn't in Kathmandu, and keep the receipt. There is international phone service available in Dhunche and a useful area map is available at the Hotel Langtang View. Most of the newer part of town serves district government functions as well as tourists. The older, charming Tamang area of town is below and worth a wander. The trail will be described to Landslide/Pairo, near the junction with the trail from Syabrubensi.

From **Dhunche,** combine a shortcut to the road with a visit to the Tamang Heritage Museum, situated in Dhunche below the newer part of town. Look for the archway advertising "Welcome to Tamang Museum" from the main road near the hotels and opposite a bus ticket stand. From here, head down the stairs to the red-roofed building below. The path continues from the museum, passing just above the lower village to the road. Otherwise, take concrete steps heading directly down from Dhunche's market area and pass the village development office to the road below. Another option is to head through town, following the main road. Just after the first hairpin turn (where there is a small Shiva temple and a road continuing straight to a bottled water factory and then on to the Gosainkund trail), a small trail descends steeply to reach the road below where a powerline also crosses the road.

There are more shortcuts along the way to avoid long road switchbacks. Walk or ride the road 3½–4 miles (6 km) to **Thulo Bharku,** with a tea shops and a restaurant, reached in **1½ hours** or less from Dhunche.

A road linking Thulo Bharku and Thulo Syabru is being constructed and may make the following trekking route redundant, at least in places where the road and trail coincide.

From Thulo Bharku, the trail leads up the hill to the right of the road. Pick it up after crossing a stream with a nearby water-powered mill. Pass behind a school compound before contouring and rising through pleasant chir pine and rhododendron forests. Pass a lodge in 25 minutes and rise above some beautifully terraced fields to the west and another simple lodge with a camping area above it. Along the way, cross several tributaries to reach the few houses of **Brabal** (7560 feet, 2304 m), in **1¾ hours** from Thulo Bharku. There is a temple, Shedup Cheling Gomba, sitting majestically on a spur splitting the two parts of this town, and a school lies just below. If the weather complies, you will have great views of Ganesh Himal and peaks to the north in Tibet. You can also see the road winding west out of the other side of the Bhote Kosi valley to cross a high ridge.

Round a bend to a rest spot with the first views up the Langtang valley in **20 minutes**. You will follow this valley floor for several days. Contour and descend another **45 minutes** to **Thulo Syabru (Syabru)** (7350 feet, 2240 m), a village commandingly strung out along a ridge (electricity is available here for recharging batteries). Notice the fine carved windows on the older houses below the newly constructed hotels for trekkers. Consider staying in one to get a sense of non-touristic life here. The fertile fields to the east and south support this region.

From Syabru, descend along the ridge toward the bottom of the village and pick up a trail that traverses the fields to the east, past a few lodges, to cross the Gopche Khola on a suspension bridge (6611 feet, 2015 m), a tributary of the Langtang Khola draining from the Gosainkund Lekh, in **40 minutes.** Climb up to a tea shop (6519 feet, 1987 m), and then descend into a lush bamboo jungle to reach the trail junction (5670 feet, 1728 m), near the Langtang Khola in less than **1 hour** from the Gopche Khola crossing. Here the trail meets the valley bottom trail from Syabrubensi and the left fork descends to Domin and out to Syabrubensi. Continue right to the east to cross a landslide near its terminus, and reach **Landslide**, also known as **Pairo**, which means "landslide" (5500 feet, 1676 m), in **20 minutes.** The trail up the Langtang valley beyond this point has already been described above.

PEOPLES OF EASTERN NEPAL: TAMANG

The Tamang, a very large and widespread hill group, are among the most recent groups to have settled along the northern border regions and higher hills, having come, it appears, from farther north and east. Tamang have retained much of their Tibetan and Buddhist heritage. They have many villages all around the Kathmandu valley, especially north, toward Helambu, and east, on the Mount Everest trek. They also populate the upper Trishuli Valley, on the Langtang trek. Tamang are well known to Himalayan climbers, who hire them for the long haul into base camps. ❖

EXPLORE: UPPER LANGTANG VALLEY

Kyangjin Gomba (12,795 feet, 3900 m) is an excellent base for exploring the idyllic upper reaches of this valley. Visit the *gomba,* which has been expanded. The newer building across from the main *gomba*'s entrance was completed in 2009. The cheese factory here was started as a Swiss project in 1955, when rounds of cheese were carried to Kathmandu over the Ganja La. (The cheese is now taken to Syabrubensi and then trucked to Kathmandu.) The original simple technology can be observed from May to October, when they produce 5000 to 7000 kg of *nak* (female yak) and *chAUmri* (yak crossbreed) cheese.

All of the suggested hikes are non-technical unless otherwise stated. Musk deer may be spotted in the forest to the south or even closer to the settlement in winter. Tibetan horses can be hired for more leisurely sightseeing, but don't take a horse higher if you couldn't walk it yourself—or if you have a headache or any other signs of AMS. You could also use one to return to Syabrubensi. You can hire tents and climbing gear and arrange guides for exploration farther up the valley or to cross the Ganja La.

⋎ *Side Trip to Lirung Glacier and Icefall. As you acclimatize, consider hiking north to reach the Lirung Glacier and icefall, a half day trip from* **Kyangjin Gomba.** *The trail can be found from the large boulder to the east of the gomba (just beside and below the boulder are* lama *quarters). The trail passes by a sleek white chorten (containing the remains of a lama). Head north, skirting along the western flank of Kyangjin Ri. After* **20 minutes** *from the white chorten, the trail divides before crossing an extensive rockslide. (The lower/left path descends to cross an outflow stream on a makeshift wooden bridge. This path can be difficult to follow due to crisscrossing grazing trails. This route contours up the gully to cross the same stream again and continues up to the lateral moraine to the east of the glacier.) The upper path crosses the rockslide area and continues up the gully to the right/east of the stream before ascending*

Dairy Development Corporation (DDC) cheese cellar (Photo by Alonzo Lyons)

sharply to a summer pasture area known as Lado (13, 661 feet, 4164 m) in another **30 minutes.** *Follow a faint trail north to the glacier, and climb the lateral moraine to the east of the glacier (14,026 feet, 4275 m) for the best views in another* **20 minutes.** *Another trail from Lado heads to a seasonal pasture area that lies to the east of the glacier known as Kimjung Kharka, and to the west of the glacier is a pasture area with a few seasonal herders huts known as Cherpache Kharka. These pasture areas and beyond are exploration opportunities in this area.*

👣 Side Trip to Glacial Lake. *Another side trip from* **Kyangjin Gomba** *is an often frozen lake that lies up the trough to the northwest of the gomba. Find the trail from behind the gomba and head north through the seasonal stone-built huts of a goTh settlement. Just beyond, a stream is visible tumbling down from the lake. The trail up to the lake will be to the left/west of this streambed. Descend to cross a stream on a wooden bridge. The lake is above, just beyond the embankment to the north. The trail heads west and after 10 minutes from the bridge, it ascends to the north along a ridge (at this point, the trail might be faint). Round a crest and then contour down to the lake (13,212 feet, 4027 m) in under* **40 minutes** *from the gomba. Langtang Lirung and Kimshung tower above.*

STREAM BIRDS IN NEPAL

Several conspicuous bird species can be found along fast-flowing streams throughout Nepal.

The ibisbill (*Ibidorhyncha struthersi*), length 1¼ feet (39 cm), is a gray wader with black forehead and face and a long decurved red bill. Shy, it breeds in gravelly river beds, such as those near Kyangjin in the upper Langtang valley. It winters on stony riverbeds in foothills.

The brown dipper (*Cinclus pallasii*), or *dubulke charo*, length nearly 8 inches (20 cm), is a plump, all-brown, short-tailed bird that bobs up and down while standing on boulders. It can feed by walking underwater on the streambed.

The plumbeous redstart (*Rhyacornis fuliginosus*), length 5½ inches (14 cm), is robinlike. It constantly pumps its tail up and down, and makes short flights after insects flying over the water. The male is slate blue with a reddish tail; the female is pale gray with a white rump.

The white-capped redstart, or river chat (*Chaimarrornis leucocephalus*), or *taukecharo*, length 7½ inches (19 cm), is a handsome maroon and black bird with a contrasting white cap. Both sexes are alike in appearance. It fans and pumps its tail as it flies from one rock to another.

The blue whistling thrush (*Myiophoneus caeruleus*), or *kalchande*, length 13 inches (33 cm), is a blue-black thrush with a bright yellow bill. It has a beautiful whistling song and harsh alarm call, both of which penetrate the sound of rushing water.

Nepal has four species of forktails (*Enicurus* spp.), or *kholedobi*, length 5–10½ inches (13 to 27 cm). Black and white birds with long, forked tails, they are shy and fly off quickly, making a harsh alarm call, when disturbed. Three species can be readily seen along the Bhurungdi Khola near Birethanti on the Thak Khola trek. ❖

For ambitious campers, Thang Demo rewards their efforts. (Photo by Tokozile Robbins)

🏕 Side Trip to Kyangjin Ri and Menchamsu. *A 1-hour climb to the north up the relatively small hill behind Kyangjin Gomba popularly known as Kyangjin Ri offers a breathtaking vantage point. Find the trail near the cheese factory and just behind the stone enclosure with a blue-topped government building. (Or, meet the trail from above the middle area of the lodge cluster and ascend.) Climb through boulders and then zigzag across the face before reaching the rocky crest of Kyangjin Ri, locally known as Brana Chumbo (14,209 feet, 4331 m), festooned with prayer flags. You can see the prayer flags as you ascend. From Kyangjin Ri, follow the ridge higher to* **Menchamsu** *(15,095 feet, 4601 m), a superlative viewpoint with more prayer flags in another hour. Take care to stay on the trail in this area as there are steep drop-offs due to erosion.*

A slightly more gradual ascent to Menchamsu would be to head up the gully to the east of Kyangjin Ri's hill and follow the gully all the way up to a saddle (14936 feet, 4553 m) in 1¾ **hours.** *From the saddle traverse the ridgeline to the southwest to Menchamsu in another* **20 minutes.** *This trail might be difficult to find at times due to erosion and an abundance of grazing paths that cut up the hillside.*

🏕 Side Trip to Tsergo Ri Viewpoint. *The trail to Tsergo Ri can be seen from the lodges of Kyangjin Gomba as it zigzags up a ridge to the northeast. To reach this trail, head east out of town through grassland and over a boulder field to cross an* **alluvial fan** *(no bridge) in* **20 minutes.** *Beyond the fan, the trail to Tsergo Ri branches north and ascends steeply up the ridgeline (while the trail to Langsisa Kharka continues east). After another* **45 minutes** *the trail divides. Take the upper path for the direct* route to Tsergo Ri, which continues along the ridgeline. (The lower path heading right is the more circuitous route that contours around the mountain to Digyabsa Kharka and Yala Kharka and then gains Tsergo Ri from the southeast. This route is described below; however, it is not recommended as it is not in wide use and therefore not clear and the area is overrun with pasturing trails.) Reach the seasonal huts of **Dacha Pesa** (13,763 feet, 4195 m) in under **1 hour** from the alluvial fan.

Continue ascending along the ridgeline. Tsergo Ri, soaring above, is marked by prayer flags. This section from Dacha Pesa to the summer pasturing area of Thang Demo is exceptionally steep. Continue along the ridgeline and a little over **1 hour** from Dacha Pesa, the trail diverges again. Take the left/north trail to continue on the direct route and reach the huts of **Thang Demo** (15,019 feet, 4578 m) 5 minutes beyond. The Ganja La, the pass leading to Helambu, is to the south across the valley and flanked between Naya Kanga, the trekking peak summit to its west side, and Pangen Dopku to its east. From the huts of Thang Demo, water can be found with a nearby camping area about 650 feet (200 meters) to the northeast through a patch of boulders, GPS coordinates, N 28° 13.047', E 085° 35.630'.

Catch the trail continuing to Tsergo Ri above the huts. It ascends between two boulder fields, heading east, and then directly through the boulders of the merged boulder fields and up to a ridge (15,869 feet, 4837 m) where there might be water in ¾–**1 hour** from Thang Demo. **Tsergo Ri** is due south from here. Head south along the ridge and up through boulders to reach the summit (16,368 feet, 4989 m), N 28° 12.788', E 085° 36.022' in less than **30 minutes** (less than 1½ **hours** from **Thang Demo** or 3½–4 **hours** from **Kyangjin Gomba**). Enjoy unrivaled views in every direction. The surrounding peaks may suggest climbs to the experienced, and ice axes and crampons can be rented in Kyangjin Gomba; however, trekking peaks are regulated and require a special permit and guide.

Alternatively, Tsergo Ri can be reached via Yala Kharka, the seasonal settlement to the peak's southeast. This route is not clear and not widely used. Nevertheless, for the adventurous a description from the **alluvial fan** crossing 20 minutes outside of Kyangjin Gomba follows: From the fan crossing, the trail to Tsergo Ri branches north and ascends steeply up the ridgeline. After **45 minutes** the trail forks. (The upper path is the recommended and more direct route to Tsergo Ri, which continues along the ridgeline and is described above.) Take the right path for Digyabsa and traverse east around the mountain, crossing several streams along the way, to just below **Digyabsa** where the trail then ascends steeply to the huts above (14,308 feet, 4361 m) in **45 minutes** from the fork (or 1½ **hours** from the crossing of the alluvial fan). From the upper end of the huts, continue contouring east around the mountain, gradually ascending before crossing a stream named the Chubi Chu and climbing steeply to the north to **Yala Kharka** (15,456 feet, 4711 m), N 28°12.563', E 085° 36.868', in a little over **1 hour** from Digyabsa. Again cross the Chubi Chu, heading west out of Yala Kharka, climbing up to a ridge and then heading northwest while keeping to the ridge as much as possible and then heading north up to the **Tsergo Ri** summit in 1½ **hours** from Yala Kharka.

◆ Side Trip, Kyangjin Gomba to Langsisa Kharka. Another option is to head up the valley to **Langsisa Kharka**, the next-to-last summer pasturing settlement. This is a long, beautiful hike up the valley, but even at Langsisa Kharka the glaciers are viewed from afar and a closer look would take a few more hours. Reaching Langsisa Kharka and returning to Kyangjin makes for an arduous, full day, and food and headlamps should be brought along. It would be best to bring shelter and supplies to camp at Langsisa or along the way.

SACRED VALLEY

There is a big reddish rock at Langsisa Kharka that, according to legend, is that color because a holy man living outside the valley lost his yak and tracked it to this place. The yak died here (Langsisa means "place where the yak [*lang*] died"), and the *lama*, wanting its hide, skinned it and spread the skin on a rock to dry. But the skin stuck and remains there on the rock to this day! This is the legend of the discovery of the Langtang valley. *Tang* means "to follow," hence the name Langtang.

Before, this place was considered a *beyul*, or hidden valley, and is hence considered sacred. Theoretically, no animals should be slaughtered in this valley. However, carnivores get around this by bringing in meat from animals killed outside the valley, and items such as tinned fish can be found on restaurant menus. ◈

From **Kyangjim Gomba**, head east from the lodges to cross an alluvial fan (12,723 feet, 3878 m) **20 minutes** beyond, and continue on to reach the abandoned STOL airstrip (12,569 feet, 3831 m), flanking it to the north. In **30 minutes,** reach the north (right) bank of the Langtang Khola and continue upstream. Another **40–45 minutes** brings you to **Chadung**, a summer settlement (12,950 feet, 3947 m), and less than **1 hour** more brings you to a second, **Numthang** (13,081 feet, 3987 m) where cheese is produced during the summer months.

Lateral and terminal moraines of the West Langtang Glacier loom ahead. Contour around its south terminus, cross a slide on the moraine, and climb to 13,556 feet (4132 m) where the huts of Langsisa Kharka and views farther up the valley can be seen. Descend slightly to reach the goTh of **Langsisa Kharka** (13,484 feet, 4110 m) in just over **1 hour.** Consider camping here away from the crowds at Kyangjin Gomba. Ahead lie a few more huts and the main Langtang Glacier and the Tibetan border, a hard day's climb away (some trekking maps are grossly in error regarding the border).

To the south lies beautiful Ganchenpo Peak and the terminus of the East Langtang Glacier. Up this valley lies a difficult pass leading to the region east of Helambu. The first recorded crossing was probably by H. W. Tilman in 1949. There are many places to explore; however, there is no bridge across the river here, and from the bridge below Kyangjin Gomba it is a rough traverse up along the south side of the river to reach this area.

A few miles farther up the valley to the southeast, two big rock gendarmes stand a hundred feet above the glacier. They are said to represent Shakyamuni (the Buddha) and Guru Rimpoche (considered by Tibetan Buddhists to be "the second Buddha," and the bearer of the dharma to Tibet).

EXPLORE: GANJA LA

For experienced parties, the high pass known as Ganja La (16,805 feet, 5122 m) leads to Helambu. Mountaineering experience and the ability to use a rope and ice ax might be necessary here. The route over **Ganja La**, usually a **3-day trip**, is normally possible from May to November, sometimes longer in dry years. Parties should be prepared for cold at any time of the year. It is always best to have someone along who is familiar with the route. This is a strenuous trip to substantial altitudes where food, fuel, and shelter must be carried for several days.

To reach the trailhead for Ganja La from the Langtang valley, follow the main route from **Kyangjin Gomba** toward Langtang village for a few hundred yards (meters) down the old moraine to where the main trail swings west down the valley. Another trail leads off (to the south) near here and descends directly to the Langtang Khola, which can be crossed on a steel box bridge. This is reached in **15 minutes** from Kyangjin Gomba. Downstream on the south (right) bank are a few huts and meadows (Tshona Kharka). Pick up a trail at the edge of the forest behind the meadows and climb in an easterly (upriver) direction through birch and rhododendron forest. A guide would be useful from here for continuing to the Ganja La, and parties need to be self-sufficient for at least three days as there are no facilities until Tarke Ghyang in Helambu (described below).

RETURN JOURNEY VARIATION: LANGTANG TO SYABRUBENSI VIA THE HIGH ROUTE

On the return down the Langtang valley from Kyangjin Gomba, there are several possible linkup routes to avoid backtracking. You can descend to Syabrubensi from Landslide/Pairo, if you came from Dhunche, or vice versa; head up to Syabru from Pairo and out to the roadway at Dhunche (this route was described above in reverse); or from Syabru you can ascend to the pilgrimage site of holy Gosainkunda and on to Helambu, described below. Alternatively, you can take the high route from Rimche to Syabrubensi, described as follows.

If you came to Langtang without visiting Syabrubensi, consider varying your exit by following the Langtang valley downstream, high on the north side, to Syabrubensi. This

BUTTERFLIES OF THE SUBALPINE AND ALPINE ZONES

Paris peacock
(Papilo paris)
*(Photo by
Tokozile Robbins)*

In spring and summer, butterflies are common in the subalpine and alpine zones, feeding on the nectar of the numerous blooming flowers. Common blue Apollo, queen of Spain fritillary, and common yellow swallowtail are frequently seen; the latter two species are also found in subtropical and temperate zones. Nepal is home to some 653 species of butterflies (2006 list), six of which are endemic to Nepal, i.e., not seen elsewhere. ❖

route has become less popular with trekkers, who take the quicker valley-bottom trail to Syabrubensi, described earlier. The high route is recommended for those preferring to take a trail away from the bulk of trekkers. Descend on the usual route from Ghora Tabela, and reach the trail junction at **Rimche,** by the lodge misnamed Ganesh View (8202 feet, 2500 m). The left fork descends to the bridge over the Langtang Khola and out via the quickest route to Syabrubensi; it has already been described above. The right fork ascends through open, steep country where you might spot some interesting animals, such as ghoral or serow. Reach Syarpa or **Sherpagaon** (8225 feet, 2507 m) in less than **1 hour.** There are lodges here.

Continue contouring and climbing along the steep valley wall for **1½ hours** until you round a ridge to an oak and blue pine forest and the valley of the main Bhote Kosi. Rarely, red panda have been spotted in this forest. A **40-minute** descent brings you to **Khangjim** (7480 feet, 2280 m), previously an old Tibetan refugee settlement and comprised of Tibetans as well as Tamang residents. The trail from Khangjim directly to Syabrubensi leaves below the middle of the village. Avoid a fork heading to the right as you descend through fields and the trail forks again in less than 5 minutes. The lower trail leads to Syabrubensi.

Descend steeply and in 45 minutes from Khangjim come to a junction. The right fork continues to Wangal, the left to Syabrubensi. Proceeding to the left, the trail then contours above the river to reach the older part of Syabrubensi that is on the east side of the Bhote Kosi and north of the Langtang Khola, **1½ hours** from Khangjim.

Cross the Bhote Kosi on a suspension bridge to continue on to the newer part of Syabrubensi on the western side of the Trishuli River. A hot springs lies below along the banks of the Trishuli River. It has five concrete bathing pools which may or may not have water but are likely to be in disrepair and a bit polluted. Buses to Kathmandu depart three times daily at 7 AM, 7:30 AM, and the last bus departs around 9 AM after first arriving from Thambuchet (times are subject to change).

GOSAINKUND

(Map No. 6, Page 297)

The Gosainkund area is the location of several sacred lakes and a pilgrimage destination that lies south of a major ridge between Helambu and the Langtang valley to the north and the Trishuli Khola to the west. This region is sparsely populated. Trekkers can visit this area from Dhunche or Syabrubensi, reached by road from Kathmandu, or from the Langtang valley trek via Syabru. It is spectacular, especially in the spring when rhododendrons are in bloom. If conditions permit, cross the Laurebina La pass to link up with Helambu.

TO GOSAINKUND LAKES AND BEYOND TO HELAMBU

The following is a description of a trek from Dhunche, up the Trishuli valley to the sacred lakes of Gosainkund, and beyond to Helambu. Another starting point to Gosainkkund is Syabru, reached from Syabrubensi or on return from a visit to the Langtang valley, and this link-up will be described as well. Such a circuit is an excellent short trek from Kathmandu. It is not feasible in the winter, when snowfall makes the high passage a mountaineering expedition. The route from Syabru to Gosainkund is recommended over the more direct route from Dhunche, which ascends steeply and is a greater concern with regard to acute mountain sickness (AMS). However, the less preferred, more direct route from Dhunche to Gosainkund will be described first.

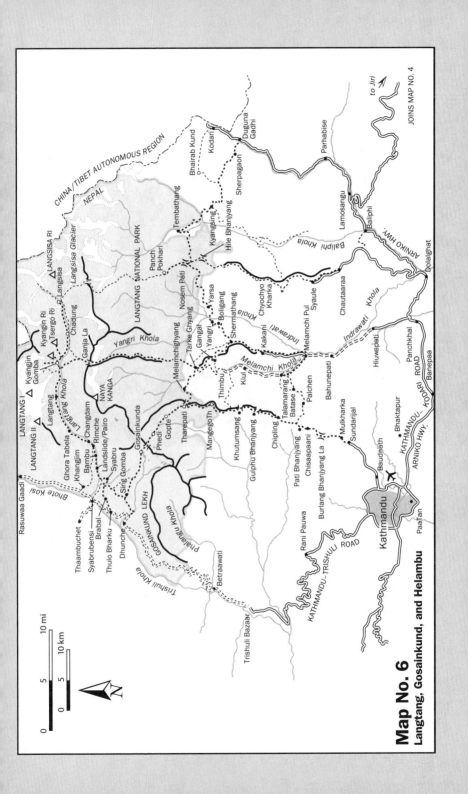

Map No. 6
Langtang, Gosainkund, and Helambu

The high settlement of Sing Gomba (Photo by Tokozile Robbins)

ALTERNATE
ROUTE

Dhunche to Sing Gomba

Reach **Dhunche** (6595 feet, 2010 m) by vehicle from Kathmandu as already described in the Langtang section. If going all the way to Laurebina La, the pass, from Dhunche, keep in mind that it is a climb of 8530 feet (2600 m). The first 330 feet (1000 m) is exceptionally steep, and water is scarce. From Dhunche, the route begins at the first hairpin turn near a small Shiva temple on the motor road out of the east end of town. Instead of turning along with the main road, continue straight on a feeder road that goes to a mineral water bottling plant. The trail begins from the plant, passing on the uphill side and contouring before descending to cross the Trishuli Khola, also known locally as the GaTTekhola (6430 feet, 1960 m) to the true right on a suspension bridge. The stream is just a small tributary of the Bhote Kosi, the major river in this valley from Tibet. Continue up the bank of the stream to a tea shop and lodge in a few minutes. Proceed by climbing up a gully to reach the crest, then with more climbing reach **Derali** (8776 feet, 2675 m), where there is a lodge, in **2½–3 hours** from Dhunche.

The trail is found to the north of the lodge. Continue climbing steeply, avoiding a left fork that heads down to Bharku, before passing an army post to reach Dimsa, known in Tamang language as Thomje (10118 feet, 3084 m), with a basic lodge in **1¼ hours** from Derali. Pass through oak forests to reach an impressive fir and rhododendron forest before arriving at the lodges of **Sing Gomba/Chandan Bari** (10,840 feet, 3304 m) in **1 hour** where the trail from Syabru coming from the Langtang valley route ties in. The cheese factory here began in 1971 and is worth a visit. A red panda reserve lies to the northeast. ❖

ALTERNATE ROUTE

Syabru to Sing Gomba

From **Syabru** (7350 feet, 2240 m), climb past the school to the signpost at the upper end of town. The right fork leads west to Brabal and on to Dhunche. For Sing Gomba, head left up the east side of the ridge by an army post and pass a *chorten* below the Health Clinic and Trekker's Aid Station sponsored by The Mountain Fund (www.mountainfund.org). The trail then switchbacks up in the forest, passing a national park building in 15 minutes. Continue on switchbacks, taking the upper fork at junctions and the bigger trail where you have a choice, generally along the ridgeline. Pass through an open area with prayer flags and *chorten* and then by a couple of seasonal tea shops to reach a lodge at **Dursakang** (8720 feet, 2658 m) in **1¼ hours** from Syabru.

Shortly beyond Dursakang, the trail divides; stay left and reach another lodge just above. There is no water available between the lodges at Dursakang and Probang Danda. Continue past one *chorten* and then others, climbing through magnificent oak, hemlock, and spruce, about **45 minutes** farther. The trail diverges just beyond the last *chorten*. Take the right fork and stay to the widest trail as much as possible. Reach the lodges of **Probang Danda** (10,459 feet, 3188 m), spectacularly perched on the ridge, in **1 hour.** Camping is possible here, and phone service is available. There are impressive views of Ganesh Himal and the Langtang peaks from this vantage.

A trail descends to Brabal from the lodges. Instead, ascend along a ridge, and just up from the lodges the trail forks. Stay right (to the west side of the ridge) for Sing Gomba (the fork to the left heads directly to Cholang Pati, farther along the route to Gosainkund and bypassing Sing Gomba). Continue on a wide trail through an enchanting forest of rhododendrons and large fir trees draped with moss. Just before reaching **Sing Gomba** (also known as Chandan Bari), pass to the left of a fenced compound, head west to reach the collection of year-round lodges, a little-used *gomba*, and an impressive cheese factory in **1 hour.**

FORESTS OF THE SUBALPINE ZONE

The subalpine zone, territory between the upper temperate zone and the timberline, of Nepal extends from 10,000–13,800 feet (3000–4200 m) in the west and 12,500 feet (3800 m) in the east.

Forests of Himalayan silver fir (*Abies spectabilis*) are widespread and are often superseded above 11,500 feet (3500 m) by birch (*Betula utilis*), or *bhoj patra*, which grows up to the treeline. Birch is deciduous, with oval leaves that are woolly-haired below, and white to gray-brown bark. Rhododendron forests or shrubberies often replace other forests in wetter places, while junipers (*Juniperus* spp.), coniferous shrubs with berrylike, fleshy fruit, occur in drier areas. Bamboo (*Arundinaria* spp.and *Bambusa* spp.) is common in the understory of high rainfall areas and sometimes forms pure stands. Some of the least disturbed forests occur in this zone, although trekkers and mountaineers are posing severe threats. ❖

There are no mountain views from Sing Gomba (10,840 feet, 3304 m). There is a red panda reserve to the northeast. (Note to those heading in the other direction, from Sing Gomba to Syabru: the trail heads to the right/east by the last lodge rather than down which leads to Dhunche.) ◈

From Sing Gomba, pass the temple and ascend on a wide trail through a former burn area. The slope is covered with *Piptanthus nepalensis* shrubs with yellow flowers during the summer. Follow along the south side of the ridge through a juniper, rhododendron, and fir forest, and cross to the north side of the ridge to reach **Cholang Pati** (11,873 feet, 3619 m) in **1¼ hours.** The trail is joined here by one coming up directly from Syabru that bypasses Sing Gomba. There are lodges here open during the trekking season, and the view of Ganesh and Langtang Himals is worth a rest if not an overnight. Farther to the west, Himal Chuli and Manaslu dominate the sky, and beyond you can make out the Annapurnas, including the top of Annapurna between Machhapuchhre and Annapurna IV.

Continue for **45 minutes,** ascending to the seasonal lodges, perched on a windy ridge, called **Laurebina** (12,800 feet, 3901 m), or Laurebina Yak, with sensational views. The name Laurebina means "without walking stick," referring to the practice of pilgrims leaving their sticks behind here, for they are now in the hands of the gods as they proceed to the lakes. You can look back and see your starting point, Dhunche or Syabru. Natural water is scarce along here, but a piped water system has been constructed. Climb on, reaching a notch in the ridge (13,750 feet, 4191 m) with prayer flags and a shrine with a statue of Buddha in **45 minutes.** Beyond, cross the ridge to the south side and notice the steeper character of the valley. To the south, you see yak and sheep pastures and other trails converging. Traverse, and be careful of the precipitous drop-off from the wide trail. Turn back if snowfall has made trail conditions unfavorable.

Beyond, you begin to see the lakes. The first is Saraswatikunda, with an impressive waterfall below you, followed by Bhairavkund, and then Gosainkunda. Gosainkunda (14,374 feet, 4381 m), with several lodges operated most of the year, is reached by descending from a small crest in **1 hour** from the shrine. There is a protected Shiva shrine, bells to announce your presence to the gods, and rest houses for pilgrims. On Stephen's first visit in 1970 there was only a simple stone hut, a freestanding *lingam* , a sign of Shiva often regarded as a phallic symbol (which scholars debate), and *nandi* "bull", made more powerful with the eerie howls of a jackal in the late afternoon. *Gosain* means "priest," and *kunda* is "lake."

Every year during the full moon between mid-July and mid-August, the festival of Janai Purnima is held at Gosainkunda. At this time, thousands of pilgrims and devotees come to bathe in this lake and to pay homage to Shiva; many of them experience symptoms of acute mountain sickness (AMS).

There are several legends, all similar, concerning the formation of this lake and its significance. One story is that the gods were churning the ocean, hoping to obtain from it *amrit*, the water of immortality. They extracted an unmanageable burning poison from the seas and turned to Shiva, who had come to the foothills to meditate. Realizing that the poison might harm the gods, Shiva disposed of it by drinking it. The poison caused him a great deal of pain and thirst, as well as a blue discoloration of his neck. To relieve the fever and suffering, Shiva traveled to the snows of Gosainkund. He thrust his trident, or *trisul*, into the mountainside and three streams of water sprang forth and collected in the hollow beneath, producing Gosainkund Lake. Shiva stretched along the lake's edge and drank its waters, quenching his thirst. There is an oval-shaped rock beneath the

The icy waters of Gosainkund Lake (Photo by R.C. Sedai)

surface near the center of the lake; worshipers say they can see Shiva reclining on a bed of serpents there. Legend also has it that the lake is connected via subterranean channels to the Kumbheswar Mahadev Temple in the Kathmandu valley.

In good weather, consider climbing the hill behind the lodges to lookout points. Or circumambulate the lake in a clockwise fashion, or even bathe in it if you are brave. Devotees believe that a dip in the waters helps to cleanse misdeeds and purify *karma*. There are several other smaller lakes in the vicinity that are worth discovering as well.

To continue to Helambu, contour the north side of the lake and, as you ascend, look back to see Shiva reclining beneath the surface of the waters. Regain views and pass more lakes along the way on the often snowy trail marked with cairns, to Laurebina La (15,121 feet, 4609 m) in **1–1¼ hours.** Look east into the valley that you will follow on the north side to reach Helambu. Off to the east, there is a spur coming down the main ridge that you will crest and head off to Tharepati, which is visible on the major north–south ridge beyond.

From the pass, descend to the valley below, heading southeast on the north side of the valley, skirting ice in the cold season and following a trail marked with cairns. *GoTh* frames testify to the use of this area during sheep and yak pasturing season when the vegetation is lush. Reach **Ayethang/Bhera goTh**, a simple, seasonal lodge (13,848 feet,

4221 m) near a trail junction, in **45 minutes–1 hour.** The left-hand trail, a supposed shortcut to Tharepati, contours high around the northeast side of the valley, eventually coming out on the ridge above Tharepati. This perilous route traverses steep country, where slides and ice make it unsafe. Nepalis rarely use it, and you should not either unless you chance a slip and rapid descent into the valley below.

Take the popular trail to the right and continue descending. Eventually reach scrub vegetation and a spur with a waterfall on your left. Descend to the upper, seasonal lodge with phone service at **Phedi** (12,356 feet, 3766 m, N 28°03.476' E085°27.502') in **1 hour**, with another seasonal lodge a few minutes below. Next to the upper lodge is a *chorten* built to honor those who perished when an airliner crashed nearby after it had departed from Kathmandu's Tribhuvan International Airport. The site of the accident, which happened during the monsoon of 1992, is just south of Phedi.

From the memorial *chorten*, the trail forks. Do not descend right on a trail which travels down to eventually meet a road from Trishuli Bazaar. Take the left fork to the east

PILGRIMAGE

The Himalaya are a great attraction to Nepali, Tibetan, and Indian pilgrims. Pilgrimage sites are common—a high "milk lake" (*dudh pokhari* or *kunda*), the confluence (*beni*) of sacred rivers, or an especially prominent shrine or temple. Some of the most famous pilgrimage sites for Hindus are at Gosainkunda, Dudh Pokhari, Panch Pokhari, and Baahra Pokhari. Muktinath and several other high-mountain shrines are sacred pilgrimage attractions to Hindus and Buddhists alike. Likewise, there are many shrines and temples within the Kathmandu valley—Swayambhunath, for one—that are sacred to both religious groups. Baudhnath and Pashupatinath, on the outskirts of Kathmandu city, are especially sacred to Buddhists and Hindus, respectively. All three are World Heritage Sites.

Pilgrims come to Nepal from all over southern Asia, and as travel conditions allow, from Tibet. Hindu holy men stand out clearly by their attire (or relative lack of attire, as the case may be). The occasion of Shiva Raatri is especially significant both to holy men and Indian lay pilgrims, who flock to the Kathmandu valley. Sometimes holy men may be encountered who are observing vows of silence; they sometimes go for as long as twelve years and more without speaking.

Lay pilgrims are commonly seen throughout the year on popular routes to the high-mountain shrines or lakes. For example, there are many seasonal events that attract pilgrims to and from Muktinath shrine above Thak Khola. Many of them have planned for years to come to a certain Himalayan Shaivite or Vaishnavite shrine (devoted to Shiva and Vishnu, respectively). Others seem to come on the spur of the moment: some to cleanse themselves from misdeed or misfortune; others, just for the pleasure of doing something different and unusual, or to see the country. For Hindus, water is an essential element at pilgrim shrines, and bathing is a central feature of the ritual observances. Sometimes Hindu and Buddhist shrines offer other attractions as well, such as natural gas fires, the presence of sacred fossils (*shaligram*), hot springs, an ice cave, a sacred footprint or other holy mark or memory of the gods, or a rich mythology of sacred events that adds to the attractiveness of a place. Legendary accounts of sacred pilgrimage sites and events in the Himalaya are recorded in the ancient literature of Hinduism, some works dating back over 2000 years. ❖

and descend to the lower lodge of Phedi, and then follow the rolling trail to Tharepati to the southeast from here. An Australian man who was ascending here in the winter of 1991–92 split from his companion and descended to the south in bad weather for about 2 hours, where he stayed in a cave for 43 days awaiting rescue. *Lost in the Himalaya* is an account of the ordeal. The obvious lesson is that if the weather is bad, do not split from your party into unknown terrain.

Descend a steep draw and cross a stream below the waterfall (a source of the TaDi Khola). The trail contours with repeated, strenuous ups and downs on the south-facing hillside, all the way to Tharepati. Reach Dubichaur (11,811 feet, 3600 m), a seasonal *goTh* set among juniper trees, in **45 minutes.** Look south and pick out Shivapuri, the summit of the north end of the Kathmandu valley. To the east of it are hillocks, atop one of which resides Swayambhunath Temple.

Continue to reach the **crest** of the spur you saw from near the pass (12,096 feet, 3687 m) in another **hour.** Reach **Gopte** (11,180 feet, 3408 m), a flat spot on a spur with two lodges, in **45 minutes,** or **2½ hours** from Phedi. The variety of primulas blooming in the spring between Phedi and Gopte is unparalleled.

From Gopte, the trail heads east past overhanging rocks to the left. There is more rock shelter just beyond near a tributary. Reach another lodge at **Mera Kharka** (10,908 feet, 3325m) in **30–40 minutes.** The trail continues through beautiful moss-draped rhododendron and fir forests and then comes up in the open to ascend through juniper woods to reach the first of several lodges of **Tharepati** (11,975 feet, 3650 m) in **1–1¼ hours** from Mera Kharka. There are good views to the northeast from the notch near the northeasternmost lodges. The hazardous trail from Ayethang/Bhera *goTh* mentioned in the description above comes in from the north along the ridgeline. You could walk partway along it and in **45 minutes –1 hour** ascend to a crest filled with prayer flags to gain superb views including sight of Melamchighyang village below to the east.

You have two choices at this point. Either you can traverse south along the main ridge to Pati Bhanjyang and on to Sundarijal to reach Kathmandu via the high route, or you can descend east to the Helambu village of Melamchighyang. We will describe this latter route, heading east to Tarke Ghyang and descending to Melamchi Pul Bazaar, where a bus can be found, within the Helambu section. The high route out to Sundarijal is described as a route of ascent into Helambu and can be followed in reverse to leave.

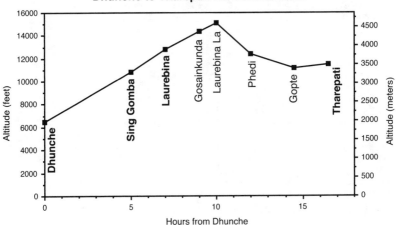

Dhunche to Tharepati via Gosainkunda

HELAMBU

(Map No. 6, Page 297)

Helambu or Helmu is the name of a region at the northern end of the Melamchi Khola valley. At one time it was a "hidden valley," or *beyul,* and considered sacred. It is still a majestic gem that receives sparse trekker traffic and is well worth a visit. The hill scenery and culture make up for the lack of spectacular, up-close mountain views, and the serene trails are a refreshing change of pace, especially when combined with treks in Langtang and Gosainkund. Helambu is derived from the local words for potato (*he*) and radish (*labu*), the two principal upland crops in that area.

The trek starts from **Sundarijal** (4560 feet, 1390 m), near drinking water and hydro-electric stations, in the northeast corner of the Kathmandu valley, and passes through Shivapuri National Park , named for Shivapuri Peak (8963 feet, 2732 m). The park encompasses 61 sq miles (159 sq km) and is a catchment area that supplies Kathmandu valley with 8 million gallons (300 million liters) drinking water per day. The sacred Bagmati and Vishnumati rivers that run through the valley have origins within the park.

Bus service to Sundarijal begins from the Old Bus Park near Ratna Park in Kathmandu and infrequent mini-van service from Shahid ("Martyr's") Gate. The bus ride takes about 1½ hours if all goes well, and you might be levied a fee for baggage. A taxi can also be hired, or you could walk, which might be a necessary option should a transport-halting strike (*bandh*) be called. Additionally, there is now daily jeep and possibly bus service from Sankhu, a Newar town farther east from Baudhnath, on to Pati Bhanjyang, which would save a day and avoid the first day's climb out of the valley.

Carrying the Book of the Dead and prayer flags to guide the soul into the afterlife in Helambu (Photo by Stephen Bezruchka)

WEAVING TRADITIONS: WOOL

Trekkers commonly come across wool weavers during their travels in the high country. Nepal has been famous for millennia as a source for woolen blankets (*raDi*) that are rainproof as a result of the felting process used. They were mentioned in the emperor Ashoka's time, the third century BCE. The local sheep's wool is very suitable for felting, and you may observe this process in your travels. The carpet industry that has become one of Nepal's biggest exports uses different wool, preferably from Tibet, but sometimes from New Zealand.

Felting is done with most woolen garments, either on a large flat stone, or on bamboo mats. Hot water is poured over the folded *raDi* on the stone, and it is walked on using the toes to fold the edges under, while holding on to support poles. This rhythmical dance is not unlike using the treadmill or stair machine in exercise centers back home, except that it usually goes on for many hours, sometimes a day! The *raDi* maker is given nutritious food, or it is believed he or she will get tuberculosis. Once completed, the *raDi* has shrunk considerably, and the garment's texture makes it hard to believe it was woven. Such wool clothing is durable, and warm, even when wet.

The wool is prepared for weaving by washing and spinning it, then using a backstrap loom, much as described for the nettle fiber in Chapter 6. Yaks are also a source of wool. The animal's outer hair is cut before the monsoon, using a sharp two-edge knife, leaving behind the soft, downlike inner layer which is plucked when the yak loses its winter coat. The yak hair is sorted and fluffed up, as is sheep's wool, and spun using a spike spindle, the twisted strands of hair feeding off rings on the arm. The outer hair makes strong, durable rope used to tie loads on animals. If you get the chance, try spinning, to appreciate the skill involved.

Formerly, natural dyes were exclusively used, but these days powdered dyes from India are often mixed with natural dyes and mordants to fix them. Natural colors are obtained from madder (plant roots), collected in the forests in winter when leaves have fallen and it is easier to spot. ❖

SUNDARIJAL TO THAREPATI

To start from the bus park at **Sundarijal**, head upstream on a wide trail and reach a large water pipe and proceed alongside it. Much of the way is along a concrete path as you ascend to reach the Shivapuri National Park office and entry counter with a nearby army post (5194 feet, 1583 m) in 30 minutes. The fee to cross through the Shivapuri National Park is 250 NRS for foreigners, 10 NRS for Nepalis. Save this ticket (valid for 7 days), as you might need to present it at a check point in Chisaapaani, especially if you are taking the Kathmandu Valley Cultural Trail (described in Chapter 9).

A few minutes beyond the entry point, proceed left at a signed junction to reach the curious-looking dam of a water reservoir in a few more minutes. Cross over the dam itself and continue uphill on concrete steps and in less than 5 minutes, a dirt trail diverges to ascend to the right while the concrete steps continue ascending to the left; both trails lead to Chisaapaani. Take the dirt track to the right to reach the first lodges of the mainly Tamang village of **Mulkharka** (5521 feet, 1683 m), in a few more minutes from the junction, **40–45 minutes** from Sundarijal (Nagi Gomba nunnery and retreat center is some 10 km away to the west). Mulkharka is widely spread out over the hillside. It takes **45–50 minutes** to ascend from the first lodges to the top end of Mulkharka village at 6562 feet (2000 m) with excellent views along the way of the Kathmandu valley behind you.

The next section passes through an isolated area of the park and is uninhabited until Chisaapaani, and water can be sparse to nonexistent as well. Don't walk this area alone, as there have been rare instances of attacks north of Mulkharka, and take care of your belongings—but you know that anyway. The trail continues up to a pass, **Burlang Bhanjyang La** (7972 feet, 2430 m), in **1–1¼ hours** from the top end of Mulkharka village. This pass marks the Shivapuri ridge, the Kathmandu valley's northern rim.

As the wide trail descends through a pleasant oak and rhododendron forest, you begin to see the snowy Himalayan giants off in the distance as you reach a covered rest area built by the Nepal Environment and Tourism Initiative Foundation (NETIF). In **35–40 minutes** of descent from the pass, reach a junction and continue to the right to gently climb to the several lodges at **Chisaapaani** (7110 feet, 2167 m), meaning "cold water," in another 5 minutes. In clear weather, there are outstanding views of the peaks to the north. (At this point, those traveling on the Kathmandu Valley Cultural Trail, see Chapter 9, will head south from Chisaapaani toward Nagarkot.)

The trail on to Helambu continues to the north to descend along a wide track sometimes used by jeeps and motorbikes. In **15–20 minutes**, take the narrower single-track path to the left away from the motor track. Continue descending for **25–30 minutes** more to meet the road again near a pair of lodges that offer a quieter location than staying in the midst of Pati Bhanjyang bazaar. Just beyond these two lodges, fork to the right from the road and descend for a few more minutes to **Pati Bhanjyang** (5722 feet, 1744 m), sitting in a saddle (less than **1 hour** from Chisaapaani), with lodges and a police post.

From here, there is a choice of two routes: One continues along the general ridge system heading north and eventually descends east to the Sherpa village of Melamchighyang. There are no permanent villages between Khutumsang and Melamchighyang on this route, but trekker accommodation is available along the way in MangegoTh and Tharepati during the popular seasons. This part of the route offers excellent views of the mountains. The other option from Pati Bhanjyang is to head east and descend to the Melamchi Khola; this route will be described in reverse, in the section that follows, for those wishing to make a circuit back to Pati Bhanjyang to walk out rather than take a bus from Melamchi Pul Bazaar.

To head north from **Pati Bhanjyang**, climb up to the left/north of the hill forming the northeast side of the saddle. In less than 5 minutes, reach a road. (Do not take the branch to the right which ascends to Thakani, a Tamang village, and beyond to Talamarang village, which will be an optional route on the return if you are doing a circuit of Helambu.)

Stay to the left, climb a little, and contour, avoiding a right fork after 25 minutes, to reach another saddle, **Thana Bhanjyang** (6027 feet, 1837 m), with a lodge and tea shops, in under **30 minutes** from Pati Bhanjyang. From here, rather than contour, the trail to Chipling climbs steeply on the ridge to the north. Reach the first lodge of **Chipling** (7169 feet, 2185 m), a hamlet scattered along the hillside, in **50 minutes**. Climb on, taking the uppermost fork at major junctions, for another 40 minutes to the crest of Joghin Danda/Lapcho Danda (8047 feet, 2453 m), with several simple lodges located before and at the crest itself. Descend through the oak forest on a trail lined with fern to the dispersed village of Thodhang Betini (7480 feet, 2280 m), in 45 more minutes. Just outside of Thodhang, the trail forks. Both lead to Gulphu Bhanjyang, the right passes a *chorten* along the way. Reach **Gulphu Bhanjyang** (6972 feet, 2125 m), a half-deserted Tamang and Gurung village that lies in a saddle, in 20 more minutes and **1¾ hours** from Chipling.

A few minutes north of Gulphu Bhanjyang, reach a clearing and a trail junction where the left branch contours while the right climbs near the ridge. Take the trail to the right and climb for 30 minutes to a seasonal lodge and continue on to another lodge (8169 feet, 2490 m) in 30 more minutes. A tea shop is 5 minutes farther up; keep to the left and ascend up to 8432 feet (2570 m) just west of the summit of the hill. Descend to the houses and trekker lodges at **Khutumsang** (8100 feet, 2469 m), situated in a pass, in 30 minutes from the tea shop and **1 hour 40 minutes** from Gulphu Bhanjyang.

Khutumsang was a place with no settlement when Stephen arrived in 1970. Now there are many lodges, and the Langtang National Park office here requires that you show your entry pass or purchase one. There are no permanent villages between this town and Melamchighyang, but trekker accommodation is available along the way in MangegoTh and Tharepati during the popular seasons.

From Khutumsang the trail ascends the hill to the north. Stay with the widest path and climb through a prickly-leaved oak forest and ascend along a ridge to the north to a simple lodge (9760 feet, 2975 m) in **1¼ hours**. Continue to climb and pass through a rhododendron and fir forest, traversing along the east side of the main ridge. Reach a notch containing a cairn and the first lodge of MangegoTh (10,908 feet, 3325 m) after climbing for another **1¼ hours** or **2½ hours** from Khutumsang. Just beyond the notch is a clearing. Continue, keeping more level, on the west side of the ridge. Another clearing with more lodges (10,604 feet, 3232 m) is reached in **20 minutes.** From the clearing, contour on the west side of the ridge to reach a notch with *goTh* (11,089 feet, 3380 m) in **30 minutes.** Cross over to the east side of the ridge and climb to reach more *goTh* (11,450 feet, 3490 m) in less than **30 minutes.** Continue from here on the west side to the ridge crest in under **1 hour** to **Tharepati** (11,975 feet, 3650 m), with lodges along the ridge crest. If you descend to the west, you pick up the trail to Gosainkund, which has already been described in the other direction. There are good views of the mountains

FLORA OF THE ALPINE ZONE

The Tibetan blue poppy
(Meconopsis horridula)
(Photo by Tokozile Robbins)

The alpine zone lies between the treeline 12,500 feet (3800 m) in the east and 13,800 feet (4200 m) in the west) and the region of perpetual snow. Shrubs grow above the treeline up to 16,000 feet (4870 m), with rhododendrons abundant in the east and junipers in the west. In the northwest and north of the Dhaulagiri–Annapurna massif, there is extensive steppe country dominated by Caragana, a low, spiny shrub typical of the Tibetan plateau. Flowers in both the subalpine and alpine grasslands produce spectacular colorful displays in late spring and summer. There is an amazing diversity of plants: gentians, anemones, saxifrages, geraniums, primulas, cinquefoils, and many others. Isolated plants are common up to 18,000 feet (5500 m). ❖

from the notch to the north (12,000 feet, 3658 m) from where the trail leads down to Melamchighyang.

THAREPATI TO SHERMATHANG AND MELAMCHI PUL BAZAAR

To reach to Melamchighyang (which lies below to the east) and the villages of upper Helambu, descend from Tharepati's northern notch. The trail heads down gently to the south for a few minutes before descending steeply to the east. It is a wide trail in a juniper, rhododendron, and birch forest with impressive fir trunks, some marked with old blazes to reassure travelers. In 1¼ **hours** come to a **cairn**, as the trail reaches a streambed (9698 feet, 2956 m). (Finding this spot is important if you are coming up from Melamchighyang, for here you would bear right/north.) The cairn should stand out, as cairns are rarely found in the forest. Turn left/east at the cairn and descend through a stretch that will be icy in the winter, and cross a stream shortly thereafter. Contour through magnificently tall rhododendron draped with moss and fern, and in less than 10 minutes reach a small *chautaaraa* and a *chorten* (9531 feet, 2905 m) above some *goTh* in a clearing. In less than 40 minutes from the *chorten*, come to a clearing and a *chautaaraa* (8465 feet, 2580 m) with a view of Melamchighyang across the tributary valley before you. Descend steeply to cross a tributary on a suspension bridge (8267 feet, 2520 m) in 15 more minutes, and continue on to **Melamchighyang** (8400 feet, 2560 m) in another 15 minutes, **1 hour 20 minutes** from the cairn. The town's name is commonly written Malemchigaon, meaning the town of Melamchi, and *ghyang* means temple in the local dialect.

The people here began calling themselves Sherpas within the last century, perhaps because of outsiders' needs to classify things. Their relationship with the Sherpas of Solu–Khumbu is distant. The languages spoken are different, though both are derived from Tibetan, and the two groups are not likely to intermarry. A more appropriate name

According to legend, this rock-sheltered hermitage was originally built by the legendary Guru Rimpoche. (Photo by Tokozile Robbins)

BIRDS OF PREY OF THE SUBALPINE ZONE

The lammergeier, or bearded vulture (*Gypaetus barbatus*), known locally as *gid-dha* (length 4 feet, 122 cm), a magnificent vulture, has a characteristic wedge-shaped tail. Rusty-white on the head and below, dark brown above, it drops bones from a height to splinter them on rocks below and then feeds on the marrow. It soars along mountain slopes on motionless wings with hardly a wing beat; it occurs from the subtropical to alpine zone 10,000–13,800 feet (3000–4200 m) in the west, to 12,500 feet (3800 m) in the east. ❖

might be *yolmo wa*, the peoples of Yolmo, "the place screened by snow mountains," or the Lama People of Helambu.

There is a *gomba* on the east end of the town, and an interesting rock hermitage on the west end. The large rocks of this shelter are claimed by locals to have been orginally assembled by Guru Rimpoche. At the north end of the village, past a large *stupa* and several smaller ones, is a well-regarded school and hostel. If you contour 5 minutes up the valley from the school, there is a small cave with a persistent trickle of water inside that is considered sacred. Purportedly, a consort of Guru Rimpoche named Kondoma bathed here during her monthly moon cycle.

Melamchighyang is a serene, beautiful locale. Try to arrange a stay in a home rather than a lodge, and admire the extraordinarily clean interiors here. Every home has a smokeless *chulo* kept spotless. The Helambu Yolmo are incredibly fastidious now, something Stephen does not recall from visits over four decades ago. Electricity lines from below supply power, and batteries might be recharged.

There are no more towns farther up this valley. To Tarke Ghyang, proceed down below the *gomba* to descend steeply on a small spur. Pass a few *chorten* to reach a crest with a tea shop, *chorten*, and prayer flags in 35 minutes (7162 feet, 2183 m). You can just make out the bridge below here, north of where the powerline crosses the river. As you descend, in less than 15 minutes come to another *chorten* and fork left to proceed underneath the powerlines. From here to the bridge, many trails intersect the route. Stick with the widest path and reach the **Melamchi/Yolmo Khola bridge** (6200 feet, 1890 m) in another 25 minutes or **1¼–1½ hours** from Melamchighyang (if going the other way, the powerlines will indicate generally the location of Melamchighyang).

There is a simple lodge on the (west) side of the Melamchi/Yolmo Khola. Legend has it that a fierce dragon once guarded this river crossing between Melamchighyang and Tarke Ghyang, requiring human sacrifice to cross. Guru Rimpoche, who brought Buddhism to these parts, subdued the monster by transforming it into a boulder, which now stands guard above the bridge near the lodge on the west side.

Cross to the east (true left) bank of the Melamchi/Yolmo Khola, and in 10 minutes reach a junction. Stay with the lower/right fork. A few minutes beyond the trail forks again. This time stay left and then cross a tributary (6397 feet, 1950 m) to reach a *gomba* (Palma Chholing Monastery) among the houses of Nakote village, **20–25 minutes** from the bridge over the Melamchi Khola. Just to the front of the *gomba* are graphically represented male and female effigies.

From the *gomba*, there are two route options. The more direct route to meet the motor road branches to the right to follow along the river, but this route is impassable in the rainy season. The usual route is to Tarke Ghyang via the left branch . This trail leads gently up to the south of the *gomba* to contour around a small spur that has a *chorten* on top. Cross a tributary with a pair of mills, one above and another below the bridge (6610 feet, 2015 m), in 10 minutes. In another 10 minutes, fork left. The right branch heads to a cave once used by the renowned, eleventh-century Tibetan ascetic Jetsun Milarepa. The route from here to this cave and *gomba* is outlined below.

Side Trip to Milarepa Cave. *To head to the cave and* gomba *in* **1 hour,** *contour to the right/south (at the branch that is 10 minutes from crossing the tributary near the two mills) to cross the Be (pronounced "bay") Khola (6709 feet, 2045 m) just beyond. Continue to contour to the south and cross a few more tributaries, and in 20 minutes pass a mani with two chorten. Just beyond, stay right and cross another stream in less than 5 minutes and descend to cross more streams to reach a trail junction in 5–10 minutes.*

The upper path at this junction ascends to Tarke Ghyang in **2¼ hours.** *It is a difficult route to follow, and asking the way is usually necessary. To continue to the cave, head right to the stupa (6460 feet, 1969 m) just below the junction. To the south of the stupa, the trail heads across the stream toward Thimbu (and the motor road). Instead, stay on the right/north side of the tributary descending to the west. Stay right at another junction a few minutes below. From here, descend steeply to reach the gomba (5896 feet, 1797 m, N 27°59.424' E085°32.099') in less than 30 minutes from the stupa.*

The cave lies behind the gomba *and behind a large prayer wheel. Both the cave and the* gomba *are kept locked and the konyer, or key custodian, may not be present. Below the* gomba *is another cave as well as a retreat center (do not disturb the residents). The lower route from Nakote to Thimbu passes just below the* gomba *compound as well and could be used as a more direct route to the cave from Nakote, depending on the season.*

To continue onward to Tarke Ghyang (from the fork 10 minutes beyond the tributary crossing with a pair of mills), take the trail to the left and in a few minutes you will reach a diminutive *chorten*. Bear left at this *chorten* and proceed steeply up a spur. Stay with the ridgeline, rather than heading into the next tributary valley, and reach a *stupa* (7546 feet, 2300 m) with a nearby simple lodge in 45 minutes. Continue ascending to pass another *stupa* (8136 feet, 2480 m) to the south of a *gomba* in 30 more minutes. You then enter a draw and climb out of it to the tight cluster of houses called **Tarke Ghyang,** a Yolmo village (8400 feet, 2560 m), in another 25 minutes (just over **2-2¼ hours** from Palma Chholing Monastery in Nakote village.

Tarke Ghyang means "temple of the 100 horses," and the town's name was taken from that of a temple established in 1727 by a *lama* called by the king of Kantipur to stop an epidemic in Kathmandu. As his reward, the *lama* asked for 100 horses, which he brought here. The local *gomba* has a curious sign in front prohibiting weapons, drunkeness, fighting, and destruction inside the temple lest the perpetrators be fined. The *gomba* was rebuilt in 1969 and follows the Bhutanese style.

A characteristic of the Helambu area is the presence of many *gomba*, each with its own lay *lama* or officiator. These *lama* are married village priests, the lineage passed from father to eldest son. They are of the Nyingmapa sect, which permits marriage unions by such *lamas*, and religion is a family affair.

The village with its tight cluster of houses, narrow lanes, and courtyards might be what a medieval village looked like ... electrified, roofed in tin, and punctured with antennas. At one time, apples became a successful cash crop around here, but the orchards were decimated by blight and have not been recultivated for fear of disease.

🌿 *Side Trip to Yangri Danda.* *For a day hike, climb above the village to the ridge-crest viewpoint of Yangri Danda (12,372 feet, 3771 m). The route starts from the former schoolhouse above the village. Just to the south of here there is a sign and steps leading to the ridge to the north as if setting out for the Ganja La, the high passage to the Langtang valley. Water is available along the way at Chomu Thang Kharka.*

The route continues to the Ganja La (16,805 feet, 5122 m) and Kyangjin Gomba several days away. To cross the pass, food, shelter, and fuel have to be carried, and the party should be experienced and equipped for snow climbing. The Ganja La is normally passable from May to November, sometimes longer in dry years.

ALTERNATE ROUTE

Tarke Ghyang to Melamchi Bazaar via Thimbu or Kiul

The direct option from Tarke Ghyang to the road is to descend to the south to the hamlet of **Thimbu** (5184 feet, 1580 m) in 2½ **hours** where the road is met. However, if the road is in disrepair, continue on to **Kiul** (4200 feet, 1280 m) in another 1–1¼ **hours**. To take this direct route out to the road, head right just after the large Hotel Tarke Ghyang at the lower end of Tarke Ghyang to descend to Thimbu. ❖

ALTERNATE ROUTE

Tarke Ghyang to Melamchi Bazaar via Shermathang

The more circuitous and scenic route from **Tarke Ghyang** contours to Shermathang (where a trail leads east to the high lakes of Panch Pokhari) before following along the ridge, the Palchowk Danda, to meet the road at Melamchi Pul Bazaar.

To continue to Shermathang, head left where the trail branches just after the stream from the lower end of Tarke Ghyang, near a *stupa* and just above the large Hotel Tarke Ghyang. The powerlines that contour along the hillside for the first hour are your guide. Pass below Shettigang (8580 feet, 2615 m), a few houses with a *gomba*, in less than 30 minutes. The trail contours in a prickly-leaved oak forest, crossing several tributaries to reach **Gangal** (8218 feet, 2505 m), with a *gomba* and lodge, on the crest of the ridge in 1½ **hours** from Tarke Ghyang. There is a nunnery here as well on a prominent spur below the village. Continue contouring, taking the uphill fork at any junctions for another 1½–1¾ **hours** to reach **Shermathang** (8491 feet, 2588 m), spread out along another notch in the ridge. Here there are three *gomba,* including one on the east side of the pass that was recently rebuilt from an 800-year-old structure. There are several lodges and a Langtang National Park check post as well. A motor road reaches Shermathang, but the monsoon rains regularly wash it out, and bus service is not yet available.

Looking back to the northwest, if you try to make out your route from Gosainkund, if you came that way, neither of the two high passes that descend into the Melamchi Khola valley are the ones you traveled. The Laurebina La is less prominent behind the ridge on the west side of the valley, where you can see your route if you came up from Kathmandu. From Shermathang, there are views of the summits to the east, including Dorje Lhakpa and an array beyond. You can head east from here to Panch Pokhari, a series of small lakes (13,156 feet, 4010 m) that are a pilgrimage site, and then continue onto the Kathmandu–Kodari Road. This option is not a well-traveled route, and there are few houses or lodges along the way; self-sufficiency in shelter, food, and fuel is required. This route description is briefly outlined below.

To continue to the bus service at Melamchi Pul Bazaar, head south, following the road out near the ridge crest, and pass a *chorten.* In 45 minutes, reach a shrine with a large, golden figure of a seated Guru Rimpoche (8215 feet, 2504 m). Shortly beyond the shrine, reach a *stupa* and two tea shops, and the end of the flat part of the ridge, and another chance to enjoy the mountain panorama. From here the route diverges. To the right is the road, and to the left is the footpath.

Follow the footpath, and in less than 30 minutes reach a *stupa* (7946 feet, 2422 m) with a pleasant vista to the south. Descend to another *stupa* in 15 minutes near the village of **Raitanyang** (7300 feet, 2225 m), in **1½ hours** from Shermathang. Just below, cross the road to another *stupa* and descend on a stony path to the right. In a few minutes the trail crosses the road again. Continue to descend on the stony path, reaching the road again in a few minutes. From here, follow the road for 15–20 minutes, then fork left on a trail that passes a row of *chorten* and a remarkably beautiful pine forest. Arrive at **Kakani** (6398 feet, 1950 m) in **35 minutes** from passing Raitanyang.

Kakani has lodges and lies in a notch in the ridge south of the school. This is not the village of the same name on the direct descent route from Tarke Ghyang to Thimbu. From Kakani, if you take the trail that descends to the west, you will reach Talamarang and the route back to Pati Bhanjyang, which is described later.

Your goal is to reach the prow at the bottom of the ridge, but the next section is a a a bit tricky. Head east from the notch along a road for 1 minute and then take a right to contour south on a footpath. Regain the prow south of a small hill in 15 minutes and fork right/west and contour toward the ridgeline to the west. Reach a *chorten* in 10 minutes. Descend steeply now on a reddish trail that will be treacherous in the monsoon or when wet (keep in mind the Nepalese maxim, *raato maato chhiplo baaTo,* "red mud, slippery trail"). Remain on the widest trail and reach another *chorten* (5857 feet, 1785 m) in less than 15 minutes.

Notice the altitude when rice paddies appear. Around 5300 feet (1600 m) is the usual upper limit in the east; rice grows several thousand feet higher in far western Nepal.

The trail crosses the road in 10 minutes and after a few minutes it reaches the road again. Follow the road now, with occasional shortcut trails. Reach **Dubhachaur** or **Pokhari Bhanjyang** (5138 feet, 1566 m), a Tamang village strung out on the ridge, in another 20 minutes (**1¼ hours** from Kakani). Continue descending. **Melamchi Pul Bazaar** lies below at the confluence of the Melamchi/Indrawati Khola. The steep

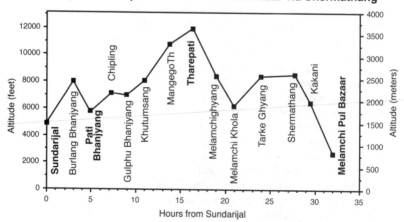

Sundarijal to Tharepati to Melamchi Pul Bazaar via Shermathang

trail follows the ridge and crosses the road several times and comes out at a long suspension bridge over the Melamchi Khola (2677 feet, 816 m) in **1½–1¾ hours** from Dubhachaur. Cross it to the TR (south) bank, and head to the left to reach Melamchi Pul Bazaar (2690 feet, 820 m) and the bus stand, or arrange basic lodging if you miss the last bus which departs at around 3 PM (times are likely to change). ❖

MELAMCHI PUL BAZAAR TO SUNDARIJAL

Alternatively, rather than taking the bus from Melamchi Pul Bazaar, if you would like to walk out to Sundarijal, head right after crossing the Melamchi Khola and follow the road 3½–4 miles (6 km) to **Talamarang** (3058 feet, 932 m), a town with simple lodging, shops, and tea houses, in **1–1¼ hours** from Melamchi Pul Bazaar.

From Talamarang there are two routes to Pati Bhajyang. The lower route follows the river but is unsuitable in the rainy season. The high route offers better views but ascends steeply to the south and follows a road for much of the time, with shortcuts along the way.

Both trails are currently little used by trekkers, and incidents have occurred to those traveling alone. Keep company if you go.

--- **ALTERNATE ROUTE**

Low Route from Talamarang to Batase

To return from **Talamarang** to Pati Bhanjyang via the lower route, head west up the Talamarang Khola's south (right) bank. The trail can be difficult to follow. Stay close to the river most of the time before ascending to the spread-out village of **Batase** (5488 feet, 1673 m) in **2¼–2½ hours** where it meets the high route from Talamarang. ❖

--- **ALTERNATE ROUTE**

High Route from Talamarang to Batase

Alternatively, to take the higher route from **Talamarang**, ascend steeply up the hill to the south, following along the road or using the footpath to make a shortcut of the road. Reach Terse (4428 feet, 1350 m) in 45 minutes and then pass through Majagaon (or Tarambra, the Tamang name) (4944 feet, 1507 m) 30 minutes later. The route diverges from the upper end of the village. Take the right/west branch to contour around the valley to cross a tributary in 30 minutes before ascending to **Batase** (5489 feet, 1673 m) in 25 more minutes, a little over **2–2¼ hours** from Talamarang. Batase is a sprawling village with no facilities other than a hostel for students and occasional foreign volunteers. (The lower route along the river ties in above Batase.) ❖

From **Batase** onward, there are many junctions and the trail can be difficult to follow. Ascend gradually and contour, keeping to the north side of the ridge, to reach the ridgetop village of **Thakani** (6004 feet, 1830 m) in **45 minutes**, with a broad view.

Reach a saddle in 15 more minutes and keep to the north of the ridge as you continue to a junction in less than 15 minutes. Take the left/upper fork and pass above the village of Kabre on a trail lined with large ferns to the hamlet of **Palchen** (6243 feet, 1903 m) at a crest in 20 more minutes, **35 minutes** from Thakani. There are magnificent views from here in clear weather. The right fork here heads off toward Chipling. Instead, keep left to cross over to the south side of the ridge and then contour west before dropping down to the trail just north of Pati Bhanjyang. Descend to **Pati Bhanjyang** in **45 minutes** from Palchen, and retrace the route described earlier to Sundarijal (reached in 3–4 hours).

RETURN JOURNEY VARIATION: SHERMATHANG TO PANCH POKHARI AND THE ROAD

For people who approach Helambu from the west or south, there are alternative means of returning to the highway through an area east of Helambu. While longer, the route offers fine scenery and a ridge route that is cooler during the hot months, along with a visit to the pristine wetland setting of Panch Pokhari ("five lakes"). Because the cirque the lakes are set in faces southeast, there are no good views of the snow-covered mountains from here. But a short climb to the crest of the cirque yields a spectacular vantage point. The trip begins from Shermathang, and self-sufficiency in food, fuel, and shelter is required for up to a week. From Panch Pokhari, you can either walk south to meet the road at Chautaaraa. or continue east to visit Bhairab Kund lake (13,074 feet, 3985 m) before descending to the road near the border with Tibet.

From the saddle where the Langtang National Park Office in **Shermathang** sits, the trail heads east into the Indrawati Khola valley to descend as it heads diagonally north. Pass Samil on the way to **Boligang** in 1½ hours. The trail is rather obscure and the villages, inhabited by Sherpas and Tamang, are notably poorer than the Sherpa villages of Helambu. Continue heading north along a better trail, which reaches the village of **Yangri** (4724 feet, 1440 m) near the confluence of streams and Indrawati Khola in **1 hour**.

Cross the branches and instead of taking a path to the right toward Bhotung, climb up through millet fields to **Yarsa** (6070 feet, 1850 m) in **1 hour**. From Yarsa, take the main path on the left, going gently up, but avoiding steeper alternative paths, pass *chorten* and clusters of houses until you come to a rushing stream in **1 hour**. Cross the stream

on a bridge and then climb steeply. Halfway up, take the steeper path (the other trail flattens out) and reach the crest in **1 hour**.

The trail continues gently up for **15 minutes** to **Haveli Dukang,** a settlement with a few permanent houses and many *goTh* and a nearby cave that locals say was used by Padmasambava (also known as Guru Rimpoche). Haveli Dukang is the last human habitation for the next several days. Panch Pokhari can be reached from here in 1 long day and should only be attempted if you have been acclimatized from a trek in the Langtang valley or elsewhere. Be vigilant of signs of AMS, (see Chapter 5).

From here, there are steep climbs and stream crossings before reaching seasonal *goTh* at a crest at **Nosem Pati** (11,909 feet, 3630 m) in **3¾ hours.** Continue gently up to the left on fine

Crossing the Ganja La
(Photo by Pat Morrow)

rock slabs to reach the saddle **Lauribina Bhanjyang** (12,270 feet, 3740 m) in **1½ hours**. There are numerous *chorten* and a trail shelter here, but water may be difficult to find.

The trail to **Panch Pokhari** runs along the left side of the ridge and is generally well built, but it has numerous ups and downs that are tiresome at that altitude. Reach a shelter to the north of the bodies of water (13,156 feet, 4010 m) in another **1–1½ hours**. The area is just above the tree line, and there are plenty of fine camping places. A Hindu shrine to Shiva and numerous prayer flags are nearby, making it a serene place, unless you are here around the full moon of August when many pilgrims arrive for the Janai Purnima festival. From the cirque crest (about 13,320 feet, 4060 m), there is a splendid view of the Jugal Mountains and much more. A route continues north from here over the difficult Tilman's Pass to reach the Lantang River valley at Langhisa Kharka, but technical skills and equipment are required as well as a good guide.

There are two ways to return from Panch Pokhari to meet the road, described as follows.

ALTERNATE ROUTE

Nosem Pati to Chautaaraa

The most direct route to the road is almost entirely along a ridge south from Lauribina Bhanjyang to Chautaaraa, where you meet the road in **3 days**. To take this route, then return to **Nosem Pati** and continue along the ridgeline to another pass at Hile Bhanjyang (12,204 feet, 3720 m). Descend south along the ridgeline to a seasonal pasture area (10,876 feet, 3315 m) and then Chyochyo Kharka (11,286 feet, 3440 m). Continue descending along the ridgeline before dropping away from the ridge to the left to the village of Phusre (7283 feet, 2220 m) and then Syaule (5249 feet, 1600 m). There might be vehicle transport available in Syaule. Otherwise, continue along the road to **Chautaaraa** (4652 feet, 1418 m) where bus service is available. ❖

ALTERNATE ROUTE

Nosem Pati to Bhairab Kund Lake and East to Meet the Highway

The other option is to head east from Nosem Pati through a rarely visited area, either camping or arranging home stay. Along the way, take a side trip to visit the sacred Bhairab Kund and eventually meet the main highway between Kathmandu and Tibet near the border town of Kodari.

To follow this route from **Nosem Pati**, head east, passing through juniper to Sanglung (7480 feet, 2280 m) and descend to cross the Balephi Khola before reaching the settlement of Tembathang (7152 feet, 2180 m) where home stay might be available. Continue on to Nimatol (7300 feet, 2225 m) and then to Kyangsing (8120 feet, 2475 m) where there is a *gomba* and possible home stay as well.

The trail ascends steeply to Nautale Kharka (11,204 feet, 3415 m) and then branches north along the ridgeline for a stiff climb to Chormu Kharka (13,156 feet, 4010 m) and on to the sacred Bhairab Kund lake at (13,074 feet, 3985 m). There is a temple near the lake but no facilities. Retrace the route south along the ridgeline before heading into the valley to the east. Descend to Sherpagaon (8202 feet, 2500 m) with home stay before descending to meet the road at Duguna Gadhi (6266 feet, 1910 m). North on the Arniko Highway toward the Friendship Bridge between Nepal and Tibet there is a natural hot springs area. ❖

9

THE TRAILS LESS TRAVELED

*Two roads diverged in a wood, and I, I took the one less traveled by,
And that has made all the difference.*

—Robert Frost

This chapter is divided into three sections. Treks in the Cultural Trails section have set-tlements along the route with home stay, community lodges, or hotels available. Routes listed in the Backcountry Treks section will also pass through settlements with similar facilities; however, these treks will at some point involve full self-sufficiency in camping, food, and fuel, for at least one night and longer depending on the route. A third section offers additional suggestions for eco-trekking in beautiful, unheralded areas.

The routes in this chapter are not for everyone and often far from outside, modern help. Considerable resilience is needed, along with a spirit of adventure and an open mind. For a first trek, it is best to consider a more established route (see Chapters 6, 7, and 8). As your experience and ambition grows, you can take on these more adventur-ous treks and beyond.

People often ask about how to get away from crowded routes that at times can seem to be nothing but a series of hotels, albeit majestically draped with extraordinary natural appeal, yet often with meager cultural interaction. Rural Nepal is rich in heritage; travel-ing away from the main tourist track and visiting nearly anywhere in the mid-hills and higher can be an immensely worthwhile endeavor. The hospitality of the hill people is unmatched, as is their spirit, and many of these areas remain relatively untouched by modernization. There are few lodges or facilities set up strictly for tourists, and trail sections may be difficult to follow; physical comfort is at a minimum. The rewards are meeting the hill people in traditional settings where often your only option will be to stay in a home, giving ample opportunity for interaction and cultural insight. With that in mind, we are tempted to say, pick any place on the map and go (or do not even bother with the map)! However, this would require more than a little experience as well as mental flexibility, endurance, and minimal language facility. You would have to arrange lodging and food in homes or stay at the occasional basically equipped lodge. If you do this, be prepared for an adventure and for a lack of facilities and ease. Usually, there will be basic to nonexistent toilet conditions. Open defecation is more often than not the ruling practice in rural settings, complicating good hygiene and general sanitation.

Rather than going out completely on your own without a guidebook, you can use the route descriptions in this chapter as a baseline for making this kind of journey. Views of the snow-clad titans might not be as up-close along these routes, but in our belief, the cultural interaction more than makes up for this, and village vistas can be just as inspir-ing. The rest is to be discovered.

Hilsa below a border settlement along the Karnali River with Nepal on the left and Tibet on the right (Photo by David Citrin)

CULTURAL TRAILS

The areas described are generally prepared for the arrival of tourists, and although few visitors might come through, home stay is often readily arranged, and there are also a few lodges along these paths with more facilities being developed.

By choosing one of these treks, you will be choosing to spread the financial benefit of tourism to lower-income areas. As on the more visited routes, we encourage the use of local products along these less-frequented trails. Do your best to eat the same fare as your hosts and support the area's farmsteads. Avoid packaged, prepared foods, which contribute to refuse that locals do not know how to deal with adequately, especially away from the main trekking venues. (Garbage is disposed of openly in villages, or otherwise stockpiled in a few locations to rot or be burned.) Be aware that monosodium glutamate (MSG), known as *TesTi pauDar* (i.e., tasty powder) or *aajinomoTo* in Nepal, may be in use, even in far-flung villages; if you prefer food without this "flavor enhancer," you can request that it not be added.

Without electronic devices impinging, there can be more interactions with people. Along the less-frequented trails, most locals will be enthusiastically pleased at your presence and will naturally be curious about who you are. Do not be surprised if you are asked many questions. We have explored Nepalese culture in depth in Chapter 3, offering guidelines for interaction. Often people will try to get your attention as you walk the trails by shouting, whistling, or yelling *"Namaste!"* from afar, or even singing. They might be trying to signal you if they think that you are going the wrong way, or they might just be excited to see you because foreigners in rural Nepal are few and far between outside of the usual routes. If the latter, try to take it in stride and realize that it is a genuine expression of interest in your presence. Most Nepali people feel that it is an honor to have a visitor.

TAMANG HERITAGE TRAIL
(Map No. 7, Page 319)

The Tamang Heritage Trail, developed and launched by the United Nations along with the Tourism for Rural Poverty Alleviation Program (UN/TRPAP) in 2005, lies west of the Langtang valley. This route takes you through mainly Tamang villages in the mid-hills that receive considerably fewer tourists than the traditional, adjoining Langtang trek (described in Chapter 8). Although the mountain views are a bit farther away, home stay enables a deeper cultural experience than can be had on the more established routes. Additionally, a trek along the Tamang Heritage Trail can be combined with the Langtang valley trek. The routes coincide at Syabrubensi or along the high route from Syabrubensi to Rimche where the trails tie in at the village of Khangjim.

The usual starting point is either Syabrubensi (one starting point for the Langtang trek as well) or Thaambuchet. There is a daily direct bus from Kathmandu to Thaambuchet; otherwise, three buses depart daily for Syabrubensi from the Baleju Bus Park (also known as Gongabu and New Bus Park).

The road rises out of the Kathmandu valley to the northeast. Enjoy refreshing sights of fertile hills along the way and the occasional symphony of cicadas (if they can be heard over the din of the bus). There are glimpses of Ganesh Himal and west to Himal Chuli and the Annapurna Range. Trishuli is a large town and the administrative center of Nuwakot District, and is less than 45 miles (70 km) (3–4 hours) by road from Kathmandu. From Trishuli, the paved road turns to a dirt road soon after climbing out of Trishuli toward Betraawati (BetrAwati) 5 miles (8 km) away. To avoid the 6–8 hour bus ride over a rough dirt road to Syabrubensi (39 miles or 63 km from Trishuli) via Dhunche, an option is to start the trek from Betraawati, and then meet the Tamang Heritage Trail at Gatlaang village in 3 days. This ambitious choice is described first below, while the details for Syabrubensi, the typical starting point, follow. Since villages along this route rarely see tourists and there are minimal facilities along this portion, it is better to start from Syabrubensi unless you are an experienced trekker with some language facility.

ALTERNATE APPROACH: BETRAAWATI TO GATLAANG

To take this option of walking in (a journey of **3 days**), disembark at the bus stop at **Betraawati** (2050 feet, 625 m). (Alternatively, a single, daily bus plies this track between Kathmandu to Pairebesi, a village 1 hour's walk ahead, from the Maccha Pokhari/Baleju Bus Park area leaving at 11 AM. The return trip leaves Pairebesi daily at 9AM. Bus times are subject to change.) Take the bridge crossing the Phalaakhu Khola to the north side where a sign announces your entry to Rasuwaa District, the location of Langtang National Park and the Tamang Heritage Trail. Rasuwaa District is named after a fort located at the border with Tibet. Over 60 percent of the inhabitants of Rasuwaa are Tamang.

Follow the road as it inclines to the left/west. A short distance (500 feet, 150 m) from the bridge, a trail to the left breaks away from the road to Dunche, which keeps climbing slightly. Follow this trail to the left, a wide double-tracked trail which drops down from the road and contours above the nearby Trishuli Khola.

In 10–15 minutes you will come to a suspension bridge across the Trishuli Khola. You can cross here to walk up the west side, then cross the Salaakhu Khola on another suspension bridge to tie in with the east-side route near Pairebesi. Otherwise, keep walking up the east side of the river, passing through the fields and houses of KaidaleTaar

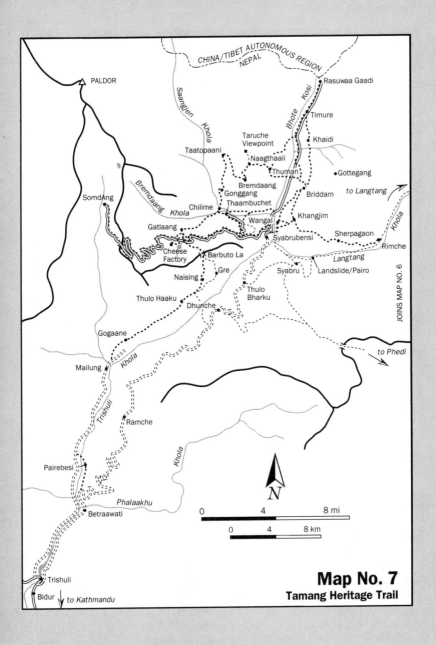

PALDOR

CHINA/TIBET AUTONOMOUS REGION
NEPAL

Rasuwaa Gaadi

Saangen Khola

Bhote Kosi

Timure

Taruche
Viewpoint

Khaidi

Taatopaani

Naagthaali

Gottegang

Bremdaang
Khola

Thuman

Bremdaang
Gonggang
Thaambuchet

Briddam

to Langtang

SomdAng

Chilime

Wangal

Khangjim

Khola

Gatlaang

Syabrubensi

Sherpagaon

Rimche

Cheese
Factory

Barbuto La

Langtang

Landslide/Pairo

JOINS MAP NO. 6

Naising

Gre

Syabru

Thulo Haaku

Dhunche

Thulo
Bharku

Gogaane

to Phedi

Mailung

Khola

Trishuli

Ramche

Khola

Pairebesi

Phalaakhu

N

0   4   8 mi

0   4   8 km

Betraawati

Trishuli

Map No. 7
Tamang Heritage Trail

Bidur   to Kathmandu

village, following the wide double track along the east side of the Trishuli Khola. The trail gradually rises to the village of Pairebesi (2230 feet, 680 m) **1 hour** from Betraawati. Simple lodges are available in Pairebesi.

From Pairebesi, take a suspension bridge to the west bank of the Trishuli River to more houses and simple lodges. You can take an immediate right to pass a row of shops,

THE TAMANG

Tamang have their own language, which is of the Tibeto-Burman family of languages and closely related to the languages of the Gurung and Thakhali. Tamang also have a distinct manner of dress, ornamentation, and craftsmanship, and many of their homes have ornately carved wooden windows and porch fronts. The Tamang comprise about 5.6 percent of the total population of Nepal, and they are the predominant inhabitants of Rasuwaa District where this trek and the Langtang valley lie. ◈

Tamang mother and daughter in traditional dress
(Photo by Alonzo Lyons)

then find your way through fields along the Trishuli Khola while gradually rising to Shanti Bazaar (2460 feet, 750 m) with several restaurants and shops. Otherwise, continue straight from the bridge and head right on the dirt road that leads up to **Shanti Bazaar** in **20–25 minutes**. (Two daily buses ply the road on the west side of the river from Maccha Pokhari/Baleju Bus Park area in Kathmandu to Shanti Bazaar. The road from Shanti Bazaar continues to Mailung, but there is currently no regular vehicle service. Road construction along this valley bottom all the way to Syabrubensi is underway. The plan is for a road that avoids the climb to Dhunche by following the river all the way to the border with the Tibet Autonomous Region.)

Reach **Simle** (2493 feet, 760 m) in **20 minutes** from Shanti Bazaar while traveling alongside the Trishuli Khola. There is good camping about halfway between Shanti Bazaar and Simle in a low-lying area near the river. From Simle, the wide track continues to contour along the Trishuli Khola for 15 minutes before climbing and then descending gradually back to the river level. As the path gradually ascends along the river, with cliffs occasionally overhanging the path, you'll pass splendid rock walls and waterfalls on both sides of the valley. On the opposite side of the river are magnificent multilevel waterfalls that have cut deeply into the rock over the years; changes in the course of the waterfalls can also be traced from the scars left behind by the previous watercourses.

One hour from Simle is ChipleTi, with landline phone service and simple lodging. A little farther along, **1 ¼ hours** from Simle, is **Mailung** (3035 feet, 925 m), a larger village than ChipleTi with a few lodges and landline phone. From here up the Trishuli Khola valley, snowy peaks in the Langtang range can be seen.

Keep to the double-track road and approximately 650 feet (200 m) from Mailung, take a trail that branches to the right, dropping from the road to cross the Nyam Khola on a wooden bridge. The service road not taken is part of the Mailung Khola hydropower project and continues ¾ mile (1.2 km) farther up the Nyam Khola.

After crossing the Nyam River, the route passes over a former rockslide and follows the Trishuli River. In 20 minutes take the trail to the left to abruptly ascend away from the river. (Just near this fork there is a basket-and-pulley system for crossing the river to a trail on the other side that leads to Dhunche.)

The trail to Gogaane heads directly and steeply up the side of the hill before contouring and ascending more gradually up the Trishuli Khola valley. It is an isolated area with no water sources from the point of departure near the river until reaching Gogaane. In 1 hour 20 minutes the trail forks (10 minutes before reaching the village); the upper trail climbs steeply and enters **Gogaane** past a school. From here it is necessary to pass through people's front landings (porches) to continue; the lower trail passes below the village and ties in on the north side. Gogaane (4888 feet, 1490 m), a Tamang village, is reached in a little over **1½ hours** from Mailung. This picturesque and rustic hamlet, with houses decorated by simple paintings around the front doors, sees few foreign visitors. There are no facilities in Gogaane.

Water is scarce between Gogaane and the next settlement, Thulo Haaku, with no facilities, and few people encountered other than herders and those out collecting wood. From Gogaane, avoid the trail that drops down steeply to a suspension bridge over the Trishuli River and on to Dhunche; instead, follow the trail that contours and climbs above the valley. About **1 hour** from Gogaane the trail levels off and then drops down slightly to cross a **stream**. Near the stream there are several large overhanging rocks favored by herders that provide shelter suitable for camping or getting out of the rain if necessary.

From the stream, the trail ascends out of the canyon and climbs steeply to a ridge, then steadily ascends while contouring north up the Trushuli Khola valley. About 30 minutes beyond the stream, you round a ridge to a view of several snow-capped peaks from the Langtang range, including Langtang I, II, and Kimshung. Pass the open, communal latrine along the side of the trail as you reach **Thulo Haaku** (6890 feet, 2100 m), in **1½ hours** from the stream (**2½ hours** from Gogaane). (If doing this trail in reverse, from Thulo Haaku to Gogaane, then avoid an upper fork 10 minutes out of Thulo Haaku on the way to Gogaane.)

Thulo Haaku is a large Tamang village with simple facilities, including a post office, monastery, secondary school, and view of Langtang peaks. Landlines that will reach overseas are available here, and some mobile networks are covered. Houses here have elaborate carvings around the doors and windows, mostly of Tibetan Buddhist motifs. The small monastery is above town nestled in a copse of trees including several grand junipers. Across the valley, the road to Dhunche can be seen about the same level as Thulo Haaku, and farther up the valley along a ridge, houses of Dhunche can be seen.

From Thulo Haaku, take the upper trail from the high end of the village. Next is Sano Haaku, visible up the valley. The first section of trail out of Thulo Haaku is a communal latrine, as on the other end of the settlement. Contour over a boulder-strewn stream and cross several more streams, some with water-powered mills and one with a cascade that is ideal for a waterfall shower.

Reach **Sano Haaku** (6562 feet, 2000 m), also a Tamang village, in approximately **25 minutes**. There is an elementary school here along with a police post. Some of the houses have elaborate carvings around windows and doors, as in Thulo Haaku.

FUNERALS

Funerals can be observed in the city and countryside at any time. Most Nepalis burn the dead, preferably at the riverside (ghaaT), within a few hours of death. Hill villagers, far from the river, prefer prominent hillsides on which to burn or bury the dead. Rai and Limbu tend to bury. The other ethnic groups prefer cremation.

Funeral parties are obvious from the presence of a white-shrouded corpse carried on a bier either prone or bound tightly into a sitting position. Male relatives at the funeral typically shave their heads; women frequently loosen their hair, letting it hang unadorned down the back. Drumming is uncommon, except on the occasion of postfunerary ceremonies held sometimes months after death to celebrate the passage of the deceased's spirit into the afterlife. Such post funerary rituals are common, for example, among the hill ethnic groups such as the Gurung, Tamang, and Thakali. These are occasions for great feasting, dancing, drinking, and serious and ancient religious rituals conducted by shamans and Bon or Buddhist monks. Such postfunerary events are sometimes known in Nepali as arghun in the hills of west and west-central Nepal. ❖

Follow the trail to the north from the upper part of town, to reach a rock imprinted with a *mantra* in Tibetan script in large colorful letters. The trail forks here with the lower fork leading to a village named Gre (described below as an alternate route). Take the upper trail to go on to Naising and the Balbuto Pass before descending to Gatlaang, a village on the Tamang Heritage Trail.

ALTERNATE
ROUTE
- -

Sano Haaku to Balbuto Pass via Gre

This path is less direct and takes longer than Sano Haaku to Naising to the Balbuto Pass.

At the trail juncture outside of **Sano Haaku** near a large rock with "*Om mani padme hum*" written in large and colorful Tibetan script, take the lower trail to Gre. The trail travels up the valley high above the Trishuli River, passing down through a canyon below Naising and crossing a stream on a concrete bridge before ascending out the other side of the canyon, continuing with occasional steep drop-offs at the trail's edge.

Cross a final ridge and pass *chorten* before descending slightly to **Gre** (6562 feet, 2000 m) in **1½ hours** from Sano Haaku. Gre is a Tamang village with few facilities other than a tea shop, school, and a *gomba* as well as a Christian church.

From Gre, a trail to Dhunche/Bharku heads east out of town and drops to the river. The steep trail to Syabrubensi can be seen across the way on the opposing hillside to the north. Perhaps unbelievably, this trail ascends up and over that ridge to the north before descending to Syabrubensi.

To head to Gatlaang, follow the trail west out of the village. It ascends steeply to **Balbuto Pass**, reached in **1½ hours** from Gre. ❖

To continue to Naising, after approximately **30 minutes** from Sano Haaku reach a ridgeline with a *mani* wall. Just beyond more *mani* walls is the town of **Naising**, a predominantly Tamang village with a Christian church established in 2003 which sits above the trail. According to locals, many people in the village fell sick and some were dying during the year 2000, and this period coincided with a visit by a Nepalese missionary. He was able to convince the villagers to convert from Buddhism to Christianity to avert further health problems.

From Naising, do not take the trail from the high end of town which leads up to grazing areas. Instead, the trail emerges from the lower edge of town and immediately forks. The trail to the right drops down to the village of Gre. Take the upper fork that snakes through fields on the way to Balbuto Pass and the Tamang Heritage Trail.

After approximately 15 minutes of gradual descent from Naising, the trail passes a few huts used for milling as it crosses a stream on a wooden bridge. The trail then begins climbing out of the canyon. After approximately 10 minutes from the bridge, avoid a faint fork that again heads to Gre. Stay on the main upper trail, which climbs steadily and steeply to the ridge top above.

Cross the ridge (8218 feet, 2505 m) and then climb gradually through a broad-leaf forest to a *mani* wall at a pass (8628 feet, 2630 m). From the pass, Gatlaang can be seen below as well as the road to SomdAng. Leave the Trishuli valley here as the trail drops down steeply to then wind along the hillside. Avoid any forks to the right that head directly to the village of Godam.

The trail passes through a few fields to emerge along the road from Syabrubensi to lead and zinc mines at SomdAng). At the point the trail meets the road, the village of Godam is approximately 450 yards (400 m) down the road itself. To continue to Gatlaang, cross the road; approximately 25 yards/22 m up on the other side of the road, the trail drops away from the road, down to the cluster of houses of **Gatlaang** (8415 feet, 2565 m) approximately 10–15 minutes away from the road crossing and **2¼ hours** from Naising.

Gatlaang is an impressive Tamang village on the Tamang Heritage Trail with closely linked houses with slate roofs. Gatlaang also has a Christian church (missionaries have been afoot in this area) as well as a school and a post office. There are two lodges here, one privately run at the top end of town and a community lodge toward the bottom. Guides can be arranged at the upper lodge. Home stay is also encouraged in this village.

The church is above the settlement by the school. Much higher above is a Buddhist *gomba* and farther above the valley and high above Gatlaang is an army post. A side trip from Gatlaang up to the *gomba* and a nearby sacred pond and cheese factory is described below.

If weather permits, the Lantang peaks are vibrant from Gatlaang. Landline phone is available here, and power sockets for charging batteries, mobile phones, and more are available in the lodges.

TRADITIONAL ROUTE: SYABRUBENSI TO GATLAANG

A bus from Syabrubensi to Thaambuchet departs Syabrubensi between 4:30 and 5 PM after first arriving from Kathmandu. The curvy road travels from Syabrubensi at 4813 feet (1467 m) and zigzags up over a pass at 7175 feet (2187 m) and down to Thaambuchet at (5800 feet) 1768 m.

Rather than take the bus, a recommended option is to hike from Syabrubensi to Thaambuchet. To do this, follow the motor road toward Tibet from the north end of Syabrubensi and along the west side of the Bhote Kosi.

Just before the road drops to cross the Chilime Khola and then the Bhote Kosi, the trail heads left/west from the road up through a canyon of the Chilime Khola valley. First pass through fields near a dwelling before dropping down to cross the **Chilime Khola** on a suspension bridge in **45 minutes** from Syabrubensi.

Backstrap looms and local wool allow for the weaving of blankets in an environmentally sustainable way. (Photo by Mary Anne Mercer)

From the bridge, follow the trail upstream/left (rather than to the right, which heads to Thuman). The trail ascends to cross a ridge and then contours to cross another nearby ridge where it then forks. The lower fork is more direct to Thaambuchet but through an area prone to landslides, and the trail might be difficult to follow. The upper fork heads to Paajungbensi (Lower Paajung) with few facilities, and from here it drops back down to the river to meet the lower trail to Thaambuchet (or continues higher along the way to upper Paajung, Bremdaang, and Taatopaani).

Eventually, reach a long suspension bridge to cross back over to the south bank of the Chilime Khola in **1 hour 10 minutes** from the previous bridge over the same river. On the other side of the bridge is the small Newar village of **Goljung Besi** (Lower Goljung) with an unusual predominance of Christians. The village of (Upper) Goljung is high above on the hillside.

Looking back from the south side of the bridge, on the other side of the river, you will notice a large Christian cross mounted atop a hillock, an unusal sight in Nepal. On a plateau just above Goljung Besi is a church as well as the neaby ruins of a former palace. Villagers say that the ruins are of an estate of a Newar king predating Prithvi Narayan Shah, the king from Gorkha District who conquered and united Nepal in the 1760s. The large, dilapidated stone structure is surrounded by fields along with more ruins built up around a nearby *pipal* tree (a sacred fig, *Ficus religiosa*). The Bodhi or Bo Tree, the tree which sheltered the Buddha as he achieved enlightenment, was a *pipal*. These trees are considered sacred to Hindus and Buddhists alike and have characteristically heart-shaped leaves. To reach the ruins, take the trail out of Goljung Besi that ascends toward

Goljung. Then head right/west away from the trail and through fields past the church to the ruins beyond.

To head directly to Thaambuchet from Goljung Besi, the trail follows from the long suspension bridge to the right along the Chilime Khola. Eventually you pass the hydropower project just before reaching the village of **Thaambuchet** (5775 feet, 1760 m) in **30 minutes**, less than **2½ hours** from Syabrubensi. There are lodges here, and electronic items can be charged. There is also a health post in the village. Tibetan refugees inhabit the upper part of town. A motor road with bus service reaches as far as Thaambuchet. Daily service includes a bus from Thaambuchet to Syabrubensi and on to Kathmandu, leaving at 7 AM; and a bus to Thaambuchet leaving Kathmandu at 6:30 AM from Baleju Bus Park.

Thaambuchet lies at the confluence of the Bremdaang Khola and the larger Saangjen Khola, and is also the location of the Chilime Hydro Power Project. From Thaambuchet, cross over the Bremdaang Khola on a suspension bridge at the upper/west end of town and pass through fields to a long *mani* wall. Head left/southwest at the *mani* wall and reach a wooden bridge to again cross the Bremdaang Khola and follow the trail upriver before ascending steeply through a forested area. (Another route continues to follow the river, crossing it a few times before steeply ascending to Gatlaang.)

Reach a large boulder with arrows pointing the way. Gatlaang can be seen up the valley. The scenic trail eventually emerges from the woods into fields and gradually ascends to Gatlaang, passing many *chorten* and *mani* walls along the way. Reach **Gatlaang** in **1 hour 35 minutes** from Thaambuchet.

🏔 *Side Trip from Gatlaang to Parvati Kund and a Cheese Factory. The trail ascends from the upper part of **Gatlaang** village, passing mani walls and then crossing a road. From there you ascend along a stream for a while before reaching a so-called "abandoned village" in 15 minutes. Many of the stone houses here are in ruins while some of the houses are still occupied. Keep ascending and reach **Parvati Kund** (8202 feet, 2500 m), in approximately **40 minutes** of steep uphill climbing from Gatlaang.*

Parvati Kund is a pond with a stone wall built around it. Inside the walled area is a ceremonial platform, along with a bathing ghaaT and chorten. Outside the rock wall is a rest area as well as a small Hindu temple containing a stone image of the goddess Parvati with Shiva. Two Buddhist chorten are located beside the temple. From Parvati Kund are commanding views of Langtang peaks and the Gosainkund range.

Across the road (which continues to mines at SomdAng) from Parvati Kund is a fenced-in apple orchard, above which sit the remains of a destroyed compound. This was previously a villa of a Nepal Army general that was demolished by Maoists (the general was away at the time).

A 5-minute walk farther along the road will bring you to a few shops. From here, a trail heads right/north to a gomba just above the hill and a nearby, newer, isolated building with a curious signboard that reads "THE COMMUNITY CREATIVITY CENTRE."

*From the left/south side of the road, a trail leads above to a **cheese factory** in **10 minutes**. Cheese and ghiu (or ghee, clarified butter) are produced here to be sold in Kathmandu. This factory is run by the governmental Dairy Development Corporation (DDC).*

Return to Gatlaang via the same route. (Another return option from here, if doing the Tamang Heritage Trail in reverse, is to follow the route described above and walk out to the road at Betraawati, 5 miles (8 km) from the large market town of Trishuli.)

GATLAANG TO THUMAN

Depart for Taatopaani at the bottom/eastern end of **Gatlaang**. A minute from leaving the village, avoid the branch that heads down steeply toward the river. Instead, continue on the gradually descending trail as it passes through fields and by rows and rows of *chorten* and *mani* walls. Pass a final *chorten* and leave the fields behind to descend through trees to the level of the river. Continue along the riverside, crossing the **Bremdaang Khola** on a wooden bridge in **1¼ hours**. The trail then follows a long *mani* wall toward Chilime. (Thaambuchet can be reached from a branch that leads right from the *mani* wall.)

From the *mani* wall, contour up the Saangjen Khola valley. (Chilime Khola is the name of the river after the confluence of the Bremdaang and Saangjen rivers.) The Chilime Hydro Power Project is visible alongside the river. (Incidentally, electricity for both Thaambuchet and Chilime arrives from Trishuli rather than this large, privately owned project.) Pass by a few houses and lodging in the lower part of Chilime, and then pass the upper settlement of **Chilime** (6000 feet, 1829 m), an enthralling village to explore, about **1½ hours** from Gatlaang. Unfortunately there may be a profuse amount of litter along the walkways.

The trail passes below Chilime to reach a suspension bridge over the **Saangjen Khola** within **20 minutes** from crossing the wooden bridge over the Bremdaang Khola.

From the east/far side of the bridge, do not ascend, but take an immediate left to follow the trail upriver for a couple of minutes before heading away from the river up through fields. After crossing through the fields, the trail branches. Take the wider trail to the right to ascend steeply. As you ascend, the houses of Chilime can be seen below as well as a bird's-eye view of the Chilime Hydro Power Project and the nearby settlement of Thaambuchet, and farther beyond Thaambuchet, the village of Goljung on the far side of the valley.

Reach **Gonggaang** (7300 feet, 2225 m) in **1 hour** from the Saangjen Khola crossing. Lodging is available. (From Gonggaang, a high trail contours down and out of the valley to the village of Paajung, and on to Syabrubensi.) Follow along the trail from the upper end of the village and ascend to round a ridge from where Taatopaani is visible high up the valley. Continue ascending through fields and trees for **1 hour** to reach the collection of lodges known as **Taatopaani** (8530 feet, 2600 m), built around a well-developed hot springs bathing area. (*Taato* means "hot" in Nepali and *paani* is "water," in other words "hot springs.") Above the lodges is the eponymous bathing area with six spouts (two each for three bathing pools) and there are dingy changing rooms nearby. Drains have to be closed before the bathing pools fill up. Keep an eye to belongings, as thieves have been known to strike here while unsuspecting bathers are enjoying the warmth of the water. Solar power is available in the lodges along with landline phones. A 5-minute walk to the northwest provides an inspiring view up the Saangjen Khola valley with a beautiful glimpse of snow-capped peaks of the Kerung Range in Tibet.

Meet the trail onward to Bremdaang by the bathing area above the lodges. Bremdaang is at a higher elevation than Taatopaani and back down the valley. Gray langurs, also known as Hanuman langurs, are an old-world monkey and likely to be seen in this forested area between Taatopaani and Bremdaang.

From Taatopaani, ascend gradually through the woods, crossing a few small streams, for 5 minutes to where the trail forks. Both branches lead to Bremdaang. The newer trail heads right to contour more gradually, while the older trail ascends steeply for 5 minutes before contouring and dropping down slightly to a meeting point with the new trail after approximately 10 minutes.

Continue to climb through the woodland, cross a small open meadow, and shortly cross a small stream and reach a fork in the trail just beyond, 30 minutes from Taatopaani.

A painted sign on a rock with an arrow pointing the way to Naagthaali might be visible. Follow the sign to take the trail to the left and ascend steeply through a forested patch to reach a rock wall surrounding the fields that abut the village of Bremdaang.

The trail passes between this wall and a large boulder topped with prayer flags. Follow along the wall to the village of **Bremdaang** (9350 feet, 2850 m) **1 hour** from Taatopaani. (Along the wall, just before reaching Bremdaang, a trail from below joins the trail from Taatopaani. If doing this route in reverse, avoid taking the trail down to the left, but continue to follow the wall to where the trail passes between the wall and a large boulder.)

Basic lodging and solar power are available in Bremdaang as well as phone service. There are elaborate carvings around the windows and doors of the houses here. A small *gomba* sits above town, along with a built-up viewpoint area where Paldor Peak can be seen. A large prayer wheel stands beside the entrance of the *gomba*. If the doors are locked, a villager can help locate the key.

Streams swell to powerful torrents during the monsoon season. (Photo by R.C. Sedai)

The trail to Naagthaali emerges from the upper part of town and winds through the trees to round a ridge with views available of the adjoining valley. The trail follows this ridge from which the Trishuli River valley can be seen as well as settlements along that valley including Dhunche. Reach a large open meadow named **Naagthaali** (10,640 feet, 3243 m) with a scattered collection of well-furnished lodges in **50 minutes** from Bremdaang.

Look for *chAUmri* here, a cross between cows and yaks. Two small *gomba*, the older stone structures surrounded by prayer flags, are located in Naagthaali; one lies at the high end of the meadow and the other is more centrally located. If the *lama* of either is present, he might let you into a throne room with Buddhist iconography. Do not be surprised if a monetary request is made. (Keep in mind that it is customary to leave a small donation when visiting religious sites.) There are caves nearby that locals say have long been used for meditation. You might need a local guide to find them in the area above and behind the uppermost lodge and higher *gomba* at the high end of the meadow.

Side Trip from Naagthaali to Taaruche Viewpoint. As advertised on a sign at a **Naagthaali** *lodge, "*Visit Taruche with kaleidoscope views of Ganesh Himal Range, Kerung Range (Tibet), Langtang Himal Range and Gosainkund Range.*" To reach Taaruche, the trail leads away from the upper end of the meadow and passes below the higher gomba. Follow the trail to ascend through pine forest, and keep to this wide trail along the ridge overlooking the Saangjen Khola valley with occasional vistas through the trees. At one point the village of Taatopaani can be seen below.*

On the way to Taaruche, there is a small, seasonal cheese-making operation in a hut among the trees below the trail. Milk is gathered and hauled up from chAUmri herders around Naagthaali, and their products are sold locally and in Kathmandu.

Emerge from the trees to contour away from the valley rim and up through open hillside, then ascend to round another ridge and pass through a lush grove of moss-laden trees including rhododendron. Water is likely to be available here. Pass out of the trees and round another ridge to reach the top of an open ridge. This area is known as **Taaruche** *(12,224 feet, 3726 m), reached in* **1½ hours** *from Naagthaali, marked with prayer flags.*

Here you will find nearly 360° immense views (if Mother Nature cooperates) and a herder's seasonal shelter. No facilities are available, but keep a lookout for grazing chAUmri. Mountain views north to Tibet, as well as west to the Ganesh Himal Range and Paldor Peak, and east to the Langtang range, are sensational. No sounds impinge but those of birds, insects, the rustling of the wind, and perhaps the occasional jingle of a bell on a grazing animal.

Note that from Naagthaali to Thuman, the trail can be unclear with several diversions. Catch the trail to Thuman at the lower end of the meadow. The trail here might be difficult to follow given the amount of heavy-footed ungulates plodding around the soft earth in a slow, never-ending search for fodder. Descend while heading northeast, and after approximately 5 minutes the trail to Thuman branches off to the right/east. This might be easy to miss as the widest trail may seem to continue on straight/northeast, but it only descends to a pasture in a few minutes where it then becomes a maze.

The right fork heads down through a grove of trees with abundant rhododendron for a few minutes, then straight across an open area (the aforementioned pasture area labyrinth is up to the left/north). Continue heading straight to descend through forest. In 30 minutes from Naagthaali, the trail emerges to cross a large, splendid meadow and continues its descent.

In another 15 minutes the trail forks. Continue straight (rather than left) and down through fields above Thuman. Pass by a school on the right and arrive at **Thuman** (7546 feet, 2300 m) in **1 ¼–1 ½ hours** from Naagthaali. Thuman is a large Tamang village with closely placed houses and elaborate wood carvings around doors and windows. Lodging and a health post are available here.

A *gomba* lies at the lower, southern end of town. The *konyer*, or keyholder, lives nearby. If you approach closer, be aware that a swarm of bees have made a home near the upper part of the *gomba*'s inner door. Trails to Taambuchet and Chilime up the Saangjen Khola valley and to Syabrubensi leave this end of town. A trail to Taatopaani that bypasses Naagthaali also branches off the same trail to Chilime. Thuman offers excellent views of Langtang. The settlement is powered by hydroelectricity from a nearby stream, and sockets are available for charging batteries, phones, and other devices. However, electricity is usually only available from evening to morning (6 PM–6 AM).

THUMAN TO BRIDDAM

The Tamang Heritage Trail offers two options from Thuman. One route is to travel north to the border town of Rasuwaa Gaadi along the trade route with Tibet and then return to the village of Briddam opposite Thuman on the other side of the valley. Another option is to head directly to Briddam from Thuman. The direct trail will be covered as an alternate route, then we will cover the longer option via Rasuwaa Gaadi.

ALTERNATE
ROUTE

Direct Route from Thuman to Briddam

Be advised that some maps need updating for this route, which steeply descends from **Thuman** at 7546 feet (2300 m) to the bridge over the Bhote Kosi (5151 feet, 1570 m) and up the other side of the valley to Briddam (7218 feet, 2200 m).

From the *gomba* at the southern end of Thuman, find the path heading down just to the north/village side of the *gomba*. Descend along a ridge past a series of *mani* walls. (Another trail leaves from the middle of Thuman just below the health post between a lodge and house. As it exits town, follow the right fork, which meets up with the trail from the *gomba* in a few minutes to descend along the ridge.)

Reach the lowest *mani* wall in 15–20 minutes. The trail to the Bhote Kosi and on to Briddam via Ling Ling village drops down from the left side of this *mani* wall toward the ridge line. From the ridge line, fork left/north away from the ridge and down through the trees in the lush gully below the fields of Thuman. Rhododendron is abundant here. (The right/south fork from the *mani* wall descends down through the Bhote Kosi valley to Syabrubensi.)

Reach the bridge over the Bhote Kosi in less than 1½ hours from Thuman. Ascend from the bridge, and reach the lower end of the village of Ling Ling in 15 minutes. To ascend to Briddam, find the trailhead after passing a *mani* wall and lodge and before reaching a small stream. The route passes behind a house, then ascends between two more houses, through a field, and steeply up to a group of prayer flags. In 40 minutes the trail meets the trail from Timure that bypasses Ling Ling. Keep ascending and round another ridge with *chorten*. Briddam can be seen over on the other side of the hill. Drop down steeply to cross a stream over a cement bridge. Pass through trees and ascend up to **Briddam** in **3¼ hours** from Thuman. ❖

Corn, a staple mid-hills crop, is sometimes roasted at the hearth and eaten plain.
(Photo by Alonzo Lyons)

The trail from Thuman to Daahaal Phedi leaves from the north end of **Thuman**, contouring through the fields to the north. The trail passes old *mani* walls and in 15 minutes
crosses the stream that is the source of electricity for both Thuman and Daahaal Phedi;
the small hydroelectric station can be seen above. Continue along the hillside, passing
more old *mani* walls, to round a ridge. The trail climbs steeply along a path cut into the
stone face of the hill. Round another ridge with a *mani* wall and descend to a fork in the
trail. A rock here has a painted sign pointing the way to "DALPHEDI/TIMURE," the upper
trail, or "TIMURE," the lower trail circumventing Daahaal Phedi.

To continue on to Daahaal Phedi, take the upper route, eventually climbing steeply
to cross another ridge marked by a *chorten*. From here, the town of Timure can be seen
up the other side of the Bhote Kosi river valley, as well as the road to Tibet. The trail then
descends to **Daahaal Phedi**, passing below the school, reached in **1 hour 10 minutes**
from Thuman. Daahaal Phedi is a small Tamang village with scattered houses and few
facilities. Continue down from the village, passing houses and then dropping through
fields directly toward the river below. Reach a resting point marked by a tall wooden
flagpole in 15 minutes.

(To bypass Daahaal Phedi for a more direct route to Timure, take the lower route
at the junction en route from Thuman, marked with the painted rock sign indicating
"TIMURE," branching right to head downhill and around the hillside. Avoid any forks
to the right that descend to the river. This route eventually passes below the houses of
Daahaal Phedi. In 40 minutes the two routes tie in again near the resting point below
Daahaal Phedi, marked by a tall wooden flagpole.)

From the resting point, the trail descends steeply to the Bhote Kosi to reach a **suspension bridge** in **30 minutes**. On the other side of the river you enter the Langtang

National Park, as indicated by a park sign. From the bridge, head upriver shortly before ascending to the motor road above through rubble created in making the road. In 15 minutes from the bridge there is a built-up hot springs area (to the left/river side of the road) with three concrete pools built in the summer of 2009. Do not be surprised if the water is too hot for bathing; perhaps a way to cool the pools will be established in the future. Other problems at these and other hot springs include people washing clothes with detergent and leaving rubbish which accumulates and becomes unsightly. If you are hoping to find a glorious bathing spot, you will likely be disappointed.

Follow the road to reach **Timure** in 40 minutes from the suspension bridge over the river or **2½ hours** from Thuman. Timure (5781 feet, 1762 m) is a prosperous village with ample lodging and phone service and many facilities including a health post, school, army post, and police post. Sockets are available and electronic equipment can be charged here. However, hydroelectricity from the GhaTTe Khola is only available from evening to morning, approximately 5 PM to 9 AM. Solar power is also available when the hydropower is off line. Timure has long prospered as a hub of the ancient trade route from Tibet, as well as being along the new motor road. Large, whitewashed *mani* walls line the center of the village. The *gomba* sits just above the settlement. To reach it, pass by the police post along the way.

To continue on to GhaTTekholaa and Rasuwaa Gaadi at the border with Tibet, meet the trail as it leaves the upper end of Timure and follows along the motor road. Reach the army post and checkpost in a few minutes. Here bags are checked; due to sensitivities in the border area, cameras and mobile phones will be confiscated and held until you return, but perhaps not under the safest of conditions.

The road follows the Bhote Kosi to reach **GhaTTekholaa** in **20 minutes** from Timure. To avoid a stretch of the road, a trail leads away from the road just where the fields of GhaTTekholaa begin. This trail passes above the fields and into the village.

GhaTTekholaa is a small, colorful BhoTiya hamlet that does not see many tourists. Most houses have traditional wooden carvings and paintings around doors and windows. The village has hydroelectric power from the nearby stream of the same name; the power plant is just above the road out of town toward Rasuwaa Gaadi.

The mantra "*Om Mani Padme Hum*" is carved in Tibetan script in big, colorful letters on a large boulder in the center of the village (looking back from the path to the Timure side). A school and a *gomba* are at the top end of the hamlet, and there are a few shops but no other facilities here. Glimpses of snowy peaks can be seen from the village up the GhaTTe Khola valley.

A trail out of the upper/north end of the village crosses a suspension bridge over the GhaTTe Khola and then drops down to the road, which continues to follow the river up to **Rasuwaa Gaadi** (5955 feet, 1815 m), reached in **20 minutes** from GhaTTekholaa.

Rasuwaa is the name of a fort built in this area in 1912. Only the foundation remains. The Rasuwaa District of Nepal, which includes the Tamang Heritage Trail and Langtang National Park, is named after this fort. It lies at the confluence of the Lendi Khola and Kerong Khola, which join to form the Bhote Kosi. The road to Tibet passes up through the Kerong River valley. On the Nepalese side, simple lodging is available along with a few shops stocked mainly with Chinese snack foods. An area for camping is available below the shops and the remains of the fort.

There is a suspension footbridge and a bridge for vehicles over the Lendi Khola. Both bridges have gates blocking free passage across. The first gate of the suspension bridge is located midway across the bridge. At this point a Chinese soldier will come to meet you to see if you have proper documents to pass into Chinese territory. The Chinese

Apples have been introduced at Khaidi village along the high route between Timure and Briddam. (Photo by Tokozile Robbins)

side is much more built up than the Nepali side and has heavy security in the presence of soldiers.

The return route to Timure is the same way, along the road. From Timure, there are two routes to reach Briddam. The lower route begins by following the road back down past the hot springs. Alternatively, there is a high route leaving from Timure village, and if you do not mind a few steep inclines and descents, then this high trail avoids the motor road and is more scenic and is 1¼–1½ hours longer.

Timure to Briddam along the High Route via Khaidi

To head to Briddam, the trail departs from **Timure** at the lower end of a mid-village *mani* wall and passes by the police post just below the *gomba*. The route follows power-lines most of the way to Khaidi as it ascends steeply uphill before contouring more gradually. Pass below a school before reaching the few houses of Khaidi (7480 feet, 2280 m) in 1¼–1½ hours from Timure. There is a tea shop here and a small veterinary clinic where animal husbandry workshops take place, but few other facilities. Fresh apples, peaches, and plums might be available depending upon the season.

(From Khaidi, a path leads a few hours higher to Gumling, where there is a *gomba*, and beyond that to a seasonal pasture area known as Braanga Kharka at about 10,500 feet (3200 m), with spectacular views. However, no facilities are available, and trekkers must be self-sufficient in food and shelter to ascend higher from Khaidi.)

Continue onward by contouring and entering a tributary valley. The trail passes above a rock face and then descends steeply down the valley wall to a bridge over the **Phenglung Khola** in **1 hour**.

The route onward from this bridge to Briddam is a lesser-traveled path with relatively few other users. The next section may be difficult to follow, as foliage often closes in on the trail; this also makes it particularly leech-infested during the monsoon season.

Ascend and contour through a wooded area. Be conscientious to follow the widest path, as there are several offshoots to the main trail. The trail eventually rounds a ridge with a *chorten* and ties in with a lower path arriving from Pelku as it descends to the Briddam Khola. Two bridges span the stream, side by side, one steel and the other cement. From this crossing (over the bridge of your choice), **Briddam** is a 5–10-minute ascent and **1¾ hours** from the Phenglung Khola crossing. ❖

Timure to Briddam along the Low Route

As you follow the motor road from **Timure**, it is possible to catch a trail that contours along the hillside above the road for some time rather than walking along the road itself. This trail can be found approximately 5 minutes downriver from the hot springs and branches to the left/east side of the road. However, this trail or parts of it will likely come into discontinuance once the road gains prominence.

Follow this trail above the road and river to reach a bridge in 1 hour from Timure. After 30 more minutes the trail branches in two. The upper path ascends to Briddam while the lower passes through the village of Ling Ling, reached in another 5 minutes.

The upper path ascends through the small village of Pelku with a tea shop and simple lodge. Keep ascending and avoid any forks along this trail that head lower. Cross a stream straddled by a prayer wheel and then round a ridge marked with prayer flags. Keep ascending and round another ridge with *chorten*. Briddam can be seen on the other side of the hill. Drop down steeply to cross a stream over a cement bridge. Pass through trees and ascend to **Briddam** (7218 feet, 2200 m) in approximately **2¾ hours** from Timure.

Briddam is a large village with lodges and many options for home stay. A number is assigned to each participating home-stay house. Signs are posted on the houses with the number as well as the names of the owners. Electricity is available 24 hours per day (power cuts notwithstanding) along with sockets for charging electronic devices.

A health post and primary school are also located here, and a *gomba* lies at the top of town. Another older and smaller *gomba* is built around an overhanging rock a few minutes farther up/east from the village. Inside, the main figure is Guru Rimpoche, also known as Padmasambava. To get to this *gomba*, follow the trail from the central village area up toward the main *gomba*. The trail branches to the right just before reaching the houses and a community center next to the main *gomba*, and passes behind the houses and through fields to this older *gomba* a few minutes beyond. ❖

W *Side Trip from Briddam Village to Gottegang Kharka. This is a long, arduous day trip from* **Briddam** *involving a 3500-foot-plus (1100 m-plus) ascent and return descent. You'll enjoy breathtaking views from the pasture at the top, while finding no facilities and scant water resources along the way, and few to no other people on the trail.*

Find the trail at the top of the village to the right of the houses that lie before the main gomba. *Pass behind the houses and to the left of the smaller, older* gomba *which is just above and marked by prayer flags. The trail ascends to reach a ridge in less than 10 minutes where it forks. Take the lower, left trail down to Briddam Khola and cross branches of the stream twice on wooden bridges before ascending steeply up the opposite hill to cross a ridge marked by prayer flags. Briefly contour to the next ridge and then ascend steeply, following this ridge to pass through lush forest abundant with rhododendron. Eventually, contour northeast through pine, enjoying views west and north along the way.*

Reach an open meadow in **2½–3 hours** *from Briddam. Seasonal* goTh *huts used by summer herders dot the meadow.* **Gottegang** *is considered to be the area at the top of the meadow. However, the trail up becomes overrun by grazing tracks. Take care to notice where you leave the main trail behind so as to be able to find it on return, especially if the weather deteriorates. Make your way up to a large rock at the top of the meadow marked with a cairn and prayer flags for the best views (11,066 feet, 3373 m, GPS coordinates, N 28° 12.537′, E 085° 23.156′). Dhunche can be seen down the valley and Naagthaali and Paldor Peak to the west, as well as the Kerong range to the north in Tibet. From Gottegang, the trail ascends farther to more* goTh *of Pangsang, but you must be self-sufficient to continue as there are no facilities.*

BRIDDAM TO KHANGJIM

The trail from Briddam to Khangjim departs from the upper, southeast corner of **Briddam** and ascends gradually to cross a ridge and then passes through an archway in 15 minutes near a rest area. From here, the wide trail gradually descends through forest.

In another 10 minutes (**25 minutes** from Briddam), reach a **fork**. The upper trail continues to Khangjim and the upper Langtang valley; the lower trail descends to Wangal and on to Syabrubensi.

ALTERNATE ROUTE ---

Direct Route to Wangal and Syabrubensi

To head directly from Briddam to Syabrubensi, where buses can be found to Kathmandu, take the right fork to Wangal and descend through a lush forested area with prime views across the valley of the Chilime Khola. Thaambuchet is the village seen at the head of the Chilime valley, alongside which lies the Chilime hydropower plant.

JEWELRY: NECKLACES AND BANGLES

Necklace designs are shared among many groups. There may be large gold beads, lac-filled for strength and lightness, strung with coral, glass, or layers of velvet circles between them. While the necklaces were once silver, the trend is away from it to gold.

A *tilhari*, a long, cylindrical, repoussé gold bead that hangs in the center of a few to a hundred strands of fine colored glass beads (seed beads), is worn by married Hindu women. Red, followed by green, are the most popular color beads.

The most commonly worn necklaces are composed of multiple strands of small glass beads (*pote*). With the availability of Czechoslovakian and Japanese beads, color choices number in the hundreds. Necklaces may be choker length with just a few strands, or may hang to the hips and have numerous strands.

The most significant color is red, the color of marriage and fertility. Among the Hindu castes, the

Various necklaces adorn this lady living south of Makalu.
(Photo by Stephen Bezruchka)

bridegroom placing a necklace of red *pote* in combination with the application of red powder (*sindur*) in the part of the hair constitutes the most important act in the wedding ceremony. The red beads are the sign of a woman whose husband is alive. When a woman becomes widowed, the beads are discarded.

BhoTiya wear big pieces of coral (often imitation) and turquoise (almost always real) as well as large black and white *dzi* beads. *Dzi* protect the wearer from stroke and lightning. They are believed to have a supernatural origin as creatures (worms) that were petrified by the contamination of human touch, but retain some of their supernatural power. BhoTiya will also wear small prayer boxes of gold and silver, often with bits of turquoise and fine filigree work. Colored, knotted strings, blessings from lamas, are also worn.

Many women wear bangles of gold, silver, and Indian glass on the wrists. Red is the most auspicious color, and the clinking is considered mildly erotic. Ankles are less commonly decorated than in the past. The Tharu in the Tarai may wear hollow or solid heavy anklets. Hill ethnic groups used to wear dragon-like (*makar* or *singha mukh*) designs. Anklets display high relief when new, but wear down over the years to become almost smooth. Some may wear similar pieces on the wrist. Gold, a divine metal, sacred to Vishnu, is rarely worn below the waist (the more impure division of the body), so these are usually silver. ❖

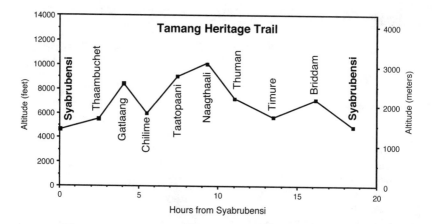

Continue descending through pine, and in less than 1 hour from the junction south of Briddam, the trail narrows and descends steeply for 15–20 more minutes before coming to a fork. The trail to the left ascends past a school and on to Khangjim; the right fork leads down to **Wangal** (5358 feet, 1633 m) a few minutes below, **1½–1¾ hours** from Briddam. Wangal has a tea shop and simple lodge with solar power but no other facilities. The trail to Syabrubensi heads south out of the village. Descend gradually following along the river below and reach the older part of **Syabrubensi** in **40 minutes**.) Here, continue up the Langtang Khola valley (see Chapter 8 for a description) or cross the Bhote Kosi on a suspension bridge to continue on to the newer part of Syabrubensi on the western side of the Trishuli River. A hot springs lies below along the banks of the Trishuli River. It has five concrete bathing pools which may or may not have water but are likely to be in disrepair and a bit polluted.

Buses to Kathmandu depart three times daily at 7 AM, 7:30 AM, and the last bus departs around 9 AM after first arriving from Thaambuchet (times are subject to change). ❖

Langtang Trek via Khangjim

To continue on to Khangjim to meet the trail to the upper Langtang valley, take the upper/left path at the **fork** which leads to Khangjim. Ascend through forest (avoid trails heading lower) before descending slightly to a ridge marked by a *chorten*; from here Khangjim is visible a short distance away. Syabrubensi is also visible far below at the confluence of the Bhote Kosi and Langtang Khola which join to form the Trishuli Khola. There are also views up the Chilime Khola valley from this point. **Khangjim** (7480 feet, 2280 m) is reached in **30 minutes** from the junction or under **1 hour** from Briddam.

Here the Tamang Heritage Trail ties in with the more popular Langtang trek. Khangjim has satellite dishes, a renovated *gomba*, as well as abundant lodging, and batteries can be recharged as well. Above town is a Tibetan refugee camp. (See the Langtang section of Chapter 8 for a continuation of route descriptions from Khangjim for either a return to Syabrubensi or a journey into the upper Langtang valley.) ❖

INDIGENOUS PEOPLES TRAIL

(Map No. 8)

This culturally diverse trail covers beautiful terrain in Nepal's mid-hills east of Kathmandu. Jointly developed by the Ramechap Economic Development Forum and the United Nations' International Labor Organization, the trail was "launched" in October 2009 by the Nepal Tourism Board but as of yet has seen few tourists. Ethnicities prevalent along this route include Sherpa, Tamang, Thami, Majhi, Newar, and Yolmo. Among these groups, the Thami and Majhi are rarely encountered on trekking routes.

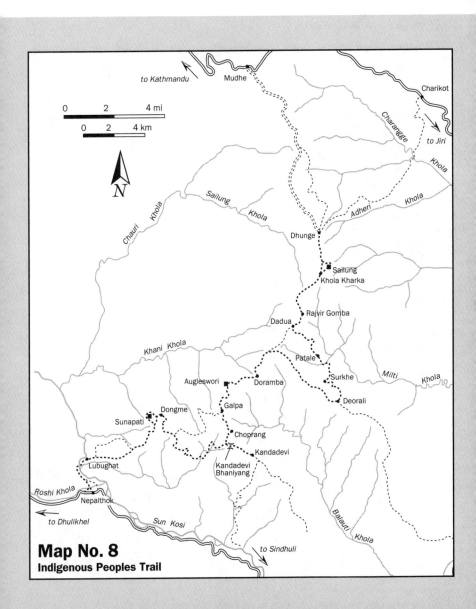

Map No. 8
Indigenous Peoples Trail

The Thami are unique to this region and, with a total Nepalese population of less than 30,000, their culture is considered endangered. The Majhi, with a Nepalese population under 75,000, traditionally make a living near rivers through fishing and as boat people, mostly in the inner Tarai along the southern belt of Nepal bordering India.

There are community lodges and home stay along the way, providing closer contact with Nepali hospitality and greater insight into ethnic lifestyles than can be found along the more developed trekking routes where interactions are more commercially oriented. This enchanting mid-hills trek is located entirely in the Mahabharat range, with picturesque vantages of the Himalaya at several hilltop lookouts and along much of the

Once off the beaten track there are many different kinds of bridges in use.
(Photo by Stephen Bezruchka)

WEDDINGS

Hindu weddings can be observed almost any time, but most are held during the months of January and February. Wedding parties travel to and from the bride's house, sometimes over a long distance and for several days. In rural villages, weddings are loud, colorful affairs accompanied by hornpipers, drummers, and dancers. Wealthy city weddings often include professional bands, and the house where the wedding feast is held is decorated with strings of lights at night. Hindu marriages are traditionally arranged by the parents of the couple; horoscopes are compared by a priest, and an auspicious date is set. Dowries are often demanded, and can be quite expensive. Child marriage is now prohibited but still occurs and was traditionally the norm among orthodox Hindus.

Buddhist weddings in the hills and mountains are less elaborate, more relaxed affairs, with great attention paid to ostentatious display and reciprocity in gift giving. Among Sherpas, for example, a wedding is preceded, sometimes years earlier, by betrothal rites and often by the birth of a child. There is much drinking and dancing. Monks from a nearby monastery attend to the actual ceremonial activities.

Today, throughout Nepal, the customs surrounding the securing of a marriage partner are relaxed compared with the past. Love marriage and marriage between castes and ethnic groups are not uncommon. Nonetheless, arranged marriages of alliance between families in proper caste or ethnic categories are regularly contracted, especially among the more orthodox Hindus. ❖

route. The highest elevation reached is 10,325 feet (3147 m), thus it is an all-season trek. However, be aware that, despite the relatively low elevation, the first part of the trek takes you to the highest point of the route in a brief period of time, with an attendant risk of AMS. People who feel mild symptoms of altitude illness should descend immediately if symptoms worsen (see Chapter 5 for more information on altitude sickness). At the other, lower end of the route, the last village, Lubughat (1755 feet, 535 m), might be excessively hot, especially outside of the winter months; fortunately it lies along the cool waters of the Sun Kosi.

DHUNGE TO KANDADEVI

The route lies mainly in Ramechap District but begins in Dolakha District at Dhunge village. A direct bus to Dhunge departs from the Old Bus Park near Ratna Park in Kathmandu between 6 and 6:30 AM (times are subject to change). The road follows the same overland route to Solu–Khumbu up to the town of Mudhe, reached in 4 hours. Here the road diverges along a rough dirt track to arrive at the hamlet of Dhunge (8123 feet, 2476 m) in less than 2 more hours with outstanding views of the broad expanse of Gauri Shankar (the mountain devoted to the God-couple Parvati, also known as Gauri, and Shiva, also known as Shankar) and more along the way. The road continues to Khola Kharka; however, the bus disgorges its contents at Dhunge and goes no farther.

From the bus stop in **Dhunge**, do not follow the road to the right/south but ascend stone steps to the southeast. Keep to the stone staircase, criss-crossing another road (which leads to a village named Ghaledanda).

🏕 **Side Trip to Caves.** *To visit two caves away from the main route, then in less than 20 minutes from* **Dhunge,** *follow the road to the left away from the ascending trail. Contour along this road and within 10 minutes pass a home with a workshop for making Tibetan Buddhist idols, which might be on display. Another 15 minutes farther along this road, take a trail that branches to the right just before crossing a small tributary. Follow the trail up this stream and shortly (**45 minutes** from Dunghe) reach a cave with an aperture in the rock called a "dharma gate." Locals believe that only the pure in heart are able to climb through the hole (there is another such "gate" at a cave closer to Sailung peak). The trail continues up the stream and in 5 minutes reaches a* **cave** *with a stalagmite that is worshipped as a shrine to Mahadev (another name for Shiva) and is purported to drip milk once every twelve years, an event celebrated by the local people.*

To continue to Kalopani from here, the trail heads upstream; keep to the right a minute from the cave, then ascend steeply up to a ridgeline (the trail to the ridgeline might be faint and difficult to find). Head left/west along the ridgeline to reach Kalopani) in **30 minutes** *from the cave.*

Continuing along the ascending trail, reach **Kalopani** (9137 feet, 2785 m) and a tea shop and basic lodging in less than **45 minutes** from Dhunge and enjoy a beautiful panorama of the snowy Himalaya to the north and east. The trail continues through rhododendron and pine and in less than 30 minutes reaches a boulder on the right adorned with scarves and flowers, locally known as DAAphe Dhunga, or "rock that looks like a *DAAphe*" (the *DAAphe*, or Impeyan pheasant, *Lophophorus impejanus*, is the national bird of Nepal). As the story goes, residents near Kailingchok Peak, across the way in Dolakha District, were in dispute with those living closer to Sailung Peak as to which peak was higher. To settle the matter, a *DAAphe* was released from each summit. Both birds flew in a straight line, and the bird released from Sailung passed above Kailingchok, whereas the bird released from Kailingchok reached a level below Sailung Peak. It is said to have landed at the very point of DAAphe Dhunga, and the boulder immortalizes the legend. (Incidentally, Kalingchok is nearly 12,100 feet [3700 m], or some 1800 feet [550 m] higher than Sailung.)

In 5 minutes beyond the boulder there is a junction with a trail leading left to another set of caves. At this junction there is a legend regarding the hillock immediately to the north, regarding a hole in the ground at the top of it. Locals say that the wishes of a petitioner will be fulfilled if the hole can be reached and rounded three times without breathing from the base of the hillock. This is a 50-yard uphill distance at an altitude of nearly 9800 feet (3000 m)!

🏕 **Side Trip to Caves.** *Take the left fork from the junction to visit three caves, a round trip of* **20 minutes,** *not including time exploring the caves. In 3 minutes the trail diverges; stay right and then stay right again in 2 more minutes to reach Devithan Cave (9636 feet, 2937 m) 1 minute beyond. The second cave, Meha Devitan, is 2 minutes farther below with a stalagmite believed to emit milk once every twelve years (similar to the cave near Kalopani). Sailung Cave is another 2 minutes below with a "dharma gate" similar to the one near Kalopani, allowing only pure-hearted supplicants to pass through. To return to the trail juncture, follow the same route in reverse.*

Continue straight from the junction. Just beyond the junction the trail branches; stay to the right. A few minutes more is a large rock; on its top is the impression of a sword said to have been used for revenge in a case of adultery. Just beyond this rock the trail diverges; again stay to the right. In another 10 minutes the trail forks again. The right fork leads directly to Khola Kharka, bypassing the summit of Sailung. The left fork reaches **Sailung Peak** (10,325 feet, 3147 m) in **1 hour** from Kalopani, passing an adorned rock said to contain Guru Rimpoche's foot imprints. Enjoy the magnificent views from either the higher peak or rounded slightly lower peak, both topped with *chorten*. On the lower peak are two other structures, used during festivals. Sailung summit is on the boundary line between Dolakha District and Ramechap District. According to locals, there are over 130 different *jaDibuTi* (medicinal herbs) found in the Sailung area.

The trail leads down to the south, and just below the summit goes by three rock formations said to represent a tiger, a mother cow, and her baby—the mother cow has come between the tiger and the calf to protect it from being devoured. **Khola Kharka** (9678 feet, 2950 m) lies **20 minutes** below Sailung, with several shops and a well-equipped community lodge just below.

The route continues southwest, following either the road or a trail that crisscrosses the road to reach **Rajvir Gomba** (8661 feet, 2640 m) in **45 minutes** where rooms might be available. Continue along the road to **Dadua** (8018 feet, 2444 m), a Sherpa village with a *thangka* painting school run by a Tamang couple, in **30 minutes** more. Follow the motor road to the south, and in just over 5 minutes the trail breaks off to the left/ southeast from the road to contour through fields on the east side of a ridge. Eventually, pass to the west side of the ridge and then generally follow the ridgeline south before descending to the right 40 minutes from leaving the road. Reach the Tamang village of **Patale** (6890 feet, 2100 m) in another 10 minutes (under **1 hour** from Dadua). There are two small *gomba* in this village. Continue along the ridgeline for 20 minutes before dropping steeply to the Patale Khola in 10 more minutes. Along the way, avoid a trail to the left that contours around the hill to a suspension bridge over the Tin Dhare Khola, unless you would like a bird's-eye view from this bridge of a waterfall below it.

Cross the **Patale Khola** (5725 feet, 1745 m) to its south side; there is no bridge. Just below this crossing, this tributary joins with the Tin Dhare tributary to form the Milti Khola. Ascend steeply, enjoying views of the waterfall on the Tin Dhare Khola across the way. In a little over 10 minutes the trail contours to the southeast. At this point, avoid trails that ascend. Cross another tributary and reach **Surkhe** (5906 feet, 1800 m), a Newar village in **30 minutes** from crossing the river. Home stay has been established here.

Contour to the southeast and cross a tributary in 15 minutes, then take the trail to the left and fork left again a few minutes farther to arrive at the Thami (also known as Thangmi) village of **Tin Ghare** (6004 feet, 1830 m) in **20–25 minutes** from Surkhe. The Thami have their own language, which is of the Tibeto-Burman family and lacks a script. They follow a shamanistic belief system with Buddhist, Bon, and Hindu influences. They are well known for weaving skills, and live mainly in Ramechap and Dolakha Districts.

To continue on to Deorali, head 5 minutes back in the direction of Surkhe up to a junction passed earlier and this time ascend to reach a school (6168 feet, 1880 m) within 10 minutes. Take the trail to the left at the school, then turn right just beyond to ascend along a deeply cut trail. Reach **Deorali** (6758 feet, 2060 m) in 35 more minutes, **50 minutes** from Tin Ghare. Deorali is a small bazaar with basic lodging that sits on a ridgeline along a motor road. Follow the road to the northwest past *chorten* and continue along the road with trail shortcuts along the way. After **1¾–2 hours** from Deorali reach a large **memorial** (7119 feet, 2170 m) built by the Maoists along the ridge top. This is the site of the so-called Doramba Massacre when

The scene from a balcony of a mid-hills village (Photo by Mark Jackson and Susan Bergin/ SAFA Himalaya Collection/Nepal)

the Nepalese Army killed nineteen people, eighteen of whom were believed to be Maoists, in August 2003.

The road continues on to Doramba bazaar, but in a few minutes from the memorial take the trail that branches to the left to descend from the road. Cross a tributary in under 30 minutes and stay to the right. Reach **Doramba Bazaar** (6739 feet, 2054 m) with a simple lodge in less than 30 more minutes, and the village with home stay 10 minutes below the bazaar (**3–3¼ hours** from Deorali). This is one of the largest Tamang settlements in Nepal. A barbed-wire fence surrounds the *gomba*, which lies on the west side of the village.

To head to Augleswori Peak and lookout point, you can ascend the hill behind the *gomba* to the road above in less than 15 minutes and then follow the road to the left. Alternatively, from the main Doramba bazaar, follow straight along the road to the south, passing a health post in 10 minutes. Another 5 minutes brings you to where the trail from the *gomba* ties in with the road. Ten minutes farther along, the road diverges. Stay with the road to the left, and a few minutes beyond follow the trail that climbs to the left side above the road. This shortcut passes near a small Hindu temple housing a rock Shiva-*lingam* where animals are sacrificed.

The trail meets back up with the road and continues to make a shortcut of the road along the way. In 30 more minutes reach a point where the trail branches to the right from the road. From here, a large boulder is visible below to the right. The local deity Augleswori Mahadev is believed to reside there. It is a 10–15-minute descent to reach this festooned boulder where ceremonies are performed during festivals.

The road does not reach the lookout point. Instead, ascend on the trail to the right to **Augleswori Peak** (7887 feet, 2404 m) in 10 minutes (**70 minutes** from Doramba) with a commanding vantage of the snowy sentinels to the northeast and the Mahabharat range and Tarai to the southwest.

There is a faint path from the lookout point to the southwest that leads down to Galpa. Otherwise, descend back to the road and follow it for 30 minutes to where a trail branches to the right to pass through a serene pine forest as it descends to **Galpa** (6519 feet, 1987 m) in just over 10 more minutes (**45 minutes** from Augleswori Peak). Galpa is a busy bazaar at a crossroads. There are restaurants, lodging, and a medical shop here.

Several roads intersect here and it might be unclear as to how to proceed from Galpa. It might be necessary to ask for the way. To continue to Kandadevi, head along the road to the left/southeast from the the point where the trail from Augleswori Peak arrives at Galpa. Descend gently before contouring and reach a few tea shops in **30 minutes**. Just beyond you begin to pass through the upper reaches of the scenic, spread-out village of **Choprang** which overlooks the broad valley below. Ascend to another set of tea shops at a pass, **Kandadevi Bhanjyang** (6693 feet, 2040 m), in **30 minutes**. Do not head to the right or left here, but follow the road, which will fork just beyond, and then stay with the wide path to the left/east. Reach the Tamang hamlet of **Kandadevi** in **35 minutes** more, **1 hour 35 minutes** from Galpa.

The Kandadevi Hindu temple complex sits just above the village, and it is here that animal sacrifices are made year-round. The tradition of sacrifice began five-and-a-half centuries ago. The eight *pujare*, individuals who do the slaughtering, reside in the village and are on a four-day rotation. The position of *pujare* is inherited and is not lucrative according to the *pujare*, most of whom consider themselves Buddhist. Sacrifices are performed when people bring the animals to the temple, and people pay as they deem fit to the *pujare* while sometimes nothing is given. The local community consumes the meat of the slaughtered animals. Twice yearly, the *pujare* are mandated by the Nepalese government to use the money collected throughout the year to purchase animals that they themselves have to offer sacrificially.

Most people bring animals in the morning around 9–10 AM, and the busiest sacrificial days are Mondays, Thursdays, and Saturdays. According to the contested interpretation of Hinduism, where sacrifice is appeasing (many Hindus are appalled by this practice), goddesses rather than gods are the recipients of animal sacrifice. The complex has the following five blood-spattered points of sacrifice, named according to the goddess to whom the sacrifice is made: Kandadevi takes sacrifices of ducks (and duck eggs) and goats; Mangaladevi, rooster (and chicken eggs); Bhairungdevi, buffalo; Komaladevi, pigeon; and Ganeshdevi, hen (and chicken eggs).

KANDADEVI TO NEPALTHOK

To travel on from **Kandadevi** to Dongme (Hildevi), return to the tea shops at **Kandadevi Bhanjyang** pass in **35 minutes** and then follow the road toward Galpa. In 5 minutes from the shops, the trail to Dongme breaks to the left/west from the road and climbs. Enter a pine forest as you reach a *chautaaraa* and prayer flag-lined *chorten* (6637 feet, 2023 m) within 15 minutes from the road. Continue to the right from the *chorten*, and in 20 minutes emerge from the forest and cross a ridge (6752 feet, 2058 m). Continue east to reach a pass (7152 feet, 2180 m) in 15 more minutes.

Sunapati hill and Dongme can be seen off in the distance to the west. Descend to the west through more pine. In less than 5 minutes take the trail to the left at a junction and reach another junction a few minutes later. Continue straight/southwest rather than ascend to the left/south or descend to the right/north. Contour along the hillside. Shiva Rock is the name given to the large boulder seen below to the left in a streambed. Reach a pass in 5 minutes and continue straight as you contour to the west. Reach houses of Saura Danda in 10–15 more minutes; from there stay left and continue to contour.

Many trails intersect the route along the way; therefore, follow the widest trail and if needed, ask locally for directions to Dongme. Reach a *mani* wall near a pond named Pangling Pokhari just below a government school in 50 more minutes. The village of **Dongme** (6503 feet, 1982 m), a cluster of houses along with a community lodge, is just beyond (**2¾ –3 hours** from Kandadevi). There is a *gomba* behind the lodge, and below the *gomba* is a *thangka* painting school.

To climb to the lookout atop of Sunapati hill, which lies to the west of Dongme village, head west between two sets of *chorten* above the government school. The path wends around to the north of the hill and then comes up to **Sunapati Peak** (7165 feet, 2184 m) from the north side in **45 minutes**, passing four *chorten* a few minutes before reaching the summit. There is a Hindu temple at the top and views in every direction with the Himalaya visible from Dhaulagiri to Rolwaling. The village of Lubughat lies over 5000 feet (1500 m) below to the west along the banks of the Sun Kosi or Gold River. The shimmering, prominent river coming in from the west is the Roshi Khola, which joins with the Sun Kosi. Just below, between Sunapati Peak and the Sun Kosi, a U.N. helicopter crashed in March 2008 and all ten people aboard perished.

Head south to descend to the **pass** along the road in **10 minutes** from Sunapati Peak. The way to Lubughat from the pass is complicated; however, a new trail is planned and may be in place by the time of publication. Otherwise, the road can be followed with the trail making shortcuts here and there, mostly following the southern ridge of the valley that was seen from atop Sunapati. **Lubughat** (1755 feet, 535 m), with a large market, is reached in **2¾ –3 hours** from the pass. Chettri, Newar, and Tamang are the predominant ethnicities here, with a few Majhi residents as well. Food and lodging is available.

A few minutes to the south of the village is a long sandy beach, and a 10-minute climb farther along the path that follows the river brings you to a Majhi village (1886 feet, 575 m). Customarily, the Majhi are riparian and most live near the waterways of the inner Tarai. The traditional occupations of the Majhi are boating and river transport,

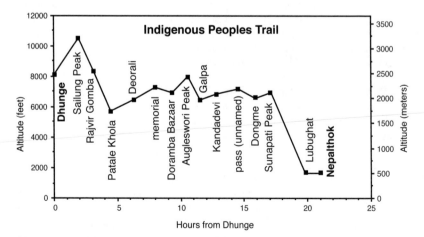

as well as fishing done primarily for their own sustenance. However, modernization of Nepal has meant a ubiquity of bridges and pollution of waterways, which make the Majhi way of life more and more obsolete. With a decreasing livelihood, they are encountering deeper impoverishment. The Majhi have one of the lowest literacy rates in Nepal but little influence in government affairs, and thus a history of being exploited by more empowered ethnicities.

To head to **Nepalthok** from Lubughat, cross to the west bank of the Sun Kosi on a suspension bridge (1765 feet, 538 m) and climb to the road above where you head left to follow the river downstream. Pass through Bandaribesi, a Tamang village, reaching the Roshi Khola in **35 minutes.** Head upstream for a few minutes to where you may have to wade across to the south bank to Nepalthok a few minutes beyond, or use a suspension bridge less than 5 minutes farther upstream. Buses are available to Banepa on the outskirts of the Kathmandu valley, passing through Dhulikhel along the way. Banepa lies on the Arniko Highway, which links the valley and the Tibet Autonomous Region of China, and there are many buses available from Banepa onward to Kathmandu.

CHITWAN CHEPANG HILLS TRAIL
(Map No. 9, Page 346)

The Chepang ethnic group (also known as Chyobang and Praja), primarily in the Chitwan Hills, previously had a system of communal ownership of land but subsequently became landless due to encroachment by other ethnic groups and an inability to document ownership. Population pressure and reduced forest size have further threatened their domain and endangered their traditional way of life. Chepang have a history of being exploited but have recently found support from the government as well as non-governmental agencies with an improvement in welfare for some members, although poverty is still endemic.

Previously, Chepang engaged in slash-and-burn agriculture and were hunter-gatherers with a nomadic lifestyle, at times subsisting on roots and general foraging. Nowadays, many Chepang have settled in villages and have adopted horticulture with progressive agricultural methods. However, many still engage in nomadic practices, especially outside of growing seasons, often relying on forest resources and even hunting with bow and arrow.

Chepang are generally animist in belief but have integrated Hindu customs into their faith and observe Hindu festivals as well; however, in some areas, it is evident that Christian missionaries have been proselytizing. Chepang have an egalitarian social framework without chieftains and little to no ranking, unlike the majority of Nepal's ethnic groups. Their own distinct language is of the Tibeto-Burman family and is one of a few, rare languages of the world that follow the duodecimal counting system with a base of twelve (rather than the decimal with a base of ten).

Other ethnicities predominant along this route include the Giripuri (subgroup of Chhetri), Magar, Bahun, and Newar. This pristine trail is an ideal choice for those seeking genuine cultural insight away from the more popular, commercialized routes. Home stay will be required, as very few tourists visit this trail and facilities have not been constructed. It is a lower-elevation trek, which makes it a pleasant option during the winter months, but it can be exceedingly hot at other times. This trek can be conveniently combined with a visit to the World Heritage Site (Natural) of Chitwan National Park.

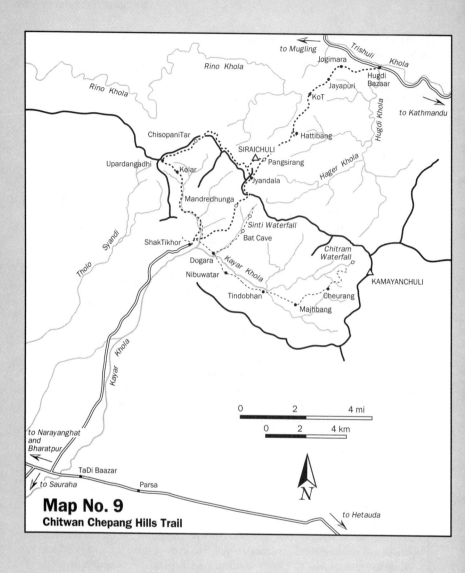

Map No. 9
Chitwan Chepang Hills Trail

HUGDI BAZAAR TO JYANDALA

The trail begins from **Hugdi Bazaar** (965 feet, 294 m), a small village located on the highway, the Prithvi Rajmarg, between Kathmandu and Pokhara. Hugdi Bazaar is 50 miles (80 km) from Kathmandu (13 miles/21 km from Mugling and 71 miles/114 km from Pokhara) and located just after the village of MajimTar and the bridge over the Hugdi Khola near its confluence with the Trishuli River. The bus journey from Kathmandu takes up to 3 to 4 hours because the steep, twisting Thangkot escarpment, encountered just after leaving the Kathmandu valley, is slow going and usually full of traffic. This highway up to Mugling, halfway to Pokhara, is the main artery out of Kathmandu for vehicles traveling east, west, and south to India. Roads are planned

346

for a direct route to the Tarai to a possible new international airport in Bara District as well as to eastern Nepal. Until these new highways are completed, this current route is likely to remain clogged with buses and trucks.

There is a small visitor information center in Hugdi Bazaar on the east/Trishuli River side of the highway. The trail ascends from the west side of the highway and follows along a ridgeline. Climb steadily to reach the first houses of **Laitak** (1870 feet, 570 m), with Chepang and Newar inhabitants, in **30 minutes**. A few minutes above is a trail signboard and small shop. Stay along the ridgeline and in 20 minutes pass a school. Just above the school, pass a small Hindu temple, and in 10 minutes pass another small shop and the start of the Bahun village of **Jogimara** (2657 feet, 810 m), **30 minutes** from Laitak. Jogimara is widely spread out along the ridgeline. After passing more shops and another school (3215 feet, 980 m), continue along the ridgeline, heading south from the school. In less than 5 minutes from the school (**30 minutes** from Jogimara), the trail splits. Do not fork to the left or right but stay straight and ascend to **Jayapuri** (3609 feet, 1100 m) with several shops in under 30 minutes from the school. Another half hour along the trail, with sounds and view of a quarry below to the north, brings you to a *chautaaraa* next to the small **Tripashwori Temple** (4298 feet, 1310 m), **1 hour** from the school.

The trail keeps along the ridge and then to the east of it to reach **KoT** (4482 feet, 1366 m) in 15 minutes from the temple. From KoT, do not fork to the right, but continue ascending south along the ridge before contouring along its west side. Avoid a branch to the left in 15 minutes; stay right and cross to the east side of the ridge for a short while and then back to the west to descend slightly to thread through fields along a notch. Continue by contouring through a slide area on the east side of the ridge. Pass a simple tea shop and follow the wide trail to reach **Hattibang** (4705 feet, 1434 m), where Magar and Chepang are prevalent, in **1 hour** from KoT (3¾ hours from Hugdi Bazaar). You have entered Chitwan District and are at roughly the same elevation as Kathmandu. Home stay is available here.

The trail departs from Hattibang from above the school at the south end of town. Take the wide path to the right/southwest and ascend for a few minutes, then descend to cross a stream (4757 feet, 1450 m) just below. Follow the stream for 20 minutes, crossing it several times. Eventually, just downstream from where two feeder streams have joined, cross to

Shamans enter into a trance and the afflicted spirit speaks about what must be done to get well. (Photo by Stephen Bezruchka)

the south or true right (TR) side. This trail to the left ascends over a boulder that will be slick if damp. The trail then follows the left/south-side feeder stream. Ascend through lush and damp subtropical vegetation, best dealt with in the morning before sunlight hits this gully.

Reach a ridge crest and rest area named **Pangsirang** (5558 feet, 1694 m) in another 25 minutes (less than **1 hour** from Hattibang); head right from here. (A 10-minute climb in the other direction, to the left/east, reveals a viewpoint (5643 feet, 1720 m) with a broad outlook, including a panorama of the mountains to the north.) Just beyond the rest area is a trail signboard providing two options: traveling directly to Jyandala village or summiting Siraichuli Peak en route. Both options are described below. However, most people prefer to reach Siraichuli around sunrise or sunset for an eye-catching light show on the snowy Himalayan range.

ALTERNATE
ROUTE

To Jyandala via Siraichuli

From the signpost, to the right is the lesser-used path that goes directly to **Siraichuli**, the highest point in Chitwan. The path ascends steeply to reach the summit (6338 feet, 1932 m, N 27° 45.740' E 084° 37.875'), in **30 minutes**. There is a small temple on top as well as a 360° commanding vantage. To head on to the Chepang village of Jyandala from here, descend steeply to the south and in 30 minutes reach a trail junction. Continue straight to cross over the ridge to descend to **Jyandala** in 10 more minutes (**40 minutes** from the summit). ◈

To bypass Siraichuli and head from the signpost at Pangsirang directly to Jyandala, a walk of **25 minutes**, take the lower, left trail. Tread carefully, as the trail passes through sections with sheer drop-offs. In 20 minutes the trail forks. Stay right and contour to **Jyandala** (5361 feet, 1634 m). Home stay is available in this Chepang hamlet.

JYANDALA TO SHAKTIKHOR

There are two routes to ShakTikhor, a large bazaar town with bus service. The more scenic route passes through prime bird-watching forest and visits the ruins of an old fort. The direct route is described as an alternative for people with less time or as part of a circuit from ShakTikhor to Jyandala.

ALTERNATE
ROUTE

Direct Route from Jyandala to ShakTikhor

To head directly to ShakTikhor from Jyandala, continue to the southwest and in 15 minutes reach a school at a pass (5459 feet, 1664 m). Enjoy another view of the mountains from here before heading down to the southwest along the west side of a ridge. ShakTikhor can be seen below in the valley floor. Reach **Mandredhunga** (4921 feet, 1500 m), a collection of boulders along the ridge, in 25 minutes (**40 minutes** from Jyandala) and continue steeply to the south along the ridgeline to a place known as Rajban (3773 feet, 1150 m) where there is a water tap, in 1 hour. Stay along the ridgeline to the south, avoid trails heading down away from the ridge, and at one point the upper part of Sinti waterfall can be seen below to the east. (See side trip description below.) In **35 minutes** reach a **crest** (3002 feet, 915 m), **1 hour 35 minutes** from Mandredhunga, from where the trail drops down to the right/west of the ridgeline. Descend along a spur through Deorali (2451 feet, 747 m) to TumaTi (1165 feet, 355 m) and cross the ShakTi Khola to **ShakTikhor** in less than **1½ hours** from the crest). ◈

NEPALI CULTURAL GROUPS: HINDU CASTES

The Hindu castes are called by the general term PahAARi (people of the hills). They inhabit the middle hills and lower valleys, generally below 6000 ft (1800 m). Each caste has an ascribed profession, but many people no longer follow the rules and nowadays, it is not unusual for Nepalis to spend several years working abroad, particulary in the Middle East and Malaysia and sending remittances home.

High Castes

Today this group includes peasant farmers, civil servants, money lenders, and school teachers, as well as people following the traditional caste occupations.

Bahun (Brahman)—the traditional priest caste. In former times, the Brahmans did not handle plows or eat certain prohibited foods (e.g., garlic, onions, tomatoes, certain kinds of meat) or consume liquor. These days, however, many of these prohibitions are ignored, even the rules against meat and alcohol. Some of these rules are still followed in the more remote and traditional rural areas. Brahmans can be grouped into those from the east (Purbiya) and those from the west (Kumaon). Offspring of irregular unions among Brahmans are termed Jaishi Bahun.

Chhetri—the traditional warrior caste. It includes much the same occupations as the Brahmans, as well as soldiers in the Gurkha armies. The erstwhile royal family was Thakuri, a subcaste of Chhetri. The term Matwali Chhetri ("those who drink liquor") refers to western peoples who are not given the sacred thread characteristic of the "twice born" castes of Brahman and Chhetri.

Menial Castes

Many men and women of the three lower menial castes no longer pursue blacksmithing, shoemaking, or tailoring but work as day laborers on the land of others or as porters for large trekking parties or merchant-traders.

Damai or Darji—tailors and musicians for Hindu weddings and festivals

Kaami—ironworkers, toolmakers, and sometimes silversmiths and goldsmiths (Sunar)

Saarki—cobblers and leatherworkers

(These are the main castes found in the Nepali hills. Many other caste groups are found among the Newar, and in the Tarai regions.) ◈

If heading from Jyandala to ShakTikhor by way of Siraichuli peak, ChisopaniTar, and Upardangadhi, ascend the hill behind the upper part of the village to the northwest and reach a trail junction at a notch (5725 feet, 1745 m) in 15 minutes. To the right it is a steep 30-minute ascent to **Siraichuli, 45 minutes** from Jyandala.

Head left from the junction for ChisopaniTar and Upardangadhi. From Jyandala to Upardangadhi, the trail passes through an isolated area with dense vegetation and no facilities. The trail can be slippery and water is scarce. Proceed with caution. Descend from the junction through a ravine, avoiding any diversions from the widest path. From here to Upardangadhi you may hear a frequent chorus of cicadas hailing your passing. This area is also well known for bird-watching. In 20–25 minutes, cross a stream (5135 feet, 1565 m). The trail leads south from here.

In 5 more minutes, come to a ridge where the trail becomes faint. Head to the right/northwest and follow along the ridge. Take care with footing, as there are sections along

INSECTS OF THE SUBTROPICAL ZONE

Cicada on a tree trunk
(Photo by Stephen Bezruchka)

Insects are particularly abundant in the subtropical zone (3300–6500 feet/ 1000–2000 m in the west, to 5500 feet/1700 m in the east). Common butterflies include the plain and common tigers and blue and peacock pansies (all four also in tropical and temperate zones) and common Indian crow (also tropical zone). Large and especially colorful species occur, such as the golden birdwing (also tropical and temperate zones), Paris peacock, and glassy bluebottle (also temperate zone). The orange oakleaf, as its name implies, closely resembles an oak leaf when its wings are closed; it is also found in tropical and temperate zones. There is a bewildering variety of other butterfly groups with evocative names such as sailors, sergeants, windmills, and Jezebels.

Cicadas are large insects that resemble the color and pattern of the tree bark on which they live. Countless numbers make a prolonged, monotonous trilling in the forest. The noise is often so loud that it has a deafening effect. Males sing by vibrating a membrane on each side of the abdomen to attract females, which are incapable of making sounds. A local saying is that "cicada has a pleasant life for it has a silent wife." There are at least four distinct sounds. One is a low-frequency rattle made in the night by the *shechshelli*, another the continuous pitch made during the day by the *jyaaUkiri*, another sounds almost electronic, and a fourth that is wavering and intermittent. Cicadas also occur in tropical and temperate zones.

Fireflies, called *junkiri (Lampyridae)*, are tiny beetles. Wingless females resemble larvae and are also called glow worms. At night, winged males flash lights on and off in flight during their courtship display. Lighting is produced by special glands in the abdomen. Each species has a distinctive glow. They also occur in tropical and temperate zones.

Stick insects *(Phasmida)* have slender bodies up to 8 inches (20 cm) long, usually green or brown. They resemble twigs or branches amazingly well and stay motionless at the first sign of danger.

Praying mantids *(Dictyoptera)* are so called because, when waiting for prey, they hold their forelegs folded in front, appearing as if in prayer. Any insect, lizard, or small bird that comes by is snapped at with lightning speed by the viselike grip of the forelegs. They also occur in the tropical and temperate zones. ❖

a cliff face with precipitous drop-offs. After nearly 1 hour of following this ridge, reach a trail junction (5676 feet, 1730 m). Avoid the trail to the left/south from here, which descends steeply to ShakTikhor. Another trail to avoid makes a level contour to the right/north. Stay with the ridgeline heading northwest.

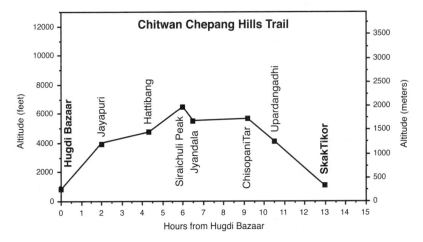

In 25 more minutes the trail diverges. Stay left and reach a resting point in less than 10 more minutes. Descend through subtropical forest to a small meadow area known as **ChisopaniTar** (5551 feet, 1692 m) in 20 minutes, or **2 hours 40–45 minutes** from Jyandala. The trail onward heads from the southwest end of the meadow (near a dilapidated structure). Traverse through a section with steep drop-offs and avoid two trails to the right within minutes of each other in less than 10 minutes from ChisopaniTar.

The trail descends steeply near or along the ridge to a notch (3878 feet, 1182 m) in 1 hour from ChisopaniTar. Contour to the west and in a little over 5 minutes reach a junction. To the left/south is the route to ShakTikhor. Continue straight to ascend to the Gurung and Chepang village of **Upardangadhi** (4029 feet, 1228 m) in less than 10 minutes (**1 ¼ hours** from ChisopaniTar, or 4 hours from Jyandala). This village was the headquarters of the Chitwan District until 1962. Ruins of a fort lie less than 10 minutes away on top of the hill to the south of the village.

The fort was built in the early 1800s by a grandson of the first king of Nepal, Prithvi Narayan Shah. The large complex (4160 feet, 1268 m) comprises 640 square meters and is surrounded by a moat and offers grand views of the surrounding area, particularly to the south, the Tarai.

To continue to ShakTikhor, follow the trail from Upardangadhi back down/east for 5 minutes to the juncture, then take the trail to the right/south. Descend, following a ridgeline, and reach a schoolhouse at the village of Kolar (3051 feet, 930 m) in 30 minutes. Continue along the ridgeline as you descend steeply to the tributary below, the ShakTi Khola (1624 feet, 495 m), in 45 minutes from Kolar.

You will have to wade aross the river several times before reaching Sampharang (1191 feet, 363 m) in 50 more minutes. In 10 minutes (**2 hours 20 minutes** from Upardangadhi), arrive at the bustling market town of **ShakTikor** (1070 feet, 326 m). There is a visitor center here next to the Chepang Museum and Chepang Development Center, which has locally produced goods on sale, including mustard seed oil and honey. The Chepang often refer to themselves as Praja or "subjects" (of the erstwhile kingdom, now of the republic).

A Hindu temple named Sri Muktinath Shivalaya is perched 50 yards (46 m) above and to the west of ShakTikhor's main market. Near the town, a regiment of Maoist guerrillas were staged for several years in a cantonment by the U.N. while politicos worked out the details of a peace process. Two side excursions from ShakTikor are described below.

Jeeps and buses can be found along the main market road for transport to the town of TaDi, located 1–1½ hours away by vehicle on the major east–west highway of Nepal, the Mahendra Rajmarg. From TaDi, transport can be found to Sauraha, a popular entry point to the World Heritage Site (Natural) of Chitwan National Park, or west to Bharatpur's modern bus station or the city of Narayanghat where transport to Pokhara and Kathmandu can be arranged.

🏕 Side Trip to Bat Cave and Sinti Waterfalls. *For this half-day excursion from* **ShakTikhor** *to a cave and scenic waterfalls, cross the ShakTi Khola and head to the southeast on a flat, wide trail. In less than* **20 minutes**, *reach houses of the Gurung village of* **Dogara** *(1076 feet, 328 m) and turn left/north here before crossing the Sinti Khola. Head up along the Sinti Khola for* **45 minutes**, *crossing it several times. The* **cave** *is on the east (true left) side of the stream. There is an upper chamber, reached by a steep set of decrepit concrete stairs without railings. Use caution! A further* **25-minute** *scramble upstream from the cave leads to twin* **waterfalls**. *Be prepared to get your feet wet, as the last 10 minutes of the journey is a scramble through the streambed.*

🏕 Side Trip to Chitram Waterfall and Majhbang. *A very few foreigners make this culturally rich 2-day side trip from ShakTikhor to Chitram Waterfall, with home stay at the Chepang village of Majhbang. However, if you wish to reach the waterfall beyond Majhbang village, the last 1½–1¾ hours is through dense subtropical forest with Himalayan giant nettle and other vegetation obscuring the trail. It is best to hire a local guide for this final section to the waterfall.*

From **ShakTikhor**, cross the ShakTi Khola and head southeast on a flat, wide trail. In less than **20 minutes**, reach houses of the village of **Dogara** (1076 feet, 328 m). Head straight/southeast to cross the Sinti Khola stream (no bridge) on a wide track. Within 10 minutes come to a fork; stay with the wide track to the right. Cross the Kayar Khola to its south (true left) side; wading is likely necessary, as there may not be a bridge. Reach DalanTar a few minutes beyond the river crossing.

Continue to Nibuwatar (1200 feet, 366 m) in less than 15 minutes and in another 30 minutes, reach Tindobhan (1427 feet, 435 m). Stay with the trail to the left which contours down to cross a tributary to its north side on a wooden **bridge** (1401 feet, 427 m) in 5 minutes, **1 hour 10 minutes** from Dogara.

Climb steeply up the hill and then follow the ridgeline with occasional views to the northeast of Chitram Waterfall in the distance. Reach the first houses of the beguiling Chepang village of Majhbang (3133 feet, 955 m) in 1¼ **hours** from the bridge. Home stay is available here. Just beyond the first houses the trail diverges. Stay to the right to arrive at more homes within 10 minutes where there are small shops and additional home-stay houses as well as a Christian church.

Otherwise, to continue directly to Chitram Waterfall, proceed left from just beyond the first group of houses, then immediately right to contour along the ridgeline. There will be another glimpse of Chitram Waterfall along the way; avoid trails that head down away from the ridgeline. In **1 hour** come to a junction at a **notch** (3510 feet, 1070 m) just after passing a Christian church (missionaries have been afoot among the Chepang). There is a water tap and small store near the pass, as well as a few houses of the Chepang village known as Cheurang, which encompasses a wide area. The waterfall that is visible off in the distance to the north of the notch is not Chitram Waterfall.

From this pass a guide would be useful. Descend to the left/northeast, and in less than 15 minutes the trail diverges. Follow the trail to the right to contour down to cross a tributary (3002 feet, 915 m), **25 minutes** *from the notch.*

From here, the trail begins to pass through thick vegetation with Himalayan giant nettle and even the occasional leech. Tread carefully, as the trail is sometimes narrow and is often overgrown with vegetation and may be damp and slippery. Climb steeply to crest a ridge (4085 feet, 1245 m) before descending through thick vegetation. Reach the waterfall viewpoint (3609 feet, 1100 m, N 27° 42.997' E 084° 40.912') in another **1½–1¾ hours.** *This viewpoint is 150 yards/meters distant from the 260-foot (80-m) waterfall, and getting closer requires traversing steep terrain that is dense with vegetation. Behind the waterfall, up and over a ridge is a large cave that is best found with the assistance of a local guide.*

THE GURUNG HERITAGE TRAIL
(Map No. 10, Page 354)

The Gurung Heritage Trail (GHT) can be done on its own, as a 3–4-day trek, or combined with the Annapurna Circuit. If the latter, the trails meet up at Khudi, an initial stopover on the circuit after a bus ride to Besisahar. Be aware that the first and last low-elevation sections of this route may be excessively warm, depending on the season.

As a precursor to the Annapurna Circuit, the GHT's scenic villages provide an inroad to the lifestyle and culture of Nepal's mid-hills, particularly of the Gurung ethnic group. Additionally, beginning by this route can be a way of conditioning the legs, lungs, and rest of the body and mind for the higher reaches of the circuit. The village panoramas with a Himalaya backdrop offer unparalleled beauty, and the cultural interaction can be even more rewarding than the views. The Gurung villages are often compact with closely built homes, and much of the trail has been laid in stone, especially around the Gurung settlements—a herculean effort.

Although the GHT enters the Annapurna Conservation Area Project (ACAP) at Pasagaon village, this route is much less developed with tourist facilities as other areas of ACAP. Home-stay lodges are available along the way, and you will generally have the same home-cooked dishes as the locals. A portion of the proceeds from the food and lodging is supposed to go toward a local-level fund for conservation and community development, and most villages have an Aamaa Samuha (or Mother's Group) dedicated to village-level development. Some of the villages are hydro-powered with electricity so electronic equipment and batteries can be charged, while most of the villages have only a solar power setup that is usually unsuitable for recharging electronic equipment.

Gurung comprise roughly 2.4 percent of the total population of Nepal. They have their own distinct language, which is closely related to Tamang and Thakali languages and is of the Tibeto-Burman family. Traditionally, the Gurung engaged in agriculture and animal husbandry, and many now serve outside the country as Gurkha soldiers.

Buses to Thumsikot/Gumle Bazaar are found in Pokhara at Rani Powa in the Mahendra Pul area. There are up to four buses per day. The first departs at 7AM and the last at 3:45 PM. The 2-hour journey offers occasional views along the way of Begnas Tal far below. The bus stops at Gumle Bazaar.

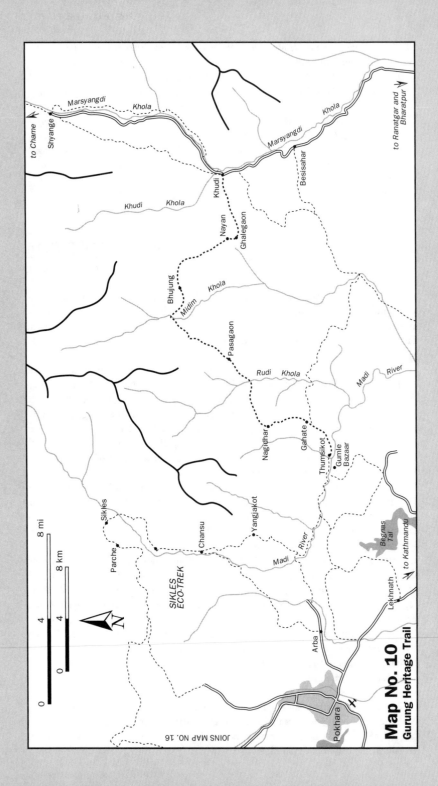

Map No. 10
Gurung Heritage Trail

to Chame

Shyange

Marsyangdi *Khola*

Khola

Marsyangdi

Besisahar

to Ranatgar and
Bharatpur

Khudi *Khola*

Khudi

Nayan

Ghalegaon

Bhujung

Midim *Khola*

Pasagaon

Rudi *Khola*

Madi *River*

Nagidhar

Gahate

Thumsikot

Gumle
Bazaar

Sikles

Parche

Chansu

Yangjakot

Madi *River*

Begnas
Tal

*SIKLES
ECO-TREK*

to Kathmandu

Lekhnath

Arba

Pokhara

N

0

4

8 mi

0

4

8 km

GUMLE BAZAAR TO BHUJUNG

To proceed from **Gumle Bazaar**, cross the Madi River on a suspension bridge (1988 feet, 606 m) and turn right, then again bear right a minute beyond and contour through Thumsikot village (2018 feet, 615 m), passing Shivalaya Temple along the way. Reach a suspension bridge (1952 feet, 595 m) over the Wardi Khola in 15 minutes and cross to the east bank. There is a market area here at the confluence of the Wardi Khola and the Madi River. Jeeps are available from here to Gahate (a ride of less than 30 minutes) and beyond to Mijure (both villages are on the GHT). Otherwise, to travel by foot, follow the road upstream along the north bank of the Madi River and then ascend away from the river. Occasionally, the footpath will make a shortcut of the road.

In about 1 hour, the trail reaches a sharp bend in the road and departs to the left to a stone laid path and *chautaaraa* (rest area) just beyond. Reach another *chautaaraa* a minute farther; just after this second rest area, at a bend in the trail, a path heads left away from the stone path. Contour up through fields for 10–15 minutes to meet the road at a ridgeline near a school and shop. Stay to the right of the road to reach the predominantly Gurung hamlet of **Gahate** (3566 feet, 1087 m) in a few more minutes, **1½–1¾ hours** from Gumle Bazaar. There is a large, pleasant *pipal* tree at a *chautaaraa* in this village providing a shady place to take a break.

As you leave the settlement, ascend past the small Mahadev Temple (Mahadev is one of Shiva's many names) and stay to the left just beyond, rather than take the stone steps to the right. Along the way you begin to see Machhapuchhare peeking over the western ridgeline and part of the Annapurna and Lamjung ranges to the north. Farther east is the Manaslu range, which will come into view as you reach a tea shop (4334 feet, 1321 m) of the small village of **Mijire**, **40 minutes** from Gahate.

Pass by a village development office and just below a health post, and contour to the right for 5 minutes, avoiding trails that descend, to reach the first house of the scat-

tered village of Pakrikot (4232 feet, 1290 m). It takes 20 to 30 minutes to walk through Pakrikot, which is situated along a ridgeline. Midway, on a hillock, is a rarely manned *gomba* surrounded by barbed wire, with a water tank nearby, along with a small Hindu temple.

The houses of Pakrikot and Nagidhar blend together, and home stay is available in both as well as solar power. Descend from Pakrikot along a ridge toward a notch and fork right at a *chorten* (left heads to a school) to reach the shops of **Nagidhar** (4134 feet, 1260 m) in less than 10 minutes, **35–45 minutes** from Mijire. A nursery school built with foreign aid lies above Nagidhar.

Head north out of the village and begin a wide arcing contour around the valley. Reach a *chautaaraa* under a tree near a defunct water tap in less than 10 minutes. Descend (rather than take the trail to the left) and in less than 2 minutes the trail

Honeyhunters use twine ladders to reach plump honeycombs that have been disarmed by smoke. (Photo by Alonzo Lyons)

A moraine lake near Manang (Photo by Pat Morrow)

divides again. Take the trail to the right and reach another *chautaaraa* (3953 feet, 1205 m) in 10 more minutes. Just beyond the path splits again. This time, stay to the left and eventually pass near a small waterfall and then below a primary school to reach another resting point (4003 feet, 1220 m) in 40–45 minutes. Descend along the ridgeline and pass a small temple (3937 feet, 1200 m) located in the spread-out village of Rabi Danda. Proceeding from here can be unclear as there are many trails. The goal is to descend to the left into the Rudi Khola valley to the river below. Aim for the spur seen from the ridgeline where there are stone steps. The Rudi Khola is reached after a steep descent of 40 minutes.

Contour upriver for 20 minutes to a **suspension bridge** (2625 feet, 800 m). Cross to the east bank of the Rudi Khola, then head left and pass a shop and houses. In a few minutes, come to a bridge to cross the Balaj Khola to the north bank. Just above are a few houses and a tea shop (2723 feet, 830 m), **2 hours 10 minutes** from Nagidhar. From here, it is a relentless **2¼–2½-hour** climb along a ridgeline to **Pasagaon** (5420 feet, 1652 m).

Enter through a traditional *kani* (gateway) which surmounts the trail. There is a *gomba* in Pasagaon. A health post and nearby *chorten* lie on a knob overlooking the village. Home stay is available, and most homes are solar powered.

Pass through another *kani* to two schools that are above town. At the far end of the high school field, the route follows a prominent stone path. Reach a *chautaaraa* in 25 minutes and bear left (rather than turning sharply to a stone path to the right). Ascend to another *chautaaraa* (6316 feet, 1925 m). Cross an open area where the trail becomes faint to then ascend steeply through isolated forest on stone steps to a **ridge crest** (6890 feet, 2100 m) in **1¼ hours** from Pasagaon. Descend into the Midim Khola valley, at first through thick, uninhabited forest and then steeply down to a wooden bridge (4298 feet, 1310 m) over a feeder stream in **1½ hours** from the ridge crest. Cross the bridge with a

view to the left of a long water cascade. Work your way across the valley, skirting be
fields, to reach a power plant (80 kw generating capacity) on the other side in **20 minutes**. Bhujung village is supplied from this station.

Cross over a deep, narrow gorge of the Midim Khola on a suspension bridge (4354 feet,
1327 m) and ascend the long, steep staircase to **Bhujung** (5331 feet, 1625 m) in **45
minutes–1 hour** from the power plant. Bhujung is one of the largest Gurung settlements
in Nepal. Home stay is available as well as electricity to recharge batteries. There is a large
Annapurna Conservation Project Area (ACAP) office located here as well.

BHUJUNG TO KHUDI

Between Bhujung and Nayan there are no facilities and much of the trail is through
uninhabited area. From Bhujung, ascend steeply to a large gateway near a high school
with a nearby student hostel and continue up stone steps to a *chautaaraa* in **45 minutes**.
From here, begin a long contour high above the valley. Cross several feeder streams before then ascending gradually. Stay with the widest trail while avoiding trails that divert
to ascend or descend. Reach a fork near a *gomba* in a grove of *utis* (alder) trees in **1½**
more **hours**.

The *gomba* is to the left of the trail along with stone steps to the majestically set village of
Ghan Pokhara which lies over 325 feet (100 m) higher. To visit Ghan Pokhara, pass by the
gomba and ascend steeply up the steps for 15 minutes. Ghan Pokhara (7093 feet, 2162 m)
lies on top of a hill with dramatic views of the mountains and surrounding landscape.

The village of **Nayan** is just beyond the fork near the *gomba*, **2¼ hours** from Bhujung.
Continue ascending gently, passing a health post, and staying left at a fork just beyond to
reach another trail junction near the Uttar Kanya Temple. To the left of the small temple
compound the trail leads to a sports ground a few minutes away, with a nearby lookout
point on the east side of Ghalegaon. To the right, the trail passes two *chorten* and shortly
thereafter forks left and ascends to the village of **Ghalegaon** (6863 feet, 2092 m), **15–20
minutes** from Nayan. Ghalegaon is a large village that locals say is the origin site of the
Gurung people. It has a magnificent setting, and home stay is possible here.

From Galaegaon to Khudi there are few facilities, and the first stretch is through uninhabited forest. Exit to the east and follow the stone laid path to the right to a *chorten* just beyond. Take the trail to the left from the *chorten* and reach another junction
in a few minutes, and again stay left (the right branch descends to Baglung Pani and

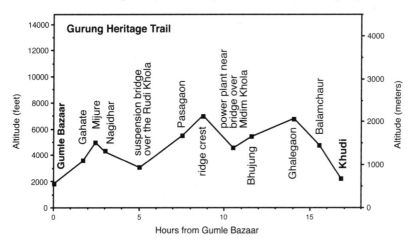

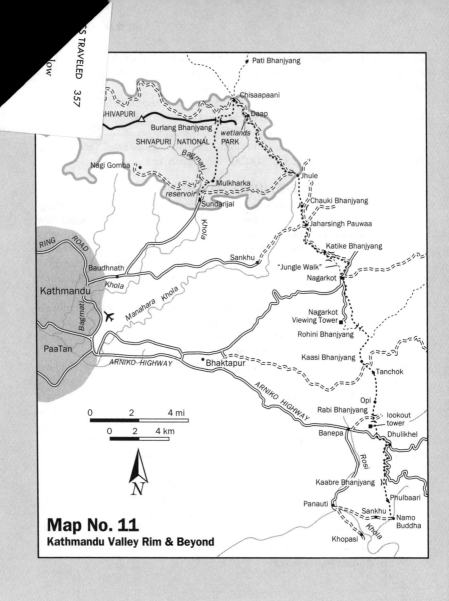

Map No. 11
Kathmandu Valley Rim & Beyond

Besisahar). Round a ridge and then descend to a bend in the road (6496 feet, 1980 m) in 10–15 minutes.

Continuing on from here, the route may be unclear. Cross the road at the bend and rather than dropping to the left to a *chautaaraa*, contour more evenly to the east through mixed vegetation. Eventually, descend to a *chautaaraa* in 20 minutes from the road. Head to the left/east rather than descend to the right/south, and pass a small temple housing several rock *lingam* in 5 minutes. Continue along a ridge, descending through mixed forest to another *chautaaraa* above the Gurung village of Mrijay in 45 minutes. Descend along the ridge and pass a *chorten* to reach a large *chautaaraa* in a few more minutes.

Continue straight/east rather than descending to the right or left and reach **Balamchaur** (4396 feet, 1340 m), the last Gurung village of this trek, in less than 5 minutes, **1 hour 35 minutes** from Ghalegaon. The inhabitants on the way to Khudi will now be predominantly Chettri and Bahun (Brahman). Pass Simpani (4167 feet, 1270 m), with a small shop and cluster of four temples; the highest temple, named Thanimai, is built around the base of a *chilaune* (*Schima wallichii*) tree. *Chilaune* means "itch" in Nepali, and if you rub sap of this tree on your skin, you will learn how it got its name. The other three temples are built to honor Ganesh, the lovers Radha and Krishna, and Mahadev (also known as Shiva).

From Simpani the trail crisscrosses the road several times on the way to Khudi. Pass through Balam (3661 feet, 1116 m) and then the hamlet of Mahatok (3051 feet, 930 m). At the lower end of Mahatok, head to the right/east to reach the small temple in honor of Mahadev near the road. Follow the road down shortly to then descend to the left along stone steps to emerge at the roadway near a hotel in **Khudi** above the old bridge over the Khudi Khola, **1¼ hours** from Balamchaur.

The trail onward from Khudi is described in Chapter 6.

THE KATHMANDU VALLEY RIM AND BEYOND

(Map No. 11, Page 358)

The Kathmandu Valley Cultural Trail is an attractive getaway option for people with time to spare in Kathmandu, perhaps before a flight home or if a regional or national strike brings vehicle transport to a standstill (keep abreast of Nepal's planned strikes at www.nepalbandh.com); generally this trek is for those with a wish to escape Kathmandu if only for a short 3-day excursion. Beautiful mountain panoramas complement the relatively fresher air once you reach the Shivapuri ridge, to the northeast of the valley, and beyond. Lodging facilities are available along the route, with camping and home stay available, too.

The first section of this trail climbs steeply to cross over the ridge to the lodges of Chisaapaani. This follows the same route to Helambu described in Chapter 8. However, from Chisaapaani, the route diverges to contour fairly evenly to the popular viewpoint hill destination of Nagarkot, perched atop a ridge. You then continue on to the large town and resort area of Dhulikhel, where economy to first-class accommodation can be found and buses to Kathmandu are available, or you can continue hiking to the religiously important site of Namo Buddha and pass through the alluring Newar town of Panauti on the way out where buses can be found for a return to Kathmandu.

Portions of the route follow the motor road, whereas much of the trail is along little-used jeep track although motorcycles will be encountered and sometimes other vehicles. The Nepal Environment and Tourism Initiative Foundation (NETIF, www.netif-nepal.org), along with a Finnish INGO, have developed the route and have set up sign posts and covered rest areas along the way.

To begin, follow the route described in Chapter 8 for Helambu, Sundarijal to Tharepati, up to the hill settlement of Chisaapaani.

CHISAAPAANI TO NAGARKOT

Meet the trail to Nagarkot at the south end of **Chisaapaani** (7110 feet, 2167 m). The Shivapuri National Park entry post is just beyond the junction of the trail from Sundarijal. You will need to show an entry ticket, valid for 7 days, or be issued a new ticket if you are coming from Langtang. Be aware that the park area between Chisaapaani and Jhule, some 3 hours away, is isolated and without facilities.

Travel south on the motor track, little used by jeeps but frequented by motorcycles. A minute up the road from the check post, pass a ceremony area on the right with a Shiva-*lingam* and an army post just beyond. The wide path continues on the northeast side of the ridge to reach a meadow. A little farther, **45 minutes** from Chisaapaani, is the wetland area known as **Daap** (6811 feet, 2076 m), an ideal camping site.

Continue east along the wide track lined with dense vegetation including many fern and rhododendron. Reach a NETIF-built water tap and rest area (6699 feet, 2042 m) at a signed crossroads in less than 40 minutes. The path to the right is another way down to Sundarijal. Take the upper route to continue along the jeep track toward Nagarkot. Reach another rest shelter (7005 feet, 2135 m) within 40 more minutes. Pass through an area thick with vegetation to a signed junction (7172 feet, 2186 m) within another 40–45 minutes.

Descend to the east/left toward Nagarkot on a wide trail. A minute below is a gate to an army post. Take the single-track trail to the left to skirt around the post. Pass through a copse of pine trees at the lower end of the base where there is a lodge at the beginning of the village of **Jhule** (6857 feet, 2090 m) in 15 minutes, or **2¼ hours** from Daap. Just below the lodge, near a house, fork left from the wide track to a single track to pass by more houses of Jhule and reach the road again and another lodge in 5 minutes (the lodges of Jhule will be quieter than the lodges of the bazaar area of Chauki Bhanjyang).

Descend along the road to the village of **Chauki Bhanjyang** (5984 feet, 1824 m) in **35 minutes** where a road from a housing development meets the path. A minute beyond, reach the road which buses ply between Sindupalchowk (Melamchi Pul) and Kathmandu. There are two lodges here. Head to the right for Nagarkot. Follow the road and over the next stretch you might encounter vehicle traffic. Keep to the widest road

A spiked collar protects this Tibetan mastiff from leopards. (Photo by Pat Morrow)

as it descends gently to the southwest. Pass through the predominantly Brahman village of Kaule (no facilities) and below a monastery complex to reach the tea shops and restaurants of **Jaharsingh Pauwaa** (5866 feet, 1788 m) in **30 minutes**. Head to the left/east and as you leave the settlement, stay with the wider road on the right rather than descend to the left. Follow this road, avoiding a road branching to the left along the way, and pass through the hamlet of Bhojeni (5807 feet, 1770 m), without facilities, and reach the market of **Katike Bhanjyang** (5676 feet, 1730 m) in **60–70 minutes** from Jaharsingh Pauwaa.

From Katike, head east from the bazaar and bear right to follow the road with trail shortcuts along the way. In less than 5 minutes, one trail that branches to the right of the road is a wide trail known locally as the "Jungle Walk" through the Kushum Community Forest. If you follow this wide trail, you will pass through vegetation dense with bamboo on the west side of the ridge to reach the market area of **Nagarkot** (6447 feet, 1965 m) just north of a secondary school in **45–55 minutes**. (Otherwise, if you stay to the narrower shortcut trails and road, you will begin reaching the hotels of Nagarkot within 30 minutes and the bazaar area in a further 20 minutes.) The highest point of Nagarkot hill station is MahÁAnkaali Temple (6463 feet, 1970 m), although some hotels have buildings that rise higher. Langtang Lirung is visible directly to the north, peeking over the Gosainkund range. To the west of Langtang are the Ganesh Himal peaks and to the right are Purba Cheche, Dorje Lhakpa, Sisa Pangma, Gauri Shankar, Numbur, and more. Bus service to Kathmandu is available from Nagarkot.

NAGARKOT TO DHULIKHEL

To continue on to Dhulikhel, follow the blacktop road from **Nagarkot**'s main bazaar to the southeast, heading toward a lookout tower on a hilltop to the south. Reach an army officer training base in 15 minutes, and bear to the left along the road. Take a wide double-track dirt path that heads left/east away from the tarmac in 5 minutes more (NETIF is planning to put a sign here indicating the way to Dhulikhel). Contour around the hillside and keep to the widest trail to pass below two lodges and reach a jeep road in 35–40 minutes. Head to the left and shortly beyond the road diverges. The road to the right ascends to a *gomba*. Instead, bear left and continue contouring. Just beyond is a lodge and water bottling plant (6430 feet, 1960 m). In a little over 5 minutes, arrive at a small tea shop of **Rohini Bhanjyang** (6463 feet, 1970 m), **60–70 minutes** from Nagarkot. This is a junction where a trail ties in from above from an army camp and lookout tower while other trails descend.

Keep straight/east rather than descend to the left or right, and ascend, gently at first, staying with the widest path to reach a junction near a ridgeline in 25 minutes. Take the jeep road to the right and follow the ridgeline. In 15 more minutes, reach a NETIF-built rest area (6588 feet, 2008 m). The trail to Kaangure and on to Dhulikhel descends steeply here to the left/south away from the road. In 15 minutes reach a signed junction (6053 feet, 1845 m). Do not head right here but continue straight to descend along the ridgeline. Reach a motor road in another 10 minutes and take it to the right/south. A tea shop of the nearby village of Kaangure is just below. Continue along the road to descend to a saddle known as **Kaasi Bhanjyang** (5446 feet, 1660 m), **1 hour 10 minutes** from Rohini Bhanjyang, and do not follow the road to the right to descend. Continue straight/south across the saddle and take the trail that branches to the left from the road to climb the hill before you.

Ascend through cultivated area and then contour on the east side of the ridge to the Tamang hamlet of **Tanchok** (5974 feet, 1821 m) in **40–45 minutes**, with the small Pemaa Choling Gomba. A *lama* of the Nyingmapa sect lives in the village. There are no facilities here. Stay to the left/southeast and skirt a hilltop to the east side. Dhulikhel comes into view ahead and below to the south, although you still have to descend the hill you are on and then ascend the hill across the way (there is not a trail that contours around that hill) before descending again to Dhulikhel.

Descend through fields and reach a motor road (5627 feet, 1715 m) in less than 20 minutes at the top of the widely scattered and predominately Chhetri village of **Opi**. Bear left and follow the road down to another road (5134 feet, 1565 m) in 20 minutes with a few shops. Head to the right on this road for a minute before turning left below a sacred *pipal* tree (*Ficus religiosa*), away from the road. As you ascend the hill, the path becomes a very wide track. Follow this track to the crest and then along the ridgeline. At one point, you can divert to the right to ascend to a lookout tower 5 minutes above (5577 feet, 1700 m) on a hilltop. The tower offers 360° views including the Kathmandu valley to the west and mountain peaks to the north and east.

After 35 minutes, as you start to descend, follow a narrower road that branches to the left away from the wide track and descend through the Chettri village of **Kaarki** with no facilities. In a few minutes, reach another road and take it to the left. Descend to the paved Arniko Highway, the highway which runs between Kathmandu (right) and Kodari (left) on the border of the Tibet Autonomous Region in 15 minutes. Follow this highway to the left to reach Dhulikhel's bus station within 10 minutes, **1¾ hours** from Tanchok. **Dhulikhel** (5052 feet, 1540 m) is a large town with many facilities, including high-end resorts, and distant mountain views.

EXPLORE: DHULIKEL TO NAMO BUDDHA AND SANKHU

To travel to the hallowed site of Namo Buddha, follow the paved road toward the east end of **Dhulikhel** to a place known locally as the "picnic spot," a grassy area where people come to relax. The road forks here. To the left is Gaikreshar Temple a short distance away. Instead, follow the bend to the right/south and leave the road to ascend through an entryway and climb the staircase that leads to Kaali Mandir (Kali Temple). Within 15 minutes reach a large statue of a seated Shakyamuni Buddha (5364 feet, 1635 m) overlooking Dhulikhel. Keep ascending to a pass (5518 feet, 1682 m) in 5 more minutes. From the pass, a trail ascends for a few minutes to the left to the hilltop temple of Kaali Mandir (5610 feet, 1710 m) with a nearby army post that guards a relay tower.

To continue on to Namo Buddha, do not fork right from the pass but follow the signs to continue straight. Immediately below the pass is a hotel, and just beyond meet

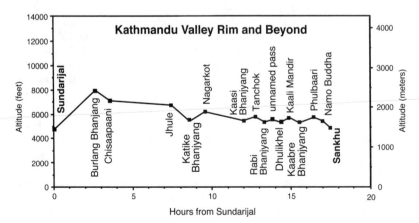

Abundant prayer flags ripple above Namo Buddha. (Photo by Alonzo Lyons)

a road and continue straight along it (rather than ascend it to the right). In another 325 feet (100 m), take the trail branching to the left with a sign for Namo Buddha. Pass through Kaabre village (no facilities) and fork left at a junction in 10 minutes. Descend to **Kaabre Bhanjyang** (4977 feet, 1517 m) in another 10 minutes, **40–45 minutes** from Dhulikhel, where there are simple restaurants and tea shops.

Follow the road to the left and in a few minutes meet a paved road that carries traffic between Sindhuli District and Dhulikhel (and in the future will connect Kathmandu with eastern Nepal rather than the current roundabout route over the Thangkot escarpment). Cross the road and ascend along a dirt trail to the left and in a little more than 5 minutes, reach another dirt road. Rather than continuing straight up this road, cross it, bearing right, and keep to the right of the gated Nepal–Japan Friendship Tree Plantation to follow a wide dirt track. Continue climbing to the Chhetri village of FaskoT (5341 feet/1628 m) in 10 minutes. There are no facilities here.

Ascend to a *stupa* (5571 feet, 1698 m) at a notch in the ridgeline in just over 15 more minutes. Do not descend right or left here, but continue straight past the *stupa* and fork to the left 20 yards (18 m) beyond. In a few minutes reach another path and continue to the left and ascend to a ridge crest at **Phulbaari** village (5718 feet, 1743 m) with no facilities, in 15 minutes from the *stupa*, **50 minutes** from Kaabre Bhanjyang. The monastery and prayer-flagged lined hilltop of Namo Buddha can be seen across the valley to the south. Continue up the ridge from Phulbaari and meet a road in 15 minutes. Take the road to the right for 20 yards (18) meters before branching to the left on a trail (the right branch is the gated compound of a large Buddhist retreat center).

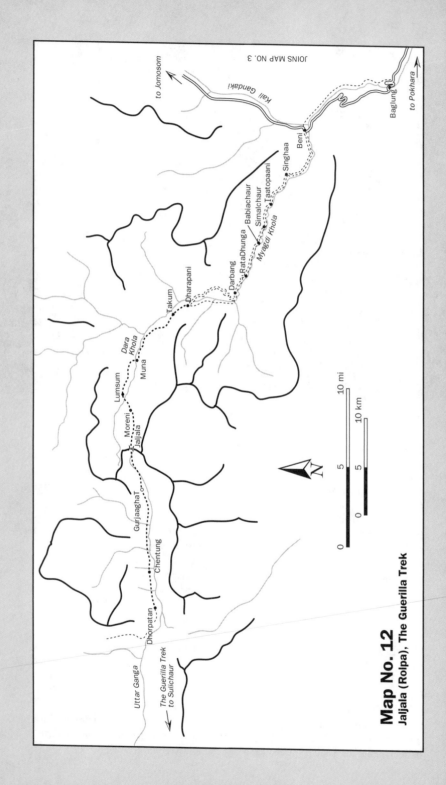

Map No. 12
Jaljala (Rolpa), The Guerilla Trek

In 5 minutes, reach a road and either follow this road to Namo Buddha or cross the road to contour above it through a grove of pine trees. Reach an area known as Chaapaa Bhanjyang with a few small shops and restaurants in 15 minutes. To the left a road winds up to a guesthouse near the monastery. To the right descend to several restaurants and shops and a few hotels of **Namo Buddha** near a *stupa* (5463 feet, 1665 m) in a few more minutes, **40 minutes** from Phulbaari.

Legend has it that Shakyamuni Buddha, in a lifetime previous to becoming the Buddha, was a prince in the surrounding area. If you climb the hill to the south (5774 feet, 1760 m), in 10–15 minutes you will find a location where, as the story goes, this compassionate prince gave up his flesh (and life) to save a tigress incapacitated by hunger and too weak to hunt for herself and her cubs. There are several points of worship along the hilltop as well as a large monastery complex and a nearby hotel, all connected and enveloped by an immense array of colorful prayer flags fluttering over the scene.

Return to Dhulikhel the way you came, or by bus, or you might be able to take a jeep to Sankhu, a town below Namo Buddha where bus service can be had to Panauti and then on to Kathmandu. To hike to Sankhu, then descend the short staircase to the immediate north of the lower *stupa* and follow the road to the left. As you approach a *chorten*, within 5 minutes, take the trail that branches to the left away from the road. Descend to the village of **Sankhu** (4803 feet, 1464 m) in 15 more minutes. There are many mandarin orange trees around this village.

The bus stand is 10 minutes farther up the road. It takes less than 40 minutes by bus to reach the historic, Newar town of Panauti which has several captivating ancient temples and is well worth a visit. Buses to Kathmandu can be arranged from Panauti's bus park, or you can travel from Panauti to the large town of Banepa, 30 minutes away by bus. Banepa lies on the Arniko Highway, where many buses to Kathmandu are available.

JALJALA (ROLPA), THE GUERILLA TREK
(Map No. 12, Page 364)

Before embarking on this trek, check with your embassy and local authorities that Dhorpatan, Rukum, and Rolpa districts are safe areas to visit. At the time of writing (May 2010) they were open and safe; however, the tentative peace process that ended the decade-long insurgency had not been completed after several years of negotiations and there had been threats of returning to arms. If the peace process fails, these areas should be avoided.

The trek follows a route that was used from west to east by a Maoist cadre during the 1996–2006 civil war to travel to Pokhara and on to Kathmandu from strongholds in Rukum and Rolpa districts where the rebellion was planned and launched. It can take up to two weeks and wends through areas that do not regularly see foreigners. Additionally, it involves a long, strenuous day between Thawang village and Jelbang village, with trail sections that have precipitous drop-offs. This journey is for the more ambitious, seasoned trekker with at least a sprinkling of language skills. It offers a chance for closer cultural interaction in a location that figures prominently in recent history. Accommodation might, at times, be challenging to arrange, especially after leaving Dhorpatan, a hunting reserve for *bharal* (blue sheep) and Himalayan tahr among other wildlife.

The Maoists' route came to light when it was used for an attack on Beni, the headquarters of Myagdi District, in 2004. After the battle, the army gave chase in helicopters as the Maoists retreated over ground. It is alleged that the Maoists then purposefully set

MAOBAADI (MAOISTS)

Communist groups in Nepal emerged from behind the scenes as part of the 1950–51 opposition that led to the downfall of the ruling Rana family of hereditary prime ministers and reinstatement of the king. In 1959, the communists won four seats in Nepal's first general election before King Mahendra's royal takeover dissolved the nascent parliament in 1960. At this point Sino-Soviet communists supported the king and his anti-democratic rule and did so until the mid-1960s while another communist group sided with the Nepali Congress party and pro-democracy forces and operated from India.

Communist factions became more extreme in the 1970s, and in the 1980s went underground. There was strict political self-censorship in Nepal before the first *jana andolan* or democracy movement in April 1990 when clandestine political parties then surfaced. After the successful movement and transition to democracy, little happened to improve the lives of the poorest. In 1992 anthropologist Stephen Mikesell predicted a rural response to Nepal's repression, akin to Peru's Shining Path guerilla movement.

Political parties who call themselves Maoist exist in Peru and other parts of the world. Immediately south of Nepal in India, there are vast political movements. Naxalite-Maoists and others work underground and control a large part of the country referred to as the 'red corridor.' Their relationship to Nepal's Maoists is dubious.

Many different parties in Nepal call themselves communist today and determining what they stand for is not easy. Although presumably sharing elemental ideology, they often behave as partisan adversaries, and even make trysts with non-communist groups before aligning with comrades from other parties. Internecine rivalries are wrought not only of jealousy but a history of broken promises and therefore legitimate distrust.

Pushpa Kamal Dahal and Baburam Bhattarai joined the communists in the 1980s as young ideologues and led a breakaway group in the mid-1990s that was not →

fire to the forest to divert attention and to disguise their escape. Scars of this burn might still be seen along the way near GurjaaghaT.

BENI TO DHORPATAN

Please be aware that after leaving Dhorpatan, the following itinerary is only approximate and times have not been precisely measured by the authors. Food and accommodation might be a challenge to arrange.

Begin the trek in Beni, a 3–4-hour bus ride west of Pokhara. Buses to Beni can be found at Pokhara's Baglung Bus Station. **Beni** (2700 feet, 823 m) is the administrative center of Myagdi District and has many facilities. The route heads west up the Myagdi Khola before crossing the Jaljala to leave this major drainage system and enter that of the Bheri Khola. To avoid the first 14 miles (24 km) of hiking, there is vehicle service from Beni along a rough road that follows the Myagdi Khola to Darbang village. The vehicle journey can take 2 or more hours and is being extended farther to Dharapani. However, if you go by vehicle, you will miss a visit to a developed hot springs along the way.

To walk in from Beni and visit the hot springs along the way, then proceed west up the Myagdi Khola. Pass many small villages, including Chutreni, Ghorsang, and Baguwa, to the tea shops of **Singhaa** (2800 feet, 914 m), reached in **1¼ hours** from Beni. In **30 minutes,** reach the first houses of **Taatopaani,** and after crossing a tributary, pass recognized as a separate party by the judicial system and thus was barred from elections in 1994. Subsequently, this party rejected the electoral process and went underground in 1995 and spawned the Unified Communist Party of Nepal (Maoist).

In western districts where the Maoists had a stronghold, they became violent toward landlords, government officials, and generally those who had participated in the elections. This violence was in part a reaction to a military operation against them in 1994–95. A "People's War" was launched in February 1996 which began as attacks on three police posts in Rolpa District and a bank in Gorkha. Dahal and Bhattari led the Maoists through the subsequent decade-long civil war and upwards of 14,000 Nepalese died.

The Maoists gained notoriety for human rights abuses, only to be outdone by the (formerly Royal) Nepal Army. At one point during the ten-year insurgency, Nepal led the world in disappeared persons (people who went missing while in custody, considered to be executed by captors). The Maoists gave women positions in battle and recruited minors for soldiers. To this day, particularly violent is the paramilitary youth wing of the party, the Young Communist League.

A second *jana andolan* led to a peace process that began in 2006. Two years later the Maoists won elections to form a democratic republic to the dismay of their Indian counterparts who did not want to accept the electoral mandate. The victory didn't last long with Prime Minister Dahal resigning over his lack of authority over the official army and the fate of the Maoist troops. At present (fall 2010) the infighting of a fractious coalition government has led to an impasse and drafting a new constitution has been delayed.

If nothing else, Maoists holding positions in government are considered to be among the least venal in Nepal's bureaucratic regime and remain a hope for ending endemic corruption. Their official website is www.ucpnm.org ◆

above a hot springs bathing area. Like similar places in other parts of the world, people with arthritis and other complaints have moved here to soak and soothe. The main part of town with simple lodges (2920 feet, 890 m) is **10 minutes** beyond. Below this part of town, by the river, are more hot springs. Follow along the road to pass through Simalchaur (3100 feet, 945 m) and continue heading up the valley, staying on the left bank and not crossing any bridges over the main river, to reach the bazaar of **Babiachaur** (3220 feet, 981 m) with a guest house with basic rooms in **1¼ hours**. Upstream, pass through Ranamang, Shastradara, and Baloti to reach RataDhunga (meaning "red rock") in **1 hour**. Reach Dharkharka in another **35 minutes**. A landslide rumbled down the south bank in September 1988, claiming the lives of over 100 people. The rock and debris washed across the river, taking out the trail on the north bank. Such major events are now considered more likely due to tectonic (mountain-building) forces than to deforestation. Nepalis are quick to rebuild the slides and reclaim farmland.

Reach the large bazaar of **Darbang** (3520 feet, 1073 m) in **40 minutes** with simple lodging and a police post. If you came by jeep you will begin walking from here unless the road onward to Dharapani has been completed. Cross the Myagdi Khola to the west (right) bank. Go past the few more hotels in the village and head north to reach Phedi, at the foot of the climb to Dharapani, in **30 minutes.** Cross the tributary Daanga Khola on a suspension bridge and pick up the trail that climbs the ridge. As you climb, on the right is subtropical forest and, on the drier left, chir pine. This results from the marked climatological changes on either side of the ridge. Reach the spectacularly situated village of **Dharapani** (5125 feet, 1562 m) in **1 hour.** Most of the houses here are single story with slate roofs. Solar power is available as well as simple lodging. Dhaulagiri is the massive mountain to the north, and off to the west is Gurja Himal, with Dhaulagiri IV and V in between. Hope to get views (unfettered by clouds) here in the morning or evening. If views elude you, don't despair; Stephen had been by several times in the mid-1970s, and it wasn't until years later that he saw the mountains unshackled by cloud.

The trail now contours high above the river, as it heads northwest toward the watershed. The views along this stretch are some of the finest in Nepal. Reach the Bahun–Chhetri village of **Takum** (5500 feet, 1676 m), another idyllic setting, in **1 hour.** Takum also has solar power; however, unlike Dharapani, most of the houses here are two-story. The predominant ethnic groups in this region are Magar, Chhetri, Kaami, Damai, and Bahun. Continue contouring through Sibang with simple lodging, and then climb up to a teashop at Maachhim. As you round a bend by a *chautaaraa* (6600 feet, 2112 m) and begin to head northwest up the tributary Dara Khola, you can look north up the Myagdi Khola valley, which drains the west side of Dhaulagiri. A trail leaves from here for a strenuous high trek that encircles the seventh-highest mountain in the world by crossing French Pass at the headwaters of this valley.

Continue on to sprawling **Phaleagaon** (6200 feet, 1890 m) in **1½ hours.** As you head up, notice that you are at the altitude limit of rice cultivation. However, nearer to Jumla, it will be growing almost 2000 feet (610 m) higher! **Muna** (6460 feet, 1969 m) is **45 minutes** beyond. Across the valley is the spectacularly perched village of Dara. Reach the suspension bridge (6200 feet, 1990 m) over the Dara Khola and cross it to the left bank. Climb up to enter a side valley and cross the tributary and climb to the basic lodges and houses of **Lumsum** (7180 feet, 2188 m) within **1½ hours.** Hydroelectricity is available in the evenings. Ask whether the next village is occupied and whether food is available, if you need to. Cross the Dara Khola again in **20 minutes,** to the right bank, and head upstream to cross another tributary and begin to climb to **Moreni** (lowest at 7820 feet, 2383 m). The houses, scattered 700 feet (213 m) up the hillside, are reached in some **40 minutes,** and they may be unoccupied in the middle of winter as the people descend to Lumsum. There may be little water along the way, so fill up at the valley bottom. Moreni is the last place to get food before Dhorpatan.

INSECTS OF THE TEMPERATE ZONE

The temperate zone is rich in insects, although there is less variety than in the subtropical zone. Temperate-zone species include praying mantis, fireflies, cicadas, beetles, bugs, bees, ants, moths, and butterflies.

Butterflies are most common in open forests, forest clearings, and grassland. Common species include the common windmill (also found in the tropical zone), indian fritillary (also in the tropical zone), painted lady, indian red admiral, and indian tortoiseshell (the last three species common from the tropical to subalpine zones). The giant honeybee, or *maahuri* (Apis dorsata), is a large bee that forms highly sophisticated colonies. Common in the Himalaya, it makes a distinctively shaped hive—a single exposed sheet of wax hanging down from beneath a rock overhang or ledge. ❖

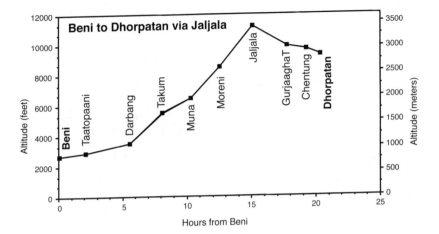

The trail heads southwest, reaching prickly-leaved oak forests, then rhododendron and birch higher up. After **2½ hours,** you reach a cluster of prayer flags and a *chorten* (11,200 feet, 3414 m). Continue to the west (don't take the left fork), pass a small spring, and reach the broad, flat plateau of **Jaljala** (to be differentiated from Jaljala mentioned later in Rolpa District) a few minutes later at a *chautaaraa*. The panorama from here takes in Machhapuchhre all the way to Churen Himal. Sunsets are supreme. There are some *goTh* here with a seasonal tea shop among them, used in the monsoon by people from Muna as they pasture their animals on the lush grass.

From Jaljala, follow the trail on the left/south side of the plateau, and don't descend into the river valley to the north. Descend some 15 minutes to reach a small saddle point (11,000 feet, 3353 m) that is the actual watershed between the Kali Gandaki and the Bheri–Karnali. Head for the valley V shape, through the pastures, and pass below a group of *goTh* to reach more in **30 minutes** from the *chautaaraa*. Beyond, cross to the right bank of the Uttar Ganga, which you will follow to Dhorpatan, and continue downvalley. Don't cross over the river 30 minutes beyond, but enjoy the rhododendron and juniper forests on the north side of the valley. Reach an open area with *goTh* in **1½ hours.** The seasonal dwellings of **GurjaaghaT** (9900 feet, 3017 m), the next cluster of *goTh* on this side of the valley, is **20 minutes** beyond. The Maoists, retreating after an attack on Beni in 2004, are alleged to have purposefully set afire the forest here as a diversion tactic for the Nepal Army helicopters pursuing them. From GurjaaghaT, cross several tributaries of the Simudar Khola on wooden bridges. As a variant side trip, you could head up this tributary valley, cross a pass and get to Gurjaakhaani, and then head back to Muna.

In **30 minutes** from GurjaaghaT, head upstream in another tributary valley to cross the Gur Gad to its right bank on a suspension bridge. Rejoin the main valley, and reach the beginning of the broad Dhorpatan valley. The way keeps to the drier north side and reaches the Tibetan village of **Chentung** (9660 feet, 2944 m) with lodging in another **hour.** The Bon-po *gomba* of this village, behind you on the hillside, follows the tradition that predated the introduction of Buddhism to Tibet. It has been much changed, so it is difficult to tell adherents apart. The best way is to see which direction they spin their prayer wheels and circumambulate *mani* walls.

Continue west and reach Nauthar, also called Chisopaani, in **35 minutes**. Here Nepalis come up from the south in the summer to grow potatoes and pasture

These Kham Magar girls near Dhorpatan wear banded cigarette wrappers in their ear lobes to make them look more Buddha-like. (Photo by Stephen Bezruchka)

animals. This agropastoral style of life is followed by many Nepalis in these parts as they farm the lowlands in the winter, grow rice in the summer, and move up with their animals to the high country in the monsoon. Cross the next tributary and go on through another Tibetan settlement before descending in **25 minutes** to **Dhorpatan** village (9416 feet, 2870 m) with lodging and the Dhorpatan Hunting Reserve (510 square miles, 1325 sq km) office, where permits will be checked or obtained. The staff monitors the trophy hunting for blue sheep (*bharal*) that is done north of here. Just beyond is the flat area called Giraaund, meaning "ground," the local term for an airstrip. The airstrip is overgrown with vegetation; planes haven't landed here for many years.

Dhorpatan is the name of the grassland area, an unusually broad, flat valley (*paaTan*) in this rugged hill country. It was once a lake that was filled in. Many Nepalis from villages to the east, south, and west live here during the summer months, when they grow potatoes and pasture animals. Their settlements are seen along the perimeter of the valley, especially on its southern aspect, and at Nauthar. When Tibetan refugees were streaming over the hills during the Chinese takeover of 1959–60, many were directed to settle in this valley by leaflet maps dropped out of airplanes. Thus began one of the four original Tibetan refugee camps set up by the Swiss in the early 1960s. While many Tibetans moved to business centers and prospered, a few remained here, content in this remoter realm of Nepal. Stephen recalls the two years that he lived here in the 1970s as some of the best times of his life.

Although there are few views from the valley floor (Annapurna can be seen some 35 miles (56 km) to the east), easy climbs of the surrounding hills provide unparalleled views. You can travel a few days to the north into blue sheep country or up into the snows of the western Dhaulagiri range. The base camps of the various expeditions at the head of the Ghustung Khola are worth visiting. A route northwest leads to Dolpo, which is one of the most sparsely populated areas of Nepal. Food and shelter must be carried for all these trips to the north.

To the west and northwest live the Kham Magar, an ethnic group with strong animistic and shamanistic traditions. Food and shelter are difficult to obtain in this area and are best carried. A 4–5-day circuit through this region can be most interesting.

After a long day down the Uttar Ganga, you reach the village of Takashera, where the flat-roofed houses are reminiscent of Thak Khola or of areas farther west. Cross the ridge up the tributary valley to the north and descend to Hukum (Hugaon), and go beyond to Maikot, on the north side of the Pelma Khola, in another very long day. The third day takes you through Puchhargaon and Yamakhar, where you meet the trail to Dolpo, which you can backtrack to Dhorpatan.

Those with less time should at least walk up one of the hills surrounding the valley for a view. The ridge crest directly south of the airstrip is the easiest viewpoint and takes less than 2 hours via one of its north-facing spurs. The view from here in clear weather extends beyond Langtang in the east! The hill to the north of the valley (13,600 feet, 4145 m) can be reached in 3–4 hours from the airstrip. Surtibang, the "writing desk" hill to the south-west, is an excellent viewpoint. Reach it by heading west for 30 minutes as the valley narrows to a bridge over the Uttar Ganga. Cross and ascend to the top (13,300 feet, 4054 m), in 4 hours from the former airstrip. Hiunchuli Patan is visible to the west. Finally, the highest of the peaks surrounding the valley, Phagune Dhuri (15,500 feet, 4724 m), lying to the northwest, can be reached from the Phagune Danda pass, on the route to Dolpo.

Other than continuing to Dolpo, which we do not describe, the return options from Dhorpatan are to retrace the same route out as followed in, or continue with the Guerila Trek to the road at Sulichaur.

EXPLORE: DHORPATAN TO SULICHAUR

The following is a brief sketch of the itinerary to continue the Guerilla Trek, with **route and walking times not reconnoitered by the authors themselves.**

The trail from **Dhorpatan** heading north goes to Dolpo. Instead, head east on a trail that passes through Masa and Bhuju with apple orchards and pastureland through an area that is well known for bird-watching. **Nisidhor** (8776 feet, 2675 m), with basic lodging, lies next to a stream and is reached in **3–4 hours** from Dhorpatan. Continue on through rhododendron forest and an area where leopards have been seen. Water may be scarce; fill up when and where you can. You cross from Baglung District into Rukum District, a district dominated by Maoists and used as a base during the war. **Takashera** (7119 feet, 2170 m) is a large Magar village near the banks of a tributary with basic lodging and telecommunication services, reached in **4½–6 hours** from Nisidhor.

There are little to no water sources between Takashera and Lukum, the next village. Climb steeply to Lukum La (10171 feet, 3100 m) and descend, being careful, as there are steep drop-offs from the trail. Pass through Lukum village, a largely Magar community

HEMP IN THE HIMALAYA

Hemp grows as a weed in a wide range of territory in Nepal. Although known as a source of intoxicants, and occasionally used this way by some people in Nepalese society, it serves other purposes as well. Seeds from the female plant are collected and pressed into oil in large hollowed-out wooden trays. The oil is commonly used for cooking out west, and it can also be used for making soap and as a liniment. Male plants growing in hot humid regions of the hills provide the best fiber. They are harvested toward the end of the monsoon; the stems are left to dry, then soaked, and the fibers pulled out with the teeth. They are then dried in the sun, beaten to soften them, and spun. Hemp is then woven into ropes and twine or made into a type of toga. ❖

with closely built houses with flat earthen roofs. These interconnected houses generally feature a bare ground floor where livestock is sheltered, while the upper level contains the living quarters. Continue down to **Rujhikhola** village (7300 feet, 2225 m) in **4–5 hours** from Takashera.

The trek from Rujhikhola to Thawang involves another strenuous uphill climb through rhododendron forest with a steep downhill section. The route passes through small settlements and terraced fields to reach **Thawang** (6562 feet, 2000 m), a village nestled between two rivers and inhabited mainly by Kham Magar, **3½–4½ hours** from Rujhikhola. Thawang was damaged during the war by mortar shells dropped from army helicopters. The hemp of the marijuana plants in the area is used for making rope, bags, and fine thread for weaving traditional clothing. Seeds are also used in making *achaar*, a pickled relish. A motor road is being built between Thawang and Holeri in the Tarai district of Dang to the south.

The next segment involves a strenuous ascent and descent with no facilities over a long day to reach the next settlement with little to no water except at the pass itself. Plan to depart early from Thawang. The path climbs uphill through rhododendron to a pass in a wetlands area known as **Jaljala** (10,367 feet, 3160 m) (to be differentiated from Jaljala pass, mentioned earlier en route to Dhorpatan from Beni) in Rolpa District in **4 hours**. Rolpa District was also a Maoist rebel base during the insurgency. Maoist soldiers were previously given weapons training in this pristine forest and grasslands area abundant with flora and fauna. There are no facilities at Jaljala, although three small temples have been erected. Views can be had of the Dhaulagiri and Annapurna ranges

Protector deities on the bridge at RaRa Lake (Photo by Robin Biellik)

and more, and nearby is Bhama Guphaa, a limestone cave. A further climb to the top of Dharampani (12,795 feet, 3900 m) offers impressive views in all directions, and locals say that even Api (23,400 feet, 7132 m) and Saipal (23,068 feet, 7031 m), the dominant peaks in the far west, can be made out.

As you descend, be aware that some parts of the path have sheer drop-offs from the trail and water might be scarce en route to **Jelbang** village (5430 feet, 1655 m), some **4 hours** or more away. A motor road is planned to Jelbang. Currently, the trek from Jelbang to the roadway at **Sulichaur** (2625 feet, 800 m) descends gently for **4–5 hours**, passing beautiful villages and terraced fields. Sulichaur has a bustling bazaar and basic lodging, and buses to Kathmandu are available (13 or more hours).

BACKCOUNTRY TREKS

The following routes will have settlements along part of the way with home stay, community lodges, and occasionally basic hotels. However, at some point, full self-sufficiency will be required in food and shelter for at least some sections of the journey. This self-reliance enables you to get beyond areas with facilities to remote areas that are more or less uninhabited. These isolated, infrequently visited areas allow closer communion with natural Nepal and a greater opportunity of encountering wildlife. An accompanying feeling of peace often results from being "away from it all," strikingly close to the mountains or alongside mesmerizing alpine lakes.

JUMLA–RARA LAKE CIRCUIT
(Map No. 13, Page 375)

At the southern edge of the Mugu District, at an altitude of almost 10,000 feet (3050 m), lies RaRa, the largest lake in Nepal. It has a circumference of almost 8 miles (13 km) and is nestled between heavily forested, steep-sided ridges that thrust up from the fault lines that riddle this section of the foot of the Himalaya. Few foreigners visit this area (only 146 were registered in 2009, 104 in 2008, and 82 in 2007).

Access to this region is from Pokhara to Beni by road and then trekking in via Dhorpatan and Lower Dolpo (2–3 weeks), or by air from an airstrip at Jumla (7660 feet, 2335 m), the headquarters of the Karnali Zone. The other nearest airfields are at Jufal near Dunai in Dolpo (5–6 days away), and KolTi in Bajura District (a 3-day trek). The flights usually pass through Surkhet or Nepalganj in the Tarai, and you might share the plane with large bags of rice from Nepal Food Corp and the U.N. Food Program, as Jumla District is regularly short on food.

A motor track now exists to Jumla from the Tarai, and thus vehicle transport is possible depending on the season and condition of the road. During the rainy season, it regularly washes out in several places and is hard going even under the best of circumstances. Generally, do not rely on this road access unless you have time to spare in the event of delays as well as a heroic ability to endure a long, arduous overland journey.

It is also possible to trek to Jumla from Surkhet to the south. This takes about a week and might offer viable alternatives for getting out of Jumla at the end of the trek. Finally, you can walk out to KolTi Airport in Bajura District in 3 days or even continue from there on to the roadway at Sanfebagar in Accham District with a possible detour through Khaptad National Park (mentioned at the end of this chapter under Additional

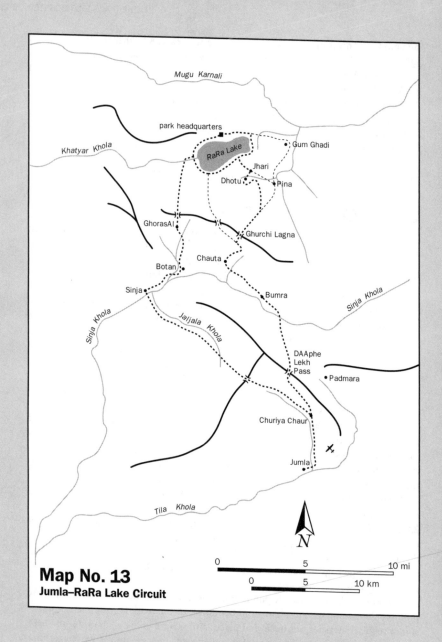

Map No. 13
Jumla–RaRa Lake Circuit

Eco-Trekking Suggestions). The route from RaRa to KolTi has been improved by local labor through the U.N.'s food for work program, although scant facilities along the way provide the bare minimum in food and lodging.

Most people fly in to Jumla Airport (also called Khalanga Airport), and the usual route from Jumla to RaRa will be described. Be aware that air service is irregular and it can be difficult to arrange return flights, either in Kathmandu or in Jumla (Jufal and KolTi). Once you arrive in Jumla, see the airline representative immediately to confirm your return flight.

From the settlement of Jumla, it is a 3-day walk to RaRa Lake. There are two variations. Most people do well to take the longer route—at least if traveling without a guide who is familiar with the shorter *lekh* (hill) route. Then the return route described follows a trail to Sinja, an interesting, historic settlement. From here, a former trade and communication route links back to Jumla. Some food must be carried no matter which route you take.

Apples, rice, wheat, potatoes, or beans may sometimes be available in the bazaar in Jumla, but food shortages are a recurring problem in this whole area. As far as possible, supplies required for trekking should be brought from Kathmandu. A local guide is advised; porters can be hired locally too, but English-speaking ones are rare and prices are likely to be high. It is essential to carry a tent when trekking in this area. Many of the people along this trek are Thakuri, the erstwhile King's caste, and have been known to be loath to allow anyone deemed below their status to enter or stay in their homes.

JUMLA TO RARA LAKE

The town of Jumla lies alongside the Tila Khola. It was the site of an attack by the Maoists during the civil war, and heavy fighting occurred throughout the town. Looking north from the Jumla bazaar, you can see most of the trail to the top of DAAphe Lekh. The trail goes just to the left of the highest point of this lekh.

Head out of the main bazaar from **Jumla** (7660 feet, 2335 m) on a wide trail along the east (left) bank of the stream, heading north. Stay on this side more or less all the time until the climbing begins. The trail up this valley passes next to the buildings of a large technical school on the way to the pass. Run by the United Mission to Nepal, this school offers educational opportunities to people in this remote region. After **1 hour** begin the ascent from the valley floor, climbing toward the right. The trail rises through a series of cultivated fields, passes close to a few scattered houses, and ascends steadily for over **1 hour.** While still well below the main tree line, the trail rises steeply for about 15 minutes, crosses a small stream, and enters one of the few clusters of blue pine trees on the open stretch of hillside. Near this spot—above the trail and slightly off to the right—is a campsite with a freshwater spring (9000 feet, 2743 m), a good place to rest and cook a morning meal. This is the last water before the pass. Don't go on in bad weather.

Ascending out of the trees, the trail opens out onto wide meadows rising gently to the north. About 15 minutes beyond the trees, the trail forks near some stone huts at **Churiya Chaur** (9875 feet, 3010 m). Take the less obvious right fork and, shortly after, reenter the forest. (The left fork is a more level main route to Sinja.) The trail emerges into high meadows, visible earlier from below, in **1½ hours** from the fork. Another **hour** on increasingly difficult rocky terrain brings you to the pass, the **DAAphe Lekh** (12,100 feet, 3688 m). The summit is marked with a small *chorten*. There is a small peak to your left (13,715 feet, 4180 m) and another to your right (13,807 feet, 4224 m). From this point you should have a fine view back down over the Jumla valley to the 15,000-foot (4500-m) ridges to the south. There is no northern view until you cross the top of the pass.

PEOPLES OF WESTERN AND FAR WESTERN NEPAL

This is the land of the ancient Malla Kingdom of the Karnali river basin. This region is literally littered with many of the cultural and historic artifacts of the Malla era, the twelfth to fourteenth centuries AD. At one time, the Malla Kingdom included portions of western Tibet as well. After its decline, the *baaisi raja* (twenty-two kingdoms) of west Nepal emerged and were not ceded to the expanding Gorkha kingdom until the nineteenth century. (Historians have postulated a relationship between the Malla kings of west Nepal and those of the Kathmandu valley just prior to the eighteenth-century Gorkha conquest, but there is no consensus.)

Along the former "royal highway" of the Malla Kingdom of west Nepal, a walking route stretching north from the inner Tarai through Jumla and into Tibet, there are various inscribed stones that scholars have used to determine the nature and extent of the Malla domain. And there are ancient shrines to be seen throughout western Nepal dedicated to the prominent local deity called "Masta." On some trails in the west, one may see carved wooden spirit effigies, festooned with bells, flowers, and strips of colored cloth, set out to appease the spirits that haunt each locale. Trekkers are admonished to respect local customs here and throughout Nepal, and to refrain from handling or taking souvenirs beyond what can be captured with a camera. Much of what is seen and admired here is sacred, and local feeling toward holy objects is not unlike the reverence and respect Westerners feel in the sanctuaries of the great cathedrals of Europe or in their hometown churches and synagogues.

One fascinating cultural feature of some of the more northerly dwelling Hindus of this region is their apparent "Tibetanization." Unlike elsewhere in Nepal, some Chhetri and Thakuri of the west and far west are indistinguishable at first glance from their Buddhist BhoTiya neighbors. They wear the same style of clothing, construct similar flat-roofed houses, and pursue the same patterns of trade and subsistence economy. Their way of living is unlike that of their more "pure" Hindu caste neighbors to the south and east, who look down upon them in some respects. The BhoTiya cultural attributes noted here, and wherever they occur among non-BhoTiya people in Nepal, are reflections of the northern mountain environment. ◈

From the *chorten*, follow the trail across the top of the ridge, winding through patchy forest to the north before dropping again into open meadows. Note carefully the spot where you emerge from the trees. If you come back this way, it is very easy to miss the opening. If you climb straight on over these meadows, you reach a different pass that leads to the village of Padmara to the southeast and a longer walk back to Jumla.

Leave the meadows, cross a small stream, follow the trail into the trees, and descend rapidly through dense, mixed forest for **2 hours**. Notice the magnificent birch trees, the bark of which is collected for use as paper. And keep your eyes open for a *DAAphe*—the multicolored national bird of Nepal. There may be *bhaTTi* for Nepali travelers along here.

Near the end of the descent, the trail drops very steeply to the **Sinja Khola**, which is immediately crossed by a bridge (8900 feet, 2713 m). Turning west, pass the *bhaTTi* of Naurighat along the north (right) bank of the river. Within the next hour, choose any suitable campsite along the valley floor by the river.

Approximately **1 hour** from the Sinja Khola bridge, the trail rises from the riverbed to pass below the village of **Bumra** (9350 feet, 2850 m). An alternative campsite could be in the vicinity of the village. Supplies can sometimes be procured from locals.

From Bumra, continue along the side of the hill, proceeding about 500 feet (150 m) above the river. Pass just above another small village within 15 minutes. After another 15 minutes, descend steeply to cross a small stream entering the main river from the north. On the valley floor, cross the main stream (9250 feet, 2819 m), and immediately climb steeply again for **30 minutes** to regain your former altitude. Within another **hour**, descend again to cross another stream entering from the north. At the foot of this descent, huddled beneath the steep rock walls on the far side of the stream, stand the few houses and small police post of **Chauta** (9000 feet, 2743 m). Splendid clay *chilim* (pipes) are made in this area and are sometimes sold at one of the shops and basic inns here. If you head downstream on the Sinja Khola, you will reach Sinja in less than a day. There is a route that returns to Chauta from RaRa Lake via Chabragaon. Hire a local guide if you wish to return this way and not do the long circuit via Sinja.

From Chauta, head north, following the trail gently uphill and crisscrossing the stream, the Chauta Khola, in a steep, narrow valley. Ascend to Bhulbule (10,270 feet, 3130 m), with a pair of simple lodges, and the RaRa Lake National Park entrance station, where you will have to pay an entrance fee if you didn't in Kathmandu. A pleasant walk through groves of large walnut trees takes you to a small *dharmsala* ("resting place") with a good, clear-flowing spring. Reach some isolated cultivated fields in 1 hour. In another 15 minutes, the trail passes out of the trees and, leaving the course of the stream, swings left onto the high, open pastures. You are now climbing again, to the pass of Ghurchi Lagna.

The wide trail proceeds almost directly westward, rising across a broad, grassy valley that runs almost at right angles to the final ridge. After you pass groups of large boulders for 30 minutes, the valley you are following splits into two distinct valleys. One heads northwest, and the other, containing the main trail, goes slightly northeast. The main trail heads up the right valley, climbing more or less north to the pass of the **Ghurchi Lagna** (11,300 feet, 3444 m), which is marked by a small stone *chorten*. The pass is some **3 hours** from Chauta.

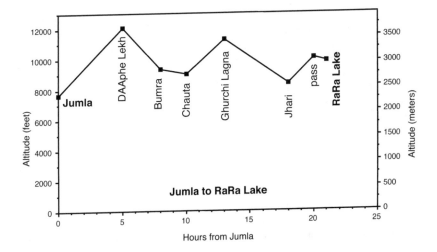

Descend 30 minutes, and take the trail branching to the left (to the right is the more circuitous route that passes through the village of Pina and on to Mugu District), and traverse, without losing much height, through young pine forest. Cross a couple of meadows, and then descend steeply to a clear stream and follow it to reach the small hamlet of Dhotu (7808 feet, 2380 m). Cross the stream and climb steeply to the north for 30 minutes to the village of **Jhari** (8350 feet, 2545 m) some **4–5 hours** from the pass.

Continue up through the village and pass some huge cedars, climb again through the forest, and emerge after about **2 hours** onto high, open pasture. Cross the easily gained summit (10,050 feet, 3063 m) and emerge at a flat area on the south side of **RaRa Lake** (9800 feet, 2987 m). Directly across, toward the northwestern side of the lake, is the building of the national **park headquarters** and staff and army accomodations. There is a simple lodge here.

The area surrounding the lake, which was designated a national park in 1975, offers spectacular scenery, although views of snow-capped peaks are limited. Magnificent examples of fir, pine, spruce, juniper, cedar, birch, and rhododendron are found in the forest. Wildlife, including bears, cats, wolves, and deer, has been observed in the area. Around the shores of the lake are some fine "Malla Stones"—pillars of rock bearing Devanagari inscriptions and figures of the sun and moon. The inscriptions probably date from the Malla kings, who reigned over much of the western Himalayan region in the twelfth century AD.

The best camping areas are on the lake's south side, which has much more diverse topography and vegetation than the north side. Meadowlands blanketed with wildflowers, virgin spruce forest full of birds, and some streams on the southwest corner of the lake make for idyllic camping. Be aware that this area has a fragile ecosystem and cannot stand the excesses of contemporary trekking development.

Legend and folklore provide the bulk of knowledge about RaRa Lake. The locals believe it is at least 1800 feet (550 m) deep. They feel it is fed from underground springs flowing from the Mugu Karnali, which is located about 1800 feet (550 m) downhill from the lake on the other side of the north *lekh*. Given its size and location near one of the main trade routes to Tibet, it is surprising that the lake does not have greater historical or religious significance. Unlike many Himalayan lakes, it is not a pilgrimage site. An annual festival in July and August commemorates the intervention of the great god Thakur, who changed the direction of the outlet of the lake. Firing an arrow to the west, he opened the western hill to form the present outlet and, taking huge quantities of earth, he filled in the eastern outlet and stamped it firmly with his great feet. His footprints, embedded in a rock, are visible to this day at the eastern end of the lake. They are the festival's main objects of interest—other than the attractive dancers and the local brew.

The lake's inaccessible location has kept many of its secrets undiscovered. The potential for discovery may be one of the most exciting aspects of this trek. A 7–8-mile circumambulation of the serene lake takes a few hours.

RARA TO JUMLA VIA SINJA

You can return to Jumla by taking a less-traveled, longer route through Sinja, the historical summer capital of the Malla Kingdom (twelfth to fourteenth centuries AD). It is necessary to bring food, shelter, and a good map or a local guide familiar with the route.

From the **RaRa Lake park headquarters** (9900 feet, 3018 m), take the shore trail southwest to the lake outlet, the **Khatyar Khola** (9780 feet, 2981 m), also called the Nisha Khola, in **45 minutes.** Do not cross the bridge here, but continue down the

BRASSWORK

Artisans from the Shakya clan of Kathmandu (their ancestors moved here eons ago) continue the centuries-old process of making the attractive small brass vessels Nepalis drink from and take to the fields. The process begins with a clay or metal mold that is covered by a thin layer of soft wax. This model is fitted by a lump of wax onto a hand-driven lathe, and the artist carves. The model is then encased in a clay-dung coating with outlets for the wax and inlets for the brass. It is heated in a charcoal oven, and then the outlets are opened to extract the wax. The mold is then fully baked. When ready, molten brass is poured into the mold.

After cooling, the molds are broken open to remove the vessel, which is finished on the hand-driven lathe, which is rotated much faster. Complicated designs are made in separate parts, which are later joined together. The decorated patterns are made by a similar process, adding wax elements with the designs embossed into the wax mold. Later the artwork is completed with fine tools. Separate sections are then joined together. To obtain the intricate floral designs often seen, wax layers containing the carved designs are pasted on the plain wax forms created as above. The same clay coating is then carried out and final finishing done by hand.

A major center for this craft in the east is in Bhojpur District west of the Arun Khola. The brasscraft is sold by weight. The brass comes from Singapore or from recycled old objects (khu). Interestingly, the biggest consumers of this dying art are in the Kathmandu valley, where the urban people have a taste for this fine craftsmanship. Elsewhere in Nepal, cheaply produced stainless steel, aluminum, and plastic ware have become commonplace. ❖

north (right) bank for **30 minutes** and then cross the stream on a bridge. One trail continues west on the south (left) bank of the *khola* after ascending a 100-foot (30-m) knoll. Instead, take the left fork (heading south) up a small valley. Climb through the woods on a sometimes indefinite trail that keeps to the western side of the valley. Reach a meadow with a *goTh* (10,740 feet, 3274 m) on a crest in **1 hour.**

Continue south, climbing steeply through oak, then birch, then rhododendron forests, to reach an alpine ridge (12,500 feet, 3810 m) in **2½ hours.** Above to the left is Chuchuemara Danda. Traverse on its west shoulder for 15 minutes and come out on a saddle above the Ghatte Khola. Descend 500 feet (150 m) to the headwaters of the river and continue down through the valley for 1 hour to **GhorasAI** (also known as Ghorasingha), site of the army guard post (10,500 feet, 3305 m), in **1½ hours** from the saddle. Here the stream turns southwest. This is an appropriate and beautiful place to camp.

From GhorasAI, the trail at first heads down the right side of the valley and then soon crosses to the left, where it is flat, to the top of the moraine wall. It recrosses the stream here and descends steeply on the right-hand side. Botan can be seen ahead on the left-hand slopes of the valley. Regardless of trails heading off to the right in the general direction of Sinja, stay in this valley, taking the fork that keeps you closest to the Sinja/Hima Khola, until you reach it.

There is an excellent campsite at the confluence of the Jaljala and Sinja Kholas. Just below here, the Sinja Khola goes through a narrow gorge. The top end of Sinja village is at the lower end of this gorge, an additional 15-minute walk. Reach **Sinja** (8000 feet, 2438 m) in **4 hours** from GhorasAI. A bridge across the Sinja/Hima Khola at this point (top end of the village and lower end of the gorge) is crossed to pick up the trail heading up the Jaljala Khola. Food and lodging might be difficult to find in Sinja, even for porters.

Sinja lies in a highly cultivated valley. To the south, on a prominent knoll, are the remains of the former capitol of this area. It is presently the site of a temple, Kankasundri. This area is well worth visiting by climbing the 400 feet (120 m) to the top of the knoll.

To return to Jumla, follow the historical route between Sinja and Khalanga, the old name for Jumla. The 2-day route through beautiful forests ascends a river valley to a *lekh* and descends to Jumla. A camp in the meadows along the way is ideal.

From Sinja, ascend the Jaljala Khola to the southeast, keeping to the south (left) bank on a good trail. Pass a few dwellings and *goTh* at Chala Chaur (9613 feet, 2930 m) and then the large pasture area of Jaljala Chaur (10,728 feet, 3270 m) to reach a high point (11,500 feet, 3505 m) in **5–6 hours**. On the far watershed, the trail descends past a few houses through forests and pastures, and from Churiya Chaur follows south along the same route you originally took out from Jumla. Reach **Jumla** (7640 feet, 2329 m) in **3 hours** from the high point.

Winnowing rice is a routine task in many villages. (Photo by Alonzo Lyons)

MAKALU BASE CAMP
(Map No. 14, Page 382)

Trekkers wishing an opportunity to visit wild cloud-forest jungle festooned with orchids, pass through Rai villages with their incredibly varied use of bamboo, or leave hill Nepal along the spine of a ridge to enter wild and sacred mountain terrain will be well rewarded in trekking to and in Makalu–Barun National Park. The park also has a surrounding conservation area where there are villages. The current park headquarters are in KhAADbari, with offices scattered throughout the region.

Makalu–Barun National Park (540 square miles, 1400 sq km) adjoins Sagarmatha National Park and lies to the east in the Arun valley watershed. It was visited by 1828 trekkers in 2009, 1371 trekkers in 2008, and only 261 in 2007. The route ascends the Arun Khola from Tumlingtar to reach the Makalu Base Camp in the upper Barun Khola valley. Ethnic groups encountered include the Tamang and Rai Hindu castes and Sherpa. Once you leave Tashigaon, the last inhabited place where food can be obtained, it takes about 5 days to reach the base camp, and fuel, food, shelter, and porters are necessary. The sense of leaving hill Nepal on the crest of a ridge from Tashigaon and crossing a high pass to enter a valley of sacred and majestic wild mountains is unparalleled in Nepal. This valley is clothed in dense forests hardly touched by people and is rich in wildlife. Two new bird species for Nepal have been found there, the slaty-bellied tesia and spotted wren-babbler.

Most people fly in to Tumlingtar's airfield. Outside of the rainy season, vehicles are now able to reach Tumlingtar from Hille, the previous starting point for those arriving overland. Other trekkers find the way in or out to Tumlingtar via Solu–Khumbu. A possible exit is to follow the Arun Khola all the way south to leave hill Nepal behind and enter the Tarai, an excellent way out during the cool winter that passes the physically and spiritually powerful junction of the Tamur, Arun, and Sun Kosi rivers that drain all of eastern Nepal's Himalaya.

TUMLINGTAR TO SEDUA VIA KHAADBARI

Tumlingtar (1500 feet, 457 m) is a long plateau with a grass airstrip, hotels nearby to the east, and the main town just north. There is now a road and vehicle transport to KhAADbari. To hike there, head east to the right of the main road, passing *chautaaraa* along the way, to reach **KhAADbari** (3500 feet, 1067 m) in 2¾ **hours**. KhAADbari is a large Newar bazaar and Sankhuwasabha District's administrative center, spread out along the ridge. The Makalu–Barun National Park office headquarters is here as well as a police check post, many shops, hotels, a hospital, and both a Wednesday and Saturday market.

Climb to the small Newar bazaar of Manebhanjyang (3700 feet, 1128 m), along the major ridge north–south. There are some simple hotels and tea shops for trekkers along the ridge. Heading toward Sedua, pass through small hamlets to reach the village of **BhoTebas** (5900 feet, 1798 m) below the ridge crest in 3½ **hours** from KhAADbari. There is simple lodging here. The trail continues close to the crest of a ridge (Chyankuti Bhanjyang), passing through **Chichila** with a tea shop in 2¼ **hours**. Look for the park signboard describing the mountain panorama. Continue in a glorious mixed broadleaf verdant forest, with moss everywhere. Don't travel alone in this forest, as incidents have occurred to solo travelers. Reach **MUDe** (6500 feet, 1981 m) with basic lodging in another 3½ **hours**. Here you can see the route toward the Makalu Base Camp, while closer to hand, Nepalis may be carrying a shrub, bound together on their backs. This is *chiraito*, a medicinal plant (*jaDibuTi*) sold at the road head.

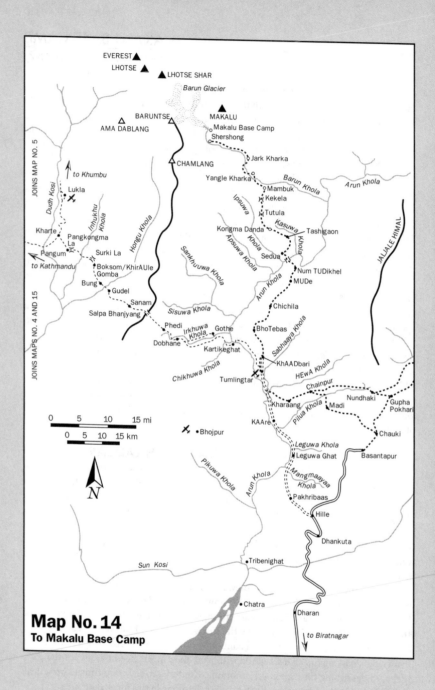

Map No. 14
To Makalu Base Camp

Head north, mostly along the west side of the ridge, sometimes on a red mud (*raato maaTo*) trail that is treacherous in the monsoon. Continue on to reach **Num TUDikhel** (4920 feet, 1500 m), on the ridge with several shops and basic lodging in **3 hours**. Leave the main north–south trail and descend steeply east through incredibly wet jungle on the east side of the valley where the sun rarely reaches to the suspension bridge over the **Arun** at 2260 feet (689 m) in **1½ hours**. Downstream are some of the more difficult kayak and rafting ventures in Nepal. Cross the torrent to the true left side and climb up relentlessly, passing a tea shop along the way, to reach **Sedua** (also known as Murmidanda) (5000 feet, 1524 m) in **3 hours**. Here there is a police post, a few shops with basic lodging and a school and park check point where you must present or obtain an entry permit.

SEDUA TO MAKALU BASE CAMP

It is good sense to hire porters who are familiar with the way to base camp; these could possibly be hired in Sedua or in Tashigaon. Make sure everyone is adequately clothed and equipped.

From **Sedua**, climb a ridge between the Ipsuwa (also called the Isuwa) Khola to the west and the Kasuwa Khola to the east, passing the hamlet of Manigaon, to a ridge crest with a shop and school at Cheksedanda (6100 feet, 1959 m). Then traverse less steeply the hillside striking northeast, entering Sherpa country, passing through Geng, above Hindrungma, and Ropessa to reach **Tashigaon** (6860 feet, 2090 m) in **3½ hours** from Sedua. This is a cluster of Sherpa homes with prayer flags, and emergency radio might be available here. A variety of trails can lead here from Sedua, all converging at the water mill below the village.

Beyond Tashigaon (literally, "luck village"), there are no settlements but the area has lots of seasonal use in the monsoon. Many trekkers continuing onward from Tashigaon report that bad weather prevents them from seeing the mountains. Good luck! There are basic lodges in Tashigaon that cater to trekkers; while here you should ask whether there are any facilities open farther on toward the Makalu Base Camp. A kerosene depot has been established, and you should not burn wood beyond Tashigaon. You might be able to rent stoves and blankets here as well. Because there are no permanent villages beyond, you must be self-sufficient for the rest of the journey. There are seven signed campsites ahead designated by the park for use by trekkers. There are minimal or no toilet facilities developed there at present. While some lodges may be in operation beyond, they are only temporary, pending new park regulations.

From Tashigaon head north, crossing a few streams, on a wide trail in a lush cloud forest, pass trees festooned with orchids, to reach a notch at 10,140 feet (3090 m). Enter the national park and descend in more open country on the west side of the ridge to Ongshisa (10,240 feet, 3121 m), with *goTh* frames. Water is a problem along here if there is no snow to melt. Continue out of the forest along a ridge crest, and look back to get a sense of climbing the backbone of hill Nepal to leave it behind. Reach **Kongma Danda**, a flat area for camping (11,420 feet, 3480 m), with water. There are overhangs that can be used as shelters to the east. It takes **4–4½ hours** from Tashigaon. Be on the lookout for altitude illness, and return should there be anything other than mild symptoms when you could wait one night at Kongma Danda. Otherwise, if AMS strikes down in the Barun, you have to ascend to get out.

Continue along the ridge, past Gongru La, (13,156 feet, 4010 m) festooned with prayer flags, with views of Makalu, Chamlang, and Baruntse, as well as Kangchenjunga and Jannu to the east, to Sano Pokhari, "little lake" (12,533 feet, 3820 m), in **2 hours**.

Peaks 6 and 7 reflect in the waters. Climb to the first of two passes, the **Tutula**, at (14,238 feet, 4340 m), in **2¼ hours**, and descend to Thulo Pokhari, the magical lake between the two passes. Climb again to the **Kekela** (13,724 feet, 4183 m), in **45 minutes** from the other pass. Westerners call the first one Shipton Pass after the first westerner to cross them. It is so signed, but we prefer the Sherpa name. Make a mental map of the route you have taken, for if returning in a whiteout, locating the snow-covered route could be a nightmare. Don't go on unless everyone is well equipped and not suffering from altitude illness.

Gaze off north into Tibet. Descend to the north, entering the fir, rhododendron, and birch forest of the Barun Khola valley, to reach **Mambuk** with spaces for camping (11,690 feet, 3563 m) in **2 hours** from the pass. The descent can be treacherous if frozen. Reach the Barun Khola at 10,380 feet (3162 m), and head upstream on the true right, south bank to reach **Jate** (or lower Mambuk) as well as an overhang in **1 hour**.

Plunge down to head up the valley in the Barun canyon, reaching Zhante before taking an hour to cross an active slide area. There is talk of rebuilding the trail to avoid this dangerous section. As the upper part of Makalu comes into view, pass Pematang, another flat area, to cross the Barun Khola and ascend to more open meadows among forests of silver fir and birch. **Yangle Kharka** (11,800 feet, 3597 m), in **3 hours** from Jate, is another designated camping site with prayer flags and a small tea shop and *gomba*. Look south at the northeast side of Peak 6 and its ice-covered neighbors. Contour along on the south side of the Barun Khola, turning into an avalanche fan through scrub alders, to **Neghe Kharka** (12,160 feet, 3706 m), a serene, powerful pasture of frames and prayer flags, and another designated campsite, **30 minutes** farther along. Guru Rimpoche stayed in a cave up high to the south and made a fist with his upturned thumb that is sculptured in one of the rocks. During the full moon of August in the monsoon, there is a festival held here, and people go up to the cave, where it is said that if you are infertile or barren and do a *puja*, you will bear children. Of the sheer cliffs to the south, the one on the right is the mother, on the left the father.

Shortly beyond, cross the Barun Khola to the true left on bridges between the huge boulders in the river (12,240 feet, 3730 m), then wind up behind in a quiet, peaceful valley, to come up to a clearing where to the south you can see two revered pregnant

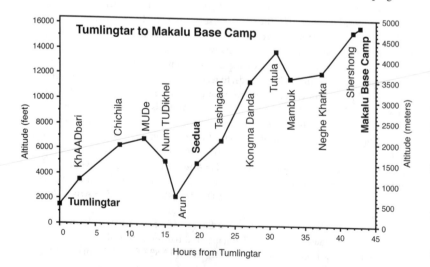

Typically children do not lack affection in the hills. (Photo by Stephen Bezruchka)

rock formations, Aama Phisum, that may account for the local fertility legends. Many waterfall slivers cascade off the canyon walls, if not frozen; one even emerges from a cave 325 feet (100 m) up. Reach the opening of Ripu Maidaan (13,040 feet, 3975 m), and then cross many tributaries to Tadosa (meaning "horse tie," where Shiva tied his steed). Continue to **Jark Kharka** (13,850 feet, 4221 m), with its roofed hut, near the upper limit of forest **2 hours** from Neghe Kharka. Be wary of altitude illness and quick to descend if necessary. Note how the valley above changes from a water worn V-shape below to a glacier scoured U-shape above.

Continue past Langmale (Yak) Kharka where a basic lodge may be in operation and kerosene supplies might be replenished if available. Then crest a ridge from where you can see the lateral moraine of the Barun Glacier, pass Merek (a string of stone enclosures and a designated campsite where there are currently no lodges), and follow a stream to **Shershong** (15,450 feet, 4710 m) in 2½ **hours**, also a campsite near a stone built dwelling. This broad plane puts you on the Schneider Khumbu Himal map.

The valley turns north. Thrushes may flock around nearby. Supplicate beneath the immense south face of Makalu in the throne room of the gods. To appreciate the 2-mile-high face, hike to a flat, sandy shelf **1 hour** up on the protected west side of a lateral moraine at 15,827 feet (4824 m). This area was the original site of the **base camp** for the 1955 French first ascent of Makalu (27,765 feet, 8463 m), an expedition where all members reached the summit! They headed northwest of here to cross a col to reach the north side of the mountain. Its name is taken from Maha-kala, meaning "the great black one," clearly appropriate for this rocky massif.

Currently, expeditions head northwest up the Barun Glacier rubble to the so-called Hillary Base Camp, a tiring day's hike up, where the views are minimal. Instead, climb up to the east, take a tent after you have acclimatized, and consider camping on the crest of the ridge (17,800 feet, 5425 m) to get the sunrise and sunset views if you can melt snow. The broad, white Kangshung (east) face of Everest can be seen, as well as Lhotse, and the flanks of their ridges reaching down into Tibet, unfamiliar views to most trekkers. Spectacular Chamlang looks very different from the peak you have been seeing. Many other hikes will suggest themselves to the energetic explorers.

The descent can be made remarkably quickly, but if you have good weather, take time to enjoy this special place.

ADDITIONAL ECO-TREKKING SUGGESTIONS

The following treks are options to consider for those wishing to explore trails and territory away from the more established routes and regions. They offer an unrivaled opportunity to experience some of unseen Nepal. We have not precisely surveyed these areas ourselves and thus only a brief outline is given, leaving much to be explored and discovered. People who choose these routes should have prior experience trekking and should be self-reliant and confident on the trails.

THE NUMBUR CHEESE CIRCUIT
(Map No. 15, Page 387)

The Numbur Cheese Circuit (NCC) is for the more ambitious trekker who is already acclimatized and is capable of full self-sufficiency away from lodging and human habitation. It is set in one of Nepal's most newly protected areas, the Gauri–Shankar Conservation Area, which was formally declared at a cabinet meeting held at Kala Pattar in December 2009 ahead of Copenhagen climate talks. The route was jointly developed by the Ramechap Economic Development Forum and the U.N.'s International Labor Organization, and "launched" in October 2009 by the Nepal Tourism Board. As of yet, the NCC has seen few tourists and involves camping for much of the journey of up to two weeks or more.

The NCC trek is located in northern Ramechap District between the Rowaling and Everest regions, and follows the major drainage valleys of the Khimti and Likhu rivers, with the Gyajo La (16,010 feet, 4880 m) between them. Another high pass, Panch Pokhari (15,108 feet, 4605 m), is crossed en route with a nearby majestic collection of five small lakes. The name of this trek is derived from Numbur Peak (22831 feet, 6959 m), a yet unclimbed peak that dominates the route which takes you to its lap. Numbur (also known as Shorong Yul Lha) is believed to be the home of the protector deity of Solu, the area to the east.

Gauri–Shankar (23,459 feet, 7150 m) is also unclimbed, and permits are not issued for this sacred mountain. It is named after the God-couple Parvati, also known as Gauri, and Shiva, also known as Shankar. Gauri–Shankar was thought at one time to be the highest summit in the world because of its visibility from afar. This trek provides a unique and striking southeastern vantage of Gauri–Shankar rather than its usual broad expanse.

Two trekking peaks of Pharchamo (20,298 feet, 6187 m) and Ramdung (19,438 feet, 5925 m) are also in this area, and many more snowy peaks provide extraordinary views to complement the adjoining alpine landscape.

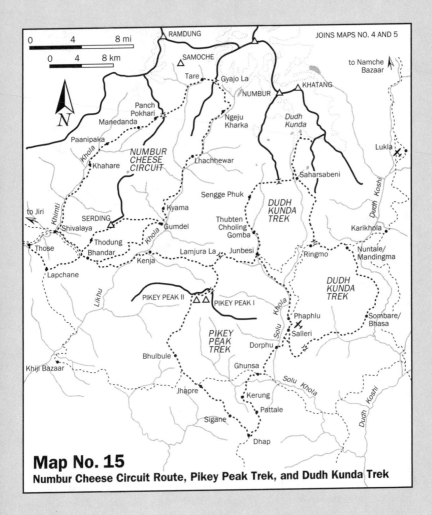

JOINS MAPS NO. 4 AND 5

0   4   8 mi

0   4   8 km

N

RAMDUNG

SAMOCHE

to Namche Bazaar

Tare

Gyajo La

NUMBUR

KHATANG

Panch Pokhari

Manedanda

Ngeju Kharka

Dudh Kunda

Paanipaka

Khimti Khola

Khahare

NUMBUR CHEESE CIRCUIT

Lhachhewar

Lukla

to Jiri

SERDING

Shivalaya

Those

Kyama

Gumdel

Sengge Phuk

Thubten Chholing Gomba

Junbesi

DUDH KUNDA TREK

Saharsabeni

Dudh Koshi

Karikhola

Thodung

Bhandar

Kenja

Khola

Lamjura La

Ringmo

Nuntale/ Mandingma

Lapchane

Likhu

PIKEY PEAK II

PIKEY PEAK I

DUDH KUNDA TREK

Solu Khola

Phaphlu

Salleri

Sombare/ Bhasa

PIKEY PEAK TREK

Dorphu

Bhulbule

Ghunsa

Khiji Bazaar

Jhapre

Kerung

Solu Khola

Pattale

Dudh Koshi

Sigane

Dhap

Map No. 15
Numbur Cheese Circuit Route, Pikey Peak Trek, and Dudh Kunda Trek

There are thirteen cheese factories along this route, most of them seasonal operations; however, the Swiss-designed plant at Thodung (10,140 feet, 3091 m) was established in 1957. Thodung Monastery is 30 minutes south of the cheese factory.

Along with the exceptional mountain vistas, this trek encompasses a variety of terrain from terraced fields to deep gorges and glacial lakes. There are a profusion of rhododendron blossoms in the springtime, and, given the area's pristine remoteness, sightings of birds of prey, musk deer, and Himalayan tahr are not uncommon. Although possible, catching sight of a prowling snow leopard is extremely rare.

This route was primarily designed for eco-camping with some home stay. The swift altitude gain warrants considerable caution, and trekkers following this route must already be acclimatized from previous excursions and stay vigilant for symptoms of AMS (see Chapter 5).

The education of rural women and girls has advanced greatly over the last few decades.
(Photo by Stephen Bezruchka)

Shivalaya has lodges and is reached in a daylong bus ride from the Old Bus Park (near Ratna Park) of Kathmandu. Or, consider disembarking at Jiri and walking from there, 3 hours away (see Chapter 7 for the route description between Jiri and Shivalaya).

NUMBUR CHEESE CIRCUIT ROUTE:

This trek begins at Shivalaya (5873 feet, 1790 m) and follows the Khimti Khola north to reach Khahare village (7136 feet, 2175 m) where home stay is available. From Khahare onward be extremely vigilant of signs of AMS due to rapid elevation gains. Climb to Paanipakha (10,187 feet, 3105 m), where camping will be necessary. Continue ascending to Manedanda (12,927 feet, 3940 m), another campsite. Ascend to Panch Pokhari (14,813 feet, 4515 m), and more camping. The trail from Panch Pokhari to Tare (13,583 feet, 4140 m) travels over the Panch Pokhari Pass (15,108 feet, 4605 m). Camping will be necessary in Tare. Continue on from Tare via the Gyajo La (16,010 feet, 4880 m) to reach Ngeju Kharka (12,106 feet, 3690 m) and more camp sites.

The trail descends from Ngeju Kharka to Lhachhewar village (8743 feet, 2665 m) where you will have an opportunity for home stay. Descend from Lhachhewar to the village of Kyama (7808 feet, 2380 m), also with home stay. Continue on from Kyama to Gumdel (7398 feet, 2255 m), again with the option of home stay. Ascend from Gumdel to Serding (11,024 feet, 3360 m) where lodging is available. Continue on to Lapchane (10,187 feet, 3105 m) via Thodung (there is a cheese factory in Thodung), intersecting the overland route from Jiri to Everest along the way. Home stay is available in Lapchane. Descend from Lapchane to Those (5758 feet, 1755 m) where there are hotels and vehicle transport to Kathmandu (9 or more hours).

SOLU TREKS
(Map No. 15, Page 387)

Both of these routes are in the southern, Solu area of Solu–Khumbu District and accessed from the main trail between Jiri and Lukla. Although near the popular Everest route, these treks are away from the beaten path and take you to previously unheralded areas. The routes offer entirely different experiences from each other.

The Pikey Peak Trek focuses on the culture of the mid-hills, the true gem of Nepal, passing through Tamang, Magar, Sherpa, Newar, and Rai areas with sensational village vistas draped in a mountain backdrop, and requires one night of self-sufficiency.

The Dudh Kunda (Milk Lake) Trek rises to a glacial lake at the base of the snowy giants, and requires four or more nights of full, self-sufficient camping. The lake lies at the lap of 22,831-foot (6959 m) Numbur Peak (also known as Shorong Yul Lha), believed to be the home of the protector deity of Solu, Khatang (22,484 feet, 6853 m), and Karyolung (21,362 feet, 6511 m). Pilgrims flock to the lake in August, and many believe that its waters can bless childless couples with fertility.

The routes tie in at Junbesi as well as Phaphlu/Salleri, and can be easily combined together (as well as with the Everest trek). Brief outlines of both are supplied below; however, **neither has been reconnoitered by the authors**.

Start either trek by flying into Phaphlu airport or arriving overland via Jiri to Junbesi village, as described in Chapter 7. (Another overland route is to Salleri via Okhaldhunga District to the south via jeep, a long ride over a rough road.)

PIKEY PEAK CULTURAL TREK

Beginning in Junbesi (8775 feet, 2675 m), the route follows the Junbesi Khola for much of the way to reach Phaphlu village (8100 feet, 2469 m) where there is an airport. Continue to the town of Salleri (7841 feet, 2390 m), Solu–Khumbu District's headquarters with many facilities. From Salleri the route leads to Dorphu and then on to Ghunsa (7710 feet, 2350 m). Continue on from Ghunsa to the Tamang village of Kerung (7874 feet, 2400 m) where there is a *gombaa* and then climb to Pattale (9318 feet, 2840 m). From Pattale continue to Sigane where there is a Hindu temple and then reach the Sherpa village of Jhapre (9252 feet, 2820 m) with a *gombaa*. The

WEAVING TRADITIONS: COTTON

Cotton originated in South Asia, and it has been grown in Nepal for at least several hundred years. Cheap imported cloth has stifled much local production. Imported yarn is spun into lively attractive patterns for producing *dhaka* cloth made into the traditional men's hat or *Topi*. The Rai and Limbu of the eastern hills are the source of this tradition, and Terhathum, south of Basantapur, is a major production center. Weaving takes place in groups near homes, with children playing about. Men make the loom, and the women weave. Inlay and tapestry patterns are continually being created, and the interplay of colors produce desirable textiles, as well as caps. Much of this material has made its way to Kathmandu and is being used by fashion designers there and exported as well. ❖

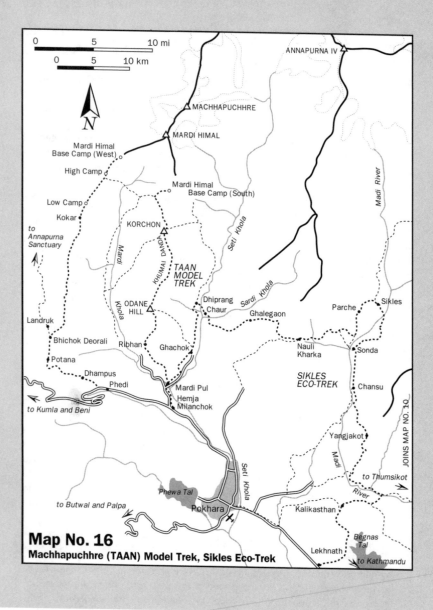

Map No. 16
Machhapuchhre (TAAN) Model Trek, Sikles Eco-Trek

route onward from Jhapre passes through Bhulbule on the way to Pikey Base Camp (11,942 feet, 3640 m). There is a tea shop in Bhulbule; however, there are no facilities at the base camp. Ascend to Pikey Peak (13,159 feet, 4010 m) with arresting views of Kanchengjunga to the east, Everest Makalu and Numbur Peak to the north, and more, including a broad vantage of the beautiful Solu valley dotted with settlements. Descend to the main Jiri–Everest route between Goyem (10,350 feet, 3155 m) and Lamjura Pass (11,580 feet, 3530 m). From here you can walk out to bus service at Bhandar, Shivalaya, or Jiri (route described in reverse in Chapter 7).

DUDH KUNDA TREK

This trek begins from Junbesi to head north to Thubten Chholing Gomba (9580 feet, 2920 m). Be extremely vigilant of AMS due to rapid elevation gains from here onward as you ascend to Sengge Phuk (12,927 feet, 3940 m). Sengge Phuk is a cave hermitage built into a rock overhang. Continue from Sengge Phuk to Bhasa Khola-Beni (12,894 feet, 3930 m) before a long ascent to Dudh Khunda lake (14,964 feet, 4561 m. Return from Dudh Khunda via Saharsabeni (12,582 feet, 3835 m) to Ringmo village (8924 feet, 2720 m) which lies on the Jiri–Everest route. Continue from Ringmo to Tragsindho (9711 feet, 2960 m) with hotels and a *gombaa*. Descend from Tragsindho to Nuntale (aka, Manidingma) (7365 feet, 2245 m) and continue on to Thulo Dhunga. From Thulo Dhunga the route reaches Sombare (aka Bhasa), a village of Khaling Rai which is a sub-group of the Rai ethnicity. Khaling Rai are well-known weavers who follow a tradition of ancestor worship and animist practices. There is a Khaling Rai museum in Bhasa. Travel on from Sombare/Bhasa to the Sherpa village of Changmanteng. A viewpoint atop nearby Rutnaki hill (11,483 feet, 3500 m) provides a panoramic feast. Continue to Ratnange and on to Phaphlu. Return flights are available from Phaphlu, or you could begin the Pikey Peak Trail (see above) or head directly to Junbesi and then out to Shivalya along the main route.

TREKS NORTH OF POKHARA
(Map No. 16, Page 390)

The Machhapuchhre Model Trek—also known as TAAN (Trekking Agents Association of Nepal) Model Trek—is one of Nepal's most newly identified treks, located in an uncrowded area of the ACAP (Annapurna Conservation Area Project) region where few tourists have previously visited. This route was jointly developed by TAAN's Pokhara Chapter, ACAP, and The Swiss National Centre of Competence in Research to provide access to a pristine area as an alternative to the well-established, more commercial trekking routes. Both it and the Sikles Eco-Trek offer an alternative to get away from the recent road building along the Annapurna Circuit while remaining in the ACAP area. There are several options for these treks, with home stay available along part of the way where you can experience the true gem of Nepal, the culture of the mid-hills. However, camping will be necessary to reach the upper heights of the Machhapuchhre Model Trek, and most visitors make arrangements for this through an agency. The following are brief, suggested itineraries, although several other route options are available.

MACHHAPUCHHRE (TAAN) MODEL TREK

The Macchapuchhre Model Trek takes you to the base of Mardi Himal (18,218 feet, 5553 m), a so-called trekking peak, and the unclimbed Machhapuchhre (22,956 feet, 6997 m) offering up-close, dramatic views of their south faces and vistas of the surrounding Himalayan giants and the Pokhara valley below. This area was once referred to as "The Other Sanctuary" by Colonel Jimmy Roberts, considered the father of trekking in Nepal. The swift altitude gain warrants considerable caution, and trekkers following this route must already be acclimatized from previous excursions and still need to be especially vigilant for signs of AMS (see Chapter 5).

There are many options in this area, including a start from Phedi, which is also an option for starting the Annapurna Sanctuary Trek. Phedi is reached by bus from Pokhara's

Baglung Bus Station. From Phedi (3750 feet, 1143 m), start trekking to pass Dhampus (5560 feet, 1695 m) and Potana (6460 feet, 1969 m) and reach the lodges of Bhichok Deorali (6922 feet, 2110 m). (Chapter 6 has details about the route from Phedi to Bhichok Deorali.)

To Mardi Himal Base Camp West. From here the route branches away from the Annapurna Sanctuary route and heads along the ridgeline to the northeast, following this skeleton itinerary: Bhichok Deorali to Forest Camp (8530 feet, 2600 m); Forest Camp to Low Camp (10,007 feet, 3050 m); Low Camp to High Camp (12,795 feet, 3900 m); High Camp to Mardi Himal Base Camp, West (14,764 feet, 4500 m). Fully self-sufficient camping is required, along with wariness of symptoms of AMS.

To Mardi Himal Base Camp South. Another option is to start the trek at the crossing of the Mardi Khola at Mardi Pul (3675 feet, 1120 m), north of Hemja Milanchok, a town along the road from Pokhara to Beni. Climb to the village of Ribhan (4692 feet, 1430 m), with home stay available; beyond this point, self-sufficient camping is required. Ascend to a viewpoint named Odane (8245 feet, 2513 m), and on to Khumai Danda (10,646 feet, 3245 m), Korchon (12,080 feet, 3682 m), and then Mardi Himal Base Camp, South (13,517 feet, 4120 m). Again, beware of the extreme altitude gains in a short period of time; trekkers should be previously acclimatized before attempting either of the above routes and must remain on the lookout for symptoms of AMS. Other options for home stay in the lower elevations of this area include the following villages: Lwang, Ghalel, Takru, Sidhing, as well as Armala, Ghachok, and Tuse Dhibrang, Misra, and Karuwa.

SIKLES ECO-TREK

This trek takes you to mainly Gurung villages that are away from the beaten track and in the shadow of the Lamjung and Annapurna ranges, with superb village and mountain vistas. This route will be especially delightful in the springtime when the rhododendrons are in bloom.

Start the trek at the crossing of the Mardi Khola (3675 feet, 1120 m) at Mardi Pul, north of Hemja Milanchok, a town along the road from Pokhara to Beni. Follow the Seti Khola past the Gurung settlement of Ghachok to Dhiprang (with hot springs a further 20 minutes upstream at Kharpaani, aka Tatopaani). Cross the Seti Khola and pass through the settlement of Chaur before crossing the Sardi Khola and ascending to the Gurung settlement of Ghalegaon (5475 feet, 1669 m) near Ghalekharkaand, then climb to a pass at Jhakarphulan (8900 feet, 2713 m, no facilities) and on to Nyaulikharka (7290 feet, 2222 m) (no facilities). Continue on to the large Gurung settlements of Parche and Sikles (6496 feet, 1980 m), overlooking the Madi River, with fine views of Annapurna II, IV, and the Lamjung Range. Follow the Madi River south down to Sonda and then Chansu (3215 feet, 980 m). Continue on to Yangjakot to Bhaise and then climb to Kalikasthan (3642 feet, 1110 m) before descending to Begnas Tal (2690 feet, 820 m) and vehicle transport back to Pokhara.

KHAPTAD OF THE FAR WEST

(Map No. 17, Page 393)

Khaptad National Park (87 square miles, 225 sq km) is widely acclaimed for the beauty of its subalpine vegetation and grassland, and renowned as the serene hermitage site of the late Khaptad Baba (also known as Swami Sachchidananda Saraswati) who

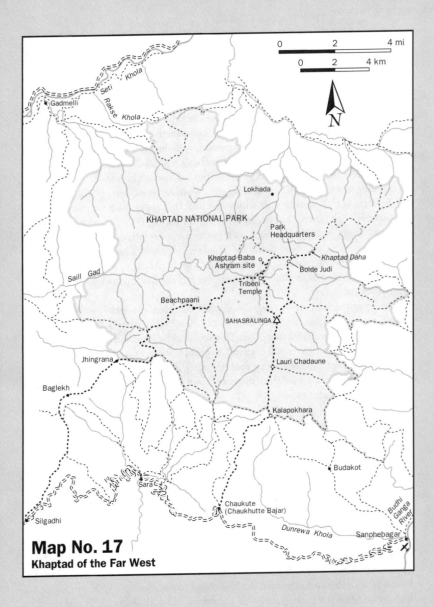

Map No. 17
Khaptad of the Far West

lived here in contemplation for half a century. Khaptad, set in the mid-hills of the far west and bordered by four districts, is remote, uninhabited, and difficult to reach. It receives a small number of foreign tourists per season (and less than 300 total since it officially opened in 1984). In 2009 only two foreigners visited, down from twenty-nine in 2008 and nine in 2007. There are only a few, spartan commercial lodges along the route, with most foreigners choosing to camp. However, several times a year a flood of local pilgrims from surrounding districts arrive for festival celebrations.

Alonzo was lucky enough to chance upon a leopard on his first visit to Khaptad in 1994. The area is an isolated massif reaching 10,584 feet (3226 m) at its highest point, Sahasralinga; it lies in far western Nepal south of the main Himalayan chain. From viewpoints in the park, the Kumoan range in India can be seen to the west, Api (23,398 feet, 7132 m) and Saipal (23,067 feet, 7031 m) to the north, and even Dhaulagiri and Annapurna to the east. Beautiful oak and rhododendron forests cover the slopes, and the rolling plateau on top consists of coniferous forests interspersed with grasslands. There is an interesting variety of bird species present, including the satyr tragopan pheasant and great parrotbill. As many as 270 species of birds are said to be found in Khaptad and over 10 percent of Nepal's flowering plants. The meadows are covered in a mass of flowers in spring and summer. Khaptad is also renowned for its jaDibuTi (medicinal herbs).

There are several sites to visit within the park that are considered sacred, including Ashutosh Sahas, a natural *lingam* formation; Khaptad Daha, a marshy pond; Nag Dhunga (Snake Rock), a boulder with snakelike indentations and striations; Sita Paila, a stone that devotees claim has Hindu Goddess Sita's foot imprint; Tribeni Temple complex, the meeting point of four districts (Accham, Bajhang, Bajura, and Doti); and the former swami's living quarters and meditation area, as well as Bolde Judi, a lookout tower.

The suggested trek begins at Silgadhi, Doti District Headquarters. From Kathmandu's Baleju Bus Station (also known as Gongabu or New Bus Park), take the bus to Dipayal (headquarters of the Far Western Zone Development Region) and on to Silgadhi (a 25-hour bus ride via Atariya, Kailali District). Silgadhi is about 1 hour by bus from Dipayal, a large bazaar town and the starting point for a trek into Khaptad National Park.

The following is a skeleton itinerary, and the area has not been precisely surveyed by the authors.

Approach Route

The trek begins in Silgadhi and leads up to Baglekh. From Baglekh continue to Jhingrana village. Jhingrana is a small hamlet with mud and stone houses. This is the Khaptad National Park entry point, with a 1000 NRS entry fee. Inquire here as to whether facilities at Beachpaani are currently open. The trail continues from Jhingrana to Beachpaani which has a seasonal tea shop and simple lodge. Continue on from Beachpaani to the park headquarters and a seasonal tea house with basic lodging as well as a government-run guest house and army post.

Return Route Options

Return via the approach route in reverse, or travel to Accham District which lies to the west of the park. To reach Accham, head in the direction of Sahasralinga, the highest point of the park, pass Lauri Chadaune and Kalapokhara along the way to Chaukute village. Chaukute is a Chettri and Brahman village with small shops and lies on the bus route between Silgadhi and Sanphebagar. Home stay can possibly be arranged in Chaukute. From Chaukute continue to Sanphebagar, a large bazaar town in Accham District with an airport and bus service to Kathmandu. Bus service between Sanphebagar and Silgadhi takes four hours or more. Alternatively, from Kalopokhara, mentioned above, another route that bypasses the road heads west through Budakot and descends to Sanphebagar.

Opposite: The view from along the route to Tsergo Ri (Photo by Tokozile Robbins)

APPENDIXES

Appendix A
FURTHER READING AND FILM

Maximum enjoyment of Nepal will come through familiarity with this country's history, culture, geography, and people. Most of the books in the following annotated list focus on areas outside of the Kathmandu valley and should help you learn more about the various regions of this country.

BOOKS

GENERAL

Lewis, Todd T., and Theodore Riccardi, Jr. *The Himalayas: A Syllabus of the Region's History, Anthropology, and Religion.* Ann Arbor, Mich.: Association for Asian Studies, 1995. The comprehensive springboard for further study.

Mayhew, Bradley. *Nepal (Country Guide).* Lonely Planet, 2006. General guide to Nepal.

McConnachie, James and David Reed. *The Rough Guide: Nepal.* London: Rough Guides, 2009. An excellent guide to the rest of the country with much helpful information.

Moran, Kerry. *Nepal Handbook.* Chico, Calif.: Moon, 2004. Much thoughtful discussion.

ANTHROPOLOGY

Bista, Dor Bahadur. *People of Nepal.* Kathmandu: Ratna Pustak Bhandar, 1996. Presents an excellent, though dated, synopsis of most of the ethnic groups found in Nepal.

Brower, Barbara. *Sherpa of Khumbu: People, Livestock and Landscape.* Delhi: Oxford University Press, 1991. A look at the yak and Sherpa society and changes brought by tourism.

Desjarlais, Robert R. *Body and Emotion: The Aesthetics of Illness and Healing in the Nepal Himalayas.* Philadelphia: University of Pennsylvania Press, 1992. Focused on Helambu.

Fisher, James F. *Sherpas: Reflection on Change in Himalayan Nepal.* Berkeley: University of California Press, 1990. A look at this legendary ethnic group seen through their eyes, interpreted by an anthropologist who first worked among them in 1964.

Kipp, Eva. *Bending Bamboo, Changing Winds: Nepali Women Tell Their Life Stories.* Kathmandu: Pilgrims Publishing, 2006. A compilation of interviews with fourteen women representing diverse situations in Nepal.

Mumford, Stan Royal. *Himalayan Dialogue: Tibetan Lamas and Gurung Shamans in Nepal.* Madison: University of Wisconsin Press, 1989.

ART

Gabriel, Hannelore. *The Jewelry of Nepal.* New York: Weatherhill, 1999. A luscious, lavish look at adornment in Nepal.

Tingey, C. *Auspicious Music in a Changing Society.* New Delhi: Heritage Publishers, 1994. A look at Nepal's traditional musicians and their bands that play at hill weddings.

ENVIRONMENT AND GEOGRAPHY

Gajurel, C. L., and K. K. Vaidya. *Traditional Arts and Crafts of Nepal.* New Delhi: S. Chand, 1999. Invaluable for understanding many of the folk processes going on around you.

Hagen, Toni. *Building Bridges to the Third World: Memories of Nepal 1950–1992.* Delhi: Book Faith India, 1994. Insight on the "development process" by one of the first long-term visitors to Nepal who played a key role in the early stages.

Hutt, Michael. *Nepal in the Nineties.* Delhi: Oxford University Press, 2002. A compendium of essays on historic developments in the 1990s.

Shakya, Sujeev. *Unleashing Nepal: Past, Present and Future of the Economy.* Penguin Books, 2010. A look at the history, current state, and possible future of Nepal's economy by the man who writes under the name Artha Beed for the *Nepali Times.* In it he covers a lot of ground, including the $15 billion in aid that has poured in over four decades, resulting in more reports (some 270,000) than results.

Shrestha, Nanda R. *Landlessness and Migration in Nepal.* Boulder: Westview Press, 1990. "Help me, I am a development victim" sets the perspective of this book.

Toffin, Gérard, ed. *Man and His House in the Himalayas: Ecology of Nepal.* New Delhi: Sterling Publishers, 1991. Architecture and human ecology.

LANGUAGE

Adhikary, Kamal R. *A Concise English–Nepali Dictionary (with transliteration and Devanagari).* Kathmandu: author, 1988. Very useful for the trekker who has mastered the basics.

Bloomfield, Andrew, and Yanki Tshering. *Learning Practical Tibetan.* Ithaca, N.Y.: Snow Lion, 1998. A useful beginning.

Hutt, Michael, Krishna Pradhan, and Abhi Subedi. *Complete Nepali with Two Audio CDs: A Teach Yourself Guide.* McGraw-Hill, 2010. A comprehensive approach to learning Nepali, from understanding to speaking and writing.

Karki, Tika B., and Chij K. Shrestha. *Basic Course in Spoken Nepali.* Kathmandu: authors, 1996. Originally written for Peace Corps volunteers; stresses the situational approach, for the serious trekker.

Lee, Hae Lyun. *Conversational Nepali.* Kathmandu: Hisi Publications, 2000. An excellent, well-organized workbook with audio materials following a situational approach to becoming conversational.

Matthews, David J. *A Course in Nepali.* London: School of Oriental and African Studies, 1998. A useful formal text for those seeking an in-depth study.

O'Rourke, Mary-Jo, and Bimal Shrestha. *Nepali Phrasebook.* Hawthorn, Australia: Lonely Planet, 2008. A useful resource.

Raj, Prakash A. *Nepali-English/English-Nepali Dictionary and Phrasebook.* Hippocrene Books, 2003.

Sherchan, Bijaya et al. *An Exercise Book on Spoken Nepali Language.* Kathmandu: School for International Training, 1994. A helpful next step.

Sherpa, Phinjo. *Sherpa Nepali English.* Kathmandu: ECO Himal 1999. The first resource on the Sherpa language.

Watters, Daniel P., and Narendra B. Rajbhandary. *Nepali in Context, A Topical Approach to Learning Nepali,* 2000. A workbook that is aptly described by its title.

LITERATURE

Dixit, Mani. *Over the Mountains*. Kathmandu: Ekta Books, 1995. An historical ethnic novel about contemporary Nepal by a prolific writer.

Dixit, Kanak Mani (illustrated by Subhas Rai). *Bhaktaprasad Bhyaguto: Adventures of a Nepali Frog*. Lalitpur: Rato Bangala Kitab, 2001. A delightful book for adults and children alike.

NATURAL HISTORY

Grimmett, Richard, Carol Inskipp, and Tim Inskipp. *Birds of Nepal*. Princeton University Press, 2000. A comprehensive field guide.

_____. *A Guide to the Birds of Nepal*. Christopher Helm Publishers Ltd., 2000. This monograph contains range and distribution maps of species, aids for identifying difficult birds, and information on bird-watching areas. A complement to *Birds of Nepal* for the keen birder.

Polunin, Oleg, Adam Stainton and Ann Farrer. *Concise Flowers of the Himalaya*. Oxford University Press, 1998. A portable wealth of photographs and descriptions of the most common species, listed in the 1984 work.

_____. *Flowers of the Himalaya*. Delhi: Oxford University Press, 1984. Together with Stainton's supplement, the best photographic record of flowering plants.

Smith, Colin. *Butterflies of Nepal (Central Himalaya)*. Bangkok: Tecpress, 1989. The long-awaited guide, with color photos, to all the species in Nepal!

Stainton, Adam. *Flowers of the Himalaya: A Supplement*. Oxford University Press, 1998. More photographs and species to extend the seminal work of Polunin and Stainton.

POLITICAL SCIENCE

Bista, Dor Bahadur. *Fatalism and Development: Nepal's Struggle for Modernization*. Sangam Books Ltd, 1994. A seminal piece that sparked much controversy with its publication; this volume and Brown's help the outsider understand current Nepal.

Mihaly, Eugene Bramer. *Foreign Aid and Politics in Nepal*. London: Oxford University Press, 1965. An early study. His conclusions make sense today.

Shrestha, Aditya Man. *Bleeding Mountains of Nepal*. IUniverse, 2001. The publisher's description says it best: "The whole book is a document of how the country is being fleeced, milked and wrenched at all times by the insiders, outsiders, donor agencies and the NGOs. It speaks of Nepal and its teeming millions squirming below the poverty line, forever exploited. It is a story of Nepal's failed development of the last fifty years, the tears behind the smile; the smile that does not reach the eyes."

_____. *Wrong We Do Right We Don't*. Ekta Books, 2005. Pre-republic account of misappropriations, abuses of power, and styles of corruption in Nepal and the challenges that lie ahead.

REGIONAL

Coburn, Broughton. *Nepali Aama: Portrait of a Nepalese Hill Woman*. Chico, Calif.: Moon, 1991. A sensitive look at life in a Gurung village, told by an old woman.

Downs, Hugh R. *Rhythms of a Himalayan Village*. New York: Harper & Row, 1980. A photo documentary of a Sherpa village in Solu—a most helpful book for understanding *Mani-rimdu* and how Sherpas may view their land.

Jefferies, Margaret, and Margaret Clarbrough. *Sagarmatha, Mother of the Universe: The Story of Mount Everest National Park*. Mountaineers Books, 1991. Information on the Khumbu.

Klatzel, Frances. *Gaiety of Spirit—the Sherpas of Everest*, Mera Publications, 2009. Kathmandu, Nepal

Messerschmidt, Don. *Muktinath: Himalayan Pilgrimage, a Cultural & Historical Guide*. Kathmandu: Sayahogi Press, 1992. A glimpse of the importance of these trekker destinations to people of South Asia.

Messerschmidt, L., F. Klatzel, et al. *Stories and customs of Manang : as told by the lamas and elders of Manang*. Kathmandu, Mera Publications, 2004.

Rogers, Clint. *Secrets of Manang: The Story Behind the Phenomenal Rise of Nepal's Famed Business Community*. Mandala, 2004. Historical background and cultural insight of the Manang community and factors responsible for their economic success.

Sakya, Karna. *Paradise In Our Backyard: A Blueprint for Nepal*. Delhi: Penguin Books India, 2009. Autobiographical details by the founder of Thamel's landmark Kathmandu Guest House and his ideas on development in Nepal.

Thapa, Manjushri. *Mustang Bhot in Fragments*. Lalitpur: Himal Books, 1992. What does a Nepali woman who was raised and educated abroad see when she returns to Nepal and works there?

RELIGION

Snellgrove, David. *Buddhist Himalaya*. Kathmandu: Himalayan Booksellers, 1995. A reprint of the 1957 edition that deals with the Solu–Khumbu region and the Buddhism of Sherpas and of Kathmandu.

TRAVELOGUES

Greenwald, Jeff. *Shopping for Buddhas*. Lonely Planet, 1996. A hilarious look at expatriate life in Kathmandu during the reign of King Birendra.

Khadka, Rajendra S. *Travelers' Tales Nepal: True Stories of Life on the Road*. Travelers' Tales, 2000. Short stories from travels in Nepal, some written by well-known people.

Lall, Kesar. *The Newar Merchants in Lhasa*. Ratna Pustak Bhandar, 2001. Travel accounts of men who conducted trans-Himalayan trade in a forgotten age without vehicle transport or mobile phones.

Murphy, Dervla. *The Waiting Land*. Overlook TP, 1990. Dervla traveled to Nepal in the 1960's and recorded her experiences in Kathmandu and in Pokhara before motor roads reached the lake-city.

Scot, Barbara J. *The Violet Shyness of Their Eyes: Notes from Nepal*. Corvallis, Ore.: CALYX Books, 2005. An endearing chronicle of the author's experience volunteering and traveling in Nepal, especially moving are insights into feminine issues.

Scott, J., and J. Robertson. *Lost in the Himalayas*. Lothian Books, 1994. What it might be like if you wander off the trail alone in the winter near Gosainkund and wait forty-three days for rescue.

Snellgrove, David. *Himalayan Pilgrimage*. Shambhala, 1988. A chronicle of travel through north-central and northwestern Nepal in the 1950s. Though scholars question his observations about hill regions, his wide range of interests and acute powers of observation make for fascinating reading.

TREKKING AND RELATED ACTIVITIES

Banerjee, Partha S. *Trekking in Nepal, Annapurna*. Milestone Books, 2007. General descriptions of main routes described on a day-by-day basis (but limited information on side and alternate routes) with photos and section-specific maps as well as a regional foldout map.

_____. *Trekking in Nepal, Everest*. Milestone Books, 2009. Also includes a DVD of the Khumbu area.

_____. *Trekking in Nepal, Langtang*. Milestone Books, 2009.

Boustead, Robin. *The Great Himalaya Trail, A Pictorial Guide*. Kathmandu: Himalayan Map House, 2009. A beautiful photojournal (including maps) of the Nepal portion of a walk along the spine of the Himalaya.

Burbank, Jon. *Culture Shock: Nepal—A Guide to Customs and Etiquitte*. Bravo Limited, 2000. Those who come to work in Nepal would do well to read this book prior to arriving.

Hawley, Elizabeth, *The Himalayan Database: The Expedition Archives of Elizabeth Hawley*, on CD (see also a website set up by Richard Salisbury, www.HimalayanDatabase.com). American Alpine Club, 2004.

Knowles, Peter, and Dave Allardice. *White Water Nepal: A Rivers Guidebook for Rafting and Kayaking*. Menasha Ridge, 1997.

Mayhew, Bradley, and Joe Bindloss. *Trekking in the Nepal Himalaya*. Victoria, Australia: Lonely Planet, 2009. Treks with general route descriptions on a day-by-day basis.

McGuinness, Jamie. *Trekking in the Everest Region*. 5th ed. Surrey, U.K.: Trailblazer Publications, 2009. A thorough guide to the area with detailed, hand-drawn route maps and several suggestions for getting off the beaten path. Written by a longtime denizen of the Himalaya.

O'Connor, Bill. *The Trekking Peaks of Nepal*. Seattle: Cloudcap Press, 1989. A climbing guide to the original eighteen "trekking" summits. (Since 2002, the Nepalese government has specified an additional fifteen "trekking peaks.")

Reynolds, Kev. *Annapurna: A Trekker's Guide*. Milnthorpe, Cumbria, U.K.: Cicerone Press, 2004. A prolific series of guidebooks by this author.

_____. *Everest: A Trekker's Guide*. Cicerone Press, 2006.

Smith, Colin. *Twenty Questions (and Answers) about Butterflies*. Kathmandu: Modern Printing Press, 2007. A brief sketch with photographs by an expatriate resident of Pokhara since the 1960s. Colin's interest in butterflies began as a hobby and blossomed into a full-time activity. He set up the butterfly collection now housed at the Annapurna Museum on the Prithvi Narayan Campus in Pokhara. Copies of this book are available at the International Mountaineering Museum in Pokhara as well as booksellers in tourist areas. Colin also leads groups on butterfly tours (www.butterflytreksnepal.com).

Thomas, Bryn. *Trekking in the Annapurna Region*. Surrey, U.K.: Trailblazer Publications, 2005. An informative guide to the area and lodges with detailed route maps.

TREKKING MEDICINE

Bezruchka, Stephen. *Altitude Illness: Prevention and Treatment*. Seattle: The Mountaineers, 2005. Another slim volume to carry with details on understanding and coping with problems at altitude.

_____. *The Pocket Doctor: Your Ticket to Good Health while Traveling.* Seattle: The Mountaineers Books, 1999. Another inexpensive, small, carry-along book to help you prepare for and deal with health problems while traveling.

Centers for Disease Control and Prevention, 2009. "CDC Health information for international travel 2010." From www.cdc.gov/travel/click on yellow book. This is updated every two years and full of useful information.

Weiss, Eric. *Wilderness 911.* Seattle: The Mountaineers Books, 2007. A comprehensive guide to medical care in the outdoors.

FILMS

NEPAL-BASED FILMS

Everest: 50 Years on the Mountain, 2003. National Geographic.

Everest (IMAX format), 2001. Directed by David Breashears, Greg MacGillivray, and Stephen Judson. Documents, with breathtaking footage, what is involved in climbing Everest. Filmed in 1996 at the same time as a tragedy unfolded on the mountain, and includes some of the rescue operation.

Himalaya, 1999. Directed by Eric Valli. Filmed in scenic Dolpo, a drama about generational struggles and yak caravans in the Himalaya.

NOVA: Lost Treasure of Tibet, 2003. Public Broadcasting System (PBS). Documentary about the technical and cultural challenges of restoring the inside of a monastery in Upper Mustang.

The People's Nepal, 2010. Jim Wills. Documentary on the decade-long civil war of Nepal, the dismantling of royal rule, and the emergence of democracy.

Secrets of Shangri-La: Quest for Sacred Caves, 2010. Pete Athans, PBS. Exploring caves in Mustang, and discovering ancient manuscripts and artwork as well as human remains.

Trailblazing: The Women of Nepal's Trekking Industry, 2005. Lisa Hoffe. Documents the pioneering spirit and determination of the fledgling few female trekking guides working in a male-dominated adventure tourism industry and a conservative mountain culture. (www.trailblazing.ca)

REGIONAL FILMS

Blindsight, 2006. Directed by Lucy Walker. A film documenting the true adventure of the attempted ascent of Lhakpa-Ri peak (7045 m) by a group of six Tibetan teens who were societal outcasts due to cultural perceptions about blindness.

Kundun ("Presence"), 1997. Directed by Martin Scorsese. A film that provides insight into Tibetan Buddhism.

Lost Horizon, 1937. Directed by Frank Capra, based on a book by James Hilton set in the Himalaya.

Michael Palin-Himalaya, 2005. Travels through Himalayan countries with brief coverage of Nepal's insurgency and a visit to Everest base camp.

Appendix B
NEPALI LANGUAGE INTRODUCTION

Nepali is an Indo-European language derived from Sanskrit. It is also one of India's official languages and is relatively easy to learn.

In what follows, the transliteration system used for Nepali words in this book is described, with a pronunciation guide to enable the reader to pronounce place-names and other words correctly. A few important phrases are given.

PRONUNCIATION

Nepali is written in Devanagari script (as are Hindi and Sanskrit), but a system of transliteration to the Roman script is used here. Many of the letters denote their usual sounds, and only the special sounds are described.

STRESS

The stress usually falls on the first syllable (**chaá mal**) unless the first syllable has a short vowel and is followed in the second syllable by a long one. Then the stress falls on the second syllable (**pa kaaú nos**). The single most common pronunciation error made by the beginning student is *not* putting the emphasis on the first syllable.

VOWELS

    a like the *a* in *balloon*. Never like the *a* in *hat*.

  aa long like the *a* in *father* or *car*.

    i like *ee* in *beer,* the short and long forms pronounced similarly.

    u like *oo* in *mood* or *root*, again with the long and short forms similar. Never like the *u* in *mute*.

    e like *a* in *skate* or like the French *e* in *café*.

  ai a diphthong with the first element like the *a* in *arise* and the second like the *y* in *city*. Together, somewhat like the *ay* in *laying*, but not like the sound of the word *eye*.

  au a diphthong in which the first element is like the *a* in *arise* and the second like the *u* in *put*.

    o like *o* in *bowl* or *go*.

aau, aai, and **eu** not diphthongs, but vowels pronounced separately one after the other.

CAPITALIZED VOWELS

Capitalized vowels (**A, E, I, O, U**) indicate nasalization of that sound. Squeeze your nostrils together and force the sound to be made high up in the mouth.

DENTAL AND RETROFLEX CONSONANTS

With retroflexed consonants, make the sound farther back in the mouth, compared to the dental, which are made much more forward.

- **t** pronounced unaspirated, with the tip of the tongue on the teeth as in the French *petite*.
- **T** like the *t* in *little*, with the tongue slightly bent back when it meets the roof of the mouth.
- **d** dental like the French *d*, in which the blade of the tongue is pressed behind the upper teeth.
- **D** pronounced with retroflexion of the tongue. Turn the tongue back in the mouth, press the underside of it against the palate, and pronounce the *d* in *dog*.
- **R** also pronounced with retroflexion of the tongue.

ASPIRATED CONSONANTS

Nepalis differentiate between aspirated and unaspirated consonants. This is quite difficult for native English speakers. Aspiration is indicated by an *h* following the consonant. Consciously avoid breathing hard or aspirating on the consonants that are not followed by an *h*.

The exception to the preceding rule in the transliteration scheme employed in this book applies to *ch* and *chh*. Only the latter is aspirated.

- **chh** press the blade of the tongue behind the upper teeth and try to say *ts*. At the same time, exert strong breath pressure so that when the tongue is released from the teeth, there is a loud emission of breath. Listen to a native Nepali speaker. It is like the *tch-h* in pi*tch* here.
- **ch** the unaspirated form as in *chalk, Chinese*.

MISCELLANEOUS

- **k** like *c* in *cat*.
- **y** like *y* in *yeast*.
- **s** like *s* in *song*.
- **j** press the blade of the tongue against the upper teeth with the tip of the tongue pointed down and say *j* as in *January*. It is somewhat like *dz* and is especially found in words coming from Tibetan dialects.
- **ph** like *f* in *full*.
- **p** less aspiration than **ph** (more like **p** than **f**).

Other consonants should present little difficulty. When two consonants come together, be sure to pronounce them individually.

QUESTIONS

The basic form is to inflect at the end of the sentence; that is, raise the pitch of your voice on the ending word.

ASKING THE WAY AND OTHER IMPORTANT PHRASES

The following is a brief introduction to asking the way as you walk along trails, together with other essential phrases. Trekkers are advised to use other resources for further language study. The spacing for the gloss of the Nepali phrases may help you change the phrases to suit your needs as you gain facility with the language.

What is the name of this town?	**yo**	**gAAU**	**-ko naam**	**ke ho?**
	this	town	of name	what is
Is this the road to Melamchighyang?	**yo**	**melamchighyang jaane**	**baaTo**	**ho?**
	this	Melamchighyang going	road is	this
Where does this trail lead to?	**yo**	**baaTo kahAAsamma**	**jaanchha?**	
	this	trail where up to	go	
Which trail goes to Ringmo?	**Ringmo**	**-samma**	**kun baaTo jaanchha?**	
	Ringmo	up to	which trail goes	
How many hours to Namche?	**Namche**	**-samma**	**kati ghanTaa**	
	Namche	up to	how many hours	
	laagchha?			
	does it take			
Where can I get food?	**khaanaa**	**kahAA**	**pAAIchha?**	
	food	where	get/available	
Where is there a hotel?	**hoTel**	**kahAA**	**chha?**	
	hotel	where	is	
Can you cook food for us?	**hami**	**-laai khaanaa pakaaunu**		
	for	food to cook can you		
	hunchha	**ki?**		
	us	or		
Where can I stay?	**kahAA basne?**			
	where stay			
Are there people in Gopte now?	**ahile**	**Gopte**	**-maa manchhe**	**chha?**
	now	Gopte	at people	are there
May we (I) stay in your house?	**tapAAIko**	**ghar**	**-maa baas pAAIchha?**	
	your	house	in stay can get	
Can I (we) stay here?	**yahAA**	**baas**	**pAAIchha?**	
	here	stay	can get	
Can I get food here?	**khaanaa**	**yahAA**	**pAAIchha?**	
	food	here	can get	
Please cook rice and lentils for me.	**daal**	**bhaat**	**pakaaunos**	
	lentils	rice	please cook	
Please give me more rice.	**bhaat**	**dinos**		
	rice	please give		
That is enough.	**pugyo**			
	enough			
How much is the cost?	**Kati**	**paisaa**	**chha?**	
	how much	money	is	
I don't eat meat.	**Ma**	**maasu**	**khAAdaena.**	
	I	meat	do not eat	
I am a vegetarian.	**Ma**	**saakaahaari hU.**		
	I	vegetarian am.		
Please don't add MSG.	**aajinomoTo**	**nahaalnus.**		
	MSG	please don't add		

GLOSSARY OF NEPALI AND TIBETAN WORDS

aaja	today
aajinomoTo	monosodium glutamate (MSG)
(also **TesTi pauDar**)	
aamaa	mother
achaar	a pickled relish
ba (or **buwaa**)	father
baasaa	language
baaTo	road or path
bAAyaa	right (direction)
bahini	younger sister
bandh	closed (in general) or a strike/shutdown enforced by protestors, with businesses and roads not likely to be open from mid-morning to sundown
beyul	hidden valley
bhaai	younger brother
bhaat	cooked rice
bharal	blue sheep
bhaTmaas	soybeans
bhaTTi	traditional Nepali inn
bhikaari	beggar
bholi	tomorrow
BhoTiya	Buddhist highlander of Nepal
bihaana	morning
chaahanu	to want
chaarpi	latrine
chang	locally brewed beer
chataamari	Newar-style pizza
chAUmri (or **zopkio**)	a cross between a yak and a cow
chautaaraa	rectangular resting platform on a trail
chhiTo	fast
chilim	clay pipe for smoking
chiso	cold (adj.) or **jaaDo** for climate
chiyaa	tea
chorten	Buddhist religious cubical/conical structure
DAADaa	ridge
daal	lentil soup poured over rice
daal bhaat tarakaari	a typical Nepali meal of lentil soup, rice, and vegetables
daaju (or **daai**)	elder brother
dAAyaa	left (direction)
dahi	yogurt
dakshiRn	south
daru (or **rakshi**)	a Thakali distilled spirit
dharma	religion (Buddhists will extend this definition to the teachings of Buddha, practice, duty, the spiritual path in general, and more)
dharmsala	rest house
Dhilo	slow
didi	elder sister

dudh	milk
du-kha	suffering
Doko	conical basket for carrying loads
drokpa	Tibetan nomad
gaahro	difficult
gahrAU	heavy (weight)
gAU	village
ghiu	clarified butter (*ghee* in India)
gomba	Tibetan Buddhist temple
goTh	shelter used by shepherds
halukaa	light (weight)
hijo	yesterday
himaal	mountain
jAAnkri	shaman
jAAR	locally brewed beer
jaDibuTi	medicinal herbs
jharanaa	waterfall
jholaa	bag
jukaa	leech
juTho	socially unacceptable, or polluting
kaani	traditional BhoTiya gateway
kahAA?	where?
kata	ceremonial scarf
kharka	pasture
khola (also kosi or nadi)	river
kiraa	insect
koThaa	room
la	pass (also bhanjyaang or deuraali)
laaligurAAs	rhododendron
lauro	walking stick
lekh	hill
lokta	bark of *daphne* plant used for making "rice" paper
loTaa	vessel for carrying water while answering nature's call
maanaa	volume measure (20 oz, 2½ cups, or 0.7 l)
maani	prayer
maayaa (or prem)	love
maTTitel	kerosene
naamlo	tumpline
namaskaar	traditional greeting (very polite and formal)
namaste	traditional greeting (less formal)
nayAA	new
paani	water
pairo	landslide
paisaa	money
paschim	west
pau	200 grams (250 grams in India)
phal	fruit
pokhari	pond
pul	bridge

puraano	old
puraano bas paark	Old Bus Park (Kathmandu)
purba	east
raamro	good
rakshi	distilled spirits
roTi	tortilla (unleavened bread)
rukh	tree
rupiyAA	smallest unit of money (about 1.4 US cents, at mid-2010 rates)
sAAjha	evening
saakaahaari	vegetarian
sAAp (or **sarpa**)	snake
saphaa	clean
shaanti	peace
shaligram	ammonite fossil
Sirdar	chief guide or manager of an expedition
solja	Tibetan salt and butter tea
stupa	a large *chorten* (see above)
taato	hot (or **garmi** for climate)
tal	lake
Tarai	the low-elevation, southernmost strip of Nepal that borders India and is an extension of the Gangetic Plain
tarakaari	vegetable dish
thangka	Buddhist scroll painting
ThAU	place
Thik	okay
Tikaa	a mark of religious or decorative significance on the forehead of Hindus
Topi	traditional men's hat of Nepal
tsampa	roasted barley flour, usually consumed by BhoTiya
Tundikhel	parade ground
tumbaa	fermented mash of millet
uttar	north
yaatraa	journey
yersa	a cluster of *goTh* in Khumbu, but also applies to other northern regions
yomori	Newar sweet pastry
zopkio	a cross between a yak and a cow (or **chAUmri**)

NUMBERS

1	ek	7	saat
2	dui	8	aaTh
3	tin	9	nau
4	chaar	10	das
5	pAAnch	100	ek saya
6	chha	1000	ek hajaar

An offering of juniper incense for the next journey (Photo by Pat Morrow)

INDEX

ABOUT THE AUTHORS

Stephen Bezruchka first went to Nepal in 1969, drawn by his interest in climbing and a desire to get close to the world's highest summits. He wrote the first edition of this guide, which was published in 1972. His fascination with Nepal soon transcended its lofty mountains to focus on the social-cultural matrix that remains a lifelong passion.

He returned to work in Nepal in the mid-1970s and in the mid-1980s. Initially he helped set up a community health project in western Nepal. Later he developed a remote district hospital as a teaching hospital for Nepali doctors and supervised the first physicians training there. He then worked with Nepali doctors to enable medical officers posted in remote district hospitals to carry out necessary surgery. Currently he spends most of his time in Nepal presenting concepts of population health to various groups.

Stephen Bezruchka has trekked far and wide in Nepal. He has climbed in the far ranges of the earth, including the Yukon, Pakistan, and China and on Everest. He is the author of *The Pocket Doctor: Your Ticket to Good Health while Traveling,* and *Altitude Illness:*

Prevention and Treatment. Of Ukrainian descent, he traveled to the Ukraine and toured outdoor museums there that reminded him of the way life continues in Nepal today. He practiced emergency medicine for thirty years and teaches at the School of Public Health at the University of Washington.

Alonzo "Lonny" Lyons first came to Nepal in the 1990s as a grassroots-level volunteer. He later earned a masters degree; however, employment as an epidemiologist did not satisfy him. Subsequently, he again traveled abroad, first to Japan and then Thailand and Nepal where wages might be low but "Gross National Happiness" is relatively high.

THE CONTRIBUTORS

Carol Inskipp, who contributed the natural history information, is an ornithologist, nature conservationist, and writer with a special interest in the birds of Nepal. Since 1977 she has made many trips to the country studying birds with her husband, Tim. Together they wrote the standard work on the distribution of birds of Nepal. Carol has also written other books and articles on Nepali birds and their conservation.

Donald Messerschmidt, who contributed the material on the people of Nepal, is an anthropologist who advised Stephen on trekking before he first came to the Himalaya, and who has continued to provide information on Nepal for subsequent editions of this book. His first experience in Nepal was with the Peace Corps in 1963. He has worked in community development, taught in the American school in Kathmandu, studied the Gurungs of west-central Nepal for his Ph.D., led treks and study tours, conducted research, and participated in scientific forums on the Himalaya.

The section on jewelry comes from the studies of anthropologist **Bronwen Bledsoe**, whose interest in Nepal began on a college study tour led by Donald Messerschmidt; it has been updated by **Hannelore Gabriel**.

Daniel Schelling, who contributed the material on geology, has been actively involved in Himalayan geological research since 1983 and did his doctoral research on the geology of the Rolwaling and the eastern Nepal Himalaya. He is presently at the Energy and Geoscience Institute at the University of Utah, conducting research throughout the Himalaya.

Dr. Jim Duff, M.D. is the founder and Director of the International Porter Protection Group (www.ippg.net), which has initiated projects for the benefit of porters' health and safety worldwide, including porter shelters, clothing banks, and rescue posts.

Declan Murphy is a long-term resident of Kathmandu working to help disadvantaged children access educational opportunities. His organization can be found at www.just-one.org.

THE MOUNTAINEERS, founded in 1906, is a nonprofit outdoor activity and conservation club, whose mission is "to explore, study, preserve, and enjoy the natural beauty of the outdoors...." Based in Seattle, Washington, the club is now one of the largest such organizations in the United States, with seven branches throughout Washington State.

The Mountaineers sponsors both classes and year-round outdoor activities in the Pacific Northwest, which include hiking, mountain climbing, ski-touring, snowshoeing, bicycling, camping, canoeing and kayaking, nature study, sailing, and adventure travel. The club's conservation division supports environmental causes through educational activities, sponsoring legislation, and presenting informational programs.

All club activities are led by skilled, experienced volunteers, who are dedicated to promoting safe and responsible enjoyment and preservation of the outdoors.

If you would like to participate in these organized outdoor activities or the club's programs, consider a membership in The Mountaineers. For information and an application, write or call The Mountaineers, Club Headquarters, 7700 Sand Point Way NE, Seattle, WA 98115; 206-521-6001. You can also visit the club's website at www.mountaineers.org or contact The Mountaineers via email at clubmail@mountaineers.org.

The Mountaineers Books, an active, nonprofit publishing program of the club, produces guidebooks, instructional texts, historical works, natural history guides, and works on environmental conservation. All books produced by The Mountaineers Books fulfill the club's mission. Visit www.mountaineersbooks.org to find details about all our titles and the latest author events, as well as videos, web clips, links, and more!

Visit www.mountaineersbooks.org to view our complete list of more than 500 outdoor titles:

The Mountaineers Books
1001 SW Klickitat Way, Suite 201
Seattle, WA 98134
800-553-4453
mbooks@mountaineersbooks.org

Leave No Trace strives to educate visitors about the nature of their recreational impacts, as well as offer techniques to prevent and minimize such impacts. Leave No Trace is best understood as an educational and ethical program, not as a set of rules and regulations.
For more information, visit www.lnt.org, or call 800-332-4100.